P9-DZN-534

Canadian Edition

The Student Writer

Editor and Critic

Barbara Fine Clouse

Peter Grevstad
Sheridan Institute of Technology and Advanced Learning

WITHDRAWN

McGraw-Hill
Ryerson
Connect. Learn. Succeed.

For my parents, Gerald and Helena

The McGraw·Hill Companies

The Student Writer: Editor and Critic
Canadian Edition

Copyright © 2011 by McGraw-Hill Ryerson Limited, a Subsidiary of The McGraw-Hill Companies. Copyright © 2008 by The McGraw-Hill Companies, Inc. All rights reserved. No part of this publication may be reproduced or transmitted in any form or by any means, or stored in a data base or retrieval system, without the prior written permission of McGraw-Hill Ryerson Limited, or in the case of photocopying or other reprographic copying, a license from The Canadian Copyright Licensing Agency (Access Copyright). For an Access Copyright licence, visit www.access copyright.ca or call toll free to 1-800-893-5777.

ISBN-13: 978-0-07-098041-9
ISBN-10: 0-07-098041-1

1 2 3 4 5 6 7 8 9 0 DOW 1 9 8 7 6 5 4 3 2 1

Printed and bound in the United States of America.

Care has been taken to trace ownership of copyright material contained in this text; however, the publisher will welcome any information that enables it to rectify any reference or credit for subsequent editions.

Vice President and Editor-in-Chief: Joanna Cotton
Publisher: Cara Yarzab
Sponsoring Editor: Karen Krahn
Marketing Manager: Margaret Janzen
Managing Editor, Development: Kelly Dickson
Developmental Editor: Daphne Scriabin, Jennifer Oliver
Editorial Associate: Marina Seguin
Senior Supervising Editor: Joanne Limebeer
Copy Editor: Ruth Bradley-St-Cyr
Proofreader: Elaine Melnick
Team Lead, Production: Paula Brown
Cover Design: Brett J. Miller/BJM Graphic Design & Communications
Cover Image: Masterfile
Interior Design: Brett Miller/ BJM Graphic Design & Communications, Greg Devitt
Page Layout: Bookman Typesetting Co. Inc.
Printer: R.R. Donnelley/ Willard

Library and Archives Canada Cataloguing in Publication Data

Clouse, Barbara Fine
   The student writer : editor and critic / Barbara Fine Clouse, Peter Grevstad. — Canadian ed.

Includes index.
ISBN 978-0-07-098041-9

   1. English language—Rhetoric—Textbooks.   2. Report writing—Textbooks.
3. Criticism—Textbooks.   I. Grevstad, Peter   II. Title.

PE1408.C556 2011   808'.042   C2010-903632-8

About the Authors

Barbara Clouse has taught all levels of college composition, first at Youngstown State University in northeastern Ohio and then at Slippery Rock University in western Pennsylvania. She has also written a number of composition texts. In addition to *A Troubleshooting Guide for Writers*, her books include *The Student Writer: Editor and Critic, Jumpstart: A Workbook for Writers, Patterns for a Purpose: A Rhetorical Reader,* and *Transitions: From Reading to Writing*, all written for McGraw-Hill. She has also developed *Cornerstones: Readings for Writers*, which is a short prose reader that is part of Primis, McGraw-Hill's custom publishing database. Barbara has also written *Progressions with Readings and Conventions* and *Expectations: A Brief Handbook and Guide to Writing* for Longman Publishers. A frequent presenter at national and regional conferences, Barbara often conducts workshops for writing teachers. McGraw-Hill authors represent the leading experts in their fields and are dedicated to improving the lives, careers, and interests of readers worldwide.

Peter Grevstad teaches Communications and General Education at Sheridan Institute of Technology and Advanced Learning in Brampton, Ontario. His teaching career began in secondary schools in the Czech Republic, in the early 1990s. He has also taught at the post-secondary level in colleges and universities in the Kingdom of Thailand, in Beijing PRC, and in Japan. For three years he was with the World University Service of Canada, in central Vietnam. His research interests include digital literacy, academic writing, Internet and research technologies in academic writing, and the immigrant experience in Canadian institutions. He has given numerous presentations at conferences and in-service events for teachers, both in Canada and overseas. He has edited both for scholarly and professional publications, and has contributed to ProQuest's CultureGrams series. This is his first book with McGraw-Hill Ryerson.

Brief Contents

PART 4
A Guide to Frequently Occurring Errors

Contents

PART 2
Patterns of Development

CHAPTER 6

Description   143

CHAPTER 7

Narration   165

CHAPTER 8

Exemplification   187

PART 4
A Guide to Frequently Occurring Errors

Thematic Contents

*Student essay
**Student essay with research

Interpersonal Relationships

Multicultural Experience

Places

Preface

The Canadian edition of *The Student Writer: Editor and Critic* is an introduction to post-secondary writing that places students at the centre of instruction by putting them in control of developing their own successful writing processes. *The Student Writer* also emphasizes helping students to become reliable critics and editors of professional writing, as well as their own texts. This emphasis on helping students become reliable critics and editors is apparent throughout the text, but it is the particular focus of the hallmark "Critique, Revise, and Edit" features that help students gain control over their writing by reading accomplished writers and creating their own best work. This important, recurring feature emphasizes both the need for writers to examine their drafts critically with their audience and purpose in mind and the need to revise in response to that critical assessment. By helping students to develop their own successful writing processes and by helping them become their own best critics, *The Student Writer* helps students become confident, capable writers.

Features

A number of features distinguish *The Student Writer: Editor and Critic* and help it fulfill its goals. Many of these features have been suggested by students and teachers.

An Emphasis on the Connection between Reading and Writing

- Strategies for reading analytically are explained and illustrated in Chapter 1.
- The instruction in how to write in response to reading in Chapter 1—including writing personal reactions, summarizing, and evaluating ideas—teaches students skills that will help them succeed in higher education and in their professional lives.
- Throughout the text, students are given many opportunities to write in response to contemporary, Canadian essays.

An Integrated Focus on the Student Writing Process

- "The Writing Process" offers extensive support at every stage of the writing process. Students are shown a variety of strategies for selecting topics, identifying audience and purpose, generating ideas, and revising. They are encouraged to sample some or all of the strategies as they work to improve their writing processes. Additionally, the "The Writing Process" includes suggestions for securing feedback from reliable readers.

- In Part 1, "Christel's Essay in Progress"—provided with commentary—illustrates the writing process that one student undertook.
- "Be a Responsible Writer" sections discuss ethical concerns associated with writing. Many of these sections have been expanded to include more help on avoiding plagiarism.
- Computer tips help students get the most out of online writing and revising.

An Emphasis on Revision

- "Critique, Revise, and Edit" sections provide strategies for evaluating drafts (to help students think like critics) and making changes (to help students work like editors). These sections help students understand the importance of revision, and they offer specific tools for revision.
- Some of the "Critique, Revise, and Edit" sections provide a close-up look at how the Canadian student writers whose essays appear in the book acted as editors to revise in response to their evaluations.
- To help students evaluate their drafts reliably (that is, to help them become reliable critics) and to help them revise accordingly, "The Writing Process" sections describe an extensive variety of revision strategies.
- Guidelines for giving and receiving reliable feedback on their drafts help students build peer response and collaborative learning techniques into their revision processes. In addition, the process guidelines accompanying writing assignments include suggestions for securing peer response.

An Emphasis on Purpose

- Writing is presented as a purposeful activity that helps people express feelings, relate experience, inform, and persuade, and the patterns of development are discussed as strategies that can be used individually, and in combination, to help writers fulfill their purposes for writing.
- "Occasions for Writing" sections note how the patterns are used across the disciplines, in the workplace, and in personal life to help students appreciate the usefulness of the patterns. This feature motivates students by showing how they can use writing to achieve a variety of purposes both in and out of the classroom.

An Emphasis on Combining the Patterns of Development

- In each chapter devoted to an essay pattern, students are shown how to combine that pattern with other patterns to help them achieve their purpose for writing.
- One or more professional essays also illustrate how to combine patterns.
- Chapter 14, "Combining Patterns of Development," explains strategies for combining patterns and offers Canadian students professional essays as examples of combining patterns to achieve a range of purposes.

A Focus on Visual Material

- An expanded discussion in Chapter 1 helps students become critical readers of visual texts. The chapter explains the components of images and shows students how to analyze and evaluate images.
- "Looking Ahead" images with related writing previews chapter contents.
- Each chapter discussing a pattern of development includes a graph, photograph, cartoon, or advertisement that makes use of the pattern. Study questions help students understand what the patterns of development contribute to the image and encourage them to consider it critically, further encouraging visual literacy.
- Graphic representations of the patterns, found in sections titled "Visualizing a [Name of Pattern] Essay," enhance text discussions of the patterns of development and provide important support for those visual learners who respond well to outline representations of textual material. These graphics help students to see the traditional five-paragraph essay, and encourage them to use an outlining strategy to develop longer pieces of academic writing.
- The design includes provocative Canadian images throughout that relate to or reinforce chapter material.

A Rich Variety of Opportunities for Reading and Writing

- Canadian student and professional essays—most at about the length instructors require of their students—offer models for writing and ideas for essays. Nearly all of the essays are Canadian, and most are current.
- *The Student Writer* has more student essays than most similar rhetorics. Reviewers consistently praised the student essays, calling them "empowering" because they are high-quality examples that represent attainable goals.
- One student essay in each pattern-of-development chapter is annotated as a study aid. The other student essays and all the professional essays are accompanied by pre-reading questions as well as questions about textual ideas and writing techniques.
- In addition to the student research paper, many other student essays draw on research sources, and are inspiring examples for students. All student essays appear in full, with MLA or APA bibliographic lists, in the OLC.
- Many of the professional essays demonstrate how to combine patterns of development to achieve various purposes for writing.
- Each chapter on a pattern of development includes an unusually generous number of writing topics, found in the Instructor Manual, including:
  - Several topics that require students to write in the pattern
  - Several topics that require students to respond to a theme evident in the readings
  - One topic that requires a response to visual material
  - One topic that is either cross-disciplinary or otherwise related to concerns outside the writing classroom
- Each professional essay is followed by a topic that students can discuss in class or write about in their journals.

Substantial Coverage of Argument

- A focus on issues and claims helps students write sound thesis statements for argumentation.
- A detailed discussion of kinds of persuasive purposes helps students establish reasonable goals for their argument papers.
- A detailed discussion of kinds of audiences helps students gear their supporting details to the level of resistance their claim is likely to meet.
- Explanations of logical, emotional, and ethical appeals and combining patterns of development help students address their audiences and argue their claims effectively.
- A full-colour casebook of images—advertisements, news photographs, cartoons, and diagrams—offers students insight into the ways arguments can be made in visual form.
- Authentic student essays (with source material online) illustrate effective argumentation.
- "The Writing Process" features help students move from idea generation through to proofreading.

Coverage of Research

- The Canadian edition of *The Student Writer* features two full chapters on research: Chapter 16, "Conducting Research," and Chapter 17, "Writing with Sources and Using Formal Documentation." These chapters feature:
  - Coverage of electronic research tools
  - Coverage of using the Internet to conduct research and of evaluating Internet sources
  - Full-colour annotated screenshots showing examples of library computer catalogues, periodical databases, and online search engines
  - Coverage of plagiarism, including online plagiarism
  - Full-colour, recent annotated MLA works-cited entry models with accompanying images of source material, showing students where to find citation information in a source
  - Updated guidelines from the seventh edition of the *MLA Handbook for Writers of Research Papers*
  - Information on APA style from its most current update
  - Colour-coded models accompanying every MLA and APA citation entry
  - Discussion of using sources in a brief essay to support students' ideas and of using sources as the primary detail in a traditional research paper
  - A thorough explanation of the research process
  - Information on field research
  - A discussion of how to read sources strategically
  - A student research paper in the Argument style

Coverage of Portfolios, Essay Examinations, and Writing about Literature

- The purposes of and requirements for a writing portfolio, including the self-reflection essay can be found in Chapter OLC-1 on the Online Learning Centre.

- Chapter OLC-2, also on the Online Learning Centre, explains how to write about literature. It includes instruction in reading and writing about literature, an annotated student essay in response to a poem, and a short story and poem with accompanying writing topics.

A Focus on Improving Style and Correcting Sentence-Level Errors

- "Writing Tools" and other special notes point out issues of style, organization, punctuation, and diction evident in the readings.
- Part 4, "A Guide to Frequently Occurring Errors" is a ready reference for students working to correct sentence-level mistakes. It includes concise explanations, exercises, and "ESL Notes" for students who use English as a second language.
- Chapter OLC-3, on the Online Learning Centre, on the parts of speech gives students a quick guide to supplement the explanations of grammar and usage in "A Guide to Frequently Occurring Errors."

The Canadian Edition

- Student and professional essays are on contemporary issues in Canadian and global societies.
- Chapter 14 focuses on combining patterns of development.
- Coverage of plagiarism is expanded in the "Be a Responsible Writer" sections and in the new research chapters.
- The coverage of research pays special attention to electronic research on databases.
- Chapter OLC-4 on document design, on the Online Learning Centre, helps students create effective PowerPoint slides, Web sites, and charts and diagrams for essays.
- "Occasions for Writing" sections highlight ways to use the patterns beyond the writing classroom: across the curriculum, in the workplace, and in daily life.
- A focus on analyzing visual material, discussed in Chapter 1, in the opening "Looking Ahead" images and accompanying writing assignments, in the casebook of visual arguments in Chapter 15, and in the new, colourful design that incorporates many additional images.

Supplements

- **Instructor's Manual:** Prepared by the author, Peter Grevstad, Sheridan Institute of Technology and Advanced Learning, the Instructor's Manual provides strong support for instructors and includes Chapter goals, classroom activities, journal prompts, homework activities, and answers to questions following the readings and grammar exercises.
- **Microsoft® PowerPoint® slides:** Prepared by Bronwen Welch, Camosun College, these slides offer a great visual complement for lectures.
- **Connect Catalyst:** Access to Connect Catalyst accompanies each new copy of *The Student Writer*. Available at www.mcgrawhillcatalyst.ca, Connect Catalyst offers course management and peer review tools, interactive tutorials, diagnostic tests, and thousands of electronic grammar exercises and activities.
- Additional textbook chapters are available through the Online Learning Centre at www.mcgrawhill.ca/olc.clouse.

Acknowledgments

I am indebted to the team at McGraw-Hill Ryerson, an exceptionally smart, energetic group dedicated to developing the highest-quality textbooks. A very special thanks to Christel Webb, who kindly agreed to share her writing process, and her successful research paper about palliative care nursing, with us for the Canadian edition of *The Student Writer*. Many thanks are also due to student writers from all across Canada, who submitted excellent essays to the McGraw-Hill Ryerson Power of Words competition. Many of these Canadian student essays found their way into this textbook. All of the student writing included in this edition is inspiring for both readers and writers, and the essays help us to understand issues and topics which are currently under discussion in academic institutions from coast to coast.

I am also indebted to the following reviewers, whose sound counsel informs this revision. I very much appreciate the gift of their time and expertise:

Anita Agar, *Sheridan Institute of Technology and Advanced Learning*
Anne MacKenzie-Rivers, *George Brown College*
Bronwen Welch, *Camosun College*
Christina Sommerfeldt, *University of Alberta*
D. M. Bridge, *Mount Royal College*
Deborah Torkko, *Malaspina University*
Dennis R. Nighswonger, *Lakehead University*
Diane Lehtinen, *Confederation College*
Elisabeth MacDonalde-Murray, *Brandon University*
Eloise L. Richardson, *Lakehead University*
Gill Teiman, *York University*
Gisele Baxter, *University of British Columbia*
Heather Barfoot, *Niagara College*
Jane Ann McLachlan, *Conestoga College*
Janice Stewart, *University of British Columbia*
Jennifer Clary-Lemon, *University of Winnipeg*
John LeBlanc, *UBC – Okanagan*
Karen Manarin, *Mount Royal College*
Marilyn Boyle-Taylor, *Seneca College*
Marlet Ashley, *Kwantlen Polytechnic University*
Megan Otton, *Langara College*
Melanie Fahlman Reid, *Capilano University*
Moira Langley, *Kwantlen Polytechnic University*
Norma-Jean Nielsen, *Canadore College*
Paula Crooks, *Conestoga College*
Paula Pedwell, *Georgian College*
Sarika P. Bose, *University of British Columbia*
Sue Adams, *Sheridan Institute of Technology and Advanced Learning*
Susan Johnston, *University of Regina*
Tim Brownlow, *Malaspina University*
Todd Karnas, *Memorial University*
Trisha Yeo, *George Brown College*
Wendy Shilton, *University of Prince Edward Island*

Guided Tour

Part 1 of *The Student Writer* introduces you to strategies for critical reading and to the stages of the writing process. **Part 2** provides chapters on the patterns of development, and **Part 3** shows you how to use the patterns in argument, in research papers, in literary analyses, and more. **Part 4** is a guide to correcting errors in grammar, punctuation, and mechanics.

Brief Contents

Looking Ahead sections begin every chapter in Parts 1, 2, and 3. These images with accompanying questions will help stimulate your thinking as you begin the new chapter, and give you an opportunity to practice your visual analysis skills.

Written with the kind of supportive tone often found in a writing workshop, *The Student Writer* puts you in control of your own writing process. Each chapter in Part 2 has a **"The Writing Process"** section that will help you at every stage of the writing process. **"Determining Purpose"** sections guide you in setting up your work, and **"Critique, Revise and Edit"** sections help you to look critically at your own drafts and revise them effectively.

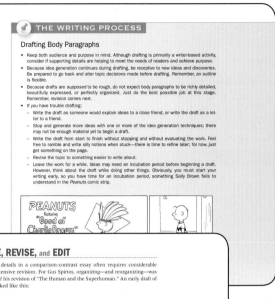

THE WRITING PROCESS

Drafting Body Paragraphs

- Keep both audience and purpose in mind. Although drafting is primarily a writer-based activity, consider if supporting details are helping to meet the needs of readers and achieve purpose.
- Because idea generation continues during drafting, be receptive to new ideas and discoveries. Be prepared to go back and alter topic decisions made before drafting. Remember, an outline is flexible.
- Because drafts are *supposed* to be rough, do not expect body paragraphs to be richly detailed, beautifully expressed, or perfectly organized. Just do the best possible job at this stage. Remember, revision comes next.
- If you have trouble drafting:
  – Write the draft as someone would explain ideas to a close friend, or write the draft as a letter to a friend.
  – Stop and generate more ideas with one or more of the idea generation techniques; there may not be enough material yet to begin a draft.
  – Write the draft from start to finish without stopping and without evaluating the work. Feel free to ramble and write silly notions when stuck—there is time to refine later; for now, just get something on the page.
  – Revise the topic to something easier to write about.
  – Leave the work for a while. Ideas may need an incubation period before beginning a draft. However, think about the draft while doing other things. Obviously, you must start your writing early, so you have time for an incubation period, something Sally Brown fails to understand in the *Peanuts* comic strip.

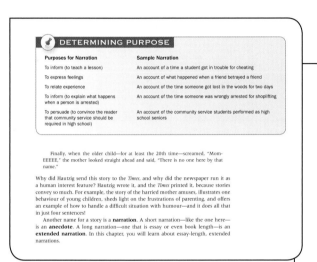

DETERMINING PURPOSE

Purposes for Narration	Sample Narration
To inform (to teach a lesson)	An account of a time a student got in trouble for cheating
To express feelings	An account of what happened when a friend betrayed a friend
To relate experience	An account of the time someone got lost in the woods for two days
To inform (to explain what happens when a person is arrested)	An account of the time someone was wrongly arrested for shoplifting
To persuade (to convince the reader that community service should be required in high school)	An account of the community service students performed as high school seniors

Finally, when the older child—for at least the 20th time—screamed, "Mom-EEEEE," the mother looked straight ahead and said, "There is no one here by that name."

Why did Hautzig send this story to the *Times*, and why did the newspaper run it as a human interest feature? Hautzig wrote it, and the *Times* printed it, because stories convey so much. For example, the story of the harried mother amuses, illustrates one behaviour of young children, sheds light on the frustrations of parenting, and offers an example of how to handle a difficult situation with humour—and it does all that in just four sentences!

Another name for a story is a **narration**. A short narration—like the one here—is an **anecdote**. A long narration—one that is essay or even book length—is an **extended narration**. In this chapter, you will learn about essay-length, extended narrations.

CRITIQUE, REVISE, and EDIT

Organizing the details in a comparison-contrast essay often requires considerable thought and extensive revision. For Gus Spirtos, organizing—and reorganizing—was a primary part of his revision of "The Human and the Superhuman." An early draft of paragraph 2 looked like this:

Early draft

Superman and Batman were the products of different inspirations. In 1938, Jerry Siegel and Joe Schuster envisioned an immensely powerful character with super powers and abilities. This character became Superman, a hero motivated by idealism, who was "more powerful than a locomotive." Unlike Superman, Batman was created with the human element in mind. In 1939, Bob Kane envisioned a hero motivated by avenging the murder of his parents. The public responded to the concept of revenge. It still responds to this concept, as urban society becomes increasingly violent. Whereas Batman is a warrior fighting a never-ending battle against crime, Superman is an idealistic role model who fights crime for high idealistic purposes.

The paragraph is structured well enough: The first sentence is the topic sentence indicating that the point of contrast is the different inspirations. However, Gus felt that the details were "squashed" into the paragraph. He also felt that using the point-by-point pattern in the paragraph made it hard to develop points. He kept feeling the need to alternate back and forth too quickly. At his teacher's suggestion, Gus reorganized to create two paragraphs. Compare the above version with paragraphs 2 and 3 in the final essay. Does the final version work better? Should Gus have made other changes?

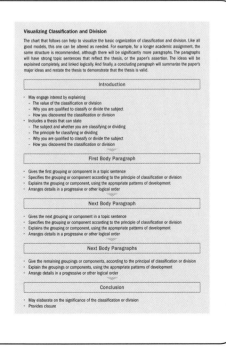

Visualizing Classification and Division

The chart that follows can help to visualize the basic organization of classification and division. Like all good models, this one can be altered as needed. For example, for a longer academic assignment, the same structure is recommended, although there will be significantly more paragraphs. The paragraphs will have strong topic sentences that reflect the thesis, or the paper's assertion. The ideas will be explained completely, and linked logically. And finally, a concluding paragraph will summarize the paper's major ideas and restate the thesis to demonstrate that the thesis is valid.

Introduction

- May engage interest by explaining
  – The value of the classification or division
  – Why you are qualified to classify or divide the subject
  – How you discovered the classification or division
- Includes a thesis that can state
  – The subject and whether you are classifying or dividing
  – The principle for classifying or dividing
  – Why you are qualified to classify or divide the subject
  – How you discovered the classification or division

First Body Paragraph

- Gives the first grouping or component in a topic sentence
- Specifies the grouping or component according to the principle of classification or division
- Explains the grouping or component, using the appropriate patterns of development
- Arranges details in a progressive or other logical order

Next Body Paragraph

- Gives the next grouping or component in a topic sentence
- Specifies the grouping or component according to the principle of classification or division
- Explains the grouping or component, using the appropriate patterns of development
- Arranges details in a progressive or other logical order

Next Body Paragraphs

- Give the remaining groupings or components, according to the principal of classification or division
- Explain the groupings or components, using the appropriate patterns of development
- Arrange details in a progressive or other logical order

Conclusion

- May elaborate on the significance of the classification or division
- Provides closure

Diagrams of the patterns of development reinforce the text discussion of each pattern by helping to visualize how the pattern works in an essay.

Essays written by professional authors—including Pre-Reading sections focus on comprehension and analysis—and by other students—including the Christel's Essay in Progress feature in Chapters 2–5—provide real-life examples that illustrate the concepts presented in the text.

CRITICAL READING PROFESSIONAL ESSAYS

Pre-reading

1. People seem to value the concept of being busy, or over-scheduled. Why is this?
2. Western culture's focus on productivity may lead to losses in other areas of life. Consider what might be lost as we rush from one task to another.
3. Many people pride themselves on juggling many obligations, and call it multi-tasking. Is this really an effective way to manage professional and social commitments?

Our Schedules, Ourselves
Jay Walljasper

1   DAMN! You're 20 minutes—no, more like half an hour—late for your breakfast meeting, which you were hoping to scoot out of early to make an 8:30 seminar across town. And, somewhere in there, there's that conference call. Now, at the last minute, you have to be at a 9:40 meeting. No way you can miss it. Let's see, the afternoon is totally booked, but you can probably push back your 10:15 appointment and work through lunch. That would do it. Whew! The day has barely begun and already you are counting the hours until this evening, when you can finally go home and happily, gloriously, triumphantly, do nothing. You'll skip yoga class, blow off the neighborhood meeting, ignore the piles of laundry and just relax. Yes! . . . No! Tonight's the night of the concert. You promised Nathan and Mara weeks ago that you would go. *DAMN!*

2   Welcome to daily grind circa 2003—a grueling 24-7 competition against the clock that leaves even the winners wondering what happened to their lives. Determined and sternly focused, we march through each day obeying the orders of our

actually get everything done that we had planned before collapsing into bed at night.

3   On the job, in school, at home, increasing numbers of North Americans are virtual slaves to their schedules. Some of what fills our days are onerous obligations, some are wonderful opportunities, and most fall in between, but taken together they add up to too much. Too much to do, too many places to be, too many things happening too fast, all mapped out for us in precise quarterhour allotments on our Palm Pilots or day planners. We are not leading our lives, but merely following a dizzying timetable of duties, commitments, demands, and options. How did this happen? Where's the luxurious leisure that decades of technological progress was supposed to bestow upon us?

4   The acceleration of the globalized economy, and the accompanying decline of people having any kind of a say over wages and working conditions, is a chief culprit. Folks at the bottom of the socioeconomic ladder feel the pain most sharply.

CRITICAL READING STUDENT ESSAY

"Media Stereotyping of Muslims as Terrorists," the following student essay, includes research material as part of its supporting details. Be sure to consider how that research helps the writer achieve his purpose.

Student Essay with Research

Media Stereotyping of Muslims as Terrorists
Thomas Baird

1   Because the media shape what we believe, the negative portrayal of an ethnic group or social class by the media can be detrimental. Nazi Germany understood this correlation and manipulated it to undermine Jews with anti-Semitic propaganda. Whereas the Nazis were confined to radio broadcasts and pamphlets, today's media can spread an image instantly anywhere in the world via satellites. Although anti-Semitic portrayals have lessened substantially, media stereotyping of Muslims is at an all-time high. Through the deliberate portrayal of the Islamic faith as one of violence, the media, including Hollywood films, succeed in stereotyping Muslims as radical terrorists.

2   Depicting Muslims almost exclusively as terrorists is one way Hollywood stereotypes Muslims. In the movie *True Lies*, for example, Palestinian Muslims are portrayed as murderous terrorists plotting to kill thousands of innocent Americans. The Muslim group is called "Crimson Jihad," and their ultimate goal is to incinerate Miami with an atomic bomb. The intervention of Arnold Schwarzenegger's commando-like character is required to prevent these radicals from accomplishing this unspeakable act. In one scene, an Uzi tossed down a flight of stairs unintentionally cuts down a roomful of Arabs. Intended to be comical, this scene was surely offensive to Arab Muslim viewers. The terrorists are viewed as inhuman because their goals include mass murder, yet the accidental murder of a roomful of Muslims is supposed to stir laughter.

3   *Executive Decision* is another movie that employs Muslim characters as villains. In this movie, Muslims hijack a passenger jet, terrorize passengers, kill a flight attendant, and prepare to unload enough lethal nerve gas to kill the millions of residents of Washington, D.C., and the neighboring East Coast. Throughout the movie, Islam itself is equated with violence. At one point, a

Notice that Baird begins with a generalization, and that he develops the first paragraph with historical examples, before he presents his thesis in the last sentence.

Again, there is a generalization in the topic sentence, followed immediately by an example from a Hollywood film.

Here, Baird continues to use examples to develop the thesis that Hollywood films portray Muslims as villainous individuals.

Christel's Essay in Progress: REVISING THE FIRST DRAFT

Christel was pleased with her first draft, which appears on page 88. She knew it needed work, but felt that she had a good start with her thesis, and strong support for her argument that there must be more support for palliative care in Canada. Christel worked with a peer editor, and the editor reviewed her draft using the following questions:

1.   What is the thesis of the essay?

The thesis for this draft of the essay is that there is no benefit to palliative care. However, the essay goes on to offer criticism of the health care system, and indicates that there is neither enough funding nor enough training, given that Canada has an aging population. Would you consider changing the thesis in a future draft of the essay?

2.   Is there anything that does not relate to the thesis?

Can you distinguish between end-of-life care and palliative care? Are they the same? If they are, then the essay is fine, but perhaps readers would be confused about the differences between end-of-life care for Canada's elderly (and aging) population, and end-of-life care for any Canadian who might be suffering from a terminal illness like cancer or AIDS. Should this be explained in the introduction?

medical interventions and patient DNR (do no resuscitate) orders? oxygen, heart pumps, or feeding?

could say more about provincial funded system. Are there public e sector?

h ideas is not clear?

t population. Does this relate to nsidering the elderly? Or are we ng-term or palliative care?

o provide an anecdote, or a sta tention and make them want to evelops.

lative care can be a waste of resources—is mirrored in the conclusion. You suggest that palliative care is "a burden." It might be necessary to detail how this burden affects families, patients, and health care professionals. Be more specific.

8.   What is the best part of the essay?

The essay flows well logically, and presents an argument around most Canadians don't think much about, until they have to arra terminally ill or elderly relative. For this reason, people should s notice.

9.   What is the weakest part of the essay?

The thesis. It could use revision for unity, and it needs to be m terms of what the paper will address. Are you convinced there is

10.   Is the focus sufficiently narrow, so that the central issue is examine

The paper should focus, perhaps, on only one type of patien elderly and the terminally ill will be considered, there needs to b

With an aging population, Statistics will increase by 33% by the year 202 the aging population, there is an i 2008 the CHPCA noted that "in 2007 nosed by a physician as having a ch more deaths. "Chronic diseases ac specially educated health profession specialized care. Doctors and nurse palliative care.

---

ionals help, since so known as palia affects more than rvivors of the dying system, and health

ain due to disease re their loved ones n Canada are not ze the life that the g oxygen therapy, nd limited medical hese decisions for e. However, family

PARAGRAPH 1
Christel revised the thesis of the paper. While it does seem more general, it is clearer in that it identifies the topic and controlling idea, and provides a grammatically correct preview for the five-paragraph essay

PARAGRAPH 2
The first body paragraph is much clearer. It defines the main goals of palliative care, and provides specific examples of choices patients and families make in a

PARAGRAPH 4
In the third body paragraph, Christel has added more detail with reference to the stresses that medical personnel experience caring for terminally ill patients. This helps to further the argument that there should be better training, and increased funding for this sector in Canada's health care industry

PARAGRAPH 5
Christel's conclusion for her five-paragraph essay includes references to the ideas which she has modified in her paper, restates the thesis, and identifies the consequences of ignoring or not funding this important public service.

4   The health care professionals necessary to deliver end of life care are under substantial psychological strain, watching people die every day. This leaves them feeling defeated and helpless, as palliative care goes against the principles of healing. There are not enough support programs for these health care workers, which would assist them in meeting the challenges surrounding palliative care. There are also ethical issues with which care providers have to struggle. Palliative care may be contradictory to medical staff's personal beliefs. Furthermore, alternatives in palliative care may be against medical personnel's personal beliefs. For example, there are many moral and ethical issues surrounding medically assisted death.

5   There are considerable issues surrounding end-of-life care, including the patients' wishes and strain on individuals as families suffer loss. Financially straitened health care providers may be unable to provide this type of care in addition to regular patient care. The burden that this type of care places on health professionals can cause "professional and emotional stress [which] may result due to repeated exposure to pain and suffering, failed attempts to alleviate that suffering, repeated deaths, distress and existential of patients and families" (Sabo, 2008). The effect of this continuing stress may lead to compassion fatigue and caregiver burnout. Canadians need to evaluate possible access to alternatives allowing life to end sooner, if they wish, therefore easing the burden felt by all involved. Palliative care can cause needless further suffering to the patient, and strain on provincial health care systems and health care professionals, making it an ineffective service as it exists today to Canadians.

Reprinted by permission of Christel Webb.

Each chapter on a pattern in Part 2 also includes a
photograph, diagram, cartoon, or **advertisement**
that makes use of the pattern, and study questions
that help you read the visual critically.

Print advertisement for the Toyota Prius, a car that runs on a combination of gasoline and electricity.

Why is Description Important?

Description adds an important dimension to our lives because it moves our emotions and expands our experience. When we read descriptions of beautiful places and scenes, we are uplifted; when we read newspaper accounts of the devastation of wars and natural disasters, we are saddened. Description expands our experience by taking us to places we might not otherwise know much about, which explains the popularity of descriptive travel essays in magazines and newspapers. Description can also give us a fresh appreciation for the familiar. For example, a description of a neighbourhood park can help someone who passes it every day rediscover its beauty.

In "Weren't We All So Young Then?" an essay for her regular Newsweek column, Anna Quindlen wrote about the attack on the World Trade Center in 2001 as a defining moment that marked a loss of innocence for people in her generation. She begins her essay with this description:

> Nightfall is as dramatic as the city itself in the days surrounding the winter solstice. The gray comes down fast, pearl to iron to charcoal in a matter of minutes, muting the hard edges of the buildings until in the end they seem to disappear, to be replaced by floating rectangles of lantern yellow and silvered white. In the space of an hour the city turns from edge to glow, steel to light.
>
> Because of this effect it is possible, at least when the moon is on the wane, to stand on Greenwich north of Canal and imagine that in the darkness to the south stand the Twin Towers of the Trade Center. It is just that someone has forgotten to put the lights on, leaving the two giants to brood invisible in the night.

🖊 OCCASIONS FOR WRITING

Description in the Classroom

You may be surprised by how important description is across the disciplines. For example, in a paper for an advertising class, students might describe the persuasive visuals in print advertisements. For a history class, student writers might describe the conditions in a 1920s sweatshop. For an art exam, one might describe the technique of a particular artist. Think about three classes you are taking this term or expect to take soon. How might description be part of the reading and writing for those classes? What would be lost if the descriptive component were eliminated from the classes?

Description in Daily Life

Description is important to the writing students do in personal life. Diary, journal, or blog entries might include descriptions of people and scenes. Vacation letters and emails to friends and family will describe places writers visit. And in a toast for a friend's award banquet, a speaker might describe that person's best traits. *If you were involved in an auto accident and had to complete an accident report for your insurance company, how might you use description? Which of the purposes of writing would the description fulfill?*

Description on the Job

Description is often used on the job. Engineers and architects, for example, write descriptions of building sites. Campus admissions officials write promotional materials describing a campus or academic program. Police officers describe crime scenes and suspects in their reports. Social workers describe domestic situations. Nurses describe patient symptoms. Pharmacists describe how to take a particular medicine. *How do travel agents use description? What about newspaper reporters? What job do you hope to pursue after finishing school? How would description be useful in this job?*

Occasions for Writing boxes in each chapter of
Part 2 explore the pattern discussed in a variety of
contexts, and demonstrate how it can be used to
achieve a range of writing aims.

The Research Process

Whether using sources to supplement personal ideas in an essay or writing a research paper, you want to work efficiently. Efficient procedures are particularly important these days to manage the explosion of information made possible by the Internet. The procedures explained in this chapter can help you plan a timeline for creating a paper as well as help to locate, analyze, and organize sources. Some of the procedures are suitable for finding sources to support personal ideas in an essay; others will help you write a research paper.

Create a Timeline for a Research Paper

A research paper is a complex assignment that cannot be completed quickly. You should create a timeline to manage your time and stay organized while working through the planning, research, drafting, and citation phases of a paper. Using the chart below, set deadlines for each step in the research process based on the amount of time assigned to complete a paper. Keeping these deadlines in mind will help you to stay on track and avoid last-minute panic.

Completion Date	Step in Process
	Choose a broad topic (see page 381).
	Narrow the topic and draft a preliminary thesis (and, if necessary, have the topic or thesis approved by the instructor) (see pages 382–384).
	Locate sources in the library, on the Internet, and through field research (see pages 384, 391, and 396).
	Compile a working bibliography (see page 398).
	Evaluate sources (see page 399).
	Take notes (see page 401).
	Create an outline (see page 408).
	Write a first draft (see page 408).
	Check in-text documentation and create a works-cited or references page (depending on whether you are using MLA or APA style) (see pages 419–442).
	Revise and edit a second draft (see pages 442–443).
	Format and submit your final paper (see page 453).

Research coverage in Chapters 16 and 17 provides comprehensive overview of the research process, including extensive coverage of electronic research tools, MLA and APA citation, drafting and editing essays with sources, and more.

Expanded coverage of **avoiding plagiarism** in both print and electronic contexts will help you maintain a high ethical standard for your writing.

What to Document

In the sections that follow, you will find extensive coverage of how to give credit properly for outside sources in writing. Providing this credit is called **documentation**.

Every time you use the words, ideas, or opinions of others, you must document that material. You must document facts that are not common knowledge, including statistics, references to studies, descriptions of experiments, an author's original ideas, an author's opinion, and an author's conclusion—regardless of whether this material appears in a paper as quotation, paraphrase, or summary. Each of these methods of incorporating others' ideas must be documented with a citation, and referenced correctly in the appropriate documentation style.

Facts that are common knowledge need not be documented. Thus, you don't need to document that John A. MacDonald was the first Prime Minister of Canada, that gravity holds the planets in orbit, or that plants bend toward the sun. Nor do you need to document dates that are not debatable, such as the date Canada became a country, or common sayings, such as "Fools rush in where wise men fear to tread."

If in doubt about whether to document a point, err on the side of caution. It is better to document too much than to document too little and plagiarize as a result. Of course, instructors can advise when you are unsure.

How to Avoid Plagiarism When Paraphrasing

One of the most common forms of plagiarism occurs when a student paraphrases a passage from a source but does not sufficiently alter the author's words and style. Even when you properly acknowledge that the material is borrowed, you will still be guilty of plagiarism if the paraphrase is too close to the original. Consider the following example, which includes a passage from a textbook and a student paraphrase of it that qualifies as plagiarism:

> From *The American Tradition in Literature*, 11th edition, by George and Barbara Perkins, page 553:
>
> A former orator, Red Jacket (or Sagoyewatha) was skilled in humorous and sarcastic speeches in defence of the traditions of the Five Nations of the Iroquois, of which his Seneca tribe was a part.

Student paraphrase considered plagiarism	A former orator, Sagoyewatha, also known as Red Jacket, was skilled in witty and sarcastic speeches on behalf of the Five Nations of the Iroquois, of which his Seneca tribe was a member (Perkins and Perkins, 553).

If you want to include the exact words of another writer, it is necessary to use quotation marks. Do not use a thesaurus, or change every third word of a source, and think that the original source is now changed sufficiently. For further coverage of paraphrasing, see page 403.

How to Avoid Online Plagiarism

Be particularly careful of plagiarism when downloading sources. It is very easy to copy sections from an online source and paste them into a paper, forgetting to use

CALVIN AND HOBBES © 1995 Watterson. Dist. by Universal Press Syndicate. Reprinted with permission. All rights reserved.

CHAPTER 1

The Connection between Reading and Writing

Looking Ahead

Reading is an important part of all your college and university classes, including the writing class you are currently taking. This chapter discusses the importance of reading for students, explains how reading and writing are connected, and describes procedures to follow when reading important material.

To preview this chapter, consider the answers to these questions:

- Why is reading so important in higher education?

- What point about reading does the Calvin and Hobbes cartoon make?

- How is the importance of reading reflected in the cartoon?

The connection between reading and writing is a strong and important one, especially for college and university students. For one thing, writing in response to reading is the most important way scholars, including student scholars, communicate with one another. Teachers, students, and researchers write about their findings, debate important issues, and discuss matters of interest in scholarly journals, newsletters, listservs, electronic message boards, books, student newspapers, and research papers. Other teachers, students, and researchers read these materials and write their responses, and so the conversation continues.

Students are frequently asked to read material and then write in response to what they read, as they are part of a community of writers, a group of people who read and react in writing in order to share ideas, report on developments, and argue points of view. In addition, writing in response to reading is an important part of college and university life because it helps students grapple with ideas and determine reactions to them. In short, writing in response to reading helps students learn.

Finally, the more we read, the more aware we become of readers' needs. You can bring this awareness to writing and do a better job of using the words and details that best address particular readers. You also become more sensitive readers of your own drafts. This sensitivity helps you judge what changes you should make. In other words, students become more reliable critics, and better editors of their own writing.

Reading Analytically

College and university reading must be **analytical reading**. To read analytically, pay close attention to ideas, evaluate their merit, and consider how they relate to other ideas you have encountered, both in and out of the classroom. Question assumptions, draw conclusions, form opinions, test ideas, weigh things out, judge the significance of points, reconsider, and perhaps change your mind about important scholarly and social issues.

Step 1: Preview the Material

Before reading, preview the material in the ways described below. Previewing is helpful because it gives the reader a sense of what the reading is about, it piques interest in the material, and it improves reading comprehension.

1. Consider the title and author, for they may hint at what you can expect. Some titles will be a good indication of content, and some will not. You may have heard of the author or read something else by him or her. Together or separately, the author and title may suggest how important the piece is, whether it will be humorous or serious, and whether it aims to inform or persuade.
2. Read headings, picture captions, and bold and italicized type. Look at pictures, charts, and lists. These offer clues to content and will suggest how the piece is organized.
3. Read the introductory paragraph and the first sentence of all other paragraphs. This preview reveals the selection's main points. It can also suggest how challenging the material is, address a level of interest in the subject, and remind you of your familiarity with the text's ideas.

Based on a preview, reflect on expectations for readings. What questions will the reading answer? What information will it provide? What will it communicate? Consider expectations, keep an open mind, and allow for the possibility that the author may go in an unexpected direction and not meet initial expectations.

Step 2: Read Thoughtfully

Analytical reading is thoughtful reading that requires active engagement with the material. Generally, it requires reading a selection more than once; a particularly challenging piece may need several readings. Specifically, you should do the following:

1. Determine the author's thesis.
2. Consider the intended audience and purpose.
3. Distinguish between facts and opinions.
4. Make inferences: Consider what the author may imply.
5. Make connections: Connect ideas within the reading, and connect ideas to issues in the world outside the text.
6. Assess the quality of the material and the arguments in it.
7. Draw conclusions based upon a close reading.
8. Highlight and annotate the text while reading (see SQ3R later in this chapter).

Determine the Author's Thesis

The **thesis** is what the reading is about; it is the main idea the author wants to convey. Sometimes the thesis is specifically stated near the beginning or at the end of an essay in one or more sentences. Sometimes it is implied rather than stated, and students must determine the main points from the evidence in the text. Either way, to be an analytical reader, you must identify the main points of what you are reading. (For a more detailed explanation of the thesis of an essay, see page 51.)

Consider the Intended Audience and Purpose

What audience is the author writing for, and why? Was the piece written for readers of a metropolitan newspaper, specialists who subscribe to a professional journal, parents of teenagers, or undergraduate students? Does the author want to convey information, share an experience, persuade the reader to think a certain way, or call the reader to action? While reading, consider how the author addresses the needs of the intended audience and works to achieve his or her purpose for writing. For example, consider the strategies the writer uses to engage the reader's interest, look for ideas that are particularly relevant to the audience, and notice the language the author uses to fulfill his or her purpose. Use some of these strategies to respond to some of the author's ideas in academic writing.

Distinguish between Facts and Opinions

A **fact** has already been proven or it can be proven: "It is a *fact* that genetic testing can tell people whether they will contract certain diseases." An **opinion**, on the other hand, is a belief or judgment, so it cannot be proven: "It is my *opinion* that people are better off not knowing whether they are going to get certain diseases." Writing is often a blend of fact and opinion, and an analytical reader is careful to distinguish between the two. A skilful writer can make an opinion seem like fact, so read critically. For example, consider this statement:

> It is a fact that transparency in campaign finance, which is favoured by most of the electorate, is necessary to restore faith in the political system.

Is it really a fact that campaign finance reform is favoured by most of the electorate? Maybe it is, and you can find this out with a bit of research. Is it a fact that the reform is necessary to restore faith in the political system? No, this is an opinion—even though it is presented as a fact.

Many people think that facts are better than opinions, but this is not uniformly true. Both facts and opinions are important. When trying to decide whom to vote for, voters gather facts about the candidates and read editorial opinions about who is likely to do the best job. Together, the facts and opinions can help voters decide. Also, a reasoned, well-supported opinion is extremely valuable, particularly because so much in life cannot be proven. For example, is cloning a good idea? No facts say yes or no, but thoughtful essays offering opinions on the implications of cloning can help readers decide.

Facts also form the basis for well-reasoned opinions. However, facts can be misleading. Statistics seem compelling—but they can steer a reader in the wrong direction if they are not current. Results of research studies seem like solid evidence—but they can be incomplete or outdated, or from a study that many scientists find faulty.

Thus, to be an analytical reader, you must identify facts and the opinions, and determine how reliable the facts are and how well reasoned and supported the opinions are.

Make Inferences

When you make an **inference**, you read between the lines. That is, you think beyond what is overtly *stated* to draw conclusions about what is *suggested*. Consider the following passage:

> Last week MPs voted overwhelmingly for a bill supporting physician-assisted suicide. The importance of the legislation is historic, as no prior law had legalized physician-assisted suicide. By passing a law allowing the practice, MPs sent a strong message to those who want it criminalized.

One can read between the lines to infer that legislators faced strong lobbying against physician-assisted suicide. The passage does not explicitly say so, but the clue is there: The lawmakers were trying to send a message, and the logical recipients of that message are people who oppose physician-assisted suicide.

To be an analytical reader, make inferences, but make reasonable ones. Inferences must be supported by the text. It is not reasonable, for example, to infer from the above passage that some policymakers are anti-life. Nothing in the passage supports that notion.

Make Connections

Analytical readers relate information—both facts and opinions—to their own experience and knowledge. For example, when the author of "School Is Bad for Children" on page 7 says that in school a child learns to feel "worthless [and] untrustworthy," you might be reminded of a time you lost self-confidence when, say, an essay earned a low grade.

In this case, personal experience bears out what the author says. You may also be able to relate what the author says to something you have learned. A fact or concept learned in an educational psychology class, for example, may relate to an idea in "School Is Bad for Children," perhaps by exemplifying it, lending it credence, or refuting it.

When you connect readings to your knowledge and experience, you remember the information better because you relate it to what you already know and have experienced. Thus, the reading ceases to be an isolated text and becomes an integral part of understanding. Such connections can also provide topics for student writing.

Assess the Quality of Source Material

People tend to trust the printed word, often believing that anything published in print or online is reliable. However, much published material is untrustworthy, so an analytical reader does not believe everything s/he reads. Evaluate the quality of the material by asking questions like these:

- Is the thesis adequately supported? Are there enough convincing details to explain or prove the thesis?
- Is the author offering facts, opinions, or both? Is the author stating opinions as facts? Is the author an expert? Are statistics and other information current (i.e. last five years)? Are opinions backed up with evidence?
- Is the treatment of controversial issues fair and balanced, or does the author ignore opposing viewpoints? (For more on dealing with opposition views, see raising and countering objections on page 355.)
- What is the source of details? Is the author writing from personal experience, from observations, or from research findings? Are the sources for the author's details reliable? Read and evaluate the source text's bibliography to determine reliability.

Draw Conclusions

Reflect on the reading and draw conclusions. Agree or disagree with the author. What is the significance of the material? How can the ideas be applied? For example, when reading "School Is Bad for Children" (page 7), either agree with the author's belief that students should work collaboratively, or disagree with his notion that students should evaluate their own work. Also, decide whether the essay's significance lies in the important implications it has for education reform. Make inferences using the author's assertions. Evaluate assertions from the reading, and relate the author's ideas to personal experience.

Highlight and Annotate the Text

Thoughtful reading should be done with a highlighter pen and a pencil in hand, to mark the text while reading. Marking a text will stimulate thinking about it, provide a record of observations so they are available for class discussions and written responses, and highlight main points as a study aid. The following strategies can help to mark a text productively. In addition, an example of a marked text appears on page 7.

1. Underline or highlight the thesis and main points. Avoid marking too much; the goal is to emphasize the most important ideas.
2. If reading for a specific purpose, underline, highlight, bracket, or checkmark the points that will help achieve that purpose. For example, while reading an essay to

write a paper about, note any ideas that can be paper topics. Develop and use a system of symbols for notation, comment, or summary.

3. Jot down responses—such as conclusions, areas of agreement and disagreement, personal associations and connections, and questions—in the margins. Note passages in the text that stimulate the most thinking. Write responses in one margin and summarize text ideas in the other. Highlight unclear or confusing passages, and prepare to raise questions about them in class.

Step 3: Review and Write for Study and Retention

You need to remember textbook material and other assigned readings important enough to require analytical reading. A good way to review is to return to the text and follow these guidelines:

1. Reread the underlined or highlighted material. Think about each point. Is everything clear? Is the significance of the main points clear? Does the author support or explain everything? Reread the relevant paragraphs to ensure understanding.

2. Review and reflect upon marginal notes. Are there any questions that remain unanswered? If so, ask those questions in class.

3. Writing is an excellent way to "set" information and to do deep learning. Write a summary of the selection, following the guidelines on page 12, and then write a summary that reacts to the selection. Also, write an outline of the piece that includes the most important ideas, or write test questions for the selection and then answer them.

Study Tip: The SQ3R Reading Strategy

SQ3R is a helpful strategy for academic success. It is a five-step process that closely relates the process described above. Critical reading and writing are recursive, or ongoing processes. SQ3R is useful for students because the process can be internalized, eventually becoming automatic. The process requires a text, and writing tools.

SQ3R is a reading strategy developed by Johnson (1971). A professor of Psychology, Johnson decided that his students would have better results in their studies if they engaged in reading actively, and used a process referred to as elaboration. This is a term borrowed from cognitive psychology. Its core idea indicates that the more readers engage in, and make knowledge connections while reading, the greater their reading retention will be, and the better their academic results will be. This strategy encourages students to elaborate their schema, or systems of knowledge and reference, to improve their comprehension of new material. There are five recursive steps in the process: Survey, Question, Read, Recite, and Review. The five steps in the process reflect the suggestions above. Here's how they work.

To **Survey**, you skim titles, headings and subheadings, review questions, study guides, topic sentences, the introductory paragraph, and the concluding paragraph. You highlight these with a highlighter pen, to establish the reading's organization and structure. This also aids in prediction of content in the reading, and helps you in other steps in the process.

In step two, **Question**, you examine questions that have been assigned or form questions of your own, which hopefully you will be able to answer by the end of the reading session. Student readers and writers may form questions based upon titles, subtitles, captions, and topic sentences. You should record questions in the form of marginal notes on the text, or on a separate sheet of paper or note card, using the Cornell Method to compare notes from reading with lecture notes (see http://lsc.sas.cornell.edu/Sidebars/Study_Skills_Resources/cornellsystem.pdf). Alternatively, you could store their questions electronically, either in a document, or online in the Course Management System your institution uses.

Step three, **Read**, requires that you proceed through the text methodically. You should continue to highlight the text's main ideas and key vocabulary, and record questions and responses either in the text's margins (best) or on note cards. You should read complex passages slowly, or aloud, if need be, in order to assure understanding. It is best to read in blocks of 30–40 minutes, to ensure maximum concentration and retention.

Step four, **Recite**, requires that you put your notes, questions, answers, and responses to the reading into an oral form. This is valuable, as it checks comprehension, and continues to allow you to make connections between what you are reading and what you have heard in lectures, and to link these with knowledge of the subject you may already have. It also serves as a study aid, when you are preparing for a test or examination.

Finally, you **Review** (and Revise if necessary). This step is closely associated with the Survey and the Recite stages of active reading. You prepare summaries or study guides for material you have read, and use these materials to prepare for formal assessments in the way of quizzes, tests, or examinations. If you have applied the strategy successfully, you will be better prepared for, and more successful in your studies.

A Sample Marked Text

The following example gives you an idea of how analytic readers can mark a text. Notice that main ideas are underlined and that reactions, questions, and personal connections are recorded in the margins.

CRITICAL READING PROFESSIONAL ESSAY

School Is Bad for Children

John Holt

1   Almost every child, on the first day he sets foot in a school building, is smarter, more curious, less afraid of what he doesn't know, better at finding and figuring things out, more confident, resourceful, persistent and independent than he will ever be again in his schooling—or, unless he is very

unusual and very lucky, for the rest of his life. Already, by paying close attention to and interacting with the world and people around him, and without any school-type formal instruction, he has done a task far more difficult, complicated, and abstract than anything he will be asked to do in school, or than any of his teachers has done for years. He has solved the mystery of language. He has discovered it—babies don't even know that language exists—and he has found out how it works and learned to use it. He has done it by exploring, by experimenting, by developing his own model of the grammar of language, by trying it out and seeing whether it works, by gradually changing it and refining it until it does work. And while he has been doing this, he has been learning other things as well, including many of the "concepts" that the schools think only they can teach him, and many that are more complicated than the ones they do try to teach him.

2   In he comes, this curious, patient, determined, energetic, skilful learner. We sit him down at a desk, and <u>what do we teach him</u>? Many things. First, that <u>learning is separate from living</u>. "You come to school to learn," we tell him, as if the child hadn't been learning before, as if living were out there and learning were in here, and there were no connection between the two. Secondly, that <u>he cannot be trusted to learn and is no good at it</u>. Everything we teach about reading, a task far simpler than many that the child has already mastered, says to him, "If we don't make you read, you won't, and if you don't do it exactly the way we tell you, you can't." In short, <u>he comes to feel that learning is a passive process, something that someone else does to you, instead of something you do for yourself.</u>

Sexist: What about females?

3   <u>In a great many other ways, he learns that he is worthless, untrustworthy, fit only to take other people's orders, a blank sheet for other people to write on</u>. Oh, we make a lot of nice noises in school about respect for the child and individual differences, and the like. <u>But our acts, as opposed to our talk, say to the child, "Your experience, your concerns, your curiosities</u>, your needs, what you know, what you want, what you wonder about, what you hope for, what you fear, what you like and dislike, what you are good at or not so

good at—all this <u>is of not the slightest importance, it counts for nothing</u>. What counts here, and the only thing that counts, is what we know, what we think is important, what we want you to do, think, and be." <u>The child soon learns not to ask questions</u>—the teacher isn't there to satisfy his curiosity. Having learned to hide his curiosity, he later learns to be ashamed of it. Given no chance to find out who he is—and to develop that person, whoever it is— <u>he soon comes to accept the adults' evaluation of him</u>.

Yes! I've seen this happen many times.

4   He learns many other things. <u>He learns that to be wrong, uncertain, confused, is a crime. Right Answers are what the school wants, and he learns countless strategies for prying these answers out of the teacher, for conning her into thinking he knows what he doesn't know</u>. He learns to dodge, bluff, fake, cheat. <u>He learns to be lazy</u>. Before he came to school, he would work for hours on end, on his own, with no thought of reward, at the business of making sense of the world and gaining competence in it. In school he learns, like every buck private, how to goldbrick, how not to work when the sergeant isn't looking, how to know when he is looking, how to make him think you are working even when he is looking. He learns that in real life you don't do anything unless you are bribed, bullied, or conned into doing it, that nothing is worth doing for its own sake, or that if it is, you can't do it in school. He learns to be bored, to work with a small part of his mind, to escape from the reality around him into daydreams and fantasies—but not like the fantasies of his preschool years, in which he played a very active part.

School becomes a game.

Yes, just do the minimum to get by.

5   <u>The child comes to school curious about other people, particularly other children, and the school teaches him to be indifferent</u>. The most interesting thing in the classroom—often the only interesting thing in it— is the other children, <u>but he has to act as if these other children, all about him, only a few feet away, are not really there</u>. He cannot interact with them, talk with them, smile at them. In many schools he can't talk to other children in the halls between classes; in more than a few, and some of these

This guy really hates teachers.

in stylish suburbs, he can't even talk to them at lunch. Splendid training for a world in which, when you're not studying the other person to figure out how to do him in, you pay no attention to him.

6   In fact, he learns how to live without paying attention to anything going on around him. *Nice sarcasm.* You might say that school is a long lesson in how to turn yourself off, which *I disagree here.* may be one reason why so many young people, seeking the awareness of the world and responsiveness to it they had when they were little, think they can only find it in drugs. Aside from being boring, the school is almost always ugly, cold, inhuman—even the most stylish, glass-windowed, $20-a-square-foot schools.

7   And so, in this dull and ugly place, where nobody ever says anything very truthful, where everybody is playing a kind of role, as in a charade, where the teachers are no more free to respond honestly to the students than the students are free to respond to the teachers or each other, where the air practically vibrates with suspicion and anxiety, the child learns to live in a daze, saving his energies for those small parts of his life that are too trivial for the adults to bother with, and thus *No! Lots of kids thrive in this environment.* remain his. It is a rare child who can come through his schooling with much left of his curiosity, his independence, or his sense of his own dignity, competence, and worth.

8   So much for criticism. What do we need to do? Many things. Some are easy—we can do them right away. Some are hard, and may take some time. Take a hard one first. We should abolish compulsory school attendance. At the *No way!* very least we should modify it, perhaps by giving children every year a large number of authorized absences. Our compulsory school-attendance laws once served a humane and useful purpose. They protected children's right to some schooling, against those adults who would otherwise have denied it to them in order to exploit their labor, in farm, store, mine, or factory. Today the laws help nobody, not the schools, not the teachers, not the children. To keep kids in school who would rather not be there costs the schools an enormous amount of time

and trouble—to say nothing of what it costs to repair the damage that these angry and resentful prisoners do every time they get a chance. Every teacher knows that any kid in class who, for whatever reason, would rather not be there not only doesn't learn anything himself but makes it a great deal tougher for anyone else. As for protecting the children from exploitation, the chief and indeed only exploiters of children these days *are* the schools. Kids caught in the college rush more often than not work 70 hours or more a *Kids still need protection.* week, most of it on paper busywork. For kids who aren't going to college, school is just a useless time waster, preventing them from earning some money or doing some useful work, or even doing some true learning.

9   Objections. "If kids didn't have to go to school, they'd all be out in the streets." No, they wouldn't. In the first place, even if schools stayed just the way they are, children would spend at least some time there because *Jobs aren't that plentiful.* that's where they'd be likely to find friends; it's a natural meeting place for children. In the second place, schools wouldn't stay the way they are, they'd get better, because we would have to start *Get real!* making them what they ought to be right now—places where children would *want* to be. In the third place, those children who did not want to go to school could find, particularly if we stirred up our brains and gave them a little help, other things to do—the things many children now do during their summers and holidays.

10   There's something easier we could do. We need to get kids out of the school buildings, give them a chance to learn about the world at first hand. It is a very recent *I agree.* idea, and a crazy one, that the way to teach our young people about the world they live in is to take them out of it and shut them up in brick boxes. Fortunately, educators are beginning to realize this. In Philadelphia and Portland, Oregon, to pick only two places I happen to have heard about, plans are being drawn up for public schools that won't have any school buildings at all, that will take the students out into the city and help them to use it and its people as a learning

EXERCISE READING "IF WE'RE SO EQUAL, WHY AREN'T WE HAPPY?" ANALYTICALLY

1. When you previewed the essay, you formed expectations for its content. Were your expectations accurate? Explain.

2. When you read the essay thoughtfully, you should have drawn some conclusions about it. Give two of them.

3. Did you have any trouble distinguishing facts from opinions? Though Wente does not use a scholarly approach, she does refer to a critical book, and to an academic study. State one fact that is in the essay. State one opinion that is in the essay. Is the essay balanced?

4. What is your assessment of the quality of the essay? Why?

5. To review and write for retention, write and answer two test questions on the essay's content.

6. Review your markings in the essay. If you were asked to evaluate the author's ideas in an essay, which of your markings would help you generate ideas? ●

Analyzing Visual Content

On television, in movies, on billboards, in store windows, in grocery store aisles, on the sides of buses, on cereal boxes, in magazines and newspapers, in textbooks, on the Internet—visual content is everywhere. Like the written word, pictures, maps, drawings, photographs, and charts convey meaning and are constructed for a purpose. To consider visual content thoughtfully, you can apply much of what you have learned about *reading* words analytically to *viewing* images analytically. In the next sections, you can read about how to analyze advertisements, photographs, and charts and graphs by answering these questions:

*   What is the *topic* of the image?
*   Who is the intended audience?
*   What is the *purpose* of the image?
*   What are the *components* of the image? How do they help the image achieve its purpose?
*   What can you *infer* from the image?
*   What is the importance of any *text* that accompanies the image?
*   Is the information conveyed in the image and text *accurate or misleading*?

Refer to this list of questions to approach an image analytically.

Analyzing Advertisements

Because advertisements routinely try to influence thinking and behaviour, knowing how to analyze them is important. If you do not consider advertisements thoughtfully, you can too easily fall victim to their persuasive strategies. Consider, for example, the advertisement for Obay, and then study the answers to the analysis questions.

What is the topic of the image? The topic is Obay, a fictitious pharmaceutical.

Who is the intended audience? The audience is parents with teenage children.

What is the purpose of the image? The purpose is to convince parents to make decisions for their children. Note, the message is intended to be ironic. Discovering this requires close inspection.

What are the components of the image? How do they help the image achieve its purpose? The image is of a father with his son. A bottle of medication figures prominently. The image's direct communication style establishes that parents who care for their children will consider using the product.

What can you infer from the image? The viewers of this ad can infer that responsible parents do not let their children make their own decisions, and medicate them so that they will obey their parents and follow the decisions that parents make.

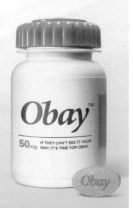

My son used to have his own hopes and aspirations. Now he has mine.

Thanks, Obay™!

Obay™
50mg IF THEY CAN'T SEE IT YOUR WAY, IT'S TIME FOR OBAY.

Obay

From the makers of WhyBecauseISaidSo.™

What is the importance of any text that accompanies the image? The text is very important because it makes explicit the notion that Obay will help parents to control their children's decision-making. Note, this is not a serious advertisement!

Once you have analyzed the advertisement by answering the questions, you can see that the ad has an ironic take on an emotional appeal that attempts to persuade parents to make decisions for their teenagers. Since presumably most parents are deeply concerned about their children's happiness and success, the ad can be very persuasive.

Analyzing Photographs

Whether candid or posed, photographs convey information to achieve a particular purpose. In textbooks, photographs convey meaning about a subject under study. For example, a photograph of politicians meeting in 1864 in Charlottetown to discuss Canadian Confederation can encourage patriotism. Photographs in newspapers and magazines can move emotions and incite viewers to act. For example, a magazine article about famine in Africa may include photos of starving children. These photos can move readers to send contributions to a famine relief agency.

To practice analyzing photographs, consider the photograph of Hurricane Katrina victims, and then study the answers to the analysis questions.

What is the topic of the image? The topic is the victims of Hurricane Katrina in New Orleans.

Who is the intended audience? Since the photograph appeared in *Newsweek* and on MSNBC's website, the audience is the people who read such material. This generally means middle-class individuals with at least a high school diploma.

What is the purpose of the image? The image serves to inform readers of the death, pain, sadness, and devastation associated with Hurricane Katrina. The purpose may also be to arouse emotions and gather sympathy for the plight of the hurricane victims.

What are the components of the image? How do they help the image achieve its purpose? The components include a weeping woman with a cut knee, a shrouded corpse, partial images of onlookers, and floodwater. The image may convey the photograph's message with more power than words because of its poignancy and starkness.

What can you infer from the image? Because the purpose of news photographs is largely to inform the viewer, much can be inferred from them. Here you can infer that the woman may be mourning the loss of the person who has died, although that cannot be known for sure from the photo. Also, since her leg wound is not bandaged, you can infer that medical care has not been administered to her. Finally, since the corpse remains on the ground, you can infer that procedures for removing the dead are going slowly.

What is the importance of any text that accompanies the image? The caption accompanying the photograph is very important because it confirms and expands upon the

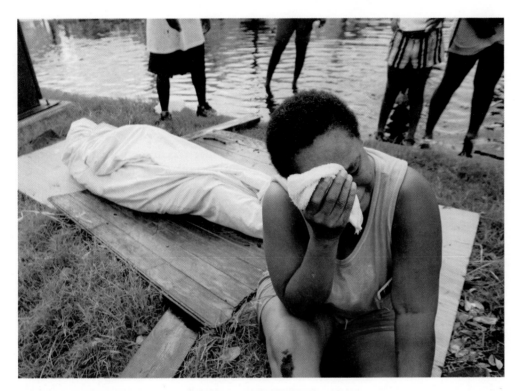

Very Dire Straits

As rising floodwaters took lives in New Orleans, residents struggled to find dry land, food, and drinking water. Search and rescue teams continued to look for survivors across the region on Aug. 31, two days after Hurricane Katrina came bearing down on the Gulf Coast. Residents of several cities report that bodies still have not been collected. Many in need of medical attention remain stranded by water or impassable roads. From Texas to Alabama, hundreds of thousands of refugees simply tried to make do. Many have lost their homes. There's no electricity or running water in many areas, and in most cases no communication. It will be some time before any sense of normalcy returns to this part of the world.

content of the photograph. The caption explains that the image is representative of a very big problem: in the wake of Katrina, bodies remain in the street; people are without shelter, electricity, running water, and communication; medical attention is not forthcoming; and the situation is not likely to improve significantly very soon. The title of the photograph, "Very Dire Straits," summarizes the situation.

Is the information conveyed in the image and text accurate or misleading? The information is accurate and conveys a true sense of post-Katrina suffering. Not all news reporting is entirely accurate, but you can usually trust major news sources to do their best to offer the truth.

Photographs can incite people to action. After Hurricane Katrina, many photographs like the one in this chapter appeared in newspapers and magazines and on websites. The power of these images was partly responsible for the outpouring of private contributions and other aid that went to the Gulf region after the hurricane.

Analyzing Charts and Graphs

Charts and graphs convey a great deal of information succinctly, and they often show how individual pieces of information relate to each other. You encounter charts, line graphs, and bar graphs often in textbooks, where they can either summarize information in the text or convey new information. Charts and graphs are also common in newspapers and magazines and on the Internet, where they often give a visual representation of the information in articles and essays.

To practice analyzing charts and graphs, consider the accompanying bar graph from Statistics Canada, and then study the answers to the analysis questions.

Percentage of population at each document proficiency level,[1] population aged 16 and over, Canada and jurisdictions, 2003

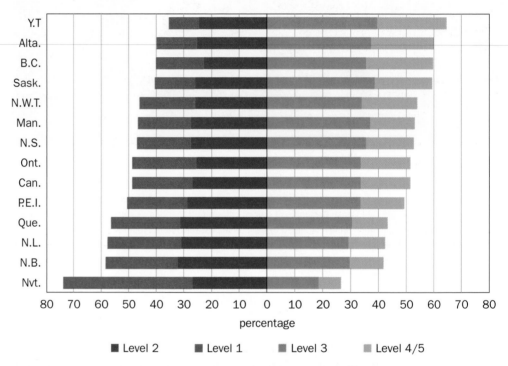

1. Document proficiency reflects the skills needed to understand forms or graphics, such as job applications, maps and timetables. Level 1 denotes the lowest proficiency level; Level 5, the highest. Since only a small proportion of the population actually reached Level 5, whenever results are presented by proficiency level, Levels 4 and 5 are combined. Level 3 is generally considered the minimum desired level of competence.

Notes: This chart contains certain estimates with relatively high coefficients of variation. Please see Table D.5.13 for more details. PCEIP's D5 indicator was developed to present information from the 2003 International Adult Literacy and Skills Survey. PCEIP 2007 presented an overview of the literacy domains (prose proficiency, document proficiency, numeracy, and problem-solving), then focused on prose proficiency. In the PCEIP June 2008 updates, the D5 series was continued and presented information on numeracy.

Chart source: Adapted from Human Resources and Skills Development Canada and Statistics Canada. 2005. *Building on our Competencies: Canadian Results of the International Adult Literacy and Skills Survey 2003.* Catalogue no. 81-617-XIE, Chart D.5.10, Table D.5.13, Ottawa. Updated December 16, 2008.

What is the topic of the image? Percentage of population at each document proficiency level,[1] population aged 16 and over, Canada and jurisdictions, 2003.

Who is the intended audience? The audience is college students in a political science, graphic arts, or communications class.

What is the purpose of the image? The purpose of the image is to indicate visual literacy of Canadians, and perhaps to indicate how institutions should communicate with them.

What are the components of the image? How do they help the image achieve its purpose? The graph breaks down the Canadian population by province, and examines adults age 16 and over regarding their understanding of complex graphics and images.

What can you infer from the image? We can infer that to some extent visual literacy differs by province. There are five levels of document proficiency, and these differ by province.

What is the importance of any text that accompanies the image? The legend and title are important for interpreting the graph, but the caption is a summary of information the reader could figure out. It is, therefore, helpful.

Is the information conveyed in the image and text accurate or misleading? The source is Statistics Canada, a highly respected institution, so there is no reason to consider the information misleading or unreliable. However, without knowing when the data were compiled, you cannot know how current the information is.

Take a moment to imagine conveying the information in the graph in text form, and you can see that an important function of graphs and charts is to convey substantial amounts of information in a brief, easily grasped form.

EXERCISE ANALYZING VISUAL CONTENT

Directions: The following advertisement is for the Lance Armstrong Foundation, a support group for people living with cancer and for those who care about them. The popular yellow wristbands shown in the advertisement, and sold by the foundation to make money, are generally worn by people who support the foundation's goals. Study the advertisement, and answer the following questions.

1. What is the purpose of the advertisement? Who is the targeted audience?

2. The advertisement includes both picture and text. What is the role of each? How does each help the ad achieve its purpose?

3. Does the advertisement appeal more to the reader's emotions or intellect? Explain.

4. What assumptions does the ad make? ●

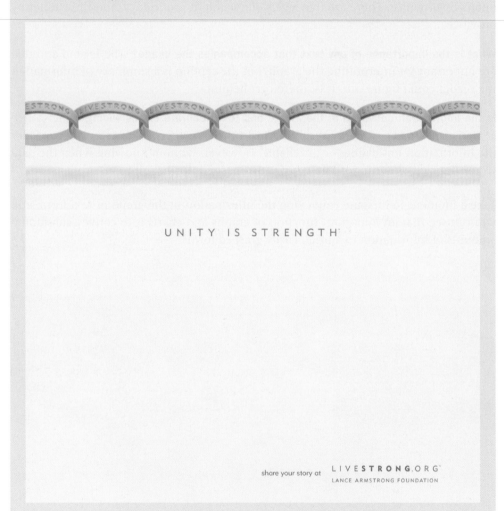

CHAPTER 2

Getting Started

Looking Ahead

Sometimes writers get lucky, and the light bulb of inspiration burns brightly. Unfortunately, inspiration is overrated; it just can't be counted on to appear when you need it. Therefore, you need strategies for discovering ideas in the absence of inspiration, and that is what much of this chapter is about. Before learning about those strategies, take some time to consider how writers come up with ideas by answering these questions:

- How do writers usually discover ideas for writing?

- Have you ever experienced writer's block? If so, what did you do about it?

Many students believe that writers are born, not made. After all, either you were born a writer, or you were not—and no amount of instruction will change that fact. This is an incorrect assumption. Students who write well learn to work with rules and conventions, and edit and revise carefully, which leads to success in academic writing.

Certainly, some people are born writers, but the fact is that the rest of us can learn to *become* excellent writers. Here is what it takes:

1. **Use available resources:** Your instructor, the writing centre staff, and your classmates can help. Follow your instructor's advice and ask questions when you are uncertain. Visit your writing centre if you need extra help, or want a sensitive reader to respond to your drafts (but not to correct your work; that's *your* job). Work collaboratively with classmates by brainstorming ideas and reacting to each other's work in progress. And remember one of the most important resources: mistakes! When you make errors, you learn from them. If you do not understand why something is a problem, ask your instructor for clarification.

2. **Remember that writing is a *process*:** It takes time and planning. You will start and stop, write and rewrite, go forward and double back. You will write multiple drafts, change approaches, revise wording, and rearrange ideas. Sometimes you will start over. You will have brainstorms and you will experience writer's block. In short, you cannot expect to write a polished piece at first sitting, any more than you can expect to plan a big event—such as a wedding—quickly.

3. **Think of yourself as a critic and an editor:** You are not expected to produce your best work in a first draft; you are expected to produce first drafts that are rough and then revise them until they are polished. Thus, you should think of yourself as a *critic*, as someone who will assess early drafts to determine their strengths and weaknesses. You should also think of yourself as an *editor*, as someone who can make the changes in a draft that critical assessment calls for.

4. **Respect your learning style:** Understand your preferences and use them to your advantage. If you prefer group work to individual work, form a writers' group and meet regularly, either in person or online, to brainstorm ideas and share drafts to obtain peer response. If you prefer lectures to textbooks, have someone read your draft aloud so you can listen for its strengths and weaknesses. If you favour pictures and diagrams over words, use mapping (page 47) rather than freewriting (page 34) to generate writing ideas. If you are a methodical planner, outline in detail before drafting. If you prefer to plunge right in, draft first without editing, and then outline to order the chaos.

The Writing Process

Ask 20 successful writers what they do when they write, and you could get 20 different answers, because different people approach their writing in different ways. Ask one successful writer what happened when he or she wrote 20 different pieces, and once again, you could get 20 different answers, because the same person does not always use the same strategies. Thus, we can make two important points about the writing process. First, there is no *one* process and different approaches can work equally well. Second, the same person does not always use the same procedures—an individual may adjust the process for a number of writing projects.

Now what if we told you it is possible to identify steps in the writing process? "Ah," you might say, "this is not as tricky as I was starting to think. I just learn the steps and perform them in order, right?" Not quite. Writing is recursive. The nature of the writing process is such that writers often find themselves stepping back before going forward again. Suppose you have shaped a topic and generated ideas, and you begin to consider ways to arrange your ideas. However, while you are arranging, you discover a relationship between your ideas that had not occurred to you before. This discovery prompts you to go back and shape your topic and thesis a bit differently, and perhaps to add a section to a paper, or revise the thesis entirely. You have stepped back before going forward, which illustrates that the writing process is not linear (advancing in a straight line through a series of steps) but **recursive** (advancing with some doubling back and more advancing—perhaps in a new direction).

Six Steps of the Writing Process

Even though writers do different things, in different orders, when they write, most successful writers turn their attention to these six stages:

1. Generating ideas, establishing purpose, and identifying audience (Chapter 2)
2. Ordering ideas (Chapter 3)
3. Writing the first draft (Chapter 3)
4. Revising (improving content, organization, and the expression of ideas) (Chapters 4 and 5)
5. Correcting errors (grammar, spelling, capitalization, and punctuation) (Chapters 20–27)
6. Proofreading (making corrections to the final copy)

Although successful writers attend to these six steps, they differ in the way they handle each one. Furthermore, they attend to these areas in different orders, and sometimes they attend to two areas at once. This variety explains the different approaches to writing.

In order to discover the process that works best, you need to understand each of the six steps, become aware of the various approaches to handle each of them, and experiment to learn which approaches work best for you.

Now look again at the list of six steps, but this time let's group them to shed more light on the writing process.

WRITER-BASED	*Prewriting*	*1. Generating ideas, establishing purpose, and identifying audience (Chapter 2)* *2. Ordering ideas (Chapter 3)*
	Writing	*3. Composing the first draft (Chapter 3)*
READER-BASED	*Rewriting*	*4. Revising (Chapters 4 and 5)* *5. Correcting errors (Chapters 20 – 27)* *6. Proofreading*

As the diagram illustrates, the six steps in the process can be divided into two groups: *writer-based activities* and *reader-based activities*. In other words, as writers move from idea to finished piece, they first concentrate on what **they want** for their writing and then focus on what their **readers need** from their writing. Of course, during writer-based activities, the reader is still considered, just as the writer's goals are still a concern during reader-based activities. The division really represents the primary focus of each of the six steps of the process.

The chart also shows that the six steps can be grouped into three categories: **prewriting** (performing activities prior to writing the first draft), **writing** (composing the first draft), and **rewriting** (making changes in the first draft to get the piece ready for a reader). Prewriting and writing are primarily writer-based activities, while rewriting is primarily reader-based, in anticipation of the audience.

As you study the chart, remember the recursive nature of the writing process. You may not always move sequentially through the steps; instead, your work on one step may prompt you to consider and make changes in an area treated earlier, and these changes will affect what you do when you go forward again.

Choosing a Writing Topic

Sometimes a writing topic is determined by an instructor, a boss, or a situation. A music appreciation instructor might tell students to write an essay about the origins of jazz; a boss might tell an employee to write a report summarizing ways to cut the budget by 10 percent; an incorrect bill might prompt a consumer to write a letter to a company's billing department. When a writing topic is not determined explicitly, and a suitable topic does not strike you right away, try the strategies explained next.

Pay Attention to the World around You

Read local and campus newspapers, either in print or online. Events, issues, controversies, and concerns reported in the news can become essay topics. Tax hikes, civic projects, curriculum changes, pending legislation, demonstrations, and actions of elected officials or citizens or students in response to these issues and events can suggest interesting, worthwhile topics. For example, an article in a campus newspaper about an increase in reported cases of cheating might prompt students to write an essay on why students cheat or what can be done to reduce the amount of cheating.

Consider what you have been learning in classes. Perhaps you just heard a lecture on business ethics in your business management class. That might prompt an essay about truth in advertising. What have you seen on television or heard on the radio lately? Did you watch a reality TV show and decide that the reality trend has finally gone too far? You could write an essay about the prevalence of cruelty in reality TV.

Listen to people and conversations around you. If you hear your roommate complain about her high credit card bills, you might be prompted to write about the ethics of banks marketing their credit cards to students. If a parking lot attendant reminds you to lock your car, you might be prompted to write about crime on campus.

Respond to Writing Prompts

You can discover topics by filling in the blanks in key sentences like these:

1. I'll never forget the time I _____.
2. _____ is the most _____ I know.
3. After _____, I was never the same again.
4. Post-secondary education can best be described as _____.
5. Is there anything more frustrating (interesting/exciting) than _____
   _____?
6. This world can certainly do without _____.
7. What Canada needs is _____.
8. _____ made a lasting impression on me.
9. After _____, I changed my mind about _____.
10. My biggest success (failure) was _____.
11. Life with _____ is _____.
12. Life would be easier if only _____.
13. I get so angry (annoyed/frightened) when _____.
14. _____ is better (or worse) than _____.
15. The main cause of _____ is _____.
16. The main effect of _____ is _____.
17. Most people do not understand the real meaning of _____.
18. The best way to do _____ is _____.

Narrowing a Broad Topic

To keep a topic manageable, writers have to narrow it to something suitable for the required or desired length of an essay. For example, whole books are written on advertising, so "advertising" is not narrow enough for an essay. "Truth in advertising" is narrower, but it still covers a great deal of territory. "Truth in television advertising to children" is narrower still, but consider how much more manageable this topic is:

Truth in television advertising of children's toys

Shaping a suitable topic can involve a series of narrowing's, or topic restrictions. Suppose you have been assigned the topic of unemployment. You must narrow the broad topic to something that can be managed in a reasonable length. You could narrow first by deciding to write about the causes and effects of the unemployment rate in Canada. It is unlikely that one essay could say everything about the causes and effects of unemployment, though, so another restriction is necessary. You might settle on a discussion either of the causes or of the effects. These are more focused, but they still take in quite a bit, so another restriction is in order. Perhaps you could discuss the effects of a parent's unemployment on the family. Such a topic would be narrow enough for treatment in a single essay. The following diagram illustrates the process.

Narrowing a Topic

Unemployment

Causes and effects of unemployment in Canada

Either the causes *or* the effects of unemployment

The effects of a father's unemployment
on a family

To narrow a topic, apply the following procedures.

Freewrite

Freewriting shakes loose ideas by freeing writers from worry about correctness, organization, and even logic. To freewrite, write nonstop for five or ten minutes. Record *everything* that comes to mind, even if it seems silly or irrelevant. DO NOT STOP WRITING FOR ANY REASON. If you run out of ideas, then write names of your family members, or write, "I don't know what to say," or write the alphabet—write anything! You will not share your freewriting with a reader, so you can say what you want and disregard spelling, grammar, neatness, and form. Just jot your ideas down any way you can. After five or ten minutes, read over your freewriting, and you will likely find at least one idea for a writing topic. Here is an example that yields several broad topics:

> *I have to find a writing subject. Let's see, there's politics and school, but politics is boring and school is done to death (and it's going to kill me, ha-ha). What else? Television, there ought to be a lot there. The shows, the commercials, the sex and violence. I could do something with arguing about the violence. Pop culture is possible too, especially MTV. I haven't watched it for a while but it used to be really racy. What about soaps? Let's see, what else? A B C D E F G H What else? My friends, my family. I could write about Dad—he'd be a book, not an essay. Especially if I write about his drinking—no, better not. I could write about Janet's accident and the courage she showed or I could write about courage in general. That could be hard. I don't know, what else? Teachers roommates studying grades? Stress? I should have enough now.*

Below is a sample of freewriting on the topic of soap operas, inspired by the writing prompts on page 33.

> *Soap operas have been around a long time. They are hugely popular. They're on day and night. Lots of different kinds of people watch them. Even very bright,*

professional people who you would think have better things to do. What now?
ABCDE. Let's see. Soaps are interesting to some people and entertaining to others,
but why I don't know because I think they are pretty stupid. Have you ever
really listened to these things? Must be a reason people like them. Maybe several
reasons. Entertainment? People are bored? Lots of famous actors started on soaps.
I can't think of who, though. At 1:00 half my residence hall meets to watch
<u>All My Children</u>. Some people even schedule their classes around their favourite
soaps. Good grief. My mother used to call them her "stories."

This freewriting could lead to several narrow topics: why soap operas are popular, the people who watch soap operas, and the steps people will take to ensure they do not miss their soap operas.

Write a List

Listing can help during brainstorming and prewriting. Write a broad topic at the top of a page, and below it list every aspect of the topic you can think of. Do not evaluate the worth of the items; just list everything that occurs to you. A list for the broad topic "leaving home for higher education" might look like this:

<u>Leaving home for college or university</u>

- *Locating a school*
- *Planning where to live*
- *Responsibilities for students*
- *Independence*
- *Chores and homework*
- *Managing a budget*
- *Residence or apartment living*
- *Living alone versus living with a roommate*
- *Working while at school*
- *Transportation*

Sometimes one list is enough. For example, you might look at the list above and decide to write about "independence," perhaps focusing on ways students can cope with it, and how it is different from living at home with family. Other times, you may need a second list to narrow a topic further. For example, you could look at the first list and narrow "independence." That is a step in the right direction, but "independence" is still broad. You could try a second list, which might look something like this:

<u>Independence</u>

- *Peer pressure*
- *Coping with roommates*
- *Managing time and money*
- *Tackling homework*
- *Effects on studies*
- *Communication with parents*
- *Personal responsibility*

CALVIN AND HOBBES © 1992 Watterson. Reprinted with permission of UNIVERSAL PRESS SYNDICATE. All rights reserved.

A second list could lead the writer to one of several narrow topics. For example, studying this list could lead to writing about ways a college student can deal with independent living.

EXERCISE CHOOSING AND NARROWING A WRITING TOPIC

1. Identify five broad topics from the program you study that you could write an essay about. If you cannot arrive at five after some thought, try one or more of the techniques described in this chapter.

2. Using three of your responses to number 1, shape three narrow essay topics. If necessary, use one or more of the techniques described in this chapter.

3. Below are five broad writing topics. Select two of them and write one narrow topic for each. Use any of the techniques described in this chapter.
    a. studying for exams
    b. team sports
    c. technology
    d. difficult decisions
    e. interesting (or unusual) people ●

Christel's Essay in Progress: DISCOVERING A WRITING TOPIC

Throughout this chapter and through to Chapter 5, students will have the opportunity to see how student writer Christel Webb approached a semester-length writing project. In Christel's Communications course, students were asked to select a topic at the beginning of the semester. This topic would move through four stages: brainstorming, outlining, writing as an informal, five-paragraph essay and finally the development of a research-based APA-style report for submission at the end of the semester.

Christel realized that the world around her, especially her experiences as a student in a nursing program, would help move her project forward, as the topic she works on is of great personal interest, and relevant to the work she will do when she finishes her studies. Her first assignment was to determine her topic, audience, and purpose. Next, she continued the project with a formal, numbered outline. Then, Christel drafted her paper as an informal, five-paragraph essay. And finally, she used the informal essay as a starting point for a much longer, APA research paper.

She began the project with an analysis of audience and purpose, and decided on the following, based on her answers to these questions:

Generally speaking, whom would you identify as the audience for this project (apart from your classmates and me)?

> *My audience would be anyone within the health care field and people possibly facing death, as well as the baby boomer generation and their children. Most adult Canadians know that boomers are a very large population, and that society will have to deal with this issue in the near future.*

And next, what is your purpose for this project?

> *The purpose of my project was to learn more about palliative care so I could determine if it was an area I wanted to specialize in as a nurse. Secondly, I wish to find others interested and/or working in it and learn about their experiences. Finally, I wanted to evaluate how effective end-of-life care is, and whether it should be funded by the government.*

BRAINSTORMING

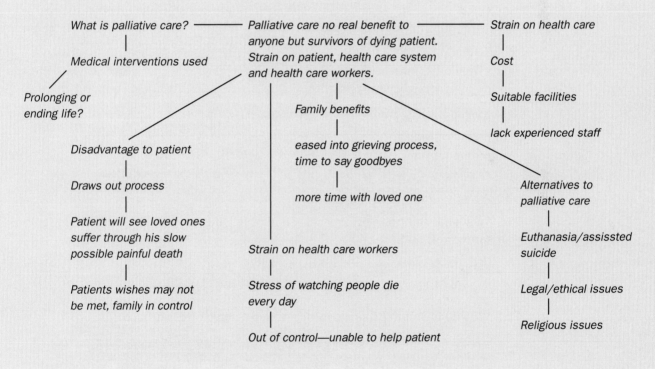

Establishing Purpose

Once you have narrowed your topic to a manageable scope, ask yourself why you are writing a particular piece. The answer will establish your purpose. In general, writers can establish one or a combination of these four purposes for their writing:

1. To express feelings or ideas to the reader and/or to relate experiences
2. To inform the reader of something

3. To persuade the reader to think or act a certain way
4. To entertain the reader

Sometimes a writing situation dictates purpose. For example, an instructor may ask students to write an informational research paper, or they may need to write a letter of complaint to convince a customer service representative to refund money for a faulty product.

Whether or not a writing situation determines purpose, you must be clear about the reason for writing because it influences the nature of the piece. Suppose you are writing about the economic and health challenges surrounding decisions about palliative care, as Christel is. If the purpose is to relate experience, you might include accounts of what it is like to care for an aging or terminally ill relative, along with descriptions of common emotional reactions to these events. If the purpose is to inform readers that palliative care can be expensive for families, it may be necessary to suggest situations families face, and to identify solutions to the problems that arise. If the purpose is to persuade readers that palliative care is very expensive, then you need examples. Note that Christel's essay does not lend itself to the purpose of entertainment. The four general purposes listed above are useful categories, but you need to be more specific when establishing a purpose. Ask why you want to express ideas—to inform, to persuade, to entertain—and what effect you want to have on readers. Here are some examples for writing about palliative care in Canada.

1. Why do I want to express issues around, or relate real experiences? What effect do I want to have on my reader?

   Palliative care is important to me, since we all die, and each person has their own needs and wishes at the time of death. I feel that palliative care is important and essential. I also feel that as a nursing student it is an honour and privilege to provide care to a dying patient and be able to share that time with them and their family.

2. Why do I want to inform readers about the issues surrounding palliative or long-term care?

   Everyone is and will be affected by the death of a loved one, so it is important to know what kind of care is available and the intent of that care.

3. Why do I want to persuade readers that palliative care is needed?

   I want to persuade them that palliative care is a service that has a great impact on all involved, but that it may or may not be an affordable service offered to all Canadians.

4. Why do I want to entertain my reader with stories about end-of-life care?

   I planned to allow readers the opportunity to think about the topic and possibly pull from their own experiences with death. This is a rather serious topic, and not entertaining. However, it's a frank discussion about the realities of terminal illnesses.

QUESTIONS FOR ESTABLISHING PURPOSE

A piece of writing can have any one or a combination of these purposes: to express feelings or ideas, to relate experience, to inform or persuade, and even to entertain. Consider the following when identifying purpose:

1. What ideas, feelings, or beliefs can I communicate to my reader?

   Why do I want to express these ideas? How do I want my reader to react to these ideas or feelings?

2. What experiences do I want to relate?

   Why do I want to relate these experiences? How do I want my reader to react to the experiences?

3. Of what can I inform my reader?

   Why do I want readers to know this information? How do I want readers to react to this information?

4. Of what can I convince my readers?

   Why do I want to convince readers? How do I want readers to think or act?

5. Can I entertain my reader?

   Why do I want to entertain? How do I want readers to respond?

Using a Pattern of Development

Part 2 of this book explains patterns of development, which are ways to think about essay topics and approaches. The patterns are as follows:

- Description (explaining what something looks, sounds, feels, smells, or tastes like)
- Narration (describing chronologically)
- Exemplification (using examples)
- Process analysis (explaining how something is made or done)
- Comparison-contrast (showing similarities and differences)
- Cause-and-effect analysis (explaining the reasons something occurs and the results of the event)
- Definition (explaining what something means)
- Classification (explaining categories)
- Argumentation (convincing a reader to think or act a particular way)

A good way to narrow a topic is to consider how these patterns can be used to think about broad topics. Do so by asking the questions in the following chart. (You may not be able to answer every question for every topic.)

CONSIDERING PATTERNS OF DEVELOPMENT TO NARROW A TOPIC

Description (Chapter 6): Can I describe my topic? What does my topic look, sound, feel, taste, or smell like? What are the main characteristics of my topic?

Narration (Chapter 7): Can I relate a story about my topic? What is the significance of the story?

Exemplification (Chapter 8): What examples illustrate my topic? What do the examples say about the topic?

Process Analysis (Chapter 9): Can I explain how my topic works or how it is made or done?

Definition (Chapter 10): Can I explain what my topic means? Does everyone agree about the meaning?

Classification and Division (Chapter 11): Can my topic be broken down into categories or parts? What do they say about the topic?

Comparison-Contrast (Chapter 12): With what can I compare or contrast my topic? What do the similarities and differences say about the topic?

Cause-and-Effect Analysis (Chapter 13): What are the significant causes or effects of my topic? Should the causes be encouraged? Are the effects positive or negative? Who is affected?

Combining Patterns of Development (Chapter 14): How can more than one pattern (i.e. narration and process analysis) be used to develop an academic essay?

Argumentation (Chapter 15): What controversies or arguments surround my topic? What do people disagree about?

Here is an example of how considering the patterns of development can help narrow a topic. The broad topic is "palliative care," from Christel's essay-in-progress.

1. Can I describe my topic?

    I can describe the issue of dying and end-of-life care, and the strain on patients, the health care system, and health care workers. As well, I can indicate that palliative care exists because there are no alternatives, like assisted death or euthanasia, for Canadians.

2. Can I tell a story about my topic? What is the significance of the story?

    When my grandmother died it was peaceful, and she was not hooked up to machines. Her daughters and two of her grandchildren were around her. She planned everything, and her wishes were all granted. But I was concerned by the use of morphine during the final stages of her life. I wanted to find out more about the topic of palliative care, i.e. what is involved and the medical and social intents.

3. What examples illustrate my topic? What do the examples say about the topic?

My grandmother's death helped me to see the positive side of palliative care. Other people's dissatisfaction with a loved one's death (i.e. patient left in pain) shows the negative side of this issue. I would also like to provide examples about people (i.e. doctors and nurses) who participate in palliative care. I could also consider those involved in alternatives like doctor-assisted death.

4. Why is the topic significant?

The topic is significant to me as I am a nursing student and it may be an area that I could specialize in. As well, the increase in number of people aging in our population and the demands that places on the health care system make this topic important.

5. Can you compare or contrast anything in the topic?

The cost of keeping people in acute-care beds in hospital is tremendous compared to being cared for at home. Levels of care may differ from hospital to home care, with limited access to specialists and possible dependence on family to assist in the care.

6. What do the similarities/differences in acute and palliative care say about the topic?

The differences include the level of care, which should be the same no matter where provided, as the needs of the patient may be the same depending on the condition or disease. The cost should not determine the level of care, and patients should determine their needs and wishes. As well, acute care is curative and palliative care is not to cure, but to live while dying.

7. What are the significant causes or effects of my topic? Should the causes be encouraged? Are the effects positive or negative? Who is affected?

The significant effects of palliative care are on the patients and their families, the health care system and health care professionals.

8. Can I explain what my topic means? Does everyone agree about the meaning?

Palliative care is living while dying. People are still alive and need the opportunity to live their lives even though they will die in the near future. This care is provided to patients once they have been determined to be terminally ill and no curative treatment can affect the outcome. This care can include pain and symptom management, as well as physical, emotional, or spiritual issues. It considers the person as a whole: mind, body, and soul.

9. Can my topic be broken down into categories or parts? What do they say about the topic?

    Palliative care can be broken down into categories of how and where delivered (i.e. hospital acute care facilities, hospice, long-term care facilities, and in-home). As well, I can consider what takes place and what level of care is available at each type of facility. The categories allow meeting most people's wishes, i.e. where they want die. Finally, it is important to communicate that there are options available to dying people.

10. What controversies or arguments surround my topic?

    Some of the controversies that surround palliative care are the use of morphine in the final stages of death, and the fact that it hastens death. Also, some believe palliative care extends not only life but also suffering.

The answers Christel provides suggest many narrow topics, including these:

1. *A comparison of palliative and other long-term care.*
2. *The benefits of palliative care for patients and their families*
3. *The problems associated with the time and expense of palliative care*
4. *The perceptions of end-of-life care in certain communities*
5. *An argument for or against palliative care and honouring families' wishes*

Identifying and Assessing Audience

In addition to establishing a purpose for writing, you must identify an audience—the readers you are writing for. Like purpose, audience shapes writing. Readers are not necessarily like writers, and they are not like each other. Readers have different backgrounds, different circumstances, different beliefs, and different needs. You must consider those differences in order to meet readers' needs and achieve purposes for writing. For example, an essay about college or university life may need considerable explanatory information if you are writing for people who have never attended higher education. However, such information would not be necessary in an essay for classmates. Similarly, you may wish to convince the administration to improve an orientation program, despite claims that there is no money to do so. You must then show that the program's cost is affordable. Such cost information might not be necessary if you are writing to persuade the student council to run the program and the council has the money. To convince the council, though, you might discuss how such a program could increase student support for council-sponsored activities, a fact you would not need to include in writing aimed at the administration.

You might think that because you are in a writing class your audience is an instructor. Of course, you are right. Yet writing teachers understand that student writers need experience writing for a variety of audiences, so they are willing to assume the identities and perspectives of different readers. Thus, you should write for different audiences. You can also identify an audience as "the average, general reader"—someone who knows something about a subject but less than you do. Think of the average, general reader as the typical reader of a large daily newspaper.

QUESTIONS FOR IDENTIFYING AND ASSESSING AUDIENCE

To decide on a suitable audience for student writing, ask yourself these questions:

1. Who could learn something from my writing?
2. Who would enjoy reading about my topic?
3. Who could be influenced to think or act a certain way?
4. Who shares an interest in my topic?
5. Who would find my topic important?
6. Who needs to hear what I have to say?

Once you have identified an audience, you must assess the typical members of this audience and provide details to meet readers' needs to help achieve their purpose. These questions can help, because it is very important to anticipate the audience for a paper. This guides the approach to audience and shapes purpose.

1. What does the reader already know about the topic?
2. What information will the reader need to appreciate opinions in my writing?
3. Does the reader have any strong feelings about the topic?
4. Is the reader interested in the topic, or will I have to arouse interest?
5. How receptive will the reader be to opinions in the essay? Why?
6. Will the reader's age, gender, level of education, income, job, politics, backgrounds, or religion affect his or her reaction to the topic?

Discovering Ideas to Develop Topics

Many people believe that ideas come in a blinding flash of inspiration, in some magic moment of discovery that propels the writer forward and causes word upon wonderful word to spill onto the page. Yes, such moments occur from time to time, but they are the exception rather than the rule. More typically, you cannot depend on inspiration, because it does not make scheduled appearances. Often it does not arrive at all.

So what should you do in the absence of inspiration? Fortunately, there are strategies to start the flow of ideas. Logically enough, these strategies are called idea generation techniques, and they are discussed next.

Freewriting

You know about freewriting to find and narrow a topic. (See page 34.) You can also freewrite to discover ideas to develop a narrow topic in a first draft. You simply follow the procedure you learned to write down everything that occurs to you about a narrow topic, without censoring. You shift direction and pursue ideas as far as possible; they can be flip, serious, or angry.

After freewriting, you should read your work. It will be rough, but you will notice at least one or two ideas that can be polished and developed in essays. Underline them. They may be enough to get you started. If not, you can freewrite again, this time focusing on the ideas you underlined.

"Go do something, honey. <u>Then</u> you can write in your journal."

© The New Yorker Collection 2002 Victoria Roberts from cartoonbank.com. All Rights Reserved. Reprinted by permission.

Listing

In addition to helping narrow a topic (see page 33), listing can help generate ideas to develop topics. You should write every idea that occurs to you about a narrow topic in a column. Don't stop to evaluate the ideas; just press on until the list seems comprehensive. Review the list, and cross out any ideas that the essay will not address. This can lead to a "scratch outline." If other ideas occur, add them to the list.

Here is a list one student wrote to find ideas for an essay about the trauma students experience when families move to new towns, and students have to change schools:

> *Students love old schools*
> *Comfortable with friends—know them many years*
> *At new school, students are outsiders*
> *Everyone belongs to a clique*
> *Sleepless nights for weeks before moves*
> *~~Parents try to reassure them~~*
> *Students know they will never see old friends again*
> *Scared to leave familiar for unknown*
> *New school may be unwelcoming*
> *~~I resented my parents for transplanting me~~*
> *~~I became argumentative with my parents~~*
> *Students fall behind in schoolwork at new school*
> *Students who move don't get on teams at new schools*

Some of the ideas in the list are crossed out because the writer decided he did not wish to work with these ideas after all, probably because they focused on his personal relationship with his parents. Rather, he wanted to concentrate on the adjustment to the new school and relationships with classmates.

After the writer eliminated ideas unsuited to his purpose, he reviewed his list and added new ideas. After this step, the list looked like this:

> *Love old school*
> *Comfortable with friends—know them many years*
> *New students are outsiders*
> *Everyone belongs to a clique*
> *Sleepless nights for weeks before the move*
> ~~*My parents tried to reassure me*~~
> *Students know they'll never see old friends again*
> *Scared to leave familiar for unknown*
> *New school may be unwelcoming*
> ~~*I resented my parents for transplanting me*~~
> ~~*I became argumentative with my parents*~~
> *Students fall behind in schoolwork at new school*
> *Students who move don't get on teams at new schools*
> ~~*New math teacher tried to help me adjust*~~
> *At new school students feel like a freak*
> *Students skip lunch because they don't know anyone to sit with*
> *Students are popular & respected at old school*
> *New school was old, needed repair—describe ugly classrooms*
> *Math & science classes may be way ahead of old ones & grades suffer*

The student will not necessarily include all of the points, examples, and details in the list in the essay. Instead, the list can provide a starting point.

Some student writers like to turn their idea generation list into a scratch outline to guide their writing of a first draft. A scratch outline organizes idea generation material by grouping related ideas together, like this:

> *Before Move*
> *loved old school*
> *comfortable with friends—know them many years*
> *sleepless nights for weeks before the move*
> *never see old friends again*
> *scared to leave familiar for unknown*
>
> *After Move*
> *Classmates*
> *New student is an outsider*
> *everyone belongs to cliques*
> *stared at like a freak*
> *skipped lunch cause have no one to sit with*
> *The new student is a nobody instead of popular & respected*
>
> *Basketball*
> *New students often do not make team*
> *can't go to games & cheer for a team they felt no loyalty toward*
>
> *Surroundings*
> *new school was ugly*
> *new school was old & needed repairs*
> *describe classrooms*
>
> *Schoolwork*
> *Students fall behind*
> *math & science classes way ahead and grades suffer*

Answering Questions

Answering questions about your topic is another way to develop ideas. Some of the most useful questions are the standard journalist's questions: Who? What? When? Where? Why? How? You can shape these questions to suit your topic. Some or all of the following questions can help student writers generate ideas.

QUESTIONS FOR GENERATING IDEAS

1. Who is involved?
2. Who is affected?
3. Who is for (or against) it?
4. Who is interested in it?
5. What happened?
6. What does it mean?
7. What causes it?
8. What are its effects?
9. What is it like (or different from)?
10. What are its strengths (weaknesses)?
11. What are its parts?
12. When does it happen?
13. When will it end (or begin)?
14. When is it important?
15. Why does it happen?
16. Why is it important?
17. Why is it interesting?
18. Why is it true?
19. Where does it happen?
20. How does it happen?
21. How does it make people feel?
22. How does it change things?
23. How often does it happen?
24. How is it made?
25. How should people react to it?

Here are some questions a student asked herself for an essay about government regulation of the food supplement industry. Notice that the writer shaped questions to suit her narrow topic.

1. What happened?

    A young woman became seriously ill with kidney failure after taking a supplement for weight loss from a health food store. She almost died.

2. Why did it happen?

    The product interacted with medication she was taking. There are no warnings on these products about drug interactions.

3. Who else could this happen to?

    Many people could become seriously ill from food supplements if they are taking medication or have medical conditions—like polycystic kidney disease—that they don't realize they have.

4. What should be done about it?

    The Ministry of Health should determine the safety of food supplements. They should require warning labels when drug interactions or adverse effects can occur.

5. Why is it important?

   People can die. The young woman is permanently disabled. Recent reports say kava can cause liver damage.

6. What else could happen?

   Sometimes people pay money for supplements that don't work because claims are made that aren't proven. Reports now say that St. John's Wort, which people take for depression, is not helpful.

7. Who is affected?

   People who take food supplements or use weight-loss products and who take prescription drugs or have medical conditions they may be unaware of.

Writing a Concept Map

Mapping can help you narrow a topic (see page 33). It can also help you discover ideas to develop that topic. Just write your narrow topic in the centre of a page and circle it. Alternatively, look for an online concept-mapping tool if you prefer to write with the assistance of technology. Below is an example of narrowing a topic for an essay on a specialized aspect of nursing.

Next, let your thoughts flow freely and record all the ideas that occur to you, circling and connecting the ideas as appropriate. Do not pause to evaluate ideas; just go with the flow of your thoughts. Here is a map to generate ideas for an essay about palliative care:

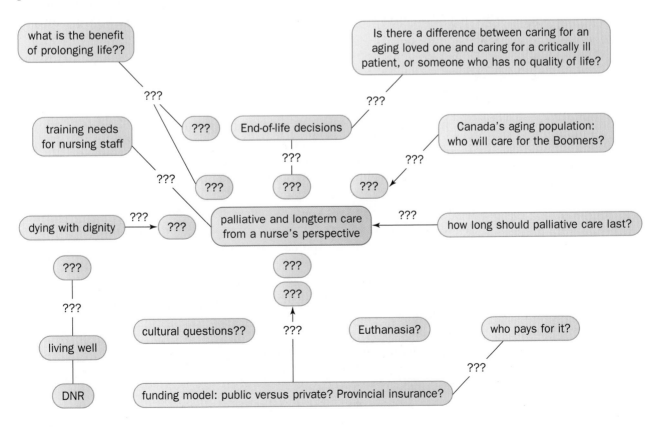

Investigate Sources Electronically

Use a campus library, or an online library, or the Internet to discover facts, expert opinions, statistics, and studies to spur ideas. Perform a webquest, which is a general search for information on the Internet. Keep a record of sources you've used, in a folder on your Internet browser or in a document. When you use source material, be sure to handle it responsibly by following the conventions explained in Chapter 17.

Interviewing people is another way to discover ideas to include in your writing. You might interview a subject expert who teaches at your institution, or someone in industry who can answer questions related to the paper you are writing. Remember to document the interview in the appropriate style.

Keep a Journal or an Online Blog

A journal, paper or electronic, is not a diary that records the events of your day; a journal is a place to respond to those events, to write on how you feel about them and to reflect on your thoughts and feelings. You can explore strong emotions and perhaps deal with them. You can also be creative and experiment with writing styles. When you write in your private journal, you are writing for yourself, so you need not worry about grammar, spelling, and other matters of form.

Journals can be handwritten in a notebook of your choosing, or they can be a separate computer file, or even blogged on the Internet. Either way, date and begin each entry on a new page. Write each day or two, and soon journal writing will become a rewarding habit. Then, when you need ideas for writing topics or details to develop a topic, scan your journal for ideas.

Your instructor may give you topics from time to time, but most often, you can write about whatever you wish. If you need ideas for journal entries, consult the following chart.

TOPICS FOR JOURNAL WRITING

1. Freewrite by beginning with the first thought that comes to mind.
2. Write about someone you admire.
3. Write an article or editorial you've seen in print or online.
4. Write about your feelings about undergraduate studies.
5. Explore your goals for the coming year.
6. Explain where you see yourself five years from now.
7. React to a book you recently read or a movie you recently saw.
8. Write about a problem you have and explore possible solutions.
9. Write about your best attribute.
10. Record a vivid childhood memory.
11. Write about an event in the news that caused strong emotions.
12. Write about family relationships.
13. Describe your writing process.
14. Write about a change you would like to make in your community.
15. Write about a valued possession.

To practice writing in the patterns, try these prompts:

16. *Describe* a painting, a commercial advertisement, or a valued possession.
17. *Narrate* an account of a time you learned a valuable lesson.
18. Use examples to *illustrate* a personality trait of someone you care about.
19. Explain how to do something that you do well (*process analysis*).
20. Compare or contrast the person you are now and the person you would like to be (or the person you used to be).
21. Explain the *effects* of an important decision you made.
22. Explain the different kinds of friends (*classification*), and explain what kind of friend you are.
23. Write a definition of education, and explain what kind of education you want.
24. Identify one change that would make your school a better place, and *argue* for that change.

Work Collaboratively

Many of the idea generation techniques can be adapted for use with two or more people. For example, to list collaboratively, one person acts as the recorder. Group members mention whatever ideas occur to them, and the recorder writes the ideas down in list form. The comments of one person often stimulate other people to come up with ideas.

You can also answer questions collaboratively. One person asks another person questions about the topic. The person answering records his or her responses for possible inclusion in the draft. Collaborative learning is a powerful writing strategy because another person can often think of many more questions than the writer can. Discussion or wiki tools in course websites are perfect places to write collaboratively. Mapping, too, can be done collaboratively. In this case, one person is assigned to write or create a poster while everyone else brings up ideas and suggests where to connect them. Like list writing, concept mapping is a productive collaborative technique because one person's thoughts will inspire another. There are many concept map tools available online, and it may be faster for students to work this way.

Pre-write Online

1. Freewrite "blindfolded" by turning down the brightness on your monitor until you cannot see what you write. Students can also freewrite with the monitor turned off. There will be many typographical errors, but your inability to see your writing will deter you from censoring yourself and allow your thoughts to flow freely.
2. Create a file with the questions in the charts on pages 43 and 46. You can call up that file whenever you want to use these questions for prewriting. Rename and save the file for each project you begin.

3. Use email or instant messaging to work collaboratively with other writers to generate ideas. Create a chat room for a study group, or a private group on Facebook. Determine meeting times for online chatting.

4. Surf news sites for writing topics. Some helpful Canadian sites include CBC news, (http://www.cbc.ca/news/), The Globe and Mail (http://www.theglobeandmail.com/), CTV news (http://www.ctv.ca/). You may also wish to bookmark local news and information sites on your browser. Consider, also, international news organizations, such as the BBC, The Independent Online, *The Washington Post*, or *New York Times* to get a balanced perspective on issues.

 THE WRITING PROCESS

Breaking through Writer's Block

All writers experience writer's block from time to time, so when it happens to you, first recognize that you are not alone. Then take action.

- Take a break. Go for a walk, listen to music, call a friend—relax, and when you return to your writing, the block may be gone.

- Force yourself to write or create something, because all writing stimulates thinking. Write a poem, draw a picture, or write the reasons you are having trouble writing. Fill a page or the computer screen with nonsense if you must, but keep writing. Ideas may surface.

- Allow time for ideas to surface. If you expect too much too soon, the pressure can cause a block.

- Accept rough ideas. Nothing is polished in the early stages of writing, so look for the *possibilities* your rough ideas offer. Do not self-censor, and investigate possibilities thoroughly.

- Try a different idea generation technique. Freewriting may usually work for you, but mapping may be more productive this time. Try a technique you have never used before. Or combine techniques. Follow listing with answering questions and see what happens. Consider using online graphic organizers, like Cmap (http://cmap.ihmc.us/) to get your mind off the block, and to learn how to use an online tool.

- Consider what people who disagree with you might say, and use their ideas as a departure point. This may lead to something interesting to explore.

- Write about what you know. You may have trouble coming up with ideas because you do not know enough about your topic. Do a webquest to learn more. Surveying information online helps to build knowledge about a topic.

 EXERCISE ESTABLISHING PURPOSE, IDENTIFYING AUDIENCE, AND DISCOVERING IDEAS

1. *Directions:* For an essay about campus life, do the following:
   a. First, develop a narrow topic about campus life, using one or more of the techniques described in this chapter. Then establish a purpose for an essay on this topic by answering the questions on page 39.
   b. Establish the audience by answering the questions on page 43.
   c. Determine the nature of the audience by answering the questions on page 43.
   d. Using any two techniques described in this chapter, generate at least five ideas that could be included in an essay with the topic from item a.

2. When you responded to question 1 on page 36 you identified five broad topics that you could develop into an essay. (If you did not complete this exercise, do so now.) For each of these topics, discover at least four ideas worthy of inclusion in an essay. Try at least two different idea generation techniques.

3. Which idea generation technique(s) worked best? Which are you likely to use in the future?

4. *Collaborative Activity.* Assume you are writing an essay about your proudest or most embarrassing moment.
   a. What moment will you write about?
   b. Team up with a classmate and work collaboratively to discover ideas by taking turns asking each other questions about your topics.
   c. Next, work together to develop maps for each of your topics.
   d. Do you find collaborative idea generation to be productive? Why or why not? ●

Develop a Preliminary Thesis

The thesis of a paper is both the first and the last thing you write, as it can change or improve during the writing process. Your thesis is the section of your paper that states what your topic is and explains what will be addressed in the paper. Appearing early in the essay, your thesis lets your reader know your writing topic, controlling idea, and ideas addressed in an essay. A good thesis identifies an important question, explores a contradiction, or identifies and examines a change. Here is an example:

The current film rating system does little to help parents make wise choices for their children.

Topic: The current film rating system

Controlling idea: It is confusing and does little to help parents decide what their children should watch.

A basic thesis must also preview an essay's main sections by indicating ideas you will cover, after your topic and controlling idea. Here is an example:

Working mothers have changed the character of the Canadian family by contributing a second paycheque, by popularizing daycare, and by creating a new division of labour in the home.

Topic: Working mothers

Controlling idea: Working mothers have changed the Canadian family.

Preview of the paper: The contribution of a second paycheque; the popularization of daycare; a new division of labour in the home

The thesis is important to both the writer and the reader. It is important because it is the guiding force of an essay. Everything in an essay must help develop the thesis or prove that it is valid. The thesis is important to your reader because s/he develops expectations according to what your thesis promises your essay will be about.

Remember, a thesis may not necessarily answer all questions surrounding an issue, but its scope should allow you to explore complex topics with a good focus. Often, general reading and research into a topic help you find a thesis. Alternatively, writing topics supplied by an instructor lead students to a thesis that meets the requirements of an assignment.

Because the thesis is so important, writers should not begin a first draft without one. However, first drafts are tentative, so thesis statements in first drafts can be equally tentative. In fact, the early version of a thesis—the one that guides and focuses a first draft—is often a preliminary thesis because, like everything else in a first draft, it is subject to change. Exploring topics, questions, changes, or contradictions may in fact lead a student writer to a thesis that they would not have considered previously.

Determine the Qualities of an Effective Thesis

1. **State your topic and your controlling idea about that topic.** Consider this thesis:

> More and more high school students are working while they attend school, but this trend is not a healthy one.

Both the topic and the central point are clear.

Topic:	High school students who work
Controlling idea:	It is not healthy for high school students to work.

Here is another example. This thesis includes the topic, the controlling idea, and a preview of the main ideas of the essay. This example works for an informal, five-paragraph essay. The thesis for a longer, academic paper is more developed and complex, and not constructed in such a formulaic manner.

> More and more high school students are working while they attend school, but this trend is not a healthy one because students are distracted from their studies, unable to participate in normal teenage activities, and jeopardize their health.

Be sure the controlling idea is clearly stated.

Unclear:	Although there are pros and cons on both sides of the issue,
Controlling idea:	I have decided how I feel about equal opportunity employment legislation.
Better:	Although there are pros and cons on both sides of the issue, equal opportunity employment legislation does more harm than good.
Unclear:	A number of provinces are evaluating equal opportunity employment legislation,
Controlling idea:	Creating a great deal of public debate.
Better:	Provinces that have eliminated equal opportunity employment legislation undermine the goals of equal rights initiatives.

2. **Limit a thesis to one topic and the ideas that develop it.** A thesis with multiple topics or many controlling ideas, will force you to write about too much, producing an unclear paper.

Two topics:	The violence on television has an adverse effect on children, as does the blatant sexuality in music videos.
Better:	The violence on television has an adverse effect on children.
Better:	The blatant sexuality in music videos has an adverse effect on children.
Two controlling ideas:	Divorce would be less traumatic if custody laws were revised and if lawyers advised their clients more carefully.
Better:	Divorce would be less traumatic if lawyers advised their clients more carefully.
Better:	Divorce would be less traumatic if custody laws were revised.

3. **Avoid broad statements.** A thesis that is too broad will force a writer into a vague, superficial discussion that will never satisfy a reader because it will never get beyond obvious statements. The following thesis statement is too broad:

   The role of women has changed drastically in the last 50 years.

   Fifty years is a long time; to discuss in depth all the changes in that time span would require more pages than the typical undergraduate essay runs. This statement could lead to a bookshelf full of writing! If the essay were to be a more manageable length, you could do little more than skim the surface and state the obvious. Below is a more suitable thesis, one that is sufficiently narrow:

   The leadership roles of women in provincial politics have changed dramatically in the last 10 years.

4. **Express your controlling idea in specific words.** The reader relies on the thesis for a clear indication of what the essay is about. Consider this thesis:

   It is interesting to consider the various meanings of *love*.

   The word *interesting* is vague, so the reader cannot be sure what the writer's controlling idea is. In the following revision, the point is stated in specific words, so the reader has a clear sense of the focus of the essay.

Better:	We apply the word *love* to a broad spectrum of emotional experiences.

5. **Avoid factual statements.** Factual statements leave the writer with nothing to say.

Factual statement:	The city's public works department is considering a rate increase.
Better:	The public works department's proposed rate increase is unnecessary and will affect taxpayers directly.

6. **Write a thesis so it is not an announcement.** A thesis such as "This paper will show why I have always hated team sports" is an announcement. In some disciplines, particularly some of the sciences and social sciences, the announcement is acceptable, but in English composition classes and many of the Humanities, it is considered poor style.

Announcement:	I will explain why the local board of education should consider magnet schools.
Better:	The local board of education should consider magnet schools.
Announcement:	The next paragraphs will present the reasons Canadians value youth.
Better:	Canadians value youth for surprising reasons.

7. **Avoid expressions such as "in my opinion," "I believe," "I think," and "it seems to me."** *You* are writing the paper, so it is obvious that you are expressing what you think. Such expressions make the student writer seem uncertain. Academic discourse is formal and objective.

Uncertain:	In my opinion, the Women's Centre performs a valuable service on campus and deserves a budget renewal.
Better:	The Women's Centre performs a valuable service on campus and deserves a budget renewal.

 THE WRITING PROCESS

Thesis Statements

How to Draft a Preliminary Thesis

- Study idea generation material to identify a narrow topic and controlling ideas and central points to make about a topic. If you are unable to identify these elements, then continue with idea generation until you can.
- If you cannot get anything down, try filling in these blanks: My topic is _____, and my controlling idea is _____.
- Do not worry about writing a statement that has all the qualities of an effective thesis. State your topic and controlling idea as best you can. Afterwards, you can rework your preliminary thesis to improve it.

EXERCISE THE THESIS

1. In the following preliminary thesis statements, identify the topic and the controlling idea.
    a. No experience is more exasperating than taking preschool children to the grocery store on a Saturday to do a week's worth of shopping.
    b. Some 20th century leaders embody the meaning of courage.
    c. Television news does not adequately inform the viewing public.
    d. No one is more skilled at diplomacy than people who make their living selling clothes.
    e. Many people believe a little white lie can be better than the truth, but even these seemingly harmless fibs can cause trouble.

2. In the following preliminary thesis statements, identify the topic, the controlling idea, and the main ideas to be developed in the essay.
    a. Socrates Pappas would make an excellent mayor because he is an experienced manager, he is fiscally conservative, and he is well connected in the provincial legislature.
    b. Different communication styles and different agendas make it challenging for men and women to communicate effectively.
    c. Her eccentricity, her courage, and her personal life would make Lady Mary Pellatt, the founder of the Girl Guides of Canada, the subject of an entertaining movie.
    d. The speed limits on our highways should be 80 km/hr to save lives and reduce the cost of automobile insurance.
    e. The student production of *Macbeth* is a big hit because of its excellent production values and daring direction.

3. Decide whether each of the following thesis statements are acceptable or unacceptable. If the thesis is unacceptable, explain what the problem is.
    a. There are many game shows on television.
    b. Schools should not be funded by property taxes.
    c. I would like to explain why I am an avid reader.
    d. Higher education is in need of reform.
    e. College students can learn to handle stress if they follow my advice.
    f. My Christmas cruise to the Bahamas was nice.
    g. The Non-traditional Student Centre and the International Student Union are two university organizations that serve students well.
    h. My parents own a beach house.
    i. This essay will explain the best way to choose a major.
    j. I do not think that reality shows deserve their bad reputation.
    k. For today's young people, the shopping mall offers a variety of entertainment options.
    l. The wise woman learns how to manage her own finances, and she learns how to take care of her car.

4. Rewrite the unacceptable preliminary thesis statements from number 3 to make them acceptable.

5. When you completed number 1 in the exercise on page 50, you shaped a topic about campus life, established a purpose, identified an audience, and generated some ideas. Now review that material and develop a compatible preliminary thesis. Do you need to revise your topic, audience, or purpose? Do you need to eliminate some of the ideas you generated or generate additional ideas? Explain.

6. *Collaborative Activity.* Below are four broad topics. With a classmate, select two of them and narrow them so that you are treating a topic manageable in 500–1000 words. Write a preliminary thesis for an essay about each.

    Example: Saturday morning cartoons: If parents took the time to watch Saturday morning cartoons with their children, they would be surprised by how violent these programs really are.

    a. Aboriginal land claims
    b. Bilingual education
    c. Canadian immigration
    d. College and university ratings ●

THE WRITING PROCESS

Sequence

- Recognize that you need not complete writing steps in the order they are presented here. Decide on audience, purpose, a preliminary thesis, and develop ideas in whatever sequence works the best for you.

- Remember the recursive nature of writing. You may often go back to a stage and alter something you worked on earlier before moving forward. This means that you need to plan your time wisely to ensure sufficient time to let your writing "rest" before returning to it with fresh eyes and fresh ideas.

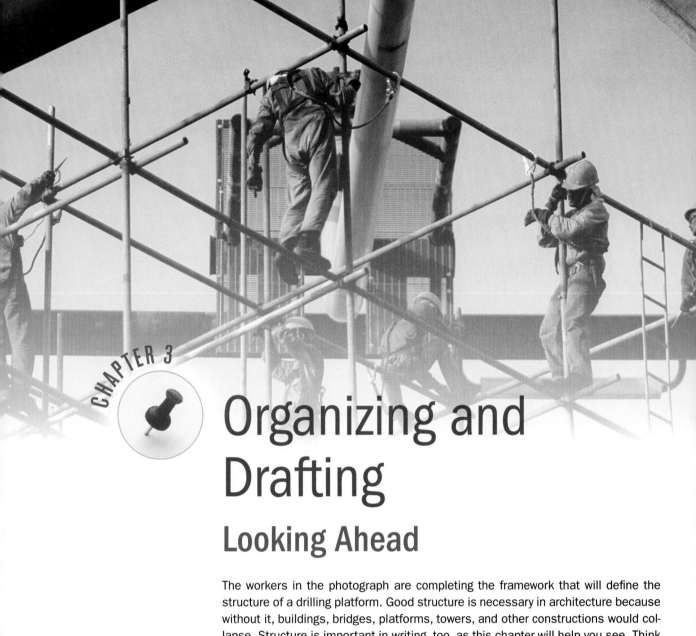

CHAPTER 3

Organizing and Drafting

Looking Ahead

The workers in the photograph are completing the framework that will define the structure of a drilling platform. Good structure is necessary in architecture because without it, buildings, bridges, platforms, towers, and other constructions would collapse. Structure is important in writing, too, as this chapter will help you see. Think of other times when structure is important, and list them. Think of instances when structure is not very important, and list those as well.

Prewriting can seem disorganized because you may engage in circular thinking, run into dead ends, double back over the same path, and test offbeat relationships. Illogical and inefficient though it may seem, this part of the writing process is productive for discovering ideas. However, you cannot expect readers to follow such twists, turns, repetitions, and leaps. Once you have generated ideas and determined which of them you will develop, you are obligated to meet the needs of the audience by presenting those ideas in an orderly, logical way. This chapter will help you do that as you write first drafts.

THE WRITING PROCESS

Evaluating Ideas

- Before determining a logical order for ideas in an essay, decide which ideas from your idea generation material you will include in your first draft. To decide, consider audience, purpose, and a preliminary thesis.
- Include ideas that meet the needs of the particular audience, and set aside those that do not.
- Include ideas that help achieve a purpose for writing, and set aside those that do not.
- Include the ideas that relate to the topic and central point presented in a preliminary thesis, and set aside those that do not.
- As a result of thinking about what ideas to include, you may decide to change the audience, purpose, or preliminary thesis.

Ordering Ideas

The next sections explain three common strategies for ordering ideas.

Chronological Order

Chronological order is time order. You begin with what happened first, move to the second event, on to the third, and so on. Chronological order is used most often for narration, when writers want to tell a story by presenting events in the order they occurred. It is also used for explaining how to do something, when the steps must be given in the order they are performed. Suppose you are writing an explanation of the best way to shop in an outlet store. Here is how you can arrange ideas in chronological order.

Preliminary thesis:	To save money shopping in an outlet store, plan ahead and proceed with caution.
First idea	Do some homework. Find out what certain items cost at full price.
Second idea	Write a shopping list to buy only what you plan to and avoid impulse buying. Decide what you are willing to pay and vow not to exceed that amount.
Third idea	Walk around the store to assess the quality of the merchandise. Look at the price tags of items on your list. Are the items really a bargain? Do they exceed the amount you planned to spend?

Talk to a sales clerk to find out whether the merchandise is high quality or imperfect.
Inquire about the return policy.

Fourth idea   Try on all clothing.
Check every item carefully for defects.

Spatial Order

With **spatial order**, readers and writers move across space in some specific way, such as from top to bottom, outside to inside, near to far, or left to right. Spatial order is often used to describe something. Suppose you want to describe your residence room for a friend considering living on campus. Here is how you can arrange your ideas in a spatial order that moves around the room in clockwise direction.

Preliminary thesis:	A dormitory room has *none* of the comforts of home.
Standing at the door and looking to the left	Describe the bunk beds: institutional and uncomfortable.
To the right of the beds	Describe the window: greying curtains, filmy windows, depressing view of power plant.
To the right of the window	Describe the two dressers: too small, scratched, broken drawer, old-fashioned.
To the right of the dressers	Describe the two study desks: facing each other, goose-neck lamps, hard wooden chairs, too small for desktop computers, no bookshelves, uneven legs.
To the right of the desks	Describe the closet: room for hanging clothes for a 3-year-old, only one shelf, funhouse mirror on the door.

Progressive Order

With **progressive order**, writers move from the *least* compelling idea to the *most* compelling idea according to how important, surprising, convincing, representative, interesting, or unusual the ideas are. With the most compelling points at the end, writers leave readers with a strong final impression. Or you can arrange your ideas from the most to least compelling, for the strongest possible opening. A third variation is to open *and* close with the strongest points. Of course, how compelling an idea is will often vary from audience to audience. For example, the idea that an increase in the provincial sales tax will benefit schools may not be a compelling reason for a senior citizen on a fixed income to vote for the tax, but it is likely to be a compelling reason for parents of young children. Progressive order is most often used when writers want to persuade readers to think or act in a particular way. Suppose you are writing to convince parents of young children that schools should offer classes in conflict resolution. Here is how you could arrange your ideas in a progressive order.

Preliminary thesis:	Beginning in first grade, schools should offer conflict resolution courses.
Least compelling idea	The courses are inexpensive to run.

Somewhat more compelling idea	The courses will help students resolve their own disputes and free teachers from this distraction.
Even more compelling idea	Students will learn skills that will eventually aid them in their personal lives and in the workplace.
Most compelling idea	Studies show that the classes are likely to reduce the amount of lethal and nonlethal violence in schools.

EXERCISE ORDERING IDEAS

Directions: For each preliminary thesis, decide whether chronological, spatial, or progressive order would be suitable. Be prepared to explain your choice. (In some cases, more than one arrangement can be effective.)

1. The events that network news programs do *not* report are often more important than the stories they *do* report.

2. The new office tower downtown is not designed with the architecture of surrounding buildings in mind.

3. Since the attacks on the World Trade Center and Pentagon on September 11, 2001, many Americans have a better sense of what is important in their lives.

4. The first vacation I took with my husband was a comedy of errors.

5. The subdivision on the edge of town is perfect for families with young children.

6. Public transit should be declared an essential service, and the workers not allowed to strike.

7. Now that it has been restored, the lobby of Bicksford Inn has an inviting Victorian charm.

8. With the right tools and materials, anyone can build a sturdy bookcase.

9. There are three effective ways to deal with a bully.

10. After my 3-year-old twins' birthday party, my backyard looked like the site of a natural disaster. ●

Outlining

Once writers have a sense of the best ordering strategy for ideas, they can arrange ideas using that order with the help of an outline. Many student writers resist outlining because they see it as time-consuming, difficult, and unnecessary. Yet outlining does not deserve this reputation. Because it helps organize ideas before drafting, outlining can ensure the success of an essay and make drafting easier. If you do not order and group ideas with some kind of outline, prior to drafting, you will have to order and group your ideas as you draft, which complicates the drafting process, and makes the writing process longer.

Outlines can be detailed or sketchy, formal or informal. Long, complex essays often call for formal, detailed outlines, while briefer pieces can be planned with less detailed, more informal outlines.

The ideas to include in an outline will come from brainstorming and prewriting. However, since outlining stimulates thought, new ideas may occur to you, which you can include in your outline. Similarly, outlining may lead students to reject some prewriting ideas, and that is fine, too.

The Formal Outline

The **formal outline**, which is the most detailed, structured outline, allows writers to plot all main and supporting ideas. This outline uses Roman numerals, letters, and Arabic numbers. Main ideas are designated with Roman numerals; supporting ideas to develop a main idea are designated with capital letters; points to develop supporting ideas further are designated with Arabic numbers. The format looks like this:

Preliminary Thesis

I. Main idea
   A. Supporting detail
   B. Supporting detail
   C. Supporting detail
II. Main idea
   A. Supporting detail
      1. Further development
      2. Further development
   B. Supporting detail

Here is an example of a formal outline written for an essay about the attitudes of children toward food. Note that each main and supporting idea is stated in a complete sentence. Also, note that the ordering strategy is a progressive order.

Thesis: Children can develop healthy eating habits and body image, and parents can make mealtimes and food choices more enjoyable.

I. Parents should make mealtimes pleasant.
   A. Keep conversation enjoyable.
      1. Avoid discussing problems.
      2. Avoid arguments about food.
   B. Serve balanced meals and let children choose quantities.
   C. Avoid eating in front of the television.
II. Parents should not forbid children to eat certain foods.
   A. Children will want what they cannot have.
   B. Reasonable amounts of sugar and fat are not harmful.
III. Parents should stress health and fitness.
   A. Teach nutrition.
   B. Serve healthy foods.
   C. Exercise with children.
   D. Set an example.
IV. Parents should praise children for their behaviour, not their appearance.
   A. Children should take pride in what they do, not in how thin they are.
   B. Those with a tendency toward carrying more weight need to like themselves.

Students may prefer writing a formal outline with phrases rather than with sentences, as in this excerpt of a phrase outline for an essay on the causes of eating disorders.

V. Poor self-image
   A. Caused by media emphasis on thinness
   B. Caused by self-hatred

Should you have trouble completing your outline, you may need to go back to prewriting to generate additional ideas.

Outline Cards

To outline using cards, you need several large index cards (or use sheets of paper). Use one card to plan each paragraph. On each of the cards, list ideas in the order they will appear in the paragraph the card represents.

One advantage of cards is flexibility: You can shuffle paragraph cards into different sequences to examine alternative arrangements.

The Outline Worksheet

The outline worksheet, like outline cards, allows writers to plot organization in as great or as little detail as required. While it is not as easy to rework parts of the hard copy outline when the worksheet is used (this is the advantage of cards), it is easy to get a clear overview of your organization (this is one advantage of the formal outline). A better strategy is to develop a template similar to the one below, and work on an electronic copy in a word processing program.

Below is a sample outline worksheet. To use it, fill in the blanks with the amount of detail that works for the assignment. If you have trouble filling in the blanks, return to idea generation.

SAMPLE OUTLINE WORKSHEET

Introduction
Detail to generate reader interest

_____

_____

_____

Preliminary thesis and ideas to address in an essay

_____

_____

_____

Paragraph
Main idea

_____

_____

Supporting details

_____

_____

_____

Paragraph

Main idea

_____

_____

Supporting details

_____

_____

_____

_____

(*Note:* The number of paragraph sections will correspond to the number of paragraphs planned for the first draft.)

Conclusion

Detail to provide closure

_____

_____

_____

_____

Here is a sample outline worksheet for an essay about the attitudes of children toward food.

SAMPLE OUTLINE WORKSHEET

In each paragraph, writers provide detail that supports that paragraph's main idea, as well as supporting or reinforcing the thesis itself. Paragraphs should indicate, in their conclusions, the relationship between the ideas in the paragraph, and the essay's main contention, or argument, to satisfy reader questions about the thesis.

Introduction

Detail to generate reader interest   *Give statistics on number of overweight and unhealthy children in Canada.*

_____

Preliminary thesis *Children can develop healthy eating habits and body image, and parents can make mealtimes and food choices more enjoyable.*

Paragraph

Main idea *Parents should stress health and fitness.*

Supporting details *Teach nutrition, serve healthy foods, exercise with children, set example.*

Paragraph

Main idea *Parents should make mealtimes pleasant.*

Supporting details *Keep conversation enjoyable, serve balanced meals, let children choose quantities, avoid eating in front of television.*

Paragraph

Main idea *Parents should not forbid children to eat certain foods.*

Supporting details *Children will want what they can't have. Reasonable amounts of sugar and fat are not harmful.*

Paragraph

Main idea *Parents should praise children for their behaviour, not appearance.*

Supporting details *Children should be proud of what they do, not how thin they are. Heavier-set children need to like themselves as much as slimmer children might.*

Conclusion

Detail to provide closure *Explain how important it is for children to have healthy attitudes about food, and reiterate the thesis statement to demonstrate how the point has been proven.*

The Outline Tree

An outline tree helps writers visualize the relationships among ideas. It also helps determine where more ideas are needed. The following example uses ideas discovered in the mapping process on page 47.

To develop an outline tree, first write a preliminary thesis. Then place the first branches of the tree, using your main ideas.

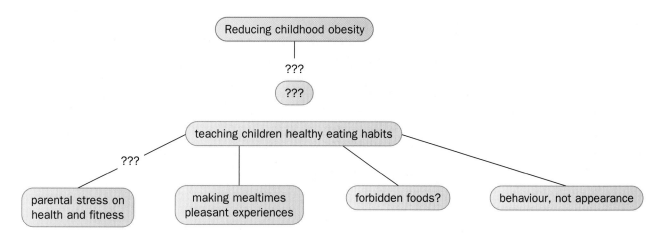

Each of the first branches will be the main idea of one or more paragraphs. Next, build the tree by adding additional branches.

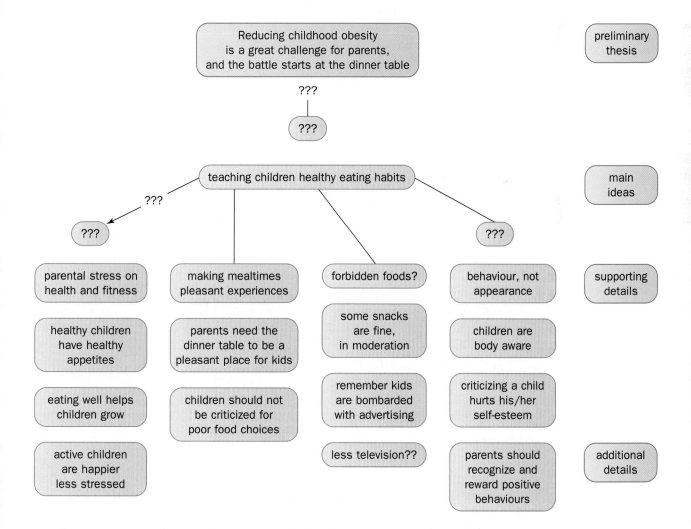

Notice that this tree grows downward, rather than up. The first level of branches gives the main ideas. The branches after the first level represent supporting details to develop main ideas. Students can study outline trees to determine where detail is needed. For example, studying the outline tree on the previous page reveals that supporting details are needed to develop the main point that reducing childhood obesity is a significant challenge for parents. If details about, say, forbidden foods cannot be developed, then this idea should be eliminated, or combined with the idea of making mealtimes a pleasant experience.

The Scratch Outline

We learned about the scratch outline in the reading about idea generation on page 44. This outline is for writers who prefer to come to the first draft knowing only the main ideas that will be discussed and maybe the order they will be presented in. The outline does not usually include much of the detail that will develop the main ideas, so writers who use it must have in mind how their ideas will be supported, or they must be capable of developing the ideas as they draft.

An example of a scratch outline appears on page 45. It shows how to turn an idea generation list into a scratch outline that groups related ideas. Some scratch outlines offer even less organizational guidance. The following scratch outline for an essay on why schools should ban cell phones is such an outline. This outline lists ideas; the numbers give the order in which the ideas will be written in the draft. The ordering strategy seems to be progressive.

> 3   *students leave class to place calls*
> 2   *ring in class*
> 5   *have games on them played in class*
> 6   *used to cheat—instant messaging, store answers*
> 4   *one kid used the phone to order pizza in study hall*
> 1   *distracting*
> 7   *used to get in trouble (drug dealing)*

THE WRITING PROCESS

Outlining

- Recognize that, in general, the more detailed an outline is, the more smoothly the first draft will go. If you have trouble drafting, return to the outline and see if additional idea generation is needed.
- Be aware that as you outline, you may make discoveries about your preliminary thesis, ideas, audience, or purpose. Always respond to good ideas, whenever they occur. Be prepared to adjust the thesis. Christel's outline and informal essay feature different ideas as her work progressed.
- To check organization, try writing a formal outline after the draft.
- Remember that the kind of outline that works best may vary with the difficulty and complexity of a writing task. A scratch outline may work well to plan an essay examination answer, but a formal outline will work better for a research paper.

Christel's Essay in Progress: OUTLINING

In Chapter 2, we met Christel Webb, who was attempting to determine a topic, audience, and purpose for a semester-length essay project. She had a tentative thesis, which she revised at each stage of her writing process, based on critical reflection and peer and instructor suggestions. Christel has developed ideas (on pages 36–37 and 40–42) for an essay about the need for increased understanding of and funding for palliative care in Ontario. Evaluate the thesis at this stage in the writing process. Can the thesis be changed for style, or for logical flow?

Topic: Palliative Care

Introduction

Note: this is the first phase of Christel's semester writing project. Her investigation into palliative care is very elementary at this point. For further development of this project's ideas, please see the draft informal essay on pages 88–89, and the completed report, which uses research, on page 136. Christel followed a recursive writing process, and her thesis and major ideas changed significantly over the semester.

When a patient is knocking on death's door, how can health care professionals help, since death is inevitable? There are health professionals that assist in this end-of-life care, also known as palliative care. There are significant issues that surround this type of care and it affects more than just the dying patient.

Thesis Statement: Death, dying, and the care associated with it have no benefit to anyone but the survivors of the dying patient, because there is significant strain on the dying patient, the health care system, and the health care worker providing care.

Body

I. The dying patient is under significant physical and emotional strain
   A. Patient watches family and loved ones suffer over their impending death
   B. Medical interventions may or may not ease dying patient
      1. May end life sooner and cross line into euthanasia/assisted suicide
      2. Options available to patients, example, Do Not Resuscitate (DNR) orders, medical assisted death
      3. Evidence that palliative care does not end life sooner
      4. May extend life and prolong suffering
      5. Evidence that palliative care does not extend life or prolong suffering
   C. Patient may not have final wishes met
   D. Palliative care plan may interfere with patients' care plans
      1. Evidence that patients' wishes are addressed, example, Do Not Resuscitate (DNR) orders
      2. Patient may not have access to the services they wish, example assisted death
II. Palliative care, as it is currently structured, puts more strain on the health care system
   A. High costs associated with keeping patient in hospital or hospice
      1. Estimated cost to facilitate this care
   B. Lack of suitable facilities in Canada
      1. Very little availability of hospice care centres
      2. Hospice care mainly disease specific, example cancer and aids

3. Not enough room in hospitals, taking beds from other patients
4. Discuss overcrowding

C. Lack of experienced health care workers, able to deliver palliative care effectively
1. Special education and skills necessary to address this type of care
2. Type of education and skills

III. Health care workers administrating palliative care to patients under substantial strain

A. Health care workers under psychological stress dealing with death and dying every day
1. Short-term mental health issues for workers
2. Long-term mental health issues for workers
3. Programs in place to address these issues

B. Health care workers are left feeling defeated and hopeless
1. Palliative care goes against principles of healing and health prevention, the outcome is always death

C. Health care workers struggle with ethical issues surrounding end-of-life care
1. Moral and ethical issues of palliative care
a. Personal ethics and beliefs
2. Moral and ethical issues with alternatives to palliative care
a. Personal ethics and beliefs

Conclusion

Palliative care causes more suffering to the patient, strain on the health care system, and health care workers, making it an ineffective service to provide for Canadians.

Reprinted by permission of Christel Webb.

EXERCISE YOUR ESSAY IN PROGRESS

Directions: After completing this exercise, save your responses. They will be used again in this chapter, and later as you work towards a completed essay.

1. Assume you have won a writer's contest. As the winner, you may write a four-page, typed essay that will be published in the magazine or the website of your choice. You may write on any topic. What topic will you write about? (Use the idea-generation techniques described in Chapter 2 if you have trouble narrowing a topic.)

2. For what purpose will you write this article? (If necessary, determine your purpose by answering the questions on page 39.)

3. In which magazine or on which site will you publish your article?

4. Who are the typical readers of this magazine or site? (If necessary, answer the audience assessment questions on page 43.)

5. Generate as many ideas as you can to include in this article. Try using at least two of the idea generation techniques described in Chapter 2.

6. What ordering strategy do your ideas suggest? Select the outlining technique that most appeals to you, and outline your ideas.

7. Now, select a different outlining technique, and outline your ideas a second time.

8. Do you like one of the outlining techniques better than the other? If so, which one, and why? ●

Writing the First Draft

After prewriting, you can write your first draft. Drafting, which moves writers out of prewriting and into the writing stage, is writer-based because the focus is on expressing ideas the best way you can. However, it is also partially reader-based because as writers draft they give some thought to a reader's needs.

A first draft, often called a **rough draft**, is an effort to transform ideas and an outline into an essay. This early effort is tentative, subject to changes of every kind. It will have errors and rough spots, but it provides material to shape until the desired product is achieved. By the time the final essay *is* complete, writers may have made so many changes that it bears little resemblance to the original draft.

Structuring the Essay

Think of an essay as having three parts: a beginning, a middle, and an end.

The beginning: The opening paragraph or paragraphs are the **introduction**. The introduction should create interest in the essay so the reader wants to read on. The introduction always includes the thesis, to let the reader know the topic, as well as the central points the writer will make about that topic. Introductions also provide a preview of the primary sections and topics in an essay.

The middle: The middle of an essay is composed of **body paragraphs**. These are the heart of the essay because they explain or prove the thesis. In other words, this is where writers include ideas to *develop* the thesis. A body paragraph always has a **topic sentence** that states the main idea of the paragraph. Body paragraphs also include concluding statements, which help the reader to see the connection between an individual paragraph and the thesis for the entire essay,

The end: The final paragraph or paragraphs are the **conclusion**. The conclusion brings the essay to a satisfying finish.

CRITICAL READING STUDENT ESSAY

This draft of a student essay illustrates basic essay structure. The marginal notes call your attention to the structural features discussed throughout the rest of this chapter. Note: this is also an example of an informal essay, as it is developed without research. In further chapters, examples of research papers will demonstrate the incorporation of secondary research materials in the academic writing process.

Read the selection below, entitled "Portrait of an Achiever." Then, use the form that follows it to complete an outline of the essay. Evaluate the arrangement of the elements in the essay, and consider where or how this paper could be improved. Note, this essay is informal, as it does not use research. Consider how this essay might be improved were it less anecdotal and incorporated research materials.

Portrait of an Achiever

Aaron Palumbo

PARAGRAPH 1

This is the introduction. It works to engage interest and present the thesis, which is the last sentence of the paragraph. The thesis presents Hugh as the topic. The central point is that his determination is the key to his ability to solve problems.

1. He is one of the greatest achievers of our time. His achievements, however, have gone unnoticed because the average person would not recognize them as such. This unsung achiever is named, Hugh. He was born with no left arm, so everyday activities can be a big problem for him. But problems do not get Hugh down. He just solves them, no matter how much time or energy it takes. The key to Hugh's ability to overcome everyday problems is his determination.

PARAGRAPH 2

This is a body paragraph. The first sentence is the topic sentence, which gives the main idea of the paragraph as Hugh learning to tie his shoes. The rest of the paragraph explains the determination Hugh showed to learn to perform the task.

2. One of Hugh's biggest problems was learning to tie his shoes. He would sit for hours trying to tie the knot that was so simple, yet so impossible. No matter how hard he tried, he just could not get it right. After seven years of practice and frustration, Hugh was finally able to tie that knot with one hand. The astonishing movements of his fingers as he tied the knot were almost miraculous. It took him seven years to train his fingers, but he never gave up, no matter how frustrated he became.

PARAGRAPH 3

This is a body paragraph. The first sentence is the topic sentence, which gives the main idea of the paragraph as Hugh not letting his abilities conflict with his interests. The rest of the paragraph gives two examples of how Hugh avoided the conflict.

3. Hugh's interests always seem to conflict with his abilities, but not for long because he does not allow this conflict to stand in his way. He always finds some way to overcome his disability and eliminate the interest-ability conflict. For example, Hugh loves baseball. He spent an entire summer in his backyard devising a method that allows him to play with one hand. With one lightning speed motion, he can catch the ball in the glove, toss both the glove and the ball a few feet into the air, retrieve the ball from the air, and throw it to another player. Hugh also enjoys building objects out of wood. The first problem he encountered with the hobby was how to hold the nail while hammering. The solution was another exercise in determination: Hugh taught himself to steady the nail between his toes while he hammered it into the wood. At first, the method was literally painful, but perfection came after months of practice (and several smashed toes).

PARAGRAPH 4

This is another body paragraph. The first sentence, the topic sentence, gives the main idea as Hugh learning to swim. The rest of the paragraph tells what caused Hugh to learn to swim.

4. Hugh's inability to swim was yet another problem that he had to overcome. For years, he thought that he could not swim with one arm, so he never tried. It was not until someone was drowning in Lake Erie that Hugh decided he would learn to swim. Much to his own surprise, he found that he could stay afloat. It was his determination to overcome fear that gave him the confidence to jump in the water and save a life that day. Of course, once he realized that he wouldn't drown, Hugh went on to practice his swimming techniques with the same determination he brings to every challenge. Now he swims farther and faster than many others do.

PARAGRAPH 5

This is the conclusion. It brings the essay to a satisfying end by noting what readers can learn from Hugh.

5. Determination can be born of challenge, but it isn't always so. Some people who face challenges just give up and wallow in self-pity or rely on others. Hugh refuses to do that. We can all draw inspiration from his example.

The complete essay, including any bibliographic references, is also available on the Online Learning Centre at www.mcgrawhill.ca/olc/clouse.

SAMPLE OUTLINE WORKSHEET

Introduction

Detail to generate reader interest

_____

_____

_____

Thesis statement

_____

_____

Paragraph 2

Main idea

_____

_____

Supporting details

_____

_____

_____

Paragraph 3

Main idea

_____

_____

Supporting details

_____

_____

_____

Paragraph 4

Main idea

_____

_____

Supporting details

_____

_____

_____

Paragraph 5

Main idea

_____

_____

Supporting details

_____

_____

_____

Conclusion

Detail to provide closure

_____

_____

_____

THE WRITING PROCESS

Crafting an Introduction

First impressions count. Have you ever dropped a course after attending only one class session? Have you ever made an excuse to walk away from a person you just met? Have you ever selected a restaurant based on its name? We do such things in response to first impressions. Because first impressions are so important, the introduction of an essay must be carefully crafted. In addition to creating a first impression that will engage the reader's interest, the introduction can serve another purpose. It can tell the reader what an essay is about by including the **thesis. It also suggests the plan for the essay, through a preview of the ideas included in the essay.** To review the purpose and qualities of a thesis, return to page 51.

To decide how to create interest and engagement in a topic, consider audience and purpose. For example, if the purpose is to inform readers about dangerous email spam, do not begin with a humorous anecdote about a piece of unsolicited pornographic email you received. However, the introduction might tell a story about a time pornographic spam reached a child. If writing a letter to the editor of a local newspaper, do not open with a graphic description of a pornographic spam, which you might do for the customer service representative of your Internet service provider.

Below are some strategies for creating interest in a topic. Each strategy is illustrated with an introduction from a student essay, and the thesis is underlined as a study aid. These approaches are possibilities. As you draft, you may find different, more suitable strategies.

Provide Background Information

Rick was always taking crazy chances. Even in elementary school, he was the one to lock himself in the teacher's supply closet or lick a metal pole in the dead of a subzero winter. By high school, Rick had moved on to wilder things, but his drinking was the biggest concern. <u>Perhaps that is why no one was really</u>

surprised when he drove off the road and killed himself the day after his 18th birthday.

Tell a Pertinent Story

Last winter while home alone, an woman tripped on the garden hose and fell in her garage when the door was down. The pain was excruciating, and she could not move. She lay there for two hours, sobbing, until her son came home. Now, she is not an old woman; she is just 45. However, that experience made her feel fearful of growing old and living alone.

Explain Why the Topic Is Important

The recent tuition hike proposed by the Board of Governors has serious implications for everyone on this campus—students, faculty, and staff alike. If tuition goes up 45 percent as expected, fewer students will be able to attend school, which will mean fewer faculty and staff will be employed. Once the cost of school becomes prohibitive for all but the wealthy, then this university will begin a downward spiral that will eventually mean its demise. There is only one way to solve economic woes. The institution must embark on an austerity program that makes the tuition hike unnecessary.

Present Some Interesting Images or Use Description

It was a cool, crisp October morning. Sunrise was complete, the countryside awake and responding to another day. As he turned and slowly made his way into the woods, he had no idea what lay ahead on the path he was to follow that day.

Present an Intriguing Problem or Raise a Provocative Question

Does a Dr. Jekyll transform into Mr. Hyde the minute he gets behind the wheel of a car? Does a kind little old lady become Mario Andretti's pace car driver the instant she hits the freeway? Does an Eagle Scout by day become a marauding motorist by night? The chances are good that this happens, because people's personalities change the moment they strap on seat belts and head out on the highway.

Present an Opposing Viewpoint

People opposed to putting warning labels on CDs with sexually explicit or otherwise offensive lyrics have their reasons. They cite free speech, and they say teens will be encouraged to buy the CDs with the advisory labels. Even so, warning labels are necessary on certain music CDs.

Establish Yourself as Someone Knowledgeable about the Topic

Racial prejudice is still a fact of North American life, no matter what people hear to the contrary. Citizens need to remember that miscegenation laws existed into the 1960s in the US. There are also many examples of how towns and cities are divided racially in North America. Most people do not understand that they have grown up in city districts in which one race predominates. This has impacts in education, and ultimately in the working world. <u>A close study of the cities of Toronto and Chicago, with demographics to support this paper's assertion, will demonstrate that prejudice, or "racialism" is still very much a fact of life in our urban spaces.</u>

Open with an Attention-Grabbing Statement

What a family doctor does not know may surprise people—or it may kill them. We assume our doctors are smart and caring, that they will do whatever it takes to keep us well. We put our trust in them and never question their advice or decisions. Unfortunately, such trust is often misplaced. <u>For the best health care, we need to learn to question our doctors carefully.</u>

Explain Your Purpose

<u>All students should contact the Dean of Academic Affairs to protest the cancellation of the artist-in-residence program.</u> If enough students express their unhappiness, the dean will be forced to reinstate the program.

Find Some Common Ground to Establish a Bond with Your Reader

No one goes through life without doing something that they later regret. In fact, we often have many regrets. Fortunately, people are often given second chances and redeem themselves. It should not be any different for people who do not commit crimes after making mistakes in their youth. Nobody should be denied a second chance. <u>Young offenders should be pardoned when they come of age.</u>

Provide an Interesting Quotation

Mark Twain said, "Man is the only animal who blushes—or needs to." <u>People may take comfort in that statement when they recall the most embarrassing moments in life.</u>

Define Something

A good teacher is someone who sees what students can do, rather than what they cannot do. A good teacher shares knowledge, helps students achieve their potential, and fosters self-esteem. <u>Without a doubt, Dr. Sorenson is a good teacher.</u>

Give Relevant Examples

<u>Sometimes telling a lie is better than telling the truth.</u> When a friend asks what you think of the hideous glasses he just paid a great deal of money for, when a grandmother asks for a verdict on the rubber chicken she lovingly prepared for a birthday, when a girlfriend asks if her dress makes her look fat—it is best to lie.

In addition to knowing some strategies for engaging your reader's interest, writers should be aware of some strategies to avoid:

1. **Avoid opening with dictionary definitions.** This approach is overused and likely to be boring.

2. **Avoid opening with tired expressions.** Expressions like "It's always darkest before the dawn" and "Fools rush in where angels fear to tread" are overused cliché expressions, and should be avoided.

3. **Avoid apologizing.** Statements like "I really don't know much about this topic" or "I doubt that anyone can understand this issue" will cause your reader to lose confidence in what you have to say.

4. **Avoid a narrow, personal focus.** Yes, students have valid life experience, but often these experiences are not sufficient evidence with which to comment generally on a problem or an issue in society. Search for objective, factual examples.

THE WRITING PROCESS

Drafting Introductions

If you have trouble drafting your introduction, try the following:

- Skip it and come back to it after drafting the rest of an essay, but jot down your preliminary thesis to guide and focus the draft.

- Keep it simple, even just one or two sentences to create interest. Plan a provisional thesis, and recognize that it may change, depending on the ideas included in the essay.

- Try explaining why the topic is important, and try giving background information, to situate an issue.

- Remember to state the topic, controlling idea, and to provide a preview of the ideas in the essay. Sometimes it is easier to do this after writing a draft.

EXERCISE THE INTRODUCTION

1. Read three articles in news magazines, online, or in newspapers. Do the introductions engage your interest? Explain why or why not.

2. Below are three introductions written by students, each in need of revision. Revise each introduction so that it stimulates interest and has a suitable thesis.

   a. It was snowing when I boarded the plane. But I was terrified. I have always been afraid of air travel, and hopefully I will someday overcome this fear.

   Some suggestions for revision: Create some images. Describe the weather in more detail. Specify the kind of airplane and explain more carefully the feeling of terror. Also, does the thesis present one or two opinions? It should only present one. Finally, though this is a personal experience, the student writer should definitely reword this passage, to make it more objective.

   b. I set the alarm two hours earlier than usual and spent the morning cleaning like crazy. At 11:00 I went to the grocery store and bought all the necessary food. All afternoon I cooked; by 5:00 I was dressed and ready; but still the first meal I cooked for my in-laws was terrible.

   Some suggestions for revision: Be more specific. What time did the alarm go off? Give an example or two of the cleaning. What food did you buy? Was it expensive? What did you cook? How bad was it? Can you find a word or words more specific than *terrible*? Again, the writer can speak more generally of the nervousness a husband or wife may feel the first time they entertain their in-laws.

   c. Does crime pay? Does justice win out? Do the police always get their man? The day a teenager shoplifted a box of candy he learned the answers to these questions.

Some suggestions for revision: Substitute more interesting questions for these trite, rather boring ones—perhaps some questions that focus on the writer's feelings, such as "How many people have wondered what a criminal feels when he or she gets caught?" Create some interest by naming the brand or type of candy and giving its price and by giving the name of the store.

3. *Collaborative Activity.* With a classmate, select one of the preliminary thesis statements you shaped when you responded to question 6 on page 56. Establish an audience and purpose, and write an introduction for an essay that might use that thesis. Feel free to alter the original thesis, and make sure to include a preview of the major ideas for the paper. ●

Body Paragraphs

As discussed previously, body paragraphs explain or prove a thesis. They are the real core of an essay because they include illustrations, descriptions, reasons, and explanations that show a thesis to be true. In other words, the body paragraphs *support* the thesis. A typical body paragraph has three parts: the topic sentence and the supporting details, and a concluding statement that relates the paragraph's ideas to the thesis statement.

The topic sentence gives the focus of the paragraph by indicating the main idea the paragraph will discuss. This main idea will be something that helps support the thesis. **Supporting details** are the information that explains, proves, or otherwise develops the idea given in the topic sentence.

Placement of the Topic Sentence

The **topic sentence** presents the main idea of the body paragraph. The topic sentence often appears first in a paragraph, indicating the paragraph's focus. When the topic sentence comes first, the supporting details that follow explain, prove, or otherwise develop the topic sentence's idea, as well as relating the paragraph's topic to the essay's thesis. Here is an example from "Portrait of an Achiever." The topic sentence is underlined as a study aid.

Thesis: The key to Hugh's ability to overcome everyday problems is his determination.

One of Hugh's biggest problems was learning to tie his shoes. He would sit for hours trying to tie the knot that was so simple, yet so impossible. No matter how hard he tried, he just could not get it right. After seven years of practice and frustration, Hugh was finally able to tie that knot with one hand. The astonishing movements of his fingers as he tied the knot were almost miraculous. It took him seven years to train his fingers, but he never gave up, no matter how frustrated he became.

When you want to begin a body paragraph with a sentence or two that links the paragraph to the one before it, your topic sentence can come *near*—rather than *at*—the beginning of the paragraph. In this case, the supporting details come after the topic sentence. The following revision of a body paragraph from "Portrait of an Achiever" is an example. The linking sentences (also known as **transition sentences**) are double-underlined, and the topic sentence is underlined. Note how the topic sentence occurs near the end of the paragraph.

> Learning to tie his shoe, throw a baseball, and hammer a nail were, indeed, remarkable accomplishments. However, they were not Hugh's biggest challenges. Hugh's inability to swim was yet another problem that he had to overcome. For years, he thought that he could not swim with one arm, so he never tried. It was not until a swimmer was drowning in Lake Erie that Hugh decided he would learn to swim. Much to his own surprise, he found that he could stay afloat. It was his determination to overcome fear that gave him the confidence to jump in the water and save a life that day. Of course, once he realized that he would not drown, Hugh went on to practice his swimming techniques with the same determination he brings to every challenge. Now he swims farther and faster than many people do.

Writers can also begin with supporting details and place the topic sentence at the end of the body paragraph. In this case, the topic sentence draws a conclusion from the supporting details, as this rewritten example from "Portrait of an Achiever" illustrates. The topic sentence is underlined as a study aid.

> Hugh loves baseball. He spent an entire summer in the backyard devising a method that allows him to play with one hand. With one lightning speed motion, he can catch the ball in the glove, toss both the glove and the ball a few feet into the air, retrieve the ball from the air, and throw it to another player. Hugh also enjoys building objects out of wood. The first problem he encountered with the hobby was how to hold the nail while hammering. The solution was another exercise in determination: Hugh taught himself to steady the nail between his toes while he hammered it into the wood. At first, the method was literally painful, but perfection came after months of practice (and several smashed toes). Hugh's interests may seem to conflict with his abilities, but he always finds a way to overcome the obstacles.

The Implied Topic Sentence

Rather than write out a topic sentence, at times writers may want to imply it instead. When a topic sentence is *implied* rather than stated, the details in the paragraph must clearly suggest the main idea of the paragraph. Here is an example of a body paragraph with an implied topic sentence. The paragraph is taken from "That Street Called Cordova" on page 86. Its thesis idea is that something was always happening on Cordova, the street where the writer grew up.

> Two hours later, I was back outside, looking for all the kids, and I ran into Ms. Berry. "What are you doing outside, Boy?" she asked. "Haven't you had enough

drama today to last you a lifetime?" I had a quick flashback to this morning. "Haven't you had enough of boyfriends to last you two lifetimes?" I replied. Her mouth dropped as she raised her hand. I don't know what I was thinking. I could do nothing but brace myself for the impact. SLAP! "Don't you ever disrespect your elders again. Now go tell your mama that I smacked your mouth, and then tell her why." My mother and Ms. Berry were like sisters, and my mother had given Ms. Berry permission to whoop us kids if she ever caught us getting out of line when she wasn't around. I felt like crying, but Ms. Berry would have slapped me again. So I ran. I ended up at the candy lady's house for something to take my mind off the sting. Some 'Now & Laters' did it.

Qualities of an Effective Topic Sentence

An effective topic sentence accurately states the main idea of the body paragraph, states only one main idea, and states an idea related to the thesis.

A topic sentence should accurately state the main idea of the body paragraph. If a topic sentence indicates one main idea for the paragraph, but the supporting details go in a different direction, the reader can become confused. To state the main idea as accurately and precisely as possible, be specific.

Vague:	One of Hugh's biggest problems was not a problem for most people.
Specific:	One of Hugh's biggest problems was learning to tie his shoes.

The second topic sentence gives the reader a clearer sense of what the paragraph is about.

A topic sentence should state one main idea. A topic sentence that presents more than one main idea splits the focus and gives writers too much to do in a single paragraph.

Split focus:	Online shopping offers convenience and affordability.
One main idea:	Online shopping offers convenience.
One main idea:	Online shopping offers affordability.

The first topic sentence requires supporting details about two things: convenience and affordability. The next two topic sentences are better because each focuses on only one main idea.

A topic sentence should state a main idea related to the thesis. The topic sentence idea must be clearly related to both the topic and central points stated in an essay's thesis, or the essay will wander off course.

Thesis:	Men and women communicate differently.
Related topic sentence:	Men speak directly, and women speak indirectly.
Unrelated topic sentence:	Men are concerned with action, and women are concerned with feelings.

The first topic sentence is acceptable because it focuses on both the topic (the communication styles of men and women) and the central point (the styles are different). The second topic sentence is unacceptable because it does not focus on the topic of communication.

Thesis:	Oprah Winfrey has made an impact on American literary culture.
Related topic sentence:	Thanks to Oprah's book club, more Americans are buying and reading books.
Unrelated topic sentence:	In addition, when Oprah endorses a movie, ticket sales increase.

The first topic sentence is acceptable because it focuses on both the topic (Oprah Winfrey) and the central point (she has made an impact on American literary culture). The second topic sentence is unacceptable because it does not focus on the central point that Oprah has affected American *literary* culture; it focuses on a different aspect of American culture.

Effective Supporting Details

Writers cannot expect readers to believe a topic sentence just because someone writes it on the page. A discerning reader requires evidence, ideas, information, and examples that demonstrate the truth of the idea given in a topic sentence. That is where supporting details come in. Supporting details are the evidence provided to demonstrate the truth of the topic sentence. To be effective, supporting details must be adequate in number, and relevant to the topic and thesis.

Supporting details should be adequate in number: Supporting details are *adequate* when there are enough of them to demonstrate the validity or truth of the topic sentence, and of the thesis. To provide adequate detail, remember to *show* as well as *tell*. For example, reread the following body paragraph from an early draft of "Portrait of an Achiever":

> Hugh's interests always seem to conflict with his abilities, but not for long because he does not allow this fact to stand in his way. He always finds some way to overcome his disability and eliminate the interest-ability conflict. No matter how big the problem, Hugh finds a solution. He may have to labour for months or years to overcome the conflict, but time and again he has shown that he will do it. That's why he learned how to play baseball and engage in woodworking.

Notice that the supporting details are not adequate. They do not demonstrate the truth of the topic sentence because they *tell* that Hugh overcomes the disability, but they do not *show* that (or how) he does this. As a result, readers are unlikely to believe that topic sentence. In revision, the writer added more supporting details.

> Hugh's interests always seem to conflict with his abilities, but not for long because he does not allow this fact to stand in his way. He always finds some way to overcome his disability and eliminate the interest-ability conflict. For example, Hugh loves baseball. He spent an entire summer in the backyard

devising a method that allows him to play with one hand. With one lightning speed motion, he can catch the ball in the glove, toss both the glove and the ball a few feet into the air, retrieve the ball from the air, and throw it to another player. Hugh also enjoys building objects out of wood. The first problem he encountered with the hobby was how to hold the nail while hammering. The solution was another exercise in determination: Hugh taught himself to steady the nail between his toes while he hammered it into the wood. At first, the method was literally painful, but perfection came after months of practice (and several smashed toes).

First, the writer *tells* in the topic sentence: Hugh does not let his disability stand in the way of his interests. Then the writer *shows* us what he means in the supporting details: two specific examples *demonstrate* that Hugh overcame obstacles to pursue his interests.

As you work to include adequate supporting details, avoid repeating the same idea in different ways. Such repetition makes a paragraph run longer, but it does not contribute to adequate detail. Here is an example of the kind of repetition to avoid. (The underlined sentences are repetitious.)

Weightlifting is an excellent physical activity for women. It increases bone density and thus wards off osteoporosis. <u>It really does women a great deal of good.</u> However, weightlifting helps more than women's bones, for it also builds muscle, which increases metabolic rate. The increase in metabolic rate is good because it means that more calories are burned. <u>The protection afforded bones, though, is the big benefit.</u> Still another advantage to weightlifting is the fact that muscles are strengthened and thus better able to protect various body parts. <u>A woman's stronger muscles are far better able to protect various parts of the</u> anatomy.

Supporting details should be relevant to the topic, and ultimately to the thesis: Sometimes writers are so concerned with supplying adequate detail that they overlook the need to include the *right* detail. In addition to being adequate in number, supporting details must be *relevant*, or clearly and directly related to the main idea expressed in the topic sentence, and in the thesis for the essay. Consider this paragraph from an early draft of "Portrait of an Achiever":

Hugh's inability to swim was yet another problem that he had to overcome. For years, he thought that he could not swim with one arm, so he never tried. It was not until a swimmer was drowning in Lake Erie that Hugh decided he would learn to swim. Much to his own surprise, he found that he could stay afloat. It was his determination to overcome fear that gave him the confidence to jump in the water and save a life that day. Of course, once he realized that he wouldn't drown, Hugh went on to practice his swimming techniques with the same determination he brings to every challenge. Now he swims farther and faster than many people do. Hugh can also beat me in any short distance foot race, which is a further indication that his disability does not stand in his way.

Did you notice the irrelevant sentence? The last sentence does not belong in the paragraph because it is about running—and the topic sentence focuses on swimming. In revision, the writer deleted the last, irrelevant sentence.

THE WRITING PROCESS

Drafting Body Paragraphs

- Keep both audience and purpose in mind. Although drafting is primarily a writer-based activity, consider if supporting details are helping to meet the needs of readers and achieve purpose.
- Because idea generation continues during drafting, be receptive to new ideas and discoveries. Be prepared to go back and alter topic decisions made before drafting. Remember, an outline is flexible.
- Because drafts are *supposed* to be rough, do not expect body paragraphs to be richly detailed, beautifully expressed, or perfectly organized. Just do the best possible job at this stage. Remember, revision comes next.
- If you have trouble drafting:
  - Write the draft as someone would explain ideas to a close friend, or write the draft as a letter to a friend.
  - Stop and generate more ideas with one or more of the idea generation techniques; there may not be enough material yet to begin a draft.
  - Write the draft from start to finish without stopping and without evaluating the work. Feel free to ramble and write silly notions when stuck—there is time to refine later; for now, just get something on the page.
  - Revise the topic to something easier to write about.
  - Leave the work for a while. Ideas may need an incubation period before beginning a draft. However, think about the draft while doing other things. Obviously, you must start your writing early, so you have time for an incubation period, something Sally Brown fails to understand in the *Peanuts* comic strip.

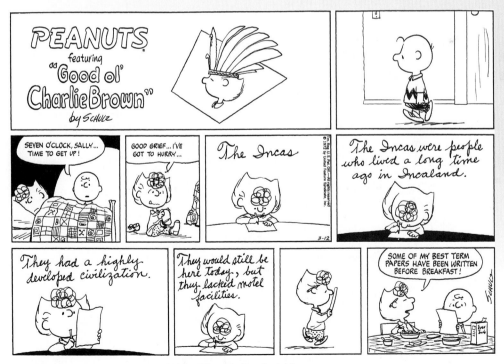

Peanuts reprinted by permission of United Feature Syndicate, Inc.

When to Begin a New Paragraph

Begin a new paragraph each time a new major point develops the thesis. Other instances when you should begin a new paragraph include the following:

- If the discussion of a point would require an overly long paragraph, writers can break up the discussion into two or more paragraphs as a courtesy to readers, who may find one very long paragraph taxing.
- A new paragraph can emphasize a point. If a point can appear in a paragraph along with other ideas but that point deserves to receive special emphasis, place it in a paragraph of its own.

EXERCISE BODY PARAGRAPHS

1. This chapter's student essay on page 86, written by a first-year student, has definite strengths as well as some problems. Read the essay and answer the questions after it.
   a. What is the thesis of "That Street Called Cordova"?
   b. Is there enough detail to demonstrate the validity of the thesis? That is, is the thesis adequately developed in the body paragraphs? Explain.
   c. What is the topic sentence for each body paragraph? Is each topic sentence relevant to the thesis?
   d. Which topic sentence receives the most development?
   e. Which topic sentence receives the least development? How do you react to the paragraph with that topic sentence?
   f. Do any paragraphs need additional supporting details because the author is telling without showing?
   g. Are any details not relevant to the appropriate topic sentence?

2. Assume you are writing an essay using one of the following thesis statements (you fill in the balnks).

   The best thing about _____ is _____.
   The worst thing about _____ is _____.

   Decide which thesis to use, and use the idea generation techniques to discover two main ideas for developing that thesis. For example, if your thesis is "The best thing about college life is meeting interesting people," writers might describe the people they meet in class and in residence. Or they might develop one paragraph about a foreign student from Zimbabwe, and another about Dr. Schwartz, the professor who creates interest in cellular biology. Develop each main point in a body paragraph.

3. *Collaborative Writing Activity.* Bring your completed body paragraphs and thesis to class, and exchange them with a classmate. After reading each other's work, write a note to the person whose paragraphs you read, answering the following questions:
   a. Are the topic sentences relevant? If not, what specifically is not relevant and why?
   b. Are all the supporting details relevant? If not, what detail is not relevant? Why?
   c. Is the supporting detail adequate in each paragraph? If not, where is the detail needed? What kind of detail should it be?
   d. Is the order of details logical? If not, what is wrong?

   When you get back your paragraphs, study your classmate's responses. Decide whether you agree with the evaluation. If not, discuss your disagreement with your instructor. ●

The Conclusion

The conclusion of an essay is important because it influences the reader's final impression. Have you ever seen a movie that starts out strong and then fizzles at the end? As you walked out of the theatre, you probably talked about the disappointing ending, not the strong beginning or middle. Writing works the same way. Even if it has a strong introduction and body, an essay with a weak conclusion, like the one in the *Luann* cartoon, will leave the reader feeling let down.

When drafting a conclusion, be sure to consider the thesis, body paragraphs, audience, and purpose. Should you summarize your main points? That depends on your body paragraphs and audience. If there are many points, the reader may find a summary helpful, but if there are only a few, the reader may find a summary unnecessary and even patronizing. Should writers end by asking readers to take a specific action? That may depend on the purpose. If the goal is to convince readers to do something, such as start a recycling program on campus, a call to action is appropriate.

The length of your conclusion will vary from essay to essay. Sometimes a single sentence ties everything up perfectly. Other times, writers need a paragraph of several sentences. A long essay or research paper may require a conclusion of more than one paragraph. No matter what the length, keep the conclusion in proportion to the rest of the essay. Short essays have short conclusions, and longer essays can have longer conclusions.

Regardless of the length of the conclusion, it is best to avoid these expressions: "in conclusion," "in summary," "to conclude," "to summarize," and "in closing." They are overused and can be flat and lifeless.

If a suitable conclusion does not immediately occur to you, try one or more of the following approaches.

Leave the Reader with an Overall Reaction

With this approach, extract from the essay an overriding impression, observation, or reaction to leave the reader with a final sense of how you, the writer, feel about things. Here is an example for an essay with the thesis "Ability grouping is harmful to many students":

> Clearly, ability grouping causes many students to feel unsuccessful, and it damages their self-esteem. That fact, alone, should be enough to prompt educators to discontinue this harmful practice.

Luann © GEC Inc. Distr. by United Feature Syndicate, Inc.

Summarize the Main Points of the Essay

Use a summary conclusion when a brief review would help the reader. If the student writer has written a relatively short essay with easily understood and easily remembered ideas, the reader does not need a summary and may grow annoyed by the repetition. On the other hand, if an essay has many ideas, some of which are complex, the reader may appreciate a final summary.

Introduce a Related Idea

An effective conclusion can include an idea not appearing elsewhere in the essay. However, the idea must be related, clearly and closely, to the ideas that appear in the body. In this way, the reader is not caught off guard by an idea that seems to spring out of nowhere. Here is an example for an essay with the thesis "With so much discussion of the advantages of computers, we tend to overlook the fact that these machines have serious disadvantages as well":

> If we overlook the drawbacks of computers, we risk becoming enslaved by these machines. Certainly, this happened with the automobile. We routinely drive even short distances, never even considering walking instead. As a result, our physical fitness suffers and we have fewer opportunities to enjoy the splendour of a beautiful day.

Make a Determination

Frequently, the ideas in the body paragraphs lead to some significant point or determination. When this is the case, use the final paragraph(s) to state and explain that point. Here is an example for an essay with the thesis "Co-workers should never attempt to become friends outside of the workplace":

> Co-workers who socialize outside of the workplace do not remain friends for long. Many regret the strain socializing creates on relationships with colleagues at work, and regret having to quit jobs. People who make this mistake claim next time they will know better.

Restate the Thesis

Restating the thesis can provide emphasis, but it can also seem dull and uninspired, so use this approach cautiously. To restate a thesis, use different language to express the idea in a new way. Or combine the restatement with another approach, as this revised conclusion of "Portrait of an Achiever" does.

Thesis: The key to Hugh's ability to overcome everyday problems is his determination.

> Determination can be born of challenge, but it isn't always so. Some people who face problems give up, wallow in self-pity, or rely on others to solve problems for them. Hugh refuses to do that. Everyone can draw inspiration from Hugh's ongoing determination to meet every problem head on and solve it.

Explain the Significance of the Topic

This approach is particularly effective when an essay tells a story and the writer wants to note why that story is important. Here is an example from an essay that tells the story of the time the author's house burned down:

> Although young people generally think they are immortal, because of a house fire, the victims no longer take safety for granted. Wherever they live, they plan an escape route in the event of fire. They also have smoke detectors, and keep chain ladders by second-storey bedroom windows.

Make a Recommendation or Call the Reader to Action

This approach is often appropriate for essays with a persuasive purpose. Here is an example for an essay with the thesis "Because there are too few organs for all the patients needing transplants, laws should govern how the limited number of organs are allocated":

> It is time to begin a letter-writing campaign to urge our Members of Provincial Parliament to indicate popular support for organ donation legislation. If enough people write, we can have equitable distribution of organs.

Explain the Consequences of Ignoring a Particular View

This approach also works well for essays with a persuasive purpose. Here is an example for the thesis used in the previous example:

> If we do not legislate organ donation provincially, then we cannot be sure that the sickest patients will be first on donation lists. Instead, the wealthy and the famous will use their influence to get organs that more appropriately belong to others.

Combine Approaches

Writers can also combine two or more strategies. For example, restate the thesis and then summarize. Or make a determination and then give an overall reaction. A related idea can appear with a restatement. Any combination of approaches is possible.

EXERCISE THE CONCLUSION

1. Locate three essays with formal conclusions. You might check the library for books of essays, weekly newsmagazines, and newspaper editorial pages online. Read the essays and answer the following questions:
    a. Does the conclusion bring the essay to a satisfying close? Explain.
    b. What approach is used for the conclusion?
    c. Is the length of the conclusion appropriate? Explain.
    d. Does the conclusion leave you with a positive final impression? Why or why not?

2. *Collaborative Activity.* The following is an essay written by a student. The conclusion has been omitted, so with two classmates, write your own. In class, take turns reading your conclusions and note the variety of approaches. You will find it interesting to see how many different ways the conclusion can be handled. ●

CRITICAL READING STUDENT ESSAY

That Street Called Cordova

Robert Howard

1   I was awakened by Ms. Berry yelling, as she threw out her boyfriend again. I hurried down from the bunk bed to join my older brothers and older sister as they watched the whole thing from the bedroom window. We laughed as she chased him down the pavement in her housecoat with rollers in her hair. "You dirty, no good, two-timing dog!" she yelled as she continued her chase. This incident was a typical start to a typical day on Cordova, where something was always happening.

2   My parents did not allow us to go off of the street, so we made up our own games with neighborhood kids. This day we played Bat on the Bounce. It was like stickball, except we used a metal bat with a tennis ball. We played it on a big dirt field in the middle of the projects. One day while I was standing off to the side watching the game, the ball I was holding rolled out of my hands and into play. I did not want the batter to trip over the ball, so I hurried to pick it up before he swung the bat. BUNNG! The bat smashed me so hard on my head that my neck snapped back. I felt my knees buckle as I fell in slow motion to the ground. My ears were ringing a thousand bells at once. I started crying, and my brothers took off after the batter, who had dropped the bat and tried to run home. They caught him at his front door and beat him up. My sister helped me to my feet. I knew that it was not that guy's fault because I walked out in front of him. But he still came to my house and apologized, and my mother made me give him a hug.

3   Two hours later, I was back outside, looking for all the kids, and I ran into Ms. Berry. "What are you doing outside, Boy?" she asked. "Haven't you had enough drama today to last you a lifetime?" I had a quick flashback to this morning. "Haven't you had enough of boyfriends to last you two lifetimes?" I replied. Her mouth dropped as she raised her hand. I don't know what I was thinking. I could do nothing but brace myself for the impact. SLAP! "Don't you ever disrespect your elders again. Now go tell your mama that I smacked your mouth, and then tell her why." My mother and Ms. Berry were like sisters, and my mother had given Ms. Berry permission to whoop us kids if she ever caught us getting out of line when she wasn't around. I felt like crying, but Ms. Berry would have slapped me again. So I ran. I ended up at the candy lady's house for something to take my mind off the sting. Some 'Now & Laters' did it.

4   I met up with my brothers just as it was getting dark. It was time to play Kissy Catchers. This game was played at sunset. All the girls hid, while the boys tried to find them. If found, the girl had to kiss the guy. I didn't like the game much because I always found the same ugly girl who lived two doors down from me. At the time, I didn't think she knew how to play very well because she always told me where she was going to hide.

The complete essay, including any bibliographic references, is also available on the Online Learning Centre at www.mcgrawhill.ca/olc/clouse.

Drafting the Title of an Essay

A good title can intrigue the reader and draw that person in. Sometimes the perfect title strikes a writer early, perhaps during idea generation or while drafting. Other times, a good title does not occur until the writer is revising.

When drafting a title, consider the content of the essay, the audience, and purpose. For example, when writing a serious piece about changing immigration laws, a humorous title would undermine the purpose. However, a humorous title might work well for an essay about everything that went wrong the first time someone met future in-laws. If the audience is a computer science instructor, indicate the contents of a piece of writing with a title like "Project Management in Networked Environments," because the reader will expect a title that previews the writing's focus.

Do not write a title that tricks or misleads the reader. If the title of an essay reads, "Making a Fortune from Home," and then the essay suggests that the joys of being a stay-at-home parent are worth a fortune, the reader will feel betrayed.

Do not refer to the title as if it were part of an introduction. For example, if the title is "The Impact of the Internet," avoid beginning with "It has changed the way we work and live." Instead, write, "The Internet has changed the way we work and live."

Finally, when drafting a title, remember the following points:

1. **Be specific.** Specific titles give readers a sense of what an essay is about. For this reason, "Understanding Email Etiquette in Business" is a much better title than "Email."
2. **Do not restate the thesis.** If the thesis is "Trying juveniles as adults is not justice," the title should not be "Trying Juveniles as Adults Is Not Justice." However, one could use "Juveniles in Adult Courts: An Alarming Miscarriage of Justice."
3. **Include humour or word play only when appropriate.** Humour and wordplay can make excellent titles for humorous, informal, or personal essays. However, they are generally not appropriate for academic and business writing, or for essays on serious topics.

Drafting Electronically

1. If your computer software has an outline feature, use it to create an outline for a first draft. In Windows, for example, click on "Format" to get a drop-down menu. Then click on "Bullets and Numbering" and then "Outline Numbered" for an outline format for use.
2. Place the outline in one window and write the draft in the other. This procedure makes it easy to refer to the outline.
3. If you have trouble writing a paragraph or two, paste in the relevant portion of the outline into the draft as a placeholder and reminder of what goes in that spot.
4. Do not forget to back up your draft frequently so you do not lose your work in the event of a power failure or hard drive crash.

Christel's Essay in Progress: FIRST DRAFT PERSUASIVE ESSAY

Using her outline and preliminary thesis, Christel wrote the following first draft of her project, as a five-paragraph essay. Please refer to her outline on page 67. Marginal text boxes call the reader's attention to some important features of this first written draft, and highlight Christel's writing process. Notice that the thesis statement includes a preview of the organization of the essay. To see how Christel developed this informal essay into an APA research paper, please see page 103. Notice how, since this process is recursive, many details, and even the thesis statement, change over the course of the project.

> *Note:* the thesis for this essay is inexact, and somewhat cumbersome. This was later revised, and appears as a stronger statement in the research paper on page 136.

When a patient is knocking on death's door how can health care professionals help, since death is inevitable? Health care professionals assist in end-of-life care, also known as palliative care. There are significant issues that surround this type of care and it affects more than just the dying patient. End-of-life care or palliative care has no benefit to the dying patient, and helps only the survivors, and there is significant strain on the health care system and the health professionals that are necessary to provide this care.

This paragraph addresses the first major idea: that palliative care strains medical resources.

The dying patient is usually under substantial physical and emotional strain due to disease progression as they enter the final stages of life. They have to endure their loved ones' watching them slowly fade away. The medical interventions accessible in Canada are not intended to end life sooner. The main goal of palliative care is to maximize the life that the patient has left. The options available to patients include Do Not Resuscitate orders, in which no heroic measures to be taken and limited medical interventions used when dying. Very often, patients cannot make these decisions for themselves and family may have to decide what is to be done. Family members have difficulty making these decisions and may not make the decision that is in the interest of the patient. There is no medically assisted death available in Canada, which would bring death sooner, therefore lessening patients' overall suffering.

Christel's second argument is addressed somewhat weakly, as this topic receives no clear mention in the thesis. The essay thesis was revised after this submission, and the content related more closely to it. See page 136 for the final draft of the paper.

In order to facilitate palliative care there needs to be availability and funding within the health care system. As the Canadian health care system is structured currently, there is not enough funding to allocate more public hospice space, and hospitals are overcrowded. Including more palliative care within these facilities will only strain them further. Also, hospice care is usually disease-specific, for example for cancer and AIDS; as well, hospice care is funded mainly through donations and by specific organizations, like the Canadian Cancer Society. With an aging population, Statistics Canada projects that the rate of deaths in Canada will increase by 33% by the year 2020 to more than 330,000 deaths per year. Not enough specially educated health professionals capable of and prepared to deal with this type of specialized care are available. Doctors and nurses only receive minimal education in the area of palliative care.

This paragraph takes up the topic of strain on the health care system, and particularly the emotional strain experienced by health professionals.

The health care professionals necessary to deliver end-of-life care are under substantial psychological strain, watching people die every day. This leaves them feeling defeated and helpless, as it goes against the principles of healing. There are not enough support programs for these health care workers to assist them with issues surrounding palliative care. There are also ethical issues that care providers have to struggle with, as palliative care may be contradictory to their own personal beliefs. As well, alternatives to palliative care may be against their personal beliefs. For example, there are many moral and ethical issues surrounding medically assisted death.

There are considerable issues surrounding end-of-life care, including patient wishes and strain on the individual as a family suffers loss. As well, there are the effects of a strained health care system unable to provide basic care, as well as the addition of palliative care. The burden that this type of care places on health professionals physically and mentally is too much to continue providing this service. Canadians need to have access to alternatives allowing life to end sooner, if they wish, therefore easing the burden felt by all involved. Palliative care causes needless further suffering to patients, strain on the health care systems and health care professionals, making it an ineffective service to provide Canadians.

In the last paragraph, Christel summarizes the content of this informal essay, and reiterates the thesis, to demonstrate that she has explored and supported the controlling idea for this paper.

Reprinted by permission of Christel Webb.

To see what Christel has done to improve this essay, by revising the thesis, and expanding ideas and examples based on research, please see page 136.

EXERCISE YOUR ESSAY IN PROGRESS

Directions: After completing this exercise, save your draft. You will use it in the next chapter as you work toward your completed essay.

1. Using one of your outlines from the exercise on page 68, write a first draft. Don't worry about getting everything down in perfect form; just write your ideas the best way you can. Skip any troublesome sections.

2. Study your draft. Does it suggest that you should return to an earlier stage in the process? If so, which one(s), and why? Return to those stages now and do what is necessary.

3. Were you comfortable writing your first draft? If not, what will you do differently the next time you draft? Why? ●

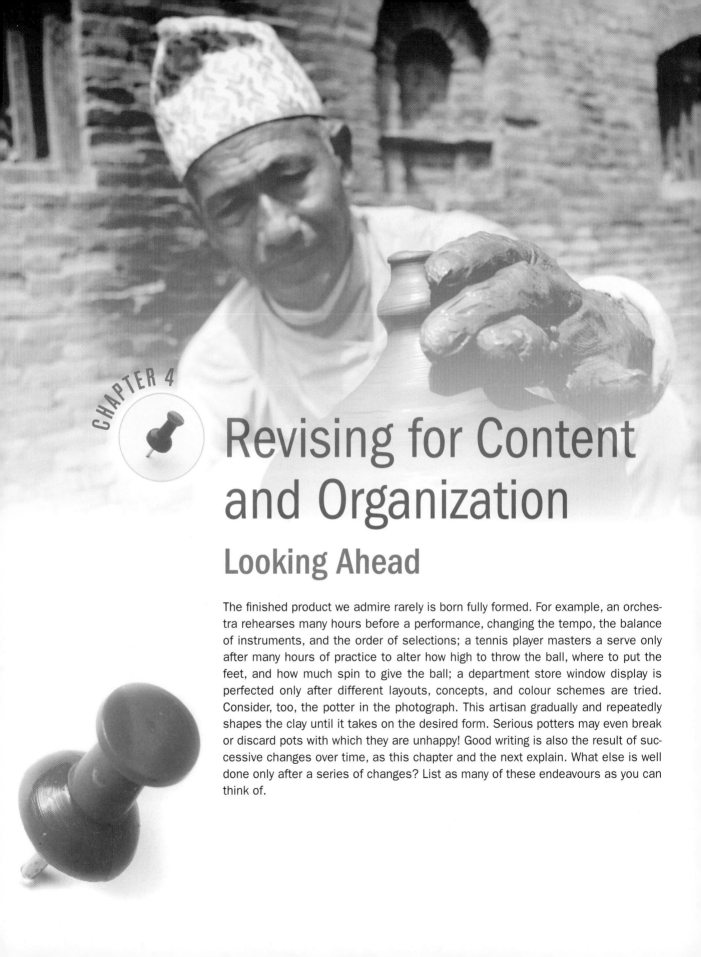

Revising for Content and Organization

Looking Ahead

The finished product we admire rarely is born fully formed. For example, an orchestra rehearses many hours before a performance, changing the tempo, the balance of instruments, and the order of selections; a tennis player masters a serve only after many hours of practice to alter how high to throw the ball, where to put the feet, and how much spin to give the ball; a department store window display is perfected only after different layouts, concepts, and colour schemes are tried. Consider, too, the potter in the photograph. This artisan gradually and repeatedly shapes the clay until it takes on the desired form. Serious potters may even break or discard pots with which they are unhappy! Good writing is also the result of successive changes over time, as this chapter and the next explain. What else is well done only after a series of changes? List as many of these endeavours as you can think of.

When reading and **editing** a draft, writers may feel overwhelmed by how rough it is. Writers may be tempted to ignore the rough spots, just correct spelling and punctuation, change a few words, and hand the essay in. However, even the roughest draft has potential, so think like a writer and read like a critic, and realize that a draft provides raw material to work with. The gaps, clumsy wording, lack of clarity, inadequate detail, and other problems will be transformed into a solid essay through the process of reworking that is **revision**.

The first draft completes the work that is primarily writer-based. With revision, student writers must make changes critically to transform writing into an essay suitable for readers. The word *revision* (re-vision) means "seeing again." The revision process calls upon writers to look again at work—but this time from the reader's point of view. If writers do not look at drafts from the reader's perspective, they can create the kind of misunderstanding illustrated in the *Non Sequitur* cartoon on the next page.

THE WRITING PROCESS

Revision

Preparing to Revise

- Put written work aside for at least several hours—a day or more if possible. The break helps you shift from writer to reader roles. Also, at this point, you know what you mean so well that you find it hard to evaluate writing objectively unless you put some distance between yourself and your draft.

- Be mindful of the audience's characteristics by listing the traits that will most affect how a reader may react to an essay. Consider age, gender, level of education, degree of resistance to a thesis, political leanings, socio-economic level, and so forth. Writers can't think like readers if they aren't clear about what that person is like.

- If a draft is handwritten, type it before beginning to revise. The draft will resemble printed matter, making it easier to view it as a reader will. Also, when work is in type, you will spot certain problems more easily. For example, a paragraph that runs only two typed lines is a visual cue that an essay may need more supporting details. (Be sure to double-space typed drafts, so there is plenty of room to add handwritten comments and corrections.)

- Ask other people to read and react to a draft, using the guidelines for reader response explained on page 102. The best way to think like a reader is to find out what other readers think.

- Ask someone to read a draft aloud. Try to listen like the audience and not the writer.

Critique, Revise, and Edit

A *critic* is a judge of both strong and weak qualities of something. For example, newspapers employ critics to review movies and write their assessments of the strong and weak aspects in movie reviews published in papers. When you revise, you must think like your critics to judge drafts and decide what is strong and what is weak. Doing so helps to determine what changes need to be made.

Non Sequitur © 2002 Wiley Miller. Dist. by Universal Press Syndicate. Reprinted with permission. All rights reserved.

An *editor* makes changes in writing. Publishing companies employ editors to make changes to improve the content, organization, and expression of ideas in manuscripts. When you revise, you must function like an editor and make the needed changes in drafts that you identify in the role of critic.

Some may think that editors focus on correcting sentence structure and mistakes with grammar, punctuation, and capitalization. However, being an editor means revising for content, organization, and expression of ideas as well. Editing for sentence structure, grammar, spelling, and punctuation should come later, when you finish making changes to improve content, organization, and expression of ideas. Why check spellings of words that may change during revision?

In Chapters 2 and 3, we learned about the qualities of an effective thesis, introduction, body paragraphs, and conclusion. When revising for content, keep these qualities, along with purpose and audience, firmly in mind. In addition, the following will help you think like a critic and work like an editor as you revise.

Evaluate and revise the thesis. Carefully reconsider the thesis. Revise, if necessary, to be sure the thesis meets the criteria in the following box. (To review any of these criteria, turn to page 52.)

EVALUATING AND REVISING THE THESIS

The thesis *should:*

- Be suited to the audience and purpose for the assignment
- Include only one topic and controlling idea, and the essay's subtopics
- Express the controlling idea in specific language

The thesis should *not:*

- Be a statement of fact or an announcement
- Include a personal expression such as "in my opinion"

Because the thesis previews the main points in an essay, state those points in the same order as they are discussed in the body paragraphs.

Evaluate and revise body paragraphs. When considering the body paragraphs, remember that the ultimate goal is to meet the needs of the audience and to achieve a purpose for writing. Revise, if necessary, to be sure body paragraphs meet the criteria in the following box. (To review these criteria, turn to page 76.)

EVALUATING AND REVISING BODY PARAGRAPHS

The topic sentences should:

- Indicate accurately the main idea of the body paragraph
- State only one main idea
- Be relevant to the thesis statement

The supporting details should:

- Be adequate by showing as well as telling
- Avoid saying the same thing in different ways
- Be relevant to the topic sentence (and, therefore, the thesis)

If detail is not adequate, it may be necessary to do more research to expand the essay's scope. You can also try adding examples or brief stories to show and not just tell. If an essay still needs further details, return to idea generation, perhaps trying a different technique this time. If idea generation does not produce optimum results, you may need to change the thesis or topic to something that you have more ideas about. Careful planning, research, and outlining, though, make a sound basis for a good paper. This is why writer-based activities discussed in previous chapters are so important.

If there is a relevance problem, try to slant the detail to make it relevant. If that does not work, alter the thesis or topic sentence to accommodate the detail, but be sure the change does not create a relevance problem elsewhere. If these strategies do not help, eliminate the irrelevant detail.

Evaluate and revise the introduction, conclusion, and title. The introduction, conclusion, and title are important because they influence the reader's initial and final reactions. Consider these elements of a draft and revise, if necessary, to be sure they meet the criteria in the following box. (To review introductions, see page 72; to review conclusions, see page 83; to review titles, see page 87.)

EVALUATING AND REVISING THE INTRODUCTION, CONCLUSION, AND TITLE

The introduction should:

- Create interest in an essay
- Be suited to the audience and purpose
- Present a controlling idea and a preview for the paper's main ideas

The conclusion should:

- Leave the reader with a positive final impression
- Be suited to the audience and purpose
- Avoid expressions such as "in conclusion" and "to summarize"
- Demonstrate how the essay has supported or proven the thesis in the introduction

The title should:

- Be suited to content, audience, and purpose
- Avoid misleading the reader or simply restating the thesis
- Be specific
- Use humour and wordplay only if appropriate

Critique, Revise, and Edit: Revising Organization

When evaluating and revising organization, keep the audience and purpose in mind, and consider the criteria in the following box. (To review ways to arrange details, turn to page 79; to review paragraphing, turn to page 76.)

EVALUATING AND REVISING ORGANIZATION

Main ideas should:

- Be arranged in a chronological, spatial, progressive, or other suitable order
- Follow logically from one to the next
- Have coherence (explained in the next section)
- Have appropriate paragraphing

A good way to check the arrangement of ideas is to outline a draft *after* having written it—even if it was outlined before. Better yet, you could do this with a partner. A close look at the outline can reveal problems with organization. To change the order of ideas and work digitally, the cut/paste function in a word processing program will expedite the process. Literally cutting and pasting a hard copy also works.

Achieving Coherence

To meet the needs of readers and achieve a purpose for writing, you must do more than simply arrange ideas logically and effectively. You must also connect ideas smoothly and show how they relate to each other. Connecting ideas smoothly and demonstrating their relationship to each other, achieves **coherence**. Two ways to achieve coherence are with transitions and repetition.

Use Transitions to Achieve Coherence

Transitions are connecting or linking words and phrases that show the relationship between ideas. Consider, for example, the following sentences taken from an essay a student wrote about what a woman experienced when she lost her job:

> For weeks she wondered what she had done wrong, until friends helped her realize that she was not necessarily responsible. The manager's explanation that "organizations change" became more acceptable to her.

The relationship between the ideas in the two sentences is not immediately clear, so the sentences are confusing. Look what happens, however, when a transitional phrase is added:

> For weeks she wondered what she had done wrong, until friends helped her realize that she was not necessarily responsible. <u>As a result</u>, the manager's explanation that "organizations change" became more acceptable to her.

The transitional phrase *as a result* signals that the ideas in the first sentence function as a cause, and the ideas in the second sentence function as the effect of that cause. By demonstrating this cause-and-effect relationship, the transition smooths the flow of ideas and helps the reader understand how the writer is connecting the two thoughts.

In addition to connecting ideas in different sentences, transitions can clarify the relationship between ideas in the same sentence:

> In her campaign speech, the MP claimed that she favoured social programs for the unemployed and the elderly; <u>however</u>, her voting record demonstrates otherwise.

The transitional word *however* signals to the reader that what comes after it is in contrast to what comes before it.

Transitional words and phrases can signal a variety of relationships. The following chart presents these relationships and some common transitions used to signal them.

TRANSITIONS

To Show	Common Transitions	Example
Addition	also, and, and then, too, in addition, furthermore, moreover, equally important, another, first, second, third	The mayor expects city council to approve her salary recommendations. *In addition,* she expects to gain support for her road repair program.
Time sequence	now, then, before, after, afterward, earlier, later, immediately, soon, next, meanwhile, gradually, suddenly, finally, previously, before, next, often	*Before* an agreement can be reached between the striking workers and management, both sides must soften their stands.
Spatial arrangement	near, nearly, far, far from, beside, in front of, beyond, above, below, to the right, around, on one side, outside, across, opposite to	As you are leaving the fair grounds, turn right on Highway 76. *Just beyond* the junction sign is the turnoff.
Comparison	in the same way, similarly, just like, just as, in like manner, likewise	The federal government must not abandon the poor. *Similarly,* it must not forget the elderly.
Contrast	but, still, however, on the other hand, yet, on the contrary, nevertheless, despite, in spite of	*In spite of* the currently depressed housing market, money can still be made in real estate.
Cause and effect	because, since, so, consequently, hence, as a result, therefore, thus	*Because of* the unusually warm weather in February, maple syrup season is early this year.
Purpose	for this purpose, so that this may occur, in order to	*In order to* hike the GST, the government must show that more money is needed to pay down the deficit.
Emphasis	indeed, in fact, surely, undoubtedly, without a doubt, certainly, truly, to be sure, I am certain	Adolescence is not a carefree time. *In fact,* it can be a very unsettled period.

To Show	Common Transitions	Example
Illustration	for example, for instance, as an illustration, specifically, to be specific, in particular	The parents complained that the school was too easy. They said, *for example*, that their children received no homework.
Summary or clarification	in summary, in conclusion, as I have shown, in brief, in short, in other words, all in all, that is	The used car she bought needed brakes, shocks, and tires. *In brief*, it was in bad shape.
Conceding a point	although, while this may be the case, granted, even though, whereas	*Even though* most Canadians can read and write, the official illiteracy rate is quite high in Canada since it accounts only for French and English literacy, not the many languages of immigrants.

Use Repetition to Achieve Coherence

Writers can also achieve coherence by repeating key words to demonstrate the relationship between ideas. Consider these sentences:

> Exam anxiety is more prevalent among students than many instructors realize. Many students who understand the material are prevented from demonstrating their knowledge.

These sentences have a relationship to each other (cause and effect), but that relationship is not revealed as clearly as it could be. In the revised version, strategic repetition solves the problem:

> Exam anxiety is more prevalent among students than many instructors realize. Such anxiety prevents many students who understand the material from demonstrating their knowledge.

The repetition of *anxiety* at the beginning of the second sentence clarifies the relationship between ideas. In addition, this repetition smoothes the flow from the first sentence to the second.

Writers can also achieve coherence by repeating a key idea rather than a key word. Consider the following sentences:

> Mr. Ferguson, driving at close to 60 miles per hour, took his eyes off the road for only a second to light a cigarette. A three-car pileup put two people in the hospital.

The relationship between these two sentences is not as clear as it should be. The repetition of a key idea can solve the problem:

Mr. Ferguson, driving at close to 60 miles per hour, took his eyes off the road for only a second to light a cigarette. <u>This momentary lapse</u> caused a three-car pileup that put two people in the hospital.

At the beginning of the second sentence, the phrase *this momentary lapse* refers to the action described in the first sentence. It repeats that idea to achieve coherence.

One other way to achieve coherence is to use synonyms to repeat an idea. Consider these sentences:

Jenny has been in bed with strep throat for a week. Her illness may force her to drop her courses this term.

Notice that the second sentence begins with *her illness*. The word *illness* is a synonym for *strep throat*, which appears in the first sentence. This synonym repeats a key idea to achieve coherence.

Use Transitions and Repetition to Achieve Coherence between Paragraphs

Writers can use transitions and repetition to link the end of one paragraph and the beginning of the next. Used this way, transitions and repetition tighten organization by demonstrating how ideas in different paragraphs are related. They also improve the flow of these paragraphs.

ACHIEVING COHERENCE BETWEEN PARAGRAPHS

Use a Transition

End of one paragraph:	The students believe that the proposed library will not meet their needs.
Beginning of next paragraph:	<u>In addition</u>, students oppose construction of the library for economic reasons.

Repeat Key Words

End of one paragraph:	Clearly, teacher burnout is a serious problem.
Beginning of next paragraph:	Unfortunately, <u>teacher burnout</u> is not the <u>only serious</u> problem facing our schools.

Repeat a Key Idea

End of one paragraph:	For the first time in years, the national divorce rate is beginning to drop.
Beginning of next paragraph:	The reasons for <u>this new trend</u> deserve our attention.

Use a Synonym

End of one paragraph:	All signs indicate that the safety forces strike will continue for at least another week.
Beginning of next paragraph:	If the <u>work stoppage</u> does last <u>seven more days</u>, the effects will be devastating.

EXERCISE COHERENCE

1. Write sentences and supply transitions according to the directions given. The first one is done as an example.
   a. Write two sentences about the way women are portrayed in television commercials. Link the sentences with a transitional word or phrase signalling contrast.

      Example: Television ads do not depict women realistically. *However,* today's commercials are an improvement over those of 10 years ago.

   b. Write one sentence about exams that has a transitional word or phrase of addition to link two ideas.
   c. Write two sentences about a television show. Link the sentences with a transitional word or phrase signalling emphasis.
   d. Write one sentence about a holiday that has a transitional word or phrase of contrast.
   e. Write two sentences that describe the location of items in the library. Link the sentences with a transitional word or phrase to signal spatial arrangement.
   f. Write one sentence about a campus issue with a transitional word or phrase for admitting a point.
   g. Write two sentences about someone you enjoy being with. Link the sentences with a transitional word or phrase of illustration.
   h. Write two sentences, each about a different family member. Link the sentences with a transitional word or phrase of either comparison or contrast.
   i. Write two sentences about what you do upon waking in the morning. Link the sentences with a transitional word or phrase to show time sequence.
   j. Write two sentences about your toughest instructor ever. Link the sentences with a transitional word or phrase of clarification.

2. In the following sentences, fill in the blanks with one or more words according to the directions given. The first one is done as an example.
   a. *Repeat key word:* I am uncomfortable with the principle behind life insurance. Basically, such insurance means I am betting some giant corporation that I will die before my time.
   b. *Repeat key word:* Over the years, the registration process has become increasingly complex, causing students to become confused and frustrated. This _____ is now being studied by campus administrators in an effort to streamline procedures.
   c. *Use a synonym for* additional week: Because so many students found it impossible to complete their term papers by Friday, Dr. Rodriguez was willing to give an additional week to work on them. _____ helped everyone feel more comfortable with the assignment.
   d. *Repeat key idea:* The Altmans returned from their weekend trip to discover that their house had been broken into and ransacked. _____ was so extensive, it took them two full days to get everything back in order.
   e. *Repeat key idea:* According to the current charter, the club's president can serve for only one term. _____ was meant to ensure that there would be frequent change in leadership. ●

Working Collaboratively: Revising With Reader Response

Nothing helps you make revision decisions more than the thoughtful responses of a reliable reader. Even professional writers make changes based on the responses of reliable readers such as editors and reviewers.

To get reader response on a draft as part of the revision process, follow one of the following procedures or use one your instructor recommends. No matter what the procedure, give the reader a clean, typed copy of a draft that has progressed past the rough-draft stage. (For an example of reader response, see page 103.)

Procedure 1

Give the reader a copy of the draft, and ask him or her to indicate the chief strengths and weaknesses in a summary comment at the end. Ask the reader to be specific, using language like this: "Good intro—it gets my interest; I don't understand the point you are making in paragraph 2—an example would help; paragraph 3 reads well, but I'm not sure how it relates to your thesis; the description at the end is vivid and interesting."

Procedure 2

Give the reader a copy of the draft, and ask him or her to write comments directly on the draft and in the margin the way an instructor might. Ask the reader to note strengths and weaknesses, and to use the same kind of specific language explained for procedure 1. Students can also share drafts through email, and use the Track Changes and Comment functions of word processing to give feedback on each other's work.

Procedure 3

Ask the reader to write specific answers to the following questions on a separate sheet of paper.

1. What is the thesis of the essay?
2. Is there anything that does not relate to the thesis?
3. Are any points unclear?
4. Do any points need more explanation?
5. Is there any place where the relationship between ideas is unclear?
6. Does the introduction engage interest?
7. Does the conclusion provide a satisfying finish?
8. What is the best part of the essay?
9. What is the weakest part of the essay?

Procedure 4

Give the reader a list of questions that reflect concerns about the draft, such as "Does the introduction arouse interest?" "Is the example in paragraph 2 detailed enough?" and "Is there a better approach to the conclusion?"

3. Are any points not clear?

    In paragraph 2 you could say more about medical interventions and patient or family options. What else exists besides DNR (do no resuscitate) orders? What about "pulling the plug" or stopping oxygen, heart pumps, or feeding? What about pain management?

4. Do any points need further explanation?

    Same for paragraph 2. Also, paragraph 3 could say more about provincial health funding in Canada, as it's a nationally funded system. Are there public hospices? Or do these only exist in the private sector?

5. Is there any place where the relationship between ideas is not clear?

    Again, paragraph 3 mentions Canada's aging population. Does this relate to the thesis at the beginning? Are we only considering the elderly? Or are we considering all Canadians who might need long-term or palliative care?

6. Does the introduction engage reader interest?

    I think it does, but the introduction could also provide an anecdote, or a statistic—something to capture the reader's attention and make them want to continue reading, to see how the argument develops.

7. Does the conclusion provide a satisfying finish?

    I'm not convinced that the thesis—which I understand suggests that palliative care can be a waste of resources—is mirrored in the conclusion. You suggest that palliative care is "a burden." It might be necessary to detail how this burden affects families, patients, and health care professionals. Be more specific.

8. What is the best part of the essay?

    The essay flows well logically, and presents an argument around a topic that most Canadians don't think much about, until they have to arrange care for a terminally ill or elderly relative. For this reason, people should sit up and take notice.

9. What is the weakest part of the essay?

    The thesis. It could use revision for unity, and it needs to be more specific in terms of what the paper will address. Are you convinced there is no benefit?

10. Is the focus sufficiently narrow, so that the central issue is examined completely?

    The paper should focus, perhaps, on only one type of patient. If both the elderly and the terminally ill will be considered, there needs to be more detail to develop the argument, with more examples, so that the reader can assess the argument and either agree or disagree with the thesis statement and the arguments in this draft of the paper.

Christel's solution Christel reviewed her peer editor's comments, and took a few days to reflect on them. She was pleased that her reader liked the draft, and moved forward confidently. The hardest part was to revise the thesis. At this point in her writing course, the task was to develop an informal essay in five paragraphs. So, while her reader suggested that she differentiate between terminal illnesses such as cancer and AIDS and end-of-life care, the challenge was to maintain the structure of the essay and the ideas she already had, without having to add too many new ideas or issues to the paper. The final draft of this paper, as an APA research report, appears in Chapter 5.

1 When a patient is knocking on death's door how can heath care professionals help, since death is inevitable? Health care professionals assist in end-of-life care, also known as palliative care. There are significant issues that surround this type of care and it affects more than just the dying patient. Palliative care has little benefit to anyone but the survivors of the dying patient, as there is significant strain on the dying patient, the health care system, and health care professionals.

PARAGRAPH 1

Christel revised the thesis of the paper. While it does seem more general, it is clearer in that it identifies the topic and controlling idea, and provides a grammatically correct preview for the five-paragraph essay

2 The dying patient is usually under substantial physical and emotional strain due to disease progression as they enter the final stages of life. Patients have to endure their loved ones watching them slowly fade away. The medical interventions available in Canada are not intended to end life sooner. The main goal of palliative care is to maximize the life that the patient has left. The options available to patients include discontinuing oxygen therapy, feeding tubes, and DNR orders, in which no heroic measures are taken and limited medical interventions are used when dying. Very often patients cannot make these decisions for themselves, and therefore family may have to decide what is to be done. However, family members have difficulty making these decisions and may not make the decision that is in the best interests of the patient. There is no medically assisted death (or physician-assisted suicide) available in Canada. Assisted suicide would bring death sooner, therefore lessening patients' overall suffering. Palliative care presents significant challenges for families, as well as for the patient at their end of life.

PARAGRAPH 2

The first body paragraph is much clearer. It defines the main goals of palliative care, and provides specific examples of choices patients and families make in a palliative care situation.

3 In order to facilitate palliative care, there needs to be availability and funding within the health care system. As the Canadian health care system is structured currently, there is not enough funding to allocate more public hospice space, and hospitals are overcrowded. Including more palliative care within these facilities will only strain their resources further. Also, hospice care is usually disease-specific, for cancer and AIDS. There are, in addition, a limited number of publicly funded and accessible hospices as hospice care is funded mainly through donations and by specific organizations like the Canadian Cancer Society. With an aging population, Statistics Canada projects that the rate of deaths in Canada will increase by 33% by the year 2020 to more than 330,000 deaths per year. Along with the aging population, there is an increase of chronic illnesses affecting Canadians. In 2008 the CHPCA noted that "in 2007, 37% of Canadians report that they have been diagnosed by a physician as having a chronic condition or illness," which in turn accounts for more deaths. "Chronic diseases account for 70% of all deaths." There are not enough specially educated health professionals capable of and prepared to deliver this type of specialized care. Doctors and nurses receive only minimal education in the provision of palliative care.

PARAGRAPH 3

In the second body paragraph, Christel introduces the argument that there is insufficient funding for end-of-life care, an issue that will become more urgent as Canada's population ages.

7 Physical and mental companionship is another term that can be used as a reason for infidelity. Although loss of interest may lead to distance between married couples, actual distance may also contribute to this factor. For example, if a spouse was away working in another city to help support the family for a long period, away with the army, or incarcerated in prison, the other spouse would be in need of companionship. This can be further evolved into marital stresses such as having no alone time due to the presence of children or family, struggles with finances and its ability to come between partners, and work related stresses, or the fact that there is someone at work to bond with. In these cases, communication, or a lack of, prohibits the intimacy married couples desperately need.

8 Spousal abuse, whether physical, psychological, or sexual, will play an important role when discussing adultery. No matter if infidelity is real or suspected, it is the reason why most couples divorce. It also causes wife-battering and wife-killing (Brand et al., 2007, p. 101). This can be the case for male victims as well. When a spouse suspects or is sure of infidelity, they may cause physical (including sexual) or psychological abuse on their adulterous spouse. Although adultery has occurred, this type of punishment is illegal. Opposite of this, a spouse that is already a victim of abuse may turn to extra-pair copulations as a way of coping with the abuse and receiving some sort of physical of psychological support.

9 One theory that is presented is the flaunting of an affair (Boylan, 1971, p.109–110). Boylan claims that the adulterous spouse would purposely flaunt an extra-marital relationship to force or influence the other spouse to obtain a divorce. This can relate to an abused woman cheating on her husband in hopes of speeding up the dissolution process of the marriage. By doing this, the wife would feel free from guilt and look better in the eyes of her friends and family for cheating on her abusive husband to end the marriage.

10 Koehler and Chisholm (2007) both try to explain why people participate in extra-pair copulations despite the negative views of them. They present the evolutionary, mechanist, and adaptationist, perspectives as well as the genetic diversity hypotheses. First, the evolutionary theory suggests males use extra-pair copulations as short-term mating to increase their offspring. Females will mate with males in extra-pair copulations to increase their offspring quality while receiving benefits from possibly both their spouse and the "superior" male involved in the affair (Koehler & Chisholm, 2007, p. 185). Brand et al. seem to support this perspective, claiming that males are more quantity orientated while females are more quality orientated. They add that females are more likely to switch mates as often as a better one comes along (Brand et al., 2007, p. 102).

11 The mechanist perspective states that individuals with high psychosocial stress are looking for instant rewards of feeling loved and gratification of risk-taking. These individuals usually fulfill this void with risky sexual activities. As for the adaptationist perspective, Koehler and Chisholm claim that in high-risk environments, individuals minimize the chance of lineage extinction by participating in many extra-marital relationships and producing an offspring before their chances are somehow "minimized," (Koehler & Chisholm, 2007, p. 189).

The adaptationist perspective is similar to the evolutionary theory, but the reasons for the extra-pair copulation are different.

12 Finally, when dealing with Koehler and Chisholm's explanations for extra-pair copulations, the genetic diversity hypothesis simply says males and females engage in extra-marital affairs and mate with as many partners as possible to increase the diversity of their offspring (Koehler & Chisholm, 2007, p.185). This stays in context with the rest of their similar ideas. Both seem to focus on evolution overall, pointing out that extra-pair copulation may be necessary for the survival of one's genetics.

...

13 Within professional counselling, infidelity debriefings have become very common today. One method a married couple may choose to reconcile their marriage is through the Modified Infidelity Debriefing Process implemented by G. A. Juhnke. This debriefing process was implemented to focus on couples' thoughts regarding the infidelity as well as their feelings associated with it to the decision of reconciliation or divorce. If the married couple experiencing infidelity chooses reconciliation, they are moved into marriage counselling (Juhnke et al., 2008, p. 309–314). Essentially, this process between the disclosure of infidelity and the decision on how to handle it is the important "make or break" period for the married couple. If a couple chooses counselling, this shows they have a positive concern for each other and a positive outcome of the infidelity. Does this prove the Modified Infidelity Debriefing Process works?

14 The first example is of Ed and MaryAnn. Married for fourteen years, Ed cheated on MaryAnn. Through the Modified Infidelity Debriefing Process, they were able to come to the reality that their marriage was worth saving. A new desire of commitment and identification in relationship changes helped enhance their marital satisfaction (Juhnke et al., 2008, p. 309).

15 The second example is of Victor and Maria. They have lived together for approximately a year now and they also work together. Maria stayed aboard a client's boat for a weekend to convince that client to commit to their company. Everyone at the firm assumed that Maria had slept with the client to bring his business and teased Victor about it. Eventually, after all of Victor's accusations and Maria's denials, they decided to attend a Modified Infidelity Debriefing Process, just for the perceived infidelity. It was not even clear if the infidelity had occurred or not, but clearly Victor could not go on assuming it did and Maria could not go on being blamed for it the rest of her life. After carefully weighing their options, they decided to stay together and pursue a marriage (Juhnke et al., 2008, p. 309).

16 When determining if one partner is willing to reconcile with another, forgiveness is a very important factor. Forgiveness may be used to restore balance and harmony within a marriage after infidelity has occurred (Gunderson & Ferrari, 2008, p. 2). According to Nelson et al., forgiveness is not given because it is deserved, earned, or a feeling, but because it is a decision made by the victim (Nelson et al., 2008, p. 377). Also, an apology may impact forgiveness. When the victim can see that the adulterer is remorseful by apologizing, it may

clear away any negative or angry feelings the victim has toward the infidel. The more the victim believes that the cheating spouse is sorry, the easier it may be for them to forgive. Apologies are used to compensate the victim for all the suffering they went through, making it easier to forgive and reconcile with their adulterous spouse. Depending on the level or romantic commitment, an apology may be the most meaningful to the victim. Forgiving is never easy, especially when the victim does not see the infidelity as unplanned or an isolated incident. This will make it harder to forgive, and in turn, harder for the couple to reconcile (Gunderson & Ferrari, 2008, p. 3–4).

17 The decision to forgive a cheating spouse may depend on the frequency of the cheating. For instance, if the infidelity was an isolated incident, the victim may believe the adulterer when they apologize; choosing to forgive faster and realizing that maybe the relationship is worth saving after all? With an isolated incident, the victim is left worrying about future cheating from their spouse. If the cheating is often or frequent, the victim is led to believe the adulterer is not really sorry and their apology is meaningless. This may result in the thought that there is no remorse and should quickly lead the victim to end the relationship. At least when a spouse cheats frequently, the victim does not have to worry about future cheating because there is less likely to be a future (Gunderson & Ferrari, 2008, p.4–5).

18 Another factor when debating reconciliation is taking into account whom the spouse cheated on the victim with. It is led to believe that if the husband had an extra-marital affair with his wife's mother or sister, forgiveness would be far less considered than if the husband were to sleep with a random woman. Also, sexually transmitted infections (STIs) are an important factor. Is a husband more likely to forgive and reconcile with his wife after discovering that because of her extra-pair copulation, she has an incurable STI such as genital herpes or HIV/AIDS? (Hyde, et al., 2006, p. 221–226). Common sense says they would most likely not reconcile.

19 In addition to the frequency of infidelity, whom the spouse cheated with, and the risk of contracting STIs, the likelihood of forgiveness is impacted by how the infidelity was discovered. Gunderson & Ferrari list four ways this can happen. First is unsolicited partner discovery. This is when the adulterer openly admits to cheating without suspicion being on them. Second is solicited partner discovery. In this discovery, the adulterer admits to the infidelity only after being suspected. Third is "red-handed" discovery. Here, the adulterer is actually caught in the act of infidelity by the victim/spouse. Fourth is unsolicited third party discovery. This happens when a third party tells the victim that they have been cheated on (Gunderson & Ferrari, 2008, p. 3–4).

20 Overall, when it comes to unsolicited partner discovery, the victim is most likely to forgive the adulterous spouse. When unsolicited third party discovery occurs, the victim is least likely to forgive the adulterous spouse (Gunderson & Ferrari, 2008, p. 3–4). Although admitting the infidelity openly is a good attempt to save a marriage, overall infidelity is still a bad idea for trying to save that same marriage. You'd still expect the victim at least to listen to their spouse's explanations and reasons in this situation. In regards to walking in on a spouse cheating or hearing the news from a third party, that is more likely

to cause anger and vengeful thoughts. The victim may realize that their cheating spouse had no intentions on telling them what was going on, leading them to believe their spouse would not want to reconcile anyways.

21 The risk of committing infidelity in the future has an impact on how individuals act today. Even if the cheating spouse has a larger loss compared to a larger net gain when dealing with adultery, the existence of punishment does not deter extra-marital affairs (Liu, 2008, p.168). Xuemei Liu reports that although punishment through the family tends to be fixed, punishment through the law is needed to achieve social efficiency. Liu claims that to discourage infidelity, the great burden of marital dissolution must be placed on the adulterer. The innocent spouse monitoring the adulterer is not only unfair, the cost is too high. Just because extra-marital affairs cannot be controlled or reduced does not mean there is no way to reduce them. Liu also states that within economic sanctions needed to punish infidels should be continued legal punishments and more alimony pay to the victim (Liu, 2008, p. 168–174).

22 Another way to deter adultery is by adding up large legal penalties with a lot of monitoring by a spouse (even though again, that is not fair to the spouse) (Liu, 2008, p.175). Although infidelity will never be conquered, there are effective strategies when trying to build immunity to it. Aside the Modified Infidelity Debriefing Process mentioned earlier and learning from the consequences listed above, a former victim of infidelity may be able to use preventative measures learned in previous relationships as well as bonding activities to deter infidelity.

23 Nelson et al. briefly describes four activities couples can do together to improve their current relationship and prevent adultery. First is getting to know your spouse's childhood role models. A person's future marital satisfaction depends on the happiness of his or her parents. Second, flexibility and intimacy are required. Stimulation can occur in all activities of everyday life, not just in the bedroom. Also, when times get rough or bad, partners should learn how to turn towards themselves for support instead of turning away. Third, the spouses must assess their commitment. Spirituality and collective ideas between them should be similar. Nelson et al. claim that commitment is the foundation to fidelity. Finally, fourth is trust and forgiveness. Without trust, there can be no forgiveness. Moreover, when hurt feelings happen again, it does not mean a lack of forgiveness, but only that further healing needs to take place (Nelson et al., 2008, p. 376). To further support what Nelson et al. say in regards to the third activity in assessing their commitment, Gunderson and Ferrari (2008, p. 2) claim that individuals are less committed and satisfied when they believe a spouse is cheating on them. In addition, individuals less committed to their partners are more likely to use adultery as a way out of their marriage. This supports the notion that adultery is a self-fulfilling prophecy when dealing with commitment and reconciliation.

24 As shown throughout this entire debate, consequences of divorce outweigh the consequences of reconciliation by a large margin. Economics such as money have the most influence over these decisions. Although there is no way to conquer infidelity, whether through a Modified Infidelity Debriefing Process, learning from past consequences with respects to adultery, or forgiveness,

couples can and probably should reconcile. As seen through the examples of Ed and MaryAnn as well as Victor and Maria, the period between disclosure of adultery and what direction to take the relationship is the most critical. Forgiveness is most common when unsolicited partner discovery occurs, the infidelity is an isolated incident, and an apology is given. Also, a partner is more likely to forgive a spouse faster with these three variables are present. The differences between males and females when dealing with infidelity are very different. Both calculate extra-marital affairs on a cost-benefit basis. When the benefits are higher then the costs, extra-pair copulation is most likely to occur.

25   In conclusion, factors such as the frequency of infidelity, weighing the cost-benefit for males and females, how the adultery was discovered, and forgiveness and apologies all showed how extra-marital mechanisms explain infidelity and prove that marriages can be reconciled. Whether or not they should be reconciled based on certain evidence is to debate by each situation's cost-benefit. Future studies relating to this question may include more complicated explanations of infidelity such as sex addictions, fantasies, and the thrill of cheating and risky sexual behaviour. One thing to keep in mind when dealing with explaining extra-marital affairs is although there are many reasons to cheat, these reasons can never be used as an excuse.

The complete essay, including any bibliographic references, is also available on the Online Learning Centre at www.mcgrawhill.ca/olc/clouse.

A Reader Response to an Essay Draft

Consider the questions from procedure 3 on page 101. Work as a peer editor, and respond to the following questions. Suggest improvements where needed.

1. What is the thesis of the essay? Reader explains his/her impression of the thesis, and makes suggestions

2. Is there anything that does not relate to the thesis?

3. Are any points not clear?

4. Do any points need more explanation?

    Readers should suggest revisions. Reader explains why he reacts as he does. Note instances where the writer can improve the essay, yet maintain an awareness of the paper's scope and topic limitations.

5. Is there any place where the relationship between ideas is unclear?

    Offer a strategy for revising ideas or arrangement in the student essay.

6. Does the introduction engage interest?

7. Does the conclusion provide a satisfying finish?

    Reader explains the reason for his/her response and suggests a possible revision. Note specific suggestion. Reader gives specific examples.

8. What is the best part of the essay?

9. What is the weakest part of the essay?

    Suggest a revision strategy

10. Is the focus of the essay clear enough? Has anything been left out? Does anything need further exploration or consideration?

    Reader offers a positive comment in summary.

EXERCISE EVALUATING A PEER'S DRAFT

Directions: Read another student's essay draft and list three of its strengths. Then list three important revisions that you would recommend to the writer, and explain why these revisions are needed. Follow the pattern above, and use the ten questions to critique and respond as an editor. Ask your peer-writing partner to do the same for you. Exchange answers to the questions, and identify your areas of agreement and disagreement. Work together to come up with lists that you can agree on. ●

EXERCISE AN ESSAY IN PROGRESS

Directions: After completing this exercise, save all revisions. Use it in the next chapter as you work towards your completed essay.

1. Review pages 92–103 and make a list of the revising techniques you would like to try—the ones that seem like they might work for you.

2. Use the techniques in your list to revise the draft you wrote in response to the exercise on page 89.

3. Did your revision activities prompt you to return to any earlier stages of the process? If so, which ones?

4. Were the revision procedures you followed helpful? If not, what will you do differently the next time you revise? Why? ●

CHAPTER 5

Revising for Effective Expression

Looking Ahead

To look ahead and consider the importance of the way we express ourselves, consider the ad shown here. The ad attempts to communicate that not all insurance plans cover retirement or financial emergencies. The two signs in the image, however, both communicate the same message, but the sign on the right is more specific. The cartoonist understands that it's not just what you say that counts, but how you say it. Politicians understand this fact as well. So do good writers.

To look ahead at the importance of effective expression, list 10 or so phrases, sentences, or expressions from advertisements, memorable political speeches, and important documents that have staying power because they are so well expressed. If you like, you can pair up with a classmate to complete this exercise.

Good ideas are not enough to keep a reader's interest. You must also express those ideas well. Thus, an important part of revising is assessing sentences and words, and making changes to express ideas as effectively as possible.

Critique, Revise, and Edit

When revising for effective expression, shape sentences so that they have energy and flow well from one to the next. The goal is to achieve a pleasing style that keeps a reader interested in what an essay has to say. The next sections will explain how to achieve this pleasing style.

Use Active Voice

In the **active voice**, the subject of the sentence *acts*. In the **passive voice**, the subject of the sentence is *acted upon*.

Active: The optometrist examined the child's eyes. (The subject, *optometrist*, performs the action of the verb, *examined*.)

Passive: The child's eyes were examined by the optometrist. (The subject, *child's eyes*, is acted upon.)

Most often, you use the active voice rather than the passive voice because it is more vigorous and less wordy, as the following examples illustrate.

Passive: The ball was thrown into the end zone by the quarterback.

Active: The quarterback threw the ball into the end zone.

Another reason to favour the active voice is that the passive may not indicate who or what performed the action.

Passive: The workers were criticized for their high absentee rate. (Who did the criticizing?)

Active: The new corporate vice president criticized the workers for their high absentee rate. (Now we know who did the criticizing.)

Although writers should usually choose the active over the passive voice, sometimes the passive voice is more appropriate, particularly when the performer of the action is either unknown or unimportant, as is often the case for writing in business, legal, and technical contexts.

Appropriate passive voice: After germination, the plants are thinned so they are spaced 10 centimetres apart. (Who thins the plants is not important.)

Appropriate passive voice: The chicken was baked until it was tough and tasteless. (The person who baked the chicken is unknown.)

Be wary when a writer or speaker uses the passive voice to hide information.

Passive voice used to conceal: I have been told that someone is stealing from the cash register. (The writer or speaker does not want to reveal who did the telling.)

Use Coordination

A word group that has both a subject and a verb is a **clause**. If the clause can stand alone as a sentence, it is an **independent clause**.

Independent clause:	this year's wheat crop was damaged by a wet fall
Subject:	this year's wheat crop
Verb:	was damaged
Sentence:	This year's wheat crop was damaged by a wet fall.

For coordination, join two main clauses in the same sentence with a comma and one of the following coordinating conjunctions ("FANBOY" words: **f**or, **a**nd, **n**or, **b**ut, **o**r, **y**et, so):

and	or
but	so
for	yet
nor	

Main clause:	the storm caused a power failure
Main clause:	we lit the candles
Sentence with coordination:	The storm caused a power failure, so we lit the candles.

The coordinating conjunction does more than join the main clauses; it also indicates the relationship between the ideas in the clauses, as the following chart explains.

USING COORDINATING CONJUNCTIONS

Coordinating Conjunctions	Relationship
And	The idea in the second main clause functions as an addition to the idea in the first main clause.

Example: The mayor urged a 14 percent budget cut, and suggested a freeze on hiring.

Coordinating Conjunctions	Relationship
But/yet	The idea in the second main clause contrasts with the idea in the first main clause.

Example: The temperatures have been warm for December, but [yet] we may have snow for Christmas.

Coordinating Conjunctions	Relationship
For	The idea in the second main clause tells why the idea in the first main clause happened or should happen.

Example: Television talk shows are popular, for viewers never tire of watching celebrities talk about themselves.

| Nor | The idea in the second main clause is a negative idea functioning in addition to the negative idea in the first main clause. |

Example: The school board cannot raise teacher salaries, nor can it renovate the high school buildings.

| Or | The idea in the second main clause is an alternative to the idea in the first main clause. |

Example: Your research paper must be handed in on time, or you will be penalized.

| So | The idea in the second main clause functions as a result of the idea in the first main clause. |

Example: Dr. Wesson was ill last week, so our midterm exam is postponed until Thursday.

When you join ideas with coordination, be sure the relationship between the ideas is clear.

Unclear: My advisor is coming at noon today, and I have a doctor's appointment this morning.

Clear: My advisor is coming at noon today, but I will miss her because of my doctor's appointment this morning.

Use Subordination

A **subordinate** or **dependent clause** has a subject and a verb, but it cannot stand alone as a sentence. It must be joined to a main clause.

Subordinate clause: because this year's wheat crop was damaged by a wet fall

Subject: this year's wheat crop

Verb: was damaged

Main clause: bread will cost more

Sentence: Because this year's wheat crop was damaged by a wet fall, bread will cost more.

For **subordination**, join a main clause and a subordinate clause in the same sentence with one of the following **subordinating conjunctions**.

SUBORDINATING CONJUNCTIONS

Subordinating Conjunctions	Relationship
because, in order that, since	To show why the idea in the main clause occurs or occurred

Example: Because the traffic signal on Darborn Street is out, cars are backed up for two blocks.

after, as, before, when, whenever, while	To show when the idea in the main clause occurs or occurred

Example: Before the city council considers tax incentives, we must be sure the city can afford them.

where, wherever	To show where the idea in the main clause occurs or occurred

Example: Janine attracts attention wherever she goes.

as if, as though	To show how the idea in the main clause occurs or occurred

Example: The mayor was speaking as if she were not facing a no-confidence vote.

if, once, provided, unless	To show under what condition the idea in the main clause occurs or occurred

Example: Unless the additional computers are purchased, we cannot compete with more wired campuses.

although, even though, though	To concede a point

Example: Although the executive apologized, the board of directors still fired him.

When you use subordination, place the idea you want to emphasize in the main clause. Notice that different ideas are emphasized in these two sentences.

Sluggish economy emphasized	Although unemployment is lower than last year, the economy is sluggish.
Lower unemployment emphasized	Although the economy is sluggish, unemployment is lower than last year.

Punctuation note: As the previous examples show, a subordinate clause at the beginning of a sentence is followed by a comma.

Achieve Sentence Variety

For a pleasing rhythm, strive for **sentence variety** by using different sentence structures. When sentences vary, you avoid the monotonous rhythm that comes from too many sentences with the same pattern. For example, the following paragraph lacks sentence variety. While reading, notice how most of the sentences are simple, with little or no subordination. The section that follows addresses this problem, and indicates how using subordination helps express complex ideas and adds variety to the passage's style.

> My son is in grade three. He told me yesterday that he was one of 12 students selected to take intensive music lessons. Greg is delighted about it. I am annoyed. I feel this way for several reasons. The music classes will be held three days a week. The students will have Music instead of their usual reading class. I believe at the third-grade level reading is more important than music. I do not want my son to miss his reading class. The teacher says Greg reads well enough for his age. I maintain that there is still room for improvement. Some people might say that learning music at an early age is a wonderful opportunity. They say students will broaden their awareness. This may be so. I do not think students should be forced into music for these reasons. They and their parents should have a choice of subjects to study, the way they do in high school.

The paragraph has an unsatisfactory rhythm because all the sentences begin the same way—with the subject. To achieve sentence variety and improve style, include a mix of sentence structures by following the suggestions below.

1. **Use coordination to combine some of your sentences.**

    Examples: Gregory is delighted to be learning music, but I am annoyed about it.

    Third graders are not ready for instrumental music, and I doubt they will profit much from it.

2. **Begin some sentences with subordinate clauses.**

    Examples: While I believe the study of music can be beneficial, I do not feel it should be taught to third graders at the expense of reading instruction.

    If my son is to learn another subject, I prefer that he choose the one he wishes to study.

3. **Begin some sentences with the *-ing* form of a verb.** The *-ing* form of a verb is the present participle, and it can appear alone, in a pair, or with a phrase.

    Examples: Sobbing, Greg explained that all his friends were taking intensive music lessons, and he wanted to also.

    Whining and crying, Greg left the room convinced that I was a cruel mother.

    Understanding his disappointment, I finally agreed to the music instruction.

    Caution: When you begin a sentence with a present participle—whether it appears alone, in a pair, or with a phrase—be sure the participle and any accompanying words are immediately followed by a sentence subject the participle can sensibly refer to. Otherwise, you will have a dangling modifier, which creates an illogical or silly sentence.

Example: Still having trouble with reading English, it is not the time for Greg to learn instrumental music.

Correction: Still having trouble with reading English, Greg is not ready to learn to play an instrument.

Explanation: In the first sentence, the participle and phrase refer to *it*, which causes the sentence to express the idea that it was having trouble with English grammar. However, Greg was the one having trouble, so the word Greg must appear as the subject just after the participle phrase.

Punctuation note: An introductory present participle—whether alone, in a pair, or with a phrase—is followed by a comma.

4. **Begin some sentences with *-ed, -en, -n, or -t* verb forms.** These are the **past participle** forms of verbs; they can function alone, in a pair, or with a phrase.

Examples: Exasperated, Greg stormed from the room.

Spent from the long discussion with Greg, I took a nap for an hour.

Stricken with grief, Greg cried for an hour because he could not take music lessons.

Frustrated and defeated, I finally allowed Greg to take instrumental music.

Caution: When you begin with a past participle, whether it is alone, part of a pair, or in a phrase, be sure the sentence subject following the structure is something the participle can sensibly refer to. Otherwise, you will have a dangling modifier, which creates an illogical sentence. Be careful with reference words!

Example: Delighted by the idea of learning a new subject, instrumental music was something Greg looked forward to.

Correction: Delighted by the idea of learning a new skill, Greg looked forward to instrumental music classes.

Explanation: In the first sentence, *instrumental music* appears just after the past participle phrase. As a result, it seems that the music class was delighted. In the revision, a subject to which the participle can sensibly refer appears after the phrase.

Punctuation Note: An introductory past participle—whether alone, in a pair, or with a phrase—is followed by a comma.

5. **Begin some sentences with *to* and the base form of the verb (the infinitive).** When *to* is used with the present-tense verb form, the structure is called an infinitive. Infinitives can appear alone, in pairs, or in phrases, but most often they appear in phrases.

Examples: To understand my reaction, you must realize that I value reading above all other subjects.

To be effective, a primary level curriculum should offer students a choice of extra subjects.

To appreciate and to accept my view, you must agree that English reading is more important than instrumental music.

Caution: When you begin a sentence with an infinitive that is not the subject of your sentence—whether it is alone, part of a pair, or in a phrase—be sure the infinitive and accompanying words are immediately followed by a subject the infinitive can sensibly refer to. Otherwise, you will have a dangling modifier, which creates an illogical sentence.

Example: To feel more secure, an alarm system was installed.

Correction: To feel more secure, I installed an alarm system.

Explanation: In the first sentence, the infinitive phrase refers to *an alarm system,* which causes the sentence to express the idea that the alarm system would feel more secure.

Punctuation note: An introductory infinitive—whether alone, in a pair, with a phrase, or with a modifier—is followed by a comma only if the infinitive and any accompanying words are followed by a main clause.

Examples: To study instrumental music in third grade, Greg would have to miss his reading class.

To study instrumental music in third grade seems foolish.

6. **Begin some sentences with a prepositional phrase.** A preposition is a word that signals direction, placement, or connection. Common prepositions include the following:

about	among	between	from	of	over	under
above	around	by	in	off	through	with
across	before	during	inside	on	to	within
along	behind	for	into	out	toward	without

A **prepositional phrase** is a preposition plus the words that are functioning with it. Here are some examples:

across the bay   of the province of Newfoundland
before the rush hour   to me
at the new shopping mall   without the slightest doubt

To achieve sentence variety, you can begin some of your sentences with one or more prepositional phrases.

Examples: For a number of reasons, I oppose instrumental music at the grade-three level.

By my standards, reading is more important than instrumental music for grade three students.

7. **Vary the placement of transitions.** Many transitions can function at the beginning, in the middle, or at the end of a sentence. To achieve sentence variety, vary the placement of transitions. (See page 97 for a chart of transitions.)

Examples: *Indeed,* Greg was disappointed that I would not allow him to take instrumental music.

He was so disappointed, *in fact,* that I felt compelled to give in.

This does not mean my belief has changed, *however.*

Punctuation note: As the above examples illustrate, transitions are set off with commas.

8. **Begin some sentences with the subject.** Sentence variety refers to mixing sentence structures to avoid monotony, so begin some sentences with the subject.

9. **Balance long and short sentences.** Follow a long sentence with a shorter one, or a short sentence with a longer one. While you need not follow this pattern throughout an essay, on occasion it can enhance rhythm and flow.

Examples:	Although I explained to Greg why I believed he was better off taking reading rather than instrumental music, he never understood my view. Instead, he was heartbroken.
	I did my best. I reasoned with him, bribed him, and became angry with him, but still I could not convince Greg that he would be better off to wait a few years before studying music.

Use Parallel Structure

For **parallel structure**, give sentence elements of equal importance serving the same function the same grammatical form. The following sentence has parallel structure:

This novel is <u>outrageous</u>, <u>offbeat</u>, and <u>shocking</u>.

The underlined words have the same function (to describe *novel*), and they all have the same degree of importance in the sentence. To emphasize this relationship, then, the words all take the same grammatical form—they are adjectives.

If sentence elements that have the same function and importance are not parallel, the result is an awkward, ungrammatical sentence, as in the following example:

Nonparallel: I have always liked <u>hiking</u> and <u>to swim</u>.

Because *hiking* and *to swim* have the same function (they have the same subject, and they are both the object of the verb *have liked*), and because they are of equal importance, they should both have the same grammatical form.

Parallel: I have always liked <u>hiking</u> and <u>swimming</u>.

Parallel: I have always liked <u>to hike</u> and <u>to swim</u>.

Faulty parallelism occurs most often when writers place items in a series or a pair, when they compare or contrast, and when they use correlative conjunctions. To ensure parallelism, follow the suggestions below.

1. **Be sure sentence elements forming a series or pair have the same grammatical form.**

Nonparallel: You can get to Toronto by <u>car</u>, <u>bus</u>, or <u>fly</u>.

Parallel: You can get to Toronto by <u>car</u>, <u>bus</u>, or <u>plane</u>.

Nonparallel: Before my first date, Mother told me <u>to be in by midnight</u>, and <u>she said I was to be a gentleman</u>.

Parallel: Before my first date, Mother told me <u>to be in by midnight</u>, and <u>to be a gentleman</u>.

2. **Be sure items compared or contrasted in a sentence have the same grammatical form.**

   Nonparallel: I love <u>a day</u> at the beach more than <u>to spend a day</u> in the country.

   The contrasted elements are not parallel because the noun phrase *a day at the beach* is contrasted to the verb phrase *to spend a day in the country.* To be parallel, the contrast should be expressed in one of the following ways:

   Parallel: I love <u>a day at the beach</u> more than <u>a day in the country</u>.

   Parallel: I love <u>spending a day at the beach</u> more than <u>spending a day</u> in the country.

   Sometimes parallelism problems crop up because the writer fails to mention the second item being compared or contrasted, as in the following sentence:

   I like small, intimate restaurants better.

   This sentence does not indicate what *small, intimate restaurants* is contrasted with. To solve the problem, add the missing contrast:

   I like <u>small</u>, <u>intimate restaurants</u> better than <u>crowded</u>, <u>noisy cafeterias</u>.

3. **Use correlative conjunctions correctly. Correlative conjunctions** are conjunctions used in pairs. The following are correlative conjunctions:

either . . . or	both . . . and
neither . . . nor	not only . . . but [also]

   To achieve parallelism with correlative conjunctions, be sure that the same grammatical structure follows both conjunctions.

   Nonparallel: I want either <u>to spend my vacation in New York City</u> or <u>in Bermuda</u>.

   Parallel: I want to spend my vacation either <u>in New York City</u> or <u>in Bermuda</u>.

   Nonparallel: The ballet was both <u>brilliantly performed</u> and <u>had lavish sets</u>.

   Parallel: The ballet had both <u>brilliant performances</u> and <u>lavish sets</u>.

EXERCISE REVISING SENTENCES

1. Five of the following sentences are in the active voice; five are in the passive voice. Rewrite those in the passive voice so they are in the active voice.
   a. The elaborate sand castle was built by Tina, Jerry, and their father.
   b. By noon, the high tide had washed away most of their creation.
   c. While I was shopping in the mall, my purse was snatched by a teenager dressed in torn blue jeans and a green sweatshirt.
   d. The police reported that someone matching that description had stolen three other purses the same day.
   e. The antique necklace I wear so often was given to me by my favourite aunt.
   f. Aunt Sadie collected antique jewellery and gave me a piece every year for my birthday.

g. A surprise birthday party was thrown for Rhoda by three of her closest friends.

h. Unfortunately, Rhoda did not arrive when she was expected, so she ruined the surprise.

i. I asked my academic advisor how to improve my calculus grade.

j. I was told by my advisor to spend two hours a week in the math lab.

2. For each general subject, write one sentence with coordination and one with subordination to demonstrate the specific relationships indicated. Try to place some of your subordinate clauses before the main clauses and some of them after. The first one is done for you as an example.

   a. *Exams:* (A) coordinate to show contrast; (B) subordinate to concede a point
      (A) I have three exams today, but I have time for lunch.
      (B) Although Dr. Manolio is known for giving difficult tests, her exams are always fair.

   b. *Spring:* (A) coordinate to show addition; (B) subordinate to show when

   c. *Your best friend:* (A) coordinate to show contrast; (B) subordinate to concede a point

   d. *Your favourite restaurant:* (A) coordinate to show an alternative; (B) subordinate to show why

   e. *Your first day of college:* (A) coordinate to show a result; (B) subordinate to show when

   f. *A miserable cold:* (A) coordinate to continue a negative idea; (B) subordinate to show under what condition

   g. *The first day of summer vacation:* (A) coordinate to show why; (B) subordinate to show when

   h. *A party:* (A) coordinate to show addition; (B) subordinate to show where

   i. *Your favourite teacher:* (A) coordinate to show why; (B) subordinate to show how

   j. *A movie you have seen:* (A) coordinate to show result; (B) subordinate to concede a point

   k. *A holiday celebration:* (A) coordinate to show contrast; (B) subordinate to show why

3. Rewrite the paragraph on page 120 to give it sentence variety. You may alter the existing wording, and you may add words (transitions, for example). Many revisions are possible. Compare your work with a partner's.

4. Rewrite the following sentences to achieve parallel structure.

   a. The boutique is known for its variety of styles, for its haughty sales clerks, and daring new designs.

   b. The police car sped up the street, its lights flashing, its siren wailing, and racing its engine.

   c. I find playing tennis to be better exercise than volleyball.

   d. Kim not only has bought a CD player but also an MP3 player.

   e. Susan is beautiful, arrogant, and has been spoiled by her parents.

   f. My neighbour wants either to resurface his driveway or be painting his house.

   g. Carlos plans to attend the university, study biology, and being accepted into medical school.

   h. Neither is the newspaper column timely nor interesting.

   i. Lisa enjoys working for a large corporation for its many chances for advancement, for its excitement, and because of its many fringe benefits.

   j. The research paper was not acceptable because it was late, it was too short, and needed typing. ●

Revising Diction

Diction is word choice. Because they convey your meaning and contribute to your style, the words you choose are very important.

Use an Appropriate Level of Diction

Levels of diction can be formal, popular, or informal, and should be suited to the audience.

A *formal* level of diction is appropriate when writing for academics and specialists. When writing a government report, an article for a scholarly academic journal, a master's degree thesis, an academic paper, or an annual report for a corporation, you would use a formal level of diction. Typically, formal diction requires strict adherence to all the rules of grammar. It includes technical language and long sentences and avoids the personal pronouns *I* and *you*, and contractions such as *don't* and *aren't*. The tone is impersonal, serious, and unemotional. Increasingly, formal diction and style are expected in all academic disciplines, even at the undergraduate level.

A *popular* level of diction is common in many magazines, newspapers, and books. Even while using popular diction, writers need to adhere to grammar rules, but can usually use contractions and the pronouns *I* and *you*. You can also express emotion and humour. The tone will usually be relaxed, and you can let your personality show through. A popular level of diction is suitable for some college writing in an English class, for example in an electronic discussion forum, or in a response to a scholarly article or text.

An *informal* level of diction is very much like the way we speak to friends. Informal diction does not include specialized terms. Sentences are short, and slang expressions may appear. Readers do not expect strict adherence to the rules of grammar. Informal diction is not acceptable for college papers (unless reproducing someone's exact words), but it is often suitable for friendly letters, email, and personal journals. When revising essays, eliminate any informal diction.

Use Words with the Appropriate Connotation

Words have both denotations and connotations. A word's **denotation** is its literal dictionary definition; a word's **connotation** refers to emotions and ideas associated with it. For example, the denotations of *excited* and *agitated* are similar, but their connotations are different. Readers associate *agitated* with a negative nervousness, and they associate *excited* with a positive enthusiasm. If writers use words with the wrong connotations, they can mislead readers and fail to achieve a purpose. For example, notice the different meanings conveyed in these sentences with verbs that have similar denotations but different connotations:

Lee *chewed* the steak.
Lee *gnawed* the steak.

When revising academic essays, pay attention to the connotations of words.

Avoid Colloquial Language

Colloquial language is informal. It includes abbreviated forms ("b-school" for "business school"), ungrammatical usages ("It's me"), informal phrases ("tough break"), and slang ("Dilberted" for "exploited by the boss"). Colloquial language is used among friends, with family, and in speech. Colloquial language is not suitable for post-secondary essays. The following examples of colloquial language present an idea of the kinds of expressions to avoid:

cool	awesome	feeling lousy	sweet
off the wall	bummed out	having a cow	chilling
back in the day	freak out	it is what it is	over the top

When revising essays, eliminate colloquial language.

Use Specific Diction

General words present a broad (and often vague) sense of ideas, whereas **specific words** present a more precise sense. Here are some examples to help appreciate the difference between general and specific words and phrases.

General Words	Specific Words
shoe	dress pumps
hat	baseball cap
woman	Mrs. Hernandez
went	stormed out
nice	colourful

Most often, you should use specific words because they give readers a more precise understanding. Consider the following sentence:

I walked across campus, feeling good about the test I just took.

The word *walked* is general and vague. More specific alternatives to *walked* that would be accurate when combined with *feeling good* include the following:

strolled	strutted	bounced
sauntered	trotted	lilted

Substituting the more specific *strutted* for *walked* gives us this sentence:

I strutted across campus, feeling good about the test I just took.

Now we have a more accurate sense of how the writer moved across campus. However, we could improve the sentence further by replacing *good,* which is also vague and general. Here are some more specific alternatives:

positive	elated	at ease	delighted	jubilant
pleased	satisfied	exhilarated	cheerful	optimistic

To work with *strutted,* the word needs to convey lots of good feeling because people strut when they are feeling very happy. For example, if we select *exhilarated,* we get this sentence:

> I strutted across campus, exhilarated by the test I just took.

This sentence is more effective than the one we started out with because it is more specific. It is also more interesting because it describes a more lifelike action.

When revising, work to make your sentences more specific by focusing on nouns and verbs. Instead of general nouns like *magazine, hat,* and *dog,* use the more specific *Newsweek, stocking cap,* and *collie.* Instead of general verbs like *said, moved,* and *drank,* use the more specific *blurted out, bolted,* and *sipped.*

Adding specific modifiers can also make a sentence more precise. For example, instead of "Cans and candy wrappers are on the floor," you can revise to get "Smashed Coke cans and crumpled Milky Way wrappers are scattered across the floor."

Of course, writers must be careful not to overdo it, because too much specific word choice, especially description, can create a bulky, overwhelming sentence, like this:

> Dozens of smashed, twisted, red-and-white Coke cans, lying bent on their distorted sides, and at least 40 crumpled, brown, wadded-up, misshapen Milky Way wrappers representing two weeks of my traditional midnight sugar intake are scattered in heaps everywhere across the green, plush-carpeted floor of my small, third-floor bedroom with its green walls and white ceiling.

Use Simple Diction

Some writers believe that effective, sophisticated sentences use obscure words of many syllables. They use *pusillanimous* when *cowardly* would do as well—even better, actually. If these writers do not have words like *egregious* or *inveigle* in their vocabularies, they pull them out of a dictionary or thesaurus and plunk them into their writing. Such writers are guilty of using **inflated language**, which is overblown usage that makes the writer seem self-important. Inflated language is wordy and full of important-sounding substitutes for common expressions, like the following:

Inflated: It would appear that the functionality of the new generation of personal computers can be demonstrated most readily by a cursory exhibition.

Better: Salespeople can show the functions of the new generation of computers with a quick demonstration.

A sentence cannot be effective if a reader cannot understand it. Remember, writers can be specific and accurate by using the wealth of simple, clear words at their disposal. Consider the following sentences taken from student essays:

> The impetuous drive of youth mellows into the steady pull of maturity.
> The car vibrated to a halt.
> Unnoticed, light filters in beneath the blinds.

These sentences are interesting and clear because of the specific word choice. Although specific, words like *filters, mellows, impetuous, drive, pull, vibrated,* and *halt* are also simple and are part of our natural, everyday vocabularies. Writers need not hunt for high-blown words, because specific yet simple words create an appealing style.

"O.K. What part of 'malignant regression and pathogenic reintrojection as a defense against psychic decompensation' don't you understand?"

© The New Yorker Collection 2000 Robert Mankoff from cartoonbank.com. All Rights Reserved. Reprinted by permission.

In addition to avoiding inflated language, keep diction simple and meaning clear by avoiding jargon. **Jargon** is the technical language of a particular profession. It is the language of insiders and should only be used when addressing an audience of specialists. Thus, use terms like *mitochondria* and *endoplasmic reticulum* when addressing cellular biologists, but for other audiences, writers need more easily understood substitutes, or need to supply definitions—something that the psychiatrist in the cartoon failed to remember.

Use Gender-Neutral, Inoffensive Language

To avoid offending members of the audience, use inclusive language and revise to eliminate offensive language in the following ways:

1. **Avoid masculine pronouns that inappropriately exclude females.**

   No: Each student should bring his catalogue to orientation.

   Yes: Each student should bring his or her catalogue to orientation.

   Yes: Each student should bring a catalogue to orientation.

   Yes: All students should bring their catalogues to orientation.

2. **Use gender-neutral titles.**

No	Yes
policeman	police officer
fireman	firefighter
waitress	server
mailman	mail carrier
chairman	chair/chairperson

   No: The committee will elect its own chairman.

   Yes: The committee will elect its own chair.

3. **Avoid assigning roles to a single gender.**

   No: Mothers worry when their children leave home.

   Yes: Parents worry when their children leave home.

4. **Avoid using terms that demean a gender.**

   No: The company promoted three girls to district manager.

   Yes: The company promoted three women to district manager.

5. **Avoid referring to women with the *-ess* suffix.**

   No: Emily is a promising young actress.

   Yes: Emily is a promising young actor.

6. **Avoid stereotypes.** A **stereotype** is a generalization that ascribes certain characteristics to all members of a group. Because stereotypes like the following are illogical and offensive, writers avoid them.

   Environmentalists are bleeding-heart liberals.
   People on welfare don't really want to work.
   Blondes have more fun.
   Men won't talk about their feelings.

   When revising, rewrite any statements that are based on stereotypes.

   No: I am opposed to art education because students are too lazy to learn academics.

   Yes: Rather than art education, I favour more classes to teach the basics of reading and mathematics.

7. **Use the designations that people prefer.** For example, use *Asian* rather than *Oriental* and *person with a disability* rather than *handicapped.*

Eliminate Wordiness

During drafting, students work to write ideas down any way they can, so being concise is not an immediate concern. However, when revising for effective expression, eliminate unnecessary words. The following tips can help:

1. **Reduce empty phrases to a single word.**

Phrase	Revision
at this point in time	now
in this day and age	now
due to the fact that	because
in many cases	often/frequently
on a frequent basis	often/frequently
has the ability to	can
being that	since
at that time	then
in the event that	if
for the purpose of	so
in society today	today
we as people	we

   Wordy: The mayor <u>has the ability</u> to alter that policy.

   Revision: The mayor <u>can</u> alter that policy.

2. **Eliminate redundancy.** A **redundancy** is a phrase that says the same thing more than once.

Redundancy	Revision
the colour yellow	yellow
circle around	circle
mix together	mix
reverted back	reverted
the reason why	the reason
the final conclusion	the conclusion
true fact	true

Wordy: The Department of National Defence felt an increased military budget would be the <u>final outcome</u>.

Revision: The Department of National Defence felt an increased military budget would be the <u>outcome</u>.

3. **Eliminate deadwood.** Words that add no meaning are deadwood, and they should be deleted.

Wordy: Joyce is a clever <u>type of</u> person.

Revision: Joyce is a clever person. [Joyce is clever.]

Wordy: A multiple-choice <u>kind of</u> question is difficult to answer.

Revision: A multiple-choice question is difficult to answer.

4. **Eliminate repetition.**

Wordy: The first car in the accident was <u>smashed and destroyed</u>.

Revision: The first car in the accident was <u>destroyed</u>.

Wordy: I <u>think and believe</u> the way you do.

Revision: I <u>think</u> [believe] the way you do.

5. **Avoid opening with *there*.**

Wordy: <u>There are</u> many things we can do to help.

Revision: We can do many things to help.

Wordy: <u>There was</u> an interesting mix of people attending the party.

Revision: An interesting mix of people attended the party.

6. **Reduce the number of prepositional phrases.**

Wordy: The decrease in violence <u>in</u> this country suggests an increase in civic values.

Revision: This country's decreasing violence suggests civic improvement.

7. **Reduce the number of *that* clauses.**

Wordy: The students asked the instructor to repeat the explanation <u>that she gave earlier</u>.

Revision: The students asked the instructor to repeat her earlier explanation.

Wordy: The book <u>that is on the table</u> is yours.

Revision: The book on the table is yours.

Note: Sometimes writers leave in words that could be cut out so a sentence works better with the sentences before and after it. The trick is to eliminate unpleasant wordiness while achieving a readable style with sentences that flow well together. Thus, whether a writer uses "Most people notice right off that Melanie is a sarcastic person" or "Most notice immediately that Melanie is sarcastic" will depend on which version reads better with the sentences before and after.

Avoid Clichés

A **cliché** is an overworked expression. At one time, a cliché was an interesting way to say something, but because of overuse, it has become dull. Below is a list of some clichés you may have heard:

black as night	free as a bird
bright-eyed and bushy-tailed	hard as nails
clear as a bell	the last straw
cold as ice	over the hill
crawl out from under	the quick and the dead
cried like a baby	sadder but wiser
drank like a sailor	scarce as hen's teeth
dry as a bone	soft as silk
first and foremost	tried but true

Avoid clichés by finding more interesting ways to express ideas. Consider this student sentence:

When my father accepted a job in Yellowknife, my heart sank.

As readers, we have no trouble determining what the writer means: He was unhappy that his father took a job in the north. Still, the cliché *my heart sank* creates two problems. First, it is vague. Just how did the writer feel? Was the writer depressed, scared, or what? Second, the sentence doesn't interest us because the cliché is dull. Consider this revision:

When my father accepted a job in Yellowknife, I lost sleep worrying about whether I could make new friends.

The revised sentence shows both the nature and the extent of the writer's negative feeling.

> **EXERCISE** REVISING DICTION
>
> 1. Revise the sentences by substituting specific words for the general ones. In some cases, substitute several words for one general word and add additional detail, as in the following example.
>
>   **Example:** The happy boy ran down the street.
>   **Revision:** The paperboy sprinted down Ford Avenue, excited that he had finished his route an hour early.
>
>   a. The room was a mess.
>   b. By afternoon, the child was feeling terrible.

    c. The food tasted awful.

    d. The way that person was driving his car almost caused an accident.

    e. The sound of that baby's cry really bothered me.

    f. The movie was very good.

    g. Carlotta watched the ballplayers practice.

2. Compose a sentence about something you saw, heard, tasted, smelled, or touched today. Revise the sentence until you are satisfied that the diction is specific enough.

3. *Collaborative Activity.* With two classmates, write the following ideas in sentences with specific diction. (You may need to revise a number of times before you are satisfied.)

    Example: the pleasant ringing of church bells
    Sentence: The melodious ring of St. John's bells announced the start of morning worship.

    a. A squirrel running back and forth across a branch
    b. The smell of brownies baking in the oven
    c. The sound of rain on a roof
    d. A woman wearing too much floral-scented perfume
    e. Walking barefoot and stepping on a sharp stone

4. Revise the sentences to eliminate wordiness.

    Example: The most frightening experience that I think I ever had occurred when I was 15.
    Revision: The most frightening experience I had occurred when I was 15.
    [My most frightening experience occurred when I was 15.]

    a. The only audible sound to be heard was the blower of the heater motor as it worked to produce a soft, low hum.
    b. The reason I feel our school is so great is that both male and female of the species have opportunities to excel.
    c. Until that day, I did not realize or consider that people such as Corey are the most dangerous of all because they are so extremely selfish.
    d. In my opinion, it seems that a physical education requirement for post-secondary students is a complete waste of time.
    e. This particular kind of sport is ideal for the person who desires exercise but is not in the best physical condition in the world.
    f. There are many reasons why beer commercials should be banned from television.
    g. The explanation of my son for why he was home late was the same explanation that he gave me last Saturday night.
    h. The tiny little package that Jimmy gave Conchetta for her birthday held the ring that was for her engagement.
    i. In the event that I am unable to join you, please start and begin to eat without my presence.
    j. There were six dogs that were roaming the neighbourhood that the dog warden found it necessary to take to the city pound.

5. Revise the sentences to eliminate the italicized clichés. Feel free to add any detail you wish.

    Example: My sixth-grade teacher was *mad as a hatter.*
    Revision: My sixth-grade teacher was so eccentric that she wore the same faded green dress from September until Christmas break.

    a. Cassandra is never bored because she is always *busy as a beaver.*

    b. *It's a crying shame* that rainy weather spoiled your vacation.

    c. Anyone who can sit through Professor James's lectures deserves a medal, because the man has a *voice that would shatter glass.*

    d. Juan is *happy as a clam* because he got an A in calculus.

    e. Poor Godfrey is so clumsy he is *like a bull in a china shop.*

6. Revise the sentences to eliminate problems with connotation, colloquialisms, and offensive language.

    a. Skinny and muscled, the bride was lovely in her designer gown.

    b. I am having trouble finding the doctor I want as a general practitioner. He must include both alternative medicine and herbal remedies in his practice.

    c. Because of the road construction on the 401, we journeyed a mere five kilometres in 30 minutes.

    d. Ralph has problems keeping a job because he is a mental case.

    e. To sell cars, a salesman must be patient and knowledgeable about his product. ●

THE WRITING PROCESS

Revising Sentences and Words

- Recognize that you cannot always replace one word with another. To convey meaning, you may have to substitute phrases and sentences for individual words.

- If you have trouble expressing an idea, imagine yourself explaining what you mean to a friend, and then write the passage the way you would speak it. If necessary, revise to improve sentences and words.

- Read a draft aloud to listen for choppiness and other problems with flow.

- Avoid using an unnatural style. Trying to impress a reader by sounding overly sophisticated, authoritative, or intellectual, writers will end up sounding pretentious. Be yourself and use your own natural style.

- Be consistent in levels of diction. If you are using a formal level of diction for, say, an upper-level research paper, maintain that level. Do not switch to a popular level here and there. Similarly, if using the popular level for an essay, do not suddenly become informal or formal.

- Avoid indiscriminate use of the dictionary and thesaurus. These are excellent tools when wisely used. However, be sure to understand both the denotations and connotations of words taken from these sources fully. Otherwise, you may lapse into a pretentious style or use words inappropriately, as pointed out in the *Shoe* cartoon.

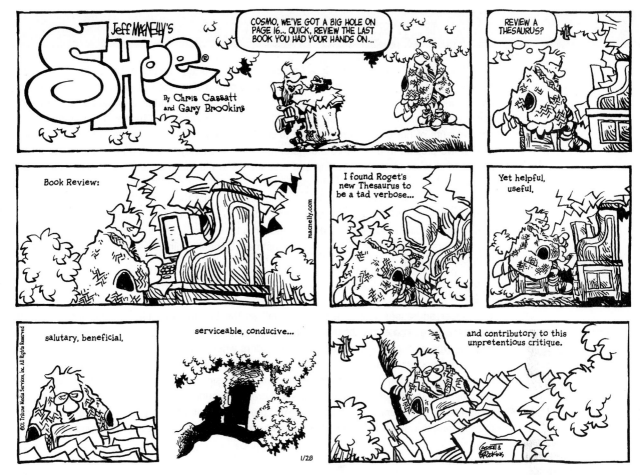

© Tribune Media Services, Inc. All Rights Reserved. Reprinted with permission.

Revising Sentences and Words Electronically

1. Use a word processing program's spelling and style checker cautiously. It may help in some ways, such as by flagging passive voice, but it can make many mistakes. Spell-checked words may be spelled correctly but be the wrong word. Evaluate the grammar suggestions carefully.

2. Use a word processing program's built-in thesaurus (right-click on a word) to find more specific alternatives for general words. Be sure to understand the connotation of words taken from this source.

3. Use the Find and Replace function to locate general words —words like *good, great, nice, awful,* and *bad.* After locating them, evaluate their appropriateness and make changes as necessary.

4. Writers who have a tendency to overuse certain words should use Microsoft Word's Find and Replace commands to tally the number of times they have used that word. For example, if a student has a tendency to use *actually* too much, s/he should go to "Find" in the drop-down Edit menu. Type in *actually* for both "Find" and "Replace." Word will tell writers how many times they have used *actually,* so they can judge if they are using it too much.

Pereira, J., Anwar, D., Pralong, G., Pralong, J., Mazzocato, C., & Bigler, J. (2008). Assisted Suicide and Euthanasia Should not be Practiced in Palliative Care Units. *Journal of Palliative Medicine, 11*(8), 1074-1076. doi:10.1089/jpm.2008.0093

Sabo, B. (2008). *Adverse Psychosocial Consequences: Compassion Fatigue, Burnout and Vicarious Traumatization: Are nurses who provide palliative and hematological cancer care vulnerable?.* (review article)(report) Retrieved from http://find.galegroup.com.library. sheridanc.on.ca/ips/infomark.do?&contentSet=IA-Documents&type=retrieve&tabID=T002 &prodId=IPS&docId=A181702081&source=gale&srcprod=ITOF&userGroupName=ko_acd_ shc&version=1.0

Solomon, M. Z. (2008). The Wisdom and Necessity of Focusing on Family. *Journal of Palliative Medicine, 11*(3), 408-409. doi:10.1089/jpm.2008.9959

Winter, L., & Mockus Parks, S. (2008). Family Discord and Proxy Decision Makers' End-of-life Treatment Decisions. *Journal of Palliative Medicine, 11*(8), 1109-1114. doi:10.1089/ jpm.2008.0039

EXERCISE YOUR ESSAY IN PROGRESS

1. Continue revising the draft you worked on for the exercise on page 113, paying particular attention to sentences and words. Then put the essay aside for a day or so. Consider seeking advice from a peer editor or a writing tutor in your school's writing centre.

2. When you return to the essay, make final revisions. Then print out the essay or type it into its final form. Proofread and submit it if your instructor asks you to.

3. If you completed all the "Your Essay in Progress" exercises, you sampled a number of writing strategies. Which of them worked well for you? ●

CHAPTER 6

Description

Looking Ahead

The descriptions on a menu have both an informational and a persuasive purpose. First, the descriptions let diners know what the various dishes are like—that's the informational purpose. Second, the descriptions are written in a way to entice diners to order food they might not otherwise bother with—that's the persuasive purpose. In this chapter, student writers will learn more about descriptive writing and its purposes. Looking ahead to that information, think of the other times we encounter written description. Do you ever order extra food or other goods just because of an appealing description? How are you persuaded?

Why is Description Important?

Description adds an important dimension to our lives because it moves our emotions and expands our experience. When we read descriptions of beautiful places and scenes, we are uplifted; when we read newspaper accounts of the devastation of wars and natural disasters, we are saddened. Description expands our experience by taking us to places we might not otherwise know much about, which explains the popularity of descriptive travel essays in magazines and newspapers. Description can also give us a fresh appreciation for the familiar. For example, a description of a neighbourhood park can help someone who passes it every day rediscover its beauty.

In "Weren't We All So Young Then?" an essay for her regular *Newsweek* column, Anna Quindlen wrote about the attack on the World Trade Center in 2001 as a defining moment that marked a loss of innocence for people in her generation. She begins her essay with this description:

> Nightfall is as dramatic as the city itself in the days surrounding the winter solstice. The gray comes down fast, pearl to iron to charcoal in a matter of minutes, muting the hard edges of the buildings until in the end they seem to disappear, to be replaced by floating rectangles of lantern yellow and silvered white. In the space of an hour the city turns from edge to glow, steel to light.
>
> Because of this effect it is possible, at least when the moon is on the wane, to stand on Greenwich north of Canal and imagine that in the darkness to the south stand the Twin Towers of the Trade Center. It is just that someone has forgotten to put the lights on, leaving the two giants to brood invisible in the night.

OCCASIONS FOR WRITING

Description in the Classroom

You may be surprised by how important description is across the disciplines. For example, in a paper for an advertising class, students might describe the persuasive visuals in print advertisements. For a history class, student writers might describe the conditions in a 1920s sweatshop. For an art exam, one might describe the technique of a particular artist. Think about three classes you are taking this term or expect to take soon. How might description be part of the reading and writing for those classes? What would be lost if the descriptive component were eliminated from the classes?

Description in Daily Life

Description is important to the writing students do in personal life. Diary, journal, or blog entries might include descriptions of people and scenes. Vacation letters and emails to friends and family will describe places writers visit. And in a toast for a friend's award banquet, a speaker might describe that person's best traits. *If you were involved in an auto accident and had to complete an accident report for your insurance company, how might you use description? Which of the purposes of writing would the description fulfill?*

Description on the Job

Description is often used on the job. Engineers and architects, for example, write descriptions of building sites. Campus admissions officials write promotional materials describing a campus or academic program. Police officers describe crime scenes and suspects in their reports. Social workers describe domestic situations. Nurses describe patient symptoms. Pharmacists describe how to take a particular medicine. *How do travel agents use description? What about newspaper reporters? What job do you hope to pursue after finishing school? How would description be useful in this job?*

DETERMINING PURPOSE

Purposes for Description	Sample Description
To entertain	An amusing description of a teenager's bedroom
To express feelings	A description of your favourite outdoor retreat so your reader understands why you enjoy it so much
To relate experience	A description of your childhood home to convey a sense of the poverty you grew up in
To inform (for a reader unfamiliar with the subject)	A description of a newborn calf for a reader who has never seen one
To inform (to create a fresh appreciation for the familiar)	A description of an apple to help the reader rediscover the joys of this simple fruit
To persuade (to convince the reader that some music videos degrade women)	A description of a degrading music video

Quindlen begins with this description to evoke an image in her readers' minds and, thereby, set the scene. As they read her column about how people have changed since the towers fell, Quindlen wants her readers to envision the haunting absence of the towers, not their horrific collapse. And that's what description does—it creates images, establishes context, and evokes a mood.

As social beings, we want to share our experience, so we write to others to describe things such as vacations, childhood homes, and people we encounter. Professionally, we are required to document many of our experiences, and it is important that we do so clearly, accurately, and objectively. We even use description to persuade others to think or act in particular ways: Advertisers describe products to persuade us to buy them; travel agents describe locales to entice us to visit them; and real estate agents describe properties to stimulate a desire to see them. As the examples in the chart above show, description enables us to entertain, express feelings, relate experience, inform, and persuade.

Combining Description with Other Patterns

Description is useful in academic writing, such as in case studies, literary analysis, and formal reports about issues or concepts in a professional field. Description frequently appears in creative, professional, and journalistic writing as well. Because description adds interest and helps readers form mental images, you will often use it with other patterns of development. To narrate a story, you might describe a person or setting to add vividness. To compare and contrast two restaurants, you might include a description of their decors; to explain the effects of not having zoning laws, you might describe what an area without zoning laws looks like; to classify kinds of jazz, you might include a description of what the different kinds of jazz rhythms sound like; to write a definition of *tacky,* you might illustrate with descriptions of tacky items. Thus, description is a good way to provide specific detail; it can often help show and not just tell. You are likely to use it frequently, in academic and professional writing, no matter what dominant pattern of development suits a writing task.

Because description can create interest in a topic, writers may use it often in introductions, regardless of the dominant pattern of development in the essay. Here is an example:

> It was a cool, crisp October morning. Sunrise was complete, the countryside awake and responding to another day. As he turned and slowly made his way into the woods, he had no idea what would happen on the path he was to follow that day.

Before Writing

When writing description, you have many decisions to make about the best details to include. The following discussion explains these decisions.

Focus Description with a Dominant Impression

Because it is not possible to describe everything about a subject in a single essay, you should settle on one *dominant impression* and describe only those features that contribute to that impression. Your approach can be either subjective (using expressive language) or objective (using language that is less emotional). Suppose the attic of your grandmother's house has intrigued you since you were a small child, and so you decide to write a descriptive essay about it. Or suppose your grandmother herself has always interested you, and so you decide to describe *her* in an essay. Either way, you cannot describe *everything* about a subject. If you tried to include every detail about your grandmother or her attic, the result would be an unwieldy essay. However, you can write about aspects that intrigued you: Perhaps your grandmother's attic is eerie, full of reminders of the past, and unusual. Pick one of these three impressions to form the dominant impression and thereby supply the central point of a description. Then describe only those features of the attic that convey the impression settled on. Similarly, if your grandmother is interesting because she is enthusiastic, eccentric, and young at heart, decide which of these three qualities will be the central point and then describe only features that convey that dominant impression. Also, decide whether to use neutral, objective language, or emotional, subjective language.

To see how description can convey one impression, read the following paragraph written by a student:

> It was late last night as she reluctantly took the steps down to the gloomy fruit cellar. Its dark, dusty shelves are located behind the crumbling basement walls. She fumbled in the dark for the lifeless screw-in light bulb and managed to twist it to a faint glow. With that the musty room was dimly lit, and long dark shadows lurked on the ceiling, outlining enlarged, misshapen jars of fruit. Water condensed and dripped from the ceiling, shattering the eerie silence. Cobwebs suspended in every corner hid their makers in a gray crisscross of lines. Hesitantly she took a step, her sneakers soaking up the black water lying five centimetres deep on the floor. A rat darted through a hole in the wall, and jars of fruit peered at her with their glassy eyes. The rotting shelves looked as if at any moment they would fall to the floor. The cold, gray walls reminded her

of an Egyptian tomb forgotten long ago. Yet mummies don't decay, and she distinctly smelled the odour of something rotting.

Use Concrete Sensory Detail

When writing subjective description, the goal is to create vivid mental images. To do that, use **concrete sensory detail**, which consists of specific words that appeal to the senses (sight, sound, taste, smell, touch). Look back at the paragraph describing the fruit cellar and notice the strong mental images created with concrete sensory detail. Take, for example, the sentence "Cobwebs suspended in every corner hid their makers in a gray crisscross of lines." The detail here is *sensory* because it appeals to the sense of sight. It is *concrete* (specific) because of specific words like *suspended* and *crisscross of lines*. This specific detail that appeals to the sense of sight creates a mental picture for the reader, much more vivid than one that would be formed from a more matter-of-fact statement like "cobwebs were in every corner, hiding their spiders."

Notice, too, that the writer appeals to more than just the sense of sight. He also includes sound (water "shattering the eerie silence"), smell ("the odour of something rotting"), and touch ("her sneakers soaking up the black water lying five centimetres deep on the floor"). While descriptions typically rely more on one sense than the others, writers convey impressions most clearly when they bring in as many senses as are pertinent. Be careful, though. Too much concrete sensory detail overwhelms a reader with mental images, as in this sentence:

> The small, fluffy, gray terrier danced and jumped with excitement and pleasure as her master took the hard, crunchy, brown dog biscuit from the large red-and-white sack.

As this overdone sentence shows, writers must recognize when enough is enough. This principle of restraint holds true in paragraphs as well. Often when there is a complex, highly descriptive sentence in a paragraph, writers should precede or follow it with a simpler, less descriptive one.

Note: Concrete sensory detail is best achieved with specific, simple diction, as in the example on the previous page.

Use Similes, Metaphors, and Personification

Similes, metaphors, and personification are forms of figurative language that can help to create vivid descriptions. A simile uses the words like or as to compare two things that are not usually seen as similar. A metaphor also compares two things not usually seen as similar, but it does so without using the words like or as. Personification grants human qualities, emotions, or sensibilities to nonliving objects, animals, or ideas. Although similes, metaphors, and personification can help create mental images for readers, writers should use them sparingly. Writers should not overwhelm readers with too much figurative language.

Consider Purpose and Audience

The purpose for description will influence the details writers select. Suppose you wish to describe your car and you want your reader to understand that the car is a

BE A RESPONSIBLE WRITER

Writing description, particularly subjective description, allows writers to use words creatively. However, being creative does not permit writers to mislead or deceive. Omitting important descriptions, for example, can give readers a false impression. When using descriptive words, use them the way a reader will. If you are renting your house for the summer and call it "deluxe," your reader will expect accommodations well above average. If the house is small, lacks air conditioning, and is in need of paint, the renter will feel deceived because such a house is not typically considered "deluxe." If you describe the flood damage to your home as "extensive," the insurance company will assume you mean that much of the house is damaged. If only the porch and garage are damaged, "extensive" is misleading.

When you describe, be a responsible writer by asking yourself these questions:

- Is the description accurate?
- Am I omitting any important features?
- Am I using descriptive words to mean what my reader will understand them to mean?

reflection of your outgoing personality. This is a subjective description. In this case, you might describe the flashy colours, custom dash, unusual hood ornament, elaborate sound system, and so forth. Now suppose you want your reader to come to a fresh appreciation of the familiar. This may be an objective description. In this case, you might describe the features of your car that show it to be a marvel of engineering. If, however, you want to convince your reader to view your car as you do (as something that does more harm than good), you might describe the features that contribute to air and noise pollution, that contribute to laziness, that can kill, and so on. This last purpose may combine description with persuasion.

Audience, like purpose, also affects detail selection. How much a reader knows about a subject, how a reader feels about a subject, how interested a reader is in a subject—these factors influence the choice of details.

Organizing Description

A thesis can note what you are describing and a dominant impression about a subject, like this:

> As a child, and now as an adult, she has always been drawn to her grandma's attic because it is filled with reminders of the past.

The thesis indicates that the writer will describe her grandma's attic and that the impression she will convey is that it is filled with reminders of the past.

When forming a thesis, express impressions in concrete, specific language. Impressions expressed in words like *nice, great, wonderful, awful, terrible,* and *bad* are vague, and do not tell the reader much. However, words like *relaxing, scenic, cheerful, depressing, congested,* and *unnerving* are specific and give readers a clearer understanding of how writers feel about what they are describing.

As an alternative, a thesis can tell readers what is described *without* specifying an impression. Instead, the reader gathers the impression from the details in the body. The thesis for such a paper would look like this:

As a child, and now as an adult, she has always been drawn to her grandma's attic.

Of course, body paragraphs form the heart of an essay. Here writers provide the descriptive details that support an impression of a subject. Writers can arrange descriptive details in several ways. If you are describing a place, **spatial order** is useful. Description can move from left to right, top to bottom, near to far, centre to periphery, or inside to outside. Sometimes a **progressive order** is effective. You can arrange details so that they build on the features that most clearly or strikingly convey impressions. A **chronological order** can even be effective at times, as when describing what you see as you move through a place or how something has changed over time.

Sometimes the best way to organize a description is by sensory impressions. For example, if you are describing a ballpark during a game, you could first describe the sights, then the sounds, next the smells, and so forth.

EXERCISE WRITING DESCRIPTION

1. Write two different dominant impressions you could use for two different descriptions of each of the following places:
    a. your bedroom
    b. a store where you shop
    c. a campus cafeteria
    d. an area outside a campus building

2. Select one of the places you used for number 1 and one of the dominant impressions you had of the place. Then mention three elements you could describe to convey that dominant impression.

3. Write one descriptive sentence for each of the items in your list from number 2. Be sure to keep your dominant impression in mind.

4. Write a simile or metaphor for each of the following:
    a. a stubborn child
    b. the sound of a lawn mower
    c. the smell of burning food
    d. the feel of cat fur

5. Write a one-sentence objective description of an item of clothing you are wearing. Then rewrite that sentence to make the description subjective.

6. *Collaborative Activity:* Form a group with three or four classmates, and together write a one-paragraph *objective* description of some part of your writing classroom. Then on a separate sheet, write a one-paragraph *subjective* description of the same aspect. Trade paragraphs with at least one other group, and note the chief strengths and weaknesses of the paragraphs you receive. ●

Visualizing a Descriptive Essay

The chart that follows can help you visualize one structure for a descriptive five-paragraph essay. Note that this five-paragraph model can be extended. Descriptive or blended essays for academic assignments, which are more formal, and likely longer, and will include documented sources. Like all good models, this one can be altered as needed.

Introduction

- Creates interest in what is being described
- Can state the thesis, which can indicate what is being described and what the dominant impression is

First Body Paragraph

- Includes objective or subjective description or both to convey the dominant impression
- Includes concrete sensory details
- May include similes, metaphors, and personification
- Arranges details in spatial, progressive, chronological, or other suitable order, such as according to sensory impressions

Next Body Paragraph

- Continues the description by conveying the dominant impression
- Includes concrete sensory details
- May include similes, metaphors, and personification
- Arranges details in spatial, progressive, chronological, or other suitable order, such as according to sensory impressions

Next Body Paragraphs

- Continue until the description is complete
- Include concrete sensory details
- May include similes, metaphors, and personification
- Arrange details in spatial, progressive, chronological, or other suitable order, such as according to sensory impressions

Conclusion

- Provides closure
- Leaves the reader with a positive final impression

CRITICAL READING STUDENT ESSAY

In the student essay, "My First Flight," the author combines description with narration to convey what it was like when he flew in his brother's ultralight plane. Notice that the author uses both objective and subjective description; consider whether he uses each appropriately. Note that this essay is from a subjective point of view, and that the voice is first person. This would also contain considerably more objective and factual detail if it were submitted for academic evaluation in a college or undergraduate course.

My First Flight

Jerry Silberman

1   The one consistent love I have had throughout my life is flying. Dreams, books, and the experiences of pilots I knew made me long to fly before I ever experienced my first flight. It was, in fact, all I talked about. Then my brother Gene bought a two-seat ultralight. For nineteen years, my feet had not left the ground. Now it was time to fly, and the experience did not disappoint.

> Note that the author provides background information, which indicates why he has chosen to describe his experience.

2   An ultralight is the most basic aircraft made. It is almost a hang glider, except that it has an engine. Its structure is made entirely of aluminum tubing, Dacron fabric, and stainless steel cables. The engine is fifty horsepower, two-cycle, two-cylinder, 503. This is the same size as the average snowmobile engine. The cockpit is open, meaning that one sits right out in the open—there are no walls, floor, or windshield. In front of the pilot are two pedals to control the rudder and a control stick for the throttle, spoilers, and elevators. The gauges consist of a tachometer, wind speed indicator, and altimeter. That is all there is to the craft. It isn't much, but, oh, the thrill it provides!

> This paragraph uses objective detail to describe the ultralight plane, for those who may not be familiar with its design.

3   On the day of my first flight, I was dressed in old jeans, a flight jacket, goggles, and a helmet. I felt more like a World War I flying ace than a modern aviator. "Clear prop" were the last words I heard until landing. Because of the engine noise, everything communicated in the air would be in sign language or by facial expression. Gene pull-started the engine. We taxied to the end of our runway and turned to face the wind. I gave Gene thumbs up to let him know I was ready. Boy, was I ready! He nodded, twisted the throttle, and we bounced over the rough field. We were airborne.

> Note the use of detail here, with the author's description of what he was wearing. He also uses a simile.

4   The only way to pinpoint exactly where one leaves the ground is by noting the extreme smoothness of air after the choppiness of the grassy field. I felt suspended. The ground dropped silently away as we climbed to clear the maples at the end of the runway. Gene's hand gripped tightly on the control stick as we skimmed thirty feet above the leaves. It felt less like we were rising above the earth, than that the earth was falling away from us. Gene banked to the right and we headed north, climbing higher and higher.

5   Suddenly, I was scared. In an instant, the reality of my situation had hit me, and there wasn't a thing I could do about it. Gene was in control, and all I could do was breathe deeply to keep from throwing up. Fortunately, as soon as we swept over another group of trees, the trauma of takeoff passed, and a

> This paragraph begins with a short, punchy sentence, as a way to transition from a description of the takeoff to note the author's sudden feelings of fear.

rush of excitement replaced it. My brain could not work fast enough to take it all in. My eyes darted left and right, trying to see everything at once, and my brain worked to process the fact that I was sitting out in the open hundreds of feet above the ground. Then I felt the most powerful rush of all: freedom! That is what flying is all about for me. I never felt more free. There were no restrictions on me as we soared high above the land.

6   Going thirty miles an hour at one thousand feet, which felt practically like hovering, we crossed empty fields, large wooded areas, and some sparsely populated streets. I could see people out in their yards and imagined them watching in awe those crazy people in their kite-like craft.

7   The day was mostly clear with just a few scattered clouds to remind us of our altitude. Lack of oxygen prevented us from climbing above the clouds, but we were close to the same level as a few of the lower ones. Clouds look different from up close and from the side. They seem more substantial, more cottony. Viewed from the air, clouds have a three-dimensional reality instead of the two-dimensional sense we get when we view them from the ground. The rays of the setting sun were diffused through the undersides, giving the clouds between us and the sun a luminescent silver base that seemed to support the puffy white foam that billowed upward from the silver.

8   The sun was a bright red ball that rolled along the horizon as we turned to head back. It gave an orange glow to the hazy horizon, and orange-tinted fog drifted below a light violet sky. It was a display that could only be witnessed from the air. The earth slowly rotated, and the great fireball lowered beneath the land.

9   Gene gave the signal that we were on our final approach for landing. I watched the ground as it rose to our level. As the craft levelled after its shallow dive, my stomach dropped. The effect of that small G-force was my last taste of flight. We were back on solid ground.

10 I have flown many times since then, and I always get the same rush of freedom and thrill from the perspective that being airborne provides. Flying intrigued me before I ever left the ground. Once I did, I was hooked.

The complete essay, including any bibliographic references, is also available on the Online Learning Centre at www.mcgrawhill.ca/olc/clouse.

Margin notes:

This paragraph uses descriptive detail to explain flying through clouds, and also uses a metaphor.

This paragraph uses another metaphor, and describes the sunset, which corresponds with the end of the flight, and the end of the descriptive essay.

EXERCISE CONSIDERING "MY FIRST FLIGHT"

1.   What is Jerry Silberman describing, and what is his dominant impression?

2.   Cite one paragraph that includes objective description, one that includes subjective description, and one that includes both.

3.   Cite two concrete sensory details that you find effective. What makes them effective?

4.   What is Jerry Silberman's purpose for writing? How does the description help him achieve that purpose? How does the narration help him achieve that purpose? ●

CRITIQUE, REVISE, and EDIT

Writing description often involves a series of revisions to get the images just right. Here, for example, is the first draft of one of Jerry Silberman's more descriptive paragraphs, followed by his first two revisions. The changes are noted in colour, with underlining to mark additions, and strikethroughs to mark deletions. Notice that with this revision, Jerry added descriptive details and used more specific word choice.

First Draft

It was a clear day, but the few clouds made us realize how high we were. Lack of oxygen prevented us from going above the clouds, but we were close to the same level as a few of the lower ones. Clouds look different from up close and from the side. The rays of the setting sun reflected off the bottoms and gave the clouds a silver glow from within. The clouds billowed upward, giving them a three-dimensional image instead of the sense of paintings we get from the ground.

First Revision

It was a clear day, but the few <u>scattered</u> clouds made us realize how high we were. Lack of oxygen prevented us from ~~going~~ <u>climbing</u> above the clouds, but we were close to the same level as a few of the lower ones. Clouds look different from up close and from the side. <u>They seem more fragile and less like thick cotton</u>. The rays of the setting sun reflected off the bottoms and gave the clouds a silver <u>tinge.</u> ~~glow from within.~~ The clouds billowed upward, giving them a three-dimensional image instead of the sense of paintings we get from the ground.

Second Revision

It was a clear day, but the few scattered clouds <u>reminded</u> ~~made~~ us <u>of</u> ~~realize~~ how high we were. Lack of oxygen prevented us from climbing above the clouds, but we were close to the same level as a few of the lower ones. Clouds look different from up close and from the side. They seem more fragile and less like thick cotton. The rays of the setting sun <u>were diffused through</u>~~reflected off~~ the<u>ir</u> <u>undersides</u>~~bottoms~~ and gave the clouds <u>between us and the sun</u> a silver tinge. The clouds billowed upward, giving them a three-dimensional <u>reality</u>~~image~~ instead of the <u>two-dimensional</u> sense of paintings we get from the ground.

In this second revision, Jerry shaped the description a bit more. However, this is still not the final version you read in the essay. After studying Jerry's revisions and final version, how would you describe his revision process?

10 And then there is the hair. On the second floor of Block 4, in a case some 20 yards long, are layer after layer of braids and tresses and curls, all gone gray now but once blond and brown and black and auburn. The hair weighs more than two tons, less than a third of what the Allied troops originally found. Hair was sold to be woven into textiles; gold fillings from teeth went to the German treasury.

11 Each display was more dreadful than the last, but the one that hit me hardest was the suitcases: a room-length mound of leather and cardboard valises once packed with the illusion that the owners were headed for a place where they could use their belongings. Names and statistics were carefully lettered outside with what looked like white shoe polish: "L. Bermann, 26.12.1886, Hamburg." As if poor Mr. Bermann ever would see his bag, or his world, again. "Sometimes visitors say, 'That's my father,' our guide told me. I scanned the mass of lost hopes and stopped short at a brown leather valise, with the name "Petr Eisler, KIND," meaning child. Petr's birth date was two days from my own.

12 As we were led from building to building along the wide, deceptively tranquil roads of the camp on this gloriously sunny day, I recognized the incongruities. The lawn was too lush ("If there had been grass, the starving prisoners would have eaten it," our guide said) and it was peaceful. The crematorium, with its tracks for the smooth delivery of bodies to ovens, has been restored. There is no shortage of grisly reminders, like Block 11 with its one-foot-square "standing cell" and its suffocating starvation cell, torturous punishment for disobedient prison laborers. A placard points out that Jakob Rosenzweig spent five nights here because he was "talking during work." Still, it's tidy—put in order—after all, a museum. "Auschwitz has a certain progression," explained one of my companions, a rabbi based in Warsaw, ushering me back into the taxi after three hours for the next part of our visit. "But Birkenau gets right away to the bones."

13 Birkenau is shorthand for KL Auschwitz II, built as an expansion to the main camp in 1941 in the nearby village of Brzezinka, a quick, two-mile drive.

14 Birkenau is where it all began and ended; where you stepped out of your boxcar and faced a lineup of storm troopers and snarling dogs and where one man would decide whether you lived temporarily or died immediately. It was called the Selection. You've no doubt seen the photographs—the ones with the Nazi officer pointing to the right (forced labor) or left (gas chamber), taking lives and splitting families. It's where Sophie had to make her unbearable choice.[2]

15 I walked down the tracks in utter silence. This camp, nearly 10 times the size of Auschwitz, has largely been left as it was, an eerie ghost town spread across an immense field with the remains of four gas chambers and crematoriums, and a sickeningly efficient reception area called the sauna, where prisoners chosen for forced labor were shaved, stripped and hosed down.

16 There are also rows of squalid barracks—one-story structures originally designed as stables, with 52 rings for horses still on the wall. They housed up to 1,000 humans each. Here the toilets were buckets, the beds triple-tiered shelves where the people were stacked like goods in a warehouse. Finally I understood the photographs of the liberation: this is where the men, or women, lay staring out at their rescuers, human cordwood too feeble to move.

17 The ovens they'd escaped are not intact. Unlike the restoration at Auschwitz, some are in clumps, ruins left by the SS when they blew them up in an attempt to destroy all evidence before retreating. Another was partly destroyed by Jewish prisoners, who somehow managed to marshal the strength of the powerless during a 1944 revolt. An enlarged photograph by the rubble puts it back together.

18 Even the ground at Birkenau is authentic—so thoroughly saturated with the remains of the prisoners' bodies, I was warned to be careful where I walked. "The ashes were dumped in the pond," I was told, "but in fact the ashes are all around here." I heard about visitors who found bits of bones in the soil sticking up near the footpaths.

19 Finally, at the far end of the grounds, we reached the memorial—a line of plaques unveiled in 1967 with the same message in 19 languages. It reads in part: "Forever let this place be a cry

of despair and a warning to humanity." That thought was echoed in my introductory conversation with Krystyna Oleska, the deputy director who has worked there for 20 years. Yes, she told me, it is difficult "but someone has to do it." Why? "Because of all those who died here."

20 She described the staff efforts to catalog prison records into a new database, to shore up the crumbling buildings, to repair the damage from acid rain, paid for mostly by international contributions organized by the Ronald S. Lauder Foundation.

21 "This is an extraordinary cemetery, the scene of a crime," she told me. "We could flatten everything, let the grass grow, and we would have in some sense fulfilled that need to commemorate. But history teaches us. The maintenance of historical knowledge is our obligation. This must never happen again."

22 I left feeling drained and shaken but curiously satisfied. I had wanted to see Auschwitz with my own eyes, not because I doubted its existence or expected to make sense of it, but to make it part of my life. "No one who has not experienced the event will ever be able to understand it," wrote Elie Wiesel, the Nobelist who survived Auschwitz. Primo Levi described winter in Auschwitz, when an icicle he'd broken off was snatched away.

23 "Why?" he asked his tormentor, who replied, "There is no why here."

[1] The tattoos were prisoner identification numbers tattooed on the arms of Auschwitz prisoners.

[2] In the William Styron novel *Sophie's Choice* (1979), a sadistic doctor in Auschwitz forces Sophie to choose in mere seconds which of her two children will live, her 4-year-old daughter or her 10-year-old son.

Considering Ideas

1. Lynn Sherr calls the words over the Auschwitz gate ("Arbeit Macht Frei" or "Work Makes You Free") cynical. Why does she think so? Do you agree? Why or why not?

2. In paragraph 3, Sherr notes, "It is very hard for the German kids" who volunteer at the museum. Why do you think it is hard for these children? Do German youth have a responsibility to see or volunteer at Auschwitz?

3. For what purpose do you think Sherr wrote "Anguished Cries in a Place of Solitude"? Where is her purpose best stated?

4. Explain the meaning of the title. Is the title a good one for this essay? Suggest a different title.

5. The essay contains a number of contrasting ideas. In the title, for example, cries are heard although the place is silent. What other contrasts do you notice in the essay? How do these contrasts help the author achieve her purpose for writing?

Considering Technique

1. Ordinarily, subjective description rather than objective description moves a reader's emotions. The description in this essay is primarily objective, yet the essay is very powerful. How do you explain the fact that so much emotion and power are conveyed by objective details rather than subjective ones?

2. Cite two examples of concrete sensory details that create clear mental images.

3. Cite one example each of a specific yet simple noun, verb, and adjective.

4. Paragraph 16 includes one simile and one metaphor. What are they? How do they add to the description?

5. In what order are the details arranged? How can you tell?

For Group Discussion or Journal Writing

In paragraph 2, Sherr notes that a particular lesson needs to be preserved. What is that lesson? Do you agree that it should be preserved? Why or why not? What other lesson from history do you think should be preserved? Why?

Pre-Reading

1. How visible are women in public and professional life? How has this changed over the last generation?

2. Do affirmative action policies work? What about equal pay legislation? Investigate these ideas and consider whether they have helped or hindered women's progress.

3. This is a piece of journalism, and though it includes statistical and anecdotal supports, there are no citations in the text. How does this change for a piece of academic writing?

Women Don't Matter: They've Been in the Workforce for a Long Time Now. They've Been Affirmative-Actioned, They've Been Studied and Mentored and Fast-Tracked. And Still...

Heather Mallick

1   She is corporate woman. A perfect employee who is highly motivated and attuned to the culture of the corporation for which she works. She puts in the hours demanded of her and then some. Well educated and expensively trained, she is immaculately dressed, keeps her family demands private, strives for the high-profile projects—as she is advised to do—and is satisfied by the way her colleagues and the corporation treat her.

2   Or at least by the way they treat her while she's not too powerful, because she is going nowhere beyond vice-president and she knows it. She will never take a genuine leading role. Unless she's Sonja Bata or Madeleine Paquin and the company belongs to her family, she will never run the show. She will not even sit on the board of directors—they have a token woman there already.

3   Women now account for 45% of the workforce in Canada. It's logical to assume that as women entered the workforce in increasing numbers, they would inevitably rise to the top. Let's call it the "trickle-up" theory. But the fact is, things have scarcely improved in recent decades for women trying to break into the top layer.

4   Look at the numbers. Two-thirds of the top 500 Canadian companies have no women directors at all. The rest don't have many: Over all, women still hold only 6.2% of board seats in Canada.

5   And of the top 500 companies, a mere 13 are headed by women. Most of them run subsidiaries of American multinationals—one could say they're in training rather than flying solo. Of the country's corporate executives and senior partners, a "small fraction" (as yet unmeasured, it seems) are women. And the stats on inside directors of top 500 companies—4% of them are women—foretell an equally dim future given that successors to CEOs in large companies most often are inside directors first.

6   These 1998 numbers, the most definitive, recent and Canadian yet compiled, come from Catalyst, a non-profit firm that exists to quantify women's progress, or lack of it, in the business world. A prior Catalyst study done with the Conference Board of Canada in 1997 provided the starting point of comparison. Women make up 43% of all managers and administrators in Canadian business and the professions, up from 29% in 1982.

7   The situation is slightly better in the U.S., where 11.2% of Fortune 500 board seats are held by women, and worse in Britain, where board seats on the FTSE 100 are only 5.9% female. How many of those British women are inside directors? An unbelievable 0.7%. This is a country where a few years ago, the banks were embarrassed by how few women executives they could present at their Christmas parties. So they hired a pile of women. Just for a few evenings, to go to the parties.

8   So what mysterious thing happens when successful senior women try to make it into the executive suite and the boardroom? They vanish into the ether. This may be the ether that apparently floats just beneath the glass ceiling. But is that ceiling made of glass? The numbers suggest that the glass ceiling is reinforced steel, floorboarded, padded and carpeted. It's the floor of the boardroom. Women are not allowed in there. Women don't matter.

9   Every now and then, they let one through the door, and the media get excited about the new stars. Carly Fiorina at Hewlett-Packard has it all! Andrea Jung runs Avon! Maureen Kempston-Darkes was put in charge of GM Canada! They're stars in an empty firmament, their presence only serving to point up how unique they are.

10   One wonders how they feel about their isolation. Trudy Eagan, vice-president and chief administrative officer of Sun Media Corp., is the only powerful woman at a company that has one claim to fame: the Sunshine Girls in its sports, sex and entertainment newspapers. She decided early on that she would always be forthright in her opinions and would do all she could to aid the progress of other women at the company.

11   Some men at Sun Media smirk and make typing gestures with their fingers when Eagan's name is mentioned. She began as a secretary. In the early '70s, Eagan points out, there was no other way in. Yet it is a stigma and is still used against her, even though she is part of core management. After Sun Media became a private company following its purchase by Quebecor last year, Eagan lost her seat on the Sun board.

12   Executive women point out that boards are mainly composed of white middle-aged men who have been plucked out of a network of friendships incubated in private school, in university, on the golf course, at the cocktail party and in other boardrooms. Women simply do not have that web of alliances.

13   Jane Pederson, director of human resources planning at Canadian Pacific Ltd., says part of the problem is that those recruiting for boards don't know where to look for qualified directors who are women. So Canadian Pacific, which has two women on its 13-member board of directors, is part of an admirable project that is compiling a database of women executives with the specific skills that corporate boards are seeking. It's a way for the two solitudes to find each other, albeit in a Petri dish rather than organically.

14   It doesn't say much for male executives that they really need an executive dating service to find a woman they can live with on their board.

15   Eagan can understand that a 60-year-old might be uncomfortable listening to an aggressive, opinionated, younger woman. "It's a generation thing. But I am appalled when I'm in meetings with late-20s and early-30s men who are arrogant, chauvinistic and outdated in their thinking."

16   Women also face a consideration that men don't every time they make a career move: Is this a place where they will always face a battle? Barbara Orser, program manager at the Conference Board's Centre of Excellence for Women's Advancement, says this is the crucial difference: Men are welcome everywhere, women go where they are welcome. She recently heard from a woman who was headhunted for a lucrative job in an engineering consulting firm. She would have been the only senior woman there. Her final interview was with the CEO, who dismissed her questions about all-male managers. He had three young daughters himself, he pointed out. Not a problem.

17   There was no explanation for the previous blanket exclusion of women, and a clear implication that it was her problem to solve. After much soul-searching, she decided against taking the job.

Whether she was right or wrong, Orser isn't sure. The problem is in the institution, not within the woman who is being asked to bend and blend.

18 And women often have to be aggressive, which then plays into the bitch/dragon-lady stereotype some men cherish as part of their rationale for sticking with a male hierarchy. Many times, Eagan has offered her opinion in meetings only to be ignored, and then five minutes later, heard the same opinion expressed by a man and taken up enthusiastically. Plenty of corporate women will find this familiar. Eagan's remedy is to always point it out, but others are worn out and will stay limp and silent.

19 A female partner in a professional services firm confirmed this in the Conference Board/Catalyst study. "Part of the male culture, which I sort of look on as a bit of a game, is to position yourself in meetings so you always speak early [because] I think there is a tendency for men to dismiss women who are very quiet."

20 Guys, eternal optimists that they are, can't figure out what the big deal is. Consider: Three-quarters of male chief executives surveyed by Catalyst said women's opportunities have increased greatly or somewhat. But only 56% of their senior women agreed with this positive spin. Senior women were more likely to report that there had been no change. In professional firms, leaders and senior women can't even agree on what they think is the proportion of women partners. The men say 21%; the women say 9%. It's a parallel world we live in.

21 Male corporate chief executives are three times as likely as female executives to believe that women simply have not been in the leadership pipeline long enough. Not enough time to get to know the ropes and make the necessary personal connections to get to the top.

22 The women were much more likely to blame cultural and work-environment barriers. One woman vice-president at a finance/insurance firm said poignantly: "When they are looking for someone to promote, they're always looking for this bright, young fellow. You have to be the cream of the crop—as a woman—to get a promotion, whereas you just have to be a reasonably good male."

23 Dianne Schwalm, senior vice-president of advertising and publicity at Warner Bros. Entertainment in Toronto, has great clout in the entertainment industry now, having spent her working life in the business. She says the fact that only excellence will be accepted from women makes it even tougher for them to enter the job-think of the upper reaches of the male-run corporation. "It's not about how you work but how you play." Are you the right type? You play the politics, watch your back, cover your ass; you identify your friends and make sure you're one step ahead of them; you play your life as a chess game.

24 Weighing all this, it seems absurd to hand-wring about how more women can get onto this glorious, hellish chessboard. The answer is to do what men do, Schwalm says. "There is no women's game to play yet. It doesn't exist."

25 So what are the reasons for men's resistance to women's advancement? Is it habit? Fear? Do men think women are smarter? Men can't have failed to notice that as soon as a profession is taken over by women, it loses all prestige. It happened to teachers, it will happen to doctors.

26 Studies show that both men and women cite the demands of family versus the workplace as a hindrance to women's advancement. Perhaps this is because the media talk about it constantly, the other barriers being duller, more complicated and less likely to start a fight between workforce women and their at-home colleagues.

27 What are women to do? When you go into the business section of a bookstore, you'd think there would be dozens of books advising women on how to win in corporate life. There aren't. There is a glut of books about women entrepreneurs—in other words, women who gave up on mainstream office life and struck out on their own. These books mask a larger failure. They also craftily subvert the debate about the structural problem of the glass ceiling, making it instead a discussion about personal choice.

28 *Fortune* magazine said it out loud: American women weren't getting to the top because of discrimination. They quoted a study showing that resistance to women managers lowers after the first handful get promoted, but resistance

reappears when women get to hold 15% of management positions. Why that threshold matters isn't clear; maybe it's a bit like saying that you don't mind one neighbourhood ex-jailbird, but you won't tolerate a halfway house full of them.

29 Here's the awful thing: *Fortune* said this in 1984. Hilary Cosell quoted the article in her book *Woman on a Seesaw*, which came out in 1985. It is one of the most prescient guides ever written to the barriers women face in office life, and highly unsettling to read now because nothing she wrote has changed.

30 Cosell quotes a woman TV executive: "Women aren't accepted, they aren't wanted and women fight every step of the way, all day, every day. If women choose to go into the corporate arena they had better be prepared to be on trial about every aspect of their looks and their personality. Worst of all, women can't even tell half the time what's going on because men have become increasingly adept at hiding what they're feeling about women executives."

31 When will women get their chance to show what they can do? At the rate we have seen up to now, I bet it will not happen in this century.

Considering Ideas

1. Mallick begins her essay with a description of a corporate "everywoman." Which details are most effective?

2. Mallick cites research from a number of sources, and compares the situation in Canada to those in the US and the UK. How do the statistics she cites bolster her argument that women are still underrepresented? Are the comparisons effective?

3. How does Mallick indicate that executive recruitment usually works for men? Is the same true for women? If not, why not?

4. Evaluate the title for this essay. Mallick ends with a tentative statement. What effect does this have?

Considering Technique

1. What does the description in paragraphs 1 and 2 contribute to the essay?

2. Which paragraphs include objective description? Why does Mallick use objective description rather than subjective description in these paragraphs?

3. What contrasts does Mallick use? What is the significance of the contrasts?

4. Mallick relies on many examples of women who have fought hard to gain entry into positions of power. Are these examples effective?

5. Mallick creates a vivid description of the "glass ceiling," a metaphor. Which details does she provide, and what is the impression she creates? Is this a subjective, or an objective description?

For Group Discussion or Journal Writing

Mallick claims, "It seems absurd to hand-wring about how more women can get into this glorious, hellish chessboard." Consider the metaphor of the business world as a chessboard. How accurate is this metaphor in terms of describing the corporate world?

WRITING TOOL

Short Paragraphs

You probably noticed that the paragraphs in "Women Don't Matter" are often short, sometimes just one or two sentences. Opinion pieces like this are written in a journalistic style—a style that often incorporates short paragraphs. Because magazine articles are printed in narrow columns, even a brief paragraph can appear long, so frequent paragraphing gives the reader's eyes a rest. In addition, in all writing, brief paragraphs can provide transition. Mallick introduces a number of ideas that she wishes to communicate. Note how this style of paragraphing supports a dense narration.

Short paragraphs can also provide emphasis. For example, Mallick's last paragraph is only two sentences long. How does this paragraph support the thesis, and function as a conclusion?

"When will women get their chance to show what they can do? At the rate we have seen up to now, I bet it will not happen in this century."

Description in an Image

The following advertisement promotes travel to Nova Scotia.

Considering the Image

1. What purpose does the description—in both the text and the picture—serve?
2. What dominant impression is conveyed by the picture? By the words?
3. Are the descriptive words objective, subjective, or both? Explain.
4. What impression do the words and picture create?
5. What audience is the advertisement targeting? How can you tell?

THE WRITING PROCESS

Description

These strategies are not meant to replace your own tried and true procedures; they are here for you to sample as you develop your own effective, efficient writing process.

Generate Ideas, Consider Audience and Purpose, and Order Ideas

- Describe a subject that you can observe.
- To establish your audience, answer the questions on page 43. In particular, consider who you want to share your perceptions with and who would come to appreciate your subject by reading your essay.
- To assess your reader's needs, consider readers' knowledge of, interest in, feelings about, and experience with the topic.
- To determine your purpose, consider whether you communicate why you perceive the subject a particular way or understand the effect your perception has on you. Will your reader appreciate this?

Draft

- When you draft, think about your dominant impression so that your descriptive details convey that impression. Also, consider your purpose, and include details that help you fulfill that purpose.

Critique, Edit, and Revise

- Revise passages that need more specific word choice or better concrete sensory detail. Remember, you may need to revise several times because description often requires a series of refinements.
- To secure reader response, see pages 101–102. In addition, ask your reader to circle words and concrete sensory details that should be reconsidered and place a check mark next to words and concrete sensory details that are particularly effective.

Correct Errors and Proofread

- Use the "Guide to Frequently Occurring Errors" for reference, and check with a writing centre tutor if you are unsure about a point of grammar, usage, or punctuation.
- Review Chapter 23, "Modifiers." Because description includes so many modifiers, this chapter is particularly relevant. In addition, refer to page 500 on using commas between coordinate modifiers and to page 516 on using the hyphen between words to form modifiers.

Remember

- Be aware that a description—even an objective description—must be more than a list. Avoid cataloguing nouns.
- Avoid shifting the vantage point. Keep the focus consistent.

CHAPTER 7

Narration

Looking Ahead

In this chapter, you will learn about narration—about telling stories, or relating situations, in time sequence. How important were stories in your childhood? Did you expect each day to end with a good story? Did you frequently hear stories of the experiences of grandparents or other relatives? Was dinner a time for family members to share stories of their day? In a brief paragraph, discuss to what extent stories were a part of your childhood. How were you affected by the stories—or lack of them?

Why is Narration Important?

Narrated stories can entertain, instruct, clarify, and persuade. They can show us how the world works, how people behave, and how events unfold. In short, stories help us understand and cope with the world. Storytelling is also academic. Think about it—a history textbook tells the story of our past so we can better understand our present. We tell young people stories with morals to help them learn important lessons. If you keep a diary, you write out the events of your life to examine and record them. Historical figures kept diaries that are important to our understanding of history. Today, you email family and friends about events that happen to you in order to share your life with them. In short, narration can fulfill any of the purposes for writing: to entertain, to express feelings, to relate experience, to inform, and to persuade.

Deborah Hautzig sent this story to the *New York Times,* where it appeared in the newspaper's "Metropolitan Diary" column in 2002:

> While shopping at Fairway, I came across a distraught-looking mother pushing a large shopping cart. She had two children in tow, about 3 and 5 years old, both of whom were whining ceaselessly. They yanked at her clothes and pleaded for candy, and her attempts to soothe them failed utterly.

OCCASIONS FOR WRITING

Narration across the Disciplines and Beyond

Narration in the Classroom

Narration is important in many kinds of classes. For instance, in a paper for a political science class, a student might narrate the sequence of events leading to the failure of the League of Nations, and its replacement with the United Nations. In an education class, students might narrate events they observed during student teaching. Science students may narrate their observations over the course of an experiment or project. Creative writers might narrate events from their own lives, or from those of characters they create. Students in business programs narrate events in case studies, while students in health care programs might narrate a sequence of events during an illness or medical procedure. *Think about your own courses and times when you have needed to use narration to complete an assignment. What was the assignment and how did narration help you do it? Why do you think narration is so useful in so many courses?*

Narration in Daily Life

Narration is perhaps the most common form of writing people do in personal life. Diaries, blogs, and journal entries include narrative accounts of events in life. Letters and emails to friends and family often include stories of things that have happened, both good and bad. And if anyone has to deliver a speech or give a toast, he or she will likely include one or more anecdotes. *Describe a recent situation in which you used narration. What were the circumstances? Which of the purposes of writing did your narration fulfill?*

Narration on the Job

Many professions require narrative writing. Police officers write arrest reports with narrative accounts of crimes. Safety workers write accident reports that narrate the causes of injuries. Social workers write narrative accounts of events in their clients' lives. Teachers write about student progress through a curriculum. Nurses document a patient's progress during treatment. *Think of other careers in which narration would be a common component. Is there a particular job you hope to pursue after finishing school? How would narration be useful in this job?*

DETERMINING PURPOSE

Purposes for Narration	Sample Narration
To inform (to teach a lesson)	An account of a time a student got in trouble for cheating
To express feelings	An account of what happened when a friend betrayed a friend
To relate experience	An account of the time someone got lost in the woods for two days
To inform (to explain what happens when a person is arrested)	An account of the time someone was wrongly arrested for shoplifting
To persuade (to convince the reader that community service should be required in high school)	An account of the community service students performed as high school seniors

Finally, when the older child—for at least the 20th time—screamed, "Mom-EEEEE," the mother looked straight ahead and said, "There is no one here by that name."

Why did Hautzig send this story to the *Times,* and why did the newspaper run it as a human interest feature? Hautzig wrote it, and the *Times* printed it, because stories convey so much. For example, the story of the harried mother amuses, illustrates one behaviour of young children, sheds light on the frustrations of parenting, and offers an example of how to handle a difficult situation with humour—and it does all that in just four sentences!

Another name for a story is a **narration**. A short narration—like the one here—is an **anecdote**. A long narration—one that is essay or even book length—is an **extended narration**. In this chapter, you will learn about essay-length, extended narrations.

Combining Narration with other Patterns

Memorable narrations often include specific, descriptive details to make the story vivid. Important details of the scene are described, as are key people and events. To appreciate the importance of description, compare these two versions of a narration:

> The child drove his tricycle down the driveway into the path of an oncoming car. Fortunately, the driver, who was speeding, was able to swerve in time to avoid a collision.

> Four-year-old Ishmael hopped on his racing red tricycle and began pedaling furiously down his driveway. By the time he reached the end, he had gathered too much speed to stop. With fear in his eyes, he screamed mightily as his out-of-control trike headed into the path of a speeding Chevy Lumina. The teenage driver, startled into action, swerved just in time to avert disaster.

Did you find the second version more interesting because of the description?

Because narration can help explain, illustrate, or support a point, it often appears in essays developed primarily with other patterns. For example, if a student writes a definition of *friendship,* and identifies loyalty as one of its characteristics, she could narrate an account of the time a best friend refused to believe rumours. The story could explain and illustrate what a writer means by *loyalty.* If a student is classifying types of teachers and establishes one type as "the authoritarian," he can tell the story of an encounter he had with an authoritarian teacher to show what that type is like. Similarly, to explain the effects of divorce on children, writers can illustrate one of the effects by narrating what happened when a father was not around when someone needed him the most. No matter what the dominant pattern of development, there is the possibility that narration can help to achieve a purpose.

For an example of combining narration with other patterns, read "The Telephone" on page 180. In this essay, the author combines narration with both description and contrast.

Before Writing

Storytelling comes naturally to us, in part because we speak, hear, read, and write stories so often. Nonetheless, when students write narration, they must choose details thoughtfully.

Answer the Journalist's Questions

One strategy that can help you choose details is to answer the standard journalist's questions: *Who? What? When? Where? Why? How?* In most cases, a reader will want to know what happened, when it happened, where it happened, why it happened, how it happened, and who was involved. If you answer each of these questions, you are likely to include the most significant information.

However, do not get carried away and include ideas not pertinent to the who, what, when, where, why, and how of a narration. We have all seen movies that drag because of unnecessary detail, action, explanation, or dialogue. Such movies are boring. To avoid boring the reader, maintain a brisk pace by including only the significant details.

You must also determine which of these significant details require emphasis. For some narrations, the *who* and *where* may deserve extended treatment, while the *why,* *when,* and *how* merit less development. Other narrations may require detailed discussion of the *why.* Purpose and audience will help determine which details to emphasize.

Describe a Person, Place, or Scene

When writers tell a story and want their readers to "be there," they can use description to help readers form a mental picture of a person, place, or scene. Description can also give narration energy and create interest. For example, in "The Telephone" on page 180, Accawi uses description to help the reader "see" the village where he lived:

> When I was growing up in Magdaluna, a small Lebanese village in the terraced, rocky mountains east of Sidon, time didn't mean much to anybody, except maybe to those who were dying, or those waiting to appear in court because they had tampered with the boundary markers on their land. In those days, there was no real need for a calendar or a watch to keep track of the hours, days, months, and years. We knew what to do and when to do it, just as the Iraqi geese knew when to fly north, driven by the

hot wind that blew in from the desert, and the ewes knew when to give birth to wet lambs that stood on long, shaky legs in the chilly March wind and baaed hesitantly, because they were small and cold and did not know where they were or what to do now that they were here.

Tell a Story for a Reason

Tell a story for a specific purpose. Perhaps it is entertaining, or perhaps it points to an important truth or teaches a lesson. Maybe it illustrates a fact of life or offers an observation. If the point of the story is strongly implied in the details, you can state the point in a thesis or in the conclusion. For example, the student author of "Canadian Refugee Policy" on page 173 explains that refugee policy has a direct impact on social work practice:

> This paper will examine Canada's historical and present refugee policies from an anti-racist perspective. Specifically, it will examine the way in which immigration discourse has viewed refugees as "foreign," "other," and a threat to Canadian society. It will conclude by discussing implications for social work practice, noting how an anti-oppressive approach reveals the structural oppression refugees face both in and out of country.

After establishing the purpose for writing, the student writer outlines what the paper will address, and situates discussion of immigration and refugee issues in a professional context.

Consider Purpose and Audience

How do writers know which of the journalist's questions to answer and which to emphasize? How do they decide whether to include dialogue or description or whether to state or imply the point of a narration? To decide, consider your purpose and audience.

Suppose you tell the story about the time you felt that your psychology instructor was unfair. If your purpose is to express anger, you might focus on yourself and your feelings. If your purpose is to convince readers that students need a grievance procedure, you might focus more on what happened. If the purpose is to inform readers that even the best professors have their bad moments, you might emphasize what happened, why it happened, and who the instructor was. For this purpose, you might also describe the instructor as typically fair, which is something you would not do for the first two purposes.

Like purpose, audience will influence what details to include and what to emphasize. Let's return to the story of the unfair psychology professor. If the reader knows little about the workings of a college classroom, the writer might include more explanatory detail than if the reader is currently attending the university. If the audience is a classmate who witnessed the incident, the writer might emphasize what happened less than if the audience were someone who did not witness the event.

Organizing Narration

Narrative details are arranged in **chronological** (time) order. Usually, writers start with what happened first, move to what happened next, and so forth. However,

that makeup: eyeliner, eyeshadow, foundation, powder, blush, lip-liner, lipstick, mascara, brow-liner. What woman has the time (or the skill) to put all that on? As if that isn't enough, the model is backlit for maximum effect.

While the above example is not a specific ad from any particular magazine, it is enough like what typically appears to be representative of actual occurrence.

Use the Right Number of Examples

How many examples to use is a key decision. If you use too few examples, they can fail to clarify a generalization and provide the necessary concreteness. If you use too many examples, you can be guilty of overkill.

You can provide just a few examples, and develop each one in great detail, or can provide quite a few examples and develop each one in far less detail. You can also provide a moderate number of examples, each developed to a degree somewhere between the other two extremes. Whatever number of examples you have, there must be enough to explain and support a generalization adequately; and to whatever degree you develop an illustration, there must be enough detail so that readers appreciate the point you are making.

Consider Purpose and Audience

Consider the purpose and audience carefully when you choose examples. Audience is an important consideration because who your reader is will affect the selection of examples. For instance, assume you are writing about why your school is superior to other schools, and you plan to present examples to illustrate some of your school's strengths. If you are writing for an academically oriented audience that does not care much for sports, you would not give the example that a football team is the league champion. Similarly, a paper aimed at parents of prospective new students would not give the example of wild parties on Saturday nights.

Taken together, purpose and audience will profoundly influence the examples you include. For instance, assume you are writing about the benefits of running. To express why you enjoy running to your friends, who think you are odd because you run four miles a day regardless of the weather, you would provide examples of the

BE A RESPONSIBLE WRITER

Being truthful and ethical are extremely important in academic writing. Sometimes writers get panicky and end up using examples irresponsibly. For instance, writers who wait until the last minute may not have time to develop solid examples from research and, in a rush to meet the deadline, they conjure up examples that mislead readers because they are not true. Remember, writers cannot conveniently make up an example to support a thesis unless the example is sufficiently representative of reality to be hypothetical, and unless the example can be substantiated.

Remember to document examples you take from sources using the conventions explained in Chapter 17. (To see how source examples are acknowledged, read "Media Stereotyping of Muslims as Terrorists" on page 195.)

When you write examples, be a responsible writer by asking yourself these questions:

- Are my actual and hypothetical examples sufficiently representative of reality?
- Are examples from outside sources properly acknowledged?

benefits runners get from this sport. However, if the purpose is to inform the average reader that running can control depression and anxiety, you might provide examples of runners who have improved their outlook by running.

Organizing Exemplification

The thesis can express a generalization, and the body paragraphs can present and develop the examples of that generalization.

When you use just a few examples, you can present and develop each one in its own body paragraph. An extended example may require more than one body paragraph for adequate development. When using quite a few examples, give each one less extensive development and group related examples together in the same body paragraph.

Often a progressive order is used for examples. If some examples are more compelling than others, save your strongest example for last in order to build to a big finish. Or begin with the second-best example to impress the reader right off with the validity of a generalization. Writers can also begin with the *best* example to impress the reader initially, while reserving the second-most-effective example for last to ensure a strong final body paragraph. Both methods work equally well.

Sometimes a chronological or spatial order is possible. Suppose the thesis is that the fans at local high school basketball games are rowdy. You could arrange examples chronologically by first giving examples of rowdiness before the game begins, then examples of rowdiness during halftime, and finally examples of rowdiness after the game. Other logical arrangements are also possible. For instance, if some examples come from firsthand experience, some from observation, and some from the experience of others, group together the examples from the same source.

EXERCISE WRITING EXEMPLIFICATION

1. Locate two published essays or articles that include examples. (You might check your textbooks, news magazines, and newspapers.) Photocopy the selections and answer these questions:
    a. Is exemplification or some other pattern the primary method of development?
    b. What is the source of the examples: personal experience, observation, research, or other?
    c. Are the examples adequately detailed? Do they support their generalization adequately? Explain.
    d. Are any of the examples hypothetical? How can you tell? If so, are they plausible?

2. For each of the following subjects, write one generalization that can be supported with examples.
    a. Education
    b. Television
    c. Sports

3. Select one of the generalizations you wrote for number 2, and establish a possible audience and purpose for an essay that uses that generalization as a thesis.

4. To support the thesis/generalization, discover one example to fit each of the categories listed below. If you are unable to think of an example for a particular category, try to come up with two for another category. Also, one example may fill

'holy war'" (2). Later in the article, he explains that the goal of his research was "to see from the inside what this *jihad* factory was producing" (3). Taken together, the comments lead the reader to believe that the author is investigating a "holy war" factory. The stereotyped image is of a barbaric institution teaching its followers such skills as firing an AK-47. However, the article actually reveals this "holy war" factory as a place where students are required to memorize the Qur'an verbatim. This is far from the gun-toting stereotype that the author originally portrays—a stereotype that reinforces the mistaken notion that all Muslims support and cultivate terrorists.

> This paragraph uses both example and definition to explain and clarify the notion of "jihad."

5   Even *Forbes* magazine, a prominent publication for entrepreneurs, published Neil Weinberg's article with the title "Leading the *Jihad.*" This article has no connection to an Islamic subject. It concerns E-Trade's chief strategist's new plan for updating technology, a plan that "involves a more adult form of *jihad*" (1). The stereotype has progressed to the point that *jihad* is used as a synonym for battle in American business lingo. In "The Islamic Doctrine of *Jihad* Does Not Advocate Violence," Mohammed Abdul Malek addresses the tendency of people to use *jihad* incorrectly: "*Jihad* is a duty of Muslims to commit themselves to a struggle on all fronts—moral, spiritual, and political—to create a just and decent society. It is not a 'holy war' against the non-believers as is commonly understood" (122). Yet the misconception persists, enabling the stereotype to prevail.

> Baird takes up one of the fundamental ideas of our society, that of justice, and notes that popular bias against Muslims can lead to negative stereotyping.

6   The stereotype is so persistent that it causes the media to abandon one of our cherished beliefs, that a person is innocent until proven guilty. When a bomb devastated the Murrah building in Oklahoma City, no suspects were immediately obvious. As is often the case, the media made unfounded accusations based on stereotypical thinking. Unconfirmed reports of Muslim suspects soon surfaced. Said Deep, author of "Rush to Judgment," feels that CNN began the attack on Muslims. He remarks, "Without citing sources, CNN reported the day after the bombing that federal authorities had arrested three men of Middle-Eastern extraction in connection with the bombing" (3). CNN, a world leader in television news broadcasting, stated unconfirmed reports of Muslim suspects based on a stereotype.

> In this last paragraph, Baird uses not only example, but also comparison, to reinforce the thesis that stereotyping is not only unreasonable, but also illogical. Note the strong ending, in the last paragraph.

7   It is difficult for many Americans to consider Islamic stereotyping unjust. The stereotype exists because some Muslims are terrorists, and because the media has drummed into the American collective consciousness that the terms *jihad* and "holy war" are synonymous. Muslim extremist groups such as al-Qaeda and Hamas call for *jihad* to declare a holy war. However, just as true Catholics do not embrace priests who sexually abuse children, true Muslims reject the ranting of extremists. We must keep in mind that misinterpretations of holy scripture occur in all religions. The misuse of *jihad* by some Muslim groups is comparable to the Roman Catholic Church's misuse of the Old Testament to justify the crusades. Islam is a religion of peace. The violence of some extremists does not justify the stereotyping of Muslims in movies and other media.

The complete essay, including any bibliographic references, is also available on the Online Learning Centre at www.mcgrawhill.ca/olc/clouse.

EXERCISE CONSIDERING "MEDIA STEREOTYPING OF MUSLIMS AS TERRORISTS"

1. What is the thesis of the essay?

2. What do you judge to be the author's purpose for writing? Do you think he achieves his purpose? Why or why not?

3. What are the sources of the writer's examples? Are the examples good ones?

4. How does the writer use research material to help him achieve his purpose for writing? ●

CRITIQUE, REVISE, and EDIT

Thomas makes a daring statement with the thesis in the last paragraph of the introduction. Evaluate the thesis, as it makes claims about Hollywood films, rather than about the media (i.e. news organizations, or Internet sites). Should the thesis take a broader focus? In paragraph 4 of his essay, Thomas extends the process of exemplification, including references to print, and then, in paragraph 6 to the news media. Would this shift—from film to news media—be better accommodated with a transition paragraph? Where should a transition paragraph appear?

CRITICAL READING PROFESSIONAL ESSAYS

Pre-reading

1. Krents is one of many writers who have directed the public's attention to issues around disabilities. Before reading, consider what it would be like to be sightless. How would your life be different if you lost this sense?

2. The essay, which first appeared in the *New York Times* in 1976, has the same title as a novel by Arthur Koestler. Koestler's novel is about a hero of the Communist revolution who is jailed for crimes he did not commit. As you read, think about why Krents chose this title.

3. Many people see those with limitations or disabilities as objects of pity. Krents, arguably, has not been limited by his disability at all. Consider how we perceive the disabled in our society, and how we can change our perceptions.

Darkness at Noon

Harold Krents

1   Blind from birth, I have never had the opportunity to see myself and have been completely dependent on the image I create in the eye of the observer. To date it has not been narcissistic.

2   There are those who assume that since I can't see, I obviously also cannot hear. Very often people will converse with me at the top of their lungs, enunciating each word very carefully. Conversely, people will also often whisper, assuming that since my eyes don't work, my ears don't either.

3   For example, when I go to the airport and ask the ticket agent for assistance to the plane, he or she will invariably pick up the phone, call a ground hostess and whisper: "Hi, Jane, we've got a 76 here." I have concluded that the word "blind" is not used for one of two reasons: Either they fear that if the dread word is spoken, the ticket agent's retina will immediately detach, or they are reluctant to inform me of my condition of which I may not have been previously aware.

4   On the other hand, others know that of course I can hear, but believe that I can't talk. Often, therefore, when my wife and I go out to dinner, a waiter or waitress will ask Kit if "*he* would like a drink" to which I respond that "indeed *he* would."

5   This point was graphically driven home to me while we were in England. I had been given a year's leave of absence from my Washington law firm to study for a diploma in law degree at Oxford University. During the year I became ill and was hospitalized. Immediately after admission, I was wheeled down to the X-ray room. Just at the door sat an elderly woman—elderly I would judge from the sound of her voice. "What is his name?" the woman asked the orderly who had been wheeling me.

6   "What's your name?" the orderly repeated to me.

7   "Harold Krents," I replied.

8   "Harold Krents," he repeated.

9   "When was he born?"

10   "When were you born?"

11   "November 5, 1944," I responded.

12   "November 5, 1944," the orderly intoned.

13   This procedure continued for approximately five minutes at which point even my saintlike disposition deserted me. "Look," I finally blurted out, "this is absolutely ridiculous. Okay, granted I can't see, but it's got to have become pretty clear to both of you that I don't need an interpreter."

14   "He says he doesn't need an interpreter," the orderly reported to the woman.

15   The toughest misconception of all is the view that, because I can't see, I can't work. I was turned down by over 40 law firms because of my blindness, even though my qualifications included a *cum laude* degree from Harvard College and a good ranking in my Harvard Law School class.

16   The attempt to find employment, the continuous frustration of being told that it was impossible for a blind person to practice law, the rejection letters, not based on my lack of ability but rather on my disability, will always remain one of the most disillusioning experiences of my life.

17   I therefore look forward to the day, with the expectation that it is certain to come, when employers will view their handicapped workers as a little child did me years ago when my family still lived in Scarsdale.

18   I was playing basketball with my father in our backyard according to procedures we had developed. My father would stand beneath the hoop, shout, and I would shoot over his head at the basket attached to our garage. Our next-door neighbor, aged five, wandered over into our yard with a playmate. "He's blind," our neighbor whispered to her friend in a voice that could be heard distinctly by Dad and me. Dad shot and missed; I did the same. Dad hit the rim; I missed entirely; Dad shot and missed the garage entirely. "Which one is blind?" whispered back the little friend.

A visually impaired snowboarder and guide. Contrary to what many people believe, those with physical impairments are often able to participate in a range of sports.

19 I would hope that in the near future when a plant manager is touring the factory with the foreman and comes upon a handicapped and non-handicapped person working together, his comment after watching them work will be, "Which one is disabled?"

Considering Ideas

1. Explain the meaning of the title. Why do you think Krents used the same title that Arthur Koestler did? Is the title a good one? Why or why not?

2. The thesis is implied rather than stated. In your own words, write out the thesis. Where in the essay is this thesis most strongly implied?

3. How does Krents distinguish between a "lack of ability" and a "disability" (paragraph 16)? Why is this distinction important to Krents?

4. What three misconceptions about blind people does Krents illustrate?

5. What do you judge to be the author's purpose? How do the examples help Krents fulfill his purpose?

Considering Technique

1. What is the source of Krents' examples?

2. In what order does Krents arrange his detail?

3. Krents uses anecdotes (brief narrations) as examples. What purpose does the basketball narration serve? What other narrative examples appear?

4. "Darkness at Noon" originally appeared in the *New York Times*. Are the examples suited to the original audience? Explain.

5. What approach does Krents take to his conclusion? Does that conclusion bring the essay to a satisfying finish? Explain.

For Group Discussion or Journal Writing

In the last paragraph of "Darkness at Noon," Krents expresses a hope for the future. How likely do you think it is that his hope will be realized? Explain.

Pre-reading

1. Despite scientific evidence, some people still express skepticism about global warming. Why would they?

2. What are some of the effects of global warming? Are they apparent in Canada?

3. Much of the carbon emissions that pollute the air are from cars. Is it possible to live without a car today?

How We Know Global Warming is Real: The Science Behind Human-induced Climate Change

Tapio Schneider

1   Atmospheric carbon dioxide concentrations are higher today than at any time in at least the past 650,000 years. They are about 35% higher than before the industrial revolution, and this increase is caused by human activities, primarily the burning of fossil fuels.

2   Carbon dioxide is a greenhouse gas, as are methane, nitrous oxide, water vapor, and a host of other trace gases. They occur naturally in the atmosphere. Greenhouse gases act like a blanket for infrared radiation, retaining radiative energy near the surface that would otherwise escape directly to space. An increase in atmospheric concentrations of carbon dioxide and of other greenhouse gases augments the natural greenhouse effect; it increases the radiative energy available to Earth's surface and to the lower atmosphere. Unless compensated for by other processes, the increase in radiative energy available to the surface and the lower atmosphere leads to warming. This we know. How do we know it?

How do we know carbon dioxide concentrations have increased?

3   The concentrations of carbon dioxide and other greenhouse gases in atmospheric samples have

been measured continuously since the late 1950s. Since then, carbon dioxide concentrations have increased steadily from about 315 parts per million (ppm, or molecules of carbon dioxide per million molecules of dry air) in the late 1950s to about 385 ppm now, with small spatial variations away from major sources of emissions. For the more distant past, we can measure atmospheric concentrations of greenhouse gases in bubbles of ancient air preserved in ice (e.g., in Greenland and Antarctica). Ice core records currently go back 650,000 years; over this period we know that carbon dioxide concentrations have never been higher than they are now. Before the industrial revolution, they were about 280 ppm, and they have varied naturally between about 180 ppm during ice ages and 300 ppm during warm periods. Concentrations of methane and nitrous oxide have likewise increased since the industrial revolution and, for methane, are higher now than they have been in the 650,000 years before the industrial revolution.

How do we know the increase in carbon dioxide concentrations is caused by human activities?

4   There are several lines of evidence. We know approximately how much carbon dioxide is emitted as a result of human activities. Adding up the human sources of carbon dioxide—primarily from fossil fuel burning, cement production, and land use changes (e.g., deforestation)—one finds that only about half the carbon dioxide emitted as a result of human activities has led to an increase in atmospheric concentrations. The other half of the emitted carbon dioxide has been taken up by oceans and the biosphere—where and how exactly is not completely understood: there is a "missing carbon sink."

5   Human activities thus can account for the increase in carbon dioxide concentrations. Changes in the isotopic composition of carbon dioxide show that the carbon in the added carbon dioxide derives largely from plant materials, that is, from processes such as burning of biomass or fossil fuels, which are derived from fossil plant

materials. Minute changes in the atmospheric concentration of oxygen show that the added carbon dioxide derives from burning of the plant materials. And concentrations of carbon dioxide in the ocean have increased along with the atmospheric concentrations, showing that the increase in atmospheric carbon dioxide concentrations cannot be a result of release from the oceans. All lines of evidence taken together make it unambiguous that the increase in atmospheric carbon dioxide concentrations is human induced and is primarily a result of fossil fuel burning. (Similar reasoning can be evoked for other greenhouse gases, but for some of those, such as methane and nitrous oxide, their sources are not as clear as those of carbon dioxide.)

How can such a minute amount of carbon dioxide affect Earth's radiative energy balance?

6   Concentrations of carbon dioxide are measured in parts per million, those of methane and nitrous oxide in parts per billion. These are trace constituents of the atmosphere. Together with water vapor, they account for less than 1% of the volume of the atmosphere. And yet they are crucially important for Earth's climate.

7   Earth's surface is heated by absorption of solar (shortwave) radiation; it emits infrared (longwave) radiation, which would escape almost directly to space if it were not for water vapor and the other greenhouse gases. Nitrogen and oxygen, which account for about 99% of the volume of the atmosphere, are essentially transparent to infrared radiation. But greenhouse gases absorb infrared radiation and re-emit it in all directions. Some of the infrared radiation that would otherwise directly escape to space is emitted back toward the surface. Without this natural greenhouse effect, primarily owing to water vapor and carbon dioxide, Earth's mean surface temperature would be a freezing −1°F, instead of the habitable 59°F we currently enjoy. Despite their small amounts, then, the greenhouse gases strongly affect Earth's temperature. Increasing their concentration augments the natural greenhouse effect.

How do increases in greenhouse gas concentrations lead to surface temperature increases?

8 Increasing the concentration of greenhouse gases increases the atmosphere's "optical thickness" for infrared radiation, which means that more of the radiation that eventually does escape to space comes from higher levels in the atmosphere. The mean temperature at the level from which the infrared radiation effectively escapes to space (the emission level) is determined by the total amount of solar radiation absorbed by Earth. The same amount of energy Earth receives as solar radiation, in a steady state, must be returned as infrared radiation; the energy of radiation depends on the temperature at which it is emitted and thus determines the mean temperature at the emission level. For Earth, this temperature is –1°F—the mean temperature of the surface if the atmosphere would not absorb infrared radiation. Now, increasing greenhouse gas concentrations implies raising the emission level at which, in the mean, this temperature is attained. If the temperature decreases between the surface and this level and its rate of decrease with height does not change substantially, then the surface temperature must increase as the emission level is raised. This is the greenhouse effect. It is also the reason that clear summer nights in deserts, under a dry atmosphere, are colder than cloudy summer nights on the U.S. east coast, under a relatively moist atmosphere.

9 In fact, Earth surface temperatures have increased by about 1.3°F over the past century. The temperature increase has been particularly pronounced in the past 20 years (for an illustration, see the animations of temperature changes at www.gps.caltech.edu/~tapio/discriminants/animations.html). The scientific consensus about the cause of the recent warming was summarized by the Intergovernmental Panel on Climate Change (IPCC) in 2007: "Most of the observed increase in global average temperatures since the mid-20th century is very likely due to the observed increase in anthropogenic greenhouse gas concentrations. ... The observed widespread warming of the atmosphere and ocean, together with ice mass loss, support the conclusion that it is extremely unlikely that global climate change of the past 50 years can be explained without external forcing, and very likely that it is not due to known natural causes alone."

10 The IPCC conclusions rely on climate simulations with computer models. Based on spectroscopic measurements of the optical properties of greenhouse gases, we can calculate relatively accurately the impact increasing concentrations of greenhouse gases have on Earth's radiative energy balance. For example, the radiative forcing owing to increases in the concentrations of carbon dioxide, methane, and nitrous oxide in the industrial era is about 2.3 Watts per square meter. (This is the change in radiative energy fluxes in the lower troposphere before temperatures have adjusted.) We need computer models to translate changes in the radiative energy balance into changes in temperature and other climate variables because feedbacks in the climate system render the climate response to changes in the atmospheric composition complex, and because other human emissions (smog) also affect climate in complex ways. For example, as the surface and lower atmosphere warm in response to increases in carbon dioxide concentrations, the atmospheric concentration of water vapor near the surface increases as well. That this has to happen is well established on the basis of the energy balance of the surface and relations between evaporation rates and the relative humidity of the atmosphere (it is not directly, as is sometimes stated, a consequence of higher evaporation rates).

11 Water vapor, however, is a greenhouse gas in itself, and so it amplifies the temperature response to increases in carbon dioxide concentrations and leads to greater surface warming than would occur in the absence of water vapor feedback. Other feedbacks that must be taken into account in simulating the climate response to changes in atmospheric composition involve, for example, changes in cloud cover, dynamical changes that affect the rate at which temperature decreases with height and hence affect the strength of the greenhouse effect, and surface changes (e.g., loss of sea ice). Current climate models, with Newton's laws of motion and the

laws of thermodynamics and radiative transfer at their core, take such processes into account. They are able to reproduce, for example, Earth's seasonal cycle if all such processes are taken into account but not, for example, if water vapor feedback is neglected. The IPCC's conclusion is based on the fact that these models can only match the observed climate record of the past 50 years if they take human-induced changes in atmospheric composition into account. They fail to match the observed record if they only model natural variability, which may include, for example, climate responses to fluctuations in solar radiation.

12 Climate feedbacks are the central source of scientific (as opposed to socio-economic) uncertainty in climate projections. The dominant source of uncertainty is cloud feedback, which is incompletely understood. The area covered by low stratus clouds may increase or decrease as the climate warms. Because stratus clouds are low, they do not have a strong greenhouse effect (the strength of the greenhouse effect depends on the temperature difference between the surface and the level from which infrared radiation is emitted, and this is small for low clouds); however, they reflect sunlight, and so exert a cooling effect on the surface, as anyone knows who has been near southern California's coast on an overcast spring morning. If their area coverage increases as greenhouse gas concentrations increase, the surface temperature response will be muted; if their area coverage decreases, the surface temperature response will be amplified. It is currently unclear how these clouds respond to climate change, and climate models simulate widely varying responses. Other major uncertainties include the effects of aerosols (smog) on clouds and the radiative balance and, on timescales longer than a few decades, the response of ice sheets to changes in temperature.

13 Uncertainties notwithstanding, it is clear that increases in greenhouse gas concentrations, in the global mean, will lead to warming. Although climate models differ in the amount of warming they project, in its spatial distribution, and in other more detailed aspects of the climate response, all climate models that can reproduce observed characteristics such as the seasonal cycle project warming in response to the increases in greenhouse gas concentrations that are expected in the coming decades as a result of continued burning of fossil fuels and other human activities such as tropical deforestation. The projected consequences of the increased concentrations of greenhouse gases have been widely publicized. Global-mean surface temperatures are likely to increase by 2.0 to 11.5°F by the year 2100, with the uncertainty range reflecting scientific uncertainties (primarily about clouds) as well as socio-economic uncertainties (primarily about the rate of emission of greenhouse gases over the 21st century). Land areas are projected to warm faster than ocean areas. The risk of summer droughts in mid-continental regions is likely to increase. Sea level is projected to rise, both by thermal expansion of the warming oceans and by melting of land ice.

14 Less widely publicized but important for policy considerations are projected very long-term climate changes, of which some already now are unavoidable. Even if we were able to keep the atmospheric greenhouse gas concentration fixed at its present level—this would require an immediate and unrealistically drastic reduction in emissions—the Earth surface would likely warm by another 0.9–2.5°F over the next centuries. The oceans with their large thermal and dynamic inertia provide a buffer that delays the response of the surface climate to changes in greenhouse gas concentrations. The oceans will continue to warm over about 500 years. Their waters will expand as they warm, causing sea level rise. Ice sheets are thought to respond over timescales of centuries, though this is challenged by recent data from Greenland and Antarctica, which show evidence of a more rapid, though possibly transient, response. Their full contribution to sea level rise will take centuries to manifest. Studies of climate change abatement policies typically end in the year 2100 and thus do not take into account that most of the sea level rise due to the emission of greenhouse gases in the next 100 years will occur decades and centuries later. Sea level is projected to rise 0.2–0.6 meters by the year 2100, primarily as a result of thermal expansion of the oceans; however, it

may eventually reach values up to several meters higher than today when the disintegration of glaciers and ice sheets contributes more strongly to sea level rise. (A sea level rise of 4 meters would submerge much of southern Florida.)

Certainties and Uncertainties

15 While there are uncertainties in climate projections, it is important to realize that the climate projections are based on sound scientific principles, such as the laws of thermodynamics and radiative transfer, with measurements of optical properties of gases. The record of past climate changes that can be inferred, for example, with geochemical methods from ice cores and ocean sediment cores, provides tantalizing hints of large climate changes that occurred over Earth's history, and it poses challenges to our understanding of climate (for example, there is no complete and commonly accepted explanation for the cycle of ice ages and warm periods). However, climate models are not empirical, based on correlations in such records, but incorporate our best understanding of the physical, chemical, and biological processes being modeled. Hence, evidence that temperature changes precede changes in carbon dioxide concentrations in some climate changes on the timescales of ice ages, for example, only shows that temperature changes can affect the atmospheric carbon dioxide concentrations, which in turn feed back on temperature changes. Such evidence does not invalidate the laws of thermodynamics and radiative transfer, or the conclusion that the increase in greenhouse gas concentrations in the past decades is human induced.

Considering Ideas

1. In your own words, write out the thesis of "How We Know Global Warming is Real." Where in the essay is that thesis best expressed?

2. The essay was written for the *Skeptic*. For what purpose do you think Schneider wrote it? Do you think he was likely to achieve his purpose with his original audience? Why or why not?

3. Do you think Schneider is fair to climate change skeptics? Explain.

4. Schneider ends the essay with the claim, "Such evidence does not invalidate the laws of thermodynamics and radiative transfer, or the conclusion that the increase in greenhouse gas concentrations in the past decades is human induced." To whom might he be speaking?

Considering Technique

1. What are the sources of Schneider's examples?

2. Does Schneider use enough examples in enough detail to support the thesis? Explain.

3. *Combining Patterns:* Schneider includes specific, factual detail. Locate at least two pieces of scientific evidence in the essay. How does specific detail help Schneider achieve his writing purpose?

4. The tone of this essay is factual and objective. Schneider does not address counter-arguments about climate change directly. Does this further the essay's thesis?

For Group Discussion or Journal Writing

How do you think that climate change skeptics would respond to Schneider's essay? Would they question the scientific evidence, or produce other arguments to support a claim that global warming and climate change are not linked to human activity?

Combining Patterns of Development

WRITING TOOL

Sarcasm

Sarcasm is saying something that seems positive or neutral on the surface, but that is really intended to be critical. Harold Krents uses sarcasm in paragraph 3 of "Darkness at Noon." When explaining that airport ticket agents use code to indicate that he is blind, Krents writes:

> I have concluded that the word "blind" is not used for one of two reasons: Either they fear that if the dread word is spoken, the ticket agent's retina will immediately detach, or they are reluctant to inform me of my condition of which I may not have been previously aware.

Krents does not really believe that people think they might go blind if they use the word or that Krents is not aware of his blindness. Instead, he is criticizing people who use euphemisms for the word "blind."

Exemplification in an Image

The following print, titled "Do Unto Others," was painted by beloved American painter Norman Rockwell (1894–1978).

Considering the Image

1. What do the people in the image exemplify?
2. What is the relationship between the people in the print and the Golden Rule written on the print? (The Golden Rule, an ethical principle in most religions, states, "Do unto others as you would have them do unto you.")
3. Rockwell organizes his examples—that is, he arranges the people—with the younger people in the foreground and the older people behind. Why do you think the artist uses that organization? Is there more to it than the need to put shorter people in the front?
4. Why are the people in the print not smiling?

THE WRITING PROCESS

Writing Exemplification

The following strategies are not meant to replace your own successful procedures. They are here for you to try as you develop your own effective, efficient writing process.

Think like a Writer: Generating Ideas, Considering Audience and Purpose, and Ordering Ideas

- For a generalization/topic you can support with examples, try these strategies:
  - Fill in the blanks in this sentence, altering words as you need to: _____ is the most _____ I know. For example, one generalization might be, "Taking a three-year-old on a car trip is the trickiest thing I know." Another might be, "Finding a reliable Internet service provider is the biggest hassle I know."
  - Take a common saying and show that it is not true. For example, provide examples to show that honesty is *not* always the best policy or that patience is *not* a virtue.
- Determine purpose by asking these questions:
  - Do I want to describe my reaction to or feelings about my topic?
  - Do I want to help my reader understand why I respond to my topic as I do?
  - Do I want to clarify the nature of my topic?
  - Do I want to convince my reader of something?
- To identify and assess your audience, answer the questions on page 43. In addition, these questions can help assess the audience:
  - Will my reader respond best to examples from any particular sources?
  - Will my reader react well to hypothetical examples?
- To generate examples, answer these questions:
  - What have I done that illustrates my generalization?
  - What have I observed that illustrates my generalization?
  - What have I learned in school that illustrates my generalization?
  - What have I read, seen on television, or heard on the radio that illustrates my generalization?
  - What have others experienced that illustrates my generalization?
  - What can I narrate or describe to illustrate my generalization?
  - What can I research to illustrate my generalization?
- Consider your idea generation material in light of your audience and purpose. Do they suggest that some of your examples are better than others? Do they suggest that a few longer, detailed examples are better than many shorter ones?
- To develop an informal outline, list your examples and number them in the order they are to appear in your draft. Be sure to have a reason for the order you have chosen, and group related examples together.

Think like a Writer: Drafting

- Draft a working thesis that expresses the generalization your examples will illustrate.
- Using your informal outline as a guide, write your draft. If you have trouble, turn your informal outline into a more detailed outline and try again.
- As you draft, think about using topic sentences, so your reader understands how the example or examples in the paragraph illustrate the thesis generalization.

Revising

- Underline the generalization your examples support. If you have not written a generalization, be sure your generalization is strongly implied. If you are in doubt, ask a reliable reader.
- Be sure your examples are adequately detailed.
- Consider how your audience is likely to react to each example and how it will achieve your writing purpose. Do you need to change any examples?
- Ask yourself whether each example is representative and whether hypothetical examples are plausible. If you have doubts, revise.
- Be sure descriptive examples include concrete sensory detail and specific words, as explained in Chapter 6. Be sure narrative examples answer the appropriate journalist's questions and include appropriate dialogue, as explained in Chapter 7.
- To obtain reader response for revision, see pages 101–102. In addition, ask your reader to write out the generalization your examples support. Also, ask your reader to do the following:
  - Place a checkmark where more detail is needed.
  - Place a question mark where something is unclear.
  - Place an exclamation point next to any particularly strong examples.

Correcting Errors and Proofreading

- Use the "Guide to Frequently Occurring Errors" for reference, and check with a writing centre tutor if you are unsure about a grammar, usage, or punctuation point.
- If you introduce examples with transitions such as *for example* or *for instance*, use commas to set off these transitional phrases. For more on commas, see page 498.
- Be sure to proofread the final copy before handing it in. If you are submitting an electronic copy, proofread from a paper copy. Be sure to read very slowly, lingering over every word and punctuation mark.

Remember

Avoid using too few examples. The cumulative impact of your examples must provide convincing support of your thesis. Thus, to support the thesis that parking is a problem on your campus, you must do more than give two examples of times you had difficulty parking—even if those examples are highly detailed.

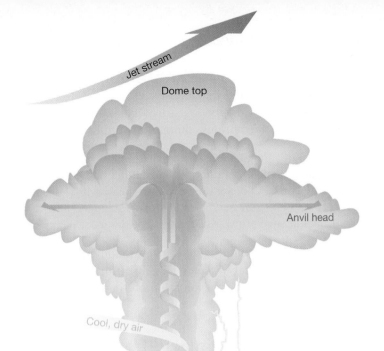

Jet stream

Dome top

Anvil head

Cool, dry air

From William Cunningham, Environmental Science, 9th Ed., p. 329. Copyright © 2007 The McGraw-Hill Companies.

CHAPTER 9

Process Analysis

Looking Ahead

People want to understand how things work, how things are made, and how things are done—that is, we want to understand the processes that are part of our lives. In fact, some of our most important scientific discoveries and some of our most useful inventions are the result of people analyzing processes to learn more about them. Our curiosity about processes may even explain why one of the most popular destinations on the World Wide Web is www.howstuffworks.com. Because understanding and examining processes is important, in class undergraduates study processes such as respiration, cell division, electrical circuit completion, photosynthesis, inflation, and checks and balances—processes often depicted in diagrams like this one from an environmental science textbook. In this chapter, you will learn about writing process analysis essays. Before doing so, consider the processes you are curious about, and list ten that you would like to learn more about. Discuss your list with a partner, and later share the list with a larger group.

When is a recipe more than a recipe? When it includes commentary along with the steps the cook should follow. Here, for example, is the first part of a chocolate chip cookie recipe that "will serve as sturdy companion through disappointment, great and small." The recipe with its commentary appeared in the *Chicago Tribune Magazine*.

> Melt 1 cup of butter. Other recipes expect you to drum your nails on the countertop while butter attains room temperature. Don't bother. Melting butter over low heat is blasphemous, but better. Remove from heat. Add 1½ cups brown sugar. Standard practice calls for a mix of white and brown. Standard practice yields unyielding cookies. Unadulterated brown sugar makes cookies more pliant and empathetic.

A recipe, like any writing that explains how something is made or done, is a **process analysis**. A process analysis can be a straightforward "this is how you do it" writing, or it can include the writer's evaluation of the process, as the above recipe does.

Why Is Process Analysis Important?

There are two kinds of process analyses, and both are important. A **directional process analysis** gives the steps in a process that the reader can perform if he or she wants to. Directional process analyses can be very helpful because they show the

---

 OCCASIONS FOR WRITING

Process Analysis across the Disciplines and Beyond

Process Analysis in the Classroom

Every academic subject involves the study of how things occur, how they are made, or how they are done, so process analysis is a common component of writing across the disciplines. In science lab reports, students often explain the process to complete an experiment. In a paper for a political science class, one might explain how a bill moves through Parliament. In a homework assignment for an electrical trades class, you might explain how to read a blueprint. In a homework assignment for a business class, you might explain how to develop a marketing report. *Think about your own courses. What processes are you likely to learn about? Look through the textbooks for those classes, and notice the processes that are explained in them. What are they? Are they directional or informational?*

Process Analysis in Daily Life

Process analysis is part of the writing we do in personal life. When you write directions to your house, you are writing process analysis, as you are when you share your homemade pizza recipe with a friend. If you email instructions to a classmate for installing and updating antivirus software, you are also writing process analysis. *Describe a situation in which you used process analysis. What were the circumstances? Which of the purposes of writing did your process analysis fulfill?*

Process Analysis on the Job

Everyone is likely to use process analysis in the workplace. Employees often write job descriptions that explain how they perform aspects of their jobs. Human resources managers write procedures for taking vacation and sick leave. Safety officers write explanations of what to do in the event of various emergencies. *How might a teacher use process analysis? A quality control manager? A nurse or physician's assistant? A religious cleric? Think of two careers not already mentioned here and note how writing process analysis might be involved.*

DETERMINING PURPOSE

Purposes for Process	Sample Process Analysis
To inform (to help the reader learn how to do something)	An explanation of how to hang wallpaper so the reader does not have to pay someone to do it
To inform of a better way to do something	An explanation of a better process for test taking so students can do better in school
To inform (by increasing the reader's knowledge)	An explanation of how computer applications work
To inform (by helping the reader appreciate the difficulty, complexity, or beauty of a process)	An explanation of how a server waits on tables so readers understand how difficult the job is
To persuade (to convince the reader that a particular way to do something is superior to another way)	An explanation of how debit cards work (to show that using a debit card is better than using cash or credit cards)

reader how to accomplish something. The directions that explain how to assemble a toy are a directional process analysis. The instructions in a biology lab manual explaining how to prepare a slide are also a directional process analysis—as are the directions for programming a cell phone, the magazine article explaining how to land the perfect job, and instructions for building a personal web page.

An **informational process analysis** explains how something is made or done, but the reader is not likely to perform the process. An explanation of how brain surgery is performed is an informational process analysis because the reader is not likely to perform brain surgery. Similarly, explanations of how the body converts carbohydrates to energy, how plants manufacture chlorophyll, and how lightning occurs are all informational process analyses. Informational process analyses are important because they add to knowledge, satisfy curiosity, and help readers appreciate complex or interesting processes.

Directional and informational process analyses can serve many purposes, as the chart above points out.

Combining Process Analysis with Other Patterns

Whenever writers need to explain how something is made or done, they will use process analysis, regardless of the dominant pattern of development. For example, while writing a definition of *federal elections,* part of the essay will explain how the parliamentary system works to elect a government. Explaining the causes and effects of anorexia nervosa, a writer may also explain by what process the condition can lead to death. Contrasting two exercise programs, you might explain how each one works.

Even when process analysis is the dominant pattern, writers are likely to use other methods of development. For example, to explain how to choose the best running shoes, one might give examples of the best ones to buy. To explain the process that causes leaves to change colour in autumn, one might include a description of the various colours of the leaves.

For an example of an essay that combines process analysis with narration, see "Wicked Wind" on page 222.

Before Writing

Most of the detail in a process analysis will be the steps in the process, but writers should not merely write out the steps in list fashion. Instead, follow these guidelines.

Include All the Important Steps

Omitting a step is a common pitfall when writing about a process with which writers are so familiar that they take steps for granted. If you omit steps in a directional process analysis, readers may not be able to perform the process properly. Suppose you are writing a directional process analysis to explain how to begin a weight-lifting program. Suppose, too, that you have been lifting weights yourself for many years. You may forget all about the step of resting between exercises because for you that step is so habitual that you do it without thinking. Omit the step, and the reader could be injured. Omitting steps in an informational process analysis means readers may fail to understand the process sufficiently. If, for instance, you are explaining how bees find food, you might indicate that scouts go out in search of food and then alert other bees to what they find. However, if you do not indicate how the scouts communicate the location of the food, your explanation of the process is incomplete, and may leave readers confused.

Explain How a Step Is Performed

To ensure that readers perform a process successfully, you need to explain how to perform one or more steps in a directional process analysis. Think again about an explanation of how to begin a weight-lifting program. If you mention the need to rest between exercises, you should also mention how long the rest period should be. Otherwise, the reader may rest too long, not work the muscle enough, or risk injury.

In an informational process analysis, you may need to explain how a step is performed to be sure readers understand the process. For example, while explaining how bees locate food, you might indicate that the insects use a dance to guide other bees to food sources. For the reader to understand the process, you must explain how that dance works. So you will explain that if the food is closer than 10 metres, the bee will dance quickly in a circle. As the distance approaches 100 metres, the dance becomes sickle-shaped. Farther than 100 metres, the dance slows and becomes a figure eight.

Explain the Significance of a Step or Why It Is Performed

You may need to explain why a step in a directional process analysis is performed if you think readers will fail to appreciate its importance and, perhaps, skip it—or perform it carelessly. For example, assume you are explaining how to find a job in a period of high unemployment, and you mention the need, after a job interview, to send a thank-you note to the interviewer. If the reader might not appreciate the importance of this step, explain that sending the note impresses the interviewer with the applicant's courtesy and follow-through.

Explain Trouble Spots and What *Not* to Do

If a step in a directional process analysis can prove troublesome, pointing out the possible problem can help the reader to avoid it. Think again about the explanation of how to find a job in a period of high unemployment. If you tell a job applicant to write a thank-you note after an interview, you can caution the person to avoid a letter that looks unprofessional, because it is written on inappropriate stationery, perhaps something with a Dilbert cartoon or picture of kittens on it. If an aspect of an informational process analysis can be difficult or troublesome, pointing out that fact can help readers appreciate the complexity of the process.

If it is feared the reader could take unnecessary or incorrect actions, a directional process analysis can point out something that should *not* be done. For example, you may want to caution your reader *not* to smile too much during a job interview because too much smiling can make an applicant seem frivolous or insincere.

Mention Necessary Items and Define Unfamiliar Terms

If a reader must assemble materials to perform a process, mention items that are needed early in a directional process analysis, so the reader can assemble them. Because it is convenient to have the items mentioned early on, most recipes begin with a list of the ingredients.

If process writing includes technical terms or other vocabulary unfamiliar to readers, provide definitions. For example, if explaining how to make the best-ever chocolate cake and indicating that the reader needs a springform pan, explain what this pan is if the reader is not likely to know. If explaining how to take blood pressure, the writer will need to define *systolic pressure* and *diastolic pressure.*

Include Examples and Description

To clarify an aspect of a process or help the reader appreciate its nature or significance, writers may need to include examples and description. For instance, while explaining how a person should behave in a job interview, you might mention the advisability of asking questions about the nature of the job. To clarify this point, provide examples of appropriate questions, such as "Will I have an opportunity to learn new skills?" and "Do you encourage additional education?" If you advise the reader to dress professionally for a job interview and pay special attention to shoes, the writer should describe appropriate footwear: Women should wear low heels and avoid open-toe shoes and sandals; men should wear brown or black dress shoes with rounded toes. If you explain how animals communicate in a paper for a linguistics class, you can illustrate the processes described with the songs of the European robin, the facial expressions of wolves, and the sounds and gestures of monkeys.

Use Visuals

Sometimes a graph, picture, chart, or drawing can help readers understand all or part of a process, particularly when the process is complex or the explanation is long. The visual cannot take the place of a written explanation of a procedure, but it can clarify the steps by providing a graphic summary. Textbooks often use visuals with process analyses to help students understand and remember explanations. This book includes essay organization charts (see page 216, for example) to help writers visualize the structure of informal and formal essays. Or consider this excerpt from a public speaking textbook. As part of the explanation of how to prepare visual aids for a speech, the author cautions to limit the number of fonts, colours, and graphics because too many can distract the audience. To prove and illustrate the point, the author includes this visual:

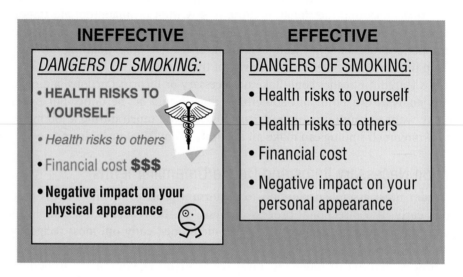

Consider Purpose and Audience

Whether explaining how to perform a step, indicating the significance of a step, noting a trouble spot, and so on, much will depend on audience and purpose. Let's say you are explaining how people can protect their credit rating, and you note that people should limit the number of credit cards they use. If the audience is college students, point out this trouble spot: Credit card companies may set up tables outside libraries on college campuses and actively recruit students to sign up for their cards, so students must resist these efforts. For an audience that is not attending college, the writer would not point out this trouble spot.

Organizing a Process Analysis

The introduction of your process analysis can include a thesis that mentions the process. It can also note the importance of understanding the process.

Thesis mentioning the process

> There is only one efficient way to clean a basement.

Thesis mentioning the process and why it is important

> Car owners can save a great deal of money if they learn to change their own points and plugs.

To create interest, the introduction can explain why understanding the process is important (if the thesis does not do this). The writer can also tell why she is qualified to explain the process, arouse the reader's curiosity about how the process is performed, or combine approaches.

The conclusion can take any of the approaches given for the introduction. However, a separate conclusion may be unnecessary if the last step in the process provides sufficient closure.

Arrange details in chronological order (see page 169) when the reader needs the steps presented in the order they are performed. Other times, chronological order is not necessary. For example, if explaining how to dress for success, the order of steps may not be significant.

If explaining what should *not* be done, do so near the step the caution is related to. For example, a cake recipe would explain not to over bake at the point baking time is mentioned. If a process analysis includes several statements of what not to do, the writer might group all the cautions together in their own paragraph.

If it is necessary to define a term, do so the first time the term is used. In order to explain a troublesome aspect of a process, do so just after presenting the step under consideration. When explaining why a step is performed, do so just before or after an explanation of the step. If necessary materials are listed, group this information together in an early paragraph, perhaps even in the introduction.

EXERCISE WRITING PROCESS ANALYSIS

1. Explain how you might use process analysis as part of each of the following essays:
    a. A definition of a *good driver*
    b. The causes and effects of premature birth
    c. A classification of the ways advertisements influence consumers

2. Think of two processes that you perform well (shoot baskets, make friends, plan a party, buy used cars, study, babysit, and so on). Then list the steps in each process, in the order they are performed, if chronological order is important.

3. Assume you will write a process analysis for each of the processes you identified for number 2, and identify a purpose and audience for each.

4. For each process, answer the following questions keeping audience and purpose in mind. Be prepared to explain your answers.
    a. Is it necessary to explain *how* any steps are performed?
    b. Is it necessary to explain *why* any steps are performed?
    c. Will the reader understand better if I explain something that should *not* be done?
    d. Are there troublesome aspects that should be explained?
    e. Are any materials needed?
    f. Should any terms be defined?
    g. Is it possible to describe anything?
    h. Is it possible to use examples?

5. *Collaborative Activity:* With two or three classmates, write a list of the processes a student should know in order to succeed in your academic program. Pick one of these processes (i.e. time management) and write an explanation of how it is performed. Think of the reader as a first-year student. ●

Visualizing a Process Analysis Essay

The chart that follows can help visualize one structure for a process analysis. Like all good models, this one can be altered as needed. *Note:* this is a basic plan for an informal, five-paragraph essay. Formal academic essays are structured differently as they include more detail, and research materials.

Introduction

- Creates interest, perhaps by noting the importance of the process, telling why you are qualified to explain the process, or arousing the reader's curiosity about the process
- States the thesis, which gives the process you will explain and which may note the importance of the process

---

First Body Paragraph

- Gives the first step in the process
- May explain how or why the step is performed
- May explain the significance of the step
- May explain what not to do or a trouble spot
- May explain items needed and unfamiliar terms
- May include examples and description
- May arrange details chronologically

Next Body Paragraph

- Gives the next step in the process
- May explain how or why the step is performed
- May explain the significance of the step
- May explain what not to do or a trouble spot
- May explain items needed and unfamiliar terms
- May include examples and description
- May arrange details chronologically

Next Body Paragraphs

- Give the remaining steps in the process
- May explain how or why the step is performed
- May explain the significance of the step
- May explain what not to do or a trouble spot
- May explain items needed and unfamiliar terms
- May include examples and description
- May arrange details chronologically

Conclusion

- Leaves the reader with a positive final impression
- Creates closure

CRITICAL READING STUDENT ESSAY

The student essay, "A Visit to Candyland," is a directional process analysis that appears with marginal notes pointing out features explained in this chapter. The author makes her feelings apparent, so you can easily tell how much she enjoys completing the process. Look for the first clue to how the author feels about the process.

A Visit to Candyland

1   You may have been to the supermarket around Christmastime and seen a gingerbread house kit. It probably involved graham-cracker slabs meant to be stuck together with thick white frosting and decorated with gumdrops. In my family, making gingerbread houses is a long-standing tradition, and one that involves far more than simply slapping some cookies and frosting together. Each year, in early December, we decide on a theme and go on to create an elaborate gingerbread structure that reflects the season and our interests. Our cardinal rule in gingerbread house making often comes as a surprise to the friends who visit to marvel at our creations: absolutely everything in the gingerbread house must be edible, and not only edible, but tasty.

2   We begin by coming up with a concept. One year, it was a crèche scene with Mary, Joseph, the baby Jesus, and various animals, shepherds, and angels. Another year, it was a covered bridge under snow, with a horse-drawn carriage. Once we've decided on a theme, we might visit the library or go on the Internet to find visual ideas we can incorporate into our design. Then, after we've done some preliminary sketches, we make a pattern, measuring carefully with a ruler to make sure each piece will fit with the others. These pattern pieces are drawn onto thin paper and then precisely cut out with sharp scissors. We've found it helps to note on each pattern piece how many need to be made—a roof, for example, is usually made of two equal rectangles, and only one pattern piece is needed.

3   The next step is to make the gingerbread. We use an old family recipe that produces a sturdy but extremely tasty gingerbread cookie, flavored with molasses, cinnamon, ground cloves, and lots of ginger. In order to make a really tough cookie, we incorporate many cups of flour into the batter. Once all the flour has been added, the dough is so dense it's almost impossible to stir, so we hand it off to my father, whose arms are the strongest. After the dough is finished it has to sit in the refrigerator for a time period ranging from several hours to a week. This cooling period makes the dough easier to handle and the finished cookie even tougher.

4   Once the dough is ready to bake, it's time to make the pieces of the house. We do this by rolling out the dough onto sheets of tinfoil. We try to avoid handling the dough too much—if it gets warm before it goes into the oven, it loses some of its resilience. The dough is rolled until it's a little less than a quarter of an inch thick. Then we place the pattern pieces onto the rolled dough. Using a small knife, we cut around the pattern piece, discarding the excess dough. After we've cut out the windows on the wall pieces, we fill the holes with broken bits of hard candy. In the oven, these candy pieces melt and harden, forming what looks like stained glass. Once that's done, we slide the tinfoil with the cookie pieces on it onto a cookie sheet and put them into the oven.

PARAGRAPH 1

The introduction provides background information. The thesis is not stated, but the paragraph suggests a focus on making gingerbread houses.

PARAGRAPH 2

The paragraph gives the first two steps in the process. The details include examples of the first step and information on how the second step is performed.

PARAGRAPH 3

The first sentence is the topic sentence. It gives the next step in the process. Some details explain why part of the step is performed.

PARAGRAPH 4

The topic sentence (the first sentence) gives the next step in the process. Notice the transitions *once the dough is ready to bake, then,* and *once that's done.*

PARAGRAPH 5

The topic sentence (the first
sentence) gives the next step
and includes a transition.

5   Seven to ten minutes later, the cookies are done, and we slide them onto wire racks to cool. After they've cooled, we peel off the tinfoil backing and admire the colored light through the little stained-glass windows. Now we're ready for the hardest part of the whole process: putting the house together. Frosting is simply not tough enough for the elaborate structures we make, so instead we use melted sugar. We sprinkle regular granulated sugar into a wide, flat pan and heat it over a medium-high flame. In a few minutes it forms a glossy, dark-brown liquid. The ends of the gingerbread pieces that are to be stuck together have to be dipped very quickly into the melted sugar and then speedily and precisely joined to their intended mates. If this process is done too quickly, there may not be enough sugar to make the pieces stick, or we may stick them on at the wrong angle. If it's done too slowly, the sugar can harden, its sticking powers completely lost. When my brothers and I were little, we were not allowed to participate in the melted-sugar operation, but now we've developed the necessary manual dexterity and nerves of steel.

PARAGRAPH 6

The topic sentence (the first
sentence) gives the next step
and includes a transition. Are
you noticing the chronological
order?

6   Now the house is assembled and ready for everyone's favorite stage: decoration. We make frosting out of butter, confectioner's sugar, and food coloring, and add a base coat to the parts of the house that seem to need it, like the roof. We generally leave the sides bare, because the dark brown gingerbread is such a pretty color, but we add details with frosting piped out of a wax-paper tube. Then we add decorations. In the past we've used raisins, cinnamon sticks, star anise, nuts, and, of course, many different kinds of candy. Necco wafers, broken in half, make particularly good shingles.

PARAGRAPH 7

The conclusion provides closure
by explaining what is done with
the gingerbread house and by
highlighting a family tradition.

7   When we're finished, we've usually consumed a substantial quantity of decorations, spoonfuls of frosting, and cookie scraps. Naturally we make gingerbread men to live in the house, but their lifespans tend to be extremely short—sometimes they don't even get frosted. We're too full to do anything but sit and admire our handiwork. A few days later, however, we host our annual holiday party, where the final part of the tradition comes into play. The youngest child at the event (apart from babies, of course) is handed an orange suspended from a red satin ribbon. This is the gingerbread wrecking ball, and it's swung at the house until total destruction has been achieved. We're always sorry to see the house ruined, but then we have the pleasure, along with our guests, of eating our annual masterpiece.

The complete essay, including any bibliographic references, is also available on the Online Learning Centre at www.mcgrawhill.ca/olc/clouse.

EXERCISES

1.   This student selection was used to demonstrate process analysis as a pattern of organization. How successful was it?

2.   To what extent do other patterns of development help the progress of this essay? Note descriptive details and examples.

3.   This essay uses the first person as a style of narration. Would it be as successful if the voice were objective, as in a recipe for assembling a gingerbread house? ●

CRITIQUE, REVISE, and EDIT

Like most student writers, the author of "A Visit to Candyland" was aware of the importance of the thesis. However, multiple attempts at a stated thesis failed to produce a version the writer was satisfied with. Here is what her early versions looked like:

Early drafts of the thesis

> To make an awe-inspiring Christmas tradition, do what my family does and create a gingerbread house every year.

> Creating a gingerbread house for Christmas can be the start of a wonderful tradition.

> Christmas should bring families together, and nothing brings my family together more than creating our annual gingerbread masterpiece.

When she repeatedly failed to draft a thesis she felt worked well with the rest of her introduction, she decided to complete her draft without a stated thesis. Afterwards, she felt her thesis was strongly enough implied, so she decided to forgo a stated thesis. What do you think of this decision? Sometimes, it may also be a good idea to proceed with the body of a paper, and to compose a thesis once it has emerged in the process of writing.

CRITICAL READING PROFESSIONAL ESSAYS

Pre-reading

1. Consider job interviews you have taken, or wish to take. What do you consider the most important factors for interview success?
2. How can one best prepare for a professional job interview?
3. Consider what the author might mean when he refers to "give" and "take" in the essay you are about to read.

The Give and Take of Successful Job Interviews

Eric Archer

1   So much of the job search process depends on your efforts—researching employers, seeking out job leads among finance colleagues and sending out resumes. And while it may feel like all the pressure is on you to disarm and dazzle hiring managers, a job interview is as much an opportunity for you to examine the potential employer as it is for the business to learn more about your financial experience and expertise.

2   Job interviewing gives you a chance to explain the talents highlighted in your resume while demonstrating your professionalism and communication

skills. At the same time, it puts you in an inquisitive role, offering you a chance to examine the work environment, management style and business culture.

3 As you approach job interviews now and in the future, keep these two questions in mind:
- What am I giving?
- What am I taking away?

The Giving

4 They say it's easier to give than to receive, but in a job interview, that's not always the case. Answering numerous questions, explaining work experiences and feeling like a puppy in a pet store window is nerve racking, to say the least.

5 The key to giving potential employers the information they need about your skills, experience and suitability to the job is preparation. The more prepared you are for questions, the more relaxed and natural you'll be, and the better you and the interviewer can determine how well you match the company and the job.

Do Your Research

6 Good interview preparation means taking time for research. Get to know as much as you can about the employer—from business operations and company history to clients, key initiatives and community involvement. Read their marketing materials and financial statements, examine their Web site and read media coverage on the organization. If there are gaps in your knowledge, talk to current and/or former employees to understand the company and demands of the position.

7 This research will give you an edge in the interview, allowing you to demonstrate the knowledge you've gathered and ask thoughtful questions about the business. In addition, it'll give you advanced insight into the organization and how the business culture aligns with your work preferences.

8 Be sure you know the names, positions and, if possible, the backgrounds of the individuals who will conduct the interview, and gather as much information as you can about the job. Show up knowing as much as you can about what the employer is looking for.

Rehearse Your Performance

9 Armed with a solid background on the company and the position, practice for the interview. Start by rehearsing your answers to standard interview questions: What are your goals? Why did you select finance as a career? What are your strengths and weaknesses? What is your most significant achievement? Why should we hire you?

10 Also, make a list of questions that are hard for you to answer on the spot, and develop succinct and compelling answers to them. Include biographical questions that explore your background, behavioral questions that examine how you've dealt with specific issues or problems in past work situations, and "what if" questions that address how you'd handle various workplace challenges.

11 You'll also want to practice speaking about your various finance roles, and your specific responsibilities and successes in each position. Practice your answers out loud to get comfortable with the language and the nonverbal communication you use to tell your story.

12 And be able to verbally quantify your results. Think "MSAP"—What have you accomplished that Made money, Saved money, Achieved something or provided Peace of mind?

13 Next, review your resume and anticipate where interviewers might have questions about your work history. If you have gaps or unusual experiences on your resume, take time to plan your explanations and identify how this relates to your professional successes.

14 With an outlined repertoire of responses in your head, you'll be less likely to get tongue-tied or ramble on without making the desired point. Rehearsing will reduce your anxiety, and give you the confidence to relax and be yourself as the questions pour in.

The Taking

15 After you've carefully prepared to give employers the information they need, it's your turn. The interview is your chance to take away as much new information as you can about the business, the workplace, the manager you'd report to, job responsibilities, career opportunities and the business culture.

16 During most interviews, you're able to examine the company and your specific interests more carefully. This is your chance to gather information that will help you decide if this is a workplace where you could find satisfaction and success.

17 Be prepared for this opportunity by planning out positive and thoughtful questions in advance. For example:

- Is it important for you to have a thorough understanding of the reporting structures or management style?
- Do you know if the job functions as part of a large team or is primarily independent work?
- Who are the other team players and what are their roles?
- Does the job offer opportunities for training, skills enhancement or professional development?
- What career path is typical for professionals hired into this position?
- Do you have questions about the business and where it is going?
- Do you have a good understanding of the clients the business serves, future growth plans, or where leadership sees the company in the years ahead?

18 Also, find out how far you can grow professionally in this role. Ask about personal management styles and what characteristics are necessary to be successful, both personal and technical. Be sure to share experiences that demonstrate you have these traits.

19 Just as a company would invest in your skills by hiring you, you are investing yourself (your time, commitment and intellectual capital) in a company by accepting a job. Be sure you leave the interview with a thorough understanding of how the business works, where it's going, and how you can be a part of its success over the long term.

Show Your Gratitude

20 After all the give and take of the interview process, both you and the interviewer should leave with a wealth of new information. As you consider what you've learned and whether you see yourself as a part of the organization, you have one more opportunity to demonstrate your professionalism: Send a sincere, customized thank-you letter, whether this is the first in a series of interviews or the only interview.

21 A brief note of appreciation for the interviewer's time can do wonders. It reminds the recipient (or recipients) of who you are, and demonstrates both your graciousness and interest in the job. Good luck!

Considering Ideas

1. For what purpose did Archer write his process analysis? Who is his intended audience?

2. What does Archer mean when he indicates that preparation is key to a successful interview? How will he present the interview advice, based upon the information in the introduction?

3. Archer explains that the interview is a blend of give and take, explaining that it is necessary to be both inquisitive and prepared. How do "giving" and "taking away" relate to interview preparation?

4. Archer uses the acronym MSAP: what does it mean, and how would it help in a job interview?

5. Archer suggests that candidates prepare for interviews. What does he suggest the candidate do? What does he imply the candidate should *not* do?

Considering Technique

1. In which paragraphs does the author do the following?
   a. Explain "giving"
   b. Explain *why* and how to research?
   c. Explain *how* to be successful in an interview?

2. Archer explains the interview process from the perspective of the applicant. Would it be helpful to explain how an interviewer would approach an interview?

3. *Combining Patterns:* Archer uses exemplification to detail questions candidates can ask during interviews. How helpful are these examples?

4. Archer uses a very personable and direct tone, addressing the candidate directly. Find at least three examples of simple diction in directions or instructions to interview candidates. How effective is this direct approach?

For Group Discussion or Journal Writing

What, if anything, did you learn about the interview process from reading "The Give and Take of Successful Interviews"? Did you find anything surprising about the interviewer's procedures?

Pre-reading

1. How important is sound in film? Is the soundtrack more important than ambient sound?

2. What makes for successful sound effects in film? Does it depend on the type of film?

3. To what extent do sound effects make a film more suspenseful? Or to what extent do sound effects help push a film's narrative forward?

Wicked Wind

Ben McGrath

1   If you want to re-create the auditory experience of being in a storm aboard a nineteenth-century British frigate, get yourself a pickup truck, some wood, a few acoustic blankets, and about a thousand feet of rope. Then drive out to the Mojave Desert and build a large wooden frame in the bed of the truck. String the rope back and forth around the frame, using a turnbuckle to make it good and taut, until all thousand feet have been spent. Face the truck head-on into a thirty-mile-an-hour wind, and lean hard on the gas pedal. Once you hit seventy, you're in business; the sound of the air meeting the lines of rope ought to approximate the shrieking of the wind in the frigate's rigging—a foretaste of what the novelist Patrick O'Brian might call "a coming dissolution of all natural bonds, an apocalyptic upheaval, a right dirty night." For added effect, try holding a barbecue grill out the window and turning it at various angles as you cruise. Muffle any peripheral truck noise, as needed, with the blankets.

2   This, at least, is the approach that Richard King came up with recently as the sound designer for *Master and Commander: The Far Side of the World,* the forthcoming adaptation of O'Brian's nautical series, set aboard the Royal Navy's H.M.S. *Surprise* during the Napoleonic Wars. King, who is forty-nine years old and a lifelong sailor, was charged not only with the task of supervising the editing of the film's soundtrack (distinct from any musical score or accompaniment) but also with recording all the individual sounds—musket fire, sloshing bilge, creaking wood—that need to be incorporated. In some cases, this requires creating the sounds from scratch.

3 Thus the trip to the desert. "Nobody wants to take their ships out in a gale," King said. "I actually tried to get myself on a ship somewhere in the world that would put itself in that situation." The Mojave, it turns out, is a convenient substitute, because it gets very windy, and the wind patterns are predictable, typically blowing from the southwest. King didn't limit his Mojave recording sessions to truck work, either. "We got some sails off a big square-rigger and took them out to the desert and built a giant framework—a mast, essentially—and rigged the sails so we could get them to flap at various intensities," he said. "So we got discrete sail flaps without any sound of water in the background."

4 King and his crew of eight editors made it a point of pride not to rely on "library" files, a standard collection of movie-ready sounds (car honks, airplanes taking off). Given that *Master and Commander* features extended battle scenes with plenty of cannon fire, forgoing the library necessitated still more ingenuity. "All the sounds I had heard in period movies of cannons going off were just big loud booms," King said. "But something O'Brian refers to a lot is the screaming of shot flying overhead." So he found a group of artillery collectors in northern Michigan who had cannons that were capable of firing vintage ammunition, and set to work re-creating the types of shot described in O'Brian's novels: round shot ("basically, their ship-to-ship—when they wanted to punch a hole in the hull"), chain shot ("two cannonballs connected by a two-foot piece of chain, which would spin around and take out the rigging and sails and mast"), grapeshot ("canisters with a number of smaller balls inside—antipersonnel weapons that would shoot across the deck to kill as many men as they could"). Then, in January, King and his crew set up a firing range at a National Guard base nearby that had all but closed for the winter. ("They had to snowplow the range for us to shoot.") They fired eighty rounds, recording both the initial explosions and, following another lead from O'Brian, the in-flight racket, which proved to be almost as loud as the booms themselves. "There was a concrete berm five hundred yards downrange which we could get behind and set up mikes and fire over," King said, "Nobody, as far as I know, had ever recorded any of this stuff. It sounded like nothing I've ever heard before." Imagine a cross between a piece of paper being ripped and a racecar speeding by.

5 Not all the work required of a sound designer is so elaborate. "The other day, I was trying to get a sound for a sail," King said. "It's kind of a mysterious scene in the film, where we look up and we see a sail, kind of loose, very softly moving in the light breeze. And I'm thinking, What would be cool there? I have a microphone in my room, and I turned on the recorder and did a *hawwwww*—a low breathing sound—and added some reverb to it. It worked."

Considering Ideas

1. The thesis of the essay is implied rather than stated. In your own words, write out the thesis.

2. For what purpose do you think McGrath wrote the essay? Who is his intended audience?

3. Why was it "a point of pride" for King that he did not use library files (paragraph 4)?

4. Make a list of at least four words or phrases that describe Richard King.

5. If you have seen *Master and Commander: The Far Side of the World,* do you have an increased appreciation for the movie because of reading the essay? If you have not seen the movie, does the essay make you want to see it? Explain.

Considering Technique

1. The essay opens with a process analysis rather than a lead-in and thesis. Why? Does that opening paragraph engage your interest in the essay? Why or why not?

2. Paragraph 4 mentions something that is *not* done. Why does McGrath include that information? How does it help him achieve his writing purpose?

3. Paragraph 4 also explains how a step is performed. How does that information help him achieve his writing purpose?

4. McGrath closes the way he opens—with a process analysis. Is the conclusion a good one? Why or why not?

For Group Discussion or Journal Writing

How important are sound effects to a movie? How aware are you of sound effects and other sound elements of a movie? If King had used library files, would it *really* have mattered much?

Combining Patterns of Development

 WRITING TOOL

Point of View

Point of view is determined by pronouns. Use the first-person pronouns *I, me, my, mine, we, our,* and *ours* to write from the point of view of the writer. Use the second-person pronouns *you, your,* and *yours* to write from the point of view of the reader. Use the third-person pronouns *he, she, it, him, her, his, hers, its, they,* and *theirs* to write from the point of view of an outsider, someone who is not you and not your reader.

First person:	To calm the dog, I reach down and offer my hand to smell.
Second person:	To calm the dog, you reach down and offer your hand to smell.
Third person:	To calm the dog, he reached down and offered his hand to smell.

Directional process analyses often use the second-person point of view because the writer is explaining to the reader a process the reader might perform. Informational process analyses often use the third-person point of view because the writer is explaining a process performed by someone other than the reader or a process the reader is not likely to perform

Finally, if you are explaining a process the way you perform it, either alone or with others, you will use the first-person point of view, as this excerpt from "A Visit to Candyland" illustrates:

> Once we've decided on a theme, we might visit the library or go on the Internet to find visual ideas we can incorporate into our design. Then, after we've done some preliminary sketches, we make a pattern.

Note, though, that academic writing assignments are almost always objective and rarely use the first person.

Process Analysis in an Image

The following picture comes from the How Stuff Works Web site (www.howstuff works.com). True to its name, the site explains how many things work, including the pop-up turkey timer shown in the picture.

Considering the Image

1. Does the picture included with the process analysis help you better understand how the pop-up turkey timer works? What, if anything, does the picture add?
2. The process analysis includes the technical term *binary*. Is the term adequately defined? Explain.
3. The process analysis concludes with a little-known fact. What does that fact add to the process analysis?

Reading Then Writing Process Analysis

1. If you play an instrument, sing, dance, paint, or otherwise practice one of the arts, do what Ben McGrath does in "Wicked Wind," and explain a process associated with the art. For example, if you paint, you can describe the process of mixing paints to achieve certain effects.
2. Like the author of "A Visit to Candyland," explain a process you complete with your family, such as trimming the Christmas tree, cooking Thanksgiving dinner, celebrating Grandma's birthday, participating in the annual park cleanup campaign, or driving to the mountains. Convey your feelings about the process.

Process Analysis beyond the Writing Classroom

Process analysis can be a helpful problem-solving strategy. To appreciate this fact, identify a problem you are currently experiencing, such as procrastination, too much time online, an unhappy job situation, smoking, or loneliness. Then write out a detailed explanation of how to solve that problem. Be specific. If you say that one step you will take to improve an unhappy job situation is to speak to a supervisor, indicate exactly what to say and when and where to say it. Also, be realistic. Do not suggest looking for another job if finding one is unlikely, given school schedules and the local economy.

Responding to Theme

1. Archer describes the interview process in "The Give and Take of Successful Job Interviews." Tell about an experience you had applying or interviewing for a job. Your essay should teach your reader something about how the job applicant should or should *not* behave.
2. Explain how much of the interview process that Archer describes in "The Give and Take of Successful Job Interviews" is applicable to Harold Krents in "Darkness at Noon" (page 198). Does Krents deserve special consideration from the interviewer? Explain and support your view.
3. The How Stuff Works Web site (www.howstuffworks.com), from which the image on page 226 is taken, is extremely popular. In fact, in 2002, *Time* magazine named it one of the 50 best Web sites. The site is successful partly because we are so

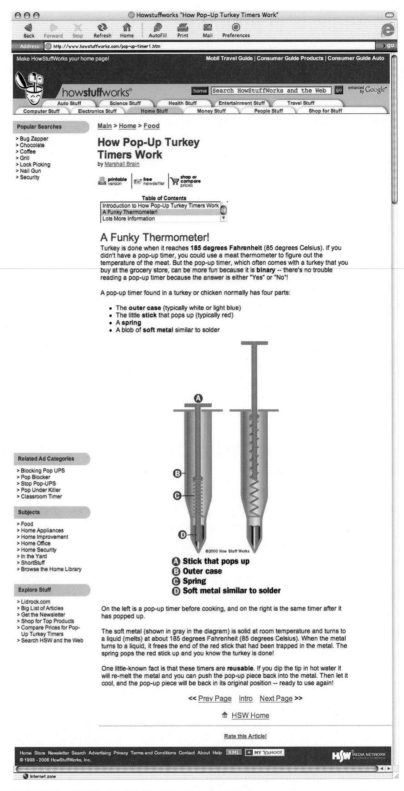

© 2003 HowStuffWorks, Inc. Reprinted by permission.

interested in learning about processes and because it explains these processes so clearly. In a brief essay, explain what process you would like to learn more about, why you would like to learn it, and how you can go about doing so.

4. *Connecting the Readings:* "The Give and Take of Successful Job Interviews" and "Wicked Wind" give insight into kinds of jobs and their challenges. Consider the kinds of work people do, and explain how we ascribe status and value to jobs. Would the interview for a corporate job and one as a housekeeper be the same? If not, how would they differ?

 # THE WRITING PROCESS

Process Analysis

Writing Process Analysis

The following strategies are not meant to replace successful procedures. They are here for you to try as you work to improve your writing process.

The student writer at work

- To come up with a topic, consider past experiences and activities. If you were involved in athletics, perhaps you can describe how to coach baseball or swimming or how to prepare mentally for a big game. If you were a tour guide, you can explain how to prepare for a hike or how to survive in the wilderness if lost.

- Use the questions on page 39 to help determine your purpose. In addition, consider the answers to these questions:
  - Do I want to inform my reader about a better way to do something or convince my reader to do something a different way?
  - Do I want to explain a process so my reader can perform it?
  - Do I want to explain a process so my reader appreciates it more?

- To identify and assess audience, answer the questions on page 43. In addition, these questions can help:
  - Who does not know how to perform the process or fully understand or appreciate it?
  - Who needs to learn a better way to perform the process?
  - Does my reader appreciate the importance or beauty of the process?
  - Has my reader had any experience with the process? Will the steps be difficult for my reader to perform or understand?
  - Does my reader need any terms defined?
  - Would my reader find visuals helpful?
  - Will my reader react well to hypothetical situations?

- To generate ideas:
  - List every step in the process—in the order it is performed if chronological order is appropriate.
  - Review your list in light of your audience and purpose. Place an "H" next to a step if you should explain **how** it is performed. Place a "W" next to a step if you should explain **why** it is performed. Place a "T" next to a step if you should explain a **troublesome** aspect. Place a "D" next to a step if you should **define** a term.
  - Make a note about anything you should describe and any visuals you should provide. Should you explain anything that should not be done?

- Turn your list of steps and letters into a formal outline. Alternatively, complete an outline worksheet.

Drafting

- Draft a preliminary thesis that states the process you are explaining and why understanding that process is important.
- Using your outline as a guide, write your draft.
- As you draft, think about using topic sentences, so your reader understands where each new step begins.

Revising

- Ask whether your introduction is likely to engage a reader's interest. Underline the statement that explains the significance of the process. If you have no such statement, be sure the significance is strongly implied throughout the piece of writing.
- Checkmark paragraphs where you explain how to perform a step, why to perform a step, or what not to do. If you have no check marks or very few, evaluate whether you need more detail.
- If you have used chronological order, check the sequence.
- If you have used any technical terms, be sure they are defined.
- Ask whether your process analysis seems boring. If so, try adding description or some lively examples. Explain the importance or beauty of the process.
- To obtain reader response for revision, see pages 101–102. In addition, ask the reader whether there are any aspects of the process that are hard to follow.

Correcting Errors and Proofreading

- Use the "Guide to Frequently Occurring Errors" for reference, and check with a writing centre tutor if you are unsure about a grammar, usage, or punctuation point.
- If you are writing a directional process analysis and want to address your reader, use the second-person pronouns *you, your,* and *yours.*
- If you do not want to address your reader directly, use the third-person pronouns *he, she, it, they, him, her, them, his, hers, its, their,* and *theirs.* Or, if you are explaining how you perform the process, use the first-person pronouns *I, me, my, mine, we, us, ours,* and *our.*
- Be careful not to mix first-, second-, and third-person pronouns inappropriately, or you will have an error called **person shift**. Here is an example of the error:

  Those who decide to take up the sport of rock climbing should do exercises to increase the strength and flexibility of *their* fingers. Many climbers learn exercises at a climbing gym, but *they* can also learn some from books on the subject. In addition, *you* can speak to a personal trainer.

  For more on point of view, see page 224; for more on person shift, see page 228.

- Be sure to proofread the final copy before handing it in. If you are submitting an electronic copy, proofread from a paper copy. Be sure to read very slowly, lingering over every word and punctuation mark.

Remember

Choose a process that is interesting or important to your reader. Avoid explaining how to wash a car or tie shoes unless you can find a way to make the process fresh, entertaining, or informative.

CHAPTER 10

Definition

Looking Ahead

In this chapter, you will learn about writing definitions, but not the kind of definitions you read in a dictionary. You will learn how to write longer definitions that go beyond dictionary definitions to include your personal sense of terms and their significance. Before beginning the chapter, try your hand at definition. Consider this picture of Venus Williams and France's Natalie Tauziat at the 2000 U.S. Open. Then, in a paragraph, write a definition of good sportsmanship. Or, if you prefer, write a definition of athletic competition.

Why is Definition Important?

To discover what a word means, you go to the dictionary, but sometimes the dictionary is not enough. A dictionary gives the meaning of a word like *fun*, but what is fun to you may not be fun to someone else, and so the full meaning of that word will vary among individuals. Some words symbolize abstractions, with subtleties that cannot all be compressed into a few lines of space in a dictionary. What, for example, does *justice* mean? Certainly, it is a concept with complexities far beyond its denotative, or dictionary definition. In addition, some words have meanings so complex that a dictionary definition can only hit the high points, leaving much unexplained. *Democracy* is such a word. Not only is its meaning complex, but it varies greatly depending on which country's democracy is referred to. In cases like these, extended definition is helpful.

Definitions of words or terms can have either denotative or connotative meanings. Denotative meanings are 'dictionary' or literal definitions and ideas. They refer, specifically, to what something is, or what something means. The connotative meaning is an associated meaning or idea related to a word or term. Connotation depends upon who, where, when and finally what is being defined. Either way, you can see that writing a definition is not as easy as opening a dictionary and recording an entry to define an idea or term. Often, in academic writing, we write extended definitions, to define not only what something is, but to suggest associated ideas, which help others understand how we see what is defined.

With online dictionaries, pocket dictionaries, collegiate dictionaries, and specialized dictionaries for specific subjects, checking the meaning of a word has never been easier. However, a dictionary does not always explain the special associations (connotations) a word has, or the significance of its meaning in society. For that, we need an **extended definition**, which goes beyond the concise formal definition in a dictionary to explain the nature of that word, including its associations, significances, nuances, or complexities.

Extended definition can serve a variety of informational purposes. Obviously, a definition can inform a reader about something not commonly understood. For example, you might define *creative accounting* for a reader who does not know what it is and who wants to learn more about illegal corporate accounting practices. An extended definition in an essay can clarify a complex, multifaceted concept such as *wisdom* or *freedom*, specifying the way you are using the word. An extended definition can also provide a fresh appreciation for something familiar. For example, an extended definition of *free speech* can give readers a new way of looking at a freedom they may take for granted. An extended definition can even comment on something beyond the subject defined. For instance, a definition of *senior citizen* can lead to an understanding of what it means to grow old in this country. In fact, a definition can serve the full range of writing purposes, as illustrated in the following chart.

Consider, for example, the term *jazz*. You probably know what jazz is when you hear it, and you could look it up in the dictionary and learn that it is "music originating in New Orleans around the beginning of the 20th century." However, to understand the characteristics of jazz, you need an extended definition, something like this excerpt from *The World of Music* by David Willoughby:

- To be jazz, the music must swing. This is the feel of jazz—the jazz rhythm.

DETERMINING PURPOSE

Purpose for Definition	Sample Definition
To entertain	A humorous definition of *commuter* that points to the humour and difficulty of having to balance work and home lives
To express feelings	A definition of *bereaved* to express how people feel after losing a loved one
To relate experience	A definition of *friendship* that includes childhood experiences with best friends
To inform	A definition of *Aboriginal* to help readers understand Canada's First Nations
To inform (to clarify a complex concept)	A definition of *courage* to help the reader understand a specific aspect of courage
To inform (and give a fresh appreciation for the familiar)	A definition of *tutor* to help the reader understand everything a tutor does for a student
To inform (and comment on something beyond the subject)	A definition of *hip-hop* that comments on the values and attitudes of young people
To persuade	A definition of *poverty* to convince the reader to do something about it

- To be jazz, the music must be improvised. Improvisation is at the heart of jazz, but much jazz music is not improvised….
- To be jazz, the rhythm must be syncopated. Although jazz has a considerable emphasis placed on syncopated rhythms, not all of it will have these off-beat rhythms….
- To be jazz, the music has to be played on certain "jazz" instruments. Some instruments, such as the saxophones (saxes), trumpets, trombones, drums, bass, and piano, are characteristically jazz instruments when they are played a certain way in a certain context….

Combining Definition with other Patterns

Definition combines readily with other patterns of development to help achieve purpose. For example, to inform a reader, you might first define *pornography* and then use cause-and-effect analysis to explain its effects. To convince your reader that even upper-middle-class people can become homeless, you can define *homelessness* and then go on to use process analysis to explain how one can become homeless. An essay on heroism can first define *heroism* and then classify the types of heroism. An essay on stress can combine three patterns by first defining *stress,* then explaining its causes, and finally noting what can be done to cope with it. An essay developed primarily with extended definition will likely draw on other patterns of development to support its points. This aspect of combining patterns is explained in the discussion of selecting detail that follows.

OCCASIONS FOR WRITING

Definition across the Disciplines and Beyond

Definition in the Classroom

Most courses introduce new terminology and important concepts, so definition will be a frequent component of post-secondary writing. In a philosophy class, for instance, you might need to define *epistemology*. Again, the purpose for writing determines the length of the definition, and which of the denotative and connotative meanings will be considered. Often, you will combine definition with another pattern. For example, in a political science class, you might be asked to define and give examples of *human rights*. In a finance class, you might need to define and explain the effects of *bear* and *bull markets*. *Look through two chapters in two textbooks for your other classes. How many terms and concepts are in boldface type and defined? Is there a glossary at the back of the book that includes definitions of important terms? How likely is it that exam questions will require you to write definitions of these terms?*

Definition in Daily Life

Definition can be an important part of personal writing. An editor of a newsletter for a religious congregation might define *charity* to encourage congregants to be more charitable. If you email a friend a recipe that calls for a Madeleine pan, you might need to define *Madeleine*. In a letter to a Member of Parliament, you might define *domestic violence* to encourage that person to support legislation to help victims of domestic violence. *How might you use definition in your personal journal? How might you use definition in a letter to the editor about Internet pornography? What purpose would the definition serve?*

Definition on the Job

Definition is often a part of workplace writing. A nutrition counsellor might define *eating disorder* in a newsletter for clients. A sales manager might define *sales resistance* for a training manual for new salespeople. A safety officer might define *disaster preparedness* in an email to all employees. *How might you use definition in the job you hope to have after graduation? For whom might you write a definition? Which of the purposes for writing will that definition fulfill?*

Before Writing

An extended definition explains the characteristics of the term being defined. When defining *anorexia nervosa*, for example, you would explain that an individual with this eating disorder tries to eat as little as possible, behaviour that can eventually lead to death (an effect). You might also explain that poor body image may be involved, along with the sufferer's compulsive need to control some aspect of his or her life. To develop these points, use some or all of the strategies explained next.

Write a Stipulative Definition

When you write a definition in an essay, what you include in the paper is just as important as what you do not discuss. You can include a **stipulative definition** to restrict the parameters of your explanation and focus your essay. If a word has more than one meaning or if its meaning includes many aspects, a stipulative definition can narrow the scope by establishing the boundaries of a definition. For example, the term *pornography* means different things to different people. To set the scope of a discussion of its meaning, it is possible include a stipulative definition like this: "Pornography is any material in any medium that sexually arouses some people but creates a threat to the well-being of others." This stipulative definition works well in a cause-and-effect essay that demonstrates the harm pornography causes to some people.

Draw on other Patterns of Development

An extended definition can include any of the patterns of development or combination of patterns. If you are asked to define *holiday spirit*, for example, you could develop the definition using one or more of the following patterns:

Description:	Use sensory details to describe how holiday spirit makes people feel, or describe the decorations, music, and foods that help create the mood that contributes to the spirit.
Narration:	Tell a story about a person who demonstrated holiday spirit.
Exemplification:	Provide examples to illustrate the nature of holiday spirit.
Process analysis:	Explain what retailers do to create holiday spirit in shopping malls.
Comparison-contrast:	Compare and contrast holiday spirit with the feelings people get on other holidays in order to clarify the nature of the spirit.
Cause-and-effect analysis:	Explain how people are affected by holiday spirit.
Classification-division:	Classify the various kinds of holiday spirit or the various ways it is manifested; divide the spirit into its components.
Argumentation:	Argue that the spirit of annual holidays is being lost to commercialism.

Compare or Contrast the Term with Related Words

Sometimes writers can clarify a term by showing how it is similar to or different from another term. For example, in "Parenthood: Don't Count on Sleeping until They Move Out," Maria Lopez compares her subject to another term: "First and foremost, a parent is a guesser." If you were defining *maturity*, you could contrast the term with a related one, like this: "Maturity is not merely adulthood, for many people over 21 lack real maturity."

Explain What Your Term Is *Not*

Sometimes, writers want to explain what your subject is *not*. For example, when defining *freedom*, you may want to say that freedom is *not* doing anything you want, it is *not* a privilege, and it is *not* necessarily guaranteed to everyone. From here, you could go on to explain what you believe freedom *is*. This technique can be useful for making important distinctions or dispelling common misunderstandings. Please see the section on the stipulative definition. If a definition is too vague, or attempts to do too much, an essay may be seen as weak and unfocused.

Visualizing a Definition Essay

The chart that follows can help visualize one structure for an extended definition. Like all good models, this one can be altered as needed. This basic plan is for an informal, five-paragraph essay. It can be expanded for a longer, academic paper. Remember, a good essay includes not only the introductory, body and concluding paragraphs. It includes specific examples, ample support, transitions, and effective topic and summary sentences.

Introduction

- Creates interest, perhaps by explaining what people believe your subject means (if you will show it means something else) or by telling an anecdote about your subject
- States the thesis, which gives the term and the characteristics you will explain or the point to be drawn from the definition

▼

First Body Paragraph or Paragraphs

- Will give the first characteristic
- May include other patterns of development
- May include a stipulative definition
- May compare or contrast the term with another term
- May explain what the term is not
- May arrange details progressively or in another logical order

▼

Next Body Paragraph or Paragraphs

- Will give the next characteristic
- May include other patterns of development
- May include a stipulative definition
- May compare or contrast the term with another term
- May explain what the term is not
- May arrange details progressively or in another logical order

▼

Next Body Paragraphs

- Give the remaining characteristics
- May include other patterns of development
- May include a stipulative definition
- May compare or contrast the term with another term
- May explain what the term is not
- May arrange details progressively or in another logical order

▼

Conclusion

- May elaborate on the significance of the definition
- Creates closure

EXERCISE WRITING DEFINITION

1. Select a concept (freedom, justice, good taste, sportsmanship, etc.), object (compact disc, microchip, etc.), person (a good teacher, a friend, etc.), or movement (environmentalism, feminism, etc.) to define.

2. What is the most distinguishing characteristic of the subject you selected for number 1? The second-most distinguishing characteristic? What patterns of development could you use to explain each of those characteristics in an essay?

3. Come up with three additional points you could make to help define the subject by answering any of the following questions that are pertinent:
    a. What story can I tell to help define my subject?
    b. What features of my subject can I describe?
    c. What examples would help define my subject?
    d. To what can I compare my subject? With what can I contrast it?
    e. What is my subject *not*?

4. Write out a thesis that includes the subject and a point that could be drawn from the definition.

5. *Collaborative Activity:* With two or three classmates, read the following paragraph and evaluate how effective it would be as an introduction for an extended definition. Be prepared to cite reasons for your view.

> Although I feel that it is not extremely difficult for two people to establish a relationship, maintaining that relationship may not be quite as easy. Undoubtedly, we all have our faults and flaws, our marks of imperfection, and as two people come to know more about each other, these flaws become more and more evident. It is the degree of emphasis placed on these flaws that determines whether or not a relationship blossoms into a true friendship. If a person is truly your friend, then even after coming to know a lot about you, he or she will still care very much for you. A true friend is fun to be with, trustworthy, and reliable. ●

CRITICAL READING STUDENT ESSAY

"Parenthood: Don't Count on Sleeping until They Move Out," appears with marginal notes that point out key features. Written to inform and express some of the author's feelings, the definition is developed with examples, many of them hypothetical. (For more on hypothetical examples, see page 191.) Ask yourself whether these examples work well to develop the definition.

Parenthood: Don't Count on Sleeping until They Move Out

Maria Lopez

1   Before I had children, I thought I had a crystal clear understanding of the word "parents." Parents were those people who fed me, clothed me, put a roof

PARAGRAPH 1

The introduction—the author engages reader interest by explaining what she used to think the term *parents* meant. The thesis (the last sentence) notes the term has come to mean something different to her. The thesis includes what will be defined and the controlling idea (the parent has the "world's most difficult job").

over my head, and took me to the doctor when I was ill. They were not, however, people who should be inquiring into my personal life, worrying about the choices I made as I grew into my teens and demanded more freedom. Most of all, they were insensitive people whose feelings could not be hurt by anything I said or did. Yes, I thought I knew all about parents—right up until the time my first child was born. That's when I discovered that my assumptions about parents were dead wrong. A parent, I've learned, is a person both blessed and cursed with the world's most difficult job.

PARAGRAPH 2

The topic sentence (the first) notes the first characteristic of the term being defined (the parent is a guesser). The rest of the paragraph is the supporting detail to develop the topic sentence. Note the use of questions to convey the sense of uncertainty and the hypothetical situations to illustrate the need for guessing.

2   First and foremost, a parent is a guesser. At best, the guess is an educated one; at worst, it's a blind shot in the dark. An educated guess, for example, would be Mom's choice of the right toy for an eight-year-old boy's birthday gift, based on what every other eight-year-old boy in the neighborhood owns. Simple, right? The educated guess, however, can get scarier: Should a child be taken to the emergency room at midnight with an earache and a fever, or can treatment safely be delayed until morning? The sleepless parent, rocking the sleepless child through the night, makes and unmakes the decision. Yes, little Jen has had earaches before, and she's usually better by morning. But what if this time is different? What if she's worse? What if she loses her hearing? But it's rainy and miserable outside. What if taking her out makes her worse? What if she has to wait hours in the emergency room? What if.... well, you get the picture. As if the educated guess isn't bad enough, though, a parent often must also be a guesser in the dark, blindly hoping that some of the guesses are the right ones. Was it right or wrong to ground the thirteen-year-old for lying? How about for screaming in her mother's face? And what's the appropriate curfew for a seventeen-year-old, anyway? How much freedom is too much? How much is too little? Is the parent encouraging rebellion and possibly dangerous behavior by being too strict or too permissive? The awful truth, of course, is seldom voiced: Parents are people who NEVER, EVER learn whether all those blind guesses were right or wrong, foolish or wise, helpful or damaging.

PARAGRAPH 3

The topic sentence (the first) gives the next characteristic (vulnerability). The supporting detail is examples. The last sentence gives another characteristic (silent sufferers) that is an effect.

3   All of this guessing helps parents become sensitive souls, exquisitely vulnerable to their offspring. The flinching probably starts with the first child's departure for kindergarten (or maybe even preschool) without a backward glance at Mom and Dad, standing tearfully at the door. Then there's that terrible moment of truth when a child first realizes that parents aren't really gods, that they don't have all the answers, even on fourth-grade homework. What can hurt worse than the astonished look on a child's face that says, "You let me down, Mom" or "I always thought you knew everything, Dad"? I'll tell you what hurts worse: the teenaged boy who finds his mother's mere presence a total embarrassment, the teenaged girl who tells her father that he doesn't understand ANYTHING, or the five-year-old who screams, "I hate you! I hate you!" Eventually, to avoid those painful scenes, many parents become silent sufferers, developing high blood pressure as well as a high tolerance for mental anguish.

PARAGRAPH 4

The last paragraph gives another characteristic in the first sentence ("anxious bargainers with God"), and the second-to-last sentence gives another characteristic ("grateful believers"). The last sentence provides the closure.

4   Finally, as they lay exhausted in the dark at midnight, or pace the floor at 3:00 a.m., many parents become anxious bargainers with God. If You just let her come home safely, God, I'll never swear at her again. If You'll just help him stop drinking, God, I promise I'll spend more time with him. Then, when the

door cracks open and footsteps creak up the stairs, every parent—whatever the religious background—becomes a grateful believer. Thankfully, we whisper, "Someday, if there's a God, you'll have a kid JUST LIKE YOU."

The complete essay, including any bibliographic references, is also available on the Online Learning Centre at www.mcgrawhill.ca/olc/clouse.

EXERCISES

1. The voice in this essay is first-person. To what extent is this a better choice than third-person? If a more objective approach were taken, how would this essay need to be revised?

2. Consider how successfully this essay demonstrates definition as a pattern of development. There is no research material, as Maria has decided to base the content on her own experience. How could Maria combine anecdotal evidence with research from academic sources? Where would research materials be appropriate?

3. Was the writer successful in defining parenthood? Does this essay make parenthood seem challenging, or unattractive? ●

CRITIQUE, REVISE, and EDIT

"Parenthood: Don't Count on Sleeping until They Move Out" has this thesis:

A parent, I've learned, is a person both blessed and cursed with the world's most difficult job.

You may have noticed when you read the essay that the author does not say anything about the blessings of parenthood. That was not the case in an earlier draft of the essay, which included this paragraph as the conclusion:

Early draft of conclusion

No matter how difficult parenting becomes, small moments surface to make the pain bearable. Your kindergartner rushes in from school and announces, "I missed you, Mommy," and you start to glow from your heart out to your skin. Your teenager tosses the car keys on the table and says, "I filled up the tank for you, Dad," and you start to think that maybe there's hope for the boy yet. We hear that more and more couples are choosing to be childless, but enough of us are becoming parents that the moments of joy must be carrying the day.

The author decided she liked the current conclusion better and opted not to revise the above paragraph for inclusion in the final version. Did she do the right thing? Should she have revised the thesis?

CRITICAL READING PROFESSIONAL ESSAYS

Pre-reading

1. Define multiculturalism as a Canadian national and social value.
2. How successful do you consider Canada's multiculturalism policy? What needs to change? What problems exist?
3. If multiculturalism is, ultimately, unsuccessful, what should replace it?

Living Better Multiculturally: In Canada, We Seem to Get the Multi Part, But How About the Culture?

Janice Gross Stein

1   Canadians today are proudly multicultural. Along with publicly funded health care, multiculturalism has become part of the sticky stuff of Canadian identity. It is relatively new, a stage in our evolution from a binational, bilingual society. An official policy of multiculturalism was first enacted in 1971, followed by the *Multiculturalism Act* in 1985. The first section of the constitution, the *Canadian Charter of Rights and Freedoms*, adopted in 1982, provides in section 27 that the Charter "should be interpreted in a manner consistent with the preservation and enhancement of the multicultural heritage of Canadians."

2   Canada is unique among Western democracies in its constitutional commitment to multiculturalism. It has also done extraordinarily well in practice. Its large cities reflect an impressive range of diversity among the many cultures that live peacefully with one another. Watching World Cup soccer in Toronto testifies to the city's cultural range and diversity. People borrowed cultures as their favourite team was eliminated and switched allegiance to another team and another cultural community. Bystanders were welcomed and invited to join Ghanaians, French, Italians, Portuguese and Koreans who took to city streets to wave flags in celebration. At its best, multiculturalism in Canada is inclusive, rather than exclusionary.

3   Canadians generally respect difference, dislike any kind of stereotyping and make a conscious—and healthy—effort to avoid giving gratuitous offence.

We are generally far more polite than our neighbour to the south and far more inclusive than many European states—Germany, France, Italy—that have old and deeply rooted cultures. We pride ourselves on having done it differently from the United States with its metaphor of a melting pot, an open society that demands assimilation and a fiercely assertive nationalism. We think that we have done better than older Europe, which treasures its past and lives uneasily with significant numbers of immigrants who are largely strangers in European cities. Generally, we do not have the squalid suburbs peopled by new immigrants that ring Paris, or the large-scale ghettoes that are visible in so many European cities. Different communities live side by side, if not exactly together, in Canada's cities, with relatively little cross-cultural violence. The record is impressive and encouraging.

4   Despite extraordinary successes, the Canadian commitment to multiculturalism is being tested in new ways. Recent immigrants to Canada are not doing as well as previous generations. Their incomes are significantly below those of Canadians with comparable skills. The commitment to multiculturalism is also being tested by worries about "homegrown" terrorism, the fear that acts of violence may be committed by Canadians against their own government. It is being tested by a resurgence of orthodoxy in Christianity, Islam and Judaism where lines of division between "them" and "us" are being drawn more sharply.

And it is being tested because Canadians are uncertain about what limits, if any, there are to embedding diverse cultures and religious traditions in the Canadian context. We know pretty well what the "multi" in multicultural means, but are much less confident about "culture." Does culture in Canada mean just a respect for pluralism and difference? Or is there more? Have we produced a broader set of shared values that must, at some point, bump up against the diversity and difference that we celebrate?

5   There is a sniff of smugness in our celebration of our successes as a multicultural society. That smugness, a culturally sanctioned political correctness, is becoming less acceptable as real divisions creep into the debate about cultural and religious difference. How far can respect for difference go? When does it constrain freedom of expression? That issue boiled over when cartoons from Denmark that Muslims considered defamatory were published, but anti-Semitic cartoons have provoked similar debates. Does respect for different cultures extend to the sanctioning of religious courts that are likely to violate the rights of women? Does freedom of expression permit one group to insult and stereotype another? And when does stereotyping subtly become incitement to hatred? Is respect for difference being polluted by a reluctance to set limits, to give positive content to what and who we are as well as to what we recognize and respect?

6   These questions are not important if multiculturalism is largely restricted to the celebration of song, dance, poetry, literature, language and food. It is these kinds of celebration that are the stuff of the official policy of multiculturalism in Canada's large cities. In Toronto, on a July weekend afternoon, residents could choose among a Brazilian street festival, the Corso Italia Toronto Fiesta or Afrofest. But multiculturalism is more than a celebration of different cultures. It is part of our collective identity and a platform for our future in the global marketplace.

7   Here we are on far more difficult terrain where we need to ask more serious questions about religious traditions and the state. How committed are "we" in Canada to the secularization of public space? Do we welcome multiple religious symbols in public squares in December or do we ban them all? How far can religious practice and celebration extend into public space? To what extent will the state, in the service of the freedom of religion, continue to allow churches, synagogues and mosques the right to exclusive interpretation of religious law when they have an impact on the fundamental rights of Canadians? The answers to these questions tell us a great deal about what we mean by culture.

8   We are not the only society that is debating these issues. And we are having several debates simultaneously. The debate in Quebec, not surprisingly, is different in its focus from in English Canada. In Quebec, multiculturalism is joined at the hip to concern about the survival of the French language and Québécois culture in North America. In continental Europe—in France and Germany, for example—the debate is louder, more strident, openly entangled in questions of how the "other" can become the self, how the stranger can become less strange. Germans speak openly of how important it is that "newcomers" learn German history and culture as well as the language. France makes no claims to multiculturalism, and openly insists on a culture of laïcité, or secularism, with an enforced dress code in its public schools. The debate in Britain is closer to our own. Britain celebrates its diversity, its many cultures, in theory if not in practice. Here too, however, a new debate has erupted in London's magazines and salons about the limits to diversity that need to be put in place so that a culture of civil disagreement, rejection of violence and engaged citizenship can be created across the country's often segregated neighbourhoods.

9   We in Canada pride ourselves that we have done better. We would not think of enforcing restrictions against Hebrew skullcaps, Christian crosses or Muslim hijabs in our public schools. On the contrary, we celebrate almost everyone's religious and national holidays. Despite our rhetoric, however, I suspect that we do draw some boundaries in Canada. We are most comfortable with those boundaries that we have enshrined over the years in the rule of law and, more recently, in the *Charter of Rights and Freedoms*. We not only celebrate differences, but we also value the human rights that define the quality of our democratic norms

and practice. So far, so good. Where we are reluctant to go, however, is the conflict between universal human rights that we treasure and different religious and cultural traditions. One obvious fault line, one that we tiptoe around, is the rights of women in different religious and cultural traditions in our midst.

10 Women in Canada are guaranteed equal treatment and an equal voice in the determination of our shared vision of the common good. We respect rights and we respect diversity, but at times the two compete. How do we mediate these disputes? What to do about private religious schools, for example, that meet government criteria by teaching the official curriculum but segregate women in separate classrooms? Or segregate women in religious worship? Should universities, for example, make space available to student groups that segregate women in worship? The University of Toronto agreed to provide space for Jewish and Islamic services that separated men from women while McGill University refused to do so.

11 Paradoxically, conflict is most intense not in those branches of religion where literal readings of text provide little room for interpretation or deviation, but rather in those that are most responsive to Canadian society even as they cherish their traditions. These conflicts are not abstract, but very personal to me. When I challenged my rabbi recently about his longstanding refusal to give women in my congregation the right to participate fully and equally in religious services, he argued: "I have not taken the position of 'separate but equal,' although I believe that a case can be made for this perspective. I have not argued for a fully egalitarian expression of Judaism, although I believe that a case can be made for this perspective. Instead, I have pressed for increased inclusion."

12 Indeed, under his leadership our congregation now permits a greater degree of involvement for women in daily services, in public readings and in leading parts of the liturgy. These are far more than cosmetic changes, but to me, as significant as these changes are, they are not enough. Women are still not counted as part of the ten people who must be present before prayers can begin. Only men count. I have had the extraordinary experience of sitting in a chapel and watching the leader of prayers count the men in the room, his eyes sliding over me as he counted. For all intents and purposes, not only did I not count, I was invisible.

13 I do not think, contrary to my rabbi, that any argument at all can be made for separate but equal treatment. These kinds of arguments have a long and inglorious history of discrimination that systematically disadvantages some part of a community. Nor is it obvious why greater inclusion should be capped short of full status, where women count as equals in constituting a prayer group. I take the Charter seriously.

14 My religious obligation clashes openly and directly with values that I hold deeply as a Canadian. Fortunately, there are congregations in the broader Jewish community in the city in which I live that are fully egalitarian. My cultural and religious community is sufficiently pluralistic that I can choose among a wide variety of options. That pluralism reflects the Canadian context in which this religious and cultural community has developed and matured.

15 A resolution of my personal dilemma may be available to me—I can vote with my feet—but the issue is public as well as private. These religious institutions that systemically discriminate against women often have legal standing and are therefore recognized, at least implicitly, by governments. How can we in Canada, in the name of religious freedom, continue furtively and silently to sanction this kind of discrimination? It is this issue that was at the core of the debate in Ontario about sharia law and orthodox Jewish courts within the framework of state-sanctioned arbitration.

16 Charitable tax status raises similar questions. If religious institutions are able to raise funds more easily because governments give a tax benefit to those who contribute, are religious practices wholly private even though they benefit from the public purse? Are discriminatory religious practices against women a matter only for religious law, as is currently the case under Canadian law, which protects freedom of religion, or should the

values of the Charter and of human rights commissions across Canada have some application when religious institutions are officially recognized and advantaged in fundraising? Does it matter that the Catholic church, which has special entitlements given to it by the state and benefits from its charitable tax status, refuses to ordain women as priests?

17 We have thus far been unwilling in Canada to ask these kinds of questions. They make us uncomfortable. They are politically incorrect. They are not respectful of different cultures and traditions. Like other societies, we in Canada live with some convenient hypocrisies. I have deliberately chosen a personal issue—the issue of women's participation in religious services in my own synagogue—to open up this difficult discussion of the desirable limits to multiculturalism and religious freedom. Some would urge silence and patience until a new social consensus emerges. Opening difficult conversations too early can fracture communities, inflict deep wounds and do irreversible damage to those who are most open to experimentation. In my own congregation, I have been counselled for the last five years to be patient. Give it time, I am told, and the synagogue will become fully egalitarian.

18 I find it hard to be patient into the indefinite future, with no commitments from my religious leadership. I worry that change will stall unless we keep a civil but difficult conversation going. There is no question that there is a conflict between equality rights, on the one hand, and the right to freedom of religion, on the other. The law recognizes that conflict, but we need to ask hard questions about the balance between them. My synagogue is ahead of comparable synagogues in the city, even though it is behind others in North America. If I am expected to be patient, almost endlessly patient, then religious leaders must be cognizant of the responsibilities of their organizations that receive charitable status and public benefit to engage with Canadian culture as it is expressed in our most fundamental laws.

19 There is, as we know, often no perfect solution when rights compete with one another. Canadians do not tolerate deliberate incitement of hatred by one group against another. The law is careful; it sets criteria of deliberate intention to spread hate and does not punish a spontaneous utterance that was not intended and willful. It does, however, quite deliberately limit freedom of speech when that speech becomes hatred and incitement to violence. What responsibilities do leaders of religious and cultural communities have, then, when some members preach the use of violence against others? Do religious and cultural leaders within these communities have an obligation to move to stop this kind of preaching when they hear it? The rule of law will take us only so far in answering these questions.

20 Religious leaders certainly have no legal obligation to do so. We are all individually responsible for our own actions. But do they have a civic obligation to do so as Canadians who share the consensus against incitement to hate and the respect for diversity? *Toronto Star* editorialist Haroon Siddiqui argues eloquently that community leaders have no special obligation. In the wake of the arrests of 17 Muslims in Toronto, he warned in June, correctly in my opinion, against assertion of collective Muslim guilt, but argued, incorrectly in my view, that community leaders have no responsibility at all for what members do. "Any time some Muslims somewhere commit an atrocity, a chorus of voices demands of Muslims everywhere: 'What do you have to say about this?' They should have to say nothing more than Christians or Jews or Hindus must for the wrongs of their co-religionists ... Muslims are also told to 'take responsibility' for their deviants, 'root out their extremists,' 'weed out the radicals, etc.' How are they supposed to do that?" Siddiqui asks. "By becoming vigilantes?"

21 These are good questions that deserve serious deliberation. Did the local imam in the mosque in Toronto, Ali Hindy, where fiery sermons inciting violence were routinely heard, have a responsibility to challenge the preacher, to dispute the interpretation of the text and to warn the young people of the risks and the dangers? I think that he did. That kind of behaviour is not vigilantism. It is responsible debate about the limits of religious freedom in a Canadian culture that abjures hate.

22 I can and do ask the same question of myself. Although the two issues—systemic discrimination against women and incitement to hatred—are different not only in degree but also in kind, I think that I do have an obligation to challenge my rabbi. My behaviour is neither vigilantism nor obstructionism, as it is frequently labelled by some in my religious and cultural community. It is designed to provoke responsible debate about the limits of religious freedom in a Canadian culture that embeds equality and human rights in our most fundamental laws. Religion tends to give a franchise to the past and, in this sense, will always reflect both the cultural and counter-cultural in the society in which it lives. That it gives a franchise to the past does not remove responsibility for engaging with the present.

23 We are at one of those hinge moments. The widespread movement of ideas and people is global, enriching of our society, and is a marvellous opportunity for Canada to grow and develop in the next few decades. A vibrant immigration is especially important as our population ages. If we are to make the most of that opportunity, however, we will have to build a deep rather than a shallow multiculturalism. Shallow multiculturalism is a veneer, official policy but not embedded practice, that can have damaging consequences for a democratic society. What I call deep multiculturalism is a resource and a strength of a democratic society in an era of globalization. It needs to be capable of meeting three core challenges.

24 First, it is important that we join the discussion of equality rights and cultural difference with explicit attention to the overlay of social and economic inequalities. Multiculturalism is shallow when social and economic inequalities reinforce and strengthen cultural difference and then fuel a sense of victimization among an impoverished minority. From this sense of grievance can grow frustration, anger and occasionally an explosion of violence. England and France, each in its own way, have recently undergone variants of this kind of experience. They each are now looking hard at the economic and social disparities among cultural and religious communities. We need to do the same in Canada.

25 Second, deep multiculturalism builds bridges across cultures. Shallow multiculturalism can strengthen each culture within its own boundaries. Each community can learn its own language, its own history, its songs, its poetry. But one community does not necessarily learn about another and then multiculturalism can have perverse effects. It can strengthen the boundaries around each community and, in so doing, help to seal one community off from another. A Home Office report, issued in England after riots broke out in three northern industrial towns in 2001, found "separate educational arrangements, community and voluntary bodies, employment, places of worship, language, social and cultural networks," producing living arrangements that "do not seem to touch at any point." Trevor Philips, chair of the Commission for Racial Equality, warned recently that much of Britain was "sleepwalking its way toward segregation."

26 How are cultural and religious communities living together in Canada's cities? Are they segregated, living side by side rather than together? How often does one join in the other's celebrations? Where do communities share public space? There are some worrying trends in multiculturalism in Canada. Some children, for example, go only to their community schools until they are ready for postsecondary education, worship at community institutions, go to community summer camps, play soccer or hockey within their own communities, and make friends only with kids who have similar cultural connections. The pattern in Britain is being replicated in some of our communities in Canadian cities. These closed patterns of associations may well not provide enough opportunity to talk across cultures. To the credit of my synagogue, that same synagogue that refuses to give women equal rights, the rabbinical leadership has been extraordinarily aware of the importance of building bridges and has been a leader in interfaith dialogue and shared services among Muslims, Christians and Jews.

27 Third, we need to make robust the meaning of "culture" in our experience of multiculturalism. We have to make explicit the contradictions between cultural and religious traditions and the rule of law

in Canada, when such contradictions exist. There are very large areas where there are no tensions at all. But where they do exist, we cannot turn away. We have to begin the uncomfortable and difficult discussion of conflict among values and work very hard to find an appropriate balance. And if we cannot find that balance—I have failed miserably thus far with my own rabbi—we need to make clear that the conflict is real and serious. We are not simply Jews or Hindus or Muslims or Christians or Indians or Pakistanis or Somalis or Germans; we are Jews and Hindus and Muslims and Christians and Indians and Pakistanis and Somalis and Germans who live—together—in Canada. That we live in Canada matters. How we live together in Canada matters. Our sense of what Canada is, our commitment to the Charter and to human rights, what Canada gives us and what we owe it, is what we collectively bring to each new cultural encounter. It is what gives meaning to Canadian culture within the tradition of multiculturalism.

Considering Ideas

1. What characteristics of multiculturalism does Stein attempt to define?
2. Stein spends the majority of the essay asking questions that she feels need to be addressed. Her specific ideas about Canadian multiculturalism do not begin until paragraph 18. What is the effect of leaving the definition so long in the essay?
3. The author uses a personal example about religious inclusion. How does the example she uses further her definition of multiculturalism?
4. Over the course of the essay, Stein develops a stipulative definition of multiculturalism. Summarize her definition.
5. Comment on the comparison of shallow and deep multiculturalism. What is Stein suggesting?

Considering Technique

1. Stein begins her essay with very strong topic sentences. What is her purpose?
2. Stein builds a definition of multiculturalism near the end of the essay. What are her three recommendations, and how do these ideas contribute to dialogue around culture in Canada?
3. Stein insists we are at a "hinge moment." What is the effect of this suggestion? How does this signal a transition in the essay?
4. How does Stein use exemplification to combine patterns in her essay?

For Group Discussion or Journal Writing

1. In paragraph 23 Stein says, "The widespread movement of ideas and people is global, enriching of our society, and is a marvellous opportunity for Canada to grow and develop in the next few decades." Agree or disagree with this idea of opportunity, citing examples to support your view.
2. Canada is known as one of the world's most diverse nations. Is it safe to assume that all Canadians are tolerant of newcomers?
3. Define the term "bigot." Consider recent events in Canadian news or culture that might suggest that Canadians are not as tolerant as they are portrayed to be.

Pre-Reading

1. Is there a stronger preference for baby girls or baby boys in Canada?
2. How do girls and boys contribute differently to families and societies?
3. Rosenberg will address what is known as a daughter "deficit." How do you usually define *deficit*, and what would you expect it to mean in this context?
4. Predict how most readers would react to the current population imbalances in developing countries.

The Daughter Deficit

Tina Rosenberg

1   In the late 1970s, a Ph.D. student named Monica Das Gupta was conducting anthropological fieldwork in Haryana, a state in the north of India. She observed something striking about families there: parents had a fervent preference for male offspring. Women who had given birth to only daughters were desperate for sons and would keep having children until they had one or two. Midwives were even paid less when a girl was born. "It's something you notice coming from outside," says Das Gupta, who today studies population and public health in the World Bank's development research group. "It just leaps out at you."

2   Das Gupta saw that educated, independent-minded women shared this prejudice in Haryana, a state that was one of India's richest and most developed. In fact, the bias against girls was far more pronounced there than in the poorer region in the east of India where Das Gupta was from. She decided to study the issue in Punjab, then India's richest state, which had a high rate of female literacy and a high average age of marriage. There too the prejudice for sons flourished. Along with Haryana, Punjab had the country's highest percentage of so-called missing girls—those aborted, killed as newborns or dead in their first few years from neglect.

3   Here was a puzzle: Development seemed to have not only failed to help many Indian girls but to have made things worse.

4   It is rarely good to be female anywhere in the developing world today, but in India and China the situation is dire: in those countries, more than 1.5 million fewer girls are born each year than demographics would predict, and more girls die before they turn 5 than would be expected. (In China in 2007, there were 1.73 million births—and a million missing girls.) Millions more grow up stunted, physically and intellectually, because they are denied the health care and the education that their brothers receive.

5   Among policymakers, the conventional wisdom is that such selective brutality toward girls can be mitigated by two factors. One is development: surely the wealthier the home, the more educated the parents, the more plugged in to the modern economy, the more a family will invest in its girls. The other is focusing aid on women. The idea is that a mother who has more money, knowledge and authority in the family will direct her resources toward all her children's health and education. She will fight for her girls.

6   Yet these strategies—though invaluable—underestimate the complexity of the situation in certain countries. To be sure, China and India are poor. But in both nations, girls are actually more likely to be missing in richer areas than in poorer ones, and in cities than in rural areas. Having more money, a better education and (in India) belonging to a higher caste all raise the probability that a

family will discriminate against its daughters. The bias against girls applies in some of the wealthiest and best-educated nations in the world, including, in recent years, South Korea, Taiwan and Singapore. It also holds among Indian immigrants in Britain and among Chinese, Indian and South Korean immigrants in the United States. In the last few years, the percentage of missing girls has been among the highest in the middle-income, high-education nations of the Caucasus: Armenia, Azerbaijan and Georgia.

7   Nor does a rise in a woman's autonomy or power in the family necessarily counteract prejudice against girls. Researchers at the International Food Policy Research Institute have found that while increasing women's decision-making power would reduce discrimination against girls in some parts of South Asia, it would make things worse in the north and west of India. "When women's power is increased," wrote Lisa C. Smith and Elizabeth M. Byron, "they use it to favor boys."

8   Why should this be? A clue lies in what Das Gupta uncovered in her research in Punjab in the 1980s. At the time, it was assumed that parents in certain societies simply did not value girls. And in important ways, this was true. But Das Gupta complicated this picture. She found that it was not true that all daughters were mistreated equally. A firstborn daughter was not typically subjected to inferior treatment; she was treated like her brothers. But a subsequent daughter born to an educated mother was 2.36 times as likely to die before her fifth birthday as her siblings were to die before theirs—mainly because she was less likely to see a doctor. It turned out that a kind of economic logic was at work: with a first-born girl, families still had plenty of chances to have a boy; but with each additional girl, the pressure to have a son increased. The effect of birth order that Das Gupta discovered has now been confirmed in subsequent studies of missing girls.

9   What unites communities with historically high rates of discrimination against girls is a rigid patriarchal culture that makes having a son a financial and social necessity. When a daughter grows up and marries, she essentially becomes chattel in her husband's parents' home and has very limited contact with her natal family. Even if she earns a good living, it will be of no help to her own parents in their old age. So for parents, investing in a daughter is truly, in the Hindi expression, planting a seed in the neighbor's garden. Sons, by contrast, provide a kind of social security. A family with only daughters will also likely lose its land when the father dies: although women can legally inherit property, in areas of north India and China, they risk ostracism or even murder if they claim what is theirs. And sons are particularly important to mothers, who acquire power and authority when they have married sons. Sons, according to Chinese custom, are also needed to care for the souls of dead ancestors.

10   What Das Gupta discovered is that wealthier and more educated women face this same imperative to have boys as uneducated poor women—but they have smaller families, thus increasing the felt urgency of each birth. In a family that expects to have seven children, the birth of a girl is a disappointment; in a family that anticipates only two or three children, it is a tragedy.

11   Thus development can worsen, not improve, traditional discrimination. This can happen in other ways too. With the access it brings to cutting-edge technology, development can also offer more sophisticated and easier options for exercising old-fashioned prejudice. In China and in the north and west of India, for instance, the spread of ultrasound technology, which can inform parents of the sex of their fetus, has turned a pool of missing girls into an ocean. The birth of girls has long been avoided through infanticide, which is still practiced often in China. But there are even more couples who would abort a pregnancy than would kill a newborn. Ultrasound has been advertised in India as "pay 5,000 rupees today and save 500,000 rupees tomorrow." In both countries, it is illegal to inform parents of the sex of their fetus, and sex-selective abortion is banned. But it is practiced widely and rarely punished.

12   Finally, because higher education and income levels generate more resources, development offers new opportunities to discriminate against living girls. After all, if people are very poor, boys and girls are necessarily deprived equally—there is little to dole out to anyone. But as parents gain the tools to help their children survive and thrive (and

indeed, all children do better as their parents' education and income levels advance), they allocate advantages like doctor visits to boys and firstborn girls, leaving subsequent daughters behind.

13 To be sure, development can eventually lead to more equal treatment for girls: South Korea's birth ratios are now approaching normality. But policymakers need to realize that this type of development works slowly and mainly indirectly, by softening a son-centered culture. The solution is not to abandon development or to stop providing, say, microcredit to women. But these efforts should be joined by an awareness of the unintended consequences of development and by efforts, aimed at parents, to weaken the cultural preference for sons.

14 The lesson here is subtle but critical: Development brings about immense and valuable cultural change—much of it swiftly—but it doesn't necessarily change all aspects of a culture at the same rate. (India and China have myriad laws outlawing discrimination against girls that are widely ignored. And how to explain the persistence of missing girls among Asian immigrants in America?) In the short and medium terms, the resulting clashes between modern capabilities and old prejudices can make some aspects of life worse before they make them better.

Considering Ideas

1. In Rosenberg's essay, Das Gupta cites numerous examples of economic and social development in India and China, but also finds that prejudice persists. Why do you think this is?

2. Examine the contradiction in paragraph 3. What might explain this?

3. How does Rosenberg define *deficit*? Does she equate it with anything else?

4. What accounts for high rates of discrimination against girls in developing nations?

5. Are there comparable examples of such discrimination in Western countries?

6. What lesson does Rosenberg offer in her conclusion?

Considering Technique

1. How does the author use cause-and-effect to further her purpose in paragraph 5?

2. Which words does Rosenberg use to refer to the gender imbalance in India and China?

3. Rosenberg cites a proverb currently used in India in paragraph 9. How does this metaphor work?

4. Rosenberg's essay reveals some surprising contradictions about development and women's attitudes toward female children. Which is her most startling example?

For Group Discussion or Journal Writing

The social and economic progress that the world has experienced in the 20th century has been breathtaking. Yet, there remain serious social and cultural problems, with, apparently, few solutions forthcoming. What will be the major social, cultural, and economic challenges for the human population in the 21st century, given that some traditional problems may persist?

WRITING TOOL

Questions

Writers can employ two kinds of questions: those that are asked and answered in print, and those that are asked in print but not answered. Janice Stein writes the second kind of question in paragraph 5:

> How far can respect for difference go?

The supporting detail in subsequent paragraphs answers the question:

> "First, it is important that we join the discussion of equality rights and cultural difference with explicit attention to the overlay of social and economic inequalities."

The second kind of question is a **rhetorical question.** A rhetorical question is asked for effect; the writer does not answer it because the answer is obvious.

Stein also asks rhetorical questions throughout the essay:

> "Is respect for difference being polluted by a reluctance to set limits, to give positive content to what and who we are as well as to what we recognize and respect"?

Because Stein asks this question before she provides a definition of multiculturalism in Canada, she does not provide an immediate answer. The answer may indeed be "yes" to this question, but Stein leaves that for the reader to decide.

Definition in an Image

This York University advertising image is part of York's "redefining the possible" campaign. How does the ad use definition as a visual construct to encourage the notion of innovative thinking?

Considering the Image

1. What subject does the advertisement define? Is there a stipulative definition included in the ad?
2. What is the purpose of the definitions in the advertisement? What does it suggest about studies at York?
3. What pattern of development helps develop the definition?

Reading Then Writing Definition

1. Using "Parenthood: Don't Count on Sleeping until They Move Out" as a guide, write a definition of *son* or *daughter.* As an alternative, write a definition of *only child, firstborn, middle child,* or *baby of the family,* whichever designation applies to you.
2. Based on the reading by Rosenberg, develop a definition of discrimination in the context of gender. Consider both connotative and denotative meanings of discrimination.

A biologist sees a pandemic.

A dietitian sees an excellent source of protein.

A philosopher sees what may have come before the egg.

QUESTION EVERY ANGLE. STUDY EVERY ANGLE. RESEARCH EVERY ANGLE. WELCOME TO THE INTERDISCIPLINARY UNIVERSITY. A WORLD WITHOUT BORDERS NEEDS AN EDUCATION WITHOUT BORDERS. AT YORK, WE BREAK DOWN TRADITIONAL BOUNDARIES AND BRING TOGETHER THINKERS FROM EVERY DISCIPLINE TO TACKLE REAL-WORLD ISSUES. WE DON'T JUST SEE THINGS IN A DIFFERENT LIGHT, WE SEE THE LIGHT IN ITS ENTIRE SPECTRUM. FOR FURTHER INFORMATION ABOUT THE INTERDISCIPLINARY UNIVERSITY, VISIT YORKU.CA.

YORK U
UNIVERSITÉ
UNIVERSITY
redefine THE POSSIBLE.

Definition beyond the Writing Classroom

Assume you are the manager of a department store and that you anticipate hiring extra salespeople to work the busy holiday period from November to mid-January. To help train these new hires, you plan to develop a manual that explains company policies and procedures. For the introduction to the manual, write a 500- to 700-word definition of "a good sales associate." Alternatively, imagine that you and your classmates have been asked to work as peer counsellors at a local high school. With a group or classmates, write a 500- to 700-word definition of "a healthy friendship" based on what you each experienced as adolescents. Remember that your audience is teenagers and your purpose is to provide helpful and compassionate guidance.

Responding to a Theme

Explain whether or not you think the York University advertisement is an effective one. Describe the characteristics of the audience the advertisement targets, and explain how well it addresses that audience and achieves its purpose.

Connecting the Readings

1. Despite remarkable progress, women in developing countries still face formidable challenges. Do multicultural societies, with their focus on accommodation and integration, address these problems any more effectively?
2. Canada has been a donor of international aid dollars, and Canadian service agencies send thousands of people overseas annually to help address the problems in developing nations. To what extent should Canadians, who come from a pluralistic society, attempt to influence more traditional cultures in developing nations?
3. Many Canadians are confident that multiculturalism defines us, and that its definition is set in stone. To what extent is this true or false?

THE WRITING PROCESS

Definition

The following guidelines are not meant to replace your own effective procedures; instead, they're here for you to try as you work to improve your writing process.

Generate Ideas, Consider Audience and Purpose, and Order Ideas

- If you need help finding a topic, try one of the following:
  - Leaf through a dictionary and consider the entries. List words you might like to explore through extended definition, and then choose one term from this list.
  - Consider your own experience. What moods or emotions have you known lately? Depression, anger, anticipation, love—these can be defined using narrations and examples from your life.
  - Think of people you have observed or interacted with recently. Coaches, teachers, salespeople, doctors—these roles can be defined using your observation and experience for details.
- To target a specific audience, answer these questions:
  - Who has a different opinion about the term than I do?
  - Who does not fully understand the term?
  - Who takes my subject for granted?
- To determine your purpose, answer these questions:
  - Am I clarifying the nature of a complex subject?
  - Do I want my reader to appreciate something taken for granted?
  - Am I informing my reader about something not well understood?
  - Am I making a statement about something related to the term?
  - Am I expressing my feelings or relating my experience?
  - Do I want to convince my reader of something?

- To generate ideas, answer all the pertinent questions:
  - What are the three most important characteristics of my subject?
  - What three words best describe my subject?
  - How does my subject work?
  - What are some examples of my subject?
  - What is my subject like and different from?
- Complete an outline worksheet. (Outline worksheets are explained on page 62.)

Draft

- As you draft, refer to your outline worksheet. Think about your audience and purpose, departing from your outline as necessary to meet the needs of your audience and fulfill your purpose.
- Use topic sentences to introduce each characteristic of the term, so your reader can follow along easily.

Revise

- Place a checkmark each time you mention a distinguishing characteristic. Do you have at least two checkmarks? Study the detail you give to explain each characteristic to be sure it is adequate. If you need more detail to develop a characteristic, consider using one of the patterns of development.
- Find the sentence or sentences that explain the significance of your definition. If you have not stated the significance, should you?
- To secure reader response, see pages 101–102. In addition, have your reader point out any place you have not adequately explained a characteristic and any place you do not move smoothly from a discussion of one characteristic to another.

Correct Errors and Proofread

- Use the "Guide to Frequently Occurring Errors" for reference, and check with a writing centre tutor if you are unsure about a grammar, usage, or punctuation point.
- Eliminate circular definitions. A **circular definition** restates the term without adding helpful information.

  Circular: Freedom of speech is being able to speak freely.

  Better: Freedom of speech is the one constitutional guarantee without which no democracy can survive because it guarantees healthy dissent and public debate on important issues.

- Don't forget to proofread your final copy. Read very slowly, pointing to and lingering over every word and punctuation mark.

Remember

Use your own writing style, not one found in dictionaries. If you write that "Holiday spirit is that seasonal mood of ebullience and feeling of goodwill and generosity characteristic of and emanating from the yearly celebration of a religious or cultural event" you will not sound natural, and you will not hold your reader's interest.

Avoid using "according to the *Canadian Oxford Dictionary*" unless citing the dictionary definition serves an important purpose—perhaps as a contrast to the definition you give.

Reprinted by permission of United Feature Syndicate, Inc.

CHAPTER 11

Classification and Division

Looking Ahead

Classification essays group items according to their characteristics, and division essays examine the components of a single item. You will learn how to write both kinds of essays in this chapter. Before doing so, however, think about the assignments post-secondary students do for credit. Sometimes students are tested, as in the opening image, but there are many other ways to assess student progress. Which kinds of assignments and assessment opportunities do your professors use to grade you? What are their components? Can they fit into categories? How can they be analyzed, using a single, or multiple organizing principles? Share your work with a classmate.

Why are Classification and Division Important?

Life is filled with information about people, places, things, devices, facts, and figures. Without some way to group and order all these elements, each new item we encounter would baffle us. Classification and division help provide a mechanism for grouping and organizing information.

Imagine a library without a division and classification system. If you wanted to read a mystery by a particular author, you would have to scan the shelves until you got lucky and came across the book. Fortunately, libraries have classification and division systems, so you can go quickly to the area where mysteries are shelved and then to the mysteries by a particular author.

Classification can serve a number of informational purposes. People often classify because ordering information makes for easier study. In biology, grouping animals into classifications such as mammals, birds, reptiles, and amphibians allows scientists to study animal life more efficiently.

Classification is also a way to clarify similarities and differences between related objects or ideas. For example, if you classify undergraduate courses for a major, they generally fall into broad categories, from which students choose. Some courses are required, and some are elective, and they can be analyzed this way. Knowing this information can help you predict the chances of success for any program you encounter.

Classification can also provide a fresh way of viewing something. For example, television programs are usually classified as dramas, situation comedies, reality shows, game shows, soap operas, variety shows, and so forth. An essay that classifies programs according to how they portray women can lead to a greater awareness of how television influences our perception of women.

Division can also serve informational purposes. A laboratory analyzes blood and reports its findings by dividing a sample into its components. Division can be a way to explain something not well understood. For example, to explain how a desktop computer works, you could divide it into its components and explain each one.

Just as grouping items aids understanding, so does identifying the components of an item. For example, upon learning that a fancy wedding cake can cost as much as $5,000, you may wonder why it costs so much. Part of the answer lies in knowing what goes into the cake. Here is that information, taken from a newspaper article:

WHAT GOES INTO A $5,000 WEDDING CAKE?

Eggs: 192

Sugar: 38 pounds

Butter: 22.2 pounds

Flour: 12.63 pounds

White chocolate: 7.7 pounds

Fresh strawberries: 17 pints

Simple syrup: 2 litres

Fondant: About 50 pounds

Fondant "tiles": Nearly 20,000

Fondant "flowers": 150

Labour: Three people working 135 hours; extra worker brought in on Saturday to help at the last minute

OCCASIONS FOR WRITING

Classification and Division across the Disciplines and Beyond

Classification and Division in the Classroom

Classification and division will likely be important components of post-secondary writing. In an exam for a speech class, you might be asked to classify persuasive rhetorical strategies, or to identify the components of an effective speech. For a biology midterm, you might be asked to divide a cell into its parts. In a paper for an advertising class, you might explain the components of a successful advertising campaign, or might classify the most successful kinds of campaigns. *How might you use classification and/or division in an education paper about remedial reading programs? In your major or in classes you are taking this term?*

Classification and Division in Daily Life

Classification and division can be a part of personal writing. To make a decision about the best benefit package to select, an employee can classify the possibilities to determine which offers the best options at the right price. In an advertisement for a garage sale, the planner can classify items she is selling according to type, such as kitchen-ware, children's clothing, and books. As fundraising chair of an organization, one can classify kinds of fundraisers to help a committee decide which kind to have. *If you had to make an extended shopping trip to many stores for many items, such as drugstore items, grocery items, and clothing, how might you write a list using classification and division?*

Classification and Division on the Job

Classification and division can be part of the writing employees do in the workplace. Investment counsellors classify the kinds of mutual funds to help their clients decide which to buy. Human resources managers divide insurance plans into their components to help employees understand their coverage. A movie reviewer for a news-paper evaluates a movie with division by considering its parts, such as the director, the actors, the script, and the cinematography. *How might you use classification and division in the job you hope to have after graduation? For whom will you write the classification and division? Which of the purposes for writing will that classification and division fulfill?*

When you group items or information according to their characteristics, you are **classifying**. When you take a single entity and break it down into its parts—the way the wedding cake is broken down—you are **dividing**. Classification and division can be performed separately, but they can also be performed together. Consider the way the telephone book's yellow pages are *classified* by service type, so there are listings for restaurants, insurance companies, automobile sales, hair salons, and so on. Then each classification is *divided* into components, so restaurant listings include Steak House, Bagels and More, and so on.

Combining Classification and Division with Other Patterns

When you classify, you set up categories. For example, to classify babysitters according to the quality of care they give, you could use these categories: the teenage sitter, the cleanliness nut, the inattentive sitter, the nervous sitter, and the elderly sitter.

DETERMINING PURPOSE

Purposes for Classification and Division

Purpose	Sample Classification and Division
To explain stages	A division of the grieving process people typically experience after the death of a loved one
To relate experience	A classification of childhood birthday parties
To inform (clarify similarities and differences)	A classification of the models of bicycles (racing, touring, dirt bikes, and so on) according to their chief characteristics (price, frame design, tire size, and so on)
To inform	A division of a good health club into its components so the reader can choose a health club wisely
To inform (bring a reader to a fresh way of viewing something)	A classification of kinds of vegetarianism
To persuade	A classification of telephone solicitors according to the reasons they take the job (those who are unprepared for other work, those who are housebound, and those who are disabled) to convince the reader to treat solicitors with more respect; or divide the job of telephone solicitation into its components to show how difficult it is and thereby convince readers to be more respectful

To explain the characteristics of the elements in the categories, you may combine patterns of development. For example, in a humorous classification of babysitters, the writer could describe the appearance of a slovenly sitter, narrate an account of the time a cleanliness nut washed the children *and* the walls, and illustrate the inattentive sitter who talked on the phone while the child wandered through the neighbourhood. To explain nervous sitters, writers could use a process analysis of the elaborate procedure they go through to guard against choking when feeding the child, and compare the elderly sitter to a doting grandparent. Lastly, you could define the perfect sitter.

Similarly, division can rely on other patterns. For example, an essay that divides the cell into its components could describe the parts and use process analysis to explain what they do.

Classification and division can also appear in essays developed primarily with other dominant patterns. An essay explaining the effects of social stratification might first explain the socioeconomic categories people fit into; an essay noting the causes of cheating among post-secondary students could begin with a classification of kinds of cheating; and an essay that explains how employers can effectively communicate with employees might divide an effective email into its parts. For an example of an essay that combines classification with definition and cause-and-effect analysis, see "The Ways of Meeting Oppression" on page 269.

Before Writing

A piece of writing can rely solely on classification or on division, but the two patterns of development are often logically used together. For example, in an essay about kinds of television shows, you might first classify the various kinds of programs—situation comedies, dramas, reality shows, game shows, and talk shows. Then you might use division to explain the parts of each kind of show. The following strategies can help you write essays that include both classification and division, or that include classification alone. Some of the strategies also apply to division used by itself.

Have a Principle of Classification or Division

To be meaningful, a classification must group elements according to some principle that provides the logic for the classification. We can classify teachers. One group could be those who lecture, one group could be those who use a question-and-answer format, and one group could be those who guide student discussion. The principle of classification in this case is instructional methods.

When you classify, you place elements in groups according to principles of classification. Supporting details can indicate what the groups are, what elements are in each group, and what the characteristics of the elements are. People who want to enrol in a yoga class have many different choices in terms of yoga classes, and each may be examined using an organizing principle, for example the effects of a type of yoga on the human body. You would describe the relevant aspects of the classes in each category (perhaps kind of poses, sequence, and degrees of difficulty for each. With division, you may or may not need a principle of division to govern what they do. If dividing toothpaste into its components to analyze what is in the product, you need no principle because you will mention every component. However, to classify successful game show hosts, you will need a principle—perhaps the qualities of the on-air personality that make the host, and by extension the show, watchable. It is not necessary to develop each grouping in equal detail, for some groupings may need more explanation than others. As long as all groupings are explained *adequately*, they need not be explained *equally*.

Be Sure All Categories or Components Conform to the Principle of Classification or Division

Suppose a task asks that students classify Canadian voters according to how they make up their minds, and you establish these categories: people who make decisions based on the issues, people who make decisions based on the personalities of the politicians, people who make decisions based on what friends and family think, and people who do not make decisions because they do not vote. The last category does not conform to the principle of classification and, therefore, should not be included.

Use Mutually Exclusive Categories

If an item can fall into more than one grouping, categories are not mutually exclusive, which is a problem that creates an unreliable classification. For instance, suppose when classifying news shows you establish these categories: cable, network, hard news, and soft news. Because these categories are not mutually exclusive, some shows can be placed in more than one group. CBC's *The National,* for instance, is both hard news and network. To classify, you need examples that work in just one group.

Explain Each Category or Component

To have an adequate amount of detail, you should do more than state what is in each category or note what the components of your subject are. Explain each category or component, perhaps with details about the characteristics of each one. The student essay in this chapter (page 261) classifies symbolism in a fairy tale to classify generational relationships.

Consider Audience and Purpose

Most things can be classified or divided according to more than one principle. To decide which principle to use, consider audience and purpose. Kinds of education curricula, for example, can be classified according to several principles, including cost-effectiveness and number of students who stay in the profession for more than five years. If the audience is college deans, you could use cost effectiveness as a principle of classification. The purpose could be to inform deans of how to structure education curricula to save money. However, if to convince members of local boards of education that they should consider the kind of program teacher applicants graduated from, then a better principle of classification will be students who stay in the profession for more than five years.

Audience and purpose will also affect supporting detail. Consider classifying home computers to inform a reader who knows little about computers. Writers may have to define terms like *RAM.*

BE A RESPONSIBLE WRITER

Responsible writers do not omit categories or items in categories to achieve their purpose. Consider the store-owner who classifies kinds of laptop computers in a sales brochure for customers. If the storeowner omits a particular kind of computer from the classification because the profit margin is low on that type, customers are given an incomplete classification—and one that steers them away from one purchasing option.

Responsible writers also do not unfairly or inappropriately classify people or things negatively. When classifying religions, for example, a responsible writer would not classify Western religions as enlightened and Eastern religions as unenlightened.

To be a responsible writer, ask these questions:

- Have I included every category and division relevant to my principle of classification or division?
- Have I included every item that belongs in each category?
- Are any of my classifications unfairly negative?

Organizing Classification and Division

The introduction of classification and division can be managed a number of ways. For example, you can explain the value of the classification or division. If you are classifying movies recently released on DVD and the audience consists of parents, you can explain that the classification is important because it helps parents choose suitable movies for their youngsters. If you are dividing sugared breakfast cereal into its components for parents, you should explain that the division is important because parents should understand what they are feeding their children. The introduction can also explain why a writer is qualified to classify or divide the subject.

The thesis can indicate the subject and state the ideas for classifying or dividing, like this:

> For those interested in losing weight, commercial weight-loss programs are available, but the best ones have the same components.

This thesis states that the best commercial weight-loss programs will be divided into their parts. The thesis can also include the principle of classification or division. For example, the following thesis states that teachers will be classified and gives the principle for classification.

> Some students classify teachers according to how they grade, but a better way to classify them is according to their teaching techniques, including lecture, discussion, and group work.

In body paragraphs, topic sentences can introduce each grouping or component as it is presented. Consider this thesis statement, and the topic sentences that follow: "Though many white lies are harmless, they may embarrass the teller, and inadvertently hurt someone." The following topic sentences could appear in a classification of white lies:

Most white lies are harmless.

At times, white lies prove embarrassing to the teller.

A small percentage of white lies are, unfortunately, hurtful.

At times, writers can arrange groups or components in a progressive order. For example, in the classification of white lies, the groupings can be arranged according to how serious the consequences of the lies are. Students can discuss the harmless lies first, then the embarrassing lies, then the hurtful ones. Sometimes writers can arrange groups in chronological order. For example, if classifying ways to discipline children, the writer can do so according to the age of a child.

To provide closure in a conclusion, indicate the value of the classification or division if this did not happen in the introduction. Otherwise, use one of the strategies explained beginning on page 83.

Visualizing Classification and Division

The chart that follows can help to visualize the basic organization of classification and division. Like all good models, this one can be altered as needed. For example, for a longer academic assignment, the same structure is recommended, although there will be significantly more paragraphs. The paragraphs will have strong topic sentences that reflect the thesis, or the paper's assertion. The ideas will be explained completely, and linked logically. And finally, a concluding paragraph will summarize the paper's major ideas and restate the thesis to demonstrate that the thesis is valid.

Introduction

- May engage interest by explaining
  - The value of the classification or division
  - Why you are qualified to classify or divide the subject
  - How you discovered the classification or division
- Includes a thesis that can state
  - The subject and whether you are classifying or dividing
  - The principle for classifying or dividing
  - Why you are qualified to classify or divide the subject
  - How you discovered the classification or division

First Body Paragraph

- Gives the first grouping or component in a topic sentence
- Specifies the grouping or component according to the principle of classification or division
- Explains the grouping or component, using the appropriate patterns of development
- Arranges details in a progressive or other logical order

Next Body Paragraph

- Gives the next grouping or component in a topic sentence
- Specifies the grouping or component according to the principle of classification or division
- Explains the grouping or component, using the appropriate patterns of development
- Arranges details in a progressive or other logical order

Next Body Paragraphs

- Give the remaining groupings or components, according to the principal of classification or division
- Explain the groupings or components, using the appropriate patterns of development
- Arrange details in a progressive or other logical order

Conclusion

- May elaborate on the significance of the classification or division
- Provides closure

EXERCISE WRITING CLASSIFICATION AND DIVISION

1. For one 24-hour period, list every classification and division that you encounter.

2. *Collaborative Activity.* List as many principles of classification as you can for an essay that classifies restaurants. Now list possible principles of division for an essay that divides restaurants into their components.

3. Identify a principle of classification or division for each of these subjects: friends, teachers, students.

4. Write a thesis for each subject and principle of classification or division from number 3. Each thesis should include words that indicate what you will classify or divide, or words that present the principle of classification or division.

5. Note the categories or components that could appear in an essay using one of the thesis statements from number 4.

6. Pick one of the categories identified in number 5, and list the elements in that category.

7. What patterns of development could you use to help explain the elements noted in number 6? ●

CRITICAL READING STUDENT ESSAY

The essay that follows was written by an undergraduate student. Mary Bowden examines three versions of the Little Red Riding Hood tale to classify types of female, intergenerational relationships. Note how the hood itself becomes the primary principle for examining how relationships change as the tale is retold.

Grandmother, What Big Lives You Have: Examining the Effects of Generational Relationships on Young Women Revealed in "Little Red Riding Hood"

Mary Bowden

1   The constituent components of the story of Little Red Riding Hood correlate with social structures and such correlation allows the authors of different versions of the tale to convey different ideas regarding social structures by transforming the narrative discourse. The story's constituent characters, Little Red Riding Hood and her Grandmother, embody the roles of women as social structures. Throughout the development of the story of Little Red Riding Hood, authors have altered the narrative discourse surrounding these two characters in such a way as to depict another structure, that of generational relationships between women. The first written account of Little Red Riding Hood, penned by Charles Perrault, depicts a traditional relationship between women of different

The introduction engages reader interest by claiming that successive writers depict female relationships in very different ways. The thesis statement identifies the organizing principle (the cloak) and indicates how the classification will work.

generations. Perrault's depiction allows modern authors, such as by Angela Carter and Roald Dahl, to depict different generational relationships by intentionally changing elements of Perrault's discourse in their new versions of the tale. By transforming the role of Little Red's cloak and her reaction to the wolf's attack, authors Charles Perrault, Roald Dahl, and Angela Carter relay the effect female generational relationships have on young women.

Paragraph 2 indicates that the riding hood is the connection between women of different generations and suggests that taking the hood cements a bond between the generations.

2   As suggested by the story's title, Little Red's riding hood is a significant symbol in the story. It represents the connection between Little Red and her Grandmother, who, in turn, represent the younger and older generations of women. Perrault explains Little Red's name as a derivation from the "little red riding hood" her grandmother had "made for her." The gift "suited the girl so extremely well that everyone called her Little Red Riding Hood" (Perrault). By beginning his narrative in this way, Perrault suggests that Little Red's character is defined by her Grandmother. The physical attributes of the hood connect it to another garment: the mantle. Mantles represent the wearer's definition of life; to "take on someone's mantle" is to take on their ideologies (2 Kings 2:13-4 KJV). Little Red taking the hood from her Grandmother suggests that she has taken on her grandmother's life-values as her own. This translates as a generational relationship in which ideologies do not change from one generation to the next. Dahl assumes the reader's familiarity of the symbolism of the hood created by Perrault's work and uses that familiarity to transform the depiction of generation relationships. He depicts Little Red rejecting the "silly hood" given to her by her Grandmother, much like a generation of women which chooses to shrug off the mantle of the past (Dahl 51). Little Red's name is altered to be "Miss Riding Hood," a transformation that solidifies her abandonment of the past (Dahl 49). She wears instead the work of her own hands: a wolf-skin coat gained through an act of violence. In choosing to sport this garment, Little Red symbolizes young women who have created ideologies totally separate from those of the past. Carter takes a different approach with the defining quality of the cloak, focusing on the red hood as a representation of the prepubescent, virginal state and the passage into womanhood. By choosing a nameless protagonist, Carter defines her heroine by her state and transition. Unlike Perrault and Dahl, who depict Grandmother's action as the sole component of the hood's defining aspect, Carter cites two components. The first is Grandmother, who makes and gifts the cloak. With it, she gives the burden of womanhood and the expectations her generation holds regarding virginity. The comparison of the garment to the "ominous if brilliant look of blood on snow" suggests the gravity and power connected to the loss of virginity (Carter 113). Following this comparison Carter denotes her protagonist as the second component of her virginal state: "She moves within the invisible pentacle of her own virginity" (Carter 113-4). Carter's protagonist represents a young woman who is defined both by the expectations of the past and her conscious acceptance of those expectations. This definition is comparable to that of Perrault's Little Red, as both protagonists accept the expectation of the past. The effects of conscious and unconscious acceptance, displayed in the works of Carter and Perrault respectively, is determined by how the protagonists face the past's expectations.

3   The virginity symbolized by the cloak serves a purpose apart from defining Carter's protagonist. Present in all three narratives, it conveys the value the younger generation puts on the female-specific customs and expectations handed down by older women. Perrault transforms the hood's symbolism to represent virginity towards the end of his narrative, as Little Red "[takes] off her clothes and [gets] into bed" (Perrault). Little Red removes her hood without any thought, naively believing her grandmother waits for her in the bed. The loss of her virginity in such a naïve manner suggests that Little Red's connection to the past has blinded her. Being a virgin is simply part of her, but is never examined for its importance as an entity. She exists by following an ideology that she did not create or consciously accept and so does not recognize its value. By rejecting a connection with the past, Dahl's Little Red also rejects the past's expectations regarding virginity. She sees innocence as a weight of the past, similar to the burden Carter's protagonist carries. Little Red compares her two garments, speaking through the voice of the narrator to depict one as a "silly hood upon her head" and herself describing the other as "My lovely furry wolfskin coat" (Dahl 51, 53). Dahl's Little Red is relieved to abandon her innocence and leaves the reader to judge whether she has lost or gained as she begs the reader to "please note / My lovely furry wolfskin coat" (Dahl 52-53). For Carter's protagonist, the dominant expectation handed down is abstinence. Carter depicts a girl who is unfamiliar with sexual experiences, who "does not know how to shiver" (Carter 114). Later however, she is awakened: "she shivered in spite of the scarlet shawl" (Carter 117). This suggests that the expectations connected to her hood are not totally binding or controlling of the protagonist; they do not prevent the protagonist's sexual awakening. Instead, the past's expectations of abstinence communicate the importance of sexual awakening to the protagonist and imply that her awakening should not occur until a time of equal importance. The wolf's threat of violence proves to be that time, as the protagonist is aware that she can only appease the wolf and save her life by sacrificing the "immaculate flesh" of a virgin. By throwing her cloak into the fire, the protagonist offers the wolf her virginity, burning up not only the fabric but the expectations of abstinence it represents. Both Dahl's and Carter's protagonists are liberated from the weight of innocence; Carter's protagonist allows innocence to serve its purpose before it is destroyed. Coupled with each protagonist's reaction to the wolf, these differences contrast the effects of the blind abandonment of the past's expectation and the conscious destruction of the same.

4   In each of the three narratives, Little Red's reaction to the wolf's attack is a direct result of her connection to her Grandmother. This reflects how the generational relationship between women affects young women's reactions. Numerous meanings are associated with the wolf and can be used to draw conclusions regarding Little Red's reaction; one of the most prominent elements the wolf represents is a threat to life. Carter's protagonist initially reacts to her precarious situation with the wolf with fear. She thinks of her knife, a symbol of violence, but "did not dare reach for it because his eyes were fixed upon her... full of Greek fire, diabolic phosphorescence" (Carter 117). Her first thought of violence is quickly assuaged by a second thought, one of the

Paragraph 3 examines the significance of the cloak as a symbol of virginity or chastity and considers the protagonist in all three versions of the tale.

Paragraph 4 uses the idea of the wolf's attack to highlight the connection between the generations in all three versions of the tale, and uses quotes from each to further the argument.

dangers associated with crossing the wolf's path. Her knowledge of the wolf, supplied by the past, is what generates the second thought and keeps this protagonist from engaging in violence. Carter inserts several paragraphs of thought between the protagonist's decision against reaching for her knife and her next action. She removes her shawl, simultaneously ending her fear. Her virginity is given up in full confidence of its effect; she laughs when the wolf suggests he will eat her. Having an understanding of the foundation of her past, the protagonist abandons her past with an accurate understanding of the results connected with doing so; thus she is able to think clearly and face her wolf without fear. She does not kill the wolf, but tames him instead. A bond between them is able to exist because the wisdom of the past not only enables her survival, but enables her to avoid destroying what threatens her. This is not the case with Dahl's Little Red, who reacts to the wolf's attack with instinct and ignorance. Little Red first speaks to the wolf as one might expect, commenting on his physical features. She deviates from this trend, mentioning his "lovely great big furry coat," the object by which she will redefine herself (Dahl 39). At the wolf's threat of eating her, Little Red shoots him point blank. Her reactions speak of a woman who is defined by the trail of carnage she creates and who responds to threats with carnal instinct. The actions Little Red takes against the wolf result in her loss of sexual innocence. Unlike Carter's protagonist who also gives up her virginity, Little Red reacts with violence, as she has no knowledge that suggests she should act otherwise. Her price for freedom is twice what Carter's protagonist pays; she is identified by the symbol of her bloody victory and must discard the symbol of her previous innocence. Unfortunately for Perrault's Little Red, the wisdom of the past cannot account for all the threats of the present. Little Red is rooted to her Grandmother, who is not able to equip her granddaughter to fully deal with wolves. Being incapable of thinking beyond the past, Little Red does not even recognize the wolf when she is staring right at him, describing his features. She is the victim of the wolf's desires and her own ignorance. Carter and Dahl depict women whose choices result in their fates; Perrault's protagonist does not recognize that she can make a choice.

5   The way in which Little Red Riding Hood reacts to the wolf's attack is a result of her connection to the past, represented by the defining elements of her name and her virginity symbolized by her hood. Authors Carter and Dahl transform the roles of these elements from Perrault's original written to depict three distinctly different generational relationships and their corresponding effects on the younger women therein. Perrault suggests that a young woman who takes on the ideologies of the women of the past will not recognize the value of the elements that define her and will be unable to cope with the threats of the present. Dahl concludes that a young woman who breaks from the past will have no wisdom to prevent her from functioning solely on carnal instincts. Finally, Carter sends the message that young women who appreciate and respect the past but are not defined by it allow themselves to apply past knowledge to issues of the present. Together these works communicate how different generational relationships affect young women's choices regarding violence, virginity, ideologies, and expectations.

The complete essay, including any bibliographic references, is also available on the Online Learning Centre at www.mcgrawhill.ca/olc/clouse.

Paragraph 5, the conclusion, reiterates the ideas considered in the paper, and the last sentence reiterates the thesis, that generational relationships affect young women's choices in each version of the tale.

EXERCISES

1. This essay attempts to classify the various intergenerational relationships in different versions of the Little Red Riding Hood tale. How successfully does the writer achieve her purpose?

2. Evaluate the thesis statement for this essay. Does the writer provide enough examples to demonstrate her thesis? Would the essay benefit from the inclusion of research? Where should the student writer use this research?

3. Mary attempts to prove that the popular children's tale has a significance beyond the simple story of a girl lost in a wood, pursued by a wolf. How does she demonstrate the sexual nature of the story, and are her examples specific enough to be convincing? ●

CRITIQUE, REVISE, and EDIT

In her essay, Mary attempts to classify the significance of the classic children's story's central symbol: the red riding hood. Identify its thesis statement in paragraph 1, and compare it with topic sentences further along in the essay. Mary claims, in paragraph 3, that "The virginity symbolized by the cloak serves a purpose apart from defining Carter's protagonist." Could the essay's thesis be revised, to reflect this central idea about intergenerational connections between women? Paragraph 4's topic sentence furthers the thesis, that Little Red Riding Hood's reactions to the wolf reflect how generational relationships determine social responses to perceived threats. Consider how the character's connection to the past is introduced in the thesis statement, and suggest an alternative thesis that might help the process of classification in this student essay.

CRITICAL READING PROFESSIONAL ESSAYS

Pre-reading

1. What are the characteristics of a good parent? Can we classify roles or activities?
2. Is parenting dependent on personality? Are some parents better than others?
3. What are components of parenthood? Name three essential activities parents need to undertake.

What Makes a Parent? It's Not Black or White

G. Fuscaldo

1 The advent of IVF and advances in reproductive technologies largely reflect the importance in our society of biological parenthood and genetic kinship. As illustrated in the controversy piece by

Merle Spriggs,[1] however, the same technology has confused our understanding of what makes a parent.

2   An embryo mix-up in Britain has resulted in a white couple giving birth to two black twins. Genetic tests have established that the wrong sperm was used to inseminate the ova of the white woman who gave birth to the twins. The two couples involved are apparently both seeking custody. Who should have parental rights and responsibilities for the twins?

3   While once it may have been obvious who a child's parents were and who had obligations and claims with regard to children, the separation of genetic, gestational, and nurturing roles now makes it impossible to "discover" who is the real parent. As Ruth Mackim points out, the question: "Which role should entitle a woman to a greater claim on the baby in the case of a dispute?" is a moral question which cannot be answered by discovery, say through a blood test, but is a matter for decision.[2] Which are the morally relevant factors and which have the greater moral weight with respect to claims over children? The same questions plague child custody disputes following disagreements between gestational surrogates and commissioning parents, same sex partners and gamete donors, and adoptive versus biological parents.

4   Many authors have grappled with these questions and the literature reveals at least four different accounts for the basis of parental rights and duties.

Biology

5   Perhaps the most intuitively appealing accounts of what defines parenthood and the most historically prominent are biological and reflect the view that a child belongs to, or is the flesh and blood of, its biological parents.[3] Difficulties arise in disputes between genetic and gestational parents because both have a biological investment in a child of their union. While the size of the physical contribution from the gestational parent is certainly greater than that from the progenitors, the fact that children share their genetic parents' blueprint, and that of a long line of kin, is also claimed to be significant.[4] Arguments over the relative importance of different biological investments in children (size v type) have failed to elucidate which factor is overriding and indeed why either entails "ownership" or parental rights and duties.[5]

Convention

6   It is often argued that in modern individualistic societies we have overemphasised the importance of biological relatedness. Anthropologists remind us that there exist many cultural groups with different parenting conventions—for example, where fosterage and surrogacy are not uncommon or where children are seen as a communal responsibility.[6] Even in our own culture it is argued that the many successful examples of couples who adopt or form blended families following divorce, show that biology is not the sole or the most important determinant of parenthood.[7] But the problem with a cultural account of parenthood and the apparently intractable nature/nurture debate, is that it is not at all illuminating in terms of who should have parental rights in the event of a dispute which challenges the current convention, as does the latest IVF mix-up.

Cause

7   A more prescriptive account for determining parenthood appeals to the claim that parents have rights and duties towards their children because they have caused them to exist.[8] This is the type of reasoning that is used to justify paternity testing to assign child welfare payments to genetic fathers in the case of an unintended pregnancy. Although a causal definition of parenthood conforms with our moral intuitions with regard to recalcitrant fathers it does not follow that only a child's genetic parents cause it to exist. It proves quite difficult where third parties are involved to explain who is the cause of a child's existence. A causal account of parenthood fails to distinguish between genes, gestation, and intention since all are involved in the existence of a child, even if not all contribute the most proximal or essential feature.[9]

Children's Welfare

8   Attempts to assign parental rights and duties on the basis of what is in the best interests of children are also unsuccessful in resolving disputes between genetic, gestational, and intended parents. There is much current debate about the need for a child to know and be raised by his or her genetic parents.[10] Evidence in support of claims that children raised in traditional genetically related families achieve better outcomes, has been presented across a range of criteria, including emotional and psychological identity, and educational outcomes.[11] To date this evidence remains unconvincing. A growing body of evidence is also available denying these claims and in support of the view that it is the quality of nurturing provided rather than the biological or ethnic relationship or gender balance in the rearing family that is important for children's welfare.[12]

9   What is clear is that many different features are sufficient to establish at least a *prima facie* claim to parenthood, but a coherent position on which of these is overriding in the case of competing claims has yet to emerge. It may be that this enterprise is doomed to fail because attempts to weigh up competing claims for parenthood are constrained by the historical and legal norm that a child have two, and only two parents (of the opposite sex).[13] Clearly for many people genetic and gestational parenthood are very important, as evidenced by the great lengths to which they will go to achieve it. At the same time the meanings attached to raising unrelated children for those who undertake this, are no less profound. Perhaps it is time to relinquish the view that genetic, gestational, and social parenthood are competing positions. We could align the social facts with an acceptance of the new scientific facts—that a child can have many different parents.

10   In the case of the IVF mix-up—parenthood is not black or white, but—black and white.

References

(1) Spriggs M. IVF mix up: white couple have black babies. J Med Ethics 2003:29:65.

(2) Mackim R. Artificial means of reproduction and our understanding of the family. In: Howell JH, Sale WF, eds. Life choices: a Hastings Center introduction to bioethics. Washington DC: Georgetown University Press, 1995: 294.

(3) Hall B. The origin of parental rights. Public Aff Q 1999;13:73-82, for a genetic account of parenthood based on self-ownership of genetic material.

(4) Discussed in Alpem KD. Genetic puzzles and stork stories: on the meaning and significance of having children. The ethics of reproductive technology. Oxford: Oxford University Press, 1992.

(5) A problem discussed in Silver LM, Silver SR. Confused heritage and the absurdity of genetic ownership. Harv J Law Technol 1998;11:593-618 at 600; and Kolers A, Bayne T. Are you my mommy? J Appl Philos 2001;18:273-85.

(6) For examples see Sault NL. Many mothers, many fathers: the meaning of parenting around the world. Santa Clara University Law Review 1998;36. www.scu.edu (accessed 23 July 2001). See also Donner WW. Sharing and compassion: fosterage in a Polynesian society. J Comp Fam Stud 1999:30:703-30 and Stone L. Kinship and gender. Boulder, GO: Westview Press, Harper Collins, 1997.

(7) Bartholet E. Family bonds, adoption and the politics of parenting. Boston MA: Houghton Mifflin, 1993.

(8) As argued by Nelson JL. Reproductive ethics and the family. New Zealand Journal of Bioethics 2000:1:4-10 and Nelson JL. Parental obligations and the ethics of surrogacy: a causal perspective. Public Aff Q 1991;5:49-61. See also Hill JL. What does it mean to be a "parent"? The claims of biology as the basis for parental rights. New York Univ Law Rev 1991;66:353-420 for an account of parenthood based on intent.

(9) For discussion of the problems with causal accounts of parental duties and rights see Blunstein J. Procreation and parental responsibility. J Sac Philos 1997;28:79-86; and reference 5: Kolers A, Bayne T.

(10) For examples see Turner AJ, Coyle A. What does it mean to be a donor offspring? The identity of adults conceived by donor insemination and

the implications for counseling and therapy, Hum Reprod 2000;15:2041-51; and Frith L. Gamete donation and anonymity. Hum Reprod 2001:16:818-24.

(11) Muehlenberg B. The case for the two-parent family. Melbourne: The Australian Family Association, 2001, and The historicity and universality of the natural family. Melbourne: The Australian Family Association, 2000 available through the association, www.family.org.au

(12) For a summary of research examining how children are affected by not living with two biological parents see Cherlin AJ. Going to extremes: family structure, children's wellbeing, and social science. Demography 1999;36:421-8. See also Baetens P, and. Brewaeys A. Lesbian couples requesting donor insemination: an update of the knowledge with regard to lesbian mother families. Hum Reprod Update 2001:7:512-19. Also Brewaeys A. Review: parent—child relationships and child development in donor insemination families. Hum Reprod Update 2001;7:38-46. For discussion of the significance of racial mismatches between parents and children see Fogg-Davis H. The ethics of transracial adoption. New York: Cornell University Press, 2002.

(13) As argued by Alta Charo R. Biological determinism in legal decision making: the parent trap. Texas J Women Law 1994;3:265-306.

Considering Ideas

1. According to the author, technology has "confused our understanding of what makes a parent." Explain how this is true in our world, where surrogacy and IVF treatments are common.

2. What are the three components of parenthood, according to the author? Are these categories fixed, or open to interpretation?

3. When Fuscaldo claims, "While once it may have been obvious who a child's parents were and who had obligations and claims with regard to children, the separation of genetic, gestational and nurturing roles now makes it impossible to 'discover' who is the real parent." Do you agree with this statement? How does Fuscaldo support this contention?

4. Paragraphs 5, 6, 7, and 8 of the reading account for the basis of parental rights and duties. Are these categories clearly defined, or are they open to question or interpretation?

Considering Technique

1. Fuscaldo uses headings in this brief article. How do they help to promote the thesis?

2. In what order does Fuscaldo arrange the components? Would there be a better way to separate the ideas?

3. *Combining Patterns.* What patterns of development does Fuscaldo use to develop each of the components of the distinctions between parenthood and kinship?

4. This is a scientific article from the *Journal of Medical Ethics*, and its presumed audience is the medical community. Would this article be as effective if it were published in a general-interest magazine? Would so much research be necessary?

For Group Discussion or Journal Writing

Contemplate both the social and the biological ideas of parenthood. Can we classify the roles of parents so easily in an age of open adoption, and IVF technologies? With significant changes in Western societies, will this problem be any less urgent?

Combining Patterns of Development

Pre-reading

1. Consider the state of interracial understanding now. Are there still oppressed people among us?

2. Identify what you know about Dr. King. If you know little, consider performing a webquest to learn more.

3. Has much changed for visible minorities in Canada since the middle of the last century?

The Ways of Meeting Oppression

Martin Luther King, Jr.

1   Oppressed people deal with their oppression in three characteristic ways. One way is acquiescence: The oppressed resign themselves to their doom. They tacitly adjust themselves to oppression, and thereby become conditioned to it. In every movement toward freedom, some of the oppressed prefer to remain oppressed. Almost 2,800 years ago, Moses set out to lead the children of Israel from the slavery of Egypt to the freedom of the promised land. He soon discovered that slaves do not always welcome their deliverers. They become accustomed to being slaves. They would rather bear those ills they have, as Shakespeare pointed out, than flee to others that they know not of. They prefer the "fleshpots of Egypt" to the ordeals of emancipation.

2   There is such a thing as the freedom of exhaustion. Some people are so worn down by the yoke of oppression that they give up. A few years ago in the slum areas of Atlanta, a Negro guitarist used to sing almost daily: "Been down so long that down don't bother me." This is the type of negative freedom and resignation that often engulfs the life of the oppressed.

3   But this is not the way out. To accept passively an unjust system is to cooperate with that system; thereby the oppressed become as evil as the oppressor. Noncooperation with evil is as much a moral obligation as is cooperation with good. The oppressed must never allow the conscience of the oppressor to slumber. Religion reminds every man that he is his brother's keeper. To accept injustice or segregation passively is to say to the oppressor that his actions are morally right. It is a way of allowing his conscience to fall asleep. At this moment the oppressed fails to be his brother's keeper. So acquiescence—while often the easier way—is not the moral way. It is the way of the coward. The Negro cannot win the respect of his oppressor by acquiescing; he merely increases the oppressor's arrogance and contempt. Acquiescence is interpreted as proof of the Negro's inferiority. The Negro cannot win the respect of the white people of the South or the peoples of the world if he is willing to sell the future of his children for his personal and immediate comfort and safety.

4   A second way that oppressed people sometimes deal with oppression is to resort to physical

violence and corroding hatred. Violence often brings about momentary results. Nations have frequently won their independence in battle. But in spite of temporary victories, violence never brings permanent peace. It solves no social problem; it merely creates new and more complicated ones.

5   Violence as a way of achieving racial justice is both impractical and immoral. It is impractical because it is a descending spiral ending in destruction for all. The old law of an eye for an eye leaves everybody blind. It is immoral because it seeks to humiliate the opponent rather than win his understanding; it seeks to annihilate rather than to convert. Violence is immoral because it thrives on hatred rather than love. It destroys community and makes brotherhood impossible. It leaves society in monologue rather than dialogue. Violence ends by defeating itself. It creates bitterness in the survivors and brutality in the destroyers. A voice echoes through time saying to every potential Peter, "Put up your sword."[1] History is cluttered with the wreckage of nations that failed to follow this command.

6   If the American Negro and other victims of oppression succumb to the temptation of using violence in the struggle for freedom, future generations will be the recipients of a desolate night of bitterness, and our chief legacy to them will be an endless reign of meaningless chaos. Violence is not the way.

7   The third way open to oppressed people in their quest for freedom is the way of nonviolent resistance. Like the synthesis in Hegelian philosophy, the principle of nonviolent resistance seeks to reconcile the truths of two opposites—the acquiescence and violence—while avoiding the extremes and immoralities of both. The nonviolent resister agrees with the person who acquiesces that one should not be physically aggressive toward his opponent; but he balances the equation by agreeing with the person of violence that evil must be resisted. He avoids the nonresistance of the former and the violent resistance of the latter. With nonviolent resistance, no individual or group need submit to any wrong, nor need anyone resort to violence in order to right a wrong.

8   It seems to me that this is the method that must guide the actions of the Negro in the present crisis in race relations. Through nonviolent resistance the Negro will be able to rise to the noble height of opposing the unjust system while loving the perpetrators of the system. The Negro must work passionately and unrelentingly for full stature as a citizen, but he must not use inferior methods to gain it. He must never come to terms with falsehood, malice, hate, or destruction.

9   Nonviolent resistance makes it possible for the Negro to remain in the South and struggle for his rights. The Negro's problem will not be solved by running away. He cannot listen to the glib suggestion of those who would urge him to migrate en masse to other sections of the country. By grasping his great opportunity in the South he can make a lasting contribution to the moral strength of the nation and set a sublime example of courage for generations yet unborn.

10   By nonviolent resistance, the Negro can also enlist all men of good will in his struggle for equality. The problem is not a purely racial one, with Negroes set against whites. In the end, it is not a struggle between people at all, but a tension between justice and injustice. Nonviolent resistance is not aimed against oppressors but against oppression. Under its banner consciences, not racial groups, are enlisted.

[1] The apostle Peter had drawn his sword to defend Christ from arrest. The voice was Christ's, who surrendered himself for trial and crucifixion (John 18:11). The wording is "Put up" rather than "Put down" or "Put away" in several biblical versions. See http://bible.cc/john/18-11.htm for various translations of this verse.

Considering Ideas

1. Explain the advantages and disadvantages of each way of meeting oppression.

2. King says that some oppressed people accept their oppression because they "would rather bear those ills they have.... than flee to others that they know not of" (paragraph 1). Why is this the case?

3. What does King mean when he says, "Under [the nonviolent] banner consciences, not racial groups, are enlisted" (paragraph 10)?

4. King says, "To accept passively an unjust system is to cooperate with that system; thereby the oppressed become as evil as the oppressor" (paragraph 3). What does King mean? Do you agree with him? Why or why not?

Considering Technique

1. Which sentence is the thesis of the essay?

2. What is King's principle of classification? In what order does King present his groupings?

3. What is the purpose of King's classification? How do you know?

4. *Combining Patterns.* What purpose does the cause-and-effect analysis in paragraphs 5–6 serve? What

purpose does the cause-and-effect analysis in paragraphs 8–10 serve?

5. *Combining Patterns.* What definition occurs in paragraph 7? What purpose does that definition serve? Which paragraphs include examples? What purpose do the examples serve?

For Group Discussion or Journal Writing

Martin Luther King, Jr., believed that nonviolent resistance was superior to violence because "violence never brings permanent peace" (paragraph 4). Are there ever times when violence is the best solution? Explain, using examples if possible.

 WRITING TOOL

The Dash

A comma signals a pause. Sometimes, however, writers want a pause that is longer, and more significant than the one a comma provides. In those cases, a dash is useful. The longer pause signalled by a dash provides emphasis or dramatic effect, as these examples from the readings illustrate:

From "What Makes a Parent? It's Not Black or White": "Anthropologists remind us that there exist many cultural groups with different parenting conventions—for example, where fosterage and surrogacy are not uncommon or where children are seen as a communal responsibility." (paragraph 6)

From "The Ways of Meeting Oppression": "So acquiescence—while often the easier way—is not the moral way" (paragraph 3).

For more on using the dash, see page 503.

Classification in an Image

The following advertisement for a coffee machine includes classification.

Considering the Image

1. What does the advertisement classify? What is the principle of classification?
2. In what way is the image part of the classification? In what way are the words part of the classification? How do the words and image work together to create the classification?
3. What audience does the advertisement target? What purpose does it hope to achieve?
4. How do the picture and words work together to help the ad achieve its purpose?

Reading Then Writing Classification and Division

1. In "What Makes a Parent? It's Not Black or White," Fuscaldo classifies types of parents, or parenting styles. Using the categories in the essay, or your own, classify types of parents in the 21st century.

2. In "The Ways of Meeting Oppression," Martin Luther King, Jr., classifies the ways to deal with oppression and notes which of the ways is best. In similar fashion, write an essay that classifies the ways to deal with one of the following: sexual harassment, gender discrimination, stress, depression, or peer pressure. Be sure to note which way is the most effective.

3. In "What Makes a Parent? It's Not Black or White." Fuscaldo begins with a general discussion of biology, genetics, and culture. The author then asks, "Which are the morally relevant factors and which have the greater moral weight with respect to claims over children?" List categories for the definition of parenthood, and consider cultural differences that may make an exact categorization problematic.

Classification and Division beyond the Writing Classroom

Assume you have accepted a job as a resident advisor in a first-year residence, beginning next fall term. You know that the new students have much to learn about college life, and you want to help them. Write a handout to put in every room that classifies and explains study techniques, so the new students understand the dos and don'ts

Responding to Theme

1. In this chapter's essay on parenting, the author identifies biology, convention, cause and child welfare as determinants for parenthood, considering biology and genetic kinship. Are there any other ways to classify parenthood? How have non-traditional families helped to change the basic classification for parenthood?

2. Cite one or more examples of oppression that you have experienced or observed, and explain how that oppression could be addressed using the nonviolent resistance that Martin Luther King, Jr., advocates in "The Ways of Meeting Oppression."

3. In an essay, explain why people buy fancy appliances, such as the Tassimo coffee maker in the advertisement.

4. *Connecting the Readings.* Harold Krents (see "Darkness at Noon," page 198) suffers humiliation and oppression, as did Japanese-Canadians placed in camps during World War II. Explain which of the ways of meeting oppression (see "The Ways of Meeting Oppression") the essay notes were used to deal with these two very different forms of oppression. Evaluate the success of these methods and comment on whether other methods would have been more successful.

 THE WRITING PROCESS

Classification and Division

The following guidelines are not meant to replace your successful procedures. They are here for you to try as you develop your own effective, efficient writing process.

Visualizing a Block style Comparison-Contrast Essay

The chart that follows can help writers visualize the block pattern of a comparison-contrast essay. Like all good models, this one can be altered as needed. If an assignment is longer than 1000 words, the student writer will adjust the paragraph structure and the topics under consideration. Remember to use an adequate number of transitions to indicate comparisons and contrasts. Also, remember to include clear topic sentences for each paragraph, as well as rich, compelling details to support not just the paragraph's topic, but also the thesis or "logical assertion" that the essay wants to prove. Finally, remember to craft effective summary statements, which may also lead the reader to the next paragraph in the essay.

Introduction

- Creates interest
- States the thesis, which can indicate the subjects under consideration; whether you are comparing, contrasting, or doing both; and the points of comparison or contrast to be discussed

First Body Paragraph or Paragraphs

- Will make and explain all the points about the first subject
- Can include other patterns

Next Body Paragraph or Paragraphs

- Will make and explain all the points about the second subject, which correspond to the points made and explained for the first subject
- Will make and explain points in the same order used for the first subject
- Can include other patterns

Conclusion

- Provides closure
- Leaves the reader with a positive final impression

Visualizing a Point-by-Point Comparison-Contrast Essay

The next chart will help visualize the point-by-point pattern of a comparison-contrast. *Note:* For an essay longer than 5 paragraphs or 500 words there will be more paragraphs and more ideas to consider in the essay.

Introduction

- Creates interest
- States the thesis, which can indicate the subjects under consideration; whether you are comparing, contrasting, or doing both; and the points of comparison or contrast to be discussed

First Body Paragraph or Paragraphs

- Will make the first point about the first subject and the corresponding point about the second subject
- Can include other patterns

Next Body Paragraph or Paragraphs

- Will make and explain the second point about the first subject and the corresponding point about the second subject
- Can include other patterns
- Continue until all the points are made about both subjects

Conclusion

- Provides closure
- Leaves the reader with a positive final impression

CRITICAL READING STUDENT ESSAY

The next essay was written by a student. "The Human and the Superhuman: Two Very Different Heroes," appears with marginal notes to point out key features. It is a contrast developed with a point-by-point pattern. Meant to inform, the essay's contrasts are also a comment on our society. See if you agree with the author's assessments of why Superman and Batman appeal to the public.

The Human and the Superhuman: Two Very Different Heroes

Gus Spirtos

1   In the late 1930s a small company in the fledgling comic book business decided to create something new and different for the public: the superhero. Two of the first characters to be created were opposites of one another. One had the powers of a god while the other was only a man, yet Superman and Batman were the mythic creations that set the stage for all who followed.

2   Superman was created in 1938 by two imaginative young men named Jerry Siegel and Joe Schuster. They wanted to create a character that was immensely powerful. What emerged was someone "faster than a speeding bullet, more powerful than a locomotive, and able to leap tall buildings in a single bound." The powers that Superman possessed created much reader interest. The story of the sole survivor of a doomed planet coming to earth to battle the forces of evil embodied the idealism people wanted during those

PARAGRAPH 1

The introduction engages interest with historical background. The thesis (sentences 2 and 3) notes that the subjects are Superman and Batman and that the two will be contrasted: One is godlike; the other is human.

PARAGRAPH 2

This paragraph begins a point-by-point pattern. The first points are made about the first subject (Superman). The points are why Superman was created, what he was like ("immensely powerful"), and why he appealed to people (he represented idealism).

post-Depression days. Although times have changed, the public still enjoys a bit of idealism once in a while, and Superman provides it.

PARAGRAPH 3

This paragraph covers the same points made in paragraph 2, but for the second subject (Batman): why he was created (for vengeance), what he was like (human, not "immensely powerful"), and why he appealed to people (he was a warrior). Note the topic sentence (the first) with its transition.

3   Unlike Superman, Batman was not created for idealistic purposes, but rather for vengeance. While Superman was flying far above society, Batman was stalking the seedy underside of Gotham, preying on the criminal element. Bob Kane created Batman in 1939 with the human element in mind. The public enjoyed the idea of having a hero as human as they. Also, the concept of revenge associated with the murder of Batman's parents struck a chord with the public's conscience. This troubled hero has become more popular than Superman in recent years because the rise in crime that is prevalent in society today has been represented in the Batman books. With urban society becoming increasingly violent, Batman's methods of combating crime have changed accordingly. Batman is not an idealistic role model, but rather a warrior fighting a never-ending battle.

PARAGRAPH 4

The topic sentence (the first) presents the last point of contrast: (one is benevolent and one is malevolent). The words "major differences" suggest progressive order. Notice that transitions help the writer move smoothly between subjects.

4   The major differences between Superman and Batman revolve around the former's benevolence and the latter's malevolence. Superman acts with restraint and exudes a noble, benevolent attitude. Criminals do not fear Superman because of his personality, but rather they fear his power. Batman, on the other hand, strikes fear into the criminal element with his methods and obvious *modus operandi:* the dark, threatening bat. Criminals are afraid of Batman simply because they don't know what he will do if he apprehends them. This psychological factor is employed by Batman because of his vulnerability. Fear makes the criminal sloppy, and that sloppiness makes it much easier for Batman to apprehend him or her. Because of Superman's obvious invincibility, he does not bother with such tactics. Also, because of Batman's methods, he is not much of a team player. He would rather work alone than with a group of his fellow costumed heroes. Superman, however, enjoys working with, and sometimes leading, his fellow superheroes. He is a group player.

PARAGRAPH 5

The conclusion creates closure by making a determination and looking to the future.

5   Superman and Batman have both survived for over 50 years. The reasons for their longevity are simple. Each was a pioneer character in the comic book medium. Superman showed readers that a man could fly. Batman showed them that being human isn't all that bad. The influence of each character on American culture will help both heroes survive at least another 50 years.

The complete essay, including any bibliographic references, is also available on the Online Learning Centre at www.mcgrawhill.ca/olc/clouse.

EXERCISES

1. This essay uses compare-contrast as a pattern of organization. How does the comparison/contrast work with respect to the subjects? Is there sufficient detail? Are the examples concrete enough?

2. The student writer of this essay builds an essay whose major point appears in the fourth paragraph. Consider this choice, and evaluate whether the essay's strongest point should appear near the conclusion, or earlier in the essay?

3. Would point-by-point or block style be more appropriate to organize this essay? Make a brief outline for both approaches. ●

CRITIQUE, REVISE, and EDIT

Organizing the details in a comparison-contrast essay often requires considerable thought and extensive revision. For Gus Spirtos, organizing—and reorganizing—was a primary part of his revision of "The Human and the Superhuman." An early draft of paragraph 2 looked like this:

Early draft

> Superman and Batman were the products of different inspirations. In 1938, Jerry Siegel and Joe Schuster envisioned an immensely powerful character with super powers and abilities. This character became Superman, a hero motivated by idealism, who was "more powerful than a locomotive." Unlike Superman, Batman was created with the human element in mind. In 1939, Bob Kane envisioned a hero motivated by avenging the murder of his parents. The public responded to the concept of revenge. It still responds to this concept, as urban society becomes increasingly violent. Whereas Batman is a warrior fighting a never-ending battle against crime, Superman is an idealistic role model who fights crime for high idealistic purposes.

The paragraph is structured well enough: The first sentence is the topic sentence indicating that the point of contrast is the different inspirations. However, Gus felt that the details were "squashed" into the paragraph. He also felt that using the point-by-point pattern in the paragraph made it hard to develop points. He kept feeling the need to alternate back and forth too quickly. At his teacher's suggestion, Gus reorganized to create two paragraphs. Compare the above version with paragraphs 2 and 3 in the final essay. Does the final version work better? Should Gus have made other changes?

CRITICAL READING PROFESSIONAL ESSAYS

Pre-reading

1. Though Carson titles her essay a fable, it has resonance in the real world. What are some of the most significant ecological problems today?

2. Carson presents her thesis through an allegory, or extended metaphor. How do you think she will attempt to create a sense of urgency around the issue of environmental degradation?

3. Are fables instructive? Would it be better to write an essay with scientific details instead?

A Fable for Tomorrow

Rachel Carson

1   There was once a town in the heart of America where all life seemed to live in harmony with its surroundings. The town lay in the midst of a checkerboard of prosperous farms, with fields of grain and hillsides of orchards where, in spring, white clouds of bloom drifted above the green fields. In autumn, oak and maple and birch set up a blaze of color that flamed and flickered across a backdrop of pines. Then foxes barked in the hills and deer silently crossed the fields, half hidden in the mists of the fall mornings.

2   Along the roads, laurel, viburnum and alder, great ferns and wildflowers delighted the traveler's eye through much of the year. Even in winter the roadsides were places of beauty, where countless birds came to feed on the berries and on the seed heads of the dried weeds rising above the snow. The countryside was, in fact, famous for the abundance and variety of its bird life, and when the flood of migrants was pouring through in spring and fall people traveled from great distances to observe them. Others came to fish the streams, which flowed clear and cold out of the hills and contained shady pools where trout lay. So it had been from the days many years ago when the first settlers raised their houses, sank their wells, and built their barns.

3   Then a strange blight crept over the area and everything began to change. Some evil spell had settled on the community: mysterious maladies swept the flocks of chickens; the cattle and sheep sickened and died. Everywhere was a shadow of death. The farmers spoke of much illness among their families. In the town the doctors had become more and more puzzled by new kinds of sickness appearing among their patients. There had been several sudden and unexplained deaths, not only among adults but even among children, who would be stricken suddenly while at play and die within a few hours.

4   There was a strange stillness. The birds, for example—where had they gone? Many people spoke of them, puzzled and disturbed. The feeding stations in the backyards were deserted. The few birds seen anywhere were moribund; they trembled violently and could not fly. It was a spring without voices. On the mornings that had once throbbed with the dawn chorus of robins, catbirds, doves, jays, wrens, and scores of other bird voices there

was now no sound; only silence lay over the fields and woods and marsh.

5   On the farms the hens brooded, but no chicks hatched. The farmers complained that they were unable to raise any pigs—the litters were small and the young survived only a few days. The apple trees were coming into bloom but no bees droned among the blossoms, so there was no pollination and there would be no fruit.

6   The roadsides, once so attractive, were now lined with browned and withered vegetation as though swept by fire. These, too, were silent, deserted by all living things. Even the streams were now lifeless. Anglers no longer visited them, for all the fish had died.

7   In the gutters under the eaves and between the shingles of the roofs, a white granular powder still showed a few patches; some weeks before it had fallen like snow upon the roofs and the lawns, the fields and streams.

8   No witchcraft, no enemy action had silenced the rebirth of new life in this stricken world. The people had done it themselves.

9   This town does not actually exist, but it might easily have a thousand counterparts in America or elsewhere in the world. I know of no community that has experienced all the misfortunes I describe. Yet every one of these disasters has actually happened somewhere, and many real communities have already suffered a substantial number of them. A grim specter has crept upon us almost unnoticed, and this imagined tragedy may easily become a stark reality we all shall know.

Considering Ideas

1. What point does Carson's contrast make? Where in the essay does she make her point known?

2. The town in the fable does not exist. Does that fact undermine the author's point? Why or why not?

3. "A Fable for Tomorrow" was published in 1962. Is the essay still relevant today? What does your answer say about the environmental movement?

4. In paragraph 4, Carson says it was "a spring without voices." Explain the significance of the phrase.

5. What is the "white granular powder" of paragraph 7?

6. Would you (or do you) pay money for food grown without chemicals? Why or why not?

Considering Technique

1. What subjects is Carson contrasting? Is the treatment of subjects balanced? Explain.

2. What pattern does Carson use to arrange her details?

3. Carson develops her discussion of the town after the blight in greater detail than she does her discussion of the town before the blight. Why does she do this?

4. *Combining Patterns.* How does Carson use narration? Description?

5. How does Carson make the transition from the first subject to the second?

6. How does Carson conclude her essay? Is the conclusion effective? Explain.

For Group Discussion or Journal Writing

Do you think we are doing enough to protect the environment? Explain.

Combining Patterns of Development

The following essay uses both comparison-contrast and exemplification (statistics) to support its contention that some Canadian cities are more dangerous than others. Note also how the essay uses crime statistics to argue that some Canadian cities are indeed more dangerous than others. Finally, the essay narrates the research process used to compile the data in the essay.

Pre-reading

1. How safe are Canada's major cities? Which sorts of crimes are on the increase?
2. Can we attribute the problems of safety in large cities to just one group? Explain your answer.
3. Which, before you read, is most likely Canada's most dangerous city? How do we know this?

The Most Dangerous Cities in Canada: *Maclean's* Exclusive Rankings of the Country's Most Crime-Ridden, and Safest, Cities

Ken MacQueen and Patricia Treble

1   The call from Victoria police dispatch comes about 11 p.m.: woman with a weapon threatening staff at Gorge Road Hospital. Acting Sgt. Peter Lane responds along with a second police vehicle, roof lights ablaze. Dispatch provides further details; Lane heaves a sigh and eases off the accelerator. "I almost hate to have you see this one," he tells a *Maclean's* reporter and photographer riding in his patrol supervisor's SUV. The woman is 78, in a dementia ward. She has been disarmed of her weapon: a pair of scissors. Sleepy old Victoria, he says, "it's such a stereotype." And so untrue, as the night would reveal.

2   Surprises emerged when *Maclean's* went searching for Canada's safest, and most dangerous communities. Toronto and Montreal, obvious crime-ridden candidates with their well-publicized racial tensions and gun and gang violence, rank well down a danger list of the 100 largest cities or regions in the country—those of 50,000 people or more. Montreal ranks 19th on *Maclean's* crime list and Toronto the Good (some stereotypes are true) is a sleepy 26th, gruesome headlines notwithstanding. The most notable result is the geographic distribution of Canadian crime. Halifax is the only eastern city in the top 10. The top nine—the Wild West—stretch from Winnipeg to Victoria.

3   The rankings are based on 2006 per capita crime rates, the most recent available from the Canadian Centre for Justice Statistics. *Maclean's* created a ranking based on aggregate results of six personal and property crimes: murder, sexual assault, aggravated assault (the most serious kind), robbery, breaking and entering, and auto theft. These are similar to the crimes measured and the criteria used by *Congressional Quarterly Press* for its annual "Crime In Metropolitan America" report. Detroit, followed by St. Louis, Mo., has the highest overall crime of major U.S. cities. Detroit's 2006 murder rate—47.3 per 100,000—is 10 times higher than Edmonton, which had the highest rate that year among major Canadian cities.

4   Canadians, though, can't be smug. We fare no better than the U.S. in other areas. The break and enter rates in Chilliwack, B.C., Victoria and Regina, for instance, rank within the top 10 per cent of all American cities. The per capita robbery rates in Saskatoon, Winnipeg and Regina would put them among the top 10 robbery-plagued metropolitan areas of the U.S. And you are far more likely to have your automobile stolen in Winnipeg or Joliette, Que., than anywhere in the U.S., including metropolitan Detroit and Las Vegas, the auto theft capitals of America. Even at that, a crime analysis this January by the Vancouver Board of Trade concludes official rates are misleadingly low: "only about one-third of actual crimes in Canada are reported to police." The board helped pressure Statistics Canada to consider an annual crime victimization survey. The last such measure estimated in 2004 there were more than eight million criminal offences—2.7 million of them violent—three times the number reported to police.

5   The top 10 high-crime cities in the *Maclean's* list are led by Regina, Saskatoon and Winnipeg in a near tie at between 146.3 and 144.6 per cent above the national average. Those are followed by Prince George, Edmonton, New Westminster, Chilliwack, Victoria, Vancouver and Halifax. The reasons a city makes the top 10 list vary. Winnipeg leads in auto theft at more than 334 per cent above the national average. Robberies plagued Saskatoon, Winnipeg and Regina, all at more than 200 per cent above average. Residents of Chilliwack, Victoria and Regina endured break-ins at rates more than 100 per cent above average. Regina and Saskatoon led in aggravated assault; Saskatoon in sexual assault. (Arthabaska, Que., which sits halfway between Montreal and Quebec City, was Canada's murder city, 2006, but ranked 21st in the overall rankings.)

6   For all that, these are hardly cities under siege. The worst of the crime is often visited upon the most vulnerable, those in the poorest postal codes. These are gathering places for the addicted, the psychiatrically disabled, and those who prey upon them. Canadians live with the consequences of releasing mentally ill people from institutions, says Allan Castle, in charge of crime analysis for the RCMP's Pacific region. "Like a lot of rights-based reasoning, it sometimes doesn't work in the interests of those whose rights are being protected," he says. "You have pockets of real disadvantage in some of these communities. Obviously [Vancouver's] Downtown Eastside is one, but there are demographic and geographic pockets in Regina, Winnipeg and Saskatoon, and other cities where there is a lot of social dysfunction, a lot of poverty, a lot of social inequity. Crime comes to those areas, always."

7   Certainly affluence helps shape Canada's statistically safest place, Caledon, Ont., a scenic, semi-rural suburb northwest of Toronto. It is, at least by the most recent numbers, a larger, real-life equivalent to such fictional television inventions as America's Mayberry, or Dog River, Sask., of *Corner Gas* fame—an idyllic world of carefree kids and unlocked doors, or more likely, of very good security systems. Caledon's policing district of almost 71,000 residents comes by its reputation honestly (naturally), with no murders or aggravated assaults in 2006. Caledon has the third-lowest level of robbery among the 100 areas and the lowest rates of break and enter, sexual assault and auto theft, combining for an overall crime rate of 107 per cent below the national average.

8   Next on the safe list is the region of Maskoutains, including the agricultural hub of St-Hyacinthe, in southern Quebec, with a crime rate almost 90 per cent below average, followed by Nottawasaga, Ont. Larger communities, like the sprawling suburban outskirts of Toronto, can also be safe havens: Halton Region, pop. 456,560, is fourth on the list, at 76.6 per cent below the national crime average, and York Region, pop. 947,096, ranks eighth.

9   The district of North Vancouver, across Burrard Inlet from the higher crime rates of Vancouver's downtown and east side, has Canada's sixth-lowest criminal activity. It, and the Edmonton suburb of St. Albert, in ninth place, are the only centres west of Ontario among Canada's top 10 low-crime communities. This begs a vexing question: what's wrong with the West?

10 Again, the issues and demographics vary from city to city, but poverty and marginalization, both

by race and neighbourhood, are often part of the mix. The top three high-crime communities also have proportionately the largest urban Aboriginal populations of any Canadian cities. Nine per cent of the populations of both Regina and Saskatoon are Aboriginal, as is 10 per cent, more than 68,000, of Winnipeg's population—most of them concentrated in the inner city. "The size of local Aboriginal populations is a big part of the picture," says University of Ottawa criminologist Ronald Melchers, whose recent research includes a study of policing in northern Saskatchewan. The Aboriginal population, which reached 1.2 million in 2006, is dramatically younger. Its median age is 27, compared to 40 for the Canadian population as a whole. Younger people commit substantially more crimes, regardless of race, says Melchers. The lack of strong Aboriginal cultural and family roots in urban centres make the young especially vulnerable to the allure of gangs, he says. "They head up a whole series of factors of risk: no single-family housing, poor parental guardianship, substance abuse issues, alcohol issues, histories of family violence." Melchers says. "When you sum it all up, the tragedy has a huge impact."

11 The gross overrepresentation of Aboriginals in custody is both an indicator of the problem and part of the reason it is perpetuated. In Saskatchewan, Aboriginal youth represent 75 to 90 per cent of all youth in open and closed custody, estimates a 2003 report by the Federation of Saskatchewan Indian Nations (FSIN). Often, they are both victimizer and victim. Nationally, Aboriginal people are three times more likely than non-Aboriginals to be assaulted, sexually assaulted or robbed. They are seven times more likely to be victims of homicide—and 10 times more likely to be charged with homicide. The FSIN report says Aboriginal people accounted for 55 per cent of Saskatchewan's homicide victims and 60 per cent of those accused of homicide between 1994 and 2000. There is little reason to believe that has improved.

12 In Winnipeg, as elsewhere, gang life is hardly limited to Aboriginal groups. The Hells Angels, a model of organization, pull the strings of more chaotic street gangs of every sort. Disaffected immigrants and refugees, scarred by the violent anarchy of places like Somalia and Ethiopia, form the nucleus of ultra-violent gangs like the Mad Cowz and the African Nation. "Sometimes people focus on the Aboriginal gangs," says Winnipeg police Chief Keith McCaskill, "but it's everything, it really is."

13 It's easy to paint a lurid picture in Canada's major cities of crime rampaging out of control. In fact, Canada's overall national crime rate hit its lowest point in over 25 years in 2006, led by a drop in property crimes in all provinces. Still, the violent crime rate, which climbed from the 1960s through the end of the last century, was unchanged. Headline-grabbing gun crimes, perhaps the biggest driver of public fear, were stable in 2006 for the fourth straight year. Almost 2,000 people in the Toronto area were victims of gun crime, one-quarter of the national total. Proportionately, however, Vancouver and Winnipeg had higher rates of gun victims, and Edmonton, followed by Abbotsford, B.C., had the highest rate of gun homicides.

14 The crime issue almost sent Canadians to the polls recently. The federal Conservatives had promised to trigger an election if their *Tackling Violent Crime Act* wasn't passed by March 1. It passed just under the wire, imposing mandatory minimum sentences for gun crimes, toughening bail restrictions, and cracking down on some repeat offenders, among other things. Though Melchers says most criminologists see removing judicial discretion in sentencing as "counterproductive," he concedes the Tories accurately read the public mood. "Crime makes political hay," he says. "I wouldn't want to be on the wrong side of that issue."

15 Last month's federal budget committed $400 million to recruit 2,500 new police officers across the country, a welcome assist to overtaxed departments. In B.C. and Alberta, for instance, a vibrant economy compounded by lofty house prices has left cities desperate for officers. Victoria's interim police chief Bill Naughton ended an interview by pleading, only half in jest, for *Maclean's* to publish the number of the department's recruiting office. The 222-person force is overwhelmed by a

growing workload, and by court rulings that have exponentially increased the time and complexity of moving a case to trial.

16   Victoria's crime rate stems in part from its role as the hub for government, tourism, entertainment and social services, says Naughton. "We triple our population during the day and, come the evening, by those coming into the entertainment district. About half the people we arrest aren't citizens of Victoria." Add to this the mild weather, which draws the homeless and fair-weather criminals from across the country, and the West Coast's "narco-centric universe," and you have the roots of much of the city's high rates of break and enters and robbery, he says. "We have over 1,200 chronic IV drug users, with probably 90 per cent of them within five to seven blocks of where we are," he says during an interview at downtown headquarters. "I think the image of Victoria the Good has long slipped into history."

17   A night on patrol with Lane proves Naughton's point. Although it's slow by the standards of a Thursday, with neither a gun call nor a stabbing as the night before, it is, as the chief had predicted, a different city after 11 p.m. Street-level dealers scuttle into the shadows as Lane cruises by. A tearful woman at a homeless shelter describes an assault. He attends the Salvation Army hostel to back up two members of the emergency response team there to pick up a man who breached probation for drug trafficking and a string of local break and enters. He doesn't know they're coming, and such an arrest can go either way. This guy proves remarkably passive, considering he faces 18 more months of federal prison time. His downfall was a urine drug test taken four days ago, one he knew he'd fail. He shrugs at the inevitability of it, offering up his hands for the cuffs. "Just a little bit of weed," he says, "a bit of coke."

18   An impressive run of street fights marks the hours before closing time at several downtown watering holes. Tempers fray, shirts are ripped, blood is spilt, pepper is sprayed. After Lane helps sort out one brawl, a smitten young woman totters up in her heels. "Can I have your number?" she coos. "Yes," says Lane, "911." A bloodied, belligerent few are cuffed and hauled to the cells to sober up. Most see the wisdom of the alternative: shut up, cool off, go home, save everybody a lot of paperwork. Besides, says Lane, looking at the bloody clothes of one still-thirsty combatant, "I don't think you'll pick up any ladies with a shirt like that."

19   As for the old woman and her scissors, that's another case to be handled off the books. Lane left her in the hospital cafeteria pouring out her life story to the responding constable, a man of much patience. "She's already in a hospital," says Lane. "If they can't handle her, what am I supposed to do, throw her in jail?" Like the chief said, crime stats don't tell the whole story.

The Worst and Best of Canada

The WORST 10 communities for each of six crimes and their percentage differences ABOVE the national rate

The SAFEST 10 communities for each of six crimes and their percentage differences BELOW the national rate

Murder

Arthabaska, Que.	302%
Kamloops, B.C.	221
New Westminster, B.C.	181
Medicine Hat, Alta.	176
Edmonton	154
Regina	138
Coquitlam, B.C.	126
Saskatoon	113
Fort McMurray, Alta.	111
Gatineau, Que.	95

Murder*

Beloeil, Que.	100%
Codiac, N.B.	100
Levis, Que.	100
Longueuil, Que.	100
Middlesex, Ont.	100
North Bay, Ont.	100
Port Coquitlam, B.C.	100
Red Deer, Alta.	100
Saguenay, Que.	100
Sarnia, Ont.	100

Auto Theft

Winnipeg	334%
Joliette, Que.	241
Chilliwack, B.C.	201
Edmonton	174
Prince George, B.C.	167
Surrey, B.C.	143
Abbotsford, B.C.	134
Regina	122
New Westminster, B.C.	112
Maple Ridge, B.C.	92

Auto Theft

Tracadie-Sheila, N.B.	67%
Nottawasaga, Ont.	69
North Bay, Ont.	70
Victoria County, Ont.	70
Halifax County, N.S.	71
Stormont, Dundas & Glengarry Counties, Ont.	74
Fredericton	74
Wellington County, Ont.	77
Oromocto, N.B.	77
Caledon, Ont.	80

Aggravated Assault

Regina	223%
Saskatoon	204
Prince George, B.C.	195
Brantford, Ont.	166
Thunder Bay, Ont.	156
Fort McMurray, Alta.	152
Edmonton	110
Red Deer, Alta.	87
Winnipeg	87
Lethbridge, Alta.	86

Aggravated Assault

Beloeil, Que.	94%
Caledon, Ont.	100
Granby, Que.	100
Middlesex, Ont.	100
Mirabel, Que.	100
Petrolia, Ont.	100
Repentigny, Que.	100
St. Albert, Alta.	100
Trois-Rivieres, Que.	100
Woodstock, Ont.	100

*Above are some of the 35 areas that had no murders in 2006

Sexual Assault

Saskatoon	93%	Arthabaska, Que.	56%
Brantford, Ont.	72	Richmond, B.C.	57
Halifax	71	Beloeil, Que.	58
Peterborough, Ont.	66	Halton Region, Ont.	58
Saint John, N.B.	59	Maskoutains MRC, Que.	60
Prince George, B.C.	54	North Vancouver, B.C.	64
Kelowna, B.C.	53	York Region, Ont.	64
Woodstock, Ont.	51	Nottawasaga, Ont.	67
Winnipeg	50	St. Albert, Alta.	69
Saguenay, Que.	50	Caledon, Ont.	81

Robbery

Saskatoon	243%	Nottawasaga, Ont.	83%
Winnipeg	221	Oromocto, N.B.	86
Regina	209	Maskoutains MRC, Que.	87
Vancouver	191	Lac-St-Jean-Est MRC, Que.	88
Halifax	186	Middlesex, Ont.	88
Montreal	133	Petrolia, Ont.	92
New Westminster, B.C.	129	Wellington County, Ont.	93
Prince George, B.C.	116	Caledon, Ont.	94
Edmonton	101	Tracadie-Sheila, N.B.	96
Burnaby, B.C.	99	Victoria County, Ont.	96

Breaking and Entering

Chilliwack, B.C.	131%	Tracadie-Sheila, N.B.	51%
Victoria	122	Wellington County, Ont.	53
Regina	104	Stroud, Ont.	53
Nanaimo, B.C.	103	Nottawasaga, Ont.	54
Burnaby, B.C.	95	Peel Region, Ont.	54
Vancouver	86	Halton Region, Ont.	54
Prince George, B.C.	85	York Region, Ont.	56
Kelowna, B.C.	74	Maskoutains, MRC, Que.	58
Saskatoon	70	Stormont, Dundas & Glengarry Counties, Ont.	58
Abbotsford, B.C.	64	Caledon, Ont.	75

Canada's Crime Map: The East-West Divide

With nine of the 10 worst crime scores belonging to cities in Manitoba, Saskatchewan, Alberta, and B.C., Halifax deprived the West of a clean sweep by taking the No. 10 spot. For comparison, Maclean's has included big cities and provincial capitals with populations over 50,000.

CRIME SCORE

Percentage above the national rate		Percentage below the national rate	
Victoria No. 8	77%	Toronto No. 26	12%
Vancouver No. 9	73	Ottawa No. 57	28
New Westminster No. 6	87	Quebec No. 50	22
Chilliwack No. 7	84	Fredericton No. 53	24
Prince George No. 4	115	St. John's No. 63	31
Calgary No. 33	2		
Edmonton No. 5	88		
Saskatoon No. 2	146		
Regina No. 1	146		
Winnipeg No. 3	145		
Montreal No. 19	34		
Halifax No. 10	72		

ON THE WEB: For more exhaustive crime statistics, go to macleans.ca/dangerouscities

Considering Ideas

1. The feature from *Maclean's* magazine is a factual exploration of safety in Canadian cities. It uses anecdotes from a night on patrol in Victoria. What is the effect of the inclusion of narration from a night on patrol?

2. This feature ends with a discussion of the study's methodology and statistics to support the article's claims. How does the inclusion of research, and the tables at the end, bolster this comparative study of safety in Canadian cities?

3. This article draws conclusions based on comparative statistics, and ranks cities. It is almost entirely factual. How does the article account for crime in some of the worst-affected communities?

4. MacQueen and Treble make frequent comparisons to some of the best (and worst) cities in the US, and also to fictitious cities immortalized on television. How do these comparisons bear out the study's conclusions?

5. While there are comparisons of cities in Canada using statistics, there are also demographic reasons for the poor community safety in some Canadian cities. These are based on expert opinion. How does this balance of fact and opinion further the compare/contrast analysis?

Considering Technique

1. MacQueen and Treble use mainly comparison/contrast to develop this article. Would it be helpful to rely on other patterns of development? Which ones?

2. Much of the information in the analysis is statistical. Would more description of community problems help to explain the reasons for the violence (or lack of violence) in some Canadian cities?

3. Much of this article is based upon empirical data. Would the inclusion of grassroots or local voices help the reader gain a better understanding of why certain communities are so plagued by crime?

4. The article's authors claim that cities are "hardly under siege." What purpose would this statement have, given that the article's statistics seem rather alarming?

For Group Discussion or Journal Writing

How would you describe the city in which you live? Which criteria do students use to measure the safety of a city? What are some practical solutions for the problems in Canadian cities? If much crime is due to disaffected youth, how can young people be rehabilitated, or how can communities prevent crime from happening?

Comparison-Contrast in an Image

Comparison-contrast is a common component of advertisements because advertisers often compare products to the competition. However, the Canadian Club advertisement uses comparison a different way.

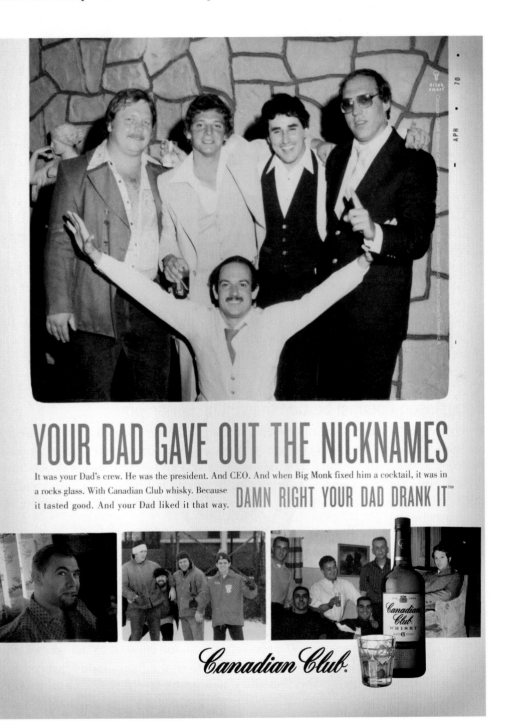

Considering an Image

1. What subjects does the advertisement consider? What is the relationship to the product? How does the comparison work? Are these subjects compared, contrasted, or both compared and contrasted? How does the ad work with implicit suggestions?
2. In what way does the advertisement say that male gender roles have changed? How have they stayed the same?
3. What assumptions does the advertisement make about the reader?
4. A comparison is at the heart of the slogan used by Canadian Club. The ad claims that "your dad gave out the nicknames." What does this suggest about men during the 60s, and men today? What does it suggest about male relationships? How have they changed?

Reading Then Writing Comparison-Contrast

1. A fable is a story, written in a simple style, with a moral or lesson. Write a fable in the style of Rachel Carson's "A Fable for Tomorrow" that compares and/or contrasts life today with life as it would be if population growth continued unchecked, if drug usage continued to escalate, or if some other problem continued unresolved. Be sure a moral or lesson is apparent.
2. Select two popular politicians, musicians, actors, or comedians with very different styles. Like Gus Spirtos did in "The Human and the Superhuman," contrast the two and explain why each appeals to the public.
3. Select two opposite types, such as the health nut and the junk food addict, the procrastinator and the planner, the impetuous and the thoughtful, or the studious and the slacker. Write a humorous contrast that shows the superiority of the one generally looked down upon.

Comparison-Contrast beyond the Writing Classroom

If you have a job, interview your boss and ask him or her to discuss the similarities and differences between your company or business and a competitor's. Then write up the comparison-contrast for a training manual that explains to new employees how the company stacks up against a competitor. If you do not have a job, interview the owner or manager of a company on campus or in the community, and complete the same assignment.

Responding to a Theme

1. In "A Fable for Tomorrow," Rachel Carson points out that we are destroying our environment. "Fable" first appeared in Carson's *Silent Spring* in 1962. Do you think our treatment of the environment has improved since the essay was published? Cite specific examples to support your view.
2. The advertisement on page 297 uses comparison and contrast to sell whisky, and uses retro graphics to send a strong message. Consider liquor industry advertisements (i.e. beer, wine, spirits) that you find in print, on television, or on radio or Internet. Write a brief essay that explains which strategies are used, and why.

THE WRITING PROCESS

Comparison-Contrast

The following strategies are not meant to replace your own successful procedures. They are here for you to try as you develop your own effective, efficient writing process.

- For a topic, consider the similarities between two subjects generally thought of as different, or consider the contrasts between two subjects generally viewed as similar. For example, an essay noting the differences between getting a degree and getting an education can clarify the real essence of education, despite the fact that "getting a degree" is commonly equated with "getting an education." Or compare apples and oranges; are they really that different, considering they are both fruit?

- Determine purpose by asking yourself these questions:
  - Do I want to clarify the nature of one unfamiliar subject by placing it next to a more familiar subject?
  - Do I want to lend a fresh insight into one subject by placing it next to another?
  - Do I want to bring one or both of my subjects into sharper focus?
  - Do I want to show that one of my subjects is superior to the other?

- To identify and assess your audience, answer the questions on page 43.

- To generate ideas, list every similarity and difference you can think of for your subjects. Write everything that occurs to you without evaluating your ideas. Use a graphic organizer to help.

- Ask whether your list suggests that you need a specific basis of comparison. If so, write that out. Then cross out and add ideas based on your basis of comparison, audience, and purpose.

- Even if you do not usually write one, remember that a formal outline makes organizing comparison-contrast easier. Be sure to check your outline for balance.

Think like a Writer: Drafting

- Draft a working thesis that mentions your subjects and whether you will compare, contrast, or both. Now draft a second working thesis that also mentions your points of comparison or contrast. Which thesis do you prefer?

- Using your outline as a guide, write your draft.

- As you draft, think about using topic sentences, so your reader understands which points and subjects you are dealing with every step of the way.

Critique, Revision, and Editing

- Consider why your comparison-contrast will interest your reader. If you do not know why, reconsider your subjects.

- Underline your thesis. Does it mention your subject and indicate whether you are comparing, contrasting, or doing both?

- Be sure you are discussing the same points for each subject of your essay.

- Read your draft aloud. If you hear awkward shifts from subject to subject or from point to point, add transitions like *similarly, in the same way, on the other hand,* or *in contrast.* Or repeat key words.

- To obtain reader response for revision, see pages 101–102. In addition, ask your reader to do the following:
  - Place a check mark where more detail is needed.
  - Place a question mark where something is unclear.
  - Place an exclamation point next to any particularly strong ideas or phrasings.

Correcting Errors and Proofreading

- Use the "Guide to Frequently Occurring Errors" for reference, and check with a writing centre tutor if you are unsure about a grammar, usage, or punctuation point.
- Use the **comparative form** of adjectives and adverbs to compare and contrast two items and the **superlative form** to compare and contrast more than two items.

Base form	Comparative form	Superlative form
old	older	oldest
eager	more eager	most eager
swiftly	more swiftly	most swiftly
good	better	best

No: Both the machinists' union and the flight attendants' union are negotiating new contracts, but the machinists have the *best* chance of receiving a pay raise.

Yes: Both the machinists' union and the flight attendants' union are negotiating new contracts, but the machinists have a *better* chance of receiving a pay raise. (Only two unions are compared, so use the comparative form.)

No: Of all the East Coast hospitals with trauma centres, our city medical centre admitted *more* burn victims.

Yes: Of all the East Coast hospitals with trauma centres, our city medical centre admitted *the most* burn victims. (More than two hospitals with trauma centres are compared, so use the superlative form.)

For more on comparative and superlative forms, see pages 493–494.

- Proofread your final copy before handing it in. If you are submitting an electronic copy, proofread from a paper copy. Read very slowly, lingering over every word and punctuation mark.

Remember

Avoid stating the obvious. For example, if you are comparing two cars, you need not mention that both cars have engines, although mentioning the size of the engines is appropriate.

Cause-and-Effect Analysis

Looking Ahead

Because we are uncomfortable with uncertainty, we want to know why events occur and what the results of events will be. Why have there been so many hurricanes lately? What will happen to the housing market if interest rates rise? Why do prescription drugs cost so much? Why doesn't your car get better mileage? How are the new scholarship guidelines affecting student recruiting? When we answer questions like these to determine the reasons for or the results of events, we engage in cause-and-effect analysis. Before learning how to write cause-and-effect analyses, consider the pictured apparatus, known as Newton's Cradle. When a ball on the end is swung as a pendulum into the next ball, the ball on the opposite end is hit away at the same speed as the first ball—but the middle balls barely move. The same phenomenon occurs if two balls are knocked into the others: Two balls on the other end are hit away at the same speed, but the middle balls barely move.

- Newton's Cradle is commonly used for demonstration in physics classes. Why would physicists be interested in the cause-and-effect relationship demonstrated by Newton's Cradle?

- Newton's Cradle is a popular desktop toy for business executives. What cause-and-effect relationship explains that popularity?

Why is Cause-and-Effect Analysis Important?

We enjoy a good mystery book or movie, but we don't necessarily like mysteries in real life. If we do not understand why something happens or what might result from an event, we don't say, "What a good mystery!" Instead, we feel unsettled, even anxious. Thus, an understanding of causes and effects helps us make sense of the world and live more comfortably in it. For example, cause-and-effect analysis can help us understand the past if we identify the causes of the stock market crash in 1929 and determine how that event is similar to, or different from, the financial crisis that occurred at the end of 2008. Cause-and-effect analysis can also help us envision the future, as when we predict the effects of the current air pollution rate on the quality of life 20 years from now.

Cause-and-effect analysis can also help us plan, make decisions, and implement important changes. For example, by considering the effect of investing a certain amount of money every month, a person can estimate the amount of money he or she will have upon retirement and decide whether to save additional money. By examining the reasons for a poor grade on a test, a student can adjust his or her study habits for the next exam. Cause-and-effect analysis even helps keep us safe. For example, an understanding of the effects of high cholesterol can lead us to avoid certain foods in order to protect our hearts.

Cause-and-effect analysis begins with a question about something we've noticed in the world around us. Academically, we may call this a research question. Causes and effects exist in a linear relationship to an event, problem, situation, or phenomenon. Causes **lead to** an event, problem, situation, or phenomenon, while effects are the **results or consequences**. You may notice effects before you identify a problem, but when you wish to analyze effects you mention the situation or problem first. Likewise, when you see a problem, you may then investigate its causes. However, when you write about the problem you identify the causes as prior to a situation. When you write cause and effect analysis, you also need to establish direct or indirect causes of a phenomenon or problem, and clearly demonstrate the relationship of causes, effects, or both, to the central issue. You will signal what you plan to prove in the thesis statement, in the order in which you will develop your analysis. Consider the relationship of causes and effects to a problem or situation this way:

Events, activities, or actions lead to …	an event, a problem, a situation, or a phenomenon in culture or society,	which may have numerous effects or consequences.

Here is an example that treats both causes and effects. Cell phones are everywhere, so naturally we are curious about the impact of this technology on behaviour. Why do people talk on their phones in restaurants and annoy other diners? How do cell phones affect automobile accident rates? How do cell phones affect the social lives of teenagers? In the following excerpt, *New Scientist* magazine even considers whether using a cell phone improves concentration (the situation or phenomenon, as above).

Hot Brains

Mobile phone users can concentrate better even when they're not using their phones, say researchers in Hong Kong. Previous studies have suggested that people's brains function better when they are exposed to microwave radiation like that emitted by mobile phones. So Chetwyn Chan and his colleagues from the Hong Kong Polytechnic University compared teenagers who owned a mobile phone with those who did not. The phone users scored higher on a test of attention, even when their phones were switched off, suggesting that the beneficial effect could be long-lasting (*NeuroReport*, vol. 12, p. 729).The researchers caution that they're not sure that using a phone causes the boost—it could simply be that mobile users tend to be better at performing several tasks at once.

When we ask why an event or action occurs or occurred—such as why cell phone users concentrate better—we are considering **causes**. When we ask what results or resulted from an event—such as what happens to concentration when people use cell phones—we are considering **effects**. The study of causes, effects, or both causes and effects is **cause-and-effect analysis**.

OCCASIONS FOR WRITING

Cause-and-Effect Analysis across the Disciplines and Beyond

Cause-and-Effect Analysis in the Classroom

Cause-and-effect analysis is one of the most frequently used patterns in college writing. For instance, in a paper for an economics class, students might explain what causes the federal government to raise and lower the prime interest rate. In a midterm history exam, student writers might explain the causes and effects of the Industrial Revolution. In a research paper for a Botany class, writers might explain the effects of logging on plant diversity. *How do you think students might use cause-and-effect analysis in an examination for an education class? In an essay for a history class? In a research paper for a psychology class? Why do you think cause-and-effect analysis is so useful in so many courses?*

Cause-and-Effect Analysis in Daily Life

Cause-and-effect analysis is very common in personal writing. For example, in a letter to the editor of a local newspaper, one might write about what may happen if voters do not pass a bond issue. In a letter to a customer service representative, one might note the reasons for dissatisfaction with a product. In a family newsletter, a writer might list the effects of a decision to move to a new city or change jobs. *When you have a difficult decision to make, how can writing cause-and-effect analysis help you make that decision?*

Cause-and-Effect Analysis on the Job

Many professions involve writing cause-and-effect analysis. A sales representative might detail the reasons for a sales decline. A human resources officer might write a report predicting the effects of changing insurance plans. A nurse will chart the effects of a particular treatment on a patient. *How might a marketing manager use cause-and-effect analysis? What about an advertising executive? A school principal?*

The chart that follows illustrates the range of purposes that cause-and-effect can serve.

DETERMINING PURPOSE

Purpose	Sample Cause-and-Effect Analysis
To entertain	A humorous account of the effects of technology on the average person
To express feelings	An explanation of the effects of being the child of divorced parents and changing households frequently
To relate experience	A narration about a boating accident that caused a fear of water
To inform	An explanation of what causes the consumer price index to rise and fall
To inform	An explanation of the effects of divorce on teenagers
To persuade (to convince the reader that your city government is not responsible for the blight downtown)	An explanation of the causes of urban blight
To persuade (to convince parents to limit the time children spend viewing television)	An explanation of the effects of watching reality television

Combining Cause-and-Effect Analysis with Other Patterns

Other patterns of development often help support cause-and-effect analysis. Exemplification is one of them. Suppose you explain the effects of moving to a new town when in seventh grade, and one of those effects was that you felt like an outsider. You could illustrate this point with the example of the time no one wanted to sit with you at lunch.

You can also use description. For example, discussing the effects of dumping industrial waste into rivers, you can describe the appearance of a river that has had industrial waste dumped into it.

Narration can also appear in a cause-and-effect analysis. Say you want to explain why there has been a call for better-trained airport security personnel in the wake of the September 11, 2001, terrorist attacks. To support this point, you can tell the story of the time a major airport was shut down because security staff had left a metal detector unplugged.

Process analysis can also be used. Assume you are explaining the long-term effects of using pesticides, and mention that pesticides work their way into the food chain. To support this point, you can describe the process, showing readers how the pesticide goes from soil to plant to animal to human.

Readers will also encounter cause-and-effect analysis in essays developed primarily with other patterns. If narrating an account of a visit to a childhood home, you might include a discussion of how you were affected by the visit. Explaining the process of batiking, you might note what causes the cracking effect in the finished art. If comparing and contrasting two cities, you might explain what causes pollution to be lower in one of them. Cause-and-effect analysis can be a part of any essay, no matter what the dominant pattern of development.

For an example of an essay that combines cause-and-effect analysis, description, exemplification, and contrast, see "Our Schedules, Ourselves" on page 314.

Before Writing

"Hot Brains," the selection from *New Scientist* magazine that opens this chapter, illustrates an important point about supporting detail in a cause-and-effect analysis: Causes and effects are not always clear cut. For that reason, the researchers mentioned in the piece allow for the possibility that cell phones do not improve concentration; instead, cell phone users may be better at multi-tasking. Keeping this example in mind and using the following strategies will help you choose details carefully.

Report Multiple Causes and Effects

A situation can have many effects; and a situation or problem can have many causes. If you overlook these multiple causes and effects, you will be oversimplifying. Consider, for example, the construction of a shopping plaza on a quiet street. The effects may be many, including increased traffic congestion, more automobile accidents, higher taxes paid to the local government, more part-time jobs for teenagers, and the need for increased police protection. If you omit discussing any of these effects, the analysis is incomplete. Now consider an announced tuition increase at your college or university. The causes for the increase are likely to be several, including a reduction in provincial subsidies, reduced enrolment, the need to pay higher salaries to attract the best professors, and rising costs generally. If you omit discussing any of these causes, the reader will fail to understand the full motivation for the increase.

Identify Underlying Causes and Effects

Some causes and effects are obvious; others are beneath the surface, so they are *underlying, or indirect* causes or effects. Be sure to identify and discuss these underlying causes and effects. For example, examining the causes of the high divorce rate, you might note the increase in two-career marriages. This would be an obvious cause. A closer examination of this cause, however, would reveal underlying causes: Two-career marriages mean less clearly defined roles, less clearly defined divisions of labour, added job-related stress, and increased competition between partners. If discussing effects, then consider underlying effects. For example, if you examine the effects of being the youngest child in a family, one obvious effect is that the youngest is considered "the baby." Look beyond that obvious effect to the underlying effects: The youngest can come to view him- or herself as the baby and hence less capable, less mature, and less strong; the youngest, viewed as a baby, may not be taken seriously by other family members.

Prove That Something Is a Cause or an Effect

You must do more than merely state that something is a cause or an effect; you must provide evidence to prove it. Remember that to have adequate detail and convince the reader, you must show and not just tell. For example, suppose while analyzing the effects of low pay for daycare workers, you note that low pay causes talented people to spurn Early Childhood Education (ECE) as a career. To back up this statement, you could survey bright students and ask them whether they would consider ECE as a career and ask them why or why not. If a significant percentage cites low pay as a reason not to choose ECE as a career, it is worth mentioning this in the essay.

Identify Immediate and Indirect Causes

Immediate causes occur near the time of an event, while *indirect* causes occur in a more distant time. For example, consider a cause-and-effect analysis of the shortage of nurses in your province. An immediate cause is that provincial funding reductions have reduced the number of nurses in local hospitals and thereby have reduced the number of nurses in the province. A more remote cause is the post–World War II baby boom that has given us record numbers of aging Canadians in need of medical care. It is tempting to assume that immediate causes are more significant than remote ones, but that is not always true. In the case of the shortage of nurses, the remote cause may be the more important one.

Reproduce Causal Chains

A **causal chain** occurs when a cause leads to an effect and that effect becomes a cause, which leads to another effect, and that effect becomes a cause leading to another effect, and so on. To understand causal chains, consider the effects of raising the cost of a stamp.

First, Canada Post raises the price of a postage stamp. What is the effect? Once the cost of the stamp goes up, it costs more to mail a letter. That is the first effect. This effect becomes a cause: It causes office expenses to rise for companies. What is the effect of this cause? The cost of doing business increases. This effect becomes a cause: It causes companies to raise the prices on their goods and services. What is the effect? Consumers cannot afford the increase, so they buy less. This effect becomes a cause: It causes the economy to slow down. Causal chains like this one are valuable parts of a cause-and-effect analysis.

CAUSAL CHAIN

Cause		Effect
Canada Post increases price of stamp	→	Cost of mailing letter increases
Cost of mailing letter increases	→	Business expenses increase
Business expenses increase	→	Cost of doing business increases
Cost of doing business increases	→	Companies raise prices of goods and services
Companies raise prices of goods and services	→	Consumers buy less
Consumers buy less	→	The Canadian economy slows

Or, in more literary terms, this proverbial rhyme about causal chains has been around since the 14th century:

> For want of a nail, the shoe was lost.
> For want of a shoe, the horse was lost.
> For want of a horse, the rider was lost.
> For want of a rider, the battle was lost.
> For want of a battle, the kingdom was lost.
> And all for the want of a horseshoe nail.

Explain Why Something Is or Is Not a Cause or an Effect

Sometimes explaining why something is a cause or effect is necessary. For example, assume that one effect of divorce on young children is to make them feel responsible for the breakup of their parents' marriage. It is necessary to explain why: Young children think that if they had behaved better, their parents would not have fought so much and would have stayed married.

Sometimes a cause-and-effect analysis must explain that something is *not* a cause or effect. Consider the causes of math anxiety among women. If the reader believes that women are genetically incapable of excelling in math, then the writer should note that this explanation is untrue and explain *why* it is not true: No studies have proved that anyone is good or bad at mathematics because of gender.

BE A RESPONSIBLE WRITER

Sometimes writers exaggerate causes or effects to achieve their writing purpose. We see this often in advertising where the effect of a new detergent is said to be "dazzling" whites or the effect of a moisturizer is said to be "a radiant, youthful appearance." We may try these products and be disappointed when we do not need sunglasses to view our white clothes or when we are not asked to show an ID when we see an R-rated movie. Clearly, such exaggeration is misleading.

Writers also mislead if they omit causes or effects to achieve their writing purpose. Perhaps you are analyzing the effects of computers on higher education because you want to convince a university to put computers in every residence room. You may be tempted to omit mentioning that students can become distracted by surfing the Internet for extended periods, because this effect does not help achieve a purpose. However, the omission contributes to an incomplete analysis. Rather than omit it, you should mention it and counter it in some way, perhaps like this: "With easy access to computers, students may be tempted to surf the Internet for extended periods. However, that is not necessarily wasted time because Net surfing offers important relaxation for students."

To be a responsible writer, ask these questions:

- Have I exaggerated any causes or effects?
- Have I identified and explained multiple causes or effects?
- Have I omitted any causes or effects?

Academic dishonesty has many causes, but its effects can be disastrous for a student. In many of the "Be a Responsible Writer" sections, we have learned ways to avoid plagiarism. In this section, it seems logical to discuss one of the chief causes of plagiarism: Many students knowingly commit acts of plagiarism because they mistakenly believe that plagiarism is a victimless offense, that it is harmless to others. However, the effects of plagiarism are actually very serious, and they can create a causal chain with effects that *can* harm other students. Honest students may not be able to compete successfully with students who cheat, and they may have lower grades as a result, causing them to lose scholarships, recommendations, and jobs. Further, students who cheat and get caught risk severe academic penalties.

Consider Audience and Purpose

Audience and purpose will determine the details to include. For example, if explaining what causes the consumer price index to rise and fall to classmates in Intermediate Economics, you need not define *consumer price index* because intermediate economics students have learned the definition already. However, a definition would be helpful to the average reader of a city newspaper because, while readers have heard of the consumer price index, they may be unsure of exactly what it is. If analyzing the effects of advertising aimed at children in order to share an experience with a child, you might narrate an account of how a child reacted to advertisements for sweetened cereal. However, if the purpose is to convince your reader that advertising should not be aimed at children, one parent's experience with one child is insufficient, so it becomes necessary to do research to find data on how children in general react to advertisements for sweetened cereal.

Organizing Cause-and-Effect Analysis

The thesis for a cause-and-effect analysis can indicate the subject, problem, situation, or phenomenon under analysis. It can also note whether you will discuss causes, effects, or both causes and effects.

Thesis indicating that the essay will analyze causes:

> To solve the problem of teenage drug abuse, we must first understand peer pressure, curiosity, and media images, which lead teenagers to take drugs.

Thesis indicating that the essay will analyze effects:

> Not everyone realizes the devastating effects unemployment has on a person's self-image, confidence, and economic situation.

Thesis indicating that the essay will analyze both causes and effects:

> The financial reasons for municipalities cutting aid to the homeless are understandable, but the social effects of this action will be devastating.

You can arrange the detail for cause-and-effect analysis a number of ways. Often a progressive order is best. In a progressive order, the most significant or obvious causes or effects are given first, and you work progressively to the least significant or obvious causes or effects. You can also move from the least significant or obvious to the most significant or obvious.

A chronological arrangement is possible if the causes or effects occur in a particular time order. If you are reproducing causal chains, a chronological order is a likely choice, since one cause will lead to an effect, which becomes a cause for yet another effect.

Sometimes you will group causes and effects in particular categories. Suppose you want to explain what causes teenagers to drop out of high school. You could group together all the causes related to home life, then peer pressure, and then the academic environment. Each section will require specific, detailed development.

The introduction of a cause-and-effect analysis can be handled in any of the ways described in Chapter 3. Another approach is to explain why understanding the cause-and-effect relationship is important. For example, to provide reasons for adolescent drug use, an introduction could provide the reasons for drug use, and note that understanding the reasons for the problem is a first step toward solving the problem.

If an essay will treat the causes of a problem, the introduction can provide a brief summary of the chief effects of the problem, before proceeding. To explain why fewer people are entering the teaching profession, an introduction can note some of the chief effects of this phenomenon: fewer qualified teachers, a decline in the quality of education, and larger class sizes. Similarly, if an essay will explain the effects of something, the introduction can note the chief causes. For example, if an essay will discuss the effects of increased tuition fees at school, an introduction can briefly explain the causes of the increase: lower enrolment generating less income, higher operating costs, or perhaps an expensive building program.

The conclusion of a cause-and-effect analysis can be handled in any of the ways explained in Chapter 3. Often a cause-and-effect analysis ends with a conclusion drawn from the cause-and-effect relationship. For example, if an essay has shown what the causes of teenage drug abuse are, it could end with the conclusion that suggests the best way to combat the problem. A summary can also be an effective way to end. If the cause-and-effect relationship is complex, with several causal chains, the reader may appreciate a final reminder of the complete picture.

EXERCISE WRITING CAUSE-AND-EFFECT ANALYSIS

1. Check textbooks in other courses, as well as newsmagazines and newspapers, for a piece of writing that includes cause-and-effect analysis. Read the selection and answer these questions:
    a. Does the cause-and-effect analysis form the primary pattern of development, or is it part of a piece developed primarily with another pattern?
    b. Are causes, effects, or both discussed?
    c. What purpose does the cause-and-effect analysis serve?

2. Pick an important decision you made sometime in your life (quitting a club or team, choosing a college or university, moving away from home, and so on). Make one list of everything that caused you to make your decision. Then make a second list of all the effects of your decision.

3. Study your list, try to identify one causal chain, and list every cause and effect in that chain.

4. Study your list again. If you were to write an essay from the list, would you treat causes, effects, or both? Why? What audience and purpose would you identify for the essay?

5. Would you note anything that is not a cause or an effect? If so, what?

6. *Collaborative Activity.* With two or three classmates, identify a problem on your campus (parking, course availability, lack of computers, overcrowded residence halls, and so on). Then make a list of all the causes of the problem and a second list of all the effects. Next, select two of the causes or effects and do the following:
    a. Identify a possible audience and purpose for a cause-and-effect analysis of the problem.
    b. Explain what supporting detail you would use to develop the selected causes or effects. ●

Visualizing a Cause-and-Effect Analysis

The chart that follows can help to visualize one structure for a cause-and-effect analysis. Like all good models, this one can be altered as needed. Like all essays, an outline for a cause-and-effect analysis needs a strong introduction, numerous examples or details, transitions between ideas, and a strong summary or conclusion. Note: the plan in the diagram is a plan for a five-paragraph essay. Academic essays are considerably longer. The basic structure is the same, however.

Introduction

- May engage interest by noting important effects if you are analyzing causes or by noting important causes if you are analyzing effects
- Includes a thesis that mentions the subject and whether causes, effects, or both will be discussed

---

First Body Paragraph or Paragraphs

- Will state the first cause or effect
- May reproduce causal chains
- May explain why something is or is not a cause or effect
- May identify underlying causes and effects or remote causes
- Will arrange details in a progressive or other logical order

---

Next Body Paragraph or Paragraphs

- Will state the first cause or effect
- May reproduce causal chains
- May explain why something is or is not a cause or effect
- May identify underlying causes and effects or remote causes
- Will arrange details in a progressive or other logical order

---

Conclusion

- May draw a conclusion from the cause-and-effect relationship
- May summarize if the cause-and-effect relationship is complex

CRITICAL READING STUDENT ESSAY

The cause-and-effect analysis, "Athletes on Drugs: It's Not So Hard to Understand," explains the reasons some professional athletes use drugs. Notice how well the author of this essay explains the causes.

Athletes on Drugs: It's Not So Hard to Understand

John Selzer

1   On June 17, 1986, Len Bias, a basketball star from the University of Maryland, was the second pick in the National Basketball Association amateur draft. Bias had everything going for him; he was a 22-year-old kid about to become a millionaire and superstar. He was on top of the world (or so it seemed). Forty hours later Len Bias was dead—from an overdose of drugs. The Len Bias story is tragic, but it is just one of many cases. Just eight days following the Bias tragedy, Cleveland Browns all-pro safety Don Rogers, then 23, died of a drug overdose. Steve Howe, once a dazzling pitcher, found himself out of baseball because of his drug problems. And the list goes on. Why? Why are professional athletes, people who have money, success, fame, and power, destroying their lives with drugs?

2   To most people the life of professional athletes is filled with glamour. All they see are the sports cars, the million-dollar contracts, and the adoring fans. People do not realize the mental anguish that is involved with being a professional athlete. The loneliness, the fear of failure, and the insecurities of their jobs are just a few of the pressures that athletes have to deal with every day. In some sports, such as baseball, basketball, and hockey, the teams play five to seven games a week, so the athletes must travel to two or three different cities. This constant travel has an adverse effect on athletes' ability to cope with daily pressures. They begin to miss family and friends, often becoming lonely and depressed. As an alternative to this depression, they turn to drugs.

3   In most cases, professional athletes of today have been the best in their sports since childhood. They have won honours and awards for their talents all through their lives. They have seldom been failures, and fear of becoming one is their worst nightmare. The athletes are surrounded by family, friends, and coaches who tell them they are the best. These people attempt to make the athletes feel flawless, incapable of making a mistake. Therefore, when players do have a bad day, they not only let themselves down but those people too. Again, in order to deal with the pressure, drugs become an option.

4   For most of today's professional athletes, sports is all they know. Many do not have a college education, and, more than likely, without sports they would not have a career. Athletes must remain above the competition to keep their jobs. In some cases, when the God-given ability is not enough, the player uses drugs for improvement. Athletes have found that some drugs, such as amphetamines, can increase their physical abilities. These drugs help the athlete to perform better, therefore giving her or him a greater chance of

PARAGRAPH 1

The introduction gives important background information. The thesis, the last sentence, indicates that the essay will discuss the causes for using performance-enhancing drugs. Notice that the introduction explains an effect—a personal tragedy.

PARAGRAPH 2

The topic sentence, the first sentence, states the first cause: the promise of fame and riches for professional athletes.

PARAGRAPH 3

The topic sentence, the first sentence, states the second cause, fear of failure, since most athletes have traditionally been the best in their chosen sports. Note the use of the transition in the second-to-last sentence.

PARAGRAPH 4

The topic sentence, the first sentence, states the next cause: professional athletes are unprepared to do anything but the sport for which they have trained. The concluding sentence presents the view that those who do not use drugs have an distinct disadvantage.

success. For example, steroids have almost become a norm in some sports. Bodybuilders and football players have discovered that these drugs speed up the development of strength and muscles. In professional football, large numbers of offensive and defensive linemen claim to have used steroids at least once in their careers. Those professional athletes who refuse to use amphetamines and steroids are no doubt at a disadvantage.

PARAGRAPH 5

The conclusion provides a satisfying ending by explaining how fans, owners, and players must take action to stop drug abuse in sports.

5   In today's sports, athletes are bigger, stronger, and faster; therefore, more injuries are occurring. Injuries are part of the game, and all players have suffered at least one in their careers. The most discomforting fact about injuries for professional athletes of today is not the pain but the drugs that are used to ease their discomfort. In many cases, coaches and trainers strongly encourage the use of such drugs. In the high-priced world of sports, time is money. Athletes cannot afford to sit out and allow their injuries to heal properly. They often turn to drugs to help speed up the healing process. Often these drugs are illegal; sometimes they are more dangerous than the injury itself, but for the athlete the use of the drug appears to be the only choice. Without the drugs, the players face the loss of thousands of dollars as well as their livelihoods.

6   The professional athlete has to deal with a great deal of pressure. As the mental struggles begin to mount and the aches and pains begin to multiply, the athlete becomes more susceptible to drug use. Drug use should never be accepted, but in the case of the professional athlete, condemning the problem will not solve it. The fans, owners, and especially the players themselves must re-examine the pressures and stop the drug problem before it destroys more people's lives.

The complete essay, including any bibliographic references, is also available on the Online Learning Centre at www.mcgrawhill.ca/olc/clouse.

EXERCISE CONSIDERING "ATHLETES ON DRUGS: IT'S NOT SO HARD TO UNDERSTAND"

1.   In paragraph 1, John expresses his thesis as a question. How well does this strategy work? Rewrite the thesis as a declarative statement. Which is better?

2.   Does the author do a good job of explaining why the factors he mentions are causes? Explain your view.

3.   Does John omit any important causes? Explain.

4.   Does John convince you that drug use by athletes is understandable? Why or why not?

5.   What strategies does John use for his introduction and conclusion? ●

CRITIQUE, REVISE, and EDIT

A student writer, Cammie Bullock, developed an essay that considered the causes for coyotes' entering cities and posing a danger to animals and humans. She read over the first draft of her essay "Mom, There's a Coyote in the Backyard!" and was concerned about her transition from discussing the threat of coyotes to pets, to discussing the threat to humans.

First draft

> Coyotes in their new habitats are coming in contact with pets and attacking them. Several years ago, a coyote killed former talk-show host Kathy Lee Gifford's small dog in the backyard of her Greenwich, Connecticut, estate. Here in St. Louis, coyotes have attacked and killed small dogs left unattended in backyards. It hasn't happened yet, but there is concern that rabies and canine distemper might spread to coyotes, which would make them more likely to attack people. Consequently, my veterinarian recommends that dog owners have their dogs vaccinated and watch out for coyotes in the daytime that might be infected. She said that in Texas, where rabies has wiped out most of the native coyotes, authorities are spreading bait with vaccine in it where the coyotes can get it, but this idea will not work for a suburban area because of domestic animals and children.

Cammie realized that the paragraph was trying to make two separate points, one about the threat to pets, and one about the threat to people. Neither point was developed well. She addressed the problem by putting each point in its own paragraph and adding detail in the first paragraph to pave the way for the second paragraph.

Second draft

> Coyotes in their new habitats are coming in contact with pets and attacking them. Several years ago, a coyote killed former talk-show host Kathy Lee Gifford's small dog in the backyard of her Greenwich, Connecticut, estate. Here in St. Louis, coyotes have attacked and killed small dogs left unattended in backyards. Although there do not seem to be any cases of coyotes attacking humans, people in Ladue have reported seeing packs of coyotes that seem to be less afraid of people.
>
> There is also concern that rabies and canine distemper might spread to coyotes, which would make them more likely to attack people. Consequently, my veterinarian recommends that dog owners have their dogs vaccinated and watch out for coyotes in the daytime that might be infected. She said that in Texas, where rabies has wiped out most of the native coyotes, authorities are spreading bait with vaccine in it where the coyotes can get it, but this idea will not work for a suburban area because of domestic animals and children.

Cammie made other changes in the next draft, but she felt the transition from the threat to pets to the threat to people was now better. What do you think? Is the transition better? Is it good enough?

CRITICAL READING PROFESSIONAL ESSAYS

Pre-reading

1. People seem to value the concept of being busy, or over-scheduled. Why is this?

2. Western culture's focus on productivity may lead to losses in other areas of life. Consider what might be lost as we rush from one task to another.

3. Many people pride themselves on juggling many obligations, and call it multi-tasking. Is this really an effective way to manage professional and social commitments?

Our Schedules, Ourselves

Jay Walljasper

1   DAMN! You're 20 minutes—no, more like half an hour—late for your breakfast meeting, which you were hoping to scoot out of early to make an 8:30 seminar across town. And, somewhere in there, there's that conference call. Now, at the last minute, you have to be at a 9:40 meeting. No way you can miss it. Let's see, the afternoon is totally booked, but you can probably push back your 10:15 appointment and work through lunch. That would do it. Whew! The day has barely begun and already you are counting the hours until evening, when you can finally go home and happily, gloriously, triumphantly, do nothing. You'll skip yoga class, blow off the neighborhood meeting, ignore the piles of laundry and just relax. Yes! . . . No! Tonight's the night of the concert. You promised Nathan and Mara weeks ago that you would go. *DAMN!*

2   Welcome to daily grind circa 2003—a grueling 24-7 competition against the clock that leaves even the winners wondering what happened to their lives. Determined and sternly focused, we march through each day obeying the orders of our calendars. The idle moment, the reflective pause, serendipity of any sort have no place in our plans. Stopping to talk to someone or slowing down to appreciate a sunny afternoon will only make you late for your next round of activities. From the minute we rise in the morning, most of us have our day charted out. The only surprise is if we

actually get everything done that we had planned before collapsing into bed at night.

3   On the job, in school, at home, increasing numbers of North Americans are virtual slaves to their schedules. Some of what fills our days are onerous obligations, some are wonderful opportunities, and most fall in between, but taken together they add up to too much. Too much to do, too many places to be, too many things happening too fast, all mapped out for us in precise quarterhour allotments on our Palm Pilots or day planners. We are not leading our lives, but merely following a dizzying timetable of duties, commitments, demands, and options. How did this happen? Where's the luxurious leisure that decades of technological progress was supposed to bestow upon us?

4   The acceleration of the globalized economy, and the accompanying decline of people having any kind of a say over wages and working conditions, is a chief culprit. Folks at the bottom of the socio-economic ladder feel the pain most sharply. Holding down two or three jobs, struggling to pay the bills, working weekends, no vacation time, little social safety net, they often feel out of control about everything happening to them. But even successful professionals, people who seem fully in charge of their destinies, feel the pinch. Doctors, for example, working impossibly

crowded schedules under the command of HMOs, feel overwhelmed. Many of them are now seeking union representation, traditionally the recourse of low-pay workers.

5 The onslaught of new technology, which promised to set us free, has instead ratcheted up the rhythms of everyday life. Cell phones, e-mail, and laptop computers instill expectations of instantaneous action. While such direct communication can loosen our schedules in certain instances (it's easier to shift around an engagement on short notice), overall they fuel the trend that every minute must be accounted for. It's almost impossible to put duties behind you now, when the boss or committee chair can call you at a rap show or sushi restaurant, and documents can be e-mailed to you on vacation in Banff or Thailand. If you are never out of the loop, then are you ever not working?

6 Our own human desire for more choices and new experiences also plays a role. Just like hungry diners gathering around a bountiful smorgasbord, it's hard not to pile too many activities on our plates. An expanding choice of cultural offerings over recent decades and the liberating sense that each of us can fully play a number of different social roles (worker, citizen, lover, parent, artist, etc.) has opened up enriching and exciting opportunities. Spanish lessons? Yes. Join a volleyball team? Why not. Cello and gymnastics classes for the kids? Absolutely. Tickets to a blues festival, food and wine expo, and political fundraiser? Sure. And we can't forget to make time for school events, therapy sessions, protest rallies, religious services, and dinner with friends.

7 Yes, these can all add to our lives. But with only 24 hours allotted to us each day, something is lost too. You don't just run into a friend anymore and decide to get coffee. You can't happily savor an experience because your mind races toward the next one on the calendar. In a busy life, nothing happens if you don't plan it, often weeks in advance. Our "free" hours become just as programmed as the work day. What begins as an idea for fun frequently turns into an obligation obstacle course. Visit that new barbecue restaurant. *Done!*

Go to tango lessons. *Done!* Fly to Montreal for a long weekend. *Done!*

8 We've booked ourselves so full of prescheduled activities there's no time left for those magic, spontaneous moments that make us feel most alive. We seldom stop to think of all the experiences we are eliminating from our lives when we load up our appointment book. Reserving tickets for a basketball game months away could mean you miss out on the first balmy evening of spring. Five p.m. skating lessons for your children fit so conveniently into your schedule that you never realize it's the time all the other kids in the neighborhood gather on the sidewalk to play.

9 A few years back, radical Brazilian educator Paulo Freire was attending a conference of Midwestern political activists and heard over and over about how overwhelmed people felt about the duties they face each day. Finally, he stood up and, in slow, heavily accented English, declared, "We are bigger than our schedules." The audience roared with applause.

10 Yes, we are bigger than our schedules. So how do we make sure our lives are not overpowered by an endless roster of responsibilities? Especially in an age where demanding jobs, two worker households or single-parent families make the joyous details of everyday life—cooking supper from scratch or organizing a block party—seem like an impossible dream? There is no set of easy answers, despite what the marketers of new convenience products would have us believe. But that doesn't mean we can't make real steps to take back our lives.

11 Part of the answer is political. So long as Americans work longer hours than any other people on Earth we are going to feel hemmed in by our schedules. Expanded vacation time for everyone, including part-time and minimum wage workers, is one obvious and overdue solution. Shortening the work week, something the labor movement and progressive politicians successfully accomplished in the early decades of the 20th century, is another logical objective. There's nothing preordained about 40 hours on the job; Italy, France, and other European nations have already cut back

working hours. An opportunity for employees outside academia to take a sabbatical every decade or so is another idea whose time has come. And how about more vacation and paid holidays? Let's start with Martin Luther King's birthday, Susan B. Anthony's birthday, and your own! Any effort to give people more clout in their workplaces—from strengthened unions to employee ownership—could help us gain much-needed flexibility in our jobs, and our lives.

12 On another front, how you think about time can make a big difference in how you feel about life . . . Note how some of your most memorable moments occurred when something in your schedule fell through. The canceled lunch that allows you to spend an hour strolling around town. Friday night plans scrapped for a bowl of popcorn in front of the fireplace. Don't be shy about shucking your schedule whenever you can get away with it. And with some experimentation, you may find that you can get away with it a lot more than you imagined.

13 Setting aside some time on your calendar for life to just unfold in its own surprising way can also nurture your soul. Carve out some nonscheduled hours (or days) once in a while and treat them as a firm commitment. And resist the temptation to turn every impulse or opportunity into another appointment. It's neither impolite nor inefficient to simply say, "let me get back to you on that tomorrow" or "let's check in that morning to see if it's still a good time." You cannot know how crammed that day may turn out to be, or how uninspired you might feel about another engagement, or how much you'll want to be rollerblading or playing chess or doing something else at that precise time.

14 In our industrialized, fast-paced society, we too often view time as just another mechanical instrument to be programmed. But time possesses its own ever shifting shape and rhythms, and defies our best efforts to corral it within the tidy lines of our Palm Pilots or date books. Stephen Rechtschaffen, author of *Time Shifting*, suggests you think back on a scary auto collision (or near miss), or spectacular night of lovemaking. Time seemed almost to stand still. You can remember everything in vivid detail. Compare that to an over crammed week that you recall now only as a rapid-fire blur. Keeping in mind that our days expand and contract according to their own patterns is perhaps the best way to help keep time on your side.

Considering Ideas

1. The thesis of "Our Schedules, Ourselves" is implied. Write out the thesis.

2. For what purpose did Walljasper write the essay? Is the situation the same for Canadians as it is for Americans?

3. According to the essay, why are we over-scheduled? That is, what causes us to do so much?

4. What are the effects of our overcrowded schedules?

5. How does the author propose solving the problem of over-scheduling? Do you think his solution is practical?

6. Explain the meaning of the title.

Considering Technique

1. The opening paragraph begins and ends with the word *damn*. Explain the effect of that strategy.

2. What metaphor do you see in paragraph 2? What simile do you see in paragraph 6? (Metaphors and similes are explained on page 147.)

3. In what way is the essay a cause-and-effect analysis?

4. *Combining Patterns*. How does the author use exemplification in paragraphs 1, 6, and 7? Why are the examples so brief? How does he use exemplification in paragraphs 12 and 13?

5. The author mentions HMOs, or Health Maintenance Organizations. Medicine is organized differently in Canada. Does this mean doctors are any less busy?

6. Why does the author tell the anecdote about Paulo Freire in paragraph 9?

7. *Combining Patterns.* How does the author use process analysis? How does he use contrast?

For Group Discussion or Journal Writing

How much of what Walljasper says applies to the lives of students? What can students do to preserve spontaneous opportunities, or to create more "downtime." Cite examples to support your view.

Combining Patterns of Development in a Cause-and-Effect Essay

Pre-reading

1. How has climate change affected Canada? What are some possibilities for the future?
2. Can Canadians learn from the Indigenous peoples in our country? What would be the consequence of ignoring traditional cultures and knowledge?
3. What can Canadians do to reduce our footprint on the ecosystem?

Canada's Crisis

Laura Blue

1   A millennium or so ago, the archipelago from Hudson Bay through Nunavut to northern Greenland was inhabited by nomadic groups we now call the Dorset people. They were, according to Inuit legend, tall and gentle folk, and they hunted from the ice edge, harpooning seals and walruses with tools made of bone and ivory. When a slight warming period hit about 1,000 years ago, the ice receded. Bowhead whales moved in from Alaskan waters, followed by seafaring hunters from the Bering Strait. With their boats, those hunters, the forebears of Canadian Inuit, eventually spread east to Greenland. For reasons still not clear, the Dorset disappeared. As with most environmental changes, the warming of northern Canada set in motion a series of complex, interrelated events that produced winners and losers.

2   As the world heats up again—this time far more rapidly—the question repeats: Who wins and who loses? Climate models are notoriously useless at predicting local effects of global change. But a massive new Canadian research project, Arctic-Net, may provide some early answers about the connections among warming, melting, ecosystem reorganization, and human response. And the results may be the best indicator the world will get about what to expect elsewhere. The Arctic will show the earliest and most severe signs of global warming—with Canadian calculations predicting a rise in mean temperature of more than 4°C between the late 20th century and the mid-21st.

3   ArcticNet, the biggest Arctic research project ever undertaken, calls on more than 100 Canadian researchers from 27 universities and five federal

departments to study just about everything in the Canadian Arctic that could be changed by global warming. "It's interesting, but pretty useless, to say the Arctic may have a three-month, ice-free summer, if you don't also look at what the impact will be on the people and industry in the north," says Louis Fortier, scientific director of the Networks of Centres of Excellence project, launched in 2004 and due to run at least seven years. The project grew out of the Canadian Arctic Shelf Exchange Study, which launched the research ice-breaker CCGS *Amundsen* in the Beaufort Sea in September 2003.

4   Ice, naturally, is central to understanding the Arctic. In the physics of climate change, the ice cover on the water is far more important than the air temperature above it. "Phase change—when there's ice—is really the key," says Rob Macdonald, a Department of Fisheries and Oceans research scientist who studies carbon and contaminant cycling.

5   The Inuit report the same thing. A hunting, fishing, and gathering people, they collect their food from the ice eight months a year. Or at least they try to. The land and sea have become noticeably less predictable in the past five to 10 years, says Sheila Watt-Cloutier, chairwoman of the Inuit Circumpolar Conference. While southern Canadians may bask in unusual winter heat, if ice is too thin to ride over and too thick to take a boat through, it is as if someone closed all the roads to the Inuits' grocery stores. "Ice and snow represent transportation, represent mobility," says Watt-Cloutier. There are more drownings from people falling through thin ice in winter and from hunters trying to cross streams in the summer that became torrents because of melting glaciers.

6   The changes in environmental cues—things like ice cover, temperature, and salinity—are reflected in other natural events. The growth rates of algae and phytoplankton change. Salmon are migrating to western Arctic waters from the northern Pacific. There is concern that Atlantic cod will encroach in the east and compete with the smaller Arctic cod, which have thrived in frigid climates with their special proteins that prevent freezing of the blood. Meanwhile, the retracting ice makes it harder for ringed seals to find breeding grounds and for polar bears to hunt.

7   That means food isn't always there even when the Inuit can travel. Wildlife may well be less adaptable to extreme changes than humans are. When polar bears can't find prey, there are few alternatives; the bears burn their own fat, releasing into their systems the contaminants stored there—pesticides and other industrial chemicals that accumulate in cool Arctic waters and build up in the food chain. Other animals are also in trouble. In February, in what should have been midwinter in the far north, Nunavut's capital city, Iqaluit, was a balmy 5°C and rainy. When the temperature dropped, a layer of ice froze over the tundra. Now there's fear that the caribou, which normally dig through snow—not hard ice—to get lichen in winter, will be underfed. So the Inuit can expect a significant change in their diet.

8   There are other human-health consequences of the shifting biology that accompanies climate variation. Warming may mean that germs reproduce faster, increasing Inuit exposure to animal diseases, such as trichinosis. Warming could probably also damage public-health infrastructure—sewage systems, water pipes, and reservoirs—as the permafrost on which it was built melts. And for Inuit communities, already reordering rapidly through modernization, the extra social dislocation brought by a warmer climate may bring stress, mental health problems, and increased substance abuse. On the positive side, frostbite may decrease, along with cardiac problems brought on by heavy exertion in extreme cold.

9   And the winners in Canada's Arctic? When the Northwest Passage finally clears enough to be a viable shipping route—probably in the next 50 years—a whole range of trade opportunities will come with it. So will resources, as fossil-fuel deposits in the ocean floor become more accessible. ArcticNet researchers are already mapping out the undersea terrain with sonar and analyzing the geopolitical implications of finding the long-sought Arctic Grail. Their proposals should help the government deal with an international legal dispute already under way: whether the Northwest Passage is within Canadian waters, subject

to domestic security and environmental regulation, or an international strait. "Our success will not necessarily be measured by the quality of science, but also in the policy," says ArcticNet executive director Martin Fortier (no relation to Louis).

10 Should Canada be doing more to mitigate the effects of climate change? Many researchers think so. The Harper government says it is committed to cutting greenhouse-gas emissions but that the Kyoto targets—a decrease of 6% from 1990 levels by 2012—are not achievable given that Canada is, by latest reckoning, 24% over the 1990 baseline. The government has announced that it will develop new "made in Canada" action plans for cutting emissions. Ultimately, once again, the problem will be figuring out which impacts count. But if ArcticNet results are meaningful, the whole world should take note of Canada's north. "It's kind of the canary in the mine shaft," says Louis Fortier. And the canary is roasting.

Considering Ideas

1. Which cause and effect relationship is Blue analyzing? For what purpose does she analyze this relationship?

2. How does the narration of the history of the Dorset people introduce the ideas about climate change and serve as a prologue to the article?

3. How does Blue create a cause and effect chain? What is the purpose of showing a sequence of related effects?

4. Does Blue address all of the effects of climate change in Canada? What about causes? Are there associated causes or effects that she should have included?

Considering Technique

1. Though the reasons for the disappearance of the Dorset people remains unclear, is it suitable to use this detail to support the contention that climate change leads to social or cultural effects?

2. How does the inclusion of statistical and research details support the thesis that the effects of climate change are already happening? Locate at least one example.

3. Paragraph 7 begins to establish the interconnectedness of the effects of global warming. It uses, primarily, anecdotal examples as evidence. Would it be more effective to use scientific evidence at this point?

4. Comment on the effectiveness of this article. Is its neutral tone compelling in terms of an argument for reducing greenhouse gases? Should there be a stronger call to action?

For Group Discussion or Journal Writing

Canada has a relatively small population compared with its size. This low density has meant abundant resources and a relatively clean natural environment. Yet, Canada also leads the world in greenhouse gas emissions, and is a major polluter. There are also issues surrounding Canada's compliance with climate change treaties. Consider a creative approach to reversing climate change in Canada, and to reducing carbon footprints. Brainstorm in a small group, and prepare to present your ideas to others.

WRITING TOOL

Specific Diction

In Chapter 5, you learned the importance of specific diction for conveying ideas as precisely as possible. In addition, specific diction gives a sentence energy and contributes to a lively style. Using specific verbs will help you achieve specific diction, as these underlined examples from "Our Schedules, Ourselves" by Jay Walljasper illustrate:

Determined and <u>sternly focused</u>, we <u>march</u> through each day <u>obeying</u> the orders of our calendars. (paragraph 2)

Friday night plans <u>scrapped</u> for a bowl of popcorn in front of the fireplace. (paragraph 12)

But time <u>possesses</u> its own ever shifting shape and rhythms, and defies our best efforts to <u>corral</u> it . . . (paragraph 14)

Cause-and-Effect Analysis in an Image

Pay attention to advertisements, and you will notice how often cause-and-effect analysis appears as a component. The United Way of Canada's ad considers the effects of donating to this charitable organization.

Considering the Image

1. The advertisement considers both causes and effects. What causes are considered? What effects?
2. What audience does the advertisement hope to reach? How can you tell?
3. What is the purpose of this advertisement?
4. How does the photograph help the advertisement achieve its purpose?
5. What causal chain is suggested in the advertisement?

Reading Then Writing Cause-and-Effect Analysis

1. In "Our Schedules, Ourselves" Jay Walljasper says that we need to change the way we view time. Explain how you view time, and give the reasons you have that view.
2. In "Athletes on Drugs: It's Not So Hard to Understand," the author discusses the causes of drug abuse among athletes. Explain the causes of some other problem behaviour, such as cheating on exams, smoking, overeating, shoplifting, or road rage.

Cause-and-Effect Analysis beyond the Writing Classroom

Write an analysis of the causes and effects of procrastination among students, and explain how to avoid the problem. The essay should be suitable for inclusion in a handbook to help first-year students make a successful adjustment to college. If you need help with ideas, interview other students to learn about their experiences with procrastination.

Responding to Theme

1. The student author of "Athletes on Drugs: It's Not So Hard to Understand" explains why athletes turn to drugs. What do you think can be done to solve the problem? Describe a specific plan to address the issues in the student's essay and any other issues you find pertinent.

2. The United Way of Canada advertisement suggests that donations help lift people out of poverty. It also suggests that a lack of education limits everyone's life opportunities. This raises the question of government support for higher education. How much should higher education cost, and what are the benefits (effects) for a society with an educated population?

3. *Connecting the Readings.* Although we understand the risks, we often do things that are not good for ourselves. We smoke, drink, drive too fast, eat poorly, over-schedule, and otherwise compromise our health and well-being. In an essay, explain why. You can draw on the ideas in "Athletes on Drugs: It's Not So Hard to Understand," "Our Schedules, Ourselves," and your own experiences and observations.

 THE WRITING PROCESS

Cause-and-Effect Analysis

Try the following guidelines, or rely on your own tried-and-true procedures if you prefer.

Generate Ideas, Consider Audience and Purpose, and Order Ideas

- If you need help finding a topic, try one of the following:
  - Think of something you do well or do badly, such as run track, do math, make friends, or play the piano. Then consider why you do this activity well or badly and how your ability or lack thereof has affected you.
  - Identify something about your personality, environment, or circumstances, and assess how this factor has affected you. You could analyze the effects of poverty, shyness, a large family, moving, and so forth.
- To establish and assess your audience, answer the questions on page 43.
- To determine your purpose, answer the questions on page 39.
- To generate ideas, try the following:
  - List every cause and/or effect you can think of. Do not censor yourself; write down everything that occurs to you.
  - To discover underlying causes and effects, ask *why?* and *then what?* after every cause and effect in your list. For example, if you listed difficulty making friends as an effect of shyness, ask *then what?* and you may get the answer "I was lonely." This answer could be an underlying effect of your shyness. If you listed "strong legs" as a reason for your success at running track, ask *why?* and you may get the answer "I lifted weights to increase leg strength." This would give you an underlying cause. Asking *then what?* will also help you discover causal chains.
  - Number your causes and effects in the order you will write them up in your draft. Remember that a progressive order is often effective.
  - Ask yourself why understanding the cause-and-effect relationship is important. The answer can be stated in your introduction, thesis, or conclusion.

Draft

- As you draft, refer to your list of numbered causes and effects. Think about your audience and purpose, and consider why understanding the cause-and-effect relationship is important.
- Use topic sentences to introduce each cause or effect, so your reader can follow along easily.

Revise

- Identify the words in your thesis that indicate what cause-and-effect relationship will be analyzed and the words that indicate whether causes, effects, or both will be discussed.

- To determine whether you should add detail, answer these questions about each cause and effect:
  - How do I prove that this is a cause or effect? Is the proof adequate?
  - Is there an underlying cause or effect? If so, should it be included?
  - Is there a remote cause? If so, should it be included?
  - Is this part of a causal chain? If so, should the chain be reproduced?
  - Is there anything my reader mistakenly thinks is a cause or effect?
- Read your draft aloud. If you hear awkward shifts, add transitions. In a cause-and-effect analysis, you will probably use transitions of addition, such as *also, furthermore,* and *in addition,* and transitions of cause and effect, such as *consequently, as a result, for this reason,* and *therefore.*
- To secure reader response, see pages 101–102. In addition, have your reader ask *why?* and *then what?* after all your causes and effects. If doing so leads your reader to any underlying causes or effects you should discuss, ask your reader to note them on the draft.

Correct Errors and Proofread

- Use the "Guide to Frequently Occurring Errors" for reference, and check with a writing centre tutor if you are unsure about a grammar, usage, or punctuation point.
- Recognize that "the reason is because" is redundant since "the reason" *means* "because." If you have used this expression, change it to either "the reason is that" or simply "because."

  No: Financial aid cheques were late this term. <u>The reason is because</u> the computer centre experienced systems problems.

  Yes: Financial aid cheques were late this term. <u>The reason is that</u> the computer centre experienced systems problems.

  Yes: Financial aid cheques were late this term <u>because</u> the computer centre experienced systems problems.

- Proofread your final copy. If you are submitting a paper copy, check with your instructor about whether you can ink in minor corrections.

Remember

Do not assume that an earlier event caused a later one. Enrolment may have declined at your college after a tuition increase was instituted, but you cannot automatically assume that one caused the other. Other factors may have been involved. Perhaps the job outlook became brighter, so more high school graduates went to work rather than to college.

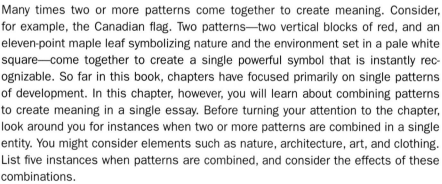

CHAPTER 14

Combining Patterns of Development

Looking Ahead

Many times two or more patterns come together to create meaning. Consider, for example, the Canadian flag. Two patterns—two vertical blocks of red, and an eleven-point maple leaf symbolizing nature and the environment set in a pale white square—come together to create a single powerful symbol that is instantly recognizable. So far in this book, chapters have focused primarily on single patterns of development. In this chapter, however, you will learn about combining patterns to create meaning in a single essay. Before turning your attention to the chapter, look around you for instances when two or more patterns are combined in a single entity. You might consider elements such as nature, architecture, art, and clothing. List five instances when patterns are combined, and consider the effects of these combinations.

Why is Combining Patterns Important?

To achieve a purpose for writing, you have the option of combining patterns of development. In fact, you are likely to combine patterns frequently, which is why each pattern chapter in Part Two of this text also includes discussions and readings that show how to combine patterns to achieve the full range of writing purposes. Though it is entirely possible to craft a piece of writing that follows just one pattern of development (i.e., a recipe, procedural manual, description of a holiday destination, or sentences that develop an example), it is more common that writing combines patterns to achieve various purposes.

As the examples in the chart below show, you can combine patterns to entertain, express feelings, relate experience, inform, and persuade, all at the same time. Look back through this book and review some of the sample essays by both students and professional writers, and find at least one example of a piece of writing that combines patterns of development. Evaluate why the writer has decided to combine patterns, and consider how effective the piece of writing would be if it were developed with only one rhetorical pattern.

In a travel piece written for *worldweb.com*, the writer describes winter in various parts of Canada, and provides examples of Canadian geography. A primary purpose for this travel piece is to convince readers to visit Canada in winter.

> The coolest season in the world is a Canadian winter—and not just because it gets so darned cold here. Simply put, Canada is a big place with unlimited wintertime possibilities. The country spans from Newfoundland and the Atlantic Ocean to Vancouver Island and the Pacific, with borders that reach from the 41st parallel in the south to the frigid Arctic Circle up north. Encompassing mountains, prairies and great lakes, its breadth begets a terrain and climate so varied that when it comes to weather— more specifically winter weather—almost anything can happen.
>
> Climatic variety aside, in most parts of the country people will battle hostile weather conditions and slippery roads for almost six months of the year (November to April). That's half a lifetime spent zipping up, buttoning down and trudging through the snow.
>
> Naturally, locals have come to cope with this fate in two different ways: fight or flight. While some tend to hibernate with the bears or fly south with the birds, there are others who live for these conditions. These winter warriors have taken an otherwise gruelling experience and turned it into a fun-filled season of big air, cross-country treks, and fantastic winter festivals.
>
> So don't be intimidated by those sub-zero temperatures and massive snowdrifts— that's half the fun—bundle up and jump into a Canadian winter. It may bring about something unexpected, especially for the adventurous.

Although the excerpt is brief, it includes three patterns of development to help the author inform travellers that Canada is a desirable winter destination. The writer compares winter weather in various regions of the country, describes how Canadians meet winter challenges, and attempts to convince tourists that it's worth a visit to Canada in winter.

OCCASIONS FOR WRITING

Combining Patterns across the Disciplines and Beyond

Combining Patterns in the Classroom

Every course that involves writing will present the opportunity to combine patterns. For a psychology exam, you might need to define operant conditioning and use process analysis to explain how it works. In an art-appreciation homework assignment, you might need to divide colour into its properties and explain the effects of each of those properties on a painting. In a paper for a communications class, you might classify the problems associated with intercultural communication, give examples of those problems, and explain their causes and effects. *Skim a chapter in one of your textbooks, and identify the various patterns of development in that chapter. How does each of those patterns help you understand and learn important content?*

Combining Patterns in Daily Life

In personal writing, writers are likely to combine patterns. For example, in a letter about travels, a friend might describe a hotel and narrate an account of a museum tour she took. A condolence note might give examples of the deceased's good deeds and how he or she affected others. A recipe sent to a friend will explain the process for making a dish, and it might describe what the finished product should look like. *How might you combine patterns in a letter to the editor of your campus newspaper, in which you try to convince students and faculty to donate money to a famine relief agency? What about in an email to a friend to tell that person how you are?*

Combining Patterns on the Job

When we write on the job, we often combine patterns. In a company newsletter, a profile of the employee of the month might narrate a story about a time the employee did something helpful to the company, and it might give examples of the employee's accomplishments. In a quarterly report, a district sales manager might contrast earnings for two quarters and explain a process for improving sales. *What writing will you do routinely on the job you hope to have after graduation? What patterns might you combine to complete that writing? How will those patterns help you achieve your purposes for writing?*

DETERMINING PURPOSE

Purposes for Combining Patterns

Purpose	Sample Pattern
To entertain	An amusing narration about a first job with a description of the boss, and an explanation of the process mistakes an employee made
To express feelings	A blog entry about a child's wedding that contrasts how someone felt with how they thought they would feel and that explains the effect of the child's wedding on a parent
To relate experience	A description of the benefits from practicing meditation with a definition of meditation and an explanation of how the process of meditation works
To inform	An explanation of the process whereby a certain type of pension increases savings and a contrast of the plan with other pension plans
To persuade	A definition a school breakfast program, with examples of its benefits to persuade readers to support a local program

Before Writing

The principles learned for selecting detail for each pattern still apply when you combine those patterns. However, when writers combine patterns, they generally rely more heavily on one pattern than the others. That is, they will likely have a *primary pattern* and one or more *secondary patterns*. For example, to convince your readers to support a recycling program, you might draw on description to create images of the litter that results when the community does not recycle, and might also use cause-and-effect analysis to explain the economic and ecological benefits of recycling. If you decide that the cause-and-effect analysis is more likely to persuade an audience than a description would, cause-and-effect analysis will be the primary pattern, so principles for selecting detail for cause-and-effect analysis will govern the writing process more than the principles for selecting descriptive detail.

Similarly, when you combine patterns, you may also use more than one organizing principle for details. To convince readers to support a recycling program, you might describe the litter problem using a spatial order and then give the economic and ecological effects of recycling using a progressive order. Because essays that combine patterns can be more complex than ones that rely on a single pattern, taking time to outline is particularly helpful.

If you have trouble generating ideas for a "blended" essay, consider the questions below. They will help in the brainstorm and the outline stages, and increase your chances for writing success.

1. What can I describe?
2. What can I narrate?
3. What illustrations can I give?
4. What process can I explain?
5. What can I compare or contrast?
6. What causes or effects can I explain?
7. What can I define?
8. What can I classify or divide?

EXERCISE COMBINING PATTERNS

1. For a letter to provincial legislators asking them to fund prenatal classes for low-income parents, how might you use each of these patterns? Which one is likely to be the primary pattern?
   a. Exemplification
   b. Contrast
   c. Cause-and-effect analysis

2. For a research paper for a criminal justice class about the nature and extent of looting following natural or human-made disasters, how might you use each of these patterns? Which one is likely to be the primary pattern?
   a. Classification-division
   b. Exemplification
   c. Definition

3. For a report to a supervisor about using virtual reality for training customer service representatives, how might you use each of these patterns? Which one is likely to be the primary pattern?
   a. Process analysis
   b. Cause-and-effect analysis
   c. Narration

4. For a paper giving guidelines for dealing with classroom bullies for an education class, how might you use each of these patterns? Which one is likely to be the primary pattern?
   a. Definition
   b. Exemplification
   c. Division

5. For a report for the school board on the benefits of school uniforms, how might you use each of these patterns? Which one is likely to be the primary pattern?
   a. Description
   b. Contrast
   c. Cause-and-effect analysis ●

CRITICAL READING STUDENT ESSAY

In the following student essay, the author combines classification, cause-and-effect analysis, and process analysis for a light-hearted discussion of that great global pastime: television viewing. Annotations in the margin point out the essay's key features.

The Many Ways to Watch a Show

Cindy Apostolos

PARAGRAPH 1

This introduction gives background information. The thesis is the last sentence.

1   Whether you live with a roommate, a spouse, your birth family, or your boyfriend or girlfriend, you have probably gotten into an argument over the television. Very little creates the potential for petty disagreement more than people sitting down on the couch for an evening of televised entertainment. Most people think arguments about television come solely from decisions over *what* to watch: *24* or *The Real World*? *CSI* or *Boston Legal*? While arguments about programming choice are common, they are not the only kind, and they are not the most problematic. No, the real trouble comes when people disagree about *how* to watch television. People differ greatly in how they enjoy their shows, and when conflicting types of viewers share the same TV, sparks can fly.

PARAGRAPHS 2–4

These paragraphs are classification. The lighthearted tone makes it clear that the writer's purpose is to entertain. Notice the specific word choice, such as "revved-up," "nanosecond," and "slurping."

2   The most difficult type of television viewer to get along with is the television tyrant. The tyrant is not content to sit back and watch one show. This revved-up multitasker wants to watch five or six programs at once. He or she monopolizes the remote control and switches back and forth between

channels at lightning speed. Once one show goes to commercial, the tyrant instantaneously switches to another. If that show gets boring for even a nano-second, the tyrant is on to something else. This frequent switching is all well and good for the hyperactive tyrant, who seems to have a much shorter atten-tion span than the average human, but for the rest of us, it creates a chaos of unfinished sentences and unresolved plots.

3   At least the tyrant is paying attention to the television. Another type of viewer, the chatterbox critic, is focused on something else entirely: the words coming out of his or her own mouth. This is the viewer who is always telling everyone else in the room when "the good parts" of a movie are coming up, the same one who is compelled to comment on how stupid a plot line is, how unrealistic a setting is, and how overexposed an actor is. The chatterbox critic cannot watch anything without giving his or her running commentary, analyzing what is on the screen, or generally letting you know you are not capable of watching television by yourself and reaching your own conclusions.

4   Another type of viewer who can make an hour of watching television unpleas-ant is the zealot. With laser focus, the zealot hones in on a program and refuses to respond to any other stimuli, no matter how compelling. Phones and doorbells are left for others to answer because the zealot refuses to break concentration, even if what is on the screen is nothing more interesting than a soap commercial. The zealot refuses all munchies and drinks, seeing them as a distraction. Worse, the zealot will not allow others in the room to snack because crunching, slurping, and paper rustling are too distracting. Nor will the zealot allow anyone to talk for any reason. Even the briefest whispered remark is met with the zealot's annoyed "Shhhhhhhh."

PARAGRAPH 5

This paragraph, which is developed with cause-and-effect analysis, explains the cause of conflict. Notice how the transitional sentence that opens paragraph 5 helps move the essay from classification to cause-and-effect analysis.

5   With such different types of television viewers, it is easy to see how conflicts can arise. Imagine a chatterbox critic sitting down next to a zealot during the zealot's favorite show. (Zealots tend to like hour-long dramas like *Lost;* if you are a nonzealot, consider yourself warned.) Or imagine a chatterbox critic who cannot synchronise commentary to the tyrant's frantic channel surfing. Mismatched viewers invite clashes.

6   Short of living alone or watching television in a sealed, empty room, what should a television viewer do to ensure peaceful, pleasant viewing? Here are a couple tips for avoiding viewing tension.

PARAGRAPHS 6-7

These paragraphs explain a process for avoiding conflict. Notice how the transitional sentence that closes paragraph 6 helps move the essay from cause-and-effect analysis to process analysis.

7   First, know your own television type and that of the people you are with. That way, you can anticipate the reactions of those viewing with you and not be caught off guard. For example, if you are a tyrant, expect to be asked to sur-render the remote control, and do not become angered when it happens. If you are a chatterbox critic watching with a zealot, expect to be shushed fre-quently. Also, communicate your type to those around you, so the people you are watching TV with know what to expect from you. If you insist on absolute quiet during *60 Minutes,* tell your fellow-viewers in advance. You might just get the chatterbox critic you live with to quiet down—at least for an hour or so. Finally, be willing to compromise. With television, as with nearly everything, you will not always get your way. So choose your battles. Be aware of channels you do not need to surf, comments you do not have to make, and background

noise you can accept. If you are a more tolerant viewer, others will respect your annoying habits a little more.

8   Understanding a bit about yourself and those you share the cable bill with can make for a much more relaxed viewing environment. And if it does not—well, you can always read a book.

PARAGRAPH 8

The conclusion provides closure and makes an ironic comment.

The complete essay, including any bibliographic references, is also available on the Online Learning Centre at www.mcgrawhill.ca/olc/clouse.

EXERCISES

1.   This essay combines patterns of development. Cindy uses both classification and argument, to further her thesis that group television viewing is anything but peaceful. How successful is she?

2.   This essay relies on anecdotal evidence, as many of the professional essays in this book do. Would it benefit from the inclusion of research materials? How could this essay develop further, from a five-paragraph to a multiple-paragraph research essay?

3.   The essay ends inconclusively, claiming, "you can always read a book." Is this a satisfactory conclusion? Should Cindy develop a stronger conclusion that includes a suggestion or a call to action? ●

CRITIQUE, REVISE, and EDIT

Cindy Apostolos suggests, in her thesis, that people watch television in different ways. Yet, she does not identify the ways in which viewing takes place. In other words, the thesis lacks a preview of the essay's content. This is important, as this essay combines patterns of development, and the writer's purpose needs to be absolutely clear. Consider how to incorporate a preview of the main ideas from the body of the paper. Would it help if the thesis statement were longer? Suggest an alternative. The essay details the different types of viewers in body paragraphs, before suggesting, in paragraph 7, strategies for a more harmonious viewing experience. Are there sufficient details and suggestions that help Cindy to achieve her writing purpose? Note, that this is a light-hearted essay, and the essay ends ironically. Does the suggestion that "you can always read a book" help Cindy achieve her writing purpose?

CRITICAL READING PROFESSIONAL ESSAYS

Pre-reading

1. Canada is a nation built, originally, by European colonizers. What have been the effects of this?

2. Some people parody a line in the Canadian National Anthem, and claim it should read "Our home on Native land." Do you agree with this?

3. Many First Nations people continue to live in poverty in neglected communities. What should the Canadian government do to address this issue?

4. How would you define globalization? Colonization? What about the term "Post-Colonial"? How are these terms related to our identity as Canadians? How "European" are we? Should Canadians rethink our connection to the British Commonwealth?

Decolonizing in the Era of Globalization

Joyce Green

1   Canada is a creature born of capitalism and colonialism. The reality of that past is what constructs Aboriginal people. According to the United Nations Draft Declaration on Indigenous Peoples, aboriginality is defined as a relationship between those whose cultural and political orders precede a current dominant occupying population and those (I call them settler populations) who are dominant and dominating. It is the settler whose community benefits from colonization and perpetuates the foundational myths that legitimate it.

2   The political project of Canada emerged from historic imperial initiatives, and from struggles between imperial agents, back when capitalism was primarily mercantile. Its success remains grounded on the appropriation of Aboriginal lands and resources; the subordination of Aboriginal peoples; and the perpetuation of racist myths, via education, religion, political theory, and popular culture, which legitimate this entire enterprise.

3   None of this should come as a surprise to contemporary Canadians, but even the most progressive of non-Aboriginal politics have yet to engage with colonial history, much less theorise and plan policy for its consequences. Consequently, too many governments, opinion leaders, media pundits, academics and political activists treat the evidence of Aboriginal anguish (e.g. social pathologies) and resistance (e.g. Ipperwash, Oka) as decontextualized incidents or policy questions. The roots of these symptoms, however, lie in colonial history. Remedying these problems cannot occur without engaging this history.

The Race/Class Question

4   A post-colonial Canada must be a primary goal of the Left—not to "save those people," but to obtain justice, social stability, political coherence, environmental health, and economic sustainability for all of us. In other words, our (the Left's) own emancipation is to be found in a struggle for justice for all of us, and in recognizing that colonial history privileges some of us at the direct, contemporary expense of others.

5   While globalization of capital has always immiserated the vast majority of Aboriginal peoples, a racist-blind class analysis is of little use in illuminating racist-sustained oppression between Aboriginal peoples and settler Canadians. This reality makes the construction of political alliances more difficult, as Aboriginal and settler activists do not always share historical

experiences, analyses, and current political priorities.

Self-Government: Necessary but Not Sufficient

6   Typically, non-Aboriginals on the Left assume that mitigation of the colonial inheritance amounts to "self-government." In fact, self-government is a modest, insufficient, and often insular accommodation with limited political and economic capacity. Worse, so much of what the federal government proposes is simply self-administration of programs, the parameters of which are established and policed elsewhere. Further, self-government has little relevance for non-land based Aboriginals, who are the majority of the Aboriginal population. Finally, any hopes for a common, albeit differentiated, citizenship; for a collective community defined by what we hold in common rather than what separates us—requires the elements for a common citizenship in a benevolent state entity designed by and for all of us.

7   Aboriginal liberation challenges the state's claim to occupy all space for sovereignty. Land and resource reparations; tax-sharing regimes; federal, constitutional and electoral accommodations—are all part of a decolonization formula that is not cost-free. The political will of non-Aboriginals to support measures for justice has too often been directly and inversely proportional to the cost to non-Aboriginals. As National Chief of the Assembly of First Nations, Matthew Coon-Come, has asked, "Are they willing to allow First Nations peoples to share the wealth?"

8   Perhaps nowhere is this more apparent than in the case of the Lubicon Lake Cree, in Alberta. Alberta is a treaty province, where almost all First Nations are party to treaties 6, 7, or 8. The Lubicon Lake Cree, however, have a claim against the provincial and federal governments by virtue of constitutionally recognized Aboriginal rights. Although their territory falls within the Treaty 8 territory, the Lubicon band was not originally approached to sign the treaty and has subsequently had great difficulty in getting either the federal or the provincial government to take it seriously. Now, the petroleum and forest resources on the Lubicon's traditional territory are claimed by Alberta by virtue of constitutional law, especially the Natural Resources Transfer Agreement of 1930. The Alberta economy has benefited from government sale of the rights to exploit these resources, to primarily transnational corporations. The Lubicon, however, have not been party to these decisions, nor have they shared in the wealth. The United Nations Human Rights Committee (UNHRC) has accepted a Lubicon Lake Cree complaint that provincially and federally authorized oil, gas, and timber "development" on their territories destroyed the Cree economy and, hence, their traditional way of life, through which their culture is practiced. The UNHRC found Canada to be in violation of Article 27 of the International Covenant on Civil and Political Rights.

How Globalization Challenges Aboriginal People

9   The world of globalized capitalism drives not only colonial governments, but, increasingly, Aboriginal ones. Some pursue profits and capitalist methods like union-busting. Some seek an accommodation with capitalist development that might benefit indigenous communities, an example being the current agreement between the James Bay Cree and Quebec about (arguably environmentally problematic) hydro development. Those who would choose non-capitalist alternatives are at odds with the dominant culture, political ideology, and economic structure.

10   The most prominent choice for decolonization, self-government, and autonomy is by means of separate lands, institutions, and economies. This is less viable in a world of globalization. Globalization erases borders of all kinds. Boundedness is difficult to maintain because of technologies, commodities, and economic practices that are deeply seductive. We are all challenged by the hegemonies purveyed by the communications industries: witness the global incorporation of states and media into America's current madness, the "War on Terrorism."

11   The ecosphere is staggering from the effects of human activity. State sovereignty, economic

stability, and cultural viability are being redefined by the technological and regulatory practices of global capitalism. Indigenous peoples, like all others, exist in this troubling milieu.

How Should the Left Engage with Aboriginal Peoples and the Politics of Decolonization?

12 Any will by Left activists to express solidarity with Aboriginal peoples requires two difficult preconditions. First, an internal process of learning about our own complicity in racism. Second, an appreciation that there is no monolithic Aboriginal community. On some issues, with some people, there can be solidarity; on others, there may be ideological or policy differences too profound for solidarity.

13 We must know our history, and we must understand how present conditions emerge from historical yet continuing relations of privilege and subordination. To accomplish this, I support Yasmeen Abu-Laban's proposal for a Forum for a Post Colonial Future, which is similar in its mandate to South Africa's Truth and Reconciliation Commission. Then, we must challenge those conditions, including our personal complicity in them. We must understand how capitalism relies on class, racist and sexist distinctions to cloak itself. We must forge alliances, in which Aboriginal movements find us to be actual rather than theoretical allies. We need to stand in solidarity with allies without dominating, redefining, or essentializing them. In doing this, we need to be mindful of the compromises of alliance politics, while being faithful to the political principles that make our struggle worthwhile. Not every objective of every Aboriginal community or organization will be consistent with a Left (anti-capitalist, anti-racist, feminist, ecologist) analysis.

Sharing the State

14 Decolonization requires structural and procedural changes. Canadian federalism, designed so the national and provincial governments hold all the jurisdiction of the Crown according to the constitutional distribution of powers, must be transformed to include a third order, Aboriginal government jurisdiction. This in turn will challenge us all to deal with overlapping jurisdictions and political interests in ways that will have to be more collaborative, less confrontational. The reality of large urban Aboriginal populations suggests that decolonization isn't only about land-claims settlements, and new governments on those land bases. It also requires new formulae for sharing political, cultural, and economic power within mainstream communities. Fiscal arrangements that provincial and federal governments have argued about for decades will become more complex with the inclusion of Aboriginal governments, and the requirement that they are obliged to provide the conditions for citizenship rights, human rights, and Aboriginal rights to their Aboriginal constituencies.

15 In the classical legal formulation of colonialism, self-determination, or decolonization, occurs when the colonizer "goes home." The colonial relationship in Canada (and in other settler states) is between indigenous and settler populations, both permanently resident in one territory. The objective of decolonization in Canada cannot be the eviction of the colonizer. Settler populations are permanently here. Indigenous and settler people have a long history of involvement, resulting in populations whose ancestry includes both. Obviously, separation of colonizer and colonized is politically and practically impossible.

Sharing Power

16 Decolonization, however, is possible. Rather than separation, decolonization requires the inclusion of colonized peoples in institutions of power, the design of which reflects the priorities and cultural assumptions of the colonized as well as those of the colonizer. In other words, Canadian federalism, the Constitution, and public politics must reflect indigenous histories, imagination, and aspirations as thoroughly as they now reflect colonial priorities.

17 Indeed, University of Victoria law professor John Borrows argues that only "Aboriginal control of Canadian affairs" will be truly liberatory. A Borrows-like analysis would move Canada to postcolonial conditions by indigenizing—and thus,

legitimating—settler society. Progressive political movements should agree to work for this goal. "The Left" would then ideally resonate more with indigenous movements and, consequently, more indigenous people may identify with the politics of the Left. And, while forging mutually respectful, knowledgeable alliances on common issues is a good beginning, real political muscle will be developed when conditional alliances are transformed into a more coherent, stable, and focused political force—such as a structured social movement with an electoral wing.

Considering Ideas

1. Green insists that Canada is "a creature born of capitalism and colonialism." On first reading, is this a positive, or a negative idea? What is the thesis for this essay selection?

2. What does Green suggest should be the "primary goal of the Left"? What does this say about the intended audience for this essay? How do her attempts to argue in favour of a goal speak to readers who may not agree?

3. Green uses a rhetorical question in a quote by Aboriginal leader Matthew Coon-Come. Does the writer expect that the reader will agree with this question? How does the question relate to this essay's thesis?

4. In her argument, Green claims, in paragraph 10, that "The most prominent choice for decolonization, self-government, and autonomy is by means of separate lands, institutions, and economies." How practical would this suggestion be, given the size and diversity of the Canadian population?

5. How clear is Green's purpose? Is her audience only "the Left"?

Considering Technique

1. Does the introduction engage your interest? Why or why not? What strategy does Green use to engage interest?

2. *Combining Patterns.* What historical and research examples does Green include in the essay?

3. *Combining Patterns.* What are the examples of narration in this essay?

4. Green claims that "the ecosphere is staggering." How does this use of personification and metaphor further the thesis of this essay? (Metaphors and similes are explained on page 147.)

For Group Discussion or Journal Writing

Green's essay is primarily an appeal to an audience that she refers to as "the Left." Does this exclude people who have political opinions that are more conservative? Would her ideas be as welcome among "the Right"? How easy would it be, "sharing the state," and "sharing power"? Do Canadians have any other choice?

Pre-reading

1. Tyre is going to suggest that boys and girls think differently. To what extent is this true, based on your experience?

2. Do parenting styles affect how boys and girls think? Do the toys presented to boys and girls imprint behaviour?

3. Finally, are boys and girls treated differently in the classroom? Cite specific examples.

4. Before reading, consider research. This professional essay does not include formal documentation due to its style and audience. As you read, look for at least one point in the essay that needs to be supported by academic research. Would the essay have greater appeal if it included citations and references?

Boy Brains, Girl Brains

Peg Tyre

Do boys and girls learn differently? Peg Tyre combines comparison-contrast, cause-and-effect analysis, process analysis, and exemplification to report research indicating that they do. In this article that originally appeared in Newsweek *in 2005, Tyre reports on an important implication of this research for education. As you read, notice how Tyre uses multiple patterns in the same paragraph.*

1   Three years ago, Jeff Gray, the principal at Foust Elementary School in Owensboro, Ky., realized that his school needed help—and fast. Test scores at Foust were the worst in the county and the students, particularly the boys, were falling far behind. So Gray took a controversial course for educators on brain development, then revamped the first- and second-grade curriculum. The biggest change: he divided the classes by gender. Because males have less serotonin in their brains, which Gray was taught may cause them to fidget more, desks were removed from the boys' classrooms and they got short exercise periods throughout the day. Because females have more oxytocin, a hormone linked to bonding, girls were given a carpeted area where they sit and discuss their feelings. Because boys have higher levels of testosterone and are theoretically more competitive, they were given timed, multiple-choice tests. The girls were given multiple-choice tests, too, but got more time to complete them. Gray says the gender-based curriculum gave the school "the edge we needed." Tests scores are up. Discipline problems are down. This year the fifth and sixth grades at Foust are adopting the new curriculum, too.

2   Do Mars and Venus[1] ride the school bus? Gray is part of a new crop of educators with a radical idea—that boys and girls are so biologically different they need to be separated into single-sex classes and taught in different ways. In the last five years, brain researchers using sophisticated MRI and PET technology have gathered new information about the ways male and female brains develop and process information. Studies show that girls, for instance, have more active frontal lobes, stronger connections between brain hemispheres and "language centers" that mature earlier than their male counterparts. Critics of gender-based schooling charge that curricula designed to exploit such differences reinforce the most narrow cultural stereotypes. But proponents say that unless neurological, hormonal,

and cognitive differences between boys and girls are incorporated in the classroom, boys are at a disadvantage.

3   Most schools are girl-friendly, says Michael Gurian, coauthor with Kathy Stevens of a new book, *The Minds of Boys: Saving Our Sons from Falling Behind in School and Life*, "because teachers, who are mostly women, teach the way they learn." Seventy percent of children diagnosed with learning disabilities are male, and the sheer number of boys who struggle in school is staggering. Eighty percent of high-school drop-outs are boys and less than 45 percent of students enrolled in college are young men. To close the educational gender gap, Gurian says, teachers need to change their techniques. They should light classrooms more brightly for boys and speak to them loudly, since research shows males don't see or hear as well as females. Because boys are more-visual learners, teachers should illustrate a story before writing it and use an overhead projector to practice reading and writing. Gurian's ideas seem to be catching on. More than 185 public schools now offer some form of single-sex education, and Gurian has trained more than 15,000 teachers through his institute in Colorado Springs.

4   To some experts, Gurian's approach is not only wrong but dangerous. Some say his curriculum is part of a long history of pseudoscience aimed at denying equal opportunities in education. For much of the 19th century, educators, backed by prominent scientists, cautioned that women were neurologically unable to withstand the rigors of higher education. Others say basing new teaching methods on raw brain research is misguided. While it's true that brain scans show differences between boys and girls, says David Sadker, education professor at American University, no one is exactly sure what those differences mean. Differences between boys and girls, says Sadker, are dwarfed by brain differences within each gender. "If you want to make schools a better place," says Sadker, "you have to strive to see kids as individuals."

5   Natasha Craft, a fourth-grade teacher at Southern Elementary School in Somerset, Ky., knows the gender-based curriculum she began using last year isn't a cure-all. "Not all the boys and girls are going to be the same," she says, "but I feel like it gives me another set of tools to work with." And when she stands in front of a room of hard-to-reach kids, Craft says, another set of tools could come in handy.

[1] A reference to the book *Men Are from Mars, Women Are from Venus: A Practical Guide for Improving Communication and Getting What You Want in Your Relationships* by John Gray. The book discusses fundamental differences between men and women.

Considering Ideas

1. What are the chief arguments for single-sex classrooms?

2. What are the chief arguments against single-sex classrooms?

3. Why are most schools girl-friendly? In your earlier schooling, were your classrooms girl-friendly?

4. David Sadker opposes single-sex education, saying that there are more differences within genders than between them (paragraph 4). What do you think these differences are?

Considering Technique

1. The thesis of "Boy Brains, Girl Brains" is implied rather than stated. In your own words, write out the thesis. For what purpose do you think the essay was written?

2. *Combining Patterns.* The essay opens with exemplification. Does that exemplification create an effective beginning? Why or why not?

3. *Combining Patterns.* How does Tyre use cause-and-effect analysis in paragraphs 1 and 3? How does she use comparison-contrast in paragraphs 1 and 2?

4. *Combining Patterns.* How does Tyre use process analysis in paragraph 3?

5. Does Tyre treat both sides of the issue with equal emphasis and detail? Explain.

For Group Discussion or Journal Writing

David Sadker says that we can improve schools if we "see kids as individuals" (paragraph 4). Discuss several ways that teachers and administrators can see children as individuals. How well do we currently treat children as individuals?

WRITING TOOL

Quoting Authorities

Writers often draw on the words of authorities to back up their points and lend credibility to their ideas. Peg Tyre also draws on authorities to make her points and establish credibility. In paragraph 3, for example, she supports the point made earlier that boys are at a disadvantage in schools by quoting an authority:

Most schools are girl-friendly, says Michael Gurian, coauthor with Kelly Stevens of a new book, *The Minds of Boys: Saving Our Sons from Falling Behind in School and Life*, "because teachers, who are mostly women, teach the way they learn."

Students who quote and paraphrase other authors must follow a number of conventions to maintain strict academic integrity. These conventions are explained in Chapter 17. Be sure you follow them scrupulously to avoid plagiarism.

Combining Patterns in an Image

Study the following advertisement to identify the elements of both exemplification and definition that it includes.

Considering the Image

1. What persuasive purpose does the advertisement have?
2. What informational purpose does the advertisement have?
3. What element of cause-and-effect appears in the advertisement, and how does that definition help the ad achieve its purpose?
4. What element of exemplification appears in the advertisement, and how does that exemplification help the ad achieve its purpose?

Reading Then Writing with Multiple Patterns

1. All of us have felt like outsiders at times, whether it has been as the new student in school, a stranger in a roomful of people who know each other, or a new employee on the job. Use multiple patterns to tell about a time you tried to fit into a group of people when you felt like an outsider.

saying Eh! is better
than saying Huh!

i wear sneakers
not snow shoes

i wear a toque
not a fur hat

i am not a mountie
nor am i a trapper

my second car
is not a dogsled

I AM

T03862BK

snow boarding
is not our
national sport

we are
the second largest
country in the world

i don't have
a pet beaver

CANADIAN

© STARLINE PACIFIC INC.

canadians
still are
the best
hockey players

we do not
shovel snow
all year round

our parliament building
is not made of ice

canadian
back bacon
only comes from
canadian pigs

the maple leaf
is our
national symbol

2. As Peg Tyre does in "Boy Brains, Girl Brains," combine patterns to explain a way to improve education.

Combining Patterns beyond the Writing Classroom

Assume you are applying for an important job, and as part of the application process, you must write an essay explaining what you hope to accomplish in the next 10 years. Drawing on whatever patterns you need to, explain what your goals are, why they are important, and how you plan to accomplish them.

Responding to a Theme

1. In "Boy Brains, Girl Brains," arguments for single-sex education are presented. Argue for or against single-sex education in high school.
2. *Connecting the Readings*. Much is made of the problems with North American education. "Boy Brains, Girl Brains" points to one problem and "School Is Bad for Children" on page 7 points to another. Despite the many criticisms of our system of education, much is right with the way we educate our youth. Write an essay in which you discuss what is *right* with Canadian education.

THE WRITING PROCESS

Combining Patterns

The following guidelines are not meant to replace your own effective procedures. They are here for you to try as you work to improve your writing process.

Generate Ideas, Consider Audience and Purpose, and Order Ideas

- Recognize that an assigned topic may suggest certain patterns. For example, the assigned topic "*gender bias* in the media" suggests that you will define *gender bias* and give examples of its occurrence, and argue that it must end.
- If you need help narrowing your topic or generating ideas, answer the questions given earlier in this chapter, on page 328.
- If necessary, answer the "Questions for Establishing Purpose" on page 39 and the "Questions for Identifying and Assessing Audience" on page 43.
- To order ideas, assess whether the patterns combined suggest particular arrangements. For example, if you combine process analysis and cause-and-effect analysis, you will likely combine chronological and progressive orders.
- Write a formal outline, which can be particularly helpful when you are using more than one order for your ideas. Before you craft an outline, brainstorm your topic, and explore some of the ideas you generate, to see where they lead. Decide which pattern of development best suits your purpose.

Draft

- Write a preliminary thesis and use an outline to guide drafting.
- If you have trouble beginning, start with your thesis and then write the first point to develop that thesis.
- Keep the characteristics of the patterns you are using in mind as you draft.
- Alternatively, order ideas in an outline, and decide on a thesis that unifies these ideas and that suggests the best pattern of development to communicate the thesis.

Revise

- Consult the graphic visualizations of each pattern in Chapters 6–13 for a quick review of their characteristics. Revise with these characteristics in mind.
- When you move from one pattern to another, achieve coherence with transitions and repetition.
- To secure reader response, see pages 101–102.

Correct errors and Proofread

- Use the "Guide to Frequently Occurring Errors" for reference, and check with a writing centre tutor if you are unsure about a grammar, usage, or punctuation point.
- Check one extra time for the kinds of mistakes you are in the habit of making.
- Remember to proofread your final copy carefully before submitting it.

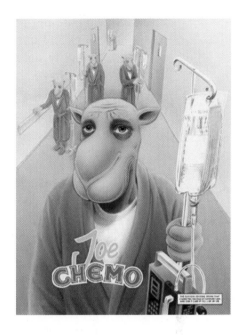

CHAPTER 15

Argumentation and Persuasion

Looking Ahead

In this chapter, you will learn strategies for argument and persuasive writing. Argumentation is a pattern of organization, and persuasion is a purpose for writing. You will learn persuasive techniques for convincing readers to think or act in a particular way. An interesting aspect of argumentation is that no matter what the issue, people will take opposing views. The images here, for example, represent opposing views. The first image is a popular Joe Camel advertisement meant to persuade people to buy Camel cigarettes. The second advertisement is a parody of Joe Camel, "Joe Chemo," meant to persuade people not to smoke Camels—or any cigarettes. Before turning attention to the chapter, consider the two advertisements, and answer the following questions:

- How does the Joe Camel ad work to persuade people to smoke Camels?

- How does the Joe Chemo ad work to persuade people not to smoke?

- What specific audience is the Joe Camel ad addressing? Is the Joe Chemo ad trying to reach the same audience?

- How well does each advertisement achieve its purpose? Explain.

Social beings are not content merely to form opinions—they are moved to express those opinions and try to convince others of their truth, the way the author of the following letter to the author of the *Globe and Mail*'s article "Disowning Canadians Abroad" does.

> The people opposing the repatriation of [Omar] Khadr are either being dishonest about their motives, are uninformed, or just plain stupid. Based on the evidence that has been released to the public, he wouldn't be convicted of this crime in the U.S. if he were to go before a legitimate court. Those opposed to this should be honest. This isn't about guilt, or even terrorism. This is about him being associated with Fundamentalist Muslims. Keep in mind that many people in this country feel equally disturbed about Fundamentalist Christians (such as the PM). The Constitution is there to protect everybody's rights, including Fundamentalist Christians and Fundamentalist Muslims. This case illustrates just how important it is to have a Constitution that protects against government persecution of minority groups regardless of whether there is a majority that supports open discrimination or not.

The letter writer has strong opinions about whether the Canadian government should support those who run afoul of the law abroad, regardless of their religious affiliation. The **issue** is help for Canadians stranded in legal limbo overseas. The belief is that all Canadians requesting assistance should be helped—this is the **claim**. Whether the writer convinces readers to agree with the claims about the issues depends, in part, on how well she argues her case. In other words, in **argumentation**, the writer offers **evidence** to support a claim about an issue. The more convincing the evidence, the more convincing the argument and the more likely readers will agree.

Written argument, to persuade successfully, depends for success on the combination of claims about issues, and the facts and/or opinions that support the claims, which in turn support a thesis and persuade readers. Remember: argumentation is a pattern of organization, and persuasion is a purpose for writing.

Why is Argumentation Important?

Argumentation, which works to convince readers to think or act a particular way, is everywhere. Magazine advertisements work to convince consumers that the surest path to popularity is using the right deodorant soap; letters from banks try to persuade clients that owning their credit cards will allow them to buy as much as they want without penalty; campaign literature works to convince citizens to vote for candidates; travel brochures aim to persuade tourists to visit Belize for the vacation of a lifetime; movie posters try to entice the public to buy a ticket to the latest James Bond film; academic Web sites urge students to attend their schools; newspaper editorials try to persuade consumers of the dangers of tax reform; public service billboards work to persuade drivers not to drink and drive; and book reviews try to convince readers of the quality—or lack of quality—of the latest bestseller.

Because so many people are trying to convince readers to adopt certain views or take certain actions, understanding how argumentation works will make writers more aware of how people are trying to move others and, thus, better able to evaluate their arguments. In addition, you will have many occasions to write argumentation yourself (as the next sections explain), so understanding the principles of argumentation is important for that reason.

OCCASIONS FOR WRITING

Argumentation across the Disciplines and Beyond

Argumentation in the Classroom

Many courses, particularly after the introductory level, require students to write argumentation. For example, for a paper in an ethics class, you might argue for an equitable procedure for allocating transplant organs. For a Canadian history paper, you might argue for or against the payment of reparations to Native Canadians. On a class Web site for a business management course, you might argue for or against the use of flextime at work. *What important issues are commonly argued in your major? In your city? How likely are you to write essays that argue claims about these issues? How might you use argumentation in the classes you are taking this term?*

Argumentation in Daily Life

In personal writing, you are likely to use argumentation often. For example, you might write a letter to the editor of a local paper to persuade readers to adopt a position on an issue, or you might write an email to convince a friend to take a day off and go to the beach. If a consumer has problems with a product he bought, he might write a letter to a customer service representative arguing for a refund. *How might you use argumentation as chair of a membership committee for a children's museum? As a member of the ticket sales committee for a theatre group? As a volunteer worker on a political campaign?*

Argumentation on the Job

The writing people do at work is likely to include argumentation. Union leaders, for example, write letters to persuade their members to vote for or against contracts. Attorneys write opening and closing arguments to convince juries; social workers write reports to convince judges to rule in clients' behalf; real estate brokers write listings to persuade people to consider buying property. *How might you use argumentation in the job you hope to have after graduation? For whom will you write the argumentation? How important will this writing be to your success on the job?*

DETERMINING PURPOSE

Determining Purpose for Argumentation

Argumentation is not fighting, and it need not involve conflict. While its purpose is to persuade, it can serve a variety of persuasive purposes, some of which are given in the following chart.

Purpose	Sample Argumentation
To reinforce an existing view and create sentiment to maintain the status quo	A report to a department supervisor explaining the benefits of the four-day work week option that the department instituted a year ago
To call readers to action	A newspaper editorial urging people to sign a petition in support of a piece of legislation
To change people's minds	A campaign brochure urging voters in a predominantly Conservative riding to vote for a Liberal candidate
To lessen an objection	An email to parents, who do not want their child to transfer to another school district, convincing them that a transfer will not be as difficult as they think
To earn support for a position	A letter to the editor of a newspaper arguing that mandatory drug testing is an invasion of privacy

Finding an Issue and Establishing a Claim

An argument essay gives evidence to support a claim about an issue. An **issue** is a concern or problem about which people agree or disagree. A **claim** is the writer's opinion about the issue. If you argue that the tax on cigarettes should be increased, the issue is the cigarette tax, and the claim is that the tax should be increased. If you argue that animals should not be used to test the safety of cosmetics, the issue is testing cosmetics on animals, and the claim is that such testing should not occur. While working to find an issue and establish a claim, be sure these are debatable and sufficiently focused.

First, an issue and claim must be debatable. That is, they must be controversial rather than a statement of fact or personal preference. We cannot argue, for example, that cigarettes are not harmful because medical science has already proven the opposite—the matter is not debatable. Nor can you argue that women look better without makeup—the matter is one of personal preference.

In addition to being debatable, an issue and claim must be sufficiently focused. How specific they should be depends on the purpose and audience. You will not be able to argue convincingly for censorship in a five-page paper for a media class. There are simply too many kinds of censorship. However, you *can* narrow an issue and claim to argue for censorship of the Internet. For an even shorter paper, you can narrow further to argue for censorship of the Internet in high schools with wired classrooms. In a letter to the editor of a campus newspaper, writers do not have space to argue convincingly against a school's new five-year plan, but can argue against the recommended annual tuition hikes. If you are a guest columnist with more space, you can argue that the five-year plan places more importance on new buildings than on quality instruction.

Consider Audience and Purpose

A piece of writing's audience will affect how to establish an issue and claim. First, you should determine which of three kinds of readers you are writing for: supportive, wavering, or hostile.

Supportive readers: These readers are already sympathetic to a claim. If a student wants a school to begin a campus-wide recycling program, supportive readers would include members of the campus environmental club. Because this audience is already on the writer's side, the purpose will focus more on moving readers to act rather than to think a certain way. Thus, rather than argue that a school should begin a recycling program, the student writer might want to argue that readers should begin a letter-writing campaign to urge the administration to begin the program.

Wavering readers: These readers are not committed to a claim but can be brought to the writer's side. They may need more information, may not yet have made up their minds, or may not care much about the issue initially. With wavering readers, you should identify the reasons for resistance and address them. Wavering readers for an argument essay urging campus-wide recycling might include students who think that recycling is too much trouble. A writer can address this concern by explaining that conveniently located recycling bins make recycling easier and that any moderate inconvenience is a small price to pay for a cleaner environment.

Hostile readers: These readers are strongly opposed to a claim or are difficult to persuade for another reason, perhaps apathy or anger. Because hostile readers are the most difficult to persuade, you must have a realistic purpose in writing for this audience. You may not be able to change these readers' minds, so you may have to settle for lessening their objections. For example, an institution's chief financial officer may be strongly opposed to recycling because the school has no money to run the program. In that case, the purpose may be to present evidence that a recycling program can be financially beneficial.

The audience will also affect the purpose of an argument essay. While writers want to convince readers to see things just as they do, this may be an unreasonable expectation. If you favour emissions targets for carbon polluters and contact oil industry executives, a realistic purpose would be to convince them of the need for stricter enforcement of existing regulations. An unrealistic purpose would be to convince them that all resource development should be banned.

Sometimes a particular audience is so opposed to a claim that the best you can hope for is that readers will consider some points and agree that they have some merit. For example, if you are writing to the president of the local teachers' union about the hardships of teachers' strikes, you cannot expect readers to come out against such strikes. However, if you present a good enough case, readers can come to understand something they never realized before and become more sympathetic to a claim. Perhaps this new understanding will influence the reader's thinking and actions in the future.

The following can help you settle on a purpose compatible with an audience.

AUDIENCE AND PURPOSE COMPATIBILITY

Audience	Possible Purpose
Is well informed and strongly opposed to a claim	To lessen the opposition by convincing the audience that some points are valid and worth consideration
Is poorly informed and opposed to a claim	To inform the audience and change their view
Would find it difficult to perform the desired action	To convince the audience that it is worth the sacrifice or convince them to do some part of what is desired
Should not find it difficult to perform the desired action	To convince the audience to perform the action
Has no interest one way or the other in the issue	To arouse interest and persuade the audience to agree

EXERCISE CONSIDERING AUDIENCE, IDENTIFYING ISSUES, AND MAKING CLAIMS

1. For each of the following claims, note whether the indicated audience is likely to be supportive, wavering, or hostile. Explain your view.
   a. In order to graduate from college or university, students should be required to perform 40 hours of community service. (*audience = college or university students*)
   b. In order to graduate from college or university, students should be required to perform 40 hours of community service. (*audience = college or university administrators*)
   c. Building a water tower on Cadillac Drive will help water reach the north quarter of the township, allowing new businesses to locate there and revitalize the area. (*audience = homeowners on Cadillac Drive*)
   d. Building a water tower on Cadillac Drive will help water reach the north quarter of the township, allowing new businesses to locate there and revitalize the area. (*audience = township administrators*)
   e. Establishing a curfew for people under 18 will help keep our youth out of trouble. (*audience = parents*)
   f. Establishing a curfew for people under 18 will help keep our youth out of trouble. (*audience = teenagers*)

2. For three of the following subjects, identify two issues suitable for consideration in an argument essay. Then make a claim about each issue.

   Example: Television
   Issue: Sexual content on prime-time television programs
   Claim: Prime-time television programs have too much explicit sexual content

   Issue: Advertising on children's programs
   Claim: Programs aimed at children under age 5 should be free of advertising

   a. Sports
   b. College life
   c. Rock music
   d. Graduation requirements
   e. Politics ●

Kinds of Support

Because an argument essay is written on a debatable issue, there is no absolute right or wrong side. In fact, all sides of the issue are likely to have some merit. To convince readers, you must support a claim to demonstrate that it is *more correct, logical, or valid* than opposing ones. Three kinds of support can help students do this: logical appeals, emotional appeals, and ethical appeals.

Logical Appeals (Logos)

To convince readers by appealing to their sense of logic, you must offer compelling reasons and evidence for your claims. **Reasons** explain why writers believe claims about issues. Suppose you are arguing that juveniles who commit violent crimes should not stand trial in adult courts. Particular reasons—why anyone should believe that juveniles should not be tried in adult courts—could include these:

- Adult courts do not offer juveniles the age-appropriate protections that juvenile courts do
- Juveniles sentenced in adult courts go to adult prisons, where they are often abused
- Adult sentences are too long for juveniles
- Juveniles sentenced in adult courts are not rehabilitated

No matter how compelling they are, reasons alone are not enough to convince thoughtful readers. For a strong logical appeal, you must back up each of these reasons with evidence. The **evidence** comprises specific facts, statistics, examples, quotations, anecdotal experience, observations, and explanations that demonstrate the basic truth of the reasons, and render these reasons logically valid. For example, to back up the reason that juveniles who are sentenced in adult courts go to adult prisons, where they are often abused, you can cite statistics about the rate of abuse of juvenile offenders by adult inmates. You could then use cause-and-effect analysis to explain that because of the abuse, the juveniles are likely to become more psychologically damaged than they were when they entered prison.

Sources of Reasons and Evidence

Reasons and evidence to support your claims can come from a variety of sources, including your own experience and observation, reading and television viewing, class lectures, the experience of others, research, and the testimony of authorities. Evidence must appeal to all readers' senses of logical correctness. Here are some examples.

Issue: Testing students for drugs

Claim: High school students should be tested regularly

Personal experience and observation: Your friend or classmate overdosed in high school. His death suggests a reason for this claim: Regular drug testing might have led to a rehabilitation that could have saved the classmate's life. As evidence to back up this reason, you can use narration to tell about the classmate, who was a regular drug user from his sophomore year until his death on the morning of high school graduation. You can then use cause-and-effect analysis to show that drug testing could have prevented the tragedy.

Reading and television viewing: A news report that over half of teenagers surveyed admitted to regular drug use suggests a reason for this claim: With drug use that common, drug testing is needed to identify users and get them help. As evidence to back up this reason, you can cite the news report as proof of how widespread adolescent drug use is and then use process analysis to explain how the testing would lead to helpful intervention.

Class lectures: Learning in a health class that drug testing has been a deterrent among Olympic athletes suggests deterrence as a reason for a claim. As evidence to back up this reason, you can cite the information as an example. You can also use a logical comparison to explain that if drug testing keeps Olympic athletes from using drugs, it can do so for high school students as well.

The experiences of others: A classmate who transferred from a private school in another province told you that he was afraid to use drugs there because of drug testing, but he felt free to use them in the new school, where no drug testing existed. This information also suggests deterrence as a reason for a claim. As evidence to back up this reason, you can cite the classmate's experience.

Research: An Internet search or library database search turns up statistics that show teenage drug use as a leading cause of violent crime. This information suggests a reason for this claim: If drug testing reduces drug use among teenagers, it will also reduce the amount of violence that plagues high schools. As evidence to back up this reason, you can use cause-and-effect analysis to show how reducing drug use will reduce the amount of violence. (Be sure to document research material according to the conventions explained in Chapter 17.) See Christel's essay in progress, or another student research paper, as an example of how to incorporate research to advance a claim and prove a thesis.

Testimony of authorities: Interviewing high school principals and drug counsellors who favour drug testing can give you additional reasons and evidence for support.

Inductive and Deductive Reasoning

In addition to giving reasons and evidence as support, an appeal to logic should show the progression of thought that led a writer to the conclusion expressed in a claim. Two frequently used patterns of reasoning are induction and deduction.

Induction: With **induction**, the progression is from specific evidence to the general conclusion given in the claim.

Specific evidence:	The number of adolescent suicide attempts is increasing.
Specific evidence:	In the last year, the local high school has reported four attempted suicides.
Specific evidence:	Guidance counsellors in high school are counselling more students for depression than ever before.
Specific evidence:	Today's high school students are under a great deal of stress.
Conclusion:	Our high school should institute a suicide prevention program.

Inductive reasoning allows writers to argue claims by showing how specific evidence (facts, statistics, cases, examples, and so on) lead to the point the writer wants to convince the reader of. Thus, to convince a reader that the local high school should institute a suicide prevention program, you could do so by stating and explaining each piece of evidence that—by way of induction—leads to the conclusion that the program is a good idea.

In inductive reasoning, a conclusion is sound only if it is based on sufficient evidence and only if that evidence is accurate, relevant, and specific. In other words, logical premises lead to a logical conclusion, and to a valid argument. Thus, you cannot reasonably conclude that today's teens are suicidal solely on the basis that there are four attempted suicides in one high school. Nor can you draw that conclusion if you are wrong about the amount of depression counsellors are seeing in teenagers.

Induction can be used in an entire essay or in part of one. Here, for example is a paragraph developed with induction. Notice that the evidence appears first, and the conclusion drawn from that evidence appears last.

evidence

Maxine Phillips reports that approximately 9.5 million preschoolers have mothers with jobs outside the house.

evidence

Many of these mothers are the sole support of their children, so they cannot stay home, although they may want to.

evidence

An alarming number, says Philips, also cannot afford quality daycare, so their children are in substandard situations, or worse—unsupervised.

evidence

Given the compelling evidence that the child's early years are key in their future intellectual and social development, we must ensure that those years are spent in sound, enriching environments that daycare can provide.

evidence

Yet, if that daycare is not affordable, large numbers of children will suffer.

conclusion

That is something we have it in our power to prevent: The federal government should subsidize daycare programs for single parents.

Deduction: A second progression of thought leading to a conclusion is deduction. **Deduction** is a form of reasoning that moves from a generalization (known as a major premise) to a specific case (known as a minor premise) and on to a conclusion. Deduction works like this:

Generalization (major premise):	Our city has a serious unemployment problem.
Specific case (minor premise):	A proposed federal infrastructure program would create 500 new jobs.
Conclusion:	If the new federally sponsored transit system is built in our city, we could put 500 people to work.

Deductive reasoning can help writers organize arguments for their claims about an issue. Suppose you want to convince readers that the city should compete for the new federal transportation infrastructure funding. You can support the claim by reproducing deductive reasoning: The city needs jobs, and the transit project will provide them. Therefore, the city needs federal funding for traffic infrastructure.

Deductive reasoning works with logical syllogism. The pattern for Aristotelian syllogism works as follows. One proposition (the conclusion) is inferred from two others. These propositions are premises. The syllogism operates on the logical basis that a major premise, combined with a minor, related premise, lead logically to a valid conclusion. The typical syllogism works with a set of at least three terms, as in the following:

> Major premise: All A are B.
> Minor premise: All C are A.
> Conclusion: All C are B.

Here is an example of how a syllogism would work:

> Major premise: All mortals die.
> Minor premise: All men are mortal.
> Conclusion: All men die.

To argue well, however, you must avoid the illogical conclusions that result from inaccurate or sweeping generalizations. Notice the problems with the following deductive reasoning:

Generalization (major premise):	All students cheat at one time or another.
Specific case (minor premise):	Lee is a student.
Conclusion:	Lee cheats.

This conclusion is illogical because the first generalization is inaccurate—all students do not cheat. This assertion cannot be proven.

Generalization (major premise):	Foreign cars are better made than Canadian-built cars.
Generalization (minor premise):	My car was made in Germany.
Conclusion:	My car is better made than Canadian cars.

This conclusion is illogical because the first generalization is sweeping—many foreign cars are not better made than Canadian cars. Remember, the conclusion is valid only when premises are valid. Remember, also, that "valid" is not a substitute for "true," as "truth" in argument is subjective.

Deduction can be used in an entire essay or in part of one. Here, for example, is a paragraph developed with deduction. Notice that the major premise appears first, followed by the minor premises and the supporting evidence. The conclusion the deduction leads to appears last.

major premise

No one argues with the fact that preschool children require a nurturing environment.

minor premise

No one disagrees either that the best nurturing environment is a stable home combined, if necessary, with a quality daycare centre.

minor premise

Lately, however, evidence suggests that many preschoolers are not getting the nurturing they need because their mothers work to make ends meet and there is too little money for adequate daycare.

evidence for minor premise

Maxine Phillips reports that over half the mothers of preschoolers are in the workforce. She also explains that many of these mothers, who are the sole support of their children, cannot afford to stop working, nor can they afford adequate daycare, so children end up in substandard environments or unsupervised.

conclusion

In light of this, the need for federally subsidized daycare becomes apparent.

Avoiding Logical Fallacies

Because any appeal to logic must have sound thinking at its core, errors in reasoning, called **logical fallacies**, will weaken an argument. If the logical fallacies are serious or frequent enough, readers will reject a claim, and the writer will not achieve the purpose for writing. In the section about induction and deduction, students learned three types of faulty logic: basing a conclusion on insufficient evidence, using sweeping generalizations, and using inaccurate generalizations. In addition, when revising, check for the following logical fallacies.

1. Do not attack an idea based on the people associated with that idea. This faulty logic is **guilt by association**.

   Example: Only Liberals oppose balancing the federal budget, and we all know the mess they've gotten this country into.

   Explanation: The people who do or do not champion an idea or action have nothing to do with the validity of that idea or action.

2. Avoid name-calling or attacks on personalities rather than ideas. This is argumentum ***ad hominem*** (to argue against the man).

   Example: The president of this college (university) is so out of touch with students that he thinks they will sit still for another tuition increase.

   Explanation: It is legitimate to criticize what people do or think, but it is unfair to attack the personalities of the people themselves.

3. Do not defend or attack an idea or action on the grounds that people have always believed that idea or performed that action.

   Example: Children have always learned to read in first grade, so why should we begin teaching them any earlier now?

   Explanation: Everything believed and done in the past and present is not always for the best. Perhaps new research in education indicates that children are capable of reading before (or after) the first grade.

4. Avoid illogical comparisons, also called **false analogy**.

Example:	The voters in this city have not passed a school levy for seven years. They will never vote for a teacher to become our next senator.
Explanation:	How voters feel about school levies has nothing to do with how they feel about a political candidate who happens to be a teacher. The comparison is not logical.

5. Do not assume that what is true for one person will be true for everybody. This is a **sweeping generalization**.

Example:	When I was a child, my parents spanked me regularly, and I turned out just fine. Clearly, there is no harm in spanking as a form of punishment.
Explanation:	It does not hold that just because one person suffered no ill effects from spanking, no one will suffer ill effects from spanking.

To avoid sweeping generalizations, writers need not avoid using evidence from personal experience. They should, however, be careful of what they conclude from this evidence. Do not make more of it than it is.

6. Do not offer an unproven statement as the truth, or you will be guilty of **begging the question**.

Example:	Unnecessary programs like Shop and Home Economics should be eliminated to balance the new school budget.
Explanation:	The importance of shop and home economics is debatable, so writers cannot assume they are unnecessary and argue from there. Writers must first prove they are unnecessary.

7. Avoid drawing a conclusion that does not follow from the evidence. This is called a **non sequitur**.

Example:	Feminism is a potent social force in the North America. No wonder our divorce rate is so high.
Explanation:	Many factors contribute to the divorce rate; no logical reason establishes feminism as the sole cause or even one cause.

8. Do not present only two options when more than two exist. This is the **either/or fallacy**.

Example:	Either you support the strike or you are opposed to organized labour.
Explanation:	The sentence ignores other possibilities, such as opposing the strike but believing the union's demands should be met, or opposing the strike but calling for further negotiations.

9. Avoid **bandwagon appeals** that argue that everyone believes something, so the reader should, too.

Example:	All the professors I spoke to in the political science department favour the trade agreement with Japan, so it must be a good idea.
Explanation:	The issue should be argued on the merits of the trade agreement, not based on who favours it.

10. Do not assume that an event that precedes another event is the cause of that event. This is called a **post-hoc fallacy**.

Example:	After students read *The Catcher in the Rye*, the number of teen pregnancies in our school increased. The book causes promiscuity.
Explanation:	Although the pregnancies followed the reading of the book, other factors may have caused the increase in the pregnancy rate.

11. Do not digress from the matter at hand by introducing a distraction, called a **red herring**.

Example:	We should not spend more money on AIDS research because so many AIDS victims chose to put themselves at risk.
Explanation:	The behaviour of some people who contract AIDS is not the issue but a distraction (red herring) meant to direct the reader's attention away from the issue—whether more money should be spent on AIDS research.

EXERCISE RECOGNIZING LOGICAL FALLACIES

Directions: Each of the following includes one or more logical fallacies. Identify what they are.

1. The proposed assisted-living facility is an unnecessary expenditure of public funds. The elderly in this city have always been cared for by family members or in nursing homes.

2. Those who favour school prayer are the same reactionaries who bomb abortion clinics.

3. The last generation has seen a marked increase in the number of working mothers, which explains the similar increase in the rate of violent crime.

4. Because football players care less about their schoolwork than their sport, the university should eliminate athletic scholarships.

5. How can any union member not vote for Chris Politician? After all, every major labour group in the country has endorsed him. ●

Emotional Appeals (Pathos)

Sound logic and compelling reasons and evidence will help you argue claims by appealing to readers' rational side. However, logical appeals are not all that influence people—emotion also plays a role. After all, when we make up our minds about something, how we *feel* about the issue can determine our decision along with what we *think* about it. For this reason, charities that seek our money often include sad pictures of hungry children along with their requests. The pictures are calculated to appeal to people's emotions. Remember, however, that while emotional appeals may communicate ideas well to an audience, they are not valid forms of evidence to support a thesis for a piece of writing.

Emotional appeals focus on readers' values and needs. For example, the belief that anyone who is willing to work hard can get ahead is a fundamental social value. To appeal to this value, an essay arguing for the election of a local political candidate can mention that the politician grew up in poverty, worked during high school to help pay the rent, and made it through university by working three jobs to pay tuition. This appeal to readers' values makes the politician seem to embody a core cultural virtue—the willingness to work hard to advance oneself, or self-reliance. This appeals to a fundamental, perhaps emotional belief that hard work brings success.

Emotional appeals also focus on needs. For example, human beings need to feel attractive. Thus, the writer of a toothpaste advertisement may claim that using the product results in fewer cavities *and* a brighter smile. Our intellect makes us understand the importance of fewer cavities, so that is an appeal to logic. However, our emotional need to be attractive makes us want a brighter smile.

The toothpaste advertisement illustrates that, together, logical and emotional appeals can be more convincing than either appeal would be alone. However, a discerning reader will recognize when emotional appeals are the sole or primary thrust of an argument, and become wary. While an appeal to emotions can be both effective and appropriate, it cannot replace appeals to logic. (For more on the responsible use of emotional appeals, see "Be a Responsible Writer" below.)

To appreciate the persuasive quality of emotional appeals, consider an essay that argues the claim that young children should not be playing organized baseball. In addition to giving reasons and evidence, the essay can include this emotional appeal to the reader's desire to protect children from emotional distress:

> To some, there is nothing more heartbreaking than watching a 6- or 7-year-old baseball player crying because he just struck out, he missed the ball, or he got yelled at by his manager. Perhaps this is old-fashioned, but some prefer games that make children laugh and leave them smiling.

Ethical Appeals (Ethos)

No matter how strong support is, writers cannot convince a reader who does not trust them. To earn reader's trust, you must establish authority and present yourself—and your supporting evidence—as reliable. The writer's ethical persona is as important as the reader's ethical values. Doing so allows you to come across as ethical, and

BE A RESPONSIBLE WRITER

Responsible writers use emotional appeals fairly and with restraint. They do not play on a reader's vulnerabilities to manipulate emotions in order to achieve their purpose. Thus, as a responsible writer, students can call upon the reader's patriotism to earn support for defence spending, but should not whip up emotions by saying that anyone who does not support the spending is unpatriotic and supports terrorists. To do so is unfair, untrue, and inflammatory. It also preys on the reader's fear of undermining the country's safety.

To be a responsible writer, ask yourself these questions when you appeal to your reader's emotions:

- What aspect of my reader's emotions, values, or needs am I appealing to?
- Is it fair to appeal to this aspect, or am I taking advantage of a vulnerability?
- Is my emotional appeal only a small part of my supporting detail?

addresses a reader's personal or public values directly. For a strong ethical appeal, present compelling reasons and solid evidence, write a well-reasoned argument that avoids logical fallacies, and avoid overusing emotional appeals. An appeal addresses the audience logically, presents major and minor premises, supports these with valid arguments from respected experts, and is free from personal, social, or religious bias, or logical fallacy. In addition, if you have knowledge or experiences that particularly qualify you to write about a subject, mention them. For example, if arguing that nursing homes should be required to install surveillance cameras in patients' rooms to help prevent abuse, explain that personal experience from volunteering in a nursing home for five years provides first-hand knowledge of the need for the surveillance.

Two other important strategies for appealing to readers' ethics are raising and countering objections, and creating goodwill.

Raising and Countering Objections

No matter what claim a writer makes about an issue, some intelligent, reasonable people will disagree. Ignoring their opposing views will weaken any position because the writer will not come across as someone who has weighed all sides before drawing conclusions. However, if writers acknowledge and come to terms with the most significant arguments on the other side, they help incline readers to accept claims because objections appear more carefully thought out. Furthermore, even if writers ignore the opposition's points, readers will have them in mind. To be convincing, then, you must deal with the chief objections head-on, to dispel some reader's disagreement. The process of acknowledging and coming to terms with opposing views is called raising and countering objections, or identifying counter-arguments. You must identify the counter-argument, and rebut it, as debaters do.

Raising and countering objections is a two-part operation. First, a writer must state the opposition's point; this is **raising the objection**. Then, it is necessary to make the point less compelling by introducing an opposing point; this is **countering the objection**.

Let's return to the paper written to convince a reader to vote for a local politician to see how raising and countering objections works. The first step is to identify a reader's most compelling objections. Let's say they are these:

- The politician lacks experience in city government.
- The politician's proposed safety forces budget is inflationary.
- The politician's health problems will undermine his effectiveness.

After identifying the chief objections, you must find a way to lessen their force, or rebut the arguments. You do this in one of two ways: by offering an equally compelling point to balance out the opposition or by showing that the opposition's point is untrue. Here are some examples:

Offering an Equally Compelling Point

Some people claim that Politician's lack of experience in municipal government will make him a poor city manager. *(objection raised)* However, while he has not had actual experience in city government, 10 years as president of a local bank have provided the politician with all the managerial skills any mayor could need. Furthermore, our current mayor, who came to the job with only five years of experience on the City Council, has mismanaged everything from Street

Department funds to the city's public relations efforts. Thus, experience in city government does not guarantee success. *(objection countered)*

Although some contend that the increased safety forces budget that Politician supports is inflationary, *(objection raised)* the fact remains that without adequate police and fire protection, we will not attract new industry to our area. *(objection countered)*

Showing That the Opposition's Point Is Untrue

Some of Politician's detractors say that he is not well enough to do the job. *(objection raised)* However, Politician's physical examination last month shows he is in perfect health and any discussion to the contrary is based on rumour and falsehood. *(objection countered)*

As the examples show, an objection is sometimes countered in a single sentence and sometimes in several sentences. If an objection is particularly compelling, you may need to devote one or more paragraphs to countering it. Usually, you need not raise and counter every objection to readers' claims. It's necessary to identify readers' most important objections and deal with those.

EXERCISE RAISING AND COUNTERING OBJECTIONS

Directions: Select one of the following claims. Assuming the audience is members of the local school board; write out two likely objections to the claim. Then explain a strategy for countering each objection.

- High school seniors should be required to pass an English proficiency test in order to graduate.
- High school seniors should not be required to pass an English proficiency test in order to graduate. ●

Creating Goodwill

If the audience includes hostile or wavering readers, an ethical appeal should involve creating some goodwill between the writer and the audience. No matter how misguided a writer think the audience's views are, a confrontational stance will only alienate these readers further, making it harder for the writer to achieve a persuasive purpose. However, establishing some common ground can make it easier for readers to consider a claim objectively. Suppose you are arguing for mandatory drug testing of high school students. You can establish common ground with hostile or wavering readers by noting that both want to ensure the safety and well-being of young people. Once readers recognize that both readers and the writer share a goal, both parties are more closely positioned and have less opposition to overcome.

A second way to create goodwill is to demonstrate an understanding of the reader's viewpoints and take them seriously. Doing so validates the reader's views and makes them less defensive and less inclined to cling to a position at all costs. For example, when arguing for mandatory drug testing of teenagers, you could say something like this to show that you understand and respect the reader's views: "Mandatory drug testing does raise important privacy issues and presents a challenge to the Charter of Rights and Freedoms, facts that make the issue a particularly thorny one."

EXERCISE ANALYZING AN ARGUMENT

Directions: Alone or as a group, select an editorial that makes an argument from a local or campus newspaper. Analyze the chief strengths and weaknesses of the editorial. Consider the following:

- How clearly the issue and claim are stated
- The logical appeals
- The sources of reason and evidence
- The emotional appeals
- The ethical appeals
- Whether the editorial achieves its purpose ●

Using the Patterns of Development

The patterns of development will help writers present the logical, emotional, and ethical appeals that support their claims. The following chart demonstrates the usefulness of the patterns by showing some of the ways a writer can use them in an essay arguing the claim that voters should elect Chris Politician.

USING THE PATTERNS OF DEVELOPMENT TO ARGUE A CLAIM

Claim: Voters should elect a local politician

Support	Pattern
The politician will eliminate the downtown blight.	**Describe** the blight so readers appreciate the importance of eliminating it.
The politician has integrity.	**Narrate** an account of a time he showed integrity.
The politician is a creative problem solver.	Give **examples** of problems he has solved creatively.
The politician has a plan for reducing the city's deficit.	Use **process analysis** to explain how the plan works.
The politician is better qualified than his opponent.	**Compare and contrast** the qualifications of the politician and the opponent.
The politician has powerful connections in provincial government.	Use **cause-and-effect analysis** to explain the benefits of having connections in the provincial government.
The politician is a political sophisticate.	**Define** political sophisticate, so readers understand the importance of being one.
The politician would be an exemplary mayor.	Use classification-division to explain the components of being mayor and show that Politician has those components.

More often than not, an argument essay will draw on multiple patterns of development. For example, to convince people to vote for a previously unelected politician, you might give examples of problems this politician has solved creatively, contrast his qualifications with those of his opponent, and explain the effects of his connections in the provincial government.

Organizing an Argument Essay

The thesis for an argument essay expresses the issue and claim. The issue must be debatable, and the claim must express a stand on the issue. Here are two examples:

Thesis:	Because these dog breeds have a history of attacking people without provocation, private citizens should be prohibited from owning Rottweilers and Pit Bulls.
Issue:	Owning Rottweilers and Pit Bulls
Claim:	Private citizens should not be allowed to own these breeds.
Thesis:	In order to graduate with a bachelor's degree, all undergraduate students should be tested for proficiency in a foreign language.
Issue:	Graduation requirements
Claim:	Bachelor's degree candidates should be tested for foreign language proficiency.

The introduction can be written with a consideration not just of the issue, but of the audience as well. See pages 344–345, and consider the typical audience. See also page 357 to help determine a combined writing purpose. In particular, you need to engage readers' interest by showing why an issue is important. For example, if arguing that college and university students should be required to become proficient in a foreign language, you could explain that globalization demands that we find ways to communicate better, and that speaking each other's language helps achieve that goal.

If a reader needs background information to understand an issue or claim, you can provide detail in the introduction. For example, if the aim to convince a reader to support term limits, a writer may need to explain what term limits are and which offices lack them. To convince a reader who does not know much about dogs that private citizens should not be permitted to own Rottweilers and Pit Bulls, you can describe the characteristics of these breeds and mention how prevalent the breeds are.

You might possess particular qualifications for writing about an issue, and can mention them in an introduction as part of an ethical appeal. For example, to convince a reader that private citizens should not be allowed to own Rottweilers and Pit Bulls, you can explain in the introduction that you volunteered in an animal shelter for five years and learned a great deal about the breeds.

To organize body paragraphs, consider how best to combine several elements:

- The pattern of reasoning—whether induction or deduction
- Reasons and evidence
- Patterns of development

- Objections to raise and counter, and other ethical appeals to make
- Emotional appeals

If all or part of the argument involves inductive or deductive reasoning (or a combination of these), that part of your essay will follow the progression characteristic of that pattern of reasoning. Following an inductive pattern, you will present specific evidence and follow it with a conclusion drawn from that evidence. When following a deductive pattern, you will write a major premise, follow it with a minor premise, and then write the conclusion. (To review these patterns, return to page 349.)

For reasons and evidence, a progressive order from the least to the most compelling point is effective because the force of an argument builds gradually. To help readers follow an argument, you can state reasons in topic sentences. To develop evidence with a particular pattern of development, use the order best suited to the pattern. Thus, narration and process analysis will follow a chronological order, and comparison-contrast will follow a subject-by-subject (block) or point-by-point order.

As part of an organizational strategy, you need to determine the most effective place to raise and counter objections. Most often, you can raise and counter opposing points in an essay outline where the objections logically emerge. Suppose you argue that children should not be allowed to play with toy guns, and explain that violent play leads to violent behaviour. At that point, you can raise and counter the objection that playing with toy guns can vent violent tendencies harmlessly and thus reduce violent behaviour with a claim that supports the initial premise.

If a claim is an unpopular one, with many objections to it, you want to raise the objections in the introduction or first body paragraphs. Then the rest of the essay can counter the objections. This strategy might be effective, for example, if arguing the unpopular claim that military service should be required of all 18-year-olds. You could explain all the reasons people are opposed to such military service, and then go on to show why your claim is more compelling.

Ethical and emotional appeals can be placed where they will have the most strategic value for an argument. If a particular emotional appeal creates a strong ending, place it in the last body paragraph or in the conclusion. If explaining why the writer is qualified to write on the issue is important for persuading a wavering reader, include that information in the introduction or first body paragraph.

Conclude with any of the strategies explained in Chapter 3. Often it is effective to restate a claim about an issue to emphasize it. When a writer includes many arguments, it is necessary to summarize them in the conclusion. Finally, the writer can craft an effective conclusion by calling readers to action, recommending a solution to a problem, or explaining what would happen if a claim were not adopted or supported.

Visualizing an Argument Essay

The chart that follows can help student writers visualize the basic structure for an argument essay. Like all good models, this one can be altered as needed. For example, an argument paper for an academic course might be considerably longer than this five-paragraph model.

Introduction

- Creates interest, perhaps by explaining why the issue is important, by providing necessary background information, or by giving your qualifications
- May state objections that will be countered in the essay
- States the thesis, which includes the issue and claim

First Body Paragraph or Paragraphs

- May give a reason to support the claim and evidence to back up the reason
- May raise and counter an objection, create goodwill, or appeal to emotions
- May include ethical appeals
- May include other patterns of development
- May arrange details in a progressive order, an inductive order, a deductive order, or any order appropriate to the pattern used

Next Body Paragraph or Paragraphs

- May give a reason to support the claim and evidence to back up the reason
- May raise and counter an objection, create goodwill, or appeal to emotions
- May include ethical appeals
- May include other patterns of development
- May arrange details in a progressive order, an inductive order, a deductive order, or any order appropriate to the pattern used

Next Body Paragraphs

- Continue until all the reasons, evidence, and other supporting details are given
- May raise and counter an objection, create goodwill, or appeal to emotions
- May include ethical appeals
- May include other patterns of development
- May arrange details in a progressive order, an inductive order, a deductive order, or any order appropriate to the pattern used

Conclusion

- May restate the claim
- May summarize the arguments
- May call the reader to action, recommend a solution to a problem, or explain what will happen if the claim is or is not adopted

CRITICAL READING STUDENT ESSAY

The following argument essay was written by a student. The reasons and evidence come from the writer's observations, experience, and consideration of the issue. In "What's for Lunch? Fast Food in the Public Schools," Cheryl Sateri argues her claim that fast-food restaurants have a place in high schools. Her supporting details are mostly reasons backed up by evidence.

What's for Lunch? Fast Food in the Public Schools

Cheryl Sateri

1   North Americans are getting fatter. Statistics and studies are not needed to prove this observation. The news media are full of stories about people suing McDonald's for making them fat, and the local mall is crowded with people who probably shouldn't "supersize" their next meal. Out of concern for the health of young people, some parents at the high school I attended tried to force healthy eating habits on students by removing snack-food and soda vending machines from the student lunchroom. These same parents are also opposing the local school board's efforts to contract with a fast-food franchise to take over part of the food service at the high school lunchroom. However, I believe that a fast-food restaurant can provide a convenient, profitable service that will improve the diets of high school students.

2   Lunchtime at my former high school (and probably at most public high schools around the country) was never a leisurely, relaxing meal. Each grade had lunch for a thirty-minute period. Students stood in line for fifteen or twenty minutes waiting for some warmed-over "pizza" or "burrito," which they then had to gulp down as fast as possible. A fast-food franchise, which likely has the experience and the equipment to serve many people quickly and efficiently, would eliminate the unreasonable wait.

3   A fast-food franchise would also offer greater variety and healthier choices. In my school cafeteria, fresh vegetables and fruits were rarely offered, but fatty, sauce-drenched mystery casseroles were. The only drinks were tiny cartons of warm milk and sugary juice drinks. However, the McDonald's franchise in my college student union offers ice-cold milk in large cartons, yogurt, fresh fruit, crispy salads, and grilled chicken sandwiches. Although I don't know what franchise would eventually move into my former high school, the school board could make healthy choices and variety a condition of the contract.

4   Along with vending machines, a fast-food franchise in the student lunchroom would keep student dollars on campus, since a portion of the profits would be returned to the school. At my high school, everyone looked forward to senior year because of off-campus lunch privileges (most seniors in good standing had a free period immediately after lunch). If students were not currently serving a detention, they were allowed to leave the building to purchase lunch. Of course, everyone walked two blocks up to the KFC or the Subway and spent their money there. If seniors could purchase such food on campus, a percentage of the money now spent off campus would go to the school's student

---

PARAGRAPH 1

The introduction creates interest with references to readily identifiable fast food restaurants. It also establishes the fact that obesity is a health issue. It then establishes that some parents want to "force" healthy eating habits on students. The thesis, the last sentence, identifies the issue (fast food availability) and the claim (that they can improve students' diets Note the use of the first-person pronoun. In an academic essay, student writers would revise this.

PARAGRAPH 2

This paragraph makes the claim that lunch periods are too brief, and that for this reason unhealthy food is prepared in advance. The writer argues that fast-food franchises are better equipped to serve fresh food quickly.

PARAGRAPH 3

The first sentence is the topic sentence. This paragraph includes personal experience to demonstrate part of the problem: Many school caterers serve unhealthy food, which is not stored properly. Evidence is developed with exemplification.

PARAGRAPH 4

This paragraph uses the author's experience and that of others to continue to prove there is a desire for franchised fast food on campus, as so many senior students partook. It advances the argument by demonstrating how franchises would help schools raise money. This is a logical appeal.

activity funds. During my senior year, funds from the vending machines helped to pay for the Club Latino's trip to Mexico. Additional funds from a franchise could help pay for more after-school sports programs or for renovating the gym, which would benefit the health of students.

PARAGRAPH 5

The conclusion includes another logical appeal (there is no money to invest in cafeterias) and a restatement of the thesis.

5 The current school lunch program is not providing convenient, healthy choices for students, nor is it helping students have a pleasant, leisurely lunch. Of course, if the food in the cafeteria were improved, vending machines and a franchise restaurant would be unnecessary. However, this would cost money, and since there is never enough money to reduce class size, I do not see the school board putting in a salad bar any time soon. As an alternative, a fast-food restaurant is an option that benefits everyone.

The complete essay, including any bibliographic references, is also available on the Online Learning Centre at www.mcgrawhill.ca/olc/clouse.

EXERCISE CONSIDERING "WHAT'S FOR LUNCH? FAST FOOD IN THE PUBLIC SCHOOLS"

1. What is the thesis of "What's for Lunch? Fast Food in the Public Schools"? What does the thesis state as the issue? As the writer's claim?

2. Which paragraph presents a problem and then argues for a particular solution? How does that strategy help the writer argue her claim?

3. What objection does the writer raise? How does she counter the objection? Does she effectively soften the objection? Explain. Should any other objections be raised and countered?

4. Does the author give enough reasons with enough evidence? Explain.

5. Does the essay include inductive reasoning, deductive reasoning, or both? How can you tell?

6. What element of ethical appeal exists in the essay? ●

CRITIQUE, REVISE, and EDIT

Cheryl makes a brave assertion in her essay, claiming in her thesis statement that "a fast-food restaurant can provide a convenient, profitable service that will improve the diets of high school students." Given her statements in the opening of the introduction ("North Americans are getting fatter") how does this contradiction work? Should there be more signposting in the paragraph to signal that despite the obesity epidemic fast-food chains can contribute to healthy eating habits? Does the contradiction work, logically, in the essay? The conclusion claims that "if the food in the cafeteria were improved, vending machines and a franchise restaurant would be unnecessary." Should Cheryl have reshaped her essay to accommodate this claim, since it seems to contradict the thesis idea that student diets would improve with fast-food offerings? Consider this idea with a partner.

CRITICAL READING PROFESSIONAL ESSAYS

Read like a Writer: Previewing Professional Essays

Before reading the following essay selections, consider and respond to the following:

1. Much has been made of the War on Terror. To what extent has this policy been effective in stopping terrorism, both in North America and abroad?

2. Do stricter immigration and border policies help protect average citizens from incidences of culturally motivated violence? Does Canada harbour international terrorists?

3. There are many claims that alleged terrorists have been abused, and even tortured, by both Canadian and American authorities. To what extent may torture be justified?

4. Does increased security in continental North America mean an increase in personal safety for average citizens? Or, is this a slippery slope to the denial of rights for average citizens?

Is Torture Ever Justified? Terrorism and Civil Liberty

The Economist, September 22, 2007

1   In every war, information is a weapon. In a "war against terrorism," where the adversary wears no uniform and hides among the civilian population, information can matter even more. But does that mean that torture can sometimes be justified to extract information?

2   The answer in international law is categorical: no. As laid down in treaties such as the Geneva Conventions, the UN Convention against Torture, and the International Covenant on Civil and Political Rights, the ban on torture or any cruel, inhuman, or degrading treatment is absolute, even in times of war. Along with genocide, torture is the only crime that every state must punish, no matter who commits it or where. Defenders of this blanket prohibition offer arguments that range from the moral (torture degrades and corrupts the society that allows it) to the practical (people will say anything under torture so the information they provide is unreliable anyway).

3   The September 11th attacks have not driven any rich democracy to reverse itself and make torture legal. But they have encouraged the bending of definitions and the turning of blind eyes. There is a greater readiness among governments that would never practise torture themselves to use information which less squeamish states have obtained—through torture.

4   Start with definitions. Most civilised people squirm at the thought of putting suspected terrorists on the rack or pulling off toenails. What if that prisoner knew the whereabouts of a ticking bomb—maybe a biological, chemical, or even nuclear one? Wouldn't a little sleep deprivation, sexual humiliation, or even water-dunking be justified to save hundreds and perhaps thousands of lives? Whatever the law says, a lot of people seem to think so.

5   In a BBC survey of 27,000 people in 25 countries last October, more than one out of three people in nine of those countries, including America, considered a degree of torture acceptable if it saved lives. Opposition was highest in most European and English-speaking countries. Another poll in 2005 by the Pew Research Centre found that nearly half of all Americans thought the torture of suspected terrorists was sometimes justified.

6   The Republican presidential hopefuls, Rudy Giuliani and Mitt Romney, support the "enhanced" interrogation of suspects in the event of an imminent attack. Dick Cheney, America's vice-president, recently suggested that "dunking" a

terrorist in water to save lives was a "no-brainer." The ensuing uproar led him to backtrack, claiming that he was not, of course, referring to "water-boarding," or simulated drowning, a technique regarded as tantamount to torture and banned in the American army's own interrogation manual.

I'll tickle you into submission

7   One objection to allowing moderate physical pressure is the difficulty of knowing where to draw the line. If stress positions and sleep deprivation do not work, do you progress to branding with red-hot irons and beating to a pulp? And can you rely on interrogators to heed such distinctions? It is the danger of a slippery slope that makes opponents of torture insist on a total ban.

8   Israel is the only country in modern times to have openly allowed "moderate physical pressure" as a "last resort." Since interrogators used such methods anyway, it was argued, passing an explicit law would at least make it possible to set out some limits. But in 1999, citing the slippery-slope argument, Israel's Supreme Court ruled that torture could never be justified, even in the case of a ticking bomb. It went on to outlaw techniques such as sleep deprivation, exposure to extremes of hot and cold, prolonged stress positions, hooding, and violent shaking.

9   In the 1970s Britain used similar techniques against suspected terrorists in Northern Ireland. These were banned in 1978 following a case brought by the Republic of Ireland to the European Court of Human Rights. Although not torture, such methods did amount to inhumane treatment, the court ruled. In 2002 the International Criminal Court for ex-Yugoslavia in The Hague decided that prolonged solitary confinement constituted torture. Such rulings did not prevent America from resorting to such harsh techniques when interrogating suspects in Afghanistan, Iraq, and Guantanamo Bay, however. Former detainees in those places have spoken of severe beatings, water-boarding, excruciating stress positions, mock executions, sleep deprivation, and much else besides.

10   Administration lawyers argued that since al-Qaeda and its Taliban allies were not a state party to the Geneva Conventions they were not covered by its ban on torture and other maltreatment. True, America had ratified (in 1988) the Convention against Torture, but that applied only to acts carried out on American soil, they said. And though America's own 1994 federal statute against torture did cover acts by Americans abroad, this applied only to full-blown torture, not lesser abuses.

11   In the notorious "torture memos" drawn up by the Department of Justice and the Pentagon in 2002 and 2003, the same lawyers sought to restrict the normal definition of torture—"severe pain or suffering"—to extreme acts equivalent to "serious physical injury, organ failure, or even death." Furthermore, as a wartime commander in chief whose main duty was to protect the American people, the president had the power to override both domestic and international law, they argued. After being leaked in 2004 most of these memos were "withdrawn," though not the one on the president's wartime powers.

12   Mr Bush and his colleagues have always said that America neither authorises nor condones torture. "We don't do torture," the president famously said. But Mr Bush has been vaguer about the grey area between torture and more moderate pressure. Soon after suspected terrorists were first sent to Guantanamo in January 2002 he said that America's armed forces would treat the detainees "humanely" in a manner "consistent with the Geneva Conventions"—but only "to the extent appropriate and consistent with military necessity."

13   Not until the Supreme Court's ruling in Hamdan in 2006 did the administration accept that all detainees, wherever held, were protected by Common Article 3 of the Geneva Conventions, which bans all forms of cruel, inhuman, or degrading treatment as well as torture. The 2005 Detainee Treatment Act, incorporating an amendment by Senator John McCain, already prohibited such treatment by American soldiers anywhere in the world. But it did not apply to the CIA.

Co-operating with torturers

14   Yet it is the CIA that has been responsible for the "extraordinary rendition" of suspects to clandestine prisons in third countries for "enhanced"

interrogation (whether by that country's agents or the CIA itself) amounting at times, many suspect, to torture. The programme's existence was not officially confirmed until Mr Bush announced last year the transfer to Guantanamo of the last 14 "high-value" detainees then being held in so-called "black sites" around the world. Of some 100 suspected terrorists believed to have been "rendered" over the past six years, 39 remain unaccounted for, Human Rights Watch, a New York-based lobby, says.

15 In July [2007], Mr Bush set out new broad guidelines for interrogations under a resumed CIA programme. He says the newly authorised techniques now comply fully with the Geneva Conventions' ban on "outrages upon personal dignity, in particular humiliating and degrading treatment" as well as torture. Even if true (which is hard to know because the details have not been disclosed), the programme itself with its enforced disappearances and black sites, which even the International Red Cross is not allowed to visit, violates basic tenets of international law.

16 Even if a country bans torture, how should it treat information that others have extracted this way? In 2004 Britain's Court of Appeal ruled that information acquired through torture was admissible as evidence in court. David Blunkett, then Britain's home secretary, welcomed the ruling. Although the government "unreservedly" condemned torture, he said, it would be "irresponsible not to take appropriate account of any information which could help protect national security and public safety." But the ruling was later overturned by the House of Lords.

17 A separate question is whether governments should use information extracted under torture by others for counter-terrorist purposes, even if it is not admissible as evidence. Most probably agree with Mr Blunkett that it would be irresponsible not to. But a case can be made that this is, in effect, condoning the use of torture by allies.

18 Britain has also run into trouble when trying to deport suspected foreign terrorists against whom it has not got enough evidence to secure a conviction in court. Under international law, a country must make sure that the person it wishes to expel is not in danger of being tortured or subjected to other abuse in the receiving country. In 2005 the UN's special rapporteur on torture criticised Britain for relying on "diplomatic assurances" that deportees would not be tortured. Charles Clarke, who had succeeded Mr Blunkett as home secretary, retorted that the rights of the victims of the London Tube bombings that year mattered more than those of the perpetrators. The UN should "look at human rights in the round," he said, "rather than simply focusing all the time on the terrorist." Fine—except that no British court had convicted these suspects as terrorists.

19 To date, 144 countries have ratified the Convention against Torture. (The holdouts include such usual suspects as Sudan, North Korea, Myanmar, and Zimbabwe, but also India.) And yet, the UN's special rapporteur told the Security Council in June, torture remains widespread. Amnesty International noted cases of state-sponsored torture or other inhumane treatment in 102 of the 153 countries included in its 2007 report. The worst offenders were China, Egypt (both of which are parties to the convention), Myanmar, and North Korea, along with several African countries. America's transgressions are trivial by comparison. The worry, argues Kenneth Roth, director of Human Rights Watch, is that when America breaks the rules it encourages others to do the same.

20 Why does torture endure? Part of the reason, argues Michael Ignatieff, a Canadian writer, may be that it is at times motivated not so much by a desire to extract vital information but by something baser, such as an urge to inflict pain, exact revenge, or even just for fun. That seems to have been part of the motivation of the Americans who abused prisoners in Abu Ghraib, for example. But torture may also endure because it sometimes works.

They'll say anything

21 Many critics of torture claim that it is ineffective as well as repugnant. Since people will say anything just to stop the pain, the information gleaned may not be reliable. On the other hand, if people do say anything under torture, you might expect some of what they say to be true and therefore—if those being tortured really

are terrorists—useful to the authorities. Torture certainly helped induce Guy Fawkes to betray his co-conspirators after they had tried to blow up King James I and the British Parliament on November 5th 1605.

22 Asked recently about the CIA's use of enhanced interrogation in secret prisons, George Tenet, the CIA's director until 2004, replied that the agency's widely condemned rendition programme had saved lives, disrupted plots, and provided "invaluable" information in the war against terrorism. Indeed, while denying the use of full-blown torture he said that the programme on its own was "worth more than the FBI, the CIA, and the National Security Agency put together have been able to tell us."

23 Mr Ignatieff, for his own part, sees no trumping argument on behalf of terrorists that makes their claims to human rights and dignity prevail over the security interests—and right to life—of the majority. Yet he continues to advocate a total ban. "We cannot torture, in other words, because of who we are," he says. He knows that many will disagree.

Considering Ideas

1. The essay's first paragraph ends with a question: "But does this mean that torture can sometimes be justified to extract information?" While it isn't a direct statement, what does it suggest that the article's thesis might be?

2. Cite three examples of international legislation and agreements that bolster this article's thesis that torture is not justified. How is the issue problematized in terms of national security?

3. Would the assertion that torture must never be justified be acceptable to this article's audience? What are some counter-arguments? Are they addressed in this piece?

4. The article attempts to strike a balance between the tenets of international law and immediate social concerns surrounding national security. How successfully does it do this?

Considering Technique

1. This article is unsigned, yet part of a series. Would its thesis and its logical assertions be more acceptable were the article attributed to a single author? Does it seem more editorial than argumentative?

2. The writer develops a definition for torture in paragraph 4, and does so with questions, rather than declarative assertions. Would it be more effective to use a dictionary definition of torture?

3. The writer uses counter-arguments or objections to this article's thesis in paragraphs 10 and 15. Paragraph 10's argument is rebutted in paragraph 11, while paragraph 14's is answered in the same paragraph. Is there enough evidence to assume that both objections are effectively countered?

4. This essay relies mainly on exemplification, citing international agreements. To what extent are the examples valid?

5. The article appeals mostly to logic with items of a legal nature, and does not include many emotional appeals. Would its thesis be stronger or weaker if there were emotional appeals?

For Group Discussion or Journal Writing

The Economist's article cites international legislation that prohibits torture, using examples of UN conventions. Are these pieces of legislation enough to protect the public from violent acts of terrorism? Can torture ever be justified if there were a legitimate national security risk? Cite examples from the text.

Pre-reading

1. Instead of a thesis statement in the first paragraph, Dershowitz poses a question: "should law enforcement be authorized to torture suspects who are thought to have information about a ticking bomb?" Why do you think the author chose such a tentative statement?

2. Torture warrants are nothing new, and, historically, were encoded in law. Should there be legislation permitting the use of torture? When and how?

3. Would torture warrants increase, or decrease the actual amounts of torture? Would they be effective in combating domestic and international threats?

4. Do a webquest, and identify issues surrounding the use of torture in recent conflicts.

The Case for Torture Warrants

Alan M. Dershowitz

1   Now that it has been disclosed that our government had information of "undetermined reliability," from an agent whose code name is Dragonfire, that New York City may have been targeted for a 10 kiloton nuclear weapon, the arguments for empowering law enforcement officials to do everything necessary to prevent a catastrophic terrorist attack are becoming more compelling.[1] In the immediate aftermath of the September 11th attacks, FBI officials leaked a story about their inability to obtain information from suspected terrorists by conventional means, such as buying the information by offers of cash or leniency, or compelling the information by grants of immunity and threats of imprisonment for contempt of court. Those who leaked the story suggested that there may come a time when law enforcement officials might have to resort to unconventional means, including nonlethal torture. Thus began one of the most unusual debates in American legal and political history: should law enforcement be authorized to torture suspects who are thought to have information about a ticking bomb?

2   This ticking bomb scenario had long been a staple of legal and political philosophers who love to debate hypothetical cases that test the limit of absolute principles, such as the universal prohibition against the use of torture which has long been codified by international treaties. The ticking bomb case has also been debated, though not as a hypothetical case, in Israel, whose security services long claimed the authority to employ "moderate physical pressure" in order to secure real time intelligence from captured terrorists believed to know about impending terrorist acts. The moderate physical pressure employed by Israel was tougher than it sounds, but not nearly as tough as the brutal methods used by the French in interrogating suspected terrorists during the Algerian uprisings. The Israeli security service would take a suspected terrorist, tie him to a chair in an uncomfortable position for long periods of time with loud music blaring in the background, and then place a smelly sack over his head and shake him violently. Many tongues were loosened by this process and several terrorist acts prevented, without any suspects being seriously injured.

3   Torture, it turns out, can sometimes produce truthful information. The Israeli experience suggested that information obtained as a result of torture should never be believed, unless it can

be independently confirmed, but such information can sometimes be self-proving, as when the subject leads law enforcement to the actual location of the bomb.

4   Nonetheless, the Israeli Supreme Court outlawed all use of even moderate, non-lethal physical pressure. It responded to the ticking bomb scenario by saying that if a security agent thought it was necessary to use physical pressure in order to prevent many deaths, he could take his chances, be prosecuted, and try to raise a defense of "necessity." In my book *Shouting Fire,* I wrote critically of this decision on the ground that it places security officials in an impossible dilemma. It would be better if any such official could seek an *advanced* ruling from a judge, as to whether physical pressure is warranted under the specific circumstances, in order to avoid being subject to an after the fact risk of imprisonment. Thus was born the proposal for a torture warrant.

5   Actually it was a rebirth, because half a millennium ago torture warrants were part of the law of Great Britain. They could be sought only in cases involving grave threats to the Crown or the Empire and were granted in about one case a year. Judges even in those times were extremely reluctant to authorize the thumbscrew.

6   Why then should we even think about returning to an old practice that was abolished in England many years ago? The reason is because if we ever did have a ticking bomb case—especially a ticking nuclear bomb case—law enforcement officials would in fact resort to physical force, even torture, as a last resort. In speaking to numerous audiences since September 11th—audiences reflecting the entire breadth of the political and ideological spectrum—I have asked for a show of hands as to how many would favor the use of non-lethal torture in an actual ticking bomb case. The vast majority of audience members responded in the affirmative. So have law enforcement officials to whom I have spoken. If it is true that torture would in fact be used in such a case, then the important question becomes: is it better to have such torture done under the table, off the books and below the radar screen—or in full view, with

accountability and as part of our legal system? This is a very difficult question with powerful arguments on both sides. On the one hand, we have had experience with off the book policies such as President Nixon's "plumbers"[2] and Oliver North's "foreign policy initiatives."[3] In a democracy, accountability and visibility must be given high priorities. On the other hand, to legitimate torture and make it part of our legal system, even in extreme cases, risks reversion to a bad old time when torture was routine.

7   One key question is whether the availability of a torture warrant would, in fact, increase or decrease the actual amount of torture employed by law enforcement officials. I believe, though I cannot prove, that a formal requirement of a judicial warrant as a prerequisite to non-lethal torture would decrease the amount of physical violence directed against suspects. Judges would require compelling evidence before they would authorize so extraordinary a departure from our constitutional norms, and law enforcement officials would be reluctant to seek a warrant unless they had compelling evidence that the suspect had information needed to prevent an imminent terrorist attack. Moreover, the rights of the suspect would be better protected with a warrant requirement. He would be granted immunity, told that he was now compelled to testify, threatened with imprisonment if he refuses to do so and given the option of providing the requested information. Only if he refused to do what he was legally compelled to do—provide necessary information which could not incriminate him because of the immunity—would he be threatened with torture. Knowing that such a threat was authorized by the law, he might well provide the information. If he still refused to, he would be subjected to judicially monitored physical measures designed to cause excruciating pain without leaving any lasting damage. A sterilized needle underneath the nail might be one such approved method. This may sound brutal, but it does not compare in brutality with the prospect of thousands of preventable deaths at the hands of fellow terrorists.

8   Let me cite two examples to demonstrate why I think there would be less torture with a warrant

requirement than without one. Recall the case of the alleged national security wiretap being placed on the phones of Martin Luther King by the Kennedy administration in the early 1960s. This was in the days when the Attorney General could authorize a national security wiretap without a warrant. Today no judge would issue a warrant in a case as flimsy as that one. When Zaccarias Moussaui was detained after trying to learn how to fly an airplane, without wanting to know much about landing it, the government did not even seek a national security wiretap because its lawyers believed that a judge would not have granted one. If Moussaui's computer could have been searched without a warrant, it almost certainly would have been.

9   It is a great tragedy that we have to be discussing the horrors of torture. Some even believe that any discussion of this issue is beyond the pale of acceptable discourse in 21st century America. But it is far better to discuss in advance the kinds of tragic choices we may encounter if we ever confront an actual ticking bomb terrorist case, than to wait until the case arises and let somebody make the decision in the heat of the moment.

10 An analogy to the shooting down of a passenger-filled hijacked airliner heading toward a crowded office building will be instructive. Prior to September 11th it might have been a debatable issue whether the plane should be shot down. Today that is no longer debatable. But would anyone suggest that the decision should be made by a low ranking police officer? Of course not. We all agree that this should be a decision made at the highest level possible—by the President or the Secretary of Defense, if there is time to have such a dreadful decision made by accountable public figures. The use of torture in the ticking bomb case, like the shooting down of the hijacked airplane, involves a horrible choice of evils. In my view, this choice should be made with visibility and accountability, either by a judicial officer or by the President of the United States. It should not be made by nameless and unaccountable law enforcement officials, risking imprisonment if they guess wrong.

[1] Ultimately, investigators determined that Dragonfire's information was false.

[2] President Nixon's "plumbers" were a group of operatives charged with "stopping leaks." The plumbers were responsible for the 1972 break-in at the Democratic Party's national headquarters in the Watergate Hotel.

[3] Oliver North was a deputy director of the National Security Council in 1981, during the Reagan administration. He was implicated in the Irangate scandal, involving the supply of arms to Iran in exchange for U.S. hostages.

Considering Ideas

1. The thesis of "The Case for Torture Warrants" is implied. What is that thesis? What is the issue? What is the claim?

2. If you were writing the legislation authorizing torture warrants in ticking-bomb scenarios, how would you define ticking-bomb scenario?

3. What reasons does Dershowitz give to support his claim?

4. What evidence does Dershowitz give to back up his reasons? Is the evidence convincing? Explain.

5. How is Dershowitz's claim different from McCain's claim in the previous essay?

Considering Technique

1. What is Dershowitz's major premise? His minor premise? His conclusion?

2. What purpose do paragraphs 1–4 serve?

3. What element of emotional appeal do you notice in paragraph 1? How does that emotional appeal help Dershowitz achieve his writing purpose? What ethical appeal do you notice in paragraph 6, and how does it help him achieve his writing purpose?

4. What objection does Dershowitz raise in paragraph 9, and how does he counter that objection? Is the counter effective? Explain.

5. *Combining Patterns.* How is exemplification used in paragraph 8 to help Dershowitz achieve his writing purpose? How is comparison-contrast used in paragraph 2 to help him achieve his writing purpose?

For Group Discussion or Journal Writing

After reading "The Case for Torture Warrants," decide which claim is better argued and why. You are not discussing whom you agree with; you are discussing who writes the more convincing argument.

WRITING TOOL

Emphasis

Setting an idea off in a one-sentence paragraph can provide emphasis for an idea. Look back at one of the essays in this chapter, find an example of a short assertion of an idea in a one-sentence paragraph, and comment on its effectiveness.

Argumentation in Images: A Casebook

Below is a casebook of visual arguments. The images, all related to global climate change, illustrate some of the forms visual arguments can take: photojournalism pictures, political cartoons, and advertisements. As you study the images, note the different appeals they employ, and consider how the images function similarly to and differently from written arguments.

From a photo essay on climate change in *Time* magazine in 2006.

Political cartoon by Ken Catalino. By permission of Ken Catalino and Creators Syndicate, Inc.

Political cartoon by Gary Varvel. By permission of Gary Varvel and Creators Syndicate, Inc.

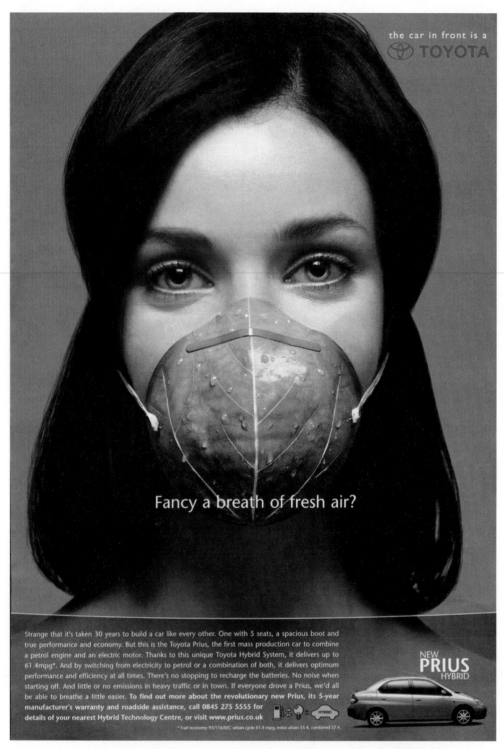

Print advertisement for the Toyota Prius, a car that runs on a combination of gasoline and electricity.

Poster for *An Inconvenient Truth*

Considering the Images

1. Write out a claim the photograph of the polar bear could support.
2. We often think of photographs as being "objective" representations of reality. Does the photograph of the polar bear make an emotional appeal? How?
3. Describe the claims in the two political cartoons. How do they use humour to bolster their claims?
4. Which of the three appeals—logical, emotional, and ethical—does the "Drowning of the Penguins" cartoon make? How is this cartoon similar to the photograph of the polar bear?
5. Describe the audience you think the Prius advertisement is targeting.
6. The facemask is made from a vegetable leaf. How does that image help the advertisement fulfill its persuasive purpose?
7. The poster for *An Inconvenient Truth*, the movie about Al Gore's campaign against global warming, is a visual depiction of the argument advanced in the film, that global warming poses a grave threat to the planet. How does the poster make its visual argument?

Reading Then Writing Argumentation

1. Making the opposite claim to that argued in "What's for Lunch? Fast Food in the Public Schools," argue against allowing fast food in public schools. As an alternative, argue for or against allowing vending machines in public schools.
2. Making the opposite claim to that argued in Dershowitz's article, argue against the use of torture in interrogation. As an alternative, argue for torture only in certain cases.

Argumentation beyond the Writing Classroom

Pick an issue currently being debated on your campus or among people your age, and write an argument that could be published as a letter to the editor of your campus newspaper or as a guest editorial. Be sure to articulate the issue, your claim, and the support for your claim. As an alternative, choose an issue being debated in your community or in the nation, and write an argument that could be published as a letter to the editor of the local newspaper or as a guest editorial.

Responding to a Theme

1. Before the terrorist attacks of September 11, 2001, we had little reason to debate the use of torture, as the essays by *The Economist* and Dershowitz do. Discuss something else that has changed dramatically since the attacks, and explain how North American society or values have been affected by that change.
2. Automobiles are a major source of air pollution. The advertisement on page 372 draws on that fact by emphasizing that the Prius automobile is good for the environment. Assume that Parliament is considering a bill that would reduce highway speed limits to 80 kilometres per hour, provide monetary incentives to employers with carpooling programs, increase the gasoline tax by 10 percent, and increase income tax rates to build high-speed trains in all major metropolitan areas. How do you think the average Canadian's life would change?

THE WRITING PROCESS

Argumentation

These guidelines are merely suggestions you can try as you develop your own effective, efficient writing process. They are not meant to replace other successful procedures.

Generate Ideas, Consider Audience and Purpose, and Order Ideas

- For an issue and claim, try the following:
  - Choose an issue you are interested in and know something about.
  - Review your campus and local newspapers for controversial issues and aims that are important to you or that you have an opinion about.
  - Fill in the blank: It is wrong that _____. If, for example, you complete the sentence by saying that "students cannot strike," you can argue that students should be permitted to strike.
  - Freewrite about an issue to discover claims you can make.
- To identify your audience, ask these questions:
  - Who thinks the issue is important but hasn't made up his or her mind? Who *should* think the issue is important?
  - Who disagrees with my claim?
  - Who could be convinced to agree with me?
  - Who could be convinced to take an action I favour?
- To assess your audience, answer these questions:
  - Is my audience supportive, wavering, or hostile?
  - Why is my audience supportive, wavering, or hostile?
- To determine your purpose, answer these questions:
  - Can I lessen opposition?
  - Can I convince my readers to agree with me?
  - Can I change my readers' minds about some aspect of my issue?
  - Can I convince my readers to take a particular action?
- List reasons that support your claim. Then list reasons to oppose your claim. Study the first list for reasons and evidence; study the second list for objections to raise and counter.
- To generate ideas for logical appeals, answer these questions:
  - Why is the issue important?
  - What would happen if my claim were adopted?
  - What would happen if my claim were *not* adopted?
  - What story can I tell to support my claim? What examples can I provide?
  - What comparisons or contrasts can I make to support my claim?
  - Do any cause-and-effect relationships support my claim?
- To generate ideas for ethical appeals, answer these questions:
  - What qualifies me to write about the issue?
  - What objections are my readers likely to have? How can I counter those objections?
  - What common ground do I share with my readers?
- To generate ideas for emotional appeals, answer these questions:
  - What needs and values are important to my readers?
  - How can I appeal to those needs and values?
- Review your idea generation material, and list the ideas to include in your first draft. From that list, develop an outline, but before you do, consider the following:
  - Whether some or all of your support follows an inductive or deductive pattern

    – Whether some or all of your support should follow a progressive order

    – What the best places are to raise and counter objections

Draft

- Draft a working thesis that mentions your debatable issue and claim.

- Using your outline as a guide, write your draft. If you have trouble writing your introduction, explain why the issue is important, and/or why you are qualified to write about the issue. If you have relevant personal experience, you can open with a brief narration that reflects the issue and points to your claim.

- If you have trouble writing your conclusion, try explaining what would happen if your claim were—or were not—adopted. If appropriate, call for your readers to take a particular action.

- As you draft, think about using topic sentences to state the reasons for your claim.

Revise

- Keep the characteristics of your audience firmly in mind as you revise. Be sure your reasons, evidence, emotional appeals, and ethical appeals are geared to the characteristics of your readers.

- Use transitions to move smoothly from reason to evidence, and from evidence to the next reason.

- Examine the evidence that supports each of your reasons. If you have only a sentence or two, consider how the patterns of development can help you include more evidence.

- Ask whether you have raised and countered objections. If not, consider doing so.

- If your audience is wavering or hostile, think about what you have done to create goodwill.

- If some of your evidence comes from research, be sure to follow the conventions explained in Chapter 17.

- To obtain reader response for revision, see pages 101–102. In addition, ask your reader to explain whether your argument is convincing and why.

Correct Errors and Proofread

- Use the Part 4 "Guide to Frequently Occurring Errors" for reference, and check with a writing centre tutor if you are unsure about a point of grammar, usage, or punctuation.

- When writing an argument, note that you will have many occasions to refer to people in general. When you do, be careful to use pronouns correctly by modeling these examples. For more on pronouns, see Chapter 22.

    – If a *person* objects to the content of a television program, *he or she* [not *they*] should write the sponsor.

    – *People* often object to the content of a television program. When *they* [not *you*] do, *they* [not *you*] should write the sponsor.

    – If *someone* objects to the content of a television program, *he or she* [not *they*] should write the sponsor.

    – *Everybody* who objects to the content of a television program should write the sponsor [not *their* sponsor].

    – *Anyone* who objects to the content of a television program should write the sponsor [not *their* sponsor].

- Be sure to proofread the final copy before handing it in. If you are submitting an electronic copy, proofread from a paper copy. Be sure to read very slowly, lingering over every word and punctuation mark.

Remember

Avoid clauses such as "most knowledgeable people agree," "as anyone can see," and "anyone who understands the issue believes." Phrases like this will alienate readers who disagree, do not see, or fail to believe, making it harder to achieve a purpose.

    Do not argue both sides of an issue. Raise and counter compelling objections, but do not present all the arguments on one side of the issue and then all the arguments on the other side. Your purpose is to argue for just one side.

© 1989 Watterson. Reprinted with permission of UNIVERSAL PRESS SYNDICATE. All rights reserved.

CHAPTER 16

Conducting Research

Looking Ahead

Calvin, the little boy in the Calvin and Hobbes cartoon, does not appreciate the value of research. Nevertheless, research is such an important component of education—particularly higher education—that students learn about it both in this chapter and in the next one. Although you learn about research here in an undergraduate writing class, make no mistake—research matters in every subject you study. Before beginning the first of the research chapters, consider the importance of research by responding to the following:

- Why should post-secondary students learn how to research?

- Think about the topics for the subject you major in. What issues or topics are actively being researched in these fields of study? Why is research important?

- What are three subjects students will take before graduation that will likely require them to write and to incorporate research findings?

Peg Tyre wrote "Smart Moms, Hard Choices" for *Newsweek* in 2006 to consider the decisions women make about whether to pursue careers or to stay at home full-time to raise their children. Tyre did research in order to present all sides of the issue. Although much of the discussion about the subject had been sparked by the newly released book *Mommy Wars,* Tyre went beyond that single source and addressed the topic from a variety of perspectives.

Here is an excerpt that includes some of the information she gathered in her research:

> While the raw emotionalism of the debate is compelling, economists and sociologists who study women in the work force complain that books like *Mommy Wars* can obscure an important reality: *most* women with children work outside the home. Women who are most likely to stay home with their children are younger than 24 and have obtained high-school diplomas, according to the U.S. Census. Older, more educated moms are more likely to keep working. When women quit to raise kids, they rarely retire for good. According to a report issued in December by the Census, 75 percent of women with school-age children are employed or looking for work. By the time their children are 12 or older, that number rises to 80 percent. "The nature of the economy," says Kathleen Gerson, a New York University sociologist, "means that only a very tiny percentage of women—very wealthy ones," can afford to leave the work force entirely.
>
> Which is not to say that the landscape for working moms isn't changing. While the number of working moms rose dramatically in the 1970s and 1980s, those numbers peaked at 73 percent in 2000. Since then, the number of working mothers has dropped about 1.6 percent.

Tyre's article is strengthened by a quotation, census data, statistics, and the perspective of economists and sociologists who did not contribute to *Mommy Wars.* All this information provides credibility and depth.

Research writing is among the most important writing you will do, both in school and in the workplace. This chapter and the next one will help you master the research process so you can sift through the wealth of resources to find information on a topic and use that information responsibly. You will learn how to use the tools of research, including a campus library and the Internet, to discover authoritative information on any topic. You will also learn how to integrate that information into your writing and document it in the proper form.

When to Research

Because we are curious, and because we are always learning, we do research to discover information. You probably already do a considerable amount of research, or fact-finding, without realizing it. When you question friends to learn which courses they recommend taking, you are researching—as you are when you check the classified advertisements for the best prices on used cars, call local electronics stores to find the best place to purchase a DVD burner, and use the Internet to learn how to fix a leaking faucet. In addition, researching and including source material is a common component of writing done in most college and university courses. Sometimes you will include a source or two in an essay to support their own ideas, and sometimes you will use sources extensively, to write a research paper.

Using Sources in an Essay to Support Your Own Ideas

Information gathered through research can help support the main points of an essay written for almost any purpose.

- **Important statistics:** For a paper arguing in favour of maintaining a gun registry, written for a criminal justice class, you can research to discover the number of handgun deaths per year in Canada.
- **Specialized procedures or technical information:** For an essay explaining a procedure for matching organs and donors, written for an ethics class, you can research the procedures currently used to decide which patients receive the limited number of available organs.
- **Background information:** For a paper about the dangers of some herbal remedies, written for a health class, you can research why Health Canada may not regulate these remedies.
- **The view of an authority:** For a paper explaining the benefits of vegetarianism, written for a nutrition class, you can research what the Canada Food Guide says about a vegetarian diet.
- **Relevant explanation:** For a paper about teacher preparation, written for an education class, you can research the effectiveness of alternative certification programs.
- **Supporting detail:** For a paper about the drawbacks of legalized gambling, written for an urban sociology class, you can research the negative effects of gambling on towns that have casinos.

For two examples of essays that use sources to support the author's ideas, see pages 136 and 261.

Using Sources in a Research Paper

The academic research paper presents a thorough exploration of a topic. Unlike an essay, which uses sources to support a student's own ideas, the research paper requires writers to investigate and accurately present a range of sources on a topic.

- For a labour studies course, you can write a research paper about the effectiveness of collective bargaining.
- For an environmental science course, you can write a research paper about the effects of beach erosion on sea turtles.
- For a nursing course, you can write a research paper about the effects of the provincial nursing shortage on nurses' work environments.
- For a childcare class, you can write a research paper about the effects of daycare on toddlers' socialization processes.
- For a psychology class, you can write a research paper about the causes of depression in college students and its effect on them.

For an example of a research paper, see page 445.

The Research Process

Whether using sources to supplement personal ideas in an essay or writing a research paper, you want to work efficiently. Efficient procedures are particularly important these days to manage the explosion of information made possible by the Internet. The procedures explained in this chapter can help you plan a timeline for creating a paper as well as help to locate, analyze, and organize sources. Some of the procedures are suitable for finding sources to support personal ideas in an essay; others will help you write a research paper.

Create a Timeline for a Research Paper

A research paper is a complex assignment that cannot be completed quickly. You should create a timeline to manage your time and stay organized while working through the planning, research, drafting, and citation phases of a paper. Using the chart below, set deadlines for each step in the research process based on the amount of time assigned to complete a paper. Keeping these deadlines in mind will help you to stay on track and avoid last-minute panic.

Completion Date	Step in Process
	Choose a broad topic (see page 381).
	Narrow the topic and draft a preliminary thesis (and, if necessary, have the topic or thesis approved by the instructor) (see pages 382–384).
	Locate sources in the library, on the Internet, and through field research (see pages 384, 391, and 396).
	Compile a working bibliography (see page 398).
	Evaluate sources (see page 399).
	Take notes (see page 401).
	Create an outline (see page 408).
	Write a first draft (see page 408).
	Check in-text documentation and create a works-cited or references page (depending on whether you are using MLA or APA style) (see pages 419–442).
	Revise and edit a second draft (see pages 442–443).
	Format and submit your final paper (see page 453).

Choose a Broad Research Paper Topic

Because it is necessary work on a research paper for an extended period, be sure to choose a topic that is of interest, so you do not become bored. Perhaps you are curious about the American civil rights movement in the 1960s, or maybe you wish you knew more about the international space program. A research paper presents the perfect opportunity to indulge curiosity.

If an interesting topic does not emerge immediately, try some of these strategies:

1. Browse through newspapers and magazines for ideas. Check out some of the newspapers, journals, and magazines listed at www.aldaily.com or in a national newspaper's Web site.
2. Review class notes for topics and issues a professor has discussed.
3. Ask a professor for the Web sites or names of journals and organizations in her field.
4. Consider what you have read lately, for personal interest. Have you read about the dropping of the atomic bomb on Hiroshima at the end of World War II in history class? Have you come across a newspaper article on Internet fraud? Either of these topics can be excellent starting points.
5. Leaf through a general-knowledge encyclopedia like *The Canadian Encyclopedia* Online, The Canadian Reference Centre, Electric Library, Quick Canadian Facts, *Encyclopedia Canadiana*, or the *World Book Encyclopedia*. Online, browse a Canadian database, such as LexisNexis or Galenet's Canadian Periodical Index (CPIQ). Alternatively, peruse sites such as howstuffworks.com, globalissues.org, or the Web site for a national or international organization or institution that interests you.
6. Before searching databases, surf the Internet, especially general reference sites. For a good starting point, visit www.refdesk.com or www.allonesearch.com. In addition, type a broad subject, such as "education," into a public search engine such as www.yahoo.ca or www.google.ca and see what surfaces. Remember, though: this phase of the research project is a webquest, and the sources found on the Internet will likely not be peer-reviewed, and so may not be acceptable for inclusion in a research paper for a post-secondary academic course.

Some topics are not suitable for a research paper and should be avoided. If you are uncertain about the suitability of a topic, consult with an instructor. Here are some cautions:

1. Avoid topics that do not require research because they have been thoroughly documented, with few recent discoveries or controversies. These are subjects like "the circulatory system" and "the life of John A. MacDonald." General biographies of well-known individuals are not focused enough to be suitable topics, as famous lives are well documented.
2. Avoid topics that lack scientific foundation, such as UFOs, the Bermuda Triangle, reincarnation, and ESP.
3. In the event that you have no Internet access, avoid topics that are very current or regional because finding print sources for these can be difficult.

4. Be aware that some instructors prefer students to avoid religious topics. If such a topic is of interest, be sure to talk it over with a professor.
5. Avoid topics that have little academic significance. Instead of researching the many moods of rapper 50 Cent, students would do better to research how hip-hop music has shaped popular culture.

Narrow the Topic

Broad topics like "media violence" cover so much territory that you cannot treat them adequately in a standard research paper. Narrower topics like "the effects of cartoon violence on preschoolers" allow for a more in-depth discussion at a manageable length. When moving from broad topic to narrow topic, remember these guidelines.

Understand the Purpose for Writing

Has an instructor asked students to write a problem–solution paper, an argumentation paper, or an explanatory report? Notice how differently the broad topic "televised violence" can be narrowed based on the purpose of the assignment:

Problem–solution paper:	How parents can limit their preschoolers' exposure to televised violence
Argumentation paper:	Why the government should limit the violence on television
Explanatory report:	The nature and amount of violence on primetime network television

Understand the Terms of the Assignment

Are there requirements for length, kinds of sources, or number of sources? When is the paper due? Answers to questions like these will help you make decisions about how to narrow. Consider the broad topic "pollution." If you are expected to submit a six-page paper in three weeks, you do not want to research the topic of "industrial pollution"—that involves too many kinds of pollution in too many industries. Even the narrower topic of "automobile emissions" would probably be too broad. Writing about "the effectiveness of Canada's legislation limiting automobile emissions," however, may work very well.

Use Strategies for Narrowing a Topic

In Chapter 2, you learned strategies for narrowing a broad topic, including freewriting, writing a list, considering the patterns of development, and mapping. Use one or more of these strategies to help narrow a research paper topic. For example, you might use mapping to help narrow the broad topic "televised violence":

Possible narrow topic:	Most attempts to regulate the amount of violence children view on television have been ineffective.

Skim Source Materials

Students can get ideas for narrowing a broad topic by skimming source materials in the following ways:

1. Review the tables of contents of books on a broad topic. Find books using a school library's online catalogue.
2. Using the previewing strategies explained in Chapter 1, skim encyclopedia articles on a broad topic, either in the library or online.
3. Look up your broad topic in an online periodical index or in a Canadian subject guide in an online library. The titles of articles on a topic can suggest ways to narrow, and often database search engines suggest related topics, and sort the results by category and source type.
4. Type in a broad topic into a favourite search engine and into www.findarticles. com. The titles that come up will suggest ways to narrow a topic.
5. Note that the campus library will probably have ProQuest, InfoTrac, EBSCOhost, Gale Net, LexisNexis, or some other online database listing magazine and journal articles. Topics and subtopics given there can suggest ways to narrow a topic. Some even recommend related searches, which may be helpful to students.

Draft a Preliminary Thesis

Based on a narrow topic, draft a preliminary thesis to guide research. (To review the information on drafting a preliminary thesis, return to pages 51–54.) A preliminary thesis focuses research by helping you decide what material will be useful (and, therefore, what material to take notes on) and what material you can pass by. Here are three examples of suitable preliminary thesis statements:

> Religious schools offer a positive alternative to traditional public schools.

> Preschoolers exposed to televised violence are more aggressive with their siblings and peers.

> Paying women to be stay-at-home mothers would reduce the number of people on welfare.

Always remember that the preliminary thesis is subject to change in light of information research brings forth. Thus, if during research you discover that certain kinds of religious schools work better than others, you can revise the thesis:

> Religious schools that specialize in educating students using religious precepts offer a positive alternative to traditional public schools.

Use the Library to Locate Sources

The information in the next sections will help you locate sources to supplement your own ideas in an essay or for a research paper. However, before getting under way, you should familiarize yourself with the campus library and its resources. Check to see whether the library offers a guided tour or a library-use workshop. Taking the tour or participating in the workshop will save you significant time by showing you how to locate the sources you need as efficiently as possible. You should also become familiar with your library's Web site to learn how to navigate it, and to learn whether it provides extra help, for example in documentation of sources with an online referencing program.

Consider the Kind of Information You Need

Perhaps you need a statistic or quotation to supplement your own ideas by backing up one of your points. Or maybe you are seeking historical background about an issue to use in the introduction of an essay you are writing on that issue. When writing a research paper, you may be looking for all the causes of the high divorce rate in Canada. Keeping research needs in mind will help you decide what to look at and what to pass by.

Use the Library Catalogue to Locate Books

You can find books on your topics by using a library's computer catalogue, which contains information on every book the library has. In most libraries, this electronic catalogue (or database) has replaced the card catalogue. This makes searching faster and often more convenient, since most libraries allow access to their computer catalogue both at terminals in the library and via the library's web page, allowing you to work from home.

The computer catalogue can be searched by author, by title, by ISBN (International Serial Book Number), by keyword, or by a subject term listed in the Library of Congress Subject Headings (LCSH), the Canadian Subject Headings (CSH) list, or by subject headings in an academic or journalistic database. The LCSH is usually located near a computer catalogue terminal. (the Library of Congress system of headings is used in most academic libraries, though the Dewey decimal system is still used in some public libraries.) Alternatively, you may search a database that uses common subject terms. Not all databases have this feature, however.

When first looking for sources for a research paper, or to supplement ideas in an essay, you will probably search a catalogue via subject entries. A search of this kind is similar to the keyword search you may already be familiar with from search engines such as Google or Yahoo! To search by subject, follow the directions on the computer catalogue screen, or ask a librarian. If unsure what word to use to start a search, consult the LCSH or CSH index for library topic headings. Once you have searched for a chosen term, you will get one or more screens listing the titles of books that the library has on the topic. See the figure below for an example of how this screen can look (but note that no two computer catalogues look exactly the same!).

Many academic library catalogues let users perform advanced searches, in which you can specify the type of material returned in the search, such as books, maps, dissertations, or scores, or dates between which you want to search.

When performing a subject search, you may have to experiment with the words you choose. For example, suppose you have a research topic on how corporations

Results of a Computer Catalogue Search.

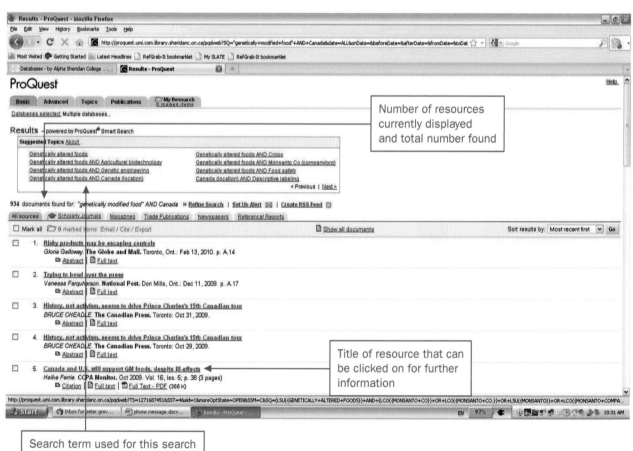

Screen capture courtesy of Sheridan Institute of Technology and Advanced Learning

have profited from genetically modifying the food we eat. If you use the too-broad "food," you end up with over 12,000 entries. There would be even more results in an Internet search, which is why it is less efficient for academic purposes. However, if you use the too-narrow "corporations and genetically modified food," you might end up with only one entry. Using the phrase "genetically modified foods" produces a more acceptable number of entries. Be sure to experiment with numerous variations of the keyword to ensure optimum results.

The computer catalogue entry for a specific book contains many useful pieces of information, including the call number of the book (which gives the location of the book in the library); its availability; bibliographic information such as the title, author, publisher, and date of publication; and related terms. Usually, you can access this additional information by clicking on the title of the book on the results page.

See the figure below for the information for a scholarly work found during our search on "global warming."

If the catalogue is not computerized, you will use the traditional card catalogue. Like the computer version, the card catalogue profiles every book in the library three ways: by author, by title, and by one or more subjects. Some catalogues compile all the cards together, and some catalogues have two parts. First, the catalogue file of books is alphabetized according to author and title; second, the subject file arranges books alphabetically by subjects.

Entry for a Book Listed in a Computer Catalogue.
This screen provides detailed information on a particular book in the library, including its subjects, bibliographic information, and call number.

Screen capture courtesy of Sheridan Institute of Technology and Advanced Learning

Use Reference Works

When looking for specific information—perhaps a particular statistic—turn to reference works. These works may be online, on CD-ROM or in a specific area of the library's reference room. Useful works include the following:

- *Information Please Almanac* and *Facts on File* give statistics and information on current events.
- *Hansard* has information about what has transpired in Parliament.
- Statistics Canada reports give information on population and Canadian institutions and social and demographic trends.
- *Current Biography* and *Webster's New Biographical Dictionary* have articles on people you may need information about.

Some of the most useful reference works are encyclopedias. Be sure to look at both the general-knowledge encyclopedias, such as *Encyclopedia Britannica,* and the relevant specialty encyclopedias, like *Encyclopedia of Economics.* You can find the names of specialty encyclopedias under the appropriate subject headings of the computer catalogue. Here is a partial list:

Canadian Encyclopedia
Canadian Encyclopedia Timeline
Canadian Oxford Dictionary
Concise Dictionary of Canadianisms
Dictionary of Canadian Place Names
Dictionary of Canadian Quotations
Dictionnaire des canadianismes
Encyclopedia Canadiana
Encyclopedia of Canada's Peoples (2006)
Encyclopédie du Canada
Encyclopedia of American Ethnic Groups
Encyclopedia of Economics
Encyclopedia of Education
Encyclopedia of Feminism
Encyclopedia of Film and Television
Encyclopedia of Judaica
Encyclopedia of Psychology
Encyclopedia of World Art
International Encyclopedia of Social Sciences
World Encyclopedia of Film

Encyclopedias are designated in the computer catalogue with "Ref." before the call number. They are shelved in the reference room.

Many library catalogues also include links to online encyclopedias. Some of these online encyclopedias are available for general use (such as the *Britannica* concise, available from Yahoo! Education), while others require a password to access. Passwords can generally be obtained from a reference librarian at an institution.

Use Indices and Databases to Locate Periodical Material

Periodicals are magazines, newspapers, and journals that are published at regular intervals. They are important to the researcher because they contain the most current material available on a subject—unlike books, they are updated frequently. Periodicals are also peer-reviewed, or at least edited, which attempts to ensure that the source is credible, authoritative, and up-to-date.

Types of Periodicals

General periodicals are magazines and newspapers meant for the average reader. They include daily newspapers like *The Globe and Mail* and *The Wall Street Journal* and magazines like *Maclean's, Newsweek,* and *Sports Illustrated.* Think of general periodicals as the publications anyone can buy at a newsstand. These periodicals rarely provide in-depth treatment of a subject, as they are meant for the average reader.

Often such periodicals have extensive Web sites that include archives. For example, cbc.ca is updated throughout the day with world and regional news. Sites like the *New York Times* also allow researchers to search archives of articles dating back as far as 1851. Some sites provide full text for articles less than a week old and abstracts (or summaries) of articles older than one week. Full text of articles older than one week can usually be purchased.

Journals are periodicals published by scholarly, professional organizations like the Canadian Association for the Study of International Development, which publishes the *Canadian Journal of Development Studies,* and the Canadian Philosophical Association, which publishes *Dialogue: Canadian Philosophical Review.* Academic journals are not available at a local newsstand but by subscription only. The treatment of subjects in journals is more detailed because it is for readers knowledgeable in the given field. However, this fact should not discourage you from using journal articles, because they can be understood by post-secondary students. In fact, their more detailed discussions usually make them more satisfying than magazine articles. They are also documents that post-secondary professors expect their students to use for formal research assignments.

Use Periodical Indices

One way to find both general periodical and scholarly journal articles is with indices. Indices catalogue magazine and journal articles, most often by topic, so they are often the easiest way to find material related to a subject. Indices are generally available in print form, on CD-ROM, and through online, searchable databases. While this last format will probably be the one you use most frequently in your research, keep in mind that some articles written prior to 1985 might not be available through an electronic database. Students should refer to a print index such as *The Readers Guide to Periodical Literature* or *The Canadian Periodical Index* to find those articles.

Online databases like EBSCOhost and ProQuest that will lead students to periodicals differ in their specifics, but most allow students to search by title, author, or keyword. The figure below shows the results of a keyword search of an online database using the search term "genetically engineered foods."

When searching an online database like EBSCOhost, keep in mind that the variety and number of keywords researchers use will affect the number and relevance of total results. After having completed a search, click on the title of an article to view complete citation information. The figure below shows what this can look like.

Results of an Online Periodical Database Search.
This page shows the periodicals found in a search for "genetically modified foods."

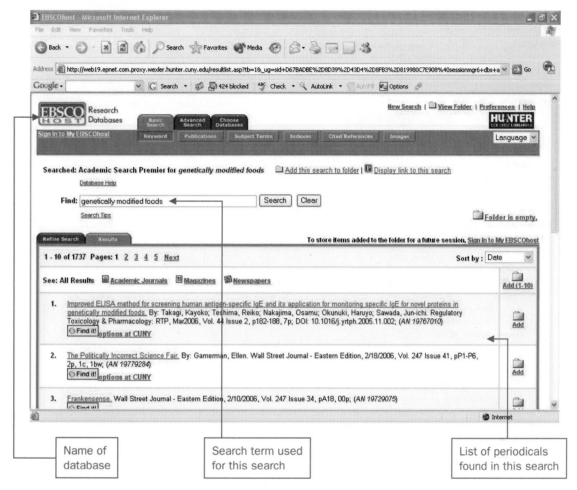

Reprinted with permission from EBSCO Host.

Often students can link directly to the full text of an article from a search results page. However, if the page does not offer a link, researchers should be able to find a print version of the complete piece in a library or obtain a copy through interlibrary loan.

Different libraries will use various online databases. However, here is a list of some of the most popular ones:

- EBSCOhost accesses articles from more than 3,000 popular and scholarly periodicals in every academic subject. An important advantage of this useful resource is that it gives access to whole articles rather than abstracts.
- ProQuest's online Canadian indexes list thousands of periodicals. An abstract is included for most articles. Abstracts are useful because they allow students to judge how helpful the article is likely to be. Beware, though, that in some cases a search result will only offer an abstract and citation for an article. Neither will help in research writing. Ensure that search results only include full text results.
- ProQuest Newspaper Abstracts indexes the *New York Times*, *Wall Street Journal*, *Christian Science Monitor*, *Washington Post*, and *Los Angeles Times*.

Detailed Citation of an Article in an Online Periodical Database.

This page gives further information on a listed article, including its publication information.

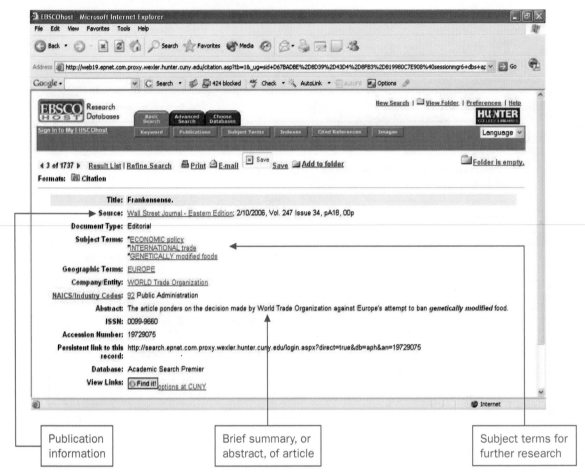

Reprinted with permission from EBSCO Host.

- InfoTrac indexes articles from over 1,100 magazines, journals, and newspapers by subject, title, and author. It is particularly helpful for very current topics.
- LexisNexis provides full-text articles from over 5,600 news, business, legal, and medical publications. It is particularly useful for searching Canadian newspapers and magazines.

Ask your librarian which databases are most useful for your topic.

To discover useful journal articles, check the online or print indices appropriate to a subject. In addition, check the abstracts and bibliographies. As touched on previously, an **abstract** lists articles by subject matter and provides a brief summary of each article's content in addition to information about where the article can be found. A **bibliography** includes both books and journal articles. The following is a list of some of the most common indices, bibliographies, and abstracts that may be available in print, on CD-ROM, or on an online database.

ABC-CLIO (American history)
Agricultural Index
Applied Science and Technology Index

Art Index
Bibliography of Modern History
Bibliography on Women
Biological Abstracts
Business Periodicals Index
Chemical Abstracts
Drama Bibliography
Energy Index
Engineering Index
ERIC (education)
Film Index
General Science Index
Historical Abstracts
Humanities Index
Index to Economic Journals
Index to Religious Periodical Literature
International Bibliography of Geography
International Nursing Index
MLA Bibliography
Music Index
Nursing Literature Index
PAIS International (public and social policy, social sciences)
Philosopher's Index
PsycInfo
PubMed (biomedicine)
Social Science Index
Sociological Abstracts
Women: A Bibliography

Use the Internet to Locate Sources

The Internet can sometimes seem like the biggest library in the world—a vast virtual hall containing billions of facts and opinions. Perfect for a researcher, right? Yes, the Internet can be a useful tool when used for careful research because it contains a variety of text, visual, and multimedia files that can be quickly searched. However, the Internet has many disadvantages. The changing nature of the World Wide Web means that a site someone read yesterday might be gone tomorrow. Furthermore, quality control can be an issue, as *anyone* can post *anything* to a web site. For instance, fiction can be presented as fact, images can be modified and tampered with, and 14-year-olds can masquerade as doctoral students in psychology.

So how do researchers traverse this minefield of information? Let's start by examining the entry points for research: basic and metasearch engines.

Searching the Internet

Basic search engines sift through the vast amounts of information and return the most relevant sites according to keywords. Metasearch engines sort through several basic search engines at once. No single search engine covers the millions of pages available on the Internet, so use a few when beginning research. Also, search engines come and go with some frequency, so check with a reference librarian to learn whether there is a new search engine to try.

Some search engines break subject areas down into categories and subcategories. For example, go to www.yahoo.com, where it becomes evident that Yahoo! allows users to search within directories such as arts, culture, news, reference, and business, among others. Google Book Search (http://books.google.com) allows researchers to search the full text of certain books.

Basic Search Engines		Metasearch Engines	
Google	www.google.com	**Metacrawler**	www.metacrawler.com
Yahoo!	www.yahoo.com	**Dogpile**	www.dogpile.com
MSN	www.msn.com	**Mamma**	www.mamma.com
Altavista	www.altavista.com	**Ixquick**	www.ixquick.com
Lycos	www.lycos.com		

The following figure shows the home page of the popular search engine Google.

The Home page of Google.
Google is one of the most popular search engines on the Internet.

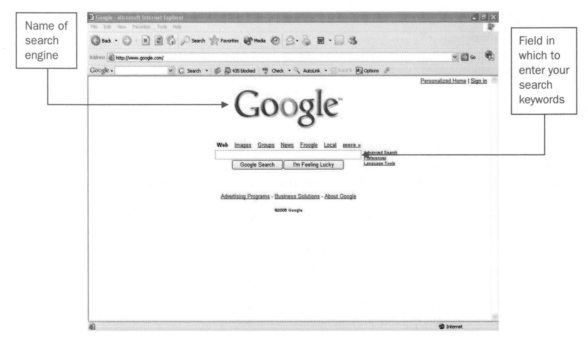

© Google Inc. and used with permission.

Search engines are powerful research tools when they are used correctly. The key to getting the best results from an Internet search is the keyword or keywords used to focus a search. As with the search terms researchers use for a library catalogue search, you want a keyword or keywords that are neither too broad nor too narrow. Be sure to spell keywords correctly and use relevant terminology to ensure that a search retrieves the most relevant results.

Students should also familiarize themselves with the following commands. Use them with keywords to search precisely and to weed out irrelevant results.

- **Quotation marks.** Keywords enclosed in quotation marks denote an exact word or phrase. So, to use a search engine to look for only the complete phrase *genetically modified foods,* with those exact words in that exact order, a researcher would enclose it in quotes: "genetically modified foods."
- **AND, OR, and NOT.** Using these words, in all-capital letters, between keywords tells a search engine how to look for them. AND stipulates that both terms should be present in a source (genetically AND food, for example). OR stipulates that at least one of the terms should be present (food OR produce), NOT excludes any source that includes that term (food NOT human).
- **+ and – signs.** The + and – signs function just like the AND and NOT commands. Include a + sign between two keywords, without spaces, to stipulate that both should be present in a source (genetically+food). Include a – before a term, again without a space, to exclude sources that include it (food–human).

Experiment with these commands to understand how they function. Once researchers have mastered them, they will save a great deal of time and improve overall Internet research skills.

Once you have entered keywords and conducted a search, the search engine will return a list of results. The figure below shows what this list can look like using Google. Clicking the links the search engine produces will take researchers directly to a web page.

Google Results Page.
This shows the web pages Google found after a search for "genetically modified" AND "foods."

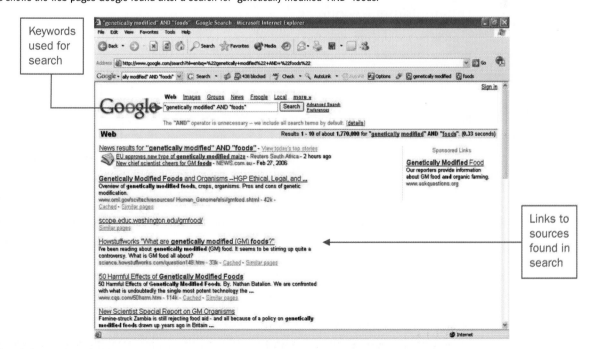

© Google Inc. and used with permission.

Evaluating Internet Sources

Internet sources present a special challenge because the quality of the material varies so greatly. An editor may or may not have checked the facts or assessed the logic of web pages. When evaluating Internet sources, ask the following questions:

1. Who is sponsoring the Web site? Generally, you should work with informational sites (ones whose purpose is to present information). Sites sponsored by universities, the government, or research foundations are likely to be more reliable than for-profit sites. In addition, pages associated with major news and media organizations like the CBC or *The Globe and Mail* are reliable.
2. Can the sponsor of the page be verified? Look for a phone number or postal address. Check the sponsor's credentials on the web or in a print source. Does the sponsor have a particular bias? For example, a page sponsored by Planned Parenthood will have pro-choice leanings.
3. When was the site last updated? The date may appear on the page. A very old page may no longer be reliable. In Internet Explorer, students can see the dates some sites were created and revised by clicking "File" and then "Properties."
4. Does the site include links to credible sites? A site full of dead links or links to questionable sites may not be current or reliable.
5. Does the site look professional? Are there grammar, usage, or spelling errors? Is the page attractively designed? A page that looks shoddy may include shoddy information.
6. Can information on the site be verified in a print source? Controversial or surprising information should be confirmed for accuracy.

The figure on page 395 compares two Web sites—one reliable and credible, the other questionable.

Other Internet Resources

Searching for documents and sites relevant to a topic is not the only way to use the Internet as a research tool. Part of the appeal of the Web is that it allows people from all over the world to interact and communicate through email, listservs, newsgroups, and blogs.

Email: Email is very useful for conducting interviews with experts on a topic. Because an email interview does not require scheduled, face-to-face time, an electronic interview format allows researchers and writers to question people who do not live nearby or who might not be able to spare the time for an in-person or phone interview. Also, email interviews provide students with an accurate record of an expert's response to questions.

When conducting an email interview, be considerate of the interviewee. Many people are wary about unsolicited questionnaires. Send a brief email first, asking permission to send additional questions. In this initial email, describe the research project and personal interest in the work of the interviewee. Be polite and professional in follow-up emails, and always send a thank-you email after the interview.

Listservs and newsgroups: Electronic discussion groups such as listservs and newsgroups can be an excellent resource for conducting interviews and surveys. Topics for

A Comparison of Two Web Sites.

Here are two web pages, the first one reliable and credible, and the second questionable in the accuracy of its content. When evaluating Web sites, look for information about the site's sponsor, the date it was last updated, and the general quality of its design and presentation.

Reprinted with permission from WashingtonPost.com.

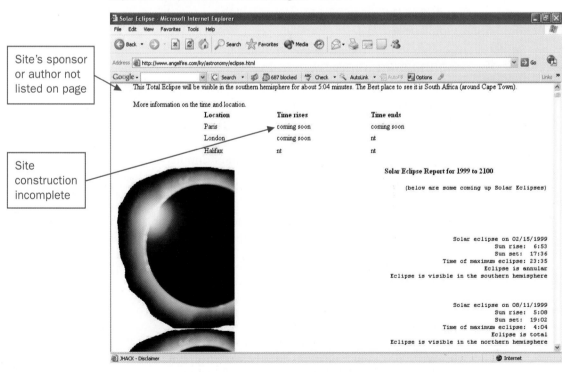

such groups range anywhere from child rearing to snowboarding, and most anyone can join any list or group. Once students have subscribed to a list, they can post questions to the group via email. Keep in mind that most group members have a great deal of knowledge about the group topic, and that broad or general questions that can be answered by other methods of research should not be posed to such groups. For example, the question "How do you learn to snowboard?" might be ignored by members of a snowboarding listserv, but the more specific question "What types of bindings are best for freestyling?" should elicit some helpful responses.

Blogs: Weblogs, or blogs, are not interactive like email, listservs, and newsgroups; however, they can still be useful during the research process. Many experts in a variety of fields maintain blogs, and researchers might find helpful book or article suggestions within these diary-like sites. Be careful about incorporating firsthand information from these sites within a paper, however. Blog entries can be based more on opinion than on fact and can contain strong biases.

Do Field Research

So far, students have read about research that leads them to what other people have discovered about a topic. **Field research**, on the other hand, is inquiry that leads the student writer to her *own* firsthand findings. The most practical field research for students to conduct is interviews and surveys. Topics based on campus and local issues are well suited to interviews and surveys, but those based on topics with a larger scope—such as international politics—may not be. After all, students, professors, and local leaders will be more available to interact with students than world leaders would be.

Conduct an Interview

Many people on or near campus can be worth interviewing. For instance, medical professionals have important perspectives on topics such as the AIDS epidemic and physician-assisted suicide; local businesspeople can speak authoritatively on increasing the provincial sales tax; school board members have information about the advantages and disadvantages of teachers' unions; and classmates can discuss their experiences with test anxiety.

These guidelines can help students conduct an interview:

1. Decide whether open or closed questions will be more useful. **Open questions** allow for unlimited response; **closed questions** limit the responders' answers.

   Open question: How will the proposed tuition increase affect you?

   Closed question: The proposed tuition increase will likely (a) cause me to drop out of school, (b) cause me to reduce my course load, (c) have no effect on me.

2. Make an appointment ahead of time.
3. Write out your questions in advance in order to be prepared and do not waste the interviewee's time. Although not required to do so, researchers can send the interviewee the questions ahead of time, so the person can prepare.

4. Although the interviewer will have prepared questions, allow the interviewee to go in unexpected directions if doing so yields useful information.

5. Take careful notes. If necessary, ask the interviewee to repeat to get the words just right. If possible, take a tape recorder and ask permission to use it.

6. Get permission to quote the interviewee, and document according to the form given on page 437.

7. Alternatively, conduct an "interview" via email, allowing the subject to write responses to questions. This is a useful strategy when the interview subject is very busy, or if the topic is technical or complex.

Conduct a Survey

A survey is a questionnaire, a set of questions designed to gather information from a group of people. There are different kinds of surveys. In the social sciences, for example, surveys are conducted according to strict, rigorous procedures. Here, however, we are using a more informal methodology.

Surveys are useful when researchers want to get the general opinion or reaction of a particular group. For example, a student may want to know how high school teachers feel about alternative schools or to learn how much television post-secondary students watch. When conducting both surveys and interviews, be sure subject choices do not overlap. In addition to asking for answers, interviewers may want respondents to indicate their age, gender, or other information in order to classify and to compare responses. For example, if surveying students to learn whether they experience test anxiety, a researcher might want to learn their class rank to see if seniors are more likely to be anxious than first-year students.

When surveying people, remember these guidelines:

1. Include a cover letter explaining who you are and what the purpose of the survey is.

2. Write clear questions. Test them out on people to be sure they are clear.

3. Decide whether open or closed questions will be more useful. Open questions such as "Explain your experience with test anxiety" can give you answers that are difficult to interpret and tally. It might be more productive to write closed multiple-choice or scale questions like these:

How often do you experience test anxiety?

a. Never
b. Every time you take a test
c. About half the time you take a test
d. Less than half the time you take a test
e. More than half the time you take a test

If you experience test anxiety at least half the time you take a test, rate the typical level of your anxiety.

mild		*severe*		*debilitating*
1	*2*	*3*	*4*	*5*

4. If using closed questions, be sure the choices do not overlap. For example, "less than half the time" and "rarely" overlap and undermine the usefulness of answers.

5. Keep value judgments out of questions. If a question reads, "Have you ever engaged in the immoral practice of plagiarism?" a respondent will be forced to admit to being immoral if answering yes. Instead, write, "Have you ever quoted a passage without using quotation marks?"

6. Be sure respondents are a representative sample of the group under consideration. Thus, if the campus is ethnically diverse, try to represent all ethnicities when surveying students about test anxiety. Also, use enough respondents. Asking 10 students about test anxiety will not tell anyone much about the student body, but asking 50 may yield reliable information about how many members of this group experience the problem.

7. Use email or a class discussion Web site, if possible, for the convenience of respondents.

Compile a Working Bibliography

A **working bibliography** is a list of potentially useful sources—sources you should look at closely later, when taking notes. To compile a working bibliography, follow these steps:

1. Look up the subject in the computer or card catalogue, and make a paper card or an electronic record for any book or research item that looks promising. Although some people place their working bibliography on notebook paper or in a computer file, index cards may also work. The wise researcher writes up the cards to follow the appropriate works-cited forms, which are given beginning on page 421. The following are examples of bibliography cards. The first card is for a book in print form; the second is for an online article.

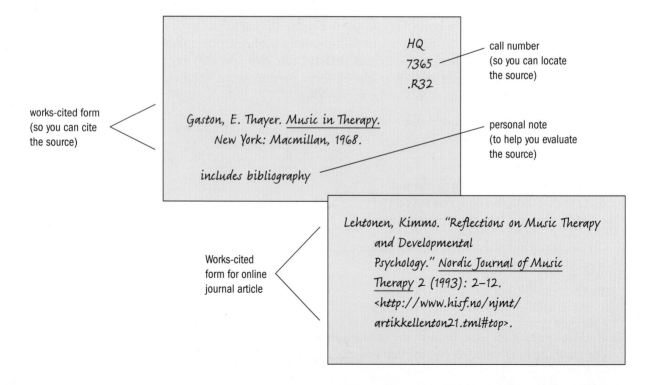

2. Look up the topic in the appropriate indices, bibliographies, databases, and abstracts, and make bibliography entries for promising sources, following the forms beginning on page 423. Alternatively, if the online library has a reference storage system like RefWorks, transfer records out of a search into a citation management program that stores bibliographic detail, and links to the articles discovered while researching.

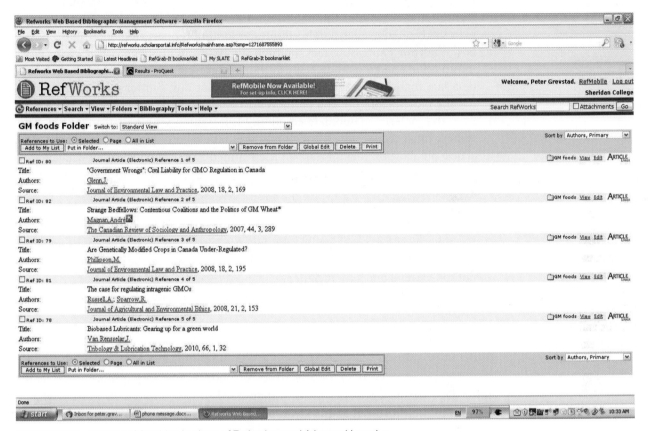

Screen capture courtesy of Sheridan Institute of Technology and Advanced Learning

3. Check the Internet if appropriate, and make bibliography entries for promising sources, following the form beginning on page 425.

Admittedly, individuals will decide what to include in a working bibliography based on flimsy evidence: whether the title of the source sounds promising. For this reason, students should err on the side of caution, making a card for any source that holds even a slight chance of usefulness. Students can discard sources later if they prove disappointing. Again, a citation management program helps with this. If a student writer decides that a promising source is anything but, the source can be deleted from the reference file for the project.

Evaluating Sources

Before taking notes, evaluate sources to determine which of them are good enough to take notes on. Answering the following questions can help.

1. Is the material recent enough? For some topics (such as General Sherman's Civil War strategy), older material may be fine, but other topics (such as the ethics of cloning) require the most up-to-date materials available. Many instructors suggest student writers use sources that are no more than five years old.

2. Does the author have suitable credentials? On the back cover, in the preface, or on the last page of a book, students can learn such things as an author's educational background and degrees earned, the relevant work or research history, institutional affiliation, the publications authored, and awards received. Similar material is often available in headnotes or footnotes of articles in journals.

3. Is the author expressing fact, opinion, or both? Remember, a fact is verifiable information and an opinion is the author's interpretation of the facts. Thus, it may be a fact that the stock market is at a three-year low, but an opinion that it will decline more before the end of the year.

4. Does the material manipulate emotions? Is it written with a particular bias? If so, writers must recognize a source's bias and take it into account. For example, an article on abortion that appears on the Planned Parenthood Web site will give one perspective on a controversial subject, while one on a right-to-life Web site will give another.

5. Is the material sufficiently scholarly, complete, and accessible? Skim to see if it includes references to relevant research. Look at the table of contents, index, and headings to check coverage. Read a few paragraphs to be sure the writing is not too technical or difficult to understand. At the same time, be sure the material is not too general and superficial.

6. Is the source useful? Does it include material needed and helpful for the research project?

Read Sources Strategically

If students read all of their sources word for word before taking notes, they would never get their papers done. Instead, they need to read *strategically* to find what is relevant to their research as quickly as possible. The first step is to determine the usefulness of a source. These strategies can help:

1. Read the title and major headings. If there is a table of contents, look it over. If there is an index, look up important words and phrases. If any of these suggest information relevant to the research, the source may be useful.

2. If there is a preface or introduction, or chapter or unit summaries, read them quickly. If they touch on a paper's topic, the source may be useful.

3. Read the first sentence of every paragraph in an article and of every paragraph of a relevant chapter in a book, looking for an indication that the rest of the material is relevant to a topic.

4. Read the last paragraph of an article or relevant chapters of a book, looking for key ideas.

5. Note boldface, italicized, and underlined terms. Are any of these keywords for the topic?

6. Note graphics and read captions looking for indications that the material is relevant to the topic.

Once it is determined that a source is useful, the writer can read, highlight, and annotate the relevant sections carefully and take notes according to the strategies explained next.

Take Notes

Some people who take notes for a research paper prefer to use small index (recipe) cards, and some people prefer to use their computers.

If using index cards:

1. Avoid the temptation to fill each card. Instead, write one piece of information per card, as in the following figure, in order to shuffle note cards into a suitable order later when it is time to organize the paper.
2. On each card, indicate the source and page number the note is taken from, or the URL if the source is online, to document the material in a paper. Forgetting to do this means students will have to locate sources all over again to document them.
3. Be sure to have an entry in the working bibliography for each source. Remember too that a citation management system linked to an online library is a great way to store records, and ultimately to make bibliography preparation simple and rapid.

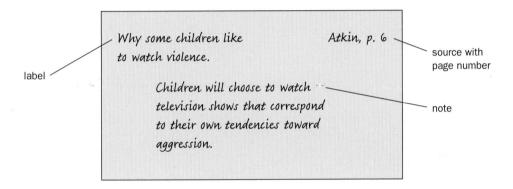

4. Label each card to categorize its content. Labels such as "Historical background," "Teen pregnancy rate," and "Possible solution" will help to organize index cards.
5. If quoting, be sure to use quotation marks.
6. Use ink, because pencil can blur and fade.

Working Electronically:

1. Using a laptop means that you can input notes in the library. Otherwise, you will need to write by notes by hand and enter them later onto your computer.
2. Put all the notes in one file, create separate files for different headings or subtopics, or place each note in a separate file. Consider which method best lends itself to cutting and pasting notes into a draft.
3. Keep backup copies of all notes on a CD or USB/flash drive, in case of hard drive or power failure. Losing all notes is a catastrophic setback.
4. Keep each item of information separate with page breaks or new files. The goal is to be able to rearrange notes easily into a draft.

5. Document by indicating the source and page number a note is taken from or the URL for an online source.
6. Label each note to categorize its content.

If most sources are online, students may be tempted to cut and paste directly from the Web site into notes—and from notes into the paper. This practice is dangerous because it often leads to plagiarism, as explained on pages 418–419. Students should paraphrase, summarize, and quote as they take notes, as it is expected that there will be instances of each in the final draft of a paper.

For an essay that uses sources to support the student writer's ideas, take notes using index cards or the computer. Photocopying or downloading and annotating are too cumbersome a process to use for sources for a research paper because students are unable to extract notes easily and to shuffle or cut and paste them. Also, writers would have to work out paraphrases, quotations, and summaries as they draft, rather than as they take notes, which makes drafting more time-consuming.

If you photocopy or download and print out sources:

1. Be sure the source and page numbers are on the photocopy. Write all the bibliographic information on the front or back of the photocopy if you are not using cards or an electronic reference manager.
2. Underline or highlight the useful information, but avoid marking too much, to avoid trouble extracting ideas needed when drafting the paper.
3. In the margins, label underlining, or highlighting to indicate its content.
4. Take time to reflect on the material highlighted or underlined. In the margins or on an attached sheet, write responses to the source, or indicate how you might use the source in your paper.
5. Review the SQ3R reading strategy from the early pages of this book. It really works!

There are four kinds of note taking students should know: paraphrase notes, quotation notes, summary notes, and personal notes.

Before we examine types of notes, let's consider the importance of quote, paraphrase, and summary. When you write a research paper, you are expected to include scholarly work by experts. Expert ideas and opinions need to be integrated into the text. But to what extent do we quote? Or paraphrase? Or summarize? A good rule of thumb is to include research or scholarly materials of a minimum one-third the length of the essay or research paper. You can of course quote expert ideas directly. However, if you only use quotation to integrate sources, a paper quickly becomes formulaic, and perhaps boring. Therefore, you need to decide which of your sources you should quote directly, and which of them you want to paraphrase (in your own words, the same length as the original text), and which to summarize (at approximately one-third the length of the original, again in your own words). Whether you quote, paraphrase, or summarize, you also need to integrate scholarly material so that your paper flows well. To do this, you need attribution phrases. Attribution phrases introduce a quote or a paraphrase or summary, and signal to the reader that the ideas that follow come from experts or from research reading. Common verbs are to note, suggest, claim, say, add, assert, and many more. Remember, however you are integrating sources, you need to mention the author's last name, to use a reporting verb in the present tense, and to adjust quoted material to integrate it into a sentence grammatically.

Paraphrase Notes

When you paraphrase, you restate an author's original ideas in your own words and style. Most of the notes should be paraphrases so that a paper has its own distinctive style. When paraphrasing, remember the following points:

- You must alter the style and wording of the original material.
- You may not add any ideas.
- You may not alter or distort the meaning of the original material in any way.

A good procedure for paraphrasing is to read the original material several times to understand its meaning. Then pretend to explain the material to a friend, and write the paraphrase in the way a student writer would form the explanation. Check to be sure that the style and wording have been altered without altering or adding to the meaning. To paraphrase a long passage, break it down into parts and write the paraphrase part by part.

To appreciate the difference between an acceptable and unacceptable paraphrase, study the following examples:

> From *Sociology* by Richard T. Schaefer, page 423: An economic system does not exist in a vacuum. Someone or some group makes important decisions about how to use resources and how to allocate goods, whether it be a tribal chief or a parliament or a dictator. A cultural universal common to all economic systems, then, is the exercise of power and authority.

Unacceptable paraphrase:	An economic system does not exist alone. A person or collection of people will make major decisions about how to use and distribute resources and allocate goods. Thus, power and authority are a cultural universal in all economies. This fact holds true regardless of whether the power or authority is benign or cruel (Schaefer 423).
Explanation:	The paraphrase is unacceptable for two reasons: The style is too close to that of the original, and the last sentence of the paraphrase includes an idea that does not appear in the original.
Acceptable paraphrase:	In every economy, one or more persons determine the use and distribution of resources and goods. Thus, economic systems do not function independently of people, and they do not function without the use of power (Schaefer 423).
Explanation:	This paraphrase has a style different from that of the original, but the meaning of the original has not been changed, nor has any interpretation been added.

When paraphrasing, you may find it useful to retain a key word or phrase from the original. If the word or phrase is part of the author's distinctive style, place it in quotation marks, as this example illustrates:

In every economy, one or more persons determine the use and distribution of resources and goods. Thus, economic systems do not function independently of people or "the exercise of power and authority" (Schaefer 423).

Quotation Notes

To ensure a paper retains a distinctive style, most of your research notes should be paraphrases. However, if a source expresses a point in a particularly effective way, or if you encounter material that is very difficult to paraphrase, then use a quotation. When quoting, remember these Modern Language Association (MLA) guidelines. Note that the advice below is subject to change, as MLA guidelines are revised and updated annually.

1. With very few exceptions (noted below), do not alter the spelling, capitalization, punctuation, or wording of anything quoted.
2. Work short quotations (those fewer than four lines in a paper) into a sentence or paragraph.
3. Set long quotations (those five or more lines in a paper) off in a particular way:
    a. Start a new line and indent the quotation 10 spaces on the left.
    b. Do not use quotation marks unless they appeared in the source, in which case use double quotation marks.
    c. Follow the introduction to a long quotation with a colon if the introduction is a complete thought.
    d. Double-space the quotation.
    e. Place the period before the parenthetical citation.
    See page 447 for an example of a long quotation in a research paper.
4. To omit some portion from the middle or end of a quotation, use an ellipsis mark (three spaced periods). Be sure when omitting words not to alter the original meaning.

Source: *Sociology* by Richard T. Schaefer, page 423: An economic system does not exist in a vacuum. Someone or some group makes important decisions about how to use resources and how to allocate goods, whether it be a tribal chief or a parliament or a dictator. A cultural universal common to all economic systems, then, is the exercise of power and authority. The struggle for power and authority inevitably involves *politics,* which political scientist Harold Lasswell (1936) tersely defined as "who gets what, when, and how."

Quotation with ellipsis mark	"A cultural universal common to all economic systems . . . is the exercise of power and authority" (Schaefer 423).

If the omission comes at the end of a sentence, use the ellipsis mark and then a period.

Quotation with ellipsis mark:	"Someone or some group makes important decisions about how to use resources and how to allocate goods . . ." (Schaefer 423).

Place the ellipsis mark in brackets ([. . .]) if the author you are quoting uses an ellipsis mark in the source. This way, readers can distinguish use of ellipses from the source's use.

5. When adding a word or phrase to a quotation to clarify something or work the quotation into a sentence, place the addition inside brackets.

Quotation with addition:	"A cultural universal common to all economic systems, then, is the exercise of power and authority [to determine how goods and resources will be used]" (Schaefer 423).

6. When part of the quoted material appears in italics, underline the part in italics.

Quotation with underlining:	"The struggle for power and authority inevitably involves politics . . ." (Schaefer 423).

7. When all or part of quoted material is itself a quotation, use single quotation marks wherever double quotation marks appear in the source. Continue to use double quotation marks to mark the place where the quoted material begins and ends.

Quotation with single quotation marks:	"The struggle for power and authority inevitably involves politics, which political scientist Harold Lasswell (1936) tersely defined as 'who gets what, when, and how'" (Schaefer 423).

8. When working the quotations into a paper with an introduction containing the word *that*, do not capitalize the first word of the quotation (unless it is a proper noun), and do not use a comma after the introduction. If the introduction in the text does not have the word *that*, then use a comma and capitalize the first word of the quotation.

Example with *that*:	Schaefer says that "an economic system does not exist in a vacuum" (423).
Example without *that*:	Schaefer says, "An economic system does not exist in a vacuum" (423).

Combining Paraphrase and Quotation

Many passages lend themselves to a combination of paraphrase and quotation, as the following example shows:

Paraphrase and quotation:	In every economy, one or more persons determine the use and distribution of resources and goods. Thus, economic systems do not function independently of people, and they do not function without the use of power. "The struggle for [this] power . . . involves politics, which political scientist Harold Lasswell (1936) tersely defined as 'who gets what, when, and how'" (Schaefer 423).

Summary Notes

A **summary** is a condensed version of a source. Like a paraphrase, a summary restates an author's ideas in your own words and style. Unlike a paraphrase, a summary gives just the main ideas of all or a large part of a source—one or perhaps many paragraphs long.

In the previous chapter, you learned the steps of the research process, including how to gather sources using the wealth of tools in a library, on the Internet, and beyond. In this chapter, you will learn to integrate research findings into writing. You will also learn how to document sources in the proper format.

Outlining

Writing a research paper is an involved process. You have many sources to deal with, along with your own ideas. You must consider all of this material to discover connections and find a way to present everything coherently. Because the undertaking is complex, you may want to write a detailed outline, even if you do not customarily do so. While outlining, consider the following:

1. Before outlining, read over written notes. Consider source material and personal notes thoughtfully. In particular, think about how your research notes support a preliminary thesis. Do research notes suggest that thesis revision is necessary?
2. Look for patterns when reviewing notes. Use patterns of development from earlier chapters to help you identify connections between ideas. Once established, arrange cards or computer notes to reflect that order. If not, study the notes until it is possible to determine an order.
3. Note ideas resulting from consideration of the ideas and order of research notes. Write those ideas out and work them into a logical order. You may want to create a concept map on a separate piece of paper, or using an online tool.
4. Using ordered ideas as a guide, write a detailed outline to guide a first draft. A formal, numbered outline may work best.
5. Ask whether it is necessary to outline an introduction and conclusion. If not, which strategy would be appropriate?
6. While outlining, be aware that an essay plan may need additional information to support or explain a point. If so, do additional research.

Writing a First Draft

Using the outline as a guide, write a first draft. If possible, use a computer to facilitate moving paragraphs, sentences, and source material around easily.

Research papers can be complex for the reader, so use organizational tools to guide the audience. Place the thesis in one of the introductory paragraphs, so readers are aware of the focus from the start; use topic sentences to make the main idea of every paragraph clear for readers; and use transitions to guide the reader from point to point. Where it is necessary to use a paraphrase, quotation, or summary, paste a computer-generated note into the draft or tape the note card on the draft copy of the paper. You may also use the Comments feature of your word processing program to make notes in the margins that will remind you where to add research.

At the draft phase, avoid stringing sources together one after another. Instead, comment on paraphrases, quotations, and summaries by analyzing them, showing their significance, indicating their relationships to something else (i.e., other research ideas and the thesis), and so forth. Here is an example of commenting on a paraphrase. Notice that the student writer comments on the source material by showing its application.

Original passage:	Behaviour inevitably adapts to conserve the scarce resource—in this case, attention and time—and to "waste" the abundant resource. Thus, for example, much of the new technology's capability has been spent on simplifying interfaces and reducing communications latencies essentially to zero; both of these conserve precious time for users. The same motive has also spawned a plethora of indexing and searching schemes, of which Google is the chief example. These are all seeking to be attention-optimizers.
Paraphrase	Nicholson identifies the scarcity of attention in the information age and human adaptations to the abundance of information and describes how information is presented through clearer means to save time. This way, the amount of attention a reader pays is maximized.
Student comment on paraphrase	Nicholson's assertions have implications for readers, for web designers, and for authors, who all compete for audience attention in an information superhighway that is increasingly busier. This will likely lead to streamlining in both quantity and information architecture, especially on the World Wide Web.

Finally, when drafting, document source material by introducing paraphrases, quotations, and summaries with present tense attribution phrases, writing parenthetical text citations, and including a works cited page. Research materials can be incorporated into sentences in the text in the following ways.

Smith (2010, p. 36)	claims, suggests, notes, offers, declares, says, argues, asserts, etc.	that dogs are better than cats.	
[Author name (date and page number in parentheses)]	[attribution phrase]	[quote, paraphrase or summary material].	
Smith	claims, suggests, notes, offers, declares, says, argues, asserts, etc.	that dogs are better than cats	(2010, p. 36).
[Author name]	[attribution phrase]	[quote, paraphrase or summary material]	[(date and page number in parentheses), followed by a period]
It has been suggested (claimed, noted, offered, declared, said, argued, asserted, etc.)	that dogs are better than cats	by Smith (2010, p. 36).	
[Attribution phrase]	[quote, paraphrase or summary material]	[author name (date and page number in parentheses), followed by a period].	

An online reference tool, like RefWorks, can facilitate the preparation of a bibliography. Every article or website or other source can be added to a folder for a research paper as you research and write. This saves time at the end of the writing process. Using an electronic citation/reference management program, which may be a feature of an institution's online library database, makes this process much easier. These issues are taken up in the next sections.

Plagiarism

When people think of plagiarism, a serious form of academic dishonesty, they often imagine students illicitly downloading papers off the Internet, or copying large passages from books and passing them off as their own work. In other words, they think of plagiarism as something intentionally dishonest. And to be sure, such behaviour is unethical, unfair, and in some cases illegal.

There are other forms of plagiarism, though, that are equally unethical but that receive much less attention. Any time a student does not give proper credit for a fact, idea, or passage in his or her writing, the result is plagiarism. Whether the absence of the citation occurred through wilful dishonesty or simply a lack of familiarity about the rules of academic honesty is beside the point. Plagiarism is plagiarism. Also, the penalty for plagiarism is severe: it can end a student's academic career.

For this reason, you must be both honest and thorough in academic writing; you must always alert readers when an idea is not your own. Of course, to do so, you must be able to recognize when such an acknowledgment is necessary.

Be a Responsible Writer

The age of the Internet has made the location of information easier than ever. We benefit from this in many ways, as the Information Superhighway is at our fingertips. It is also, though, very tempting to locate and to use obscure or net-available information in research papers, and many student writers mistakenly assume that their professors will not notice. This is an incorrect assumption. If it is easy to Google information and "borrow" it for use in a paper, it is equally easy for a professor to find the same information. Remember, your professors generally have advanced research skills, not to mention professional reading skills that allow them to identify changes in voice or academic level in written work. There are also software programs like turnitin.com, which allow professors to compare student papers with any and everything available on the World Wide Web. Students who ignore academic honesty policies do so at their peril. Plagiarism is the highest crime in academia, and is taken very seriously. A charge of plagiarism can end an academic career, so err on the side of caution. Learn to cite and reference, and review sections of your papers where you have included secondary sources to ensure you have documented properly.

Deception Detection: A Review of Nonverbal Cues

Grant Hatcher

Abstract

1   The purpose of this paper is to review the empirical research on nonverbal cues for deception detection. Nonverbal cues indicative of deception can be broken down into two categories: facial expressions and body movements. Facial expressions of fear and disgust are reliable cues of deceit; however, the effectiveness of other body movements as cues is inconclusive. Research has shown that no nonverbal cue for deception detection works all the time; therefore, these methods should not be the sole decision on which to base the veracity of a statement. Goals for future research and how this information should be applied are discussed.

2   Lying has been an interest to humans for at least 3000 years (Grubin & Madsen, 2005). One of the earlier methods used for detecting deceit was trial by ordeal. Grubin and Madsen (2005) explain that trial by ordeal involved putting suspects into a life-threatening situation and waiting for a higher power to intervene. If a higher power did become involved, then the suspect was considered innocent. One trial by ordeal method known as "floating the witch" was used by the Christian Church during the 1600s (Levack, 2004). "Floating the witch" involved binding the suspect's arms and legs and then throwing her into a body of water that was blessed by a priest. If the suspect floated, she was considered guilty because the water rejected her (Levack, 2004). If she sank, she was considered innocent, though this often led to her death.

3   Perhaps the most well known method for deception detection is the polygraph, which measures an individual's autonomic responses elicited by answering carefully constructed questions (Fiedler, Schmid, & Stahl, 2002). Despite the popularity of the polygraph, many studies have questioned its validity (see Bunn, 2007), and scientific interest in alternative methods of deception detection has increased in recent years. In the current deception detection literature, cues that have received significant research attention can be categorized into two broad types: verbal and nonverbal. The purpose of this paper is to examine the empirical research on nonverbal cues of deception detection. This review will help guide future studies through several concerns of deception detection research. As well, it will help researchers understand which nonverbal cues are indicative of lying and whether these cues can be applied in real life situations. Facial expressions and body movements are different general types of nonverbal cues, and they will be discussed separately in this paper. This distinction is necessary because measuring facial expressions involves measuring the type of movements (i.e., how the face moved) (Ekman & Friesen, 1978), while coding body movements involves simply measuring whether or not a movement occurred.

Facial Expressions

4   Facial expressions can be divided into two classes: macro versus micro expressions, and intentional versus unintentional expressions (Ekman & Friesen, 1974; Ekman & O'Sullivan, 2006). Macro facial expressions are normal facial expressions that an individual does not try to hide. They usually stay on the face for about three or four seconds (Ekman & O'Sullivan, 2006). Micro facial expressions are expressions of concealed emotions. These expressions usually last for a fraction of a second (1/25s) because when hidden emotions appear on the face, they are quickly concealed again (DePaulo et al., 2003). Ekman and Friesen (1974) called micro expressions "leakages" because even with strong attempts to hide them, the true emotions "leak" onto the individual's face. The other distinction of facial expressions, intentional and unintentional, is self-explanatory. Intentional facial expressions are expressions that are deliberately expressed; however, they may not reflect what is actually being felt (Ekman & O'Sullivan, 2006). For example, some individuals may smile in order to disguise that they are actually feeling sad. Unintentional facial expressions are real expressions that are automatic and outside of the control of the individual expressing them (Ekman & O'Sullivan, 2006). For example, smiling at something funny is often unintentional.

5   Research has shown that distinguishing between these two continuums of facial expressions can be reliable for detecting deception. There are two reasons why this is the case. The first reason is that most people cannot deliberately control all of the muscles involved in producing facial expressions. Ekman, Roper, and Hager (1980) studied the facial muscles that are activated when someone displays an unintentional facial expression. When the researchers asked the participants to generate such unintentional facial expressions deliberately, more than 75% of them were unable to do so. Ekman and his colleagues (1980) hypothesized that if most people cannot control their facial muscles then they probably cannot inhibit them either. Therefore, it would be expected that expressions should leak onto the face even if an individual is trying to conceal them (Ekman & O'Sullivan, 2006). The second reason why facial expressions can help detect lying is that several of them are universal. Ekman and his colleagues (1987) showed individuals from 10 different countries pictures of different facial expressions. There was high agreement between all cultures (range=90.4%–73.2%) in identifying the specific emotion depicted in each picture, especially for surprise, sadness, fear, disgust, and anger. It is crucial for facial expressions to be universal if they are going to be applied to deception detection because it provides internal consistency. That is, if an investigator examines an angry facial expression from one person it would be expected that any other individual would express anger in a similar way. Therefore, facial expressions are indicative of what a person is actually feeling regardless of who that individual is.

6   As mentioned above, facial expressions can be quite brief and they may involve many different muscles. In order to measure the facial expressions that an individual makes properly, Ekman and Friesen (1978) created The Facial Action Coding System (FACS). Coders who use the FACS can measure all possible facial expressions by examining the activation of 46 different

facial muscles (Sayette, Cohn, Wertz, Perrott, & Parrott, 2001). In order to measure micro, and even macro expressions, coders need to use videos in order to watch the expressions in slow motion. Every facial expression is defined by the activation of specific facial muscles. For example, the combined activation of muscle unit six (*orbicularis oculi* and *pars orbitalis*) and 12 (*zygomaticus major*) will result in an unintentional smile, whereas an intentional smile only activates muscle unit 12 (Sayette et al., 2001).

7   Many studies have substantiated the reliability of the use of FACS for deception detection (see Ekman & Rosenberg, 2005). In one such study, Frank and Ekman (1997) created a mock crime scenario in which participants had the chance to steal 50 dollars. All participants were interrogated; however, those who did decide to take the money were instructed to lie to the interrogator about stealing it. If they were able to fool the interrogator, they were allowed to keep the 50 dollars. By using the FACS, blind coders were able to detect 80% of the liars because they displayed more micro expressions of fear and disgust than the truth tellers (Frank & Ekman, 1997). Using fear and disgust as a measure for lying is effective because these emotions are positively correlated with deception apprehension; that is, the fear of being caught lying (DePaulo et al., 2003).

8   The FACS is also effective for distinguishing between intentional and unintentional facial expressions. Ekman and colleagues (Ekman, O'Sullivan, Friesen, & Scherer, 1991) had participants watch an unpleasant video of amputations and burn victims. Half of the participants were instructed to hide their negative emotions and pretend that the video was actually enjoyable (lying group). They found that the liars produced fewer unintentional smiles (M=1.62) and more intentional smiles (M=1.14) than truth tellers (M=2.49 and M=.71 respectively). Based on differences in smiles, blind detectors who applied the FACS were able to pick out the liars from the truth tellers more than 70% of the time.

9   The most current and realistic evidence for smiling and deception comes from Porter, Doucette, Woodworth, Earle, and MacNeil (2008). They examined two groups of participants: 27 criminals who were serving a sentence and 38 students who were non-offenders. In general, the offenders made significantly fewer smiles (M=.805) than the students (M=3.02). Consistent with these findings, other studies have demonstrated similar results (e.g., Granhag & Strömwall, 2002; Vrij, 1995).

10 Understanding facial expressions may be a promising method in detecting lies, but it has not gone without controversy. A meta-analysis by DePaulo and her colleagues (2003) revealed that smiles may not be a good predictor of statement veracity. They examined 27 studies that used smiling as a cue, and the effect size for smiling across these studies was exactly zero. Ekman's work has also been questioned because outside of his circle of colleagues, little research has been conducted on micro expressions and deceit. Even Ekman himself mentions that there is still more research needed to understand how facial expressions are related to deceit (Ekman & O'Sullivan, 2006). Finally, at best, the effectiveness of facial expressions for detecting deceit has been around 80% (Frank & Ekman, 1997). It would be expected that at least 20% of liars would be undetected if this method was used on its own. Therefore,

facial expressions alone should not be used for deception detection. Instead, facial expressions that leak onto an individual's face may be a clue for an interviewer to investigate something further (Ekman & O'Sullivan, 2006).

Body movements

11 Blair and Kooi (2004) explain three theories about how body movements are involved in lying: the emotional approach, the cognitive complexity approach, and the image control approach. The emotional approach suggests that liars will feel fear, nervousness, or excitement (Granhag & Strömwall, 2002). This theory predicts that even though liars will try to suppress these emotions, they will be expressed in other ways, such as more body movements (Vrij et al., 2008). The cognitive complexity approach suggests that lying is more difficult than telling the truth (Blair & Kooi, 2004). There are several reasons why this may be the case: creating and telling a lie may be less automatic than telling the truth, liars feel like they have to take extra precautions to seem believable, and they have to remember what they have already said in order to avoid contradictions. Based on this theory, liars will be concentrating on cognitive processes, which may cause them to neglect their body and make fewer movements (Vrij et al., 2008). The image control approach takes into account the fact that liars are aware that they are lying, so they try to act natural and calm (Blair & Kooi, 2004). However, in their attempt to appear calm, they over control their movements and appear unnaturally still.

12 Research indicates that there is support for all three of these approaches to deception. Granhag and Strömwall (2002) found support for the cognitive complexity and image control theories. In their study, participants watched trained actors perform a murder. Afterwards, they were separated into two groups: truth tellers and liars. During an interrogation, the truth tellers had to recall what they saw, while the liars were instructed to describe events that did not happen in the skit. Results indicated that liars made fewer gaze aversions (M=23.9) and self-manipulations (M=0.52) than the truth tellers (M=33.81 and M=1.84 respectively). Liars also made fewer head movements and trunk movements, but the difference was not statistically significant. Fewer gaze aversions supports the control approach to deception because the liar is trying to act as natural as possible and not look away from the interviewer, whereas fewer self-manipulations supports both the cognitive and control approach. Perhaps the liars are concentrating so much on lying that they do not move as much (cognitive), or they are trying to act calm, and as a result deliberately move less (control). Vrij (1995) found results that were consistent with Granhag and Strömwall (2002). He found that liars made fewer gaze aversions (M=13.73), foot and leg movements (M=6.36), and trunk movements (M=6.28) than did truth tellers (M=14.3, M=8.02, and M=6.45, respectively). Vrij, Mann, and Fisher (2006) conducted an experiment on nonverbal behaviours and lying and found support for the emotional approach. The truth tellers were interviewed and asked to recall a series of events that had happened earlier. The liars were also interviewed; however, they did not participate in the events that the truth tellers did. Instead, the liars were informed about the events that took place and had to pretend that they were involved. The results revealed only one significant finding for body movements. That is, liars shifted

their posture (*M*=4.65) more than truth tellers (*M*=3.85) during the interview (Vrij, Mann, & Fisher, 2006). Although this finding contradicts the cognitive and image control approach, the results of the liars shifting more than the truth tellers can be explained by applying the emotional theory. More shifts were the resultant behaviour of the liars' emotions of fear and nervousness.

13 One reason why Vrij, Mann, and Fisher's (2006) results contradict Vrij (1995) and Granhag and Strömwall (2002) could be level of motivation. Perhaps the liars in the Vrij et al. (2006) study were more highly motivated than were participants in the other studies. Some research has shown that different levels of motivation can produce different nonverbal behaviours (Frank & Ekman, 1997). As well, individuals who are more highly motivated to lie will likely have deception apprehension, which would cause deception cues that are consistent with the emotional approach and that conflict with the cognitive and control approaches (DePaulo et al., 2003).

14 Despite empirical support, there are studies that contradict all three theories. Sporer and Schwandt (2007) conducted a meta-analysis of 54 studies that measured multiple cues to lying. Like Vrij (1995), they found that liars produced significantly fewer arm and leg movements than did truth tellers. However, contrary to Vrij (1995) and Granhag and Strömwall (2002), they found no differences in the number of gaze aversions for truth tellers and liars. More conflicting results were found in the largest meta-analysis of cues to deception. DePaulo and her colleagues (2003) combined the information from 120 separate studies and examined 158 different cues to deception. They found no significant differences in foot and leg movements, posture shifts, and gaze aversions for liars and truth tellers. However, when they divided the studies based on high and low motivation, they found different results. The highly motivated participants made significantly less foot and leg movements (*d*=-.15) than those who had low motivation (*d*=-.02; DePaulo et al., 2003).

15 Based on differing results in the literature, it is unclear whether body movements can be used reliably for deception detection. Although some studies do provide proof (e.g., Vrij, 1995), there is also contradicting evidence (DePaulo et al., 2003). In an insightful new method for detecting deception, Vrij and his colleagues (2008) were able to exaggerate cues to deception when they increased the cognitive demands of lying. Instead of having liars give their statements normally, they were instructed to explain what happened in reverse order. This resulted in the production of more leg and foot movements (*M*=13.8) and hand and finger movements (*M*=15.41) than produced by liars who did not give their statement in reverse (*M*=6.28 and *M*=7.33, respectively). They concluded that giving a statement in the reverse order caused the liars to be more nervous, and this was reflected in their behaviour. However, before reliable conclusions can be made, more research is needed on this technique.

Discussion

16 Facial expressions, particularly of fear and disgust, have been substantiated as reliable cues to deception (Frank & Ekman, 1997). When an individual is lying, facial "leakages" may occur, resulting in a cue to detect deceit. Body movements, although inconclusive, may reveal that an individual is withholding

information. The three theories of body movements (emotional, control, and cognitive) have at least some empirical support. The promising study by Vrij and his colleagues (2008) has shown that increasing cognitive demands of a liar exaggerates nonverbal cues to deception.

17 For future research and the application of these findings in real-world deception-detection contexts, several issues need to be addressed. As DePaulo and her fellow researchers (2003) have shown, cues to deception may differ depending on the liar's motivation. In order to better understand the interaction of motivation and lying, the effects of manipulating motivation for lying and potential repercussions need to be examined more closely. That is, high and low motivation groups need to be compared to observe the cues each group displays. Another issue is that every individual is different, and this needs to be taken into consideration when attempting to detect deceit. For example, the level of attractiveness (Porter, Campbell, Stapleton, & Birt, 2002), personality characteristics (Lee, Klaver, & Hart, 2008), and verbal fluency (Vrij, Akehurst, & Soukara, 2004) of individuals can influence their ability to lie. As well, someone may display mostly nonverbal cues when lying, while another individual may show more verbal cues. In order to avoid these types of complications two steps should be taken: (1) develop an in-depth rapport with the person in question, and (2) apply more than one deception detection technique. Building rapport will provide a baseline of behaviour that investigators can use to assist in identifying potential deceptive cues and may provide insight into the types of cues the individual may elicit. Combining verbal and nonverbal measures for detection is more effective for detecting lies than either method on its own (Ekman & O'Sullivan, 1991). However, even the combination of methods is not 100% effective in determining the veracity of an individual's statement. Therefore, all possible information, such as physical evidence, DNA, and corroborating testimonies, must be factored into the decision making process. Although our understanding of the role of nonverbal cues in deception detection is incomplete, the research evidence is promising. Once these cues are more completely understood and the research is refined, nonverbal cues could be a vital key in understanding if what an individual says is a truth or a lie.

References

Blair, J. P., & Kooi, B. (2004). The gap between training and research in the detection of deception. *International Journal of Police Science and Management, 6*, 77-83.

Bunn, G. C. (2007). Spectacular science: The lie detector's ambivalent powers. *History of Psychology, 10*, 156-178.

DePaulo, B. M., Lindsay, J. J., Malone, B. E., Muhlenbruck, L., Charlton, K., & Cooper, H. (2003). Cues to deception. *Psychological Bulletin, 129*, 74-118.

Ekman, P., & Friesen, W. V. (1974). Detecting deception from body or face. *Journal of Personality and Social Psychology, 29*, 288-298.

Ekman, P., & Friesen, W. V. (1978). *Facial action coding system.* Palo Alto: Consulting Psychologist Press.

Ekman, P., Friesen, W., O'Sullivan, M., Chan, A., Diacoyanni-Tarlatzis, I., Heider, K., et al. (1987). Universals and cultural differences in the judgments of facial expressions of emotion. *Journal of Personality and Social Psychology, 53,* 712-717.

Ekman, P., & O'Sullivan, M. (2006). From flawed self-assessment to blatant whoppers: The utility of voluntary and involuntary behaviour in detecting deception. *Behavioural Sciences & the Law, 24,* 673-686.

Ekman, P., O'Sullivan, M., Friesen, W. V., & Scherer, K. R. (1991). Face, voice and body in detecting deception. *Journal of Nonverbal Behaviour, 15,* 125-135.

Ekman, P., Roper, G., & Hager, J. C. (1980). Deliberate facial movement. *Child Development, 51,* 886-891.

Ekman, P., & Rosenberg, E. L. (Eds.) (2005). *What the face reveals: Basic and applied studies of spontaneous expression using the facial action coding system* (*FACS*; 2nd ed.). New York: Oxford University Press.

Fiedler, K., Schmid, J., & Stahl, T. (2002). What is the current truth about polygraph lie detection? *Basic and Applied Social Psychology, 24,* 313-324.

Frank, M., & Ekman, P. (1997). The ability to detect deceit generalizes across different types of high stake lies. *Journal of Personality and Social Psychology, 72,* 1429-1439.

Granhag, P. A, & Strömwall, L. A. (2002). Repeated interrogations: Verbal and non-verbal cues to deception. *Applied Cognitive Psychology, 16,* 243-257.

Grubin, D., & Madsen, L. (2005). Lie detection and the polygraph: A historical review. *Journal of Forensic Psychiatry & Psychology, 16,* 357-369.

Lee, Z., Klaver, J., & Hart, S. (2008). Psychopathy and verbal indicators of deception in offenders. *Psychology, Crime & Law, 14,* 73-82.

Levack, B. P. (Ed.). (2004). *The witchcraft sourcebook.* London: Routledge.

Porter, S., Campbell, M. A., Stapleton, J., & Birt, A. (2002). The influence of judge, target, and stimulus characteristics on the accuracy of detecting deceit. *Canadian Journal of Behavioural Science 34,* 172-185.

Porter, S., Doucette, N., Woodworth, M., Earle, J., & MacNeil, B. (2008). Halfe the world knowes not how the other halfe lies: Investigation of verbal and non-verbal signs of deception exhibited by criminal offenders and non-offenders. *Legal and Criminological Psychology, 13,* 27-38.

Sayette, M., Cohn, J., Wertz, J., Perrott, M., & Parrott, D. (2001). A psychometric evaluation of the facial action coding system for assessing spontaneous expression. *Journal of Nonverbal Behaviour, 25,* 167-185.

Sporer, S. L., & Schwandt, B. (2007). Moderators of nonverbal indicators of deception: A meta-analytic synthesis. *Psychology, Public Policy, and Law, 13,* 1-34.

Vrij, A. (1995). Behavioural correlates of deception in a simulated police interview. *Journal of Psychology: Interdisciplinary and Applied, 129,* 15-28.

Vrij, A., Akehurst, L., & Soukara, S. (2004). Let me inform you how to tell a convincing story: CBCA and reality monitoring scores as a function of age, coaching, and deception. *Canadian Journal of Behavioural Science, Special issue: Forensic Psychology, 36,* 113-126.

Vrij, A., Mann, S., & Fisher, R. P. (2006). An empirical test of the behaviour analysis interview. *Law and Human Behaviour, 30,* 329-345.

Vrij, A., Mann, S. A., Fisher, R. P., Leal, S., Milne, R., & Bull, R. (2008). Increasing cognitive load to facilitate lie detection: The benefit of recalling an event in reverse order. *Law and Human Behaviour, 32,* 253-265.

The complete essay, including any bibliographic references, is also available on the Online Learning Centre at www.mcgrawhill.ca/olc/clouse.

What to Document

In the sections that follow, you will find extensive coverage of how to give credit properly for outside sources in writing. Providing this credit is called **documentation**.

Every time you use the words, ideas, or opinions of others, you must document that material. You must document facts that are not common knowledge, including statistics, references to studies, descriptions of experiments, an author's original ideas, an author's opinion, and an author's conclusion—regardless of whether this material appears in a paper as quotation, paraphrase, or summary. Each of these methods of incorporating others' ideas must be documented with a citation, and referenced correctly in the appropriate documentation style.

Facts that are common knowledge need not be documented. Thus, you don't need to document that John A. MacDonald was the first Prime Minister of Canada, that gravity holds the planets in orbit, or that plants bend toward the sun. Nor do you need to document dates that are not debatable, such as the date Canada became a country, or common sayings, such as "Fools rush in where wise men fear to tread."

If in doubt about whether to document a point, err on the side of caution. It is better to document too much than to document too little and plagiarize as a result. Of course, instructors can advise when you are unsure.

How to Avoid Plagiarism When Paraphrasing

One of the most common forms of plagiarism occurs when a student paraphrases a passage from a source but does not sufficiently alter the author's words and style. Even when you properly acknowledge that the material is borrowed, you will still be guilty of plagiarism if the paraphrase is too close to the original. Consider the following example, which includes a passage from a textbook and a student paraphrase of it that qualifies as plagiarism:

> From *The American Tradition in Literature,* 11th edition, by George and Barbara Perkins, page 553:
>
> > A former orator, Red Jacket (or Sagoyewatha) was skilled in humorous and sarcastic speeches in defence of the traditions of the Five Nations of the Iroquois, of which his Seneca tribe was a part.

Student paraphrase considered plagiarism	A former orator, Sagoyewatha, also known as Red Jacket, was skilled in witty and sarcastic speeches on behalf of the Five Nations of the Iroquois, of which his Seneca tribe was a member (Perkins and Perkins, 553).

If you want to include the exact words of another writer, it is necessary to use quotation marks. Do not use a thesaurus, or change every third word of a source, and think that the original source is now changed sufficiently. For further coverage of paraphrasing, see page 403.

How to Avoid Online Plagiarism

Be particularly careful of plagiarism when downloading sources. It is very easy to copy sections from an online source and paste them into a paper, forgetting to use

BE A RESPONSIBLE WRITER

Plagiarism is a form of academic dishonesty that often carries serious penalties. To avoid plagiarism, do the following:

- Always use quotation marks around someone else's exact words. As you incorporate sources, you may wish to format them differently from the text you are writing, as an extra reminder to cite the sources while preparing the final draft.
- Be sure to quote accurately. Use the ellipsis mark when omitting words in a passage you are quoting directly.
- Never add or alter meaning when paraphrasing. Be as faithful as possible to the original.
- Use appropriate wording and style when paraphrasing, to avoid writing something too similar to the source. Use synonyms wherever possible, and if you do use an exact word or term, put it in quotation marks.
- Include the author and/or title of the source with each paraphrase, quotation, or summary in an attribution phrase that introduces another author's ideas. See pages 404–405 for models that indicate how to use attributions and citations.
- Give a parenthetical citation and works cited or references entry for every paraphrase, quotation, and summary.
- Be sure to document any online or other digital source properly and completely.

quotation marks and a citation and reference. You may think you will paraphrase and document the material later and then neglect to do so. This practice is a serious form of plagiarism. Instructors will not accept carelessness as an excuse. Be particularly vigilant in documentation when using Web sites, emails, blogs, or other digital sources.

Also, note that digital sources, because they are new and always changing, can be particularly tricky to document in the proper format. See pages 433–437, 441–442 for details on correct digital documentation. Ask an instructor for guidance with any questions surrounding incorporation of sources. Not knowing how to document a source correctly does not excuse you from doing so.

Documenting Source Material

Documentation refers to the system for acknowledging that student and research writers are using the words or ideas of another person. It is also the system of conventions for noting the source of paraphrase, quotation, or summary so that readers can locate this material if they want to. (These conventions will be discussed in the next sections.) In order to document responsibly using the Modern Language Association guidelines (or another style, such as APA), students must be diligent about doing the following for every paraphrase, summary, and quotation in a paper:

1. Introduce the source material with the name of the author or source (an attribution phrase).
2. Provide a parenthetical text citation for the source material, whether that material is quoted, paraphrased, or summarized.
3. Enclose all quotations in quotation marks.
4. Provide a "Works Cited" entry in the bibliography of the paper.

How to Document Source Material Using MLA Style

The next sections explain the Modern Language Association's conventions for documenting source material. They are appropriate for papers written in the humanities (including some writing courses). These conventions include introducing paraphrases, quotations, and summaries; providing parenthetical text citations; and writing a "Works Cited" page. Keep in mind that all the rules are designed to make it clear to readers what source material students are using and where that material can be found, and thus the rules will seem more logical, and easier to remember. Also, note that the style conventions change, so check a current edition of an MLA or APA style guide in your school library, and use an approved software program to create a bibliography. Finally, once you have prepared a bibliography, check it carefully, as there may be errors in capitalization or punctuation—no reference program is perfect!

Introduce Source Material

Because a paper will include your own ideas along with those discovered in the library or on the Internet, you must distinguish what is yours from what is from a source. To do so, introduce each paraphrase, quotation, and summary with an attribution phrase that indicates its source. Consider, for example, the following passage taken from a student paper. The introductions are underlined as a study aid.

> Businesses in the United States and the world over lose great sums of money because of the alcoholic employee. Estimates of the Department of Health, Education, and Welfare and a study done by Roman and Trice show that the number of alcoholics ranges from as high as ten out of every one hundred workers to a low of three to four out of one hundred (Williams and Moffat 7). Alcoholism, as Joseph Follman states, is "a problem so far reaching and so costly [it] must have an effect upon the business community of the nation." Follman goes on to say, "The result is impaired production, labor turnover, and increased costs of operation" (78). In terms of impaired productivity, the cost in the United States alone is said to be $12.5 billion a year, as the National Council on Alcoholism estimates (Follman 81-82). Obviously, someone must pay these costs, and no doubt it is the consumer who pays higher prices for goods and services. Yet reduced productivity because of alcoholic employees and the resulting higher prices could be held in check by the sound implementation of company programs to rehabilitate the alcoholic employee.

The paragraph includes both source material and the writer's own ideas. Each paraphrase and quotation is introduced to identify it as someone else's words or ideas. A close look reveals these points about introducing source material:

- The attribution phrase is in the present tense. This **present-tense convention** is followed because printed words live on, even if they were written long ago.
- Attributions usually appear before the source material, but they can also be placed in the middle or at the end. Various placements of the attribution are illustrated in the sample paragraph above.
- The verbs used in introductions should be varied to avoid monotony. For example, instead of repeatedly writing "Smith says," use "Smith explains" (notes, reveals, demonstrates, believes, contends, and so on).

- An attribution can refer to the author of the source material ("Smith finds"), or to the credentials of the author ("one researcher believes" or "a prominent sociologist contends"), or to the title of the source ("according to *Advertising Age*").

Write Parenthetical Text Citations

In addition to introducing source material, you must cite sources of information within parentheses immediately after the material. This is true whether material is a paraphrase, a summary, or a quotation. You must document this way so readers know exactly where the material comes from.

1. When the paraphrase, quotation, or summary has been introduced with the author's name, include the page number or numbers the material appears on in the source in parentheses; place the period after the citation:

   Ruth Caldersen agrees that corporal punishment is not a legitimate form of discipline in schools (104).

2. When the introduction does not include the author's name, note this name along with the appropriate page number or numbers in parentheses:

   One high school principal remarks, "I've never known corporal punishment to improve the behaviour of unruly students" (Hayes 16).

3. When more than one source by the same author is cited in a paper, include the author's name in the attribution, and use a short form of the title in the parenthetical citation:

   Rodriguez feels that a teacher who resorts to corporal punishment is acting out of frustration (*Discipline* 86).

   The above title is a short form of *Discipline in the Public Schools*. It distinguishes the source from another of Rodriguez's works cited, *Education in an Enlightened Age*.

4. For online or other sources that do not have page numbers, place the author in parentheses. If the author is not given, place the title in parentheses:

   According to the American Academy of Pediatrics, all corporal punishment should be banned in schools ("Corporal Punishment in Schools").

Note: A citation for a long quote that is set off appears after the period. (See page 404 on long quotes.)

Write the "Works Cited" Page

In addition to introducing source material and providing parenthetical text citations, proper documentation requires students provide a "Works Cited" page (or pages) at the end of a paper. This is an alphabetical listing (by author) of all the sources from which writers paraphrased, summarized, and quoted—it is *not* a listing of all the sources consulted during your research. For an example of a "Works Cited" page, see page 452. Notice that writers list the entries alphabetically by the author's last name. If the source has no known author, alphabetize the work according to the first important word in the title (excluding *a, an,* or *the*). Double-space each entry and double-space between each entry.

The following sections present forms students should model for papers written according to the style recommended by the Modern Language Association (MLA), which is explained in the *MLA Handbook for Writers of Research Papers* (7th ed., 2009). Most humanities papers are written according to MLA guidelines. Instructors in the social sciences may want students to use the style recommended by the American Psychological Association (APA, 2009) (see page 438), while science instructors may favour the Council of Science Editors (CSE) format. When in doubt, check with an instructor. Remember that the editions of the MLA and APA and Chicago (and other) style manuals are reprinted and updated frequently in new editions. Check with your institution's reference librarian to ensure you are using the most recent documentation styles. The examples in this text are based on the most current information at time of writing.

For additional information on MLA style, go online to Purdue University's Online Writing Lab at http://owl.english.purdue.edu/ and search for the documentation style related to the assignment. Also, see the following sites: http://www.diana hacker.com/resdoc/ or McGraw-Hill's Bibliomaker at http://highered.mcgraw-hill. com/sites/0073525820/student_view0/bibliomaker.html.

Proper MLA works-cited entries require that you combine different pieces of information from a source into a single citation. The following figures will show what some of the most important citation forms look like and where you can find their various parts within a source.

To assist further in understanding which parts of a source match up with which parts of a citation, the citations in these figures are colour-coded:

- Author information is highlighted in tan.
- Title information is highlighted in red.
- Publication data is highlighted in blue.

Note that you should *not* reproduce this colouring in your own citations. It is here only for reference.

The figures are followed by a list of models of proper MLA forms. Consult these pages when preparing a "Works Cited" page.

MLA Works-Cited Entry: Book with One Author.
Students can find the information for a book citation on the book's title page and copyright page.

Author's name. Book Title. Place of Publication: Publisher, year of publication. Print.

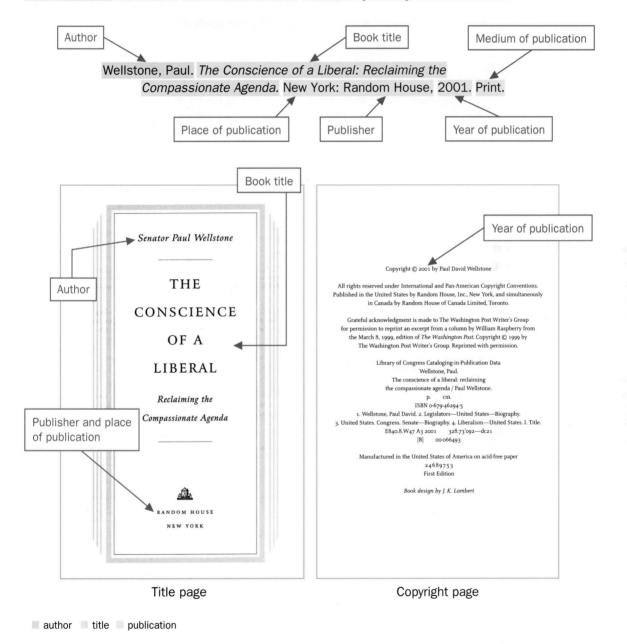

| Author | Book title | Medium of publication |

Wellstone, Paul. *The Conscience of a Liberal: Reclaiming the Compassionate Agenda.* New York: Random House, 2001. Print.

| Place of publication | Publisher | Year of publication |

Title page

Copyright page

author   title   publication

MLA Works-Cited Entry: Journal Article.

Many journals, like the one shown below, provide the information needed for a citation on the first page of an article as well as on the cover or contents page. Note that this journal uses continuous pagination, so only the volume number is needed in the citation. For citation of an article in a journal paginated by issue, see page 432.

Author's name. "Title of Article." Publication information. Print.

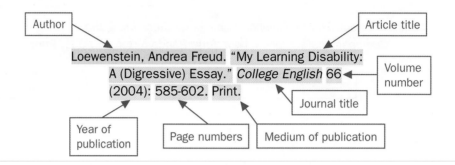

Author → Loewenstein, Andrea Freud. "My Learning Disability: A (Digressive) Essay." *College English* 66 (2004): 585-602. Print. ← Article title, Volume number, Journal title, Medium of publication

Year of publication — Page numbers

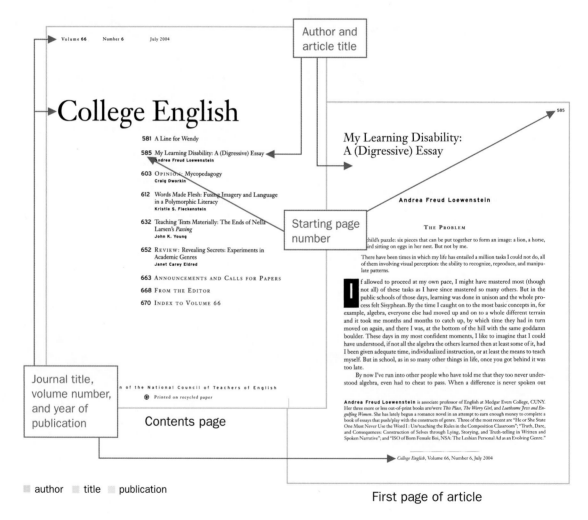

Journal title, volume number, and year of publication

Contents page

Author and article title

Starting page number

First page of article

■ author   ■ title   ■ publication

MLA Works-Cited Entry: Journal Article from an Online Database.

Citing an article accessed via an online subscription database like ProQuest or EBSCO requires information about the print version of the article and the database used.

Author's name. "Title of Document." Information about print publication. Information about electronic publication. Web. Access information including URL.

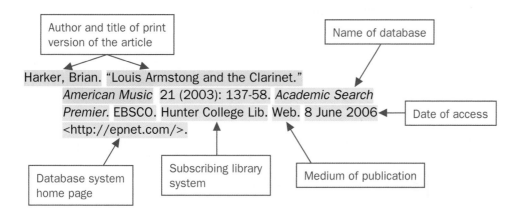

Author and title of print version of the article

Name of database

Harker, Brian. "Louis Armstong and the Clarinet." *American Music* 21 (2003): 137-58. *Academic Search Premier*. EBSCO. Hunter College Lib. Web. 8 June 2006 <http://epnet.com/>.

Date of access

Database system home page

Subscribing library system

Medium of publication

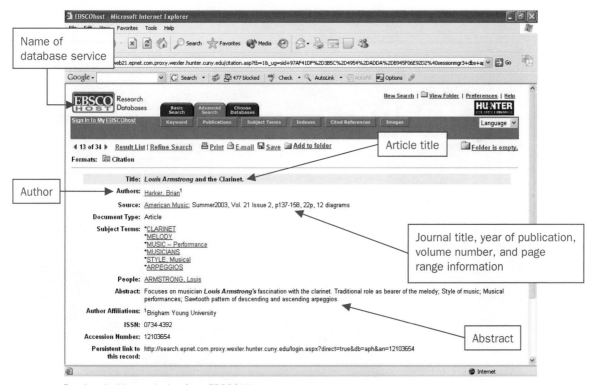

Reprinted with permission from EBSCO Host.

██ author   ██ title   ██ publication

MLA Works-Cited Entry: Scholarly Web Site.

To cite a scholarly Web site as a whole—as opposed to a single page within it—include the title of the site, the editor (if any), the version number (if relevant), the date of publication or the most recent update, the sponsoring institution (if any), the date of access for the site, and the site's URL. Students may need to click through the site a bit to find all this information.

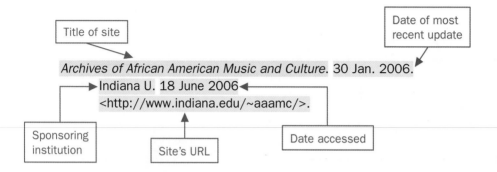

Author's name. "Title of Document." Information about publication. Date. Name of sponsoring institution.

Title of site

Date of most recent update

Archives of African American Music and Culture. 30 Jan. 2006.
Indiana U. 18 June 2006
<http://www.indiana.edu/~aaamc/>.

Sponsoring institution

Site's URL

Date accessed

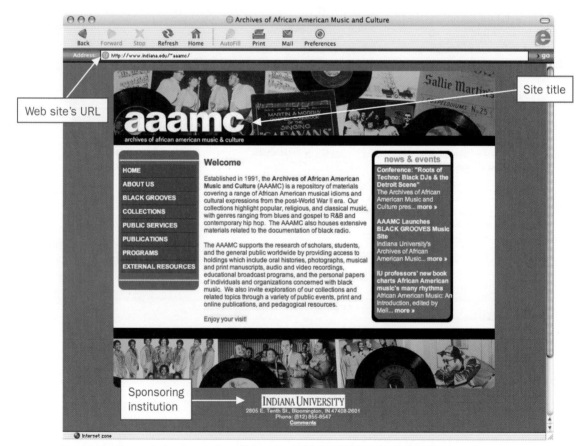

Web site's URL

Site title

Sponsoring institution

Reprinted with permission from Indiana University, Archives of African American Music and Culture.

▓ author   ▒ title   ░ publication

Elements of an MLA Works-Cited Entry: Newspaper Article.
To find the citation information for a newspaper article, look on both the page(s) the article appears on and the front page of the newspaper (where researchers will find, for example, the edition of the newspaper).

Author's name. "Title of article." Newspaper name. Complete date (day, month, year), edition: page number. Print.

Author

Article title

Elliott, Andrea. "Tending to Muslim Hearts and Islam's Future." *New York Times* 7 Mar. 2006, natl. ed.: A1+. Print.

Edition

Article page number

Newspaper title

Publication date

Medium of publication

Edition

Newspaper title

Publication date

Article title and author

author   title   publication

MLA Works-Cited Models

Below is information on formatting various types of works for inclusion in an MLA "Works Cited" page. Note that each entry includes, in addition to a sample, a colour-coded model. This model is designed to show how each part of a source fits into the citation. It should also help writers understand the underlying structure of all MLA citations.

- Author information is highlighted in tan.
- Title information is highlighted in red.
- Publication data is highlighted in blue.

Note that students should *not* reproduce this colour highlighting in their own citations. It is included here for reference only.

MLA WORKS-CITED ENTRIES: DIRECTORY TO MODELS AND SAMPLES

MLA Forms for Books

Book by One Author

Titles of books should be italicized or underlined. The city of publication, but not the state or province, should appear just before the publisher. Use the short name of the publisher—for example "Anansi" rather than "House of Anansi." The names of university presses can be shortened by using U and P instead of University and Press—for example U of Toronto P rather than University of Toronto Press.

Author's Last Name, First Name. *Title*. Publication City: Publisher, Year of
    Publication. Format ("Print" for books).

> Bakker, Karen J. *Eau Canada: The Future of Canada's Water*. Vancouver:
>   UBC P, 2007. Print.

Book by Two Authors or Three Authors

List the authors in the order in which they appear on the title page. Last name appears first for the first author only.

Book with two authors:

First Author's Last Name, First Name, and Second Author's First and Last Names.
    Title. Publication City: Publisher, Year of Publication. Print.

> Taylor, Shelley E. and Fuschia M. Sirois, *Health Psychology*, Toronto:
>   McGraw-Hill Ryerson Limited, 2009. Print.

Book with three authors:

First Author's Last Name, First Name, Second Author's First and Last Names, and
    Third Author's First and Last Names. *Title*. Publication City: Publisher, Year of
    Publication. Print.

> Davies, Dele H., Hiram E. Fitzgerald, and Vasiliki Mousouli. *Obesity in
>   Childhood and Adolescence*. Westport: Praeger, 2008. Print.

Book by More Than Three Authors

If a book has more than three authors, you may name only the first author, followed by *et al.* (short for *et alia*, meaning "and others") or you may list all the authors. If you list all the authors in the Works Cited, you can use *et al.* in the text citations.

First Author's Last Name, First Name, et al. *Title*. Publication City: Publisher, Year of
    Publication. Print.

> Potter, Patricia Ann, et al. *Canadian Fundamentals of Nursing*. Toronto: Mosby/
>   Elsevier Canada, 2009. Print.

Book by an Unknown Author

Title. Publication City: Publisher, Year of Publication. Print.

Note: In MLA style, you do not begin an entry with *Anonymous* or *Anon*.

> *Seasons of the Heart: A Windspun Collection*. Victoria: Trafford, 2004. Print.

Book by an Author with an Editor

List the author, the title, and then *Ed.* followed by the name of the editor.

Author's Last Name, First Name. *Title*. Ed. Editor's First and Last Names. Publication City: Publisher, Year of Publication. Print.

> Osborne, Mark. *How to Cheat at Managing Information Security*. Ed. Paul M. Summitt. Rockland: Syngress, 2006. Print.

Book by an Editor

Treat the editor as an author, listing his or her name first, but follow the name with *ed.* If the book has more than one editor, use the plural *eds.*

Editor's Last Name, First Name, ed. *Title*. Publication City: Publisher, Year of Publication. Print.

> MacKenzie, David, ed. *Canada and the First World War: Essays in Honour of Robert Craig Brown*. Toronto: U of Toronto P, 2005. Print.

Edition Other Than the First

Author's Last Name, First Name. *Title*. Name or Number of ed. Publication City: Publisher, Year of Publication. Print.

> Stein, Susan M., ed. *Boh's Pharmacy Practice Manual: A Guide to the Clinical Experience*. 3rd ed. Philadelphia: Wolters Kluwer Health/Lippincott Williams & Wilkins, 2009. Print.

Multivolume Work

Indicate in a citation of a multivolume work whether the citation used only one volume or all the volumes. If using only one volume, list the number of the volume used, preceded by *Vol.,* after the title. If using all the volumes, give the total number of volumes, followed by *vols.*

One volume in a multivolume work:

Author's Last Name, First Name. *Title*. Vol. Number Used. Publication City: Publisher, Year of Publication. Print.

> Reich, Warren, ed. *Encyclopedia of Bioethics*. Vol. 2. New York: Macmillan, 1995. Print.

All volumes in a multivolume work:

Author's Last Name, First Name. *Title*. Number of vols. Publication City: Publisher, Year of Publication. Print.

> Kurian, George Thomas, ed. *Encyclopedia of the World's Nations and Cultures*. 4 vols. New York: Facts On File, 2007. Print.

Selection in an Anthology

Follow the author and title of the selection with the title of the anthology. Include *Ed.* and the name of the editor.

Author's Last Name, First Name. "Title of Work." *Title of Anthology.* Ed. Editor's First and Last Names. Publication City: Publisher, Year of Publication. Page(s). Print.

> Mukherjee, Bharati. "A Wife's Story." *Women's Worlds: The McGraw-Hill Anthology of Women's Writing in English Across the Globe.* Eds. Robyn Warhol-Down, Diane Price Herndl, Mary Lou Kete, Lisa Schnell, Rashmi Varma, and Elizabeth Kowaleski. Boston: McGraw-Hill, 2008. 1722-1732. Print.

Encyclopedia Article

"Title of Entry." *Title of Encyclopedia.* Name or Number of ed. Year of Publication. Print.

> "South Asia in Canadian Literature." *Encyclopedia of Post-Colonial Literatures in English.* London: Routledge, 2005. Print.

Book with a Translator

The MLA guidelines suggest that, "To cite a translation, state the author's name first if you refer primarily to the work itself; give the translator's name, preceded by *Trans.,* after the title. If the book has an editor as well as a translator, give the names, with appropriate abbreviations, in the order in which they appear on the title page" (MLA 164).

List the author of the work, followed by the title. Place the translator's name after the title, with the abbreviation *Trans.*

Author's Last Name, First Name. *Title.* Trans. Translator's First and Last Names. Publication City: Publisher, Year of Publication. Print.

> *Voices from Canada: Focus on Thirty Plays.* Ed. Albert-Reiner Glaap. Trans. Nicholas Quaintmere. Toronto: Playwrights Canada P, 2003. Print.

More Than One Work by the Same Author

List the author's name in the first entry only. The second or subsequent entries have three hyphens followed by a period in place of the author's name. Order the citations alphabetically by title.

First entry:

Author's Last Name, First Name. *Title.* Publication City: Publisher, Year of Publication. Print.

> Ricci, Nino. *The Origin of Species.* Toronto: Doubleday Canada, 2008. Print.

Second entry:

---. *Title.* Publication City: Publisher, Year of Publication. Print.

> Ricci, Nino. *The Origin of Species.* Toronto: Doubleday Canada, 2008. Print.

> ---. *Testament.* Boston: Houghton Mifflin, 2003. Print.

Note: The MLA guidelines state that, "you have to include shortened titles if you cite two or more works by the same author, and you have to add initials or first names if two of the cited authors have the same last name" (MLA, 129). The in-text citation for these works (using example page numbers) would be (Ricci, *Origin* 22) and (Ricci, *Testament* 15).

MLA Forms for Periodicals

Author Unknown

"Title of Article." *Name of Publication* Day Month Year: Page(s). Print.

> "'I Don't Want It': A Prolife Doctor's Dilemma." *Commonweal* 135.18
> 24 October 2008: 18-19. Print.

Article from a Scholarly Journal (Continuous Pagination through Volumes)

If a journal is paginated by volume, put the volume number after the title. Put the year of publication in parentheses, followed by the page numbers of the article.

Author's Last Name, First Name. "Title of Article." *Title of Journal* Volume (Year): Page(s). Print.

Note: Since there are more than three authors, this entry could be listed either using all the names or using *et al.* to replace the names of the authors after the first author:

> Hazewinkel, Roderick R. O., *et al.* "Have Atmospheric Emissions from the
> Athabasca Oil Sands Impacted Lakes in Northeastern Alberta,
> Canada?" *Canadian Journal of Fisheries and Aquatic Sciences*
> 65.8 (2008): 1554-1568. Print.

OR

> Hazewinkel, Roderick R. O., Alexander P. Wolfe, Sergi Pla, Chris Curtis, and Kris
> Hadley. "Have Atmospheric Emissions from the Athabasca Oil Sands
> Impacted Lakes in Northeastern Alberta, Canada?" *Canadian Journal
> of Fisheries and Aquatic Sciences* 65.8 (2008): 1554-1568. Print.

Article from a Scholarly Journal (Separate Pagination in Each Issue)

If a journal is paginated by issue, include the volume and issue number. Put a period after the volume number and follow it with the issue number. In this example, the volume number is 33 and the issue number is 1-2.

Author's Last Name, First Name. "Title of Article." *Title of Journal* Volume. Issue (Year): Page(s). Print.

> Boyd, Susan C. "Community-Based Research in the Downtown Eastside of
> Vancouver." *Resources for Feminist Research* 33.1-2 (Spring-Summer
> 2008): 19-43. Print.

Article in a Magazine Published Monthly

For an article in a monthly magazine, include the month and year of publication.

Author's Last Name, First Name. "Title of Article." *Title of Magazine* Month Year: Page(s). Print.

Siddiqui, Haroon. "No Room for Bigots: How Have Canadians Managed to
Make a Go of Multiculturalism When It's in Trouble Almost Everywhere
Else? Haroon Siddiqui on the reasons to cheer (and what bothers
Muslims most about the country)." *New Internationalist* May 2009:
10-12. Print.

Article in a Magazine Published Weekly

For an article in a weekly magazine, include the day, month, and year of publication.

Author's Last Name, First Name. "Title of Article." *Title of Magazine* Day Month Year:
Page(s). Print.

Lunau, Kate. "Teens Lose Faith in Droves: Islam and Atheism are on
the Rise While Christianity Fades." *Maclean's* 13 Apr. 2009:
43-44. Print.

Article in a Newspaper

Include the day, month, and year of publication, as well as the edition if available
(*natl. ed.* or *late ed.* for example) after the date. Give a section designation along
with the page number when possible. When citing an article that appears on non-
consecutive pages, put a plus (+) sign after the first page number.

Author's Last Name, First Name. "Title of Article." *Name of Newspaper* Day Month
Year, specific ed.: Page(s). Print.

DiManno, Rosie. "Gypsies Caught in Political Crossfire: Add Canada to the List
of Nations that, to Varying Degrees, Make Pariahs of Roma." *Toronto
Star* 13 Sept. 2009: A1. Print.

Editorial

To cite a newspaper editorial, add the word *Editorial* after the title of the article.

"Title." Editorial. *Name of Newspaper* Day Month Year, specific ed.: Page(s). Print.

"Small steps toward Copenhagen." Editorial. *The Globe and Mail* 23 Sept.
2009: A18. Print.

Letter to the Editor

Bila, Bill. Letter. "'Gypsy' an insult to Czech Roma." *Toronto Star* 16 Sept.
2009: A22. Print.

MLA Forms for Electronic Sources

The following examples are based on the most recent guidelines published by the
Modern Language Association. Citation methods for electronic sources continue to be
refined and modified. For the most up-to-date information on MLA forms for electronic sources, visit http://www.mla.org.

Note: In Web site citations, the first date in the citation is the date the site was published or last modified. The second date is the date you accessed the site.

Scholarly Web Site

Begin with the title of the site (in italics), followed by the name of the editor (if relevant) and the electronic publication data: the version number (if relevant), the date of publication or most recent update, and the name of the sponsoring institution (if any). End with the date of access and the site's URL in angle brackets (< >), but be sure to cite the home or index page link as the <URL>.

Title of Site. Ed. Editor's First and Last Names. Day Month Year Posted or Last Updated. Sponsoring Institution. Day Month Year of Access. <URL>.

> *Growing Gap*. 24 Sept. 2009. Canadian Centre for Policy Alternatives. 28 Sept. 2009. <http://growinggap.ca/>.

Part of a Scholarly Web Site

When citing one page or part of a scholarly Web site, use the basic model above, but add to the beginning the author (if known) and the title of the page or part in quotes. If the author is unknown, begin with the title (in quotes).

Author's Last Name, First Name. "Title of Page or Part." *Title of Site*. Ed. Editor's First and Last Names. Day Month Year Posted or Last Updated. Sponsoring Institution. Day Month Year of Access. <URL>.

> Kerstetter, Steve. "The Affordability Gap: Spending Differences Between Canada's Rich and Poor." *Growing Gap*. Sept. 2009. Canadian Centre for Policy Alternatives. 28 Sept. 2009. <http://www.growinggap.ca/files/Spending%20Patterns,%20Low%20Incomes.pdf>.

Professional or Personal Web Site

Name the person who created the site (if there is one), the site title (italicized), the name of the associated institution (if any), date of access, and the URL in angle brackets (< >). If no title is given, use a description like *Home page* (do not underline, italicize, or place it in quotes).

Author's Last Name, First Name. *Title of Site* or Home page. Sponsoring Institution. Day Month Year of Access. <URL>.

> *Professional Writers Association of Canada*. 28 Sept. 2009. <http://www.pwac.ca/>.

Email

List the author first, then the subject line in quotation marks, followed by *Email to* and the recipient, then the date of the message.

Writer's Last Name, First Name. "Subject Line." Message to Recipient's First and Last Names. Day Month Year of Message. Email.

> Ashley, David. "Bias in Local News." Message to Karen Hirschberg. 8 Sept. 2001. Email.

Article in an Online Newspaper

Provide the following information: the author's name (if available), the title of the article (in quotation marks), the name of the newspaper (in italics), the publication date, the date of access, and the URL in angle brackets (< >).

Author's Last Name, First Name. "Title of Article." *Name of Newspaper* Day Month Year of Publication. Web. Day Month Year of Access. <URL>.

> Ibbitson, John. "Catching up to the New Canada: Ottawa Wants to Add More Seats." *The Globe and Mail* 25 Sept. 2009. Web. 29 Sept. 2009. <http://v1.theglobeandmail.com/servlet/story/LAC.20090925.IBBITSON 25ART22332/TPStory/TPComment/>.

Article in an Online Magazine

Provide the following information: the author's name (if available), the title of the piece (in quotation marks), the name of the magazine (in italics), the publication date, the medium of publication (*Web*), the date of access, and the URL in angle brackets (< >).

Author's Last Name, First Name. "Title of Article." *Title of Magazine* Day Month Year of Publication. Web. Day Month Year of Access. <URL>.

> Engelhart, Katie. "Women? In Ahmadinejad's Cabinet?" *Maclean's* 3 Sept. 2009. Web. 29 Sep. 2009. <http://www2.macleans.ca/2009/09/03/ women-in-ahmadinejad%E2%80%99s-cabinet/>.

Article in an Online Journal

Provide the following information: the author's name, the title of the work cited (in quotation marks), and the name of the journal (in italics). Next, provide the volume and issue number, separated by a period, and then the journal's year of publication, in parentheses. Indicate the number of paragraphs in the article if this information is available. Follow this with your access date and the URL in angle brackets (< >).

Author's Last Name, First Name. "Title of Article." *Title of Journal* Information about print publication. Information about electronic publication. Web. Access information including date and <URL>.

> Janssen, Patricia A., Lee Saxell, Lesley A. Page, Michael C. Klein, Robert M. Liston, and Shoo K. Lee. "Outcomes of planned home birth with registered midwife versus planned hospital birth with midwife or physician." *Canadian Medical Association Journal* 181.6-7 (15 Sept. 2009): 377-383. Web. 29 Sept. 2009. <http://www.cmaj.ca/cgi/ content/short/cmaj.081869v1>.

Material from a CD-ROM or DVD

Follow the basic instructions for citing books or parts of books, but add the term CD-ROM or DVD and the name of the vendor, if available and different from the publisher.

Author's Name (if given). "Title of Article or Section." *Title of CD-ROM or DVD*. Name of Vendor. Publication City: Publisher, Year of Publication. CD-ROM or DVD.

> "Photosynthesis." *Microsoft Encarta Multimedia Encyclopedia*. Redmond: Microsoft, 1994. CD-ROM.

> McDonald, Derek E. *Recorded History: Rock Music Encyclopedia.* Oakville: Emperor Multimedia, 2002. CD-ROM.

Work from an Online Database or Subscription Service

A citation for a work obtained from an online database or subscription service includes the print information about the work, followed by the name of the database, the name of the database service, the subscribing library, the date of access, and the URL of the service's home page.

Journal article:

Author's Last Name, First Name. "Title of Article." *Title of Periodical* Volume. Issue (Year): Page(s). *Name of Database*. Name of Database Provider. Name of Subscribing Library. Day Month Year of Access. <URL>.

> Little, Lisa. "Nurse Migration: A Canadian Case Study." *Health Services Research* 42.3 (June 2007): S1336-1354. *Academic OneFile.* Gale. Web. 19 Sept. 2009. <http://find.galegroup.com/gtx/start.do?prodId=AONE>.

> Schuurman, Nadine, Nathaniel J. Bell, Randy L'Heureux, and Syed M. Hameed. "Modelling optimal location for pre-hospital helicopter emergency medical services." *BMC Emergency Medicine* 9.6 (May 9, 2009): 6. *Academic OneFile.* Gale. SOLS - Oakville Public Library. Web. 19 Sept. 2009 <http://find.galegroup.com/gtx/start.do?prodId=AONE>.

Newspaper article:

Author's Last Name, First Name. "Title of Article." *Name of Newspaper* Day Month Year, ed.: Page(s). *Name of Database*. Name of Database Provider. Name of Subscribing Library/Web. Day Month Year of Access. <URL>.

> McKenzie, Lewis. "Canadian coverage of the military has failed to pass muster." *The Globe and Mail* 12 Feb. 2010: A21. *Canadian Newsstand Major Dailies*, ProQuest. Sheridan College Lib. Web. 13 Feb. 2010. <http://www.proquest.com/>.

If students use a personal subscription service like Yahoo! Canada or MSN, identify the service, the date of access, and either the keyword used or the topic path preceded by either *Keyword* or *Path*. If following a topic path, separate the topics with semicolons.

"Title of Document." *Title of Longer Work*. Date of Publication. Service Used. Day Month Year of Access. Keyword or Path: Keyword Used or Path Followed.

> "Photosynthesis." *World Book Online Reference Center*. 2005. America Online. 5 Nov. 2005. Path: Research and Learning; References; Encyclopedia; Site Contents; Photosynthesis.

Weblog ["Blog"] Posting

Citing Personal Weblog Entries

List the author of the blog (even if there is only a screen name available), provide the name of the particular entry you are referring to, identify that it is a weblog entry and then follow the basic formatting for a Web site as listed above.

Last Name, First Name. "Title of Entry." Weblog Entry. Title of Weblog. Date Posted.
    Web. Date Accessed <URL>.

NOTE: Give the exact date of the posted entry so your readers can look it up by date
in the archive. If possible, include the archive address for the posted entry as the URL
in your citation as you would for an online forum. If the site doesn't have a public
archive, follow the suggestion under "Listserv" citation below.

Helland, Josh. "Talking Trash: Recycling Reconnaissance." Weblog Entry.
    16 Sept. 2009. Web. 22 Sept. 2009. <http://www.takepart.com/
    blog/2009/09/16/talking-trash-blog-9-recycling-reconaissance-photos/>.

Computer Software

Give the name of the author or editor, if available, followed by the title of the software, the format (e.g., CD-ROM), the version or edition number, and standard
publication information. If downloading the software from the Internet, list the date
of access and the URL that it was downloaded from instead of the publication data.

Author or Editor's Last Name, First Name. *Software Title*. Format. Vers. or Ed.
    Number. Publication City: Publisher, Year of Publication.

ARIEL: A Reader's Interactive Exploration of Literature. CD-ROM. Vers. 1.0.
    New York: McGraw-Hill, 2004.

Online Posting to a Listserv or Newsgroup

Author's Last Name, First Name. "Title or Subject Line of Post." Online posting. Day
    Month Year of Post. List or Group Name. Day Month Year of Access. <URL>.

Devlin, Sean. "Canada at a political tipping point on climate change!" Online
    posting. 10 Sept. 2009. BC Campus Climate Network. 27 Sept.
    2009. <http://groups.google.com/group/bccampusclimatenetwork/
    browse_thread/thread/e3198f3f49f3a78f>.

Radio or Television Show

Include the specific episode title, the title of the program, the series title (if necessary—note that in the example below there is none), the name of the network that
is responsible for the show, the broadcast station and the city, and the date of the
broadcast.

Author Name. "Title of Episode." *Title of Program*. Series Title. Name of Network.
    Broadcast Station, City. Day Month Year of Broadcast. Format.

"Staying Alive." *Fifth Estate*. CBC Television, Toronto, 13 Mar. 2009. Television.

Personal Interview

List the name of the person interviewed, followed by *Personal interview* and the date
on which the interview took place.

Subject's Last Name, First Name. Personal interview. Day Month Year of Interview.

Humphrey, Neil. Personal interview. 1 May 2006.

Published Interview

List the name of the person interviewed, followed by the title of the interview (if there is a title) and *Interview by* and the name of the interviewer (if known and relevant). Then list the name and publication information for the source of the interview.

Subject's Last Name, First Name. "Title of Interview" or Interview. Interview by Interviewer's First Name and Last Name. Citation Information for Source of Interview.

> Suzuki, David. "The Venerable David Suzuki." Interview by David Leibl and Saul Landau. *Canadian Dimension* 37.1 (1 Jan. 2003): 18. *CBCA Reference*, ProQuest. Web. 30 Sept. 2009 <http://proquest.umi.com.proxy.bib.uottawa.ca/pqdweb?index=2&did=295230361&SrchMode=1&sid=1&Fmt=3&VInst=PROD&VType=PQD&RQT=309&VName=PQD&TS=1270477569&clientId=3345>.

Lecture or Speech

Speaker's Last Name, First Name. "Title of Lecture." Sponsoring Institution. Venue. City. Day Month Year of Presentation. Form of Delivery (Address, Lecture, Reading, On-stage Interview, etc.)

> Sharma, Deepak. "Accountability Agreements from a Hospital Perspective." Ryerson University. Sally Horsfall Eaton Centre for Studies in Community Health. Toronto. 13 Nov. 2008. Address.

How to Document Material Using APA Style

The methods for documenting source material explained so far have been those of the Modern Language Association (MLA). For papers written in the social sciences, instructors may want students to follow the American Psychological Association (APA) format, which is explained in the APA's *Publication Manual of the American Psychological Association* (7th ed., 2009). The APA format for handling parenthetical citations and the final list of sources is different from the MLA format.

Parenthetical Citations

In the APA format, the conventions for parenthetical citations are different from those used in the MLA format. Also, parenthetical citations for paraphrases are handled differently from those for quotations.

In the APA format, parenthetical citations include the publication date, but page numbers are *required* for quotations only. Also, *p.* or *pp.* is used before the page number(s). There is another difference as well: A comma appears between the name of the author and year, and between the year and the page number. For example, when introducing source material with the author's name, place the year of publication in parentheses after the name. For a quotation, add the page number with a *p.* in parentheses at the end.

Paraphrase

> For mutual gains bargaining to work, Haines (1991) believes that everyone involved must have extensive training in how to resolve conflict without confrontation.

In the same paragraph, references to the author do not need to repeat the publication year if it is clear that the same source is referred to.

> Mutual gains bargaining has not become popular because, as Haines points out, the required training is costly and time-consuming.

Quotation

> Haines (1991) says that for mutual gains bargaining to work, "all parties must undergo rigorous training in nonconfrontational dispute resolution" (p. 40).

For a paraphrase of the source material without the author's name, students must follow the material with the author's last name, a comma, and the publication year for a paraphrase. Add the page number for a quotation. Place this information in parentheses.

Paraphrase

> For mutual gains bargaining to work, everyone involved must have extensive training in how to resolve conflict without confrontation (Haines, 1991, p. 40).

Quotation

> For mutual gains bargaining to work, "all parties must undergo rigorous training in nonconfrontational dispute resolution" (Haines, 1991, p. 40).

List of References

Rather than a "Works Cited" page, APA format calls for a list of sources with the heading "References." The "References" page includes the same information as the "Works Cited" page, but it is presented in a different format, as the examples in the next sections illustrate. For additional information on APA style, go online to Purdue University's Online Writing Lab at http://www.owl english.purdue.edu, or to http://highered.mcgraw-hill.com/sites/0073525820/student_view0/bibliomaker.html if your online library does not have a direct export citation manager like RefWorks.

APA REFERENCE ENTRIES: DIRECTORY TO MODELS AND SAMPLES

APA Forms for Books

Book with One Author

Author's Last Name, Initial(s). (Year of Publication). *Title*. Publication City: Publisher.

> Bakker, K. J. (2007). *Eau Canada: The future of Canada's water*. Vancouver: UBC Press.

Book with Two or More Authors

First Author's Last Name, Initial(s), & Second Author's Last Name, Initial(s). (Year of Publication). *Title*. Publication City: Publisher.

> Davies, H. D., Fitzgerald, H. E., & Mousouli, V. (2008). *Obesity in childhood and adolescence*. Westport: Praeger.

Edition Other Than the First

Author's Last Name, Initial(s). (Year of Publication). *Title* (name or number ed.). Publication City: Publisher.

> Stein, S. M. (Ed.). (2009). *Boh's pharmacy practice manual: A guide to the clinical experience* (3rd ed.). Philadelphia: Wolters Kluwer Health/ Lippincott Williams & Wilkins.

Edited Book or Anthology

Editor's Last Name, Initial(s). (Ed.). (Year of Publication). *Title*. Publication City: Publisher.

> MacKenzie, D. (Ed.). (2005). *Canada and the First World War: Essays in honour of Robert Craig Brown*. Toronto: University of Toronto Press.

Item in an Anthology or Chapter in an Edited Book

Author's Last Name, Initial(s). (Year of Publication). Title of item or chapter. In Editor's Initial(s) and Last Name (Ed.), *Title of edited book* (pp. pages). Publication City: Publisher.

> Rubenstein, J. P. (1967). The effect of television violence on small children. In B. F. Kane (Ed.), *Television and juvenile psychological development* (pp. 112-134). New York: American Psychological Society.

APA Forms for Periodicals

Article from a Scholarly Journal (Continuous Pagination through Volumes)

Author's Last Name, Initial(s). (Year of Publication). Title of article. *Title of Journal volume*, page(s).

> Hazewinkel, R. O., Wolfe, A. P., Pla, S., Curtis, C., & Hadley, K. (2008). Have atmospheric emissions from the Athabasca oil sands impacted lakes in Northeastern Alberta, Canada? *Canadian Journal of Fisheries and Aquatic Sciences, 65*, 1554-1568.

Article from a Scholarly Journal (Separate Pagination in Each Issue)

Author's Last Name, Initial(s). (Year of Publication). Title of article. *Title of Journal, volume*(issue), page(s).

> Boyd, S. C. (2008, Spring-Summer). Community-based research in the downtown Eastside of Vancouver. *Resources for Feminist Research, 33*(1-2), 19-43.

Article in a Magazine Published Weekly

If the magazine has a volume number, include it after the title. If it does not, follow the title with the page numbers (as in the example below).

Author's Last Name, Initial(s). (Year, Month Day of Publication). Title of article. *Title of Magazine, volume,* page(s).

> Lunau, K. (2009, April 13). Teens lose faith in droves: Islam and atheism are on the rise while Christianity fades. *Maclean's, 122* (13), 43-44.

Article in a Magazine Published Monthly

If the magazine has a volume number, include it after the title. If it does not, follow the title with the page numbers (as in the example below).

Author's Last Name, Initial(s). (Year Month of Publication). Title of article. *Title of Magazine, volume,* page(s).

> Siddiqui, H. (2009, May). No room for bigots: How have Canadians managed to make a go of multiculturalism when it's in trouble almost everywhere else? Haroon Siddiqui on the reasons to cheer (and what bothers Muslims most about the country). *New Internationalist, 422,* 10-12.

Article in a Newspaper

Author's Last Name, Initial(s). (Year, Month Day of Publication). Title of article. *Title of Newspaper,* p(p). page(s).

> DiManno, R. (2009, September 13). Gypsies caught in political crossfire: Add Canada to the list of nations that, to varying degrees, make pariahs of Roma. *Toronto Star,* p. A1.

APA Forms for Electronic Sources

The following examples are based on the most recent guidelines published by the American Psychological Association. Citation methods for electronic sources continue to be refined and modified. For the most up-to-date information on APA forms for electronic sources, visit www.apa.org.

Document on a Web Site

Document Author's Last Name, Initial(s). (Year, Month Day of Publication). *Title of document.* Retrieved Month, Day, Year of Access, URL

> Watson, D. (2005, May 15). *Photosynthesis: How life keeps going.* Retrieved April 2, 2006, from http://www.ftexploring.com/photosyn/ photosynth.html

Article in an Online Periodical or Database with No Print Version

Author's Last Name, Initial(s). (Year, Month Day of Publication). Title of article. *Title of Periodical.* Retrieved Month Day, Year, from URL

> Merron, J. (2006, March 31). What's a nervous breakdown? *Slate.* Retrieved May 12, 2006, from http://www.slate.com/id/2139052/?nav=tap3

Article in an Online Periodical or Database with a Print and an Online Version

Author's Last Name, Initial(s). (Year, Month Day of Publication). Title of article [Electronic version]. *Title of Periodical, volume* if any, page(s).

> Engelhart, K. (2009, September 7). Women? In Ahmadinejad's cabinet? [Electronic Version] *Maclean's, 122* (34), 25. Retrieved September 29, 2009 from *Canadian Business and Current Affairs (Business) Database.*

Journal Article Accessed through a Database

Author's Last Name, Initial(s). (Year of Publication). Title of article. *Title of Journal, volume*(issue), page(s). Retrieved Month Day, Year, from Name of Database.

> Janssen, P. A., Saxell, L., Page, L. A., Klein, M. C., Liston, R. M., & Lee, S. K. (2009, September 15). Outcomes of planned home birth with registered midwife versus planned hospital birth with midwife or physician. *Canadian Medical Association Journal, 181*(6-7), 377-383. Retrieved September 29, 2009 from http://www.cmaj.ca/

Email, Newsgroups, Online Forums, Discussion Groups, Personal Interviews, and Electronic Mailing Lists

Do not include personal communications that are not archived in reference lists. They are cited within the text only. For example: L. Capri (personal communication, 4 Oct. 2001).

Tech tip: use an online guide to help with your citing and referencing. A good guide, published by St. Martin's Press, is: http://www.dianahacker.com/resdoc/home.html. McGraw-Hill also has its own Bibliomaker site: http://highered.mcgraw-hill.com/sites/0073525820/student_view0/bibliomaker.html.

Revising and Editing a Research Paper

Once you have completed a draft of a research paper, you want to revise it carefully, rewriting sections for clarity and effectiveness, checking over your documentation to ensure it is thorough and properly formatted, and finally eliminating errors of grammar and punctuation. You should expect that this process will take time. Even the best writers must go through many drafts and be vigilant in correcting careless mistakes. Alternatively, use the questions below and work with another student, or with a small group. Peer editors often notice things that research writers miss.

To help you revise and edit researched writing, ask the following questions:

1. Have I fully explained or proven my thesis? Is it backed up by sufficient evidence?
2. Have I revised for effective expression including sentence variety?
3. Is my level of diction appropriate? Have I avoided colloquialisms and clichés? Is my language gender-neutral and inoffensive?
4. Does my paper include a sufficient number and variety of sources? Are the sources current and authoritative?
5. Have I correctly documented anything in my paper that comes from another source? Are my paraphrases sufficiently changed from their original source? Have I been especially careful in documenting any online material sources I used?
6. Are the citations in my essay properly formatted for the documentation style I am using? Have I included a properly formatted "Works Cited" or "References" page at the end of my paper?
7. Have I eliminated any typos, spelling errors, or grammatical mistakes?

EXERCISE WRITING RESEARCH

1. Assume you are writing a paper on how magazine advertisements influence people to buy and are seeking explanations of specific persuasive techniques used. With this in mind, do the following:
   a. Check the computer catalogue and write two bibliography cards for two different, promising books.
   b. Refer to the list on page 387, and name the abstracts, bibliographies, and indexes to check.
   c. Check the titles named for item b, and write two bibliography cards for promising articles.

2. Examine the following excerpt from *The Reader's Guide to Periodical Literature*, and respond to the questions that follow.

Economic conditions

Displaced homemaker. A. McCarthy. Commonweal
103:38+   Ja 16 '76

Employment

Job strategies '76. N. A. Comer. Mademoiselle
82:112–15   F '76
Women on the job. McCalls   103:68+   F '76
See also
Women—Occupations

   a. What is the title of the article about economic conditions? Who is the author?
   b. In what periodical does the article appear? In what issue? On what page does the article begin?
   c. Write a bibliography card for the article.

3. Assume you are interested in the general subject "The Prime Minister of Canada." Look up the subject in a general-interest encyclopedia, and list five aspects of the general topic to explore further if working to narrow to a topic.

4. Write correct works-cited citations in MLA style for the following:
   a. A book titled *Play a Song Somebody* by Cyril Dabydeen, published by Oakville, Ontario, publisher Mosaic Press in 2004.
   b. A book edited by Patricia Lockhart Fleming, Gilles Gallichan, and Yvan Lamonde titled *History of the Book in Canada,* Volume 1, published by University of Toronto Press in 2004.
   c. An article from *The Globe and Mail,* by Kathy Flaxman titled "The orders are there, the money's not," that appeared on April 5, 2010, on page B1.
   d. An article by Andrew Potter, titled "The best thing to happen to the Liberals," that appeared in the 22 February 2010, issue of *Maclean's* on pages 38–41.
   e. An article titled "'I had never seen such a shed called a house before': The Discourse of Home in Susanna Moodie's *Roughing It in the Bush*" by Christa Zeller Thomas, that appeared in the journal *Canadian Literature,* #203, in Winter 2009 on pages 105–121.

5. Paraphrase two paragraphs from any professional essay in this book. If you like, you may include some quotations. Be sure to introduce the paraphrase and alter style but not meaning.

6. Quote directly the first sentence from any one of the professional or student essays in this book. Introduce the quotation with the author's name and *that.* Then rewrite the quotation without *that* in the introduction.

7. Quote a sentence from one of the essays in this book. Choose a long sentence, and select a few words to remove from the direct quotation. Remember to use ellipses and introduce the quotation.

8. Quote a sentence from one of the professional or student essays in this book. When there is a pronoun (i.e. it, they, he, or she) write the noun that the pronoun refers to, in brackets to introduce the quotation.

9. With a classmate, select one essay in this book. Each of you should summarize the essay. Then compare your summaries to see how they are similar and how they are different. Discuss the differences. ●

Cooper 1

Julie Cooper

Professor Hansen

English 101

4 September 2006

Genetically Modified Food: Watching What We Eat

1   When most people eat out at restaurants or in their homes, they do not stop to consider that scientists have modified the genes in many of the ingredients in their meals. The ripe tomatoes in their salads may contain fish genes, the chemical makeup of their salmon or beef entrées may have been manipulated to cause these animals to grow four times as fast as their species would develop in the wild, and the pie they enjoy for dessert might consist of apples embedded with chicken genes. Genetically altered food is not new—for years, farmers have fused strains of plants of the same species to create hybrids that were less prone to disease or more appealing in taste or appearance. What is different about many of today's genetically modified foods is that they have been re-engineered by scientists using genes from different species to create altogether new entities. Henri E. Cauvin cautions that such alterations could have far-reaching consequences, although scientific testing has not demonstrated that all such foods are unsafe for human consumption (A6). Current international regulation of genetically modified (GM) foods has been weakened by the economic and political influence of the biotech industry and an overall lack of understanding about the process of genetic engineering. New federal regulations need to be put in place to protect consumers from the uncertain environmental and health effects of genetically modified food.

Note double-spacing, heading, centred title, and page number.

The introduction gives background information.

The paraphrase helps establish the reason for author's argument. The paraphrase is introduced with the author's name and followed by a parenthetical citation.

Thesis.

Cooper 2

The source material helps establish the extent of the issue and why it is important.

The parenthetical citation includes a shortened title. There is no page number because the source is a Web site.

Note the explicit introduction showing that the information did not originate with Caplan.

2   Genetically modified crops are now widespread in the United States. According to the Campaign to Label Genetically Engineered Foods, in 1999, one fourth of crops were genetically modified, including 35% of corn and 55% of soybeans, and these figures continue to increase ("Meteoric"). Worldwide, genetically modified crops are also on the rise (Fig. 1). GM crops in the United States currently undergo field tests overseen by a division of the U.S. Department of Agriculture that determine their impact on the ecosystem and nontarget species, or species that are not directly involved in the genetic engineering. Records interpreted by Richard Caplan of the Public Interest Research Group (PIRG) show that in 1990, the USDA recognized eighty-one field site tests, and by the year 2000, 4,549 field tests were permitted, a 56-fold increase in a decade (4). Some critics argue that the development of GM foods is progressing at such a rapid rate that rigorous testing by the government cannot keep pace with the technology.

Fig. 1 Line graph indicating the global surge in genetically altered crops. Pew Initiative on Food and Biotechnology, University of Richmond, August 2004.

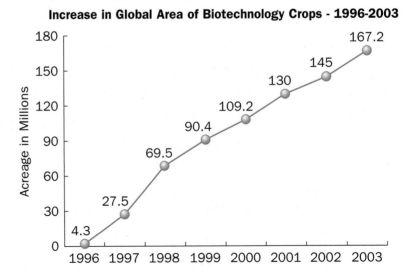

Increase in Global Area of Biotechnology Crops - 1996-2003

Source: (ISAAA) Global Review of Transgenic Crops 2003

Cooper 3

3   Environmental groups like Greenpeace and Friends of the Earth claim that the USDA has designed their regulations to promote the biotech industry at the expense of the safety of the American public. Ralph Nader, the consumer advocate and founder of PIRG, has also voiced this complaint:

> The U.S. Department of Agriculture has been handing out tax dollars to commercial corporations, including co-funding the notorious terminator-seed project, in order to protect the intellectual property of biotechnology firms from some farmers. You can expect nothing but boosterism from that corner.
>
> The creation of pervasive unknowns affecting billions of people and the planet should invite, at least, a greater assumption of the burden of proof by corporate investigators that their products are safe. Not for this industry. It even opposes disclosing its presence to consumers in the nation's food markets and restaurants. Against repeated opinion polls demanding the labelling of genetically engineered foods, these companies have used their political power over the legislative and executive branches of the government to block the consumer's right to know and to choose. (ix-xiii)

Nader's reference to the "terminator-seed project" alludes to one of the more insidious forms of genetically modified or engineered foods: an organism bred so that it is programmed to kill its own seeds, effectively eliminating a plant's ability to regenerate. The testing for this "seed suicide" technology, according to one source, was funded by the USDA and Delta and Pine Land Co. (McHughen 192). Some argue that because plants grown from terminator technology do not generate seeds for farmers to save for reuse in their next planting, it undoes the very processes in nature that have enabled agriculture to flourish since time immemorial. If plants no longer regenerate themselves, human beings will be dependent on the large biotech firms that profit, in turn, by selling them more seeds.

Side annotations:

Topic sentence.

Quotation of more than four lines is set off, introduced with a colon, and indented. The period comes before the parenthetical citation.

Notice the synthesis of sources: The McHughen paraphrase explains the Nader quotation.

The author's name is included in the parenthetical citation because it is not part of the introduction.

Cooper 4

Topic sentence.

4   Other GM foods may threaten the health of the people who consume them. This issue, which has generated great controversy in the European Union, has only recently received the same level of attention in the United States. As the PBS video *Harvest of Fear* explains, when it was revealed that the company Aventis had created a kind of GM corn called Starlink that Taco Bell used in its taco shells, many Americans were indignant. Most of them had no idea that they were regularly consuming numerous bioengineered products. Starlink corn was different from other genetically modified foods approved for the nation's dinner tables, however. In July of 2000, Larry Bohlen, a member of the environmental group Friends of the Earth, had read on the Environmental Protection Agency's website that Starlink was a kind of GM corn "not approved for human consumption . . . only animal consumption." The film goes on to explain that Bohlen decided to send twenty-three different corn-based products that he bought at his local supermarket to a laboratory to determine whether or not they had been made with Starlink corn. The lab found that Starlink corn, deemed unfit for human consumption by the EPA because it contained the Cry9C, a protein that elevates risks of allergic reaction, had entered a widely available supermarket product. These findings disturbed many consumers and made headlines in the United States. Taco Bell later vowed that they would end their use of Starlink corn in their products (Harvest).

Reintroduction makes it clear
that the paraphrase is ongoing.

5   Such concerns about the existence of allergens in genetically altered organisms (GMOs) have practical repercussions in countries far from the United States. Cauvin reports that since its discovery in Taco Bell's taco shells, Starlink corn has been found in Japan, Korea, the United Kingdom, and Denmark (*Harvest*). In Zambia, where 13 million people are presently suffering from a severe famine, an international aid effort to donate GM corn has resulted in a political standoff. Cauvin reports that Zambian officials have "banned the distribution of food produced with genetically modified organisms" (A6). Martin Teitel and Kimberly A. Wilson note that the debate has

Topic sentence

Source material is introduced
with the author's name and the
present tense.

Cooper 5

centered on the human and environmental impact of GM corn. To date, there have been no documented cases of deaths due to allergic reactions caused by genetically modified foods (47). But it has been impossible to assess whether fatalities due to food allergies have increased because of genetically modified ingredients because most foods are not labelled with detailed genetic information. Charles Arntzen of Cornell University asserts that users of GM foods have never "had so much as a headache," from genetically engineered foods, and that because these products are "science-driven" they are extremely safe (Harvest). But the assurance of scientists and biotech firms that their products are safe is not enough to calm growing fears. Mundia Sikatana, the Zambian Minister of Agriculture asks: "What else would you call an allergy caused by a substance? That substance is poisonous" (qtd. in Cauvin A6). As a result, thousands of tons of GM corn shipped to Zambia by the United States and administered by the United Nations World Food Program are sitting in freezers on the orders of the Zambian president.

6   In addition to the risk of allergic reactions in consumers, *Harvest of Fear* cautions that the GM corn offered by the United States presents a threat of cross-pollination with Zambia's non-modified varieties of corn. Such a cross-over would endanger the country's exports to the European Union, which requires the labelling of all GM products. The video explains that such contamination issues concern many members of the environmental community. They worry that if disease-resistant GM foods become dominant, they may wipe out non-modified versions of the same food, thus eliminating the variety of foods available to the human race. In some cases, such as that of B.t. corn, a GM corn that contains a toxic gene that deters corn borers and caterpillars, the diversity of the ecosystem is threatened. The gene in B.t. corn kills not only crop pests, but also a so-called "non-target species," the larvae stage of monarch butterflies that feed on the milkweed plants that grow near cornfields (*Harvest*). As Stephen Nottingham notes in his book *Eat Your*

Note the synthesis of multiple sources.

Key words in paraphrase are placed in quotation marks.

Parenthetical citation for material from one source quoted in a second source.

The reintroduction makes it clear that the paraphrase is ongoing.

Genes, "Because plants produce the toxin continuously," resistance to B.t. will develop much faster using genetically modified plants than using B.t. sprays (56). The fact that the genetic makeup of our plants can be toxic to certain species is alarming to the general public, and for good reason.

> The last sentence of the paragraph combines common knowledge and the author's evaluation.

7   One of the only ways to avoid consuming genetically modified produce is to eat organically grown plants and vegetables. Unlike genetically modified agriculture, which uses cutting-edge gene manipulation in its plants, organic farming promotes a "back to the land" philosophy, in which plants are grown naturally, using compost and other organic substances as fertilizer and little or no chemical pesticides. But even if consumers could eat organic produce exclusively, such a radical approach to protecting themselves from GMO consumption is not assured. The seeds or pollen of GMOs easily contaminate organic plants. The Campaign to Label Genetically Engineered Foods reports that in 1999, the Wisconsin-based company Terra Prima was forced to destroy 87,000 bags of organic chips at a cost of almost $150,000, after a European importer determined that they were contaminated with GM corn ("Organic"). Genetically modified foods pose legitimate threats to the organic agricultural industry. In their book *The Rubbish on Our Plates*, Fabien Perucca and Gerard Pouradier argue that the only way consumers can advance the organic movement is to encourage and reward organic farmers by patronizing their farm-stands and purchasing their products (208). If consumers send a clear economic message to the agriculture giants who devote a great deal of their financial resources to developing new GM products and the governments that allow those products on the global market, perhaps the flood of GM products can be slowed.

> Even though the source is given in the introduction, the title appears in the parenthetical citation because the source is a Web site without page numbers, and something is needed to mark the end of the paraphrase.

> Note the synthesis of source material with the author's own ideas.

> The conclusion restates the thesis to reassert the author's claim.

8   Americans are definitely interested in knowing more about whether or not the foods they eat have been genetically modified. A poll conducted by ABC News in June of 2001 revealed that 93% of 1,024 people surveyed believe "the federal government should require labels on food saying whether it's

Cooper 7

been genetically modified or bioengineered" (ABC News). The long-term environmental and health effects resulting from the growth and consumption of genetically modified foods remain unknown. This uncertainty, coupled with the eagerness on the part of the American people to know when the food they are eating has been genetically modified, suggests that a new course of action needs to be charted. The federal government is expected to protect its citizens from bioterror and biohazards. Therefore, the federal government must not give the biotech industry free reign in its creation of GMOs. New restrictions and clearer genetic labelling will give the American public the security of knowing that what they eat is good for them.

The source material helps establish the point that Americans support the writer's claim.

Cooper 8

Works Cited

"Behind the Label: Many Skeptical of Bio-Engineered Food." *ABC News*. 20
June 2001. Web. 20 Aug. 2006 <http://abcnews.go.com/sections/
scitech/DailyNews/poll010619.html>.

Caplan, Richard. *Raising Risk: Field Testing of Genetically Engineered Crops in
the U.S.* Washington: U.S. Public Interest Research Group, June 2001. Print.

Cauvin, Henri E. "Between Famine and Politics, Zambians Starve." *New York
Times* 30 Aug. 2002, natl. ed.: A6. Print.

"Genetically Modified Crops in the United States." *Pew Initiative on Food
and Biotechnology*. Aug. 2004. U of Richmond. Web. 8 June 2006
<http://pewagbiotech.org/resources/factsheets/display.php3?Fact
sheetID=2%207sep04>.

Harvest of Fear. Dir. Jon Palfreman. Prod. WGBH Educational Foundation. PBS
Video, 2001. Videocassette.

McHughen, Alan. *Pandora's Picnic Basket: The Potential and Hazards of
Genetically Modified Foods*. New York: Oxford UP, 2000. Print.

"Meteoric Growth: GE Foods Now Are Almost Everywhere You Look." The *Campaign
to Label Genetically Engineered Foods*. 2002. GE Foods Tutorial. Web. 8 Aug.
2006 <http://www.thecampaign.org/education/brochuregrowth.htm>.

Nader, Ralph. Foreword. *Genetically Engineered Food: Changing the Nature of
Nature*. By Martin Teitel and Kimberly A. Wilson. Rochester: Park Street,
1999. ix–xiii. Print.

Nottingham, Stephen. *Eat Your Genes: How Genetically Modified Food Is Entering
Our Diet*. New York: Zed, 1998. Print.

"Organic Foods at Risk." *The Campaign to Label Genetically Engineered Foods*.
2002. GE Foods Tutorial. Web. 8 Aug. 2006. <http://www.thecampaign.org/
education/brochureorganic.htm>.

Perucca, Fabien, and Gerard Pourardier. *The Rubbish on Our Plates*. London:
Prion, 1996. Print.

Teitel, Martin, and Kimberly A. Wilson. *Genetically Engineered Food: Changing the
Nature of Nature*. Rochester: Park Street, 1999. Print.

The complete essay, including any bibliographic references in MLA style, is also available
on the Online Learning Centre at www.mcgrawhill.ca/olc/clouse.

The title is centred. Double-space before the first entry.

Works cited entries are double-spaced. The first line is flush left, and a hanging indent is used on subsequent lines.

Alphabetize entries according to the author's last name. If no name appears, use the first important word in the title.

Process Guidelines

Before you submit your paper, review the following checklist on your own, with a peer editor, or with a writing tutor.

- Consider the audience for your paper. Have you considered the readers' knowledge of the topic and how the readers may respond?
- Consider your writing purpose. Will you be explaining? Have you done this clearly? Are examples and support sufficient? Have you used current scholarship? Are your claims logical? Have you used ethical sources?
- Review the thesis. Have you proven it? Do you address the thesis and demonstrate its soundness in the conclusion? Do all paragraph topic sentences support the paper's assertions and thesis?
- Revise one last time. Have you used sufficient transition words? Have you fully explained the relevance and importance of examples and research? Have you made strong connections between ideas? Have you raised and countered objections? See procedure 3 in Chapter 4.
- Review grammar, punctuation, and usage. Ask a peer editor to read your paper aloud for you. If your reader hesitates or stumbles, there may be mechanical problems at the sentence level, or ideas may not flow logically. Ask for and act on feedback. Proofread from a paper copy. Read very slowly, and consider style alternatives.

A Guide to Frequently Occurring Errors

CHAPTER 18

Word Choice

In Chapter 5, you learned much about word choice (diction), including choosing the appropriate level of diction, using specific words, choosing simple words, using gender-neutral language, avoiding wordiness, and eliminating clichés. In this chapter, you will learn about correcting errors to eliminate certain troublesome words and phrases, to eliminate double negatives, and to use commonly confused words correctly.

Troublesome Phrasings (tp)

The words, phrases, and clauses discussed next are incorrect or inappropriate in many writing situations.

Phrasings That Announce Your Intent or Opinion

1. Eliminate phrasings like *as this paragraph will explain, my paper will prove, as I will show,* and *the following paragraphs will tell.* These announcements of intent are common conventions in business, scientific, and technical writing, but in essays for the humanities, they are poor style.
2. Eliminate the phrase *in conclusion* when you have reached your last paragraph, and it is obvious that you are concluding.
3. Avoid phrases and clauses such as *I believe, in my opinion, it seems to me,* and *I think* when the ideas expressed are clearly your beliefs, opinions, and thought. Use these expressions to distinguish your ideas from those of another person.

   Avoid: *In my opinion,* the mayor's refusal to endorse the safety forces' pay raise is short-sighted.

   Use: The mayor's refusal to endorse the safety forces' pay raise is short-sighted.

   Use: The city council president believes that the mayor is right to criticize the pay raise for the safety forces, but *I believe* the mayor's refusal to endorse the safety forces' pay raise is short-sighted.

Unnecessary or Faulty Modifiers

1. Do not use *very* to intensify things that cannot be intensified. The temperature can be *hot* or it can be *very hot,* but words like *dead, gorgeous, incredible, outstanding, unique,* and *perfect* cannot be made stronger by adding *very.*

2. Avoid unnecessary qualifications using words such as *really, different,* and *particular.* They add no meaning to your sentences and make them wordy.

   Avoid: In this *particular* case, I agree.

   Use: In this case, I agree.

   Avoid: She served three *different* kinds of sandwiches.

   Use: She served three kinds of sandwiches.

3. Avoid modifying nouns and adjectives with the suffix *-type.* Find the accurate word for what you mean.

   Avoid: She likes a *desert-type* climate.

   Use: She likes a *dry* climate.

Faulty Synonyms

1. Avoid *being as* or *being that* as synonyms for *since* or *because.*

   Avoid: *Being that* final exams begin next week, I must take a leave of absence from my job to study.

   Use: *Because* final exams begin next week, I must take a leave of absence from my job to study.

   Use: *Since* final exams begin next week, I must take a leave of absence from my job to study.

2. Avoid using *expect* as a synonym for *suppose.*

   Avoid: I *expect* dinner will be ready in an hour.

   Use: I *suppose* dinner will be ready in an hour.

3. Avoid using *real* to mean *very.*

   Avoid: The weather was *real* hot in Arizona.

   Use: The weather was *very* hot in Arizona.

4. Do not use *of* to mean *have.*

   Avoid: He could *of* (should *of,* would *of*) gone if he had had the time.

   Use: He could *have* (should *have,* would *have*) gone if he had had the time.

5. Do not use *plus* as a synonym for *and* to join main clauses.

   Avoid: My car needs new tie rods *plus* the tires need to be rotated.

   Use: My car needs new tie rods; *in addition,* the tires need to be rotated.

Etc.

1. *Etc., and more, and so forth, and such* suggest that you could say more but do not want to. At times, these expressions are appropriate, but usually you *should* say whatever you *could* say, especially when providing support for an argument.

   Avoid: For his camping trip, Kevin bought a tent, a sleeping bag, a lantern, *etc.*

   Use: For his camping trip, Kevin bought a tent, a sleeping bag, a lantern, *a stove, and a first-aid kit.*

2. Do not use *etc.* with *such as*. *Such as* notes that you are listing items representative of a group, so there is no need to use *etc.* to indicate that other things are included.

Avoid: For his camping trip, Kevin bought several items, *such as* a tent, a sleeping bag, a lantern, *etc.*

Use: For his camping trip, Kevin bought several items, *such as* a tent, a sleeping bag, and a lantern.

3. Do not use *and etc. Etc.* means "and so forth"; therefore, *and etc.* means "and and so forth."

Faulty Grammar and Usage

1. Avoid referring to people with the relative pronoun *which* or *that*. Instead, use *who* or *whom*.

Avoid: Donna is the woman *which* won the essay contest.

Avoid: Donna is the woman *that* won the essay contest.

Use: Donna is the woman *who* won the essay contest.

2. Do not use *irregardless*. Use *regardless* or *irrespective of*.

3. Eliminate *the reason is because*. Use *the reason is that* or *because* instead.

Avoid: *The reason* fewer people are becoming teachers *is because* teachers' salaries are not competitive.

Use: *The reason* fewer people are becoming teachers *is that* teachers' salaries are not competitive.

Use: Fewer people are becoming teachers *because* teachers' salaries are not competitive.

4. Avoid using *so* as an intensifier unless it is followed by a clause beginning with *that*.

Avoid: After studying for midterm exams, I was *so* tired.

Use: After studying for midterm exams, I was *very* tired.

Use: After studying for midterm exams, I was *so* tired *that I slept for 12 hours.*

5. Eliminate *vice versa*. If you want to indicate that the opposite is also true, write out exactly what that opposite is.

Avoid: My mother is always criticizing me, and *vice versa.*

Use: My mother is always criticizing me, *and I am always criticizing her.*

6. Replace *a lot* and *a lot of* with *many, much*, or *a great deal of*.

Avoid: Juan earned *a lot of* respect when he told Peter he would not cheat for him.

Use: Juan earned *a great deal of* respect when he told Peter he would not cheat for him.

If you do find it appropriate to use *a lot* (in quoting dialogue, for example), remember that it is two words.

7. Use *try to* rather than *try and*.

Avoid: *Try and* understand my position.

Use: *Try to* understand my position.

> **ESL NOTE**
>
> **Idioms**
>
> An **idiom** is an expression whose meaning cannot be determined from the meaning of the words that form it. For example, *on the ropes* is an idiom that means "to be close to failure." You cannot figure out that meaning from the meaning of the words *on, the,* and *ropes.* Learning a language's idioms takes time, so be patient with yourself. Listen for idioms on television and radio and in the speech of your teachers and classmates. Look for them in newspapers and magazines. You can often learn their meaning by looking up the most important word in a dictionary; idioms with the word are often listed. For example, for *on the ropes,* you would look up "ropes." If you cannot find the idiom in the dictionary, ask someone about the meaning. Many online sites help students learn idioms. Use them sparingly in academic writing.

Double Negatives (dn)

The following words are **negatives** because they communicate the sense of *no*.

no	none	nothing	hardly
not	nowhere	no one	scarcely
never	nobody		

Be sure to use only *one* negative to express a single negative idea.

No (two negatives):	*No one* can do *nothing* to help.
Yes (one negative):	*No one* can do anything to help.
No (two negatives):	I *cannot* go *nowhere* with you.
Yes (one negative):	I *cannot* go *anywhere* with you.
Yes (one negative):	I can go *nowhere* with you.

Contractions often include a form of *not,* which is a negative.

No (two negatives):	She *can't hardly* wait for Leonard to arrive.
Yes (one negative):	She *can't* wait for Leonard to arrive.
Yes (one negative):	She can *hardly* wait for Leonard to arrive.
No (two negatives):	Henry *wouldn't* be *nothing* without you.
Yes (one negative):	Henry would be *nothing* without you.
Yes (one negative):	Henry *wouldn't* be anything without you.

A sentence can include more than one negative idea. However, only *one* negative word should express each of these negative ideas, like this:

I will not go if you do not change your attitude.

Frequently Confused Words

accept, except

Accept is a verb that means "to receive" or "to agree to":

> Mary was pleased to *accept* the scholarship.

> I *accept* the conditions of employment you explained.

Except is a preposition that means "excluding":

> *Except* for the colour, Joe liked the car.

advice, advise

Advice is a noun that means "a recommendation":

> Harriet always values Jan's *advice*.

Advise is a verb that means "to recommend":

> I *advise* you to quit while you are ahead.

affect, effect

Affect is a verb meaning "to influence":

> The trade deficit *affects* the strength of our economy.

Effect is a noun meaning "result":

> The *effects* of the drug are not fully known.

Effect is also a verb meaning "to bring about":

> The new company president plans to *effect* several changes in corporate policy.

all right, alright

Alright is nonstandard.

allusion, illusion

Allusion is a noun meaning "indirect reference":

> I resent your *allusion* to my past.

Illusion is a noun meaning "something false or misleading":

> Having money can create the *illusion* of happiness.

already, all ready

Already means "by this time":

> I would stay for dinner, but I have *already* eaten.

All ready means "prepared":

> Now that I have packed, I am *all ready* to leave.

among, between

Between is usually used to show the relationship of two things:

The animosity *between* Lee and Ann has existed for years.

Between can be used for more than two things when it means "within":

The floor *between* the stove, refrigerator, and table is hopelessly stained from years of wear.

Among is used to show the relationship of more than two things:

The friendship *among* Kelly, Joe, and Stavros began in third grade and has continued for 15 years.

amount, number

Amount is used for a unit without parts that can be counted individually:

The *amount* of suffering in the war-torn nation cannot be measured.

Number is used for items that can be counted:

The *number* of entries in the contest will determine the odds of winning the grand prize.

beside, besides

Beside means "next to":

Dad put his book down *beside* his glasses.

Besides means "in addition to" or "except for":

Besides a crib, the expectant parents bought a dresser.

I have nothing to tell you *besides* watch your step.

breath, breathe

Breath is a noun:

The skaters held their *breath* as the judges announced the scores.

Breathe is a verb:

At high altitudes it is more difficult to *breathe*.

coarse, course

Coarse means "rough":

Because wool is *coarse,* I do not like to wear it.

Course means "path," "route," or "procedure":

To speed your progress, summer school is your best *course*.

complement, compliment

Complement means "something that completes":

Red shoes will *complement* the outfit nicely.

Compliment means "praise" or "flattery":

Your *compliment* comes at the right time because I was beginning to doubt myself.

conscience, conscious

Conscience is an awareness of right and wrong:

> When in doubt, follow your *conscience*.

Conscious means "aware":

> Eleni is always *conscious* of the feelings of others.

dessert, desert

Dessert is the sweet at the end of a meal:

> Ice cream is everyone's favourite *dessert*.

Desert (deh-ZERT´) is a verb meaning "abandon":

> Kim is a good friend because he never *deserts* me in my time of need.

Desert (DEZ´-ert) is a noun meaning "dry, sandy land":

> When driving across the *desert*, a person should have a survival kit in the car.

different than, different from

Experienced readers are likely to prefer *different from*.

> June is different from her twin sister in many ways.

disinterested, uninterested

Disinterested means "impartial":

> In labour disputes, a federal mediator acts as a *disinterested* third party.

Uninterested means "lacking interest" or "bored":

> Giselle is *uninterested* in my problem because she has troubles of her own.

farther, further

Farther refers to distance:

> It is not much *farther* to the restaurant I told you about.

Further means "in addition" or "additional":

> The minister believed *further* that the tax favoured the rich.

> Any *further* discussion is a waste of time.

fewer, less

Fewer is used for things that can be counted individually:

> There were *fewer* A's on the test than I expected.

Less is used for one unit without individual members that can be counted:

> The *less* you know about what happened, the happier you will be.

human, humane

Human refers to men and women and to the qualities they possess.

> If we did not make mistakes, we would not be *human*.

Humane means "compassionate":

> Our society is not known for *humane* treatment of farm animals.

imply, infer

Imply means "to suggest something without stating it":

> Your attitude *implies* that you do not care.

Infer means "to draw a conclusion from evidence":

> I can *infer* from your sarcasm that you do not agree with me.

it's, its

It's is the contraction of *it is* or *it has:*

> *It's* unfair to accuse Lee of lying without proof.

> *It's* been three years since I saw George.

Its is a possessive pronoun:

> The dog buried *its* bone at the base of the oak tree.

lay, lie

Lay means "to put" or "to place." Both its past tense and past participle forms are *laid:*

> I always *lay* my keys on the table by the door as soon as I come into the apartment, but I must have *laid* them somewhere else last night because I cannot find them.

Lie means "to recline" or "to be in a horizontal position." Its past tense form is *lay* and its past participle form is *lain:*

> I thought I would *lie* down on the couch for an hour to rest, but I *lay* there for three hours thinking about changing my major.

loose, lose

Loose means "unfastened" or "not tight":

> Joey's *loose* tooth made it hard for him to eat corn on the cob.

Lose means "misplace":

> Every time I buy an expensive pen, I *lose* it.

passed, past

Passed means "went by":

> Summer *passed* far too quickly.

Past refers to previous time:

> The *past* week was hectic because I had to work overtime at the store and study for final exams.

precede, proceed

Precede means "to come before":

A preface *precedes* the main part of a book.

Proceed means "continue":

I am sorry I interrupted you; *proceed* with your plan.

principal, principle

Principal, as a noun, refers to a school administrator; as an adjective, *principal* means "first in importance":

The *principal* suspended the students for fighting.

The *principal* issue here is whether we can afford the trip.

Principle is a truth or a moral conviction:

My *principles* will not allow me to lie for you.

set, sit

Set is a verb that takes a direct object:

For daylight saving time, *set* your clock ahead one hour.

Sit is a verb that does not take a direct object:

Sit near the door, and I will find you when I arrive.

stationary, stationery

Stationary means "unmoving" or "unchanging":

This fan is *stationary;* it does not rotate.

Stationery is writing paper:

More men are using pink *stationery* for personal correspondence.

than, then

Than is used for comparisons:

The car I bought is more fuel efficient *than* yours.

Then is a time reference; it also means "next":

I went to university in the 1970s; students were politically active *then*.

Spade the ground thoroughly; *then* you can plant the seeds.

there, their, they're

There indicates place; it is also a sentence opener:

I thought my car was parked *there.*

There are twelve people going on the ski trip.

Their is a possessive pronoun:

Children rarely appreciate what *their* parents do for them.

They're is the contraction form of *they are:*

Lyla and Jim said *they're* coming, but I will believe it when I see them.

threw, through, thorough

Threw is the past tense of *throw:*

The pitcher *threw* the ball to third base.

Through means "finished" or "into and out of":

We should be *through* by noon.

When I drove *through* the tunnel at Windsor, I forgot to put my headlights on.

Thorough means "complete":

In the spring, many people give their houses a *thorough* cleaning.

to, too, two

To means "toward," and it is also used with a verb to form the infinitive:

After five years, Kathleen saved enough money *to* go *to* Italy.

Too means "also" or "excessively":

The child whined because he did not get to go skating *too.*

When the curtain went up, I was *too* frightened to say my lines.

Two is the number:

Lenny gets along well with his *two* roommates.

whose, who's

Whose is the possessive form of *who:*

Whose books are on the kitchen table?

Who's is the contraction form of *who is* and *who has:*

Who's going with you?

Who's been in the cookie jar?

your, you're

Your is the possessive form of *you:*

Your car is parked in a tow-away zone.

You're is the contraction form of *you are:*

Let me know when *you're* coming with us.

CHAPTER 19

Sentence Fragments (frag)

A **sentence fragment** is a word group that cannot stand as a sentence—even if you give it a capital letter and end punctuation. A fragment results under several circumstances:

- A fragment results when the subject is omitted.

  Fragment: Fans were anxious for the concert to begin. *But waited patiently.*

  Sentence: Fans were anxious for the concert to begin. But *they* waited patiently.

- A fragment results when all or part of the verb is omitted.

  Fragment: The townspeople were angry that the hotel allowed *bands* to entertain guests outdoors. *Their amplifiers up so high that the noise carried to residential districts.*

  Sentence: The townspeople were angry that the hotel allowed *bands* to entertain guests outdoors. Their amplifiers *were* turned up so high that the noise carried to the suburbs.

- A fragment results when the subject and the complete verb are omitted.

  Fragment: The bus driver and his wife spent over $500 on toys for their *children. Most of it on the two girls.*

  Sentence: The bus driver and his wife spent over $500 on toys for their *children. They spent* most of it on the two girls.

- A fragment occurs when a subordinate clause is capitalized and punctuated as a sentence.

  Fragment: *Since she was graceful as well as daring.* She was an excellent dancer.

  Sentence: Since she was graceful as well as daring, she was an excellent dancer.

For a discussion of subordinate clauses, see page 120.

Finding Sentence Fragments

If you have a tendency to write sentence fragments, go over your paper a separate time, looking just for fragments. Read each word group aloud, and ask yourself whether it sounds like a complete sentence. If you are not sure, check to see if the word group has a subject and a complete verb and does not begin with a subordinating conjunction (see below). Do not move on to the next word group until you are sure the one you are leaving behind is a sentence. For this method to be effective, you must move slowly, listening to each word group independent of what comes before and after it. Otherwise, you may fail to hear a fragment because you complete its meaning with the sentence that comes before or after it. A better idea is to do peer review. Ask a classmate to read your work aloud. Listen to their voice. If their reading sounds unsure, or if they seem puzzled with a sentence, it probably contains an error.

Subordinating conjunctions often begin subordinate clauses, and also sentence fragments, so study any word group that begins with one of them. The following are common subordinating conjunctions:

after	as if	because	for example	such as	when
although	as long as	before	if	unless	whenever
as	as soon as	especially	since	until	whether
	as though	even though	so that		while

If you compose on a computer, use the search function to locate these words in your draft. Use the Find>Replace function in Microsoft Word. Each time you locate a word group beginning with a conjunction, make sure you have a sentence rather than a fragment. Another computer tip is to isolate every word group you are calling a sentence by hitting the tab key twice before each capital letter that marks a sentence opening. Then read each word group separately to check for completeness. With word groups visually isolated this way, you are less likely to overlook a fragment by mentally connecting it to a sentence before or after it. After checking everything, reformat your draft, using the Delete key to move the text back into paragraphs.

If your computer's grammar and spelling checker highlights a sentence for you and labels it a fragment, you should still make certain that it is incomplete before revising it.

Correcting Sentence Fragments

How you correct a sentence fragment depends upon what is causing the fragment. Often, you have more than one option.

1. When the sentence subject is missing, you can correct the fragment two ways:
   a. Add the missing subject.
   b. Connect the fragment to a sentence.

Fragment:	I wanted to work full-time over the summer. *Yet could find only part-time employment.*
Add the missing subject:	I wanted to work full-time over the summer. Yet *I* could find only part-time employment.
Connect the fragment to a sentence:	I wanted to work full-time over the summer, *yet* could find only part-time employment.

2. When all or part of the verb is missing, you may be able correct the fragment two ways:
   a. Add the missing verb or verb part.

b. Change the verb form.

Fragment:	Adrian ran for the bus. *However, gone before he reached the bus stop.*
Add the missing verb or verb part:	Adrian ran for the bus. However, it *was* gone before he reached the bus stop.
Change the verb form:	Adrian ran for the bus. However, it *went* before he reached the bus stop.

3. When the subject and the complete verb are missing, you have two choices:
   a. Add the missing elements.
   b. Connect the fragment to a sentence.

Fragment:	The new Mexican restaurant was an instant hit. *Particularly with young people.*
Add the missing elements:	The new Mexican restaurant was an instant hit. *It was* particularly *popular* with young people.
Connect the fragment to a sentence:	The new Mexican restaurant was an instant hit, particularly with young people.

4. When a subordinate clause is capitalized and punctuated as a sentence, you have two choices:
   a. Change the subordinate clause to a main clause.
   b. Connect the subordinate clause to a sentence.

Fragment:	*When the curtain came down to signal intermission.* The audience stormed the concession stand.
Change the subordinate clause to a main clause:	The curtain came down to signal intermission. The audience stormed the concession stand.
Connect the subordinate clause to a sentence:	When the curtain came down to signal intermission, the audience stormed the concession stand.

ESL NOTE

The Past Participle and Passive Voice

Regular verbs have the same form for the past tense and for the past participle. The past tense form can stand alone.

Yes (past tense):	The boy walked his dog.

When you are using the past participle form for the passive voice, be sure to combine it with *am, is, are, was,* or *were.* Otherwise, you will have a sentence fragment. (In passive voice, explained on page 116, the subject *receives* the action of the verb.)

No (sentence fragment):	The child's allowance *earned* with hard work.
Yes (correct passive voice):	The child's allowance *was earned* with hard work.

Academic writing generally uses active constructions, so do not rely too heavily on passive verb forms.

CHAPTER 20

Run-On Sentences and Comma Splices (r/o, cs)

A **run-on sentence** occurs when two or more main clauses are written without correct separation. (**Main clauses**, explained on page 117, are word groups with subjects and verbs that can stand as sentences.)

Main clause:	the power was out for two days
Main clause:	most of the food in my refrigerator spoiled
Run-on sentence:	The power was out for two days most of the food in my refrigerator spoiled.

A **comma splice** occurs when two or more main clauses are separated by nothing more than a comma. It can also occur when two or more main clauses are separated by a comma and a conjunctive adverb such as *therefore* instead of with a coordinating conjunction. (For a list of conjunctive adverbs, see pages 471 and 502. **Coordinating conjunctions, or fanboys words**, explained on page 117, and are for, and, nor, but, or, yet, and so.

Main clause:	Rocco studied hard for his final exams
Main clause:	he passed them all with high marks
Comma splice:	Rocco studied hard for his final exams, he passed them all with high marks.
Comma splice:	Rocco studied hard for his final exams, therefore he passed them all with high marks.

Finding Run-on Sentences and Comma Splices

If you tend to write run-ons and comma splices, edit a separate time, checking just for these errors. Study each group of words you are calling a "sentence," and ask yourself how many main clauses there are. If there is more than one, make sure either a semicolon or a comma and a coordinating conjunction separate the clauses. When you find a run-on or comma splice, make the correction according to the guidelines in the following section.

If you compose on a computer, use the Find>Replace function to locate the conjunctive adverbs listed on pages 471 and 502. Each time you locate one of these adverbs, check for main clauses on both sides. Wherever you have main clauses on both sides, make sure you have used a semicolon before the word. (Sometimes conjunctive adverbs appear in the middle of a clause, or at the end of the second clause.)

Another computer tip is hitting the tab key twice before each capital letter marking the beginning of a sentence. The visual separation will allow you to check the number of main clauses more easily. After finding and eliminating run-ons and comma splices, reformat your text.

Again, work with a writing tutor or with another student to locate grammar and punctuation errors. If your computer's grammar checker tells you that a sentence is a run-on or a comma splice, check to make sure that the sentence is, in fact, faulty before correcting it.

Correcting Run-on Sentences and Comma Splices

Run-ons and comma splices can be corrected five ways.

1. Separate the main clauses with a period and capital letter to form two sentences.

   Run-on: The power was out for two days most of the food in my refrigerator spoiled.

   Correction: The power was out for two days. Most of the food in my refrigerator spoiled.

   Comma splice: Rocco studied hard for his final exams, he passed them all with high marks.

   Correction: Rocco studied hard for his final exams. He passed them all with high marks.

2. If the two main clauses are closely related, you can separate them with a semicolon.

   Run-on: The personnel department was praised for its efficiency all the workers received a bonus.

   Correction: The personnel department was praised for its efficiency; all the workers received a bonus.

   Comma splice: I never like to wear wool, its coarseness irritates my skin.

   Correction: I never like to wear wool; its coarseness irritates my skin.

3. Separate the main clauses with a comma and coordinating conjunction *(fanboys word—for, and, nor, but, or, yet, so).*

   Run-on: The new computer's manual is very clear Enrico learned to use the machine in an hour.

   Correction: The new computer's manual is very clear, so Enrico learned to use the machine in an hour.

   Comma splice: The hospital laid off 100 workers, most of them will be called back in three months.

   Correction: The hospital laid off 100 workers, but most of them will be called back in three months.

Run-ons and comma splices frequently occur when writers confuse the following **conjunctive adverbs** for coordinating conjunctions:

also	furthermore	indeed	nonetheless
consequently	hence	moreover	therefore
for example	however	nevertheless	thus

Conjunctive adverbs cannot be used to join main clauses with a comma; only the coordinating conjunctions can do this.

Run-on:	I was certain my interview went well therefore I was surprised when I was not among the finalists for the job.
Correction:	I was certain my interview went well; therefore, I was surprised when I was not among the finalists for the job.
Comma splice:	The party was dull, consequently I left early.
Correction:	The party was dull; consequently, I left early.

Notice that a conjunctive adverb can join main clauses when a semicolon comes before the conjunctive adverb and a comma comes after. This creates a natural pause, and links ideas correctly.

4. Change one of the main clauses to a subordinate clause.

Run-on:	My car stalls when I accelerate quickly the carburetor needs to be adjusted.
Correction:	Because the carburetor needs to be adjusted, my car stalls when I accelerate quickly.
Comma splice:	Spring is supposed to be a happy time, many people get depressed.
Correction:	Although spring is supposed to be a happy time, many people get depressed.

5. Recast the sentence.

Run-on:	The museum has a traveling exhibition that goes to local schools it is very popular with young children.
Correction:	The museum's traveling exhibition, which goes to local schools, is very popular with young children.
Comma splice:	The silver earrings are an heirloom, they have been in my family for four generations.
Correction:	Having been in our family for four generations, the silver earrings are an heirloom.

ESL NOTE

Commas and Main Clauses

In several languages, including Spanish and Vietnamese, commas can legitimately separate main clauses. If you speak one of these languages, check your written English carefully to be sure you are separating main clauses in the ways explained in this chapter.

CHAPTER 21

Verbs

Verb Forms (vb fm)

Except for *be*, English verbs have five basic forms: the base form, the present tense form, the past tense form, the past participle form, and the present participle form.

Base Form: love/hold

The base form is used with *I, we, you, they*, or a plural noun to form the present tense (to show that something occurs *now*):

> I (we, you, they, the children) *love.*
> I (we, you, they, the children) *hold.*

Present Tense Form: loves/holds

The *-s* or *-es* form is used with *it, he, she*, or a singular noun to form the present tense (to show that something occurs *now*):

> It (he, she, the child) *loves.*
> It (he, she, the child) *holds.*

Past Tense Form: loved/held

The past tense form shows that something occurred in the past:

> I (we, you, he, she, it, they, the child, the children) *loved.*
> I (we, you, he, she, it, they, the child, the children) *held.*

Past Participle Form: loved/held

The past participle form is used with *has, have, had, am, is, was*, and *were*:

> I (we, you, they, the children) *have loved/have held.*
> It (he, she, the child) *has loved/has held.*
> I *am loved/am held.*
> It (he, she, the child) *is loved/is held.*
> We (you, they, the children) *are loved/are held.*
> I (we, you, they, he, she, the child, the children) *had loved/had held.*
> I (he, she, it, the child) *was loved/was held.*
> We (you, they, the children) *were loved/were held.*

Present Participle Form: loving/holding

The present participle form adds an *-ing* to the base form. It is used with *am, is, are, was,* and *were. Note the verbs below need a direct object for the sentence to be correct.*

I *am loving/am holding.*

It (he, she, the child) *is loving/is holding.*

We (you, they, the children) *are loving/are holding.*

I (he, she, it, the child) *was loving/was holding.*

We (you, they, the children) *were loving/were holding.*

ESL NOTE

Use of Am with the Present Participle

Be sure to use *am* between *I* and the present participle.

No:	I *working* 20 hours a week at Zellers.
No:	I *is working* 20 hours a week at Zellers.
Yes:	I *am working* 20 hours a week at Zellers.

Regular Verb Forms

Regular verbs form their past tense and past participle forms by adding *-d* or *-ed* to the base form.

Base	Past tense	Past participle
work	worked	worked
talk	talked	talked

Irregular Verb Forms

The forms for **irregular verbs** vary. They are given in the dictionary entry for each verb. Following are the forms for some of them.

SOME COMMON IRREGULAR VERBS

Base	Past Tense	Past Participle	Present Participle	*-s/-es* Form
arise	arose	arisen	arising	arises
become	became	become	becoming	becomes
bring	brought	brought	bringing	brings
buy	bought	bought	buying	buys

(continued)

SOME COMMON IRREGULAR VERBS (*continued*)

Base	Past Tense	Past Participle	Present Participle	*-s/-es* Form
do	did	done	doing	does
drink	drank	drunk	drinking	drinks
fly	flew	flown	flying	flies
get	got	gotten, got	getting	gets
go	went	gone	going	goes
grow	grew	grown	growing	grows
hang (a picture)	hung	hung	hanging	hangs
hang (execute)	hanged	hanged	hanging	hangs
have	had	had	having	has
hide	hid	hidden	hiding	hides
know	knew	known	knowing	knows
lay	laid	laid	laying	lays
leave	left	left	leaving	leaves
lose	lost	lost	losing	loses
prove	proved	proved, proven	proving	proves
ride	rode	ridden	riding	rides
rise	rose	risen	rising	rises
see	saw	seen	seeing	sees
sit	sat	sat	sitting	sits
spring	sprang, sprung	sprung	springing	springs
steal	stole	stolen	stealing	steals
take	took	taken	taking	takes
tear	tore	torn	tearing	tears
throw	threw	thrown	throwing	throws
wear	wore	worn	wearing	wears
write	wrote	written	writing	writes

Forms of Be

Unlike other verbs, *be* has eight forms.

Base Form: be

The base form of *be* is used in commands and with *to, in the infinitive form:*

> *Be* careful or you will hurt yourself.

> Jan is studying *to be* a court reporter.

ESL NOTE

Incorrect Use of –d and –ed Endings

Do not add a *-d* or *-ed* ending to the past tense or past participle forms of irregular verbs.

No:	Hannah *wored* a new sweater today.
Yes:	Hannah *wore* a new sweater today.
No:	Stavros *has tored* his pants.
Yes:	Stavros *tore* his pants.

Present Tense Forms: am/is/are

I *am* the first person in my family to attend college.

Julio *is* sick with the flu.

The board members *are* interested in a fundraiser.

Past Tense Forms: was/were

The CD *was* scratched and unplayable.

We *were* uncertain about which way to go.

Past Participle Form: been

Lanie *has been* my best friend for 15 years.

The window *had been broken*.

They *have been* here before.

Present Participle Form: being

She *is being* rude to the sales clerk.

The children *are being* quiet right now.

You *were being* too sarcastic.

ESL NOTE

Use of Has, Have, or Had with Been

Be sure to use *has* or *have* with *been*.

No:	He *been* anxious about the exam.
Yes:	He *has been* anxious about the exam.
Yes:	He *had been* anxious about the exam.
No:	The children *been* good all day.
Yes:	The children *have been* good all day.
Yes:	The children *had been* good all day.

Present Tense Forms of Regular and Irregular Verbs

For the present tense, remember to use *-s* or *-es* with the base form when the sentence subject is third person - *it, he, she*, a singular noun, or a singular indefinite pronoun. (Indefinite pronouns, listed on page 477, are words like *anyone, somebody,* and *everything.*)

No: My uncle *eat* in a restaurant every night.

Yes: My uncle *eats* in a restaurant every night.

Yes: It/he/she *depends* upon you.

Yes: The soprano *sings* beautifully.

Yes: Everybody *confuses* the twins.

For more on this grammar point, see subject–verb agreement below.

Subject–Verb Agreement (s–v agr)

The rule for **subject–verb agreement** is straightforward: A present tense verb should always agree with its subject *in number.* That is, a singular subject requires a singular verb, and a plural subject requires a plural verb.

Singular subject, singular verb: The green *ink looks* difficult to read.

Plural subject, plural verbs: The *desks are* highly polished.

Most of the time, subject–verb agreement is easily achieved. However, some instances present special agreement problems, and these are discussed below. Also, if your computer's spelling and grammar checker highlights an agreement error, make certain the error does, in fact, exist before making changes.

Compound Subjects

A **compound subject** occurs when two or more words, phrases, or clauses are joined by *and, or, nor, either . . . or,* or *neither . . . nor.*

1. When the parts of a compound subject are linked by *and,* use a plural verb:

   The *lioness and her cub share* a close bond.

2. When subjects are preceded by *each* or *every,* use a singular verb:

   Each lioness and *each cub faces* starvation on the drought-stricken plain.

3. When singular subjects are linked by *or* or *nor* (or by *either . . . or* or *neither . . . nor*), use a singular verb:

   Drought or famine threatens all wildlife.

4. When plural subjects are linked by *or* or *nor* (or *either . . . or* or *neither . . .nor*), use a plural verb:

   Neither the children nor their parents are enjoying the play.

5. When a plural subject and a singular subject are joined, use a verb that agrees with the nearer subject:

Disease or predators are also a danger to newborn cubs.

Neither the scouts nor their leader is willing to camp out on such a cold night.

For a more pleasant-sounding sentence, place the plural form last:

Neither the leader nor the scouts are **willing to camp out on such a cold night.**

Subject and Verb Separated

Words, phrases, or clauses that come between the subject and verb do not affect the subject–verb agreement rule:

The *chipmunks,* burrowing under my flowerbed, also *raid* my vegetable garden.

The subject *chipmunks* is plural, so the plural verb *raid* must be used, even though the phrase *burrowing under my flowerbed* separates subject and verb. Here is another example:

One of the demonstrators *was* fined $100.

Although the phrase between the subject and verb contains the plural word *dem-onstrators,* the singular subject *one* still requires the singular verb *was, because "one" is the subject of the sentence.*

Inverted Order

When the verb appears before the subject, the word order of the sentence is **inverted**. Be sure the verb agrees with the subject and not some other word close to the verb:

Floating on the water *were three lilies.*

Sentences that begin with *there* or *here* often have inverted order, as do sentences that ask a question:

There *are* many *causes* of cancer.

Here *sits* the *box* of records.

Why *are* your *questions* so hard to answer?

Indefinite Pronouns

Indefinite pronouns refer to a member or members of a group of people, items, or ideas without specifying the particular member or members. The following indefinite pronouns are singular and require singular verbs:

anybody	either	neither	nothing	something
anyone	everybody	nobody	one	
anything	everyone	none	somebody	
each	everything	no one	someone	

Nobody ignores an insult all the time.

Everybody retaliates once in a while.

No one likes to be the butt of a joke.

Note: Although *everyone* and *everybody* clearly refer to more than one, they are still singular in a grammatical sense and take a singular verb:

Everyone is invited to the party after the show.

You may be tempted to use a plural verb with a singular indefinite pronoun followed by a phrase with a plural word. However, in this case too, the singular verb is used in formal usage:

Each of the boys *is* willing to help rake the leaves.

Neither of us *plans* to contribute a week's salary to the Christmas fund.

The following indefinite pronouns may be singular or plural, depending on the meaning of the sentence:

all	some	most
any	more	

Most of the players *are* injured.

Most of the pie *has* been eaten.

All of the bills *are* paid.

All of the food *tastes* good.

Collective Nouns

Collective nouns have a singular form and refer to a group of people or things. The following are examples of collective nouns:

audience	crew	jury
class	faculty	majority
committee	family	team

Collective nouns take a singular verb when the noun refers to the group as a single unit:

The *number* of people attending the concert *poses* a fire hazard.

The women's basketball *team is* still in contention for the provincial championship.

Collective nouns take a plural verb when the members of the group are functioning individually:

A *number* of those in attendance *seem* over 30 years old.

The *faculty have* agreed among themselves to promote tougher admissions standards.

If you prefer to use a plural verb, you can often add a phrase like "members of":

The *members of* the committee *have* agreed to a new set of membership guidelines.

Relative Pronouns

Who, whom, which, and *that* are **relative pronouns**. They refer to nouns in a sentence.

1. When the relative pronoun refers to a singular noun, use a singular verb:

   My roommate, *who is* on the cross-country team, runs at least 50 miles a week.

2. When the relative pronoun refers to a plural noun, use a plural verb:

   The advertisements, *which were* offensive to women, were pulled from the newspaper.

3. When the phrase *one of the* appears before a plural noun, use a plural verb:

   Kamie is one of the two scholarship winners *who hope* to be a veterinarian.

4. When the phrase *only one of the* appears before a noun, use a singular verb:

   Kamie is the only one of the two scholarship winners *who hopes* to be a veterinarian.

ESL NOTE

Singular Verbs and Non-count Nouns

Use a singular verb with nouns that name something that normally cannot be counted (**non-count nouns**). These are nouns like *air, baggage, hunger, honesty, water, sugar,* and *health.*

| No: | Her *wisdom surprise* me because she is so young. |
| Yes: | Her *wisdom surprises* me because she is so young. |

Tense Shifts (t. shft)

Verbs tense indicates past, present, and future time. Once you begin a sentence with a particular verb tense, maintain that tense as long as you are referring to the same period of time. Switching the tense without a valid reason creates a problem called **tense shift**. The following paragraph contains unwarranted tense shifts (the verbs are italicized to help you recognize the shifts):

> Wayne Gretzky, Rick Hansen, Catriona LeMay Doan, Steve Nash and Nancy Greene Raine all *helped* in an unusual lighting ceremony on the floor of B.C. Place just before fireworks *start* spouting from the outer rim of the B.C. Place roof. The Canadian icons *approach* the indoor cauldron together.
>
> But Gretzky, with flame *held* aloft, then *runs* out of the stadium and into a pickup truck led by a police escort. The truck *wound about* through the streets of downtown Vancouver to Jack Poole Plaza, which looks out on Burrard Inlet with the breathtaking North Shore Mountains in the background. Gretzky *arrives* and then *lights* what will be the Olympic Cauldron that *will burn* throughout the 17 days of the Games.

The verbs in this paragraph shift back and forth from present to past, interfering with an accurate representation of the action of the game. To prevent confusion about time sequence, once you use a verb tense, maintain that tense consistently and shift time only when the shift is justified.

A corrected version of the example paragraph reads like this:

> Wayne Gretzky, Rick Hansen, Catriona LeMay Doan, Steve Nash and Nancy Greene Raine all *helped* in an unusual lighting ceremony on the floor of B.C. Place just before fireworks *started* spouting from the outer rim of the B.C. Place roof. The Canadian icons *approached* the indoor cauldron together.
>
> But Gretzky, with flame *held* aloft, then *ran* out of the stadium and into a pickup truck led by a police escort. The truck *wound about* through the streets of downtown Vancouver to Jack Poole Plaza, which looks out on Burrard Inlet with the breathtaking North Shore Mountains in the background. Gretzky *arrived* and then *lit* what will be the Olympic Cauldron that *will burn* throughout the 17 days of the Games.

A shift from one tense to another is appropriate when the time frame has changed:

> When I first *began* working as a waiter, I *hated* my work. Now I *am enjoying* my job more than I *thought* possible.

In the above example, each shift (from past to present to past) is justified because each verb accurately reflects the time period referred to.

Voice Shifts (v. shft)

Active and passive voice are discussed on page 116. When a verb is in the **active voice**, the subject of the sentence *performs* the action. When a verb is in the **passive voice**, the subject of the sentence *receives* the action.

Active voice: The doctor *gave* the girl a shot.

Passive voice: The girl *was given* a shot by the doctor.

In general, avoid shifting from active to passive voice unnecessarily.

Shift: Cell phones *offer* convenience. However, other people *are* frequently *irritated* by thoughtless cell phone users.

Better: Cell phones *offer* convenience. However, thoughtless cell phone users frequently *irritate* other people.

Not all shifts from active to passive voice are inappropriate. Passive voice is useful when you do not know who performed the action, or when you want to emphasize the receiver of the action.

Appropriate passive voice: The rear bumper of my car *was dented* in the parking lot.

CHAPTER 22

Pronouns

A **pronoun** substitutes for a noun. Using pronouns helps writers and speakers avoid monotonous repetition, as the following example shows.

> **Repetition:** **The kitten licked the kitten's paw.**
>
> **Pronoun used:** **The kitten licked *her* paw.**

Pronoun–antecedent agreement (p. Agr)

Pronouns must agree with the nouns to which they refer—with their **antecedents**—in **gender** (masculine, feminine, or neutral) and **number** (singular or plural). Many times this agreement is easily achieved, as in the following example:

> *Kurt* lost *his* tennis *racket*, but *he* eventually found *it*.

The pronouns *he* and *his* are singular and masculine to agree with the number and gender of the antecedent *Kurt*, and the pronoun *it* is singular and neutral to agree with *racket*.

At times, pronoun–antecedent agreement is not as obvious as in the above sentence, and these instances are discussed next. (If your computer's grammar checker flags an agreement problem, be sure that one does, in fact, exist before making a correction.)

Compound Subjects

A **compound subject** is formed by two or more words, phrases, or clauses joined by *and, or, nor, either . . . or,* or *neither . . . nor.*

1. When the parts of the antecedent are joined by *and,* use a plural pronoun:

> *The shoes and baseball cap* were left in *their* usual places.

> *Linda, Michelle, and Audrey* finished *their* group project early.

2. When the antecedent is preceded by *each* or *every,* use a singular pronoun:

> *Every citizen and each group* must do *its* part to elect responsible officials.

> *Each school and athletic department* must submit *its* budget to the superintendent.

3. For singular antecedents joined by *either . . . or* or *neither . . . nor,* use singular pronouns:

Has *either Sean or Frank* taken *his* batting practice today?

Neither Melissa nor Jennifer has finished packing *her* bag.

4. For plural antecedents joined by *either . . . or* or *neither . . . nor,* use plural pronouns:

Neither the teachers nor the students have *their* coats.

5. If one singular and one plural antecedent are joined by *or, either . . . or,* or *neither . . . nor,* be sure the pronoun agrees with the antecedent closer to it:

Either Brian Adams or The Tragically Hip will release *their* new album soon.

Note: Placing the plural antecedent second makes a smoother sentence.

Collective Nouns

Collective nouns have a singular form and refer to a *group* of people or things. Words like these are collective nouns:

audience	committee	panel
band	group	society
class	jury	team

1. If the group is functioning as a single unit, the pronoun that refers to the collective noun is singular:

A civilized *society* must protect *its* citizens from violence.

2. If the members of the group are functioning individually, use a plural pronoun:

Yesterday the *team* signed *their* contracts for next season.

Indefinite Pronouns

Indefinite pronouns refer to a member or members of a group of people, things, or ideas without specifying the particular member or members of the group referred to. Indefinite pronouns can be antecedents.

The following indefinite pronouns are singular, and in formal usage, the pronouns referring to them should also be singular:

anybody	everyone	no one
anyone	neither	one
each	nobody	somebody
either	none	someone
everybody		

Anyone who has finished *his or her* essay may leave.

Nobody on the football team should assume that *his* position is safe.

Neither of the young mothers forgot *her* exercise class.

Note: See the discussion on gender-neutral pronouns that follows.

In formal usage, a pronoun referring to a singular indefinite pronoun is singular, even when a phrase with a plural word follows the indefinite pronoun:

Each of the boys selected *his* favourite bat.

Few and *many* are plural, so pronouns referring to them are also plural:

Many of my friends have already bought *their* tickets.

The following indefinite pronouns may be singular or plural, depending on the meaning of the sentence:

all	more	some
any	most	

Some of the book is still attached to *its* binding.

Some of the band forgot *their* sheet music.

Gender-Neutral Pronouns

The pronoun agrees with its antecedent in this sentence, but the meaning excludes women:

Each contestant must bring *his* birth certificate.

To avoid using pronouns that inappropriately exclude one gender, you have three options.

1. Use both a masculine and a feminine pronoun:

   Each contestant must bring *his or her* birth certificate.

   This option can be cumbersome if you must use *his or her, he or she,* or *him or her* often. In that case, one of the following options may work better.

2. Rewrite the sentence to make the pronoun and antecedent plural:

   All contestants must bring *their* birth certificates.

3. Rewrite the sentence to eliminate the pronouns:

   Each contestant must bring a birth certificate.

Pronoun reference (p. Ref)

If you fail to provide a clear, stated antecedent for a pronoun, you create a problem with **pronoun reference**. The most common kinds of pronoun reference problems are described below. (If your computer's grammar checker flags a reference problem, be sure that one does, in fact, exist before making a correction.)

Ambiguous Reference

Ambiguous reference occurs when your reader cannot tell which of two possible antecedents a pronoun refers to.

Ambiguous reference: **When I placed the heavy vase on the shelf, *it* broke.** (What broke, the vase or the shelf? Because of the ambiguous reference, the reader cannot tell.)

To eliminate the ambiguous reference, replace the pronoun with a noun.

Correction: **When I placed the heavy vase on the shelf, *the shelf* broke.**

Unstated Reference

Unstated reference occurs when a pronoun has no antecedent to refer to.

1. Unstated reference occurs when a pronoun refers to an unstated form of a stated word.

   Unstated reference: **Carla is very ambitious. *It* causes her to work 60 hours a week.** (*It* is meant to refer to *ambition,* but that word does not appear; *ambitious* does.)

   To correct a problem with unstated reference, substitute a noun for the pronoun.

   Correction: **Carla is very ambitious. *Her ambition* causes her to work 60 hours a week.**

2. Unstated reference occurs when *this, that, which, it,* or *they* has no stated antecedent. To eliminate the problem, supply the missing word or words.

   Unstated reference: **When I arrived at the office, *they* said my appointment was cancelled.** (*They* has no antecedent to refer to.)

   Correction: **When I arrived at the office, *the receptionist* said my appointment was cancelled.**

   Unstated reference: **At my last appointment with my advisor, I decided to major in marketing. This has made me feel better about school.** (This has no word to refer to.)

   Correction: **At my last appointment with my advisor, I decided to major in marketing. *This decision* has made me feel better about school.**

   Unstated reference: **In the newspaper, *it* says we're going to have a hot summer.**

   Correction: **The newspaper says that we're going to have a hot summer.**

3. Unstated reference occurs when *you* appears with no antecedent. To solve the problem, replace the pronoun with a noun.

   Unstated reference: **A teacher becomes frustrated when *you* do not ask questions.** (*You* has no antecedent to refer to.)

   Correction: **A teacher becomes frustrated when *students* do not ask questions.**

4. Unstated reference occurs when a subject pronoun refers to a possessive noun. To solve the problem, replace the noun with a pronoun and the pronoun with a noun.

   Unstated reference: **In Barbara Kingsolver's novels, she writes about strong women.**

   Correction: **In her novels, Barbara Kingsolver writes about strong women.**

EXERCISE PRONOUN REFERENCE

Directions: Correct the errors in the sentences to eliminate problems with pronoun reference.

1. The song lyrics were particularly offensive to women. This caused many radio stations to refuse to play it.

2. Doris explained to Philomena that she had to help clean the apartment.

3. I left the spaghetti sauce and the milk on the counter, and when I answered the phone, my cat knocked it over.

4. Frank was nervous about today's midterm examination. It made sleep impossible last night.

5. Rodney's car is double-parked. He is certain to get a ticket.

6. Dale is a very insecure person. It is his most unattractive trait.

7. The personnel director explained that I am entitled to 12 vacation days a year, which is guaranteed by the union contract.

8. By the time I arrived at the Dean's office, they had left for lunch.

9. Julius was on the phone with Roberto when he realized that he forgot to go to the bank and cash a cheque.

10. Dr. Wang is known to be a patient math instructor. It is the reason so many students sign up for his course. ●

Person shifts (p. Shft)

When you refer to yourself, you use **first-person pronouns**. When you speak to other people directly, you use **second-person pronouns**. When you refer to other people and things, you use **third-person pronouns**.

First-person pronouns	Second-person pronouns	Third-person pronouns
I	you	he
we	your	she
me	yours	it
us		they
my		his
mine		him
our		her
ours		hers
		its
		their
		theirs
		them

When using the above pronouns, be consistent in person.

Shift from third to second person:	If a football player works hard, *he* has many chances for financial aid, and *you* might even be eligible for a full scholarship.
Shift eliminated:	If a football player works hard, *he* has many chances for financial aid, and *he* might even be eligible for a full scholarship.
Shift from second to first person:	An empathetic friend is one *you* can tell your most private thoughts to. This kind of friend also knows when *I* want to be alone and respects *my* wish.
Shift eliminated:	An empathetic friend is one *you* can tell your most private thoughts to. This kind of friend also knows when *you* want to be alone and respects *your* wish.

Reflexive and Intensive Pronouns (Ref/Int Pn)

Reflexive pronouns and **intensive pronouns** end in *-self* in the singular and *-selves* in the plural. The reflexive and intensive pronouns are as follows:

Singular	Plural
myself	ourselves
yourself	yourselves
himself	themselves
herself	
itself	

Reflexive pronouns can show that the subject of the sentence did something to or for itself. They often express the idea of acting alone:

Shirley taught *herself* to play the guitar.

We solved the homework problems *ourselves*.

Intensive pronouns can emphasize the words they refer to:

I *myself* never believe politicians.

The teachers *themselves* are opposed to ability grouping.

1. Do not use a reflexive or intensive pronoun without an antecedent.

   | No: | Hector and *myself* drove 550 kilometres to Thunder Bay. |
   | Yes: | Hector and *I* drove 550 kilometres to Thunder Bay. |

2. Never use hisself or theirselves.

No:	Nick locked *hisself* out of his apartment.
Yes:	Nick locked *himself* out of his apartment.
No:	The children entertained *theirselves* for an hour.
Yes:	The children entertained *themselves* for an hour.

Pronoun Case (Case)

A pronoun's **case** is the form the pronoun takes to indicate how it functions in a sentence. Pronouns that function as the subject of a sentence or as the subject complement are in the **subjective case**. These are the subjective case pronouns:

I	he	they
we	she	who
you	it	whoever

Subjective case pronoun as subject: *We* should ask for directions.

Because the pronoun is the sentence subject, it is in the subjective case.

Pronouns that function as the subject complement are also in the subjective case. A **subject complement** comes after a linking verb and describes or renames the subject. **Linking verbs** do not show action. They are verbs like these: *am, is, are, was, were, been, seem, appear, taste, feel, smell,* and *sound.*

Subjective case pronoun as subject complement: **The person I trust is** *he.*

The subjective case pronoun *he* is used because *is* is a linking verb and because *he* renames the subject, *person.*

Pronouns that function as the direct object, indirect object, or object of a preposition are in the **objective case**. These are the objective case pronouns:

me	him	them
us	her	whom
you	it	whomever

To be in the objective case, a pronoun can be one of three kinds of objects: the object of a preposition, the direct object, or the indirect object of a verb. Let's first discuss pronouns as the object of a preposition.

A **preposition** connects words by showing how a noun or pronoun relates to another word in a sentence. A pronoun is the **object of a preposition** when it follows the preposition and is one of the words connected. A pronoun that is the object of a preposition is in the objective case.

Objective case pronoun as object of preposition: **The dog is near** *me.*

The preposition *near* connects *dog* and *me* by showing how they are related to each other—they are *near* each other.

A pronoun is the **direct object** when it follows a verb and identifies who or what receives the verb's action. A pronoun that is a direct object is in the objective case.

Objective case pronoun as direct object: **The angry child kicked** *him.*

The pronoun is in the objective case because it follows the verb *kicked* and receives its action.

A pronoun is an **indirect object** when it answers the question "to or for whom?" after the verb. A pronoun that is an indirect object is in the objective case.

Objective case pronoun   **I gave *her* the ball.**
as indirect object:

The pronoun is in the objective case because when you ask the question, "gave to whom?" the answer is *her*.

Most of the time, choosing the correct pronoun is not a problem. However, a few special circumstances present special problems. These circumstances are described below.

Pronouns in Compounds

Use subjective case for subjects and objective case for objects.

Subject: *He and I* **prefer to drive to Winnipeg.** (sentence subject)

Subject: **The ones I like are** *she and he.* (subject complement)

Object: **Police authorities gave** *them and us* **citations for bravery.** (indirect object)

Object: **Professor Whan asked** *her and me* **to help out after class.** (direct object)

Object: **Joyce sat down near** *him and her.* (object of preposition)

When a pronoun is paired with a noun, you can often tell which pronoun is correct if you mentally cross out the noun and the conjunction, leaving the pronoun. For example, which is correct?

Ricardo asked Dale and *me* to leave.

Ricardo asked Dale and *I* to leave.

Cross out *Dale and* to find out:

Ricardo asked ~~Dale and~~ *me* to leave.

Ricardo asked ~~Dale and~~ *I* to leave.

Now you can tell that the correct form is:

Ricardo asked Dale and *me* to leave.

Pronouns after Forms of *to Be*

In strict formal usage, the subjective case is used after forms of *to be (am, is, are, was, were):*

It is *I.*

The stars of the play are Carlotta and *she.*

Pronouns in Comparisons

When *than* or *as* is used to compare, some words may go unstated. You can choose the correct pronoun by mentally adding the unstated words. For example, which is correct?

Jackson works longer hours than *I.*

Jackson works longer hours than *me.*

Add the unstated words to decide:

Jackson works longer hours than I do.

Jackson works longer hours than me do.

With the unstated words added, the correct choice is clear:

Jackson works longer hours than *I*.

Sometimes the pronoun chosen affects the meaning of the sentence:

I enjoy running as much as *she*. (This sentence means that I enjoy running as much as she does.)

I enjoy running as much as *her*. (This sentence means that I enjoy running as much as I enjoy her.)

Pronouns Followed by Nouns

When a pronoun is followed by a noun, you can choose the correct form by mentally crossing out the noun. For example, which is correct?

We students resent the tuition increase.

Us students resent the tuition increase.

Cross out the noun:

We ~~students~~ resent the tuition increase.

Us ~~students~~ resent the tuition increase.

Now the choice is clear:

We students resent the tuition increase.

Who, Whoever, Whom, and Whomever

Who and *whoever* are the subjective forms and are used as subjects:

Henry is the one *who* understands Phyllis. (*Who* is the subject of the verb *understands*.)

Whom and *whomever* are the objective forms and are used for direct objects, indirect objects, and objects of prepositions.

Direct object:	**Whom did you take with you?** (Recast questions as statements: You did take *whom* with you.)
Indirect object:	**Give *whomever* you want the job.**
Object of preposition:	**Seat yourself near *whomever* you wish.**

Choosing between *who* and *whom,* or *whoever* and *whomever* can be tricky when you are dealing with questions. The choice is easier if you recast the questions into statements and then decide whether the subjective or objective pronoun is needed. For example, which is correct?

Who did you see at the concert?

Whom did you see at the concert?

Recast the question as a statement, and you see that the object pronoun is needed to function as a direct object:

You did see *who* at the concert.

You did see *whom* at the concert.

Now it is clear that the correct sentence is:

Whom did you see at the concert?

When you recast questions into statements, use the subjective *who* and *whoever* after forms of *to be (am, is, are, was, were)*. For example, which is correct?

Who was the top point scorer in the game?

Whom was the top point scorer in the game?

Recast the question as a statement:

The top point scorer in the game was *who*.

The top point scorer in the game was *whom*.

Now it is clear that the correct form is:

Who was the top point scorer in the game?

ESL NOTE

Pronoun Reference and *Who, Whom, Which, or That*

Do not use a pronoun to refer to a word that is already referred to by *who, whom, which,* or *that.*

No: I asked directions from the man who *he* was standing on the corner.

Yes: I asked directions from the man who was standing on the corner.

No: Jillian was not interested in the movie that we wanted to watch *it.*

Yes: Jillian was not interested in the movie that we wanted to watch.

CHAPTER 23

Modifiers

A **modifier** is a word or word group that describes or "modifies" another word or word group. Two kinds of modifiers are adjectives and adverbs.

Adjectives and Adverbs (ad)

Adjectives modify nouns and pronouns, and **adverbs** modify verbs, adjectives, and other adverbs.

Adjective modifying noun:	The *tired* child cried for her teddy bear.
Adjective modifying pronoun:	They are *foolish* to hike at night.
Adverb modifying verb:	The politician campaigned *vigorously* for tax cuts.
Adverb modifying adjective:	For July, the temperatures are *unusually* cool.
Adverb modifying another adverb:	Jan slept *very* soundly after final exams.

Many (but not all) adverbs end in *-ly*.

Adjective	Adverb
quiet	quietly
angry	angrily
clear	clearly
bright	brightly

1. Be sure to use adverbs to modify verbs, adjectives, and other adverbs.

   No: The audience shouted that the speaker was talking too *soft*.
   (An adjective modifies the verb *shouted*.)

   Yes: The audience shouted that the speaker was talking too *softly*.
   (An adverb modifies the verb *shouted*.)

2. Use *good* and *well* correctly. *Good* is an adjective; *well* is usually an adverb, but it is an adjective when it means "healthy."

Good as adjective: Mother keeps the *good* dishes in the attic.

Well as adverb: Julio plays the piano well, although he has never had a lesson.

Well as adjective: Grandmother has not felt *well* since March.

Use *good* after linking verbs and *well* (as an adverb) after action verbs. Linking verbs are forms of *to be* (*am, be, is, are, was, were, been, being*) and verbs such as *appear, become, feel, look, seem, smell, sound,* and *taste* when they **express a state of being** rather than action. Action verbs show movement, thought, or process. They are verbs such as *run, sit, consider, develop, organize,* and *whistle*.

Good after linking verb: The weather forecast for our vacation *is good.*

Good after linking verb: The brownies *smell good* even though they are burned.

Well after action verb: Although it is 15 years old, the television *works well.*

3. Use *bad* as an adjective and *badly* as an adverb. Be sure to use *bad* as an adjective after linking verbs.

Bad as adjective: The *bad* news is that I must cancel my trip

Bad as adjective: The teacher felt *bad* about the test results.

Badly as adverb: Parents who dance *badly* often take lessons before their children's wedding receptions.

4. Use *real* and *really* correctly. *Real* is an adjective and should not be used as an adverb. *Really* is the adverb.

Real as adjective: The *real* problem is that the company is short of money.

Really as adverb: The menu for the dinner party is *really* (not real) interesting.

Comparative and Superlative Forms of Adjectives and Adverbs

Adjectives and adverbs have a **comparative form** for comparing two elements and a **superlative form** for comparing more than two elements.

Base form: This ice cream is *sweet.*

Comparative form: This ice cream is *sweeter* than my homemade ice cream. (compares two)

Superlative form: This is the *sweetest* ice cream I have ever tasted. (compares more than two)

Most comparative and superlative forms are made by adding *-er* and *-est* or by adding *more* and *most* or *less* and *least*.

Base	Comparative form	Superlative form
slow	slower	slowest
young	younger	youngest
lucky	luckier	luckiest
beautiful	more beautiful	most beautiful
slowly	more slowly	most slowly
quickly	more quickly	most quickly
brave	less brave	least brave

1. Use comparative forms for two elements, and superlative forms for three elements.

    No: The twins are excellent runners. Of the two, Joe is the *best* sprinter, but Jim is the *best* distance runner.

    Yes: The twins are excellent runners. Of the two, Joe is the *better* sprinter, but Jim is the *better* distance runner.

    Yes: Joe is the *best* sprinter on the team, but Jim is the *best* distance runner.

2. Do not use *more* or *most* with *-er* and *-est* forms.

    No: Hannah is *more friendlier* than Marcus.

    Yes: Hannah is *friendlier* than Marcus.

3. Be aware of irregular forms. These adjectives and adverbs form their comparative and superlative forms irregularly.

Base	Comparative form	Superlative form
bad	worse	worst
badly	worse	worst
good	better	best
little	less	least
many	more	most
much	more	most
some	more	most
well	better	best

4. Recognize that some adjectives and adverbs do not have comparative and superlative forms. For example, something cannot be "the most perfect" because "perfect" is as good as something gets. These modifiers do not have comparative and superlative forms:

dead	favourite	unanimous
empty	perfect	unique
endlessly	perfectly	

    No: *Les Belles-sœurs* is my most favourite play.

    Yes: *Les Belles-sœurs* is my favourite play.

ESL NOTE

A, An, and The

A, an, and *the* are special adjectives called **articles**. The following are some of the rules for using articles.

1. Use *a* before a word that begins with a consonant sound and *an* before a word that begins with a vowel sound:

   a hat   an idea
   a baby   an uncle
   a big tree   an old movie

2. Be aware that the letter *u* sometimes has a long vowel sound and sometimes has a short sound:

   a union
   an uncle

3. Use *a* when the letter *h* is pronounced and *an* when the letter *h* is silent.

   a hairy beast
   an honest politician

4. Use *a* or *an* with *singular* words that name items that can be counted *and* whose specific identity is unknown to the reader or listener. Use *the* with *singular* words that name items that can be counted *and* whose specific identity is known to the reader or listener:

   André applied for *a* scholarship.

   André applied for *the* Perlman Scholarship.

5. Do not use *a* or *an* with plural words or with singular words that name items that cannot be counted.

   No: The gardener planted *a* trees along the fence.

   Yes: The gardener planted trees along the fence.

   No: My advisor gives me *a* helpful information.

   Yes: My advisor gives me helpful information.

6. Use *the* to point out something specific:

   A sales tax discourages new business. (This sentence says that sales taxes *in general* discourage new business.)

   The sales tax discourages new business. (This sentence says that a specific sales tax in a specific location is discouraging new business.)

Dangling Modifiers (dm)

A modifier that has no stated word in the sentence to describe sensibly is a **dangling modifier**. Dangling modifiers often create silly sentences, as this sentence with a dangling modifier illustrates:

> While basting the turkey, the sweet potatoes burned.

While basting the turkey is a modifier, but there is no word for the modifier to describe. As a result, it seems that the sweet potatoes basted the turkey.

You can correct a dangling modifier two ways. You can leave the modifier as it is and supply a word for the modifier to describe. *This word should appear immediately after the modifier.*

> **Dangling modifier:**   Listening for the telephone, the doorbell rang.

Because there is no word for *listening for the telephone* to describe, the phrase is a dangling modifier. The sentence indicates that the doorbell listened for the telephone.

> **Correction:**   Listening for the telephone, I heard the doorbell ring.

I, placed immediately after the modifier, is a word the modifier can logically describe.

A second way to eliminate a dangling modifier is to rewrite the modifier as a subordinate clause (see pages 118–120).

> **Dangling modifier:**   *Jogging along the side of the road,* a car splashed me with mud.

Because there is no word for *jogging along the side of the road* to describe, the phrase is a dangling modifier. The sense of the sentence is that the car did the jogging.

> **Correction:**   While I was jogging along the side of the road, a car splashed me with mud.

The modifier has been rewritten as a subordinate clause to eliminate the dangling modifier.

As the above examples illustrate, dangling modifiers often occur when sentences begin with an *-ing* verb form (present participle). However, a dangling modifier can also occur when a sentence begins with an *-ed, -en, -n,* or *-t* verb form (past participle) or when it begins with the present-tense verb form used with *to* (infinitive).

> **Dangling modifier (present participle):**   *While rocking the baby,* the cat purred contentedly.
>
> **Correction:**   While rocking the baby, I heard the cat purr contentedly.
>
> **Correction:**   While I was rocking the baby, the cat purred contentedly.
>
> **Dangling modifier (past participle):**   *Tired from the day's* work, weariness overcame me.
>
> **Correction:**   Tired from the day's work, I was overcome with weariness.
>
> **Correction:**   Because I was tired from the day's work, weariness overcame me.

Dangling modifier (infinitive):	*To excel in sports*, much practice is needed.
Correction:	*To excel in sports,* an aspiring athlete needs much practice.
Correction:	If an aspiring athlete wants to excel in sports, he or she needs much practice

Misplaced Modifiers (mm)

A **misplaced modifier** is positioned too far away from the word it describes. The result is an unclear, silly, or illogical sentence. (Do not rely on grammar checkers to find misplaced modifiers, as they do not identify these errors very well.)

Misplaced modifier:	The strolling musicians played while we were eating dinner *softly.*

The modifier *softly* is intended to describe *played.* However, *softly* is too far removed from *played,* so it seems to describe *were eating.* To correct a sentence with a misplaced modifier, move the modifier as close as possible to the word it describes.

Correction:	The strolling musicians played softly while we were eating dinner.

A misplaced modifier can be a word, a phrase, or a clause.

Misplaced modifier (word):	There must be something wrong with this cookie recipe, for it *only* requires a half-cup of sugar. (Placement of *only* indicates no other ingredients are needed.)
Correction:	There must be something wrong with this cookie recipe, for it requires *only* a half-cup of sugar.
Misplaced modifier (phrase):	Across the street, *playing far too wildly*, we saw the young children. (The phrase seems to describe *we.*)
Correction:	Across the street, we saw the young children *playing far too wildly.*
Misplaced modifier (clause):	We brought the rubber tree into the house *which was at least eight feet tall.* (The clause seems to describe the house.)
Correction:	We brought the rubber tree, which was at least eight feet tall, into the house.

CHAPTER 24

Punctuation

Punctuation marks aid communication because they signal where ideas end, how ideas relate to one another, which ideas are emphasized, which ideas are downplayed, and which ideas are expressed in someone's spoken words.

The Comma (,)

Writers who do not know the rules often place commas wherever they pause in speech. However, listening for pauses is an unreliable way to place commas. Computer grammar checkers are also undependable, so if you have not yet learned the rules, study the next pages carefully.

Commas with Items in a Series

A **series** is formed by three or more words, phrases, or clauses. Use commas to separate each item in the series.

Words in a series:	The gardener sprayed the *grass, trees, and shrubs* with pesticide.
Phrases in a series:	Louis Riel was passionately religious, determined to lead his people, and ultimately a tragic hero.
Clauses in a series:	Before the first day of school, *Shonda took her kindergartner on a tour of the school, she introduced him to the principal, and she bought him school supplies.*

If the items in the series are separated by *and* or *or*, do not use a comma:

The only vegetables Tom will eat are carrots or peas or corn.

Some writers omit the comma after the last item in the series, but you should get in the habit of using the comma to avoid misreading.

Commas with Introductory Elements

Elements placed before the subject are usually followed by a comma.

1. Follow an introductory subordinate clause with a comma (see page 120):

   Although she promised to meet me for lunch, Caroline never arrived at the restaurant.

2. Follow introductory phrases with a comma:

   By the end of the first half of the tournament, our team had won nine games.

3. Follow introductory adverbs with a comma. (See also page 498.)

Reluctantly, Mr. Simpson told his oldest employee that he was selling his business.

Quickly yet cautiously, the store detective moved in on the suspected shoplifter.

4. You may omit the comma after a very brief opener:

Unfortunately, the exam grades were lower than expected.

or

Unfortunately the exam grades were lower than expected.

Commas to Set off Nouns of Direct Address

The names of those directly addressed are set off with commas:

"*Dorrie*, you must get ready for school now."

"Get away from that hamburger, *you mangy dog."*

"If you ask me, *Juan,* we should turn left."

Commas with Nonessential Elements

Nonessential elements are words, phrases, and clauses that are not necessary for the clear identification of what they refer to.

Nonessential element:	Uncle Ralph, *who has been on the police force 20 years*, believes handgun legislation is the key to reducing violent crime.

Who has been on the police force 20 years is nonessential because the person it refers to (Uncle Ralph) is already clearly identified.

Essential element:	The student *who wins the state finals in speech* will get $1,000.

Who wins the state finals in speech is necessary for identifying which student will win $1,000; therefore, it is an essential element.

1. Use commas to set off nonessential clauses:

Sara Summers, *who is a senior,* was voted president of senior council.

My roommate collects pop cans, *which she stacks against the wall.*

but

Dr. Kingsley is a person *whose opinion I respect.* (Clause is essential.)

2. Use commas to set off nonessential phrases:

The sparrows, *hunting for food in the snow,* sensed the cat's approach and took off suddenly.

but

The child *playing in the sandbox* is my nephew. (Phrase is essential.)

3. Use commas to set off nonessential **appositives**. An appositive is a word or word group that renames the noun it follows.

Nonessential appositive:	My brother, an investment banker, makes $200,000 a year. (*An investment banker renames my brother,* so it is an appositive. Since it is not necessary for identification, commas are used.)

Essential appositive: My son the doctor is not as happy as my son the actor. (*The doctor* is an appositive renaming *my son*, and *the actor* is an appositive renaming the second *my son*. In both cases, the appositives are essential for identifying which son is referred to, so no commas are used.)

Commas with Interrupters

Interrupters are words and phrases that "interrupt" the flow of a sentence; they function more as side remarks than as integral parts of sentences. Often transitions interrupt flow and are considered interrupters, which is why the following partial list of interrupters includes some transitions.

after all	in fact
as a matter of fact	in the first place
by all means	it seems to me
consequently	of course
for example	to say the least
in a manner of speaking	to tell the truth

Interrupters are usually set off with commas.

Interrupter at beginning: *Of course*, not everyone shares my concern about this issue.

Interrupter in middle: The students' behaviour at the concert, *it seems to me*, was exemplary.

Interrupter at end: News broadcasts have become insubstantial, *to say the least.*

Commas with Main Clauses

1. When two main clauses are connected with a coordinating conjunction (fanboys words: for and nor but or yet, so), place a comma before the conjunction (see page 117).

   The match was over, but the spectators refused to leave.

   The garden was heavily fertilized, so the yield of vegetables was even higher than expected.

2. Do not use a comma before a coordinating conjunction linking two elements that are not main clauses.

   No: Lee asked for forgiveness, and promised to try harder.

   Yes: Lee asked for forgiveness and promised to try harder.

Commas between Coordinate Modifiers, Commas for Clarity, and Commas to Separate Contrasting Elements

Coordinate modifiers are two or more modifiers referring equally to the same word. Commas separate such modifiers when they are not already separated by *and* or *but*. (If the order of the modifiers can be reversed or if *and* can be used to join the modifiers, they are coordinate and should be separated with a comma.)

An *expensive, well-tailored* suit is a necessary investment for a young executive. (The order of the modifiers can be reversed: a well-tailored, expensive suit.)

They ate their picnic lunch under the *blossoming apple* tree. (And cannot be used between the modifiers, nor can the order be reversed.)

She is certainly a *happy and carefree* person. (No comma is needed because and is used.)

Sometimes a comma is necessary for clarity, to prevent the misreading of a sentence:

For Easter, lilies are the most popular flower. (Without the comma, a reader might read the first three words as a single phrase.)

Commas also set off an element that contrasts with what comes before it:

Dale is only lazy, not stupid.

When Not to Use a Comma

1. Do not use a comma to separate a subject and verb.

   No: The Premier-elect, promised to work to change the way public education is funded in our province.

   Yes: The Premier-elect promised to work to change the way public education is funded in our province.

2. Do not use a comma between a preposition and its object.

   No: Canada has a government of, the people.

   Yes: Canada has a government of the people.

3. Do not use a comma between a verb and its object.

   No: Carl smacked, the ball out of the park.

   Yes: Carl smacked the ball out of the park.

4. Do not use a comma between a verb and a subject complement. A subject complement, which follows a verb that does not show action, describes or renames the subject. (See also page 488.)

   No: Louise will become, a concert pianist if she continues to practice.

   Yes: Louise will become a concert pianist if she continues to practice.

5. Do not use a comma after a coordinating conjunction linking main clauses.

   No: I have tried to understand Juan but, his behaviour continues to puzzle me.

   Yes: I have tried to understand Juan, but his behaviour continues to puzzle me.

6. Do not use a comma before the first item or after the last item in a series.

   No: The math test covered, improper fractions, common denominators, and mixed fractions.

   Yes: The math test covered improper fractions, common denominators, and mixed fractions.

   No: Improper fractions, common denominators, and mixed fractions, were on the math test.

   Yes: Improper fractions, common denominators, and mixed fractions were on the math test.

7. Do not use a comma between a modifier and the word it modifies.

   No: The frayed, curtains must be replaced.

   Yes: The frayed curtains must be replaced.

8. Do not use a comma after *such as* or *like*.

   No: Kurt believes in some unusual ideas such as, reincarnation, transmigration, and mental telepathy.

   Yes: Kurt believes in some unusual ideas, such as reincarnation, transmigration, and mental telepathy.

   No: Medical technology students must take difficult courses like, physiology, biochemistry, and pharmacology.

   Yes: Medical technology students must take difficult courses like physiology, biochemistry, and pharmacology.

9. Do not use a comma between that and a direct quotation.

   No: The school board president said that, "we are considering a ten-month school year."

   Yes: The school board president said that "we are considering a ten-month school year."

The Semicolon (;)

A **semicolon** separates two main clauses not linked by a coordinating conjunction:

The canvas raft floated near the edge of the pool; it was pushed by a gentle summer breeze.

The A team wore the old uniforms; the B team wore new ones.

A semicolon should appear before a conjunctive adverb that joins two main clauses. Here is a list of conjunctive adverbs:

also	indeed	nonetheless
besides	instead	similarly
certainly	likewise	still
consequently	meanwhile	subsequently
finally	moreover	then
furthermore	nevertheless	therefore
however	next	thus

1. When you join two main clauses with a semicolon and conjunctive adverb, place a comma after the conjunctive adverb:

   The car I want to buy is a real bargain; *furthermore,* the bank is offering me an excellent financing rate.

   The test grades were low; *consequently,* Dr. Barnes allowed us to retake the exam.

2. For clarity, use a semicolon to separate items in a series that already contains commas:

   The following prairie cities have experienced phenomenal growth in the past five years: Regina, Saskatchewan; Edmonton, Alberta; and Winnipeg, Manitoba.

The Colon (:)

A **colon** is used after a main clause to introduce a word, phrase, or clause that indicates a particular example or examples or that explains.

Colon to introduce phrase that particularizes:	Four occupations were represented in the union membership: secretaries, maintenance workers, cafeteria workers, and bookkeepers.
Colon to introduce word that explains:	Rick writes soap opera scripts for one reason: money.
Colon to introduce clause that explains:	All of Terry's efforts were directed toward one goal: She wanted to be a dancer.

Do not use a colon between a verb and its object or the subject complement, or between a preposition and its object.

No: The students who will compete in the debate are: David Haynes, Lorenzo Ruiz, and Clara Jakes.

Yes: The students who will compete in the debate are David Haynes, Lorenzo Ruiz, and Clara Jakes.

Yes: The following students will compete in the debate: David Haynes, Lorenzo Ruiz, and Clara Jakes.

No: I am afraid of: heights, small rooms, and water.

Yes: I am afraid of heights, small rooms, and water.

Yes: I am afraid of these things: heights, small rooms, and water.

The Dash (—)

A **dash** (formed on the keyboard lacking a dash key with two hyphens) indicates a pause for emphasis or dramatic effect. It should be used sparingly and thoughtfully so that its emphatic or dramatic quality is not weakened by overuse. Often dashes can be used in place of commas, semicolons, colons, or parentheses; the mark used depends on the effect you want to create.

Jake told me—I can't believe it—that he would rather stay at home than go to Whistler. (Parentheses may be used instead.)

I know why Tony's bike disappeared—it was stolen from the backyard. (Semicolon or colon may be used instead.)

Vinnie is 35—although he won't admit it. (A comma may be used instead.)

Parentheses ( )

Parentheses enclose elements you want to downplay. Often parentheses signal a side comment or incidental remark:

Louise Rodriguez (you remember her) has been elected president of the Women's Action Council.

When I was in college (over 20 years ago), writing was taught very differently.

Commas or dashes often set off material that could also be enclosed in parentheses. However, commas and dashes will emphasize the material, whereas parentheses will deemphasize it.

Parentheses deemphasize:	This week's lottery prize (an incredible $12 million) will be split between two winners.
Dashes emphasize:	This week's lottery prize—an incredible $12 million—will be split between two winners.
Commas give more emphasis than parentheses but less than dashes:	This week's lottery prize, an incredible $12 million, will be split between two winners.

1. Do not place a comma before the element enclosed in parentheses.

    No: Most of the class, (easily 30 of us) felt the test was too long to complete in an hour.

    Yes: Most of the class (easily 30 of us) felt the test was too long to complete in an hour.

2. Use a period and capital letter with a complete sentence enclosed in parentheses when the sentence is not interrupting another sentence.

    No: After three days (Most of us wondered what took so long.) the winners were announced.

    Yes: After three days the winners were announced. (Most of us wondered what took so long.)

    Yes: After three days (most of us wondered what took so long) the winners were announced.

3. Place a comma or end mark of punctuation *outside* the closing parenthesis:

    The new parking deck is an imposing structure (it has 15 levels), but people have trouble finding their cars in it (a serious drawback).

4. Use parentheses to enclose numbers and letters in a list of items:

    The Citizens' Coalition has three reservations about endorsing Smith for mayor: (1) she is inexperienced, (2) she opposes increasing city taxes, and (3) she has no clear position on arts spending.

The Apostrophe (')

The **apostrophe** is used most frequently to show possession. It is also used to form contractions and certain kinds of plurals.

The Apostrophe to Show Possession

The apostrophe is used with nouns and certain indefinite pronouns (see page 483 for an explanation of indefinite pronouns) to signal possession.

1. To form the possessive of a noun or indefinite pronoun that does not end in *-s*, add an apostrophe and an *-s:*

   The *apartment's* bedroom is much too small.

   Anybody's help would be appreciated.

   The university has agreed to fund a library for *Women's* Studies.

2. To form the possessive of a *singular* noun that ends in *-s*, add an apostrophe and an *-s:*

   Charles's stolen car was found across town.

   The *business's* stock climbed three points.

3. To form the possessive of a *plural* noun that ends in *-s*, add just the apostrophe:

   The *premiers'* council on aging will examine the issue of adequate health care.

4. To show joint possession of one thing, use an apostrophe only with the last noun. To show individual ownership, use an apostrophe with every noun:

   Manuel and Louise's committee report was thorough and clear. (One report belonging to both Manuel and Louise)

   Jason's and Helen's financial problems can be solved with better money management. (Jason and Helen have separate financial problems.)

5. To show possession with a hyphenated word, use the apostrophe only with the last element of the word:

   The *editor-in-chief's* salary was cut in half after the magazine's circulation decreased dramatically.

   I have planned a surprise party to celebrate my *mother-in-law's* 60th birthday.

6. Do not use apostrophes with possessive pronouns *(its, whose, hers, his, ours, yours, theirs).*

   No: The expensive vase fell from *it's* shelf and shattered.

   Yes: The expensive vase fell from *its* shelf and shattered.

   No: The book that is missing is *her's.*

   Yes: The book that is missing is *hers.*

The Apostrophe to Indicate Missing Letters or Numbers and for Some Plurals

A **contraction** is formed when two words are joined and one or more letters are omitted. In a contraction, the apostrophe stands for the missing letter or letters.

isn't (is not)	we'll (we will)
hasn't (has not)	who's (who is, or who has)
they're (they are)	that's (that is, or that has)
we're (we are)	she'll (she will)
haven't (have not)	it's (it is or it has)
I'll (I will)	shouldn't (should not)

1. When you reproduce dialect or casual speech, use an apostrophe for missing letters in words that are not contractions:

add 'em up (add them up)

sugar 'n' spice (sugar and spice)

ma'am (madam)

2. Use an apostrophe to stand for missing numbers:

The class of '67 will hold its annual reunion the day after Thanksgiving. (The apostrophe stands for the missing *19*.)

3. Use an apostrophe and an *-s* to form the plural of letters, numbers, and words meant to be taken as terms:

If I get any more <u>D</u>'s, I will lose my scholarship.

How many <u>t</u>'s are in omit?

Mark makes his <u>3</u>'s backwards.

Janice is too polite; I am tired of all her <u>yes sir</u>'s and <u>no ma'am</u>'s.

Note: Underline or italicize letters, numbers, and words used as terms. In printed copy, these words may be set in italics. Do not underline or italicize the apostrophe and added *-s*.

ESL NOTE

Its and *It's*

Be sure to distinguish between *its* and *it's*. *Its* is a pronoun that shows ownership. Notice that it does *not* have an apostrophe:

The pen is missing *its* cap.

It's is a contraction that means "it is" or "it has":

It's difficult to predict how long the concert will last.

It's been three years since I have had a cigarette.

Its' is not an English word.

Quotation Marks (" ")

Quotation marks enclose the exact words somebody spoke or wrote. For information on this use of quotation marks, see pages 234, 404–405, and 419.

The salesclerk explained, "For eighty dollars, you can buy a wireless mouse."

"For eighty dollars, you can buy a wireless mouse," the salesclerk explained.

"For eighty dollars," the salesclerk explained, "you can buy a wireless mouse."

1. Use quotation marks to enclose the titles of short published works (poems, short stories, essays, book chapters, and articles from periodicals). Titles of longer, full-length works (books, magazines, and newspapers) are underlined or italicized:

   "Morning in the Burned House" is my favourite Atwood poem, and The Blind Assassin is my favourite Atwood novel.

   Do not use quotation marks, underlining, or italics for unpublished titles, including the titles of your own papers.

2. Use quotation marks around words used in a special sense:

   Your "humour" is not funny.

The Ellipsis Mark (. . .)

The **ellipsis mark**, which is three spaced periods, indicates that something has been purposely omitted from a quotation. Most often, writers use ellipsis marks to shorten quotations so they can use just the portion they want. The ellipsis mark indicates where the omission occurs. Ellipsis marks are often used in research papers according to specific conventions, which are explained on page 404.

When you omit part of a quotation, you must not change the meaning of the original.

Original Quotation

Women only won the right to vote gradually in Canada and remain underrepresented in Parliament as well as in provincial legislatures. . . . The first federal election in which women were able to vote and run as candidates was 1921. In that election, four women ran for office and Agnes Campbell MacPhail (1890–1954) made history as the first woman elected to the Canadian House of Commons. Between 1921 and 2006, 3402 women candidates stood in the 39 general elections and won on 426 occasions. . . . The 2008 election was one of records for women in Canadian politics. 69 or 22.4% of winning candidates in the 2008 election were women. This is both a record number and record percentage of MPs who are women.

—Women and Elections, *http://www.sfu.ca/~aheard/elections/women.html*

No: "The first federal election . . . was 1921."

Yes: "The first federal election in which women were able to vote . . . was 1921."

Notice that the three periods are evenly spaced.

To Omit the End of a Sentence

If you are omitting words from the end of a sentence, use a period followed by the ellipsis mark:

"Women only won the right to vote gradually in Canada and remain underrepresented. . . ."

To Omit the Opening of a Sentence

Do not use an ellipsis mark when material has been omitted from the beginning of a quotation. However, if you change the capitalization of the first word, place the letter in brackets.

> "[F]our women ran for office and Agnes Campbell MacPhail (1890–1954) made history as the first woman elected to the Canadian House of Commons."

To Omit a Sentence or More in the Middle

Use a period followed by the ellipsis mark:

> "Women only won the right to vote gradually in Canada and remain under-represented in Parliament as well as in provincial legislatures. . . . Between 1921 and 2006, 3402 women candidates stood in the 39 general elections and won on 426 occasions. . . ."

Brackets ([ ])

Brackets indicate that you have added a word, phrase, or sentence to a quotation that is otherwise reproduced exactly. Often brackets enclose explanatory material, as the following examples illustrate. Brackets are often used in research papers according to specific conventions, which are explained on page 404.

> "It was a Canadian [Lester B. Pearson] who first proposed a UN mission along the lines of what we have come to know as peacekeeping."

The original sentence did not give Pearson's name. The writer added it in case the reader did now know who the Canadian statesman was who developed the UN's peacekeeping role.

> "In the 1960s [well before the Internet was developed], Arthur C. Clarke [the science fiction writer who penned *2001: A Space Odyssey*] predicted that by 2000 a 'global library' would be developed."

The information in brackets, which did not appear in the original material, is explanation added to help the reader.

Brackets also enclose the Latin word *sic* to indicate that an error in the quotation appears in the original.

> "The earliest digital machines were based on vaccum [sic] tubes."

Sic indicates that *vacuum* was misspelled in the original sentence.

Italics and Underlining (ital/ul)

Italics is slanted type. Most word-processing programs allow you to use italics. If yours does not, or if you are writing by hand or on a typewriter, use underlining.

1. Italicize or underline the titles of works that are published separately (books, magazines, newspapers, plays, television and radio programs, long poems, and movies). Do not italicize or underline unpublished titles, including the titles of your own works.

   The Gum Thief by Douglas Coupland is the last novel I read, and *Maggie's Getting Married* by Norm Foster is the last play I saw.

   Shorter works, such as magazine articles, appear in quotation marks (see page 507).

2. Italicize or underline foreign words and phrases unless they have become an accepted part of the English language (laissez-faire, taco):

   Enrico graduated *magna cum laude.*

3. Italicize or underline words, letters, and numbers used as words:

   Your *3*'s look like *B*'s to me.

4. Italicize or underline words or phrases that you want to emphasize:

   What do you mean, *we* have a problem?

CHAPTER 25

Capitalization, Spelling, Abbreviations, and Numbers

Capitalization (cap)

Below are rules governing the most frequent uses of capital letters. If you are unsure whether to capitalize a word, you can consult a dictionary.

1. Capitalize proper names of people and animals:

   Harry   Rover
   Joe Popovich   Einstein

2. Capitalize names of nationalities, languages, and races:

   American   Asian   Chinese art
   Spanish   Italian architecture French cooking

3. Capitalize names of specific countries, states, regions, places, bodies of water, and so on.

   New Brunswick   Algonquin Park   North Pole
   Zimbabwe   United Counties of Prescott-Russell   Fourth Avenue
   Lake Huron   Europe   Surrey

   Do not capitalize: *the park, the beach, a large city, the town hall.*

4. Capitalize proper names and titles that precede them, but not general terms:

   Justice Walters   Chairman Mao
   Prime Minister Gandhi   Mayor Johnson
   Professor Kline   President Obama

   Do not capitalize: *the judge, a president, the chairman.*

5. Capitalize words designating family relationships only when these are not preceded by a possessive pronoun or article:

   Grandma Moses   Mum (as in I asked *Mum* to come along)
   Aunt Donna   Cousin Ralph

   Do not capitalize: *my uncle, his aunt, her mom.*

6. Capitalize specific brand names but not the type of product:

   Coca-Cola   Colgate
   Crisco   Nike

   Do not capitalize: *pop, toothpaste, oil, athletic shoes.*

7. Capitalize directions when they refer to specific geographic regions:

   the Prairies   the Middle East   the South
   the East Coast   the Pacific Northwest   the North

   Do not capitalize: *east on the 401, three kilometres south, the northern part of the province.*

8. Capitalize specific course titles and all language courses:

   History 101   Intermediate Calculus II
   French   English

   Do not capitalize studies that do not name specific courses: *math class, chemistry, drama.*

9. Capitalize the names of ships, planes, and spacecraft:

   the *Enterprise*   the *Challenger*
   RMS *Queen Elizabeth 2*   the *Titanic*

10. Capitalize the names of specific buildings, institutions, and businesses:

    the Toronto Dominion Bank   Gananoque Light & Power
    Via Rail   Brock University

11. Capitalize names of religions, sacred books, and words that refer to God:

    the Almighty   Jewish   the Qur'an
    Islam   the Holy Bible   Buddha
    Jesus Christ   Catholic   Jehovah
    the Old Testament   the Scriptures   Mohammed
    Christianity   Protestantism   the Trinity

12. Capitalize modifiers derived from proper nouns:

    French accent   Inuit art
    Franco-Newfoundlander community   Shakespearean comedy

13. Capitalize the first and the last word of a title and the first word of a subtitle after a colon. In between, capitalize everything except articles (*a, an, the*), short prepositions (*of, as, to, in, near*), and short conjunctions (*and, but, for*). You can consider "short" to be fewer than five letters.

The Gum Thief	*The Blind Assassin*
The Decline of the American Empire	*Maggie's Getting Married*
Maria Chapdelaine	*Away From Her*

Note: For discussions of capitalization rules for direct quotation, see pages 404–405.

ESL NOTE

Capitalization

Capitalization rules in your native language may differ markedly from English rules for capitalization. If you speak Arabic, Chinese, or Japanese, you may not readily see the significance of the size difference between capital and lower case letters. If you speak a Romance language, you may not be accustomed to capitalizing the names of languages, religions, nationalities, and days of the week. Be patient and focus on capital letters in your reading to become more familiar with the rules.

Spelling (sp)

A paper with frequent misspellings makes the writer seem careless, so whenever you have the slightest inkling that a word might be misspelled, check your dictionary. If you have a serious, persistent spelling problem, study the rules in this chapter, as well as the frequently confused words beginning on page 460. In addition, try these tips:

1. Check spellings *after* revising your content.
2. Buy and use the *Canadian Oxford Dictionary*, or use an online dictionary.
3. Use your computer's spellchecker—but use it with the understanding that it will not catch everything. Make sure to choose Canadian rather than American spelling from the "set language" function. A spellchecker will not flag sound-alike words that are used incorrectly—for example, *its* for *it's* or *here* for *hear.*
4. Keep a personal spelling list. Include misspelled words your instructor marks, important terms you must use in your classes, and words you frequently misspell. Study the list often.
5. Spell by syllables or parts—for example, *leth-ar-gy* or *un-bear-able.*
6. Pronounce words correctly to spell them correctly. If you mispronounce "athlete" as "ath-e-lete," you will likely include an extra *-e.*
7. Use memory tricks. For example, if you misspell *instrument* as *insturment*, think of the fact that you <u>strum</u> a guitar, which is an instrument.

Adding a Prefix

A **prefix** is one or more letters added to the beginning of a word to form a new word. Adding a prefix does not change the spelling of the base word.

un + nerved = unnerved   dis + satisfied = dissatisfied

de + emphasize = deemphasize   im + mobile = immobile

Choosing –ie and –ei

Use -i before -e except after -c, or when sounded like *a* as in *neighbour* and *weigh:*

achieve   priest   ceiling   sleigh

The rule applies when the -ie or -ei are pronounced as one syllable, but not when the letters are divided between two syllables:

deity   diet   science

Memorize these exceptions:

ancient	height	protein
caffeine	leisure	seize
either	neither	weird

Adding Endings to Words with a Final –y

Change -y to -i when there is a consonant before the -y. Keep the -y when there is a vowel before it or when adding -ing:

cry + ed = cried   enjoy + ment = enjoyment

kindly + ness = kindliness   play + ed = played

marry + ing = marrying   try + ing = trying

Memorize these exceptions:

daily	laid
drily	paid
gaily	said

Adding Endings to Words with a Final –e

Drop the silent -e if the ending begins with a vowel (*a, e, i, o, u*). Keep the silent -e if the ending begins with a consonant.

drive + ing = driving   care + ful = careful

love + able = lovable   encourage + ment = encouragement

Memorize these exceptions:

acknowledgment	judgment
argument	mileage
awful	ninth
courageous	truly

Adding –s or –es

Add an -s to form the plural of most nouns.

Singular	Plural
ship	ships
hat	hats
umbrella	umbrellas

Add an -s to most verbs to form the present tense used with *he, she, it,* or a singular noun:

He sings.

She understands.

It works.

The child sleeps.

If the word ends in -s, -x, -z, -ch, or -sh, add -es:

address + es = addresses	sandwich + es = sandwiches
fix + es = fixes	dish + es = dishes
waltz + es = waltzes	

If the word ends in a consonant and -y, change the -y to -i and add -es. If the word ends in a vowel and -y, just add -s.

Consonant and -y		Vowel and -y	
fly	flies	toy	toys
lady	ladies	key	keys

If a word ends in a consonant and -o, add -es. If it ends in a vowel and -o, just add -s.

Consonant and -o		Vowel and -o	
hero	heroes	zoo	zoos
tornado	tornadoes	ratio	ratios

Doubling the Final Consonant

When you add an ending to a one-syllable word, double the final consonant if the ending begins with a vowel *and* the last three letters of the word are consonant-vowel-consonant:

hop	hopped	run	runner
grab	grabbing	slim	slimmer

Do not double the final consonant when the one-syllable word does *not* end in a consonant-vowel-consonant:

clear	clearest	peel	peeled	fear	fearing

Here are some exceptions to memorize:

boxing	busing	sawed

When a word has more than one syllable, double the final consonant if the ending begins with a vowel *and* the last three letters of the word are consonant vowel-consonant *and* the accent (emphasis) is on the last syllable:

begin   beginner   refer   referral   regret   regretted

Do not double the final consonant if one of the conditions is not met:

commit   commitment   visit   visitor

Here are some exceptions to memorize:

cancellation   equipped   excellence   excellent

FREQUENTLY MISSPELLED WORDS

absence	definitely	leisure	receive
accessible	disastrous	license	recommend
accommodate	discipline	lightning	reference
achievement	efficient	maintenance	relieve
amateur	eighth	mathematics	restaurant
apologize	environment	mischievous	ridiculous
apparent	especially	necessary	roommate
argument	exaggerate	ninety	secretary
athlete	existence	noticeable	separate
beginning	familiar	occurrence	several
believe	February	omission	sophomore
bureaucracy	foreign	particularly	succeed
business	forty	personnel	surprise
cemetery	grammar	picnicking	thorough
column	guarantee	precede	tragedy
committee	humorous	prejudice	truly
conceive	immediately	privilege	usually
conscience	intelligence	proceed	vacuum
convenience	irresistible	pronunciation	Wednesday
criticize	judgment	psychology	weird
deceive	knowledge	quantity	villain

ESL NOTE

Spelling

If your native language does not have the same sounds that English does, mastering spelling can be more complicated for you. Spanish, for example, does not have the *-wh* sound, so Spanish speakers may spell *whether* as *wether*. Be sure to keep a personal spelling list and study it daily.

The Hyphen (-)

1. If a word is too long to fit at the end of a line, use a hyphen to divide the word between syllables. If you are unsure of the correct syllable break, check your dictionary. (Never divide a one-syllable word.)

   Note: Most word-processing programs automatically space text so that hyphens are not required.

   Duane hired a clown, a magician, and an acrobat to perform at his daughter's birthday party.

2. Use a hyphen between two or more words used to form an adjective that precedes a noun or to form a noun:

   high-interest loan

   low-cost mortgage

   state-of-the-art computer

   sister-in-law

   If the adjective follows the noun, the hyphen is usually not needed:

   The computer was *state of the art.*

   Do not use a hyphen with an *-ly* adverb:

   eagerly devoured meal

   badly reviewed play

3. Use a hyphen with the prefixes *all-, ex-,* and *self-:*

   all-inclusive

   ex-husband

   self-starter

4. Use a hyphen to separate the numerator and denominator of a fraction:

   one-half

   two-thirds

   three-fourths

5. Use a hyphen with whole numbers from twenty-one to ninety-nine, and when a number is combined with a word:

   twenty-one thousand

   thirty-three

   a nine-page letter

Abbreviations and Numbers (ab/num)

1. Use A.M. (a.m.) and P.M. (p.m.) for exact times of day. Either uppercase or lowercase is acceptable; just be consistent.

   We left home at 6:30 A.M. and arrived at 7:00 P.M.

2. Use A.D. before the year and B.C. after the year. A.D. is the abbreviation for the Latin *anno Domini.* B.C. stands for "before Christ." Use both B.C.E. and C.E. after the date. B.C.E. (before the common era) and C.E. (common era) are increasingly used as alternatives to B.C. and A.D.

   The artifact is dated 50 B.C., but it is similar to items dated A.D. 500.

   The artifact is dated 50 B.C.E., but it is similar to items dated 500 C.E.

3. Do not use periods with familiar abbreviations:

   RCMP   CSIS   NATO

   BMO   UFO   MTV

4. Recognize that some titles come before a person's name, and some come after:

   Ms. Jenkins   Mr. Hank DuBois

   Dr. Louise Garcia   Louise Garcia, MD

   Tony Minnelli, CPA   Margaret Atwood, FRSC

   Ordinarily, do not use titles both before and after a person's name.

   No: Professor Lee Morrison, Ph.D.

   Yes: Professor Lee Morrison

   Yes: Lee Morrison, Ph.D.

5. Use *U.S.* as a modifier and *United States* all other times:

   The U.S. ski team did well in the Olympics.

   The United States has a huge national debt.

6. Do not abbreviate place names, except in addresses.

   No: The Museum of Anthropology in B.C. has dozens of totem poles.

   Yes: The Museum of Anthropology in British Columbia has dozens of totem poles.

7. Although publishers and style guides differ, words rather than numbers are often used for anything that can be written in one or two words. Two-word numbers between 21 and 99 are hyphenated. Numbers that require three or more words are written with numerals (a hyphenated number is one word). Finally, any number that opens a sentence should be spelled out.

   eighteen   fourth   Twenty-five   1,503   one-third

8. Use numerals for time, addresses, measurements, percentages, page numbers, and decimals:

   5 A.M.   2' 3"   page 3

   100 Oak Street   15 percent   1.5 ounces

Credits

Photo Credits

Page 23: Colleges Ontario advertisement. Used with permission.; **25:** AP Photo/Eric Gay; **28:** Courtesy of the Lance Armstrong Foundation; **29:** © 2004 Thinkstock LLC; **57:** © Robert Garvey/Corbis; **91:** © Royalty-Free/Corbis; **115:** www.CartoonStock.com; **143:** © David Raymer/Corbis; **155:** © Michael St. Maur Sheil/Corbis; **162:** Nova Scotia Department of Tourism, Culture and Heritage; **165:** Mike Grenville; **187:** Courtesy of Russell Stover Candies; **199:** John Norris/Corbis; **206:** Collection of the Norman Rockwell Museum at Stockbridge, Norman Rockwell Art Collection Trust, Printed by permission of the Norman Rockwell Family Agency © 1961 the Norman Rockwell Family Entities; **229:** © Maiman Rick/CORBIS SYGMA; **250:** © York University 2006; **297:** © Canadian Club is a registered trademark of Canadian Club, Inc.; **301:** © Stefan Puetz/zefa/Corbis; **321:** United Way, Toronto; **325:** © iStockphoto.com/Graffizone; **339:** Starline Pacific Inc. Premiere Canadian T-Shirt Manufacturer; **341: (both)** Image courtesy of The Advertising Archives; **370:** © Dan Guravich/Corbis; **372:** Image courtesy of The Advertising Archives; **373:** Paramount Classics/Photofest © Paramount Classics.

Text Credits

NOTE: All Student Essays have been reprinted with permission from their authors.

Accawi, Anwar. "The Telephone" from *The Boy from the Tower of the Moon* by Anwar Accawi. Copyright © 1999 by Anwar Accawi. Reprinted by permission of the author.

Archer, Eric. "The Give and Take of Successful Job Interviews," AFP Exchange, Sep/Oct 2003, Vol 23, Iss 5; p. 58. Copyright © 2003 by the Association of Financial Professionals. All rights reserved. Used with permission of the Association for Financial Professionals.

Blue, Laura. "Canada's Crisis." *Time Canada*, April 3, 2006, p. 55. Copyright TIME INC. Reprinted by permission. TIME is a registered trademark of Time Inc. All rights reserved.

Carson, Rachel. "Fable for Tomorrow" from *Silent Spring* by Rachel Carson. Copyright © 1962 by Rachel L. Carson, renewed 1990 by Roger Christie. Reprinted by permission of Houghton Mifflin Company. All rights reserved.

Dershowitz, Alan. "The Case for Torture Warrants." Copyright © 2002 Alan Dershowitz. Reprinted by permission of the author.

Fuscaldo, G. "What Makes a Parent?" Reproduced from *Journal of Medical Ethics*, April 2003, p. 66, with permission from BMJ Publishing Group.

Green, Joyce. "Decolonizing in the Era of Globalization," *Canadian Dimension*, March 2002, p. 31.

Holt, John. "School Is Bad for Children," *The Saturday Evening Post*, 1969. Reprinted by permission of *The Saturday Evening Post*.

"Is Torture Ever Justified? Terrorism and Civil Liberty," *The Economist*, Sept. 22, 2007, p. 76. Copyright 2007 by Economist Newspaper Group. Reproduced with permission of Economist Newspaper Group in the format textbook via Copyright Clearance Center.

King, Martin Luther, Jr. "The Ways of Meeting Oppression," Reprinted by arrangement with the Estate of Martin Luther King, Jr., c/o Writers House as agent for the proprietor, New York, NY. Copyright © 1958 Martin Luther King Jr., copyright renewed 1986 Coretta Scott King.

Krents, Harold. "Darkness at Noon," *New York Times*, 5/26/76. Copyright © 1976 New York Times Company. Reprinted by permission.

MacQueen, Ken, and Patricia Treble. "The Most Dangerous Cities in Canada: *Maclean's* Exclusive Rankings of the Country's Most Crime-Ridden, and Safest, Cities." *Maclean's*, March 24, 2008, p. 38.

Mallick, Heather. "Women Don't Matter: They've Been in the Workforce for a Long Time Now. They've Been Affirmative-Actioned, They've Been Studied and Mentored and Fast-Tracked. And Still..." *Report on Business Magazine*, 16.8 (February 2000) cover, pp. 36–38, 40. © 2000 Globe and Mail Ltd. Reprinted by permission of the author.

McGrath, Ben. "The Wicked Wind." Copyright © 2003 Condé Nast Publications. All rights reserved. Originally published in *The New Yorker*. Reprinted by permission; Illustration by Michael Kupperman. Copyright © 2003 by Michael Kupperman. All rights reserved. Used by permission of Michael Kupperman.

Petroski, Henry. "Better to Try Than to Simply Ask Why." Copyright © 2010 by Henry Petroski. Mr. Petroski's latest book is *The Essential Engineer: Why Science Alone Will Not Solve Our Global Problems.*

Rosenberg, Tina. "The Daughter Deficit," *The New York Times*, © 2009 The New York Times. All rights reserved. Used by permission and protected by the Copyright Laws of the United States. The printing, copying, redistribution, or retransmission of the Material without express written permission is prohibited. www.nytimes.com.

Schneider, Tapio. "How We Know Global Warming Is Real: The Science Behind Human-induced Climate Change," *Skeptic*. Altadena: 2008. Vol 14, Issue 1, pp. 31ff. © Skeptic Magazine and skeptic.com.

Sherr, Lynn. "Anguished Cries in a Place of Silence," *New York Times*, 8/18/02. Copyright © 2002 New York Times Co. Reprinted by permission.

Stein, Janice Gross. "Living Better Multiculturally: In Canada We Seem to Get the Multi Part, But How About the Culture?" This essay was first published in the September 2006 *Literary Review of Canada* (Vol. 14, No. 7).

Tyre, Peg. "Boy Brains, Girl Brains," *Newsweek*, 9/19/05. Copyright © 2005 Newsweek, Inc. All rights reserved. Reprinted by permission.

Walljasper, Jay. "Our Schedules, Ourselves," *The Utne Reader*, January/February, 2003. Reprinted by permission of the Utne Magazine.

Wente, Margaret. "If We're So Equal, Why Aren't We Happy?" *The Globe and Mail*, Friday, June 12, 2009. http://www.theglobeandmail.com/news/opinions/if-were-so-equal-why-arent-we-happy/article1180751/. Reprinted by permission.

Wong, Jan. "Ten Things the Chinese Do Much Better Than We Do." Used by permission of the author.

Index

REVISING AND EDITING REFERENCE GUIDE

REVISING AND EDITING SYMBOLS

ab	incorrect or inappropriate abbreviation (p. 516–517)	sexist	sexist diction (p. 129–130)
ad	incorrect adjective or adverb (p. 492–494)	sp. dic	use specific diction (p. 127–128)
apos	apostrophe needed or used incorrectly (p. 504–506)	s-v agr	faulty subject–verb agreement (p. 476–479)
case	incorrect pronoun case (p. 488–491)	sp	spelling error (p. 512–515)
cap	capital letter needed (p. 510–512)	thesis	revise thesis (p. 51–54)
cl	cliché (p. 132)	tp	troublesome phrase (p. 456–459)
col	colloquial (p. 127)	t. sent.	topic sentence needed or faulty (p. 76–79)
con	connotation (p. 126)	t. shft	tense shift (p. 479–480)
concl	revise conclusion (p. 83–85)	trans	transition needed or faulty (p. 96–98)
cs	comma splice (p. 469–471)	var	sentence variety needed (p. 120–123)
csd	concrete sensory detail needed (p. 147)	vb fm	incorrect verb form (p. 472–476)
det	supporting detail needed (p. 76)	v. shft	voice shift (p. 480–481)
dm	dangling modifier (p. 496–497)	wdy	wordy (p. 130–132)
dn	double negative (p. 459)	ww	wrong word
fcw	frequently confused word (p. 460–465)	//	faulty parallelism (p. 123–124)
frag	sentence fragment (p. 466)	⊙	period
intro	revise introduction (p. 69, 72–75)	?/	question mark
lc	lowercase letter needed (p. 510–512)	!/	exclamation point
lev	level of diction (p. 126)	∨	apostrophe (p. 504–506)
log	faulty logic (p. 351–353)	∧	comma (p. 498–502, 504)
mm	misplaced modifier (p. 497)	∧;	semicolon (p. 502)
num	incorrect form for number (p. 517)	∨ ∨	quotation marks (p. 506–507)
punc	punctuation error (p. 498–508)	…	ellipsis mark (p. 507–508)
pass	inappropriate use of passive voice (p. 116, 468)	⊙	colon (p. 503)
p. agr.	faulty pronoun–antecedent agreement (p. 482–484)	/-/	dash (p. 503, 504)
p. ref.	faulty pronoun reference (p. 484–485)	( )	parentheses (p. 503–504)
p. shft	person shift (p. 486–487)	[ ]	brackets (p. 508)
ref/int pn	reflexive or intensive pronoun (p. 487)	-	hyphen (p. 516)
rel	unclear relevance (p. 79–80)	∿	transpose
r/o	run-on sentence (p. 469–471)	℘	delete
		?	unclear
		¶̸	do not begin new paragraph (p. 82)
		¶	begin paragraph (p. 82)
		√	good